Racism and the Tory P

Racism is an endemic feature of the Tory Party. Tracing the history of that racism, *Racism and the Tory Party* investigates the changing forms of racism in the party from the days of Empire, including the championing of imperialism at the turn of the 20th century and the ramping up of antisemitism, the imperial and 'racial' politics of Winston Churchill, the rise of Enoch Powell and Powellism, to the Margaret Thatcher years, the birth of 'racecraft' and her polices in Northern Ireland, and the hostile environment and its consolidation and expansion under Theresa May and Boris Johnson's premierships. Throughout the book, all forms of racism are addressed including the various forms of colour-coded and as well as non-colour-coded racism as they are put in their historical and economic contexts.

This book should be of relevance to all interested in British politics and British history, as well as undergraduate and postgraduate students studying the sociology and politics of racism, as well as for students of the history of the development of British racism and of imperialism and its aftermath.

Mike Cole is a writer and Emeritus Professor of Racism Studies at the University of East London, UK and in Education and Equality at Bishop Grosseteste University, Lincoln, UK. Recent books include *Trump, the Alt-Right and Public Pedagogies of Hate and for Fascism* (Routledge, 2020), *Theresa May, the Hostile Environment and Public Pedagogies of Hate and Threat* (Routledge, 2021), *Climate Change, the Fourth Industrial Revolution and Public Pedagogies* (Routledge, 2021), *Education, Equality and Human Rights*, 5th edition (Routledge, 2022) and *Equality, Education and Human Rights in the United States* (Routledge, 2022).

'An accessible and penetrating analysis of the troubling evolution of the contemporary politics of "race" in Britain. Cole illuminates how, across decades and centuries, primary definers within the Conservative Party have strategically used "race" to construct a "hostile environment". For readers located within and beyond British shores, the book provides intellectual insights into how we might investigate the toxic entanglement of "race" and nation.'

Paul Michael Garrett, *University of Galway, Republic of Ireland, author of* Social Work with Irish Children and Families in Britain *(2004) and several other books. These include* Welfare Words *(2017),* Dissenting Social Work: Critical Theory, Resistance and Pandemic *(Routledge, 2021) and (with Washington Marovatsanga)* Social Work with the Black African Diaspora *(2022)*

'Mike Cole's *Racism and the Tory Party* is essential for anyone interested in understanding the historical context for Conservative party racism. Far from being incidental or contingent on populist pragmatism, this book traces how racism has saturated the party for over two centuries. Entrenched within the party, white superiority has combined with national protectionism; stoking fears of miscegenation with attempts to improve white stock in one-nation Toryism; the attempted maintenance of Empire with colonial experimentation in Ireland; liberal multiculturalism with rampant anti-migrant policy. At a time marked by vehement nativism and increased racialisation, this book is a must read for anybody interested in understanding the current state of British political crisis.'

James Trafford, *author of* The Empire at Home: Internal Colonies and the End of Britain *(2020)*

Racism and the Tory Party

From Disraeli to Johnson

Mike Cole

Routledge
Taylor & Francis Group

NEW YORK AND LONDON

Designed cover image: © Shutterstock, 2019. ID 1494586286

First published 2023
by Routledge
605 Third Avenue, New York, NY 10158

and by Routledge
4 Park Square, Milton Park, Abingdon, Oxon, OX14 4RN

Routledge is an imprint of the Taylor & Francis Group, an informa business

© 2023 Taylor & Francis

Library of Congress Cataloging-in-Publication Data
Names: Cole, Mike, author.
Title: Racism and the Tory party : from Disraeli to
Johnson / Mike Cole.
Description: New York, NY : Routledge, 2023. |
Includes bibliographical references and index.
Identifiers: LCCN 2022034596 | ISBN 9781032056777 (hardback) |
ISBN 9781032056753 (paperback) | ISBN 9781003198673 (ebook)
Subjects: LCSH: Tory Party (Great Britain)--History. | Racism--Great
Britain--History. | Conservative Party (Great Britain)--History. |
Great Britain--Race relations--History. | Great Britain--Politics and
government--History.
Classification: LCC JN1129.T7 C65 2023 | DDC 324.241/09--dc23/
eng/20220920
LC record available at https://lccn.loc.gov/2022034596

ISBN: 978-1-032-05677-7 (hbk)
ISBN: 978-1-032-05675-3 (pbk)
ISBN: 978-1-003-19867-3 (ebk)

DOI: 10.4324/9781003198673

Typeset in Bembo
by Taylor & Francis Books

Contents

Acknowledgements

My grateful thanks are due to the following for help, advice and comments in the course of writing this book: Lyka Cole, Rita Cole, Lewis Hodder, Laura Jaffee, John MacKenzie, Alpesh Maisuria and John Simkin. I take full responsibility for any shortcomings in the analysis.

Introduction

Racism: a multifaceted reality

This book is about racism in the British Conservative (Tory) Party over more than two centuries. In a country where, as I demonstrate throughout it, historically and contemporaneously racism takes a multitude of different forms, it is important to first consider the nature of its wide parameters. Racism is directed at people because of a number of perceived 'identities', including 'race', ethnicity, nationality, religion or a combination of these. For these reasons, it is important to adopt a broad concept of racism rather than a narrow one based on skin colour and/or imagined biological inferiority alone.

Racism can be unintentional as well as intentional (the former can sometimes cause as much distress as the latter). The difference between these two forms of racism depends obviously on intention and is summed up by the epithet: you do not have to be a racist (intentional) to be racist (which can be unintentional).[1] Racist pronouncements, intentional as well as unintentional, are often introduced with 'I'm not racist but …'. Racism can be direct (open and spelt out) or indirect (rules for everyone that are racist for some); it can be overt as well as covert. Racism can be dominative (direct and oppressive), as well as aversive (exclusion, cold-shouldering[2] and avoidance of interaction).[3] Racism can also become (more) apparent given certain stimuli. Crowds at UK soccer matches are an obvious example. It should also be stressed that 'seemingly positive' attributes will probably (ultimately) have racist implications, as in 'they are good at sport' that may also have the subtext that 'they' are not good at much else or at something else. Racism can be based on genetics, a belief that some genes are inferior to others – biological racism; or culture, thinking that some cultures are not as good as others – cultural racism, or it can be a combination of both.

Racism related to skin colour is the most recognized and discussed form of racism in the UK. I refer to this as colour-coded racism. Directed towards Black and Asian communities, it has its origins in the British Empire that dates back at least to the 18th century. Racism, however, is not necessarily related to skin colour. When it is not or maybe not, I use the terms 'non-colour-coded

DOI: 10.4324/9781003198673-1

racism' and 'hybridist racism': the first to describe racism that is *not* related to skin colour; and the second to refer to racism that is not or not specifically or not necessarily related to skin colour.[4]

As far as non-colour-coded racism is concerned, we have anti-Irish racism, antisemitism; and anti-Gypsy Roma and Traveller (GRT) racism, all of which have a long history in the UK. For clarification, the GRT communities include but are not limited to English Romani Gypsies, Welsh Gypsies, Irish Travellers, Scottish Gypsy/Travellers, Travelling Show-people, Circus People, Boat Dwellers, Fairground Travellers, New Travellers and Romanis from central and eastern Europe who have arrived as refugees or asylum seekers.[5] With respect to central and eastern Europe, we have a possible conflation with xeno-racism, another but more recent form of non-colour-coded racism, in that it refers, *in the contemporary British context*, to that directed at *White* central and eastern European workers and their families.[6]

Finally, hybridist racism is the term I employ for those more recent forms of racism that can be colour-coded, non-colour-coded or a combination of both. Examples are anti-asylum-seeker racism and Islamophobia. Thus, in the year ending September 2021, the top ten countries from which people sought asylum in the UK were Iran, Eritrea, Albania, Iraq, Syria, Sudan, Afghanistan, Vietnam, Pakistan and Bangladesh.[7] Those on the receiving end of in Islamophobia are not by any means a homogenous group, since 'Muslim' includes people of many nations and colours, who speak many languages and whose only common denominator is religion and religious culture,[8] and even here, there are different varieties of the Muslim religion and associated cultures. Islamophobia can also be associated with perceived bodily features and modes of dress. For example, as Sivanandan has argued, Muslims 'are marked out not so much by their colour as by their beards and headscarves'.[9] With these examples, we can thus see the many permutations of colour and non-colour that are possible.

This brief incursion into the plethora of different forms of racism that characterize the UK both historically and contemporaneously is not merely analytical in intent. It is also important in at least four other respects. First, it demonstrates, as stressed at the beginning of this Introduction, that racism is multifaceted. It exists far and beyond the commonplace notion that racism is related only to perceived biological inferiority and confined to what White people think of, or the way they treat, or what they do to Black and Asian people. It is imperative to add that in moving beyond the 'Black/White binary', the preceding discussion should not serve to underestimate the fundamental historical and ongoing significance of colour-coded racism.

Second, it is important to bear in mind that 'racial' and cultural identities are not discreet. For example, Jewish people can be Black and/or Asian and/or central and eastern European and/or asylum-seekers; central and eastern European people can be Black and/or Asian and/or Muslim; members of Gypsy, Roma and Traveller communities can be Muslim and/or Asian and/or Black and/or asylum-seekers and/or Irish and so on.

Third, *anyone* or any combination of individuals as well as institutions can be racist towards anyone or any combination of individuals or institutions who is/are not considered part of the same perceived 'race', ethnicity, nationality, religion or a mixture of these. People can also be racist towards people who are racialized for the same reasons that they are.

Fourth, considering multiple forms of racism, and relating them to historical and contemporary changes in capitalism and accompanying political processes and practices (e.g. controls on immigration and deportations); and to economic and political developments in capitalist societies from imperialism and colonialism[10] to the present, *and not just to phenotypical appearance in an ahistorical context*, gives us a much clearer understanding of the phenomenon of racism, and crucially, makes us better equipped to combat it. Colour-coded, non-colour-coded and hybridist racism are exemplified in detail in the pages of this book.

Racialization

Racialization means categorizing people as belonging to scientifically invalid distinct 'races' (see the next main section of this Introduction) and provides a useful way to describe how this happens. In Miles' words:

> I am rigorous in believing that there is a very clear distinction between an idea and a concept ... insofar as there is an idea of 'race' that is a historical reality ... [I] use the notion of racialization to then seek to explain the origin, development and use of that idea.[11]

In its neo-Marxist variant, as developed by Robert Miles[12] and myself,[13] it is distinct from other interpretations of racialization in that it focuses on how different groups of people are racialized in different geo-political contexts related to changes in capitalism and associated political processes. In this book, I draw on and expand this version of racialization to analyze racism in the Tory Party, beginning with the discourses and policies on 'race', nation and Empire of Benjamin Disraeli in the 19th century, and ending with racism's various manifestations during the premiership of Boris Johnson in the 21st century.

Miles has argued that racialization is a *process*. As he put it, 'by talking about racialization as a process you have a perspective ... that opens the door to history,[14] in that it enables an understanding of the complexities of who gets racialized when and for what purpose, and how that changes through time.[15] Miles compares two examples of racialization, one of non-colour-coded racism, and directed at Irish people who, as we shall see later in this Introduction (see also chapter 1 of this book), were racialized in the 1850s, and one of colour-coded racism, namely of Jamaicans (and others from the Caribbean, of course), who as we shall also see in this book were racialized along with others one century later in the 1950s. As Miles puts it:

There are fundamental aspects of those two migrations, experiences, processes and all that was consequent upon them that are very similar. And if you get so tied up in the 'race relations' paradigm to see the 'black-white' dichotomy as what it was all about and that racism is only ever about that, then you have backed yourself into a huge cul-de-sac.[16]

It should be stressed here that the interests of pro-capitalist politicians and capitalists do not always correspond, nor coalesce around racialization. For example, it is often in the interests of establishment politicians to racialize certain groups of workers for greater overall control of the workforce (divide and rule) and/or for electoral gain ('British jobs for British workers'), while capitalists may prefer not to do so in their pursuit of cheap labour power, for which migrant workers are ideal, and greater profits.

Institutional racism

Institutional racism has existed in various forms throughout British history. The chapters of this book trace its development, as with racialization, from the days of the Empire to the present. Institutional racism was not acknowledged by the British state until 1999 in the aftermath of the racist murder of Black teenager Stephen Lawrence in 1993. The definition of 'institutional racism', as in the Stephen Lawrence Inquiry Report by William Macpherson, was officially quoted in the House of Commons by the then Home Secretary Jack Straw in 1999:

> the collective failure of an organisation to provide an appropriate and professional service to people because of their colour, culture or ethnic origin. It can be seen or detected in processes, attitudes and behaviour which amount to discrimination through unwitting prejudice, ignorance, thoughtlessness and racist stereotyping which disadvantage minority ethnic
> · people
>
> (Macpherson, 1999, 6.37, para 11.3)

From a neo-Marxist perspective,[17] this psychological ahistorical definition needs to have an economic, historical and political focus. It can also be enhanced by racialization. Bearing in mind the preceding analysis in this Introduction, the above definition can be reformulated as follows:

Collective acts and/or procedures in an institution or institutions (locally, nation-wide, continent-wide or globally) that intentionally or unintentionally have the effect of racializing certain populations or groups of people. This racialization process, that is not limited to skin colour and can be colour-coded, non-colour-coded or hybridist, cannot be adequately understood without reference to economic and political factors related to developments and changes, historical and contemporaneous, in national, continent-wide and global capitalism.

As we shall see in chapter 10 of this book, the existence of institutional racism was denied by the Boris Johnson Government twenty-two years later in 2021.

'Race': a social construct, not a biological reality

Ta-Nehisi Coates is correct when he states that 'Race is the child of racism, not the father'.[18] By the dawn of the 21st century, there was firm evidence from scientists studying the origins of our species that, in fact, all of humankind has its origins in the continent of Africa,[19] and as British geneticist Adam Rutherford notes, it is also accepted that there are no purebred humans, since our family trees 'are matted webs, and all lines of our ancestry get tangled after a few generations'. All racists, he adds acerbically, have African ancestors and all Nazis have Jewish forebears.[20] After just a few centuries, Rutherford concludes, referring to our family trees, we are linked to everyone else on our continent, and after a couple of millennia to everyone in the world.[21]

It is now almost universally acknowledged among the mainstream scientific and social scientific communities that 'race' is socially constructed rather than biological reality. In 1972 the evolutionary geneticist Richard Lewontin argued that 85% of human genetic diversity occurred within, rather than between, populations, with the rest associated with the broadly defined 'races'.[22] That 'race' is a social construct is explained succinctly by neuroscientist Steven Rose and sociologist Hilary Rose[23]. Rose and Rose explain that most of the diversity between populations is accounted for by the readily visible genetic variation of skin colour, hair form and so on. The everyday business of seeing and acknowledging such difference is not the same as the project of genetics. For genetics, and more importantly, for the prospect of treating genetic diseases, the difference is important, since humans differ in their susceptibility to certain diseases, and genetics can have something to say about this.[24]

However, beyond medicine, the invocation of 'race' is increasingly suspect. There has been a growing debate about the utility of the term, and an entire issue of the influential journal *Nature Reviews Genetics* (Autumn, 2004) was devoted to it. The geneticists agreed with most biological anthropologists that for human biology, the term 'race' is an unhelpful leftover. Rose and Rose argue that '[w]hatever arbitrary boundaries one places on any population group for the purposes of genetic research, they do not match those of conventionally defined races' (Rose & Rose, 2005). For example, the DNA of 'native' Britons contains traces of the multiple entries into the UK of occupiers and migrants. 'Race', as a scientific concept, Rose and Rose conclude, 'is well past its sell-by date'.[25] The popular political slogan 'one race, the human race' would appear to be accurate. 'Race' as a concept should be abandoned. For these reasons, following Miles, if I need to use the terms 'race' or 'racial', I put them in quotations.

Nation, racism and imperialism

Ernest Gellner has suggested that 'nations are the artefacts of men's convictions and loyalties and solidarities'[26] and elsewhere that nationalism '*invents* nations where they do not exist'.[27] However, as Benedict Anderson has convincingly made the case in his book, *Imagined Communities: Reflections on the Origin and Spread of Nationalism*, Gellner assimilates 'invention' to 'fabrication' and 'falsity' rather than to 'imagining' and 'creation'. 'In this way', he continues, Gellner 'implies that "true" communities exist which can be advantageously juxtaposed to nations' whereas '[i]n fact, all communities larger than primordial villages of face-to-face contact (are perhaps even these) are imagined'.[28] If Anderson is not the first nor the only person to view 'nation' as a myth,[29] it is his name that is most closely associated with the thesis of the nation as an 'imagined community'. His argument is that the convergence of capitalism and print technology on the diversity of human language created the possibility of such communities and that the myth of the 'nation state' became possible only with the decline of cosmically central religious communities and dynasties. Anderson points out that the promotion of 'official nationalism' involved considerable manoeuvrings. In the case of the Kingdom of Great Britain and Ireland at the start of the 19th century, the monarchy was Hanoverian, originating in Germany, and it ruled over the continents of the world as well as the Irish, the Welsh and the Scots. The ideologies of racism and nationalism both assert the existence of a natural division within the world's population. However, nationalism goes further in that, in claiming divisions with distinct cultural profiles and therefore capacities for self-government, it implies the existence of nation states within a given geographical area. An ideological creation of the late 18th century, nationalism posits nations as universal entities, each with its own character and destiny.[30]

Miles has described the close correspondence between 'nation' and 'race':

> Like 'nations', 'races' too are imagined, in the dual sense that they have no real biological foundation and that all those included by the signification can never know each other, and are imagined as communities in the sense of a common feeling of fellowship. Moreover, they are also imagined as limited in the sense that a boundary is perceived, beyond which lies other 'races'.[31]

While I agree with Tom Nairn about the possibility of a 'healthy nationalism',[32] for example a political movement organized around the aim of expelling an invading power (to the extent that it engaged in fulfilling its limited objective). However, the nationalism under discussion here in this book is of the morbid variety, a degenerate nationalism that, in emphasizing an imagined common stock of memory of the past and hopes for the future[33], tends to exploit senseless fears, racism and violence.[34] Miles has contended that 'English nationalism is particularly dependent on and constructed by an idea of "race", with the result that English nationalism encapsulates racism' and that 'the ideas of "race" and "nation", as in a kaleidoscope merge into one another in varying patterns, each simultaneously highlighting and obscuring the other'.[35]

Connecting 'race', 'nation' and Empire, Miles states: 'it was widely believed that the English were largely an Anglo-Saxon 'race' characterized by an inherent capacity for freedom and by an ability to create democratic institutions, capacities which they could express in many other parts of the world'.[36]

Anderson suggests that the imagining of 'nation' was greatly aided by the character of British imperialism and colonialism. Unlike Czardom, for example, it was a grab-bag of primarily tropical possessions scattered over every continent and without any long-term religious, linguistic or cultural ties with the metropole.[37] It was this factor, I would argue, that gave the imagining of the British nation its particular quality. Along with a right of 'Anglo-Saxons' to impose 'democracy' wherever they chose, there were 'the British' and the White-skinned colonials, on the one hand, and 'the natives' or 'savages' on the other. In a sense, it did not really matter where they came from; they could simply be described as 'not British' and in need of being under control of and/or looked after by superior beings. If I am right, in a very real sense, to be pro-imperialist was to be racist and (usually) vice versa.

Colour-coded racism: colonial and imperial origins

The slave trade and the colonies[38]

The slave trade was, of course, primarily about profit. Indeed, British capitalism was built on the trans-Atlantic slave trade, a major component of the establishment of the British Empire (at its height in 1922 comprising incredibly an area of approximately 13½ million square miles, populated by some 460 million human beings)[39] providing the supply source for the intense exploitation of the labour of people of colour that took place initially in Britain's colonies (and later in the homelands as the Empire came home to roost – see part 2 of this book). In 1808, when that great advocate of Empire, Benjamin Disraeli (discussed in chapter 1) was an infant, the number of enslaved Africans transported across the Atlantic since 1640 by Britain, the leading slave trading nation, reached 3.1 million.

Conditions on the slave ships were so appalling that many did not make it. They were very overcrowded with the captives in many ships held between the hold and the deck 'packed like spoons, with no room even to turn'.[40] If the sea was rough, portholes had to be closed, often leaving people gasping for breath. As Alexander Falconbridge, a surgeon aboard slave ships and later the governor of a British colony for freed enslaved Africans in Sierra Leone, put it, 'the excessive heat was not the only thing that rendered their situation intolerable. The deck ... was so covered with the blood and mucus which had proceeded from them in consequence of the flux, that it resembled a slaughterhouse'.[41]

In the three hundred years between the 16th and 19th centuries over 54,000 voyages were made across the Atlantic, with the largest proportion of those enslaved Africans (42%) who survived the journey ending up in the Caribbean.[42] Miles discusses the advantages there of slave labour over indentured labour in the first half of the 17th century. Giving the example of Barbados, the first 'black slave society',[43] he explains the benefits of the former over the latter, detailing first the indentured labour system and how between 1627 and 1640 subsistence production was switched to the production of tobacco, cotton and ginger.[44] This was controlled by 'yeoman' (small landowning) farmers with indentured labour recruited from Europe (under a legal contract binding the indentured worker to a 'master' for a fixed number of years, usually four).[45] The individual was required to work for the master in return for the costs of transport and subsistence. On termination of the contract, the indentured labourer was provided with a small plot of land.[46]

From around 1640, however, sugar production developed first and fast in Barbados, then throughout the Caribbean. The total population of the Caribbean increased dramatically from the mid-17th century owing to the arrival of enslaved Africans who joined indentured European workers in the cane fields, the former gradually replacing the latter. The cost and control advantages of slave labour over indentured labour are that the slave owners had their labour power for life rather than a fixed period. Moreover, while a deduction had to be made for the purchase price and costs of reproduction, the indefinite period of servitude and the lower costs of reproduction ensured the generation of a much higher profit for the slaveowner. This was also because of less expenditure on clothes and food since the material living standards of enslaved Africans were depressed below those of indentured labourers, and they were required to grow their own food.[47]

In attempts to maintain social control to try to prevent revolt, a complex body of law was developed over time which regulated many aspects of the lives of those enslaved and their relations with the planter class,[48] generally to establish a legal basis for human beings to be held as property, being subject to being bought and sold with minimum provision for clothing, food and shelter, and for their movement to be controlled.[49] All this flagrant inhuman treatment had to be defended ideologically. As Isabel Ringrose explains, 'Capitalism justified slavery by claiming black people were inferior to white people'[50] (scientific racism is discussed throughout the book). British people were told that Africans had no culture, no religions, no laws, no traditions – some Britons even believed that Africans had no languages.[51] This built colour-coded institutional racism into the system, where it remains today. Colonized people in Africa and the Caribbean were largely unaware of its existence in Britain, when they arrived there after

World War II, following the decline of the Empire[52] (see the second section of chapter 3 and chapter 4).

Rebellions

Enslaved Africans were by no means passive recipients of slavery. For example, Jamaica was the scene of frequent rebellions. The First Maroon War led by Queen Nanny of the Maroons took place there from 1728 to 1740.[53] One of the most notable took place from 1760 to 1761. Led by a high-ranking chieftain Ghanaian King Takyi (also known as Tacky),[54] it was an uprising among Akan and other enslaved people from Ghana that occurred in St. Mary Parish, Jamaica, against the British. The goal of the rebellion was to take control of the British island colony and create a separate Black independent nation.[55] Hundreds of enslaved Ghanaians made their way to Fort Haldane where they captured and defended the town of Port Maria from British colonial forces, who eventually crushed the rebellion after a year's resistance. Despite the King's death (his head was displayed on a pole), insurrections continued in Jamaica.[56]

King Takyi had inspired others across the island. For example, in 1831 Samuel Sharpe, a Baptist deacon, led a Christmas Day general strike for wages and better working conditions. After the strikers' demands were ignored, the strike turned to open rebellion by tens of thousands of enslaved Africans who looted and burned plantations into January 1832 before being defeated by British troops. The Baptist War was one of the largest rebellions in the British West Indies[57] and preceded the Slavery Abolition Act of 1833 that formally ended slavery in Jamaica and most other colonies in 1834.[58] According to Samuel Momodu, one of nearly a thousand volunteer historians who write for *BlackPast*, the cost of these continuing rebellions was a major factor in the British Government outlawing slavery throughout the Empire.[59]

Profits generated

Asad Rehman, Executive Director of War on Want, points out that slave traders earned £8 billion from enslaving 1.5 million people of African descent. This fuelled Britain's industrial revolution, Britain's 'bricks and mortar'.[60] Isabel Ringrose identifies some key capitalist institutions that were central to slavery and benefited from its massive profits. Eleven former governors and 16 directors of the Bank of England owned enslaved Africans or directly profited from the trade between the 18th and 19th centuries, while the Royal Bank of Scotland, Barclays Bank, Lloyds Banking Group, HSBC and Royal Mail have also been linked to slavery. As well as banking, slavery generated vast profits to construct roads, docks, canals and mines, thus generating even more profit. Slavery also allowed the slaveowners to practice 'philanthropy'. For example, Tory slaver Edward Colston, director of the Royal African Company in 1680, whose name rose to prominence during the Black Lives Matter (BLM) protests of 2020 when his statue was smashed in Bristol, invested today's equivalent of £25 million in that city – notorious for its slave-trading past – for schools, alms houses and poor-houses. Ringrose also refers to 'the heirs of slavers continuing to talk up their "charitable" work', with, for example, the Greene King pub chain and brewery, founded by owner of enslaved Africans Benjamin Greene, saying in 2020 that the company would pay reparations 'to support the BAME community'. Greene was handed around £500,000 in today's money when the slave trade was banned in 1807 for three plantations and 231 enslaved Africans, while his heirs were compensated with £400,000.[61] Moreover, through the 1980s, tax havens took more than £16 trillion in capital flows, about £13 trillion of which was in illicit flows, and about £4.5 trillion in unsustainable debt repayments.[62]

Kris Manjapra, Professor of 'History and of race, colonialism and diaspora studies' at Tufts University, explains some of the little-known and long-enduring legacies of slavery. In 1835, two years after the British government had passed the Slavery Abolition Act, somewhere in the City of London, two of Europe's most famous bankers, Nathan Mayer Rothschild and Moses Montefiore, came to an agreement with the Chancellor of the Exchequer. It was to take out one of the largest loans in history to finance the 'slave compensation package' required by the 1833 Act. They agreed to loan the British government £15m, with the government adding an additional £5m later (£20 million then is worth nearly £300 billion in 2021). One would have expected this so-called 'slave compensation' to have gone to the enslaved Africans. Instead, the money went exclusively to the 'slave-owners' for their 'lost property'. As Manjapra points out, not a single penny has ever been granted by the British state to the people it enslaved, or their descendants. Incredibly, British taxpayers paid off the loan which only ended in 2015. Manjapra concludes, 'Generations of Britons have been implicated in a legacy of financial support for one of the world's most egregious crimes against humanity'.[63]

The Empire in India and profits generated

The Empire in India also produced colossal profits. According to Rehman, £45 trillion was looted from India alone during Britain's occupation of the Indian subcontinent.[64] At the time of the so-called 'Indian mutiny' or the Indian sub-continent's first war of independence (1857–1859) (see chapter 1), there had been a British commercial interest in India since 1600 when Elizabeth 1 of England had granted a charter to the East India Company. Starting as a monopolistic trading company, it became involved in politics, acting as an agent of British imperialism. The Company was established to share in the spice trade that had been monopolized by Spain and Portugal prior to the defeat of the Spanish Armada in 1588[65] (explained in the next section). In the 1620s, the Company began using slave labour, the majority from Africa. Large-scale transportation of enslaved people mainly to the company's holdings in India and Indonesia occurred from the 1730s to the early 1750s, ending in the 1770s. Following the 'mutiny', the East India Company ceased to be a legal entity in 1873,[66] when the British Raj was established and India officially became a British colony (see chapter 1) (it remained as such until the Indian Independence Act of 1947). According to Sashi Tharoor, a former Under-Secretary General of the UN whose book *Inglorious Empire* chronicles the atrocities of the British Empire, 'India's share of the world economy when Britain arrived on its shores was 23 per cent. By the time the British left, it was down to below four per cent'. 'Why?', he asks: 'Simply because India had been governed for the benefit of Britain. Britain's rise for 200 years was financed by its depredations in India'. Tharoor adds, 'In fact, Britain's industrial revolution was actually premised upon the de-industrialisation of India'.[67]

Rehman concludes by reminding us that the slave trade and the Empire in India both contributed to the economic inequalities that have sacrificed half the world to live on less than $5 a day. He also relates everything to 'a sustainable economy ... which is not bound by the nation state, but ... is ... global'. The world's climate response needs at its core keeping temperatures below 1.5°C; food and energy as a public good, not for exploitation by private corporations. A sustainable future must also guarantee economic justice, including guaranteed basic income, social protection, universal public services and workers' rights.[68]

Non–colour–coded racism: colonial origins

Anti-Irish racism

Anti-Irish racism also had its origins in profit, in this case first-of-all for royalty and nobility. The colonization of Ireland began in 1171 when King Henry II of England invaded Ireland and declared Dublin a royal city.[69] In 1177, he pronounced his son John to be 'Lord of Ireland'.[70] There followed centuries of ruthless English rule. Henry rewarded his conquering Anglo Norman Barons with large tracts of prime Irish land. During this period the English rulers at home were much 'more interested in their possessions in sunny and fertile France than the permanently hostile and warlike environment of Ireland which suffered under the powerful English barons accordingly'.[71]

In 1533, Henry VIII broke from the Catholic Church and married Anne Boleyn and was excommunicated by the Pope. From then on, the English viewed the Irish as potential enemies who might side with the Pope, and with Catholic France and Spain.[72] The English fear was well founded, and in 1588 seven Spanish ships, miserable remnants of the once mighty Spanish Armada, anchored off Kilrush.[73] The English annihilated the combined

Spanish and Irish armies in the south of Ireland. In England, worship of the Catholic faith was banned.[74]

Religious persecution

A 400-year period of continuous religious persecution followed. The English renewed the Anglo-Norman policy of rewarding loyal supporters, who were now of course Protestant, with large areas of Irish land. They were suspicious of all Catholics and vice versa, plus in the case of Ulster, Scottish Protestant extremists, Presbyterians.[75] The stage was set for religious conflict which has lasted until now. Following the defeat of Charles I in the English Civil War in 1649, Oliver Cromwell, a fundamentalist Calvinist Puritan, put down the rebellion in Ireland – that arose because of Charles's imposition of taxes to fund his religious aim to make all of his Empire, including Ireland, Anglican.[76] His 'Model Army', a crusading force, systematically marched from the North to the South massacring any Catholic in its path.[77]

In 1685, the then King of England Charles II died and was succeeded by his Catholic brother James II, who had spent many years in Catholic France close to the King Louis XIV. A disaster for the English ruling class, this brought hopes to Ireland of a Catholic revival. The English Parliament's solution was to ask Holland's Protestant Prince William of Orange to fight his way into England and become King. James II fled to his natural Catholic power base, Ireland, where he quickly sought to massacre as many Protestants as he could. In the north, Protestants took refuge in the walled city of Derry, to which James's forces lay siege in 1689. William landed in the north of Ireland in the following year won the ensuing 'battle of the Boyne', 50 miles north of Dublin,[78] and became King of England Scotland and Ireland in 1689.

From 1704, members of the Irish parliament had to be members of the Protestant Church of Ireland and could not be Catholics or Presbyterians. No Catholic could buy land or leave their land to a single heir, and they could not inherit land from Protestants. These measures meant that by 1778 only 5% of the land in Ireland was owned by Catholics. Both Catholics and Dissenters (Protestants who did not belong to the Church of Ireland) had to pay tithes to the Church of Ireland.[79] The 18th century witnessed dire poverty in Ireland, at its worst during the famine of 1741 that killed hundreds of thousands of people. In the 1760s and 1770s, the grievances of Irish peasants boiled over into violence, and buildings were burned and cattle maimed.[80] From 1778 the laws restricting the rights of Catholics were gradually repealed, and in 1792 Catholics could practice as lawyers and marry Protestants. From 1793 Catholics could vote but were not permitted to sit as MPs.[81]

Profits drawn from the estates in Ireland

At the same time, while Ireland was in appalling poverty, English trade with Ireland was the most important branch of English overseas trade.[82] Absentee landlords took about £800,000 per year in farm rents in the early part of the 18th century, rising to £1 million, in an economy that amounted to about just £4 million. Ireland had been completely de-forested for timber exports and a temporary iron industry during the 17th century, and the estates used for export of salt beef, pork butter and cheese for England, as well as for the Royal Navy and for the sugar colonies in the West Indies. The Bishop of Cloyne in Cork, the county that supplied the produce, is cited as wondering 'how a foreigner could possibly conceive that half the inhabitants are dying of hunger in a country so abundant in foodstuffs'.[83]

In 1801, the Act of Union making Great Britain (England and Scotland) and Ireland one entity under the name of the United Kingdom of Great Britain and Ireland was passed. Under the terms of the Union, the Irish Parliament was abolished; Ireland henceforth was entitled to one hundred MPs at Westminster and 28 life peers in the House of Lords. Four Church of Ireland bishops were also permitted to sit in the Lords by rotation.[84]

Antisemitism

Jewish people have been on the receiving end of antisemitism in what is now the UK for centuries. According to Joseph Jacobs, writing for the *Jewish Encyclopedia*, there is no evidence of Jews residing in England before the Norman Conquest of 1066. Thereafter, Jews experienced racism throughout the12th century.[85] This continued into the thirteenth with the enforcement of the wearing of a badge. As Jacobs puts it, 'During the two hundred and twenty years of their stay the position of the Jews had steadily grown worse'.[86] In 1290, under an Edict of Expulsion, the entire Jewish population of England (about 3,000 people) was expelled from the country on the orders of Edward I who was under pressure having run up large debts waging war abroad and needed to negotiate a financial settlement. He thus bartered the whole Jewish population in return for the granting by Parliament of a tax of £116,000 – the largest single tax of the Middle Ages.[87] Between then and their formal return in 1655 at the invitation of Oliver Cromwell, there is hardly any official trace of Jewish people as such on English soil.[88] Cromwell appears to have given informal permission for Jewish people to reside and trade in England on condition that they did not obtrude their worship on public notice and that they refrained from making proselytes (converts).[89]

Around the middle of the 17th century, around 300 Spanish and Portuguese Jews – settled in London, and in 1701 erected the country's first purpose-built synagogue, Bevis Marks in the City of London (later to become of further historical significance in the context of Disraeli's baptism into the Anglican Church (see chapter 1). Resettlement was not a smooth process. As Paul Vallely reports, just as the relationship between 'Jew' and 'Gentile' 'had blown hot and cold during the medieval settlement, so it was in the new dispensation'.[90] Coalitions of aristocrats, Christian zealots and business people, he explains, tried to re-expel the Jews. However, the new Jewish merchants were too useful, having brought in £1,500,000 in capital that had increased by the middle of the century to £5,000,000. Wars against the Spanish were financed by these merchants, and during the Jacobite rising of 1745 (an attempt by Charles Edward Stuart to regain the British throne for his father, James Francis Edward Stuart) they offered finance and volunteers for the corps raised to defend London. At the time, their investment provided one-twelfth of the nation's profits and one-twentieth of its foreign trade.[91] As a reward, the Jewish Naturalization Act was introduced in 1753 to allow Jews to be naturalized as British citizens. It was passed by the House of Lords, though it fell in the Commons with the Tories making great outcry against this 'abandonment of Christianity'.[92]

History and the role of the individual

This book focuses in the main on individuals, primarily Tory politicians. However, I fully agree with Marx's well-known dictum: 'Men make their own history, but they do not make it as they please; they do not make it under self-selected circumstances, but under circumstances existing already, given and transmitted from the past'.[93] In other words, individuals are not completely free agents, but are constrained by the material conditions, social relations and economic laws of their time.[94] Therefore, wherever it makes sense, in this book I refer to the socio-economic circumstances in which events occur. I write 'wherever it makes sense' because I am equally convinced that Engels was right when he wrote:

> the *ultimately* determining element in history is the production and reproduction of real life. Other than this neither Marx nor I have ever asserted. Hence if somebody twists this into saying that the economic element is the *only* determining one, he transforms that proposition into a meaningless, abstract, senseless phrase.[95]

So, I will contextualize events that happen within their economic, political and social parameters wherever this is relevant. As far as individuals being people of their time, with corresponding opinions and attitudes is concerned, while what they do and say is, of course affected and constrained by the norms and values dominant during their lives, this does not exonerate them from responsibility for their actions.

Outline of chapters

Part 1: 'Race', nation and Empire

The book is divided into four parts. The first section of chapter 1 on Benjamin Disraeli, entitled 'Historical background' begins with a brief discussion of the institutional racism that saturated the UK before and during Disraeli's lifetime. This took the form of scientific racism in the 18th and 19th centuries, spawned by imperialism. I then address colour-coded racism directed at African and Asian peoples. I turn next to two major forms of non-colour-coded racism of the time, anti-Irish racism and antisemitism. Drawing on the preceding analysis, I then look at Disraeli's worldview. After a brief look at Disraeli's early life, I go on to make a distinction between a 'two nations' and a 'class divisions and class struggle' interpretation of the 1830s and 1840s. I then discuss Disraeli's 'one nation solution' contrasting this with the Marxist alternative of class struggle and socialism. In the second section I move on to an assessment of Disraeli's political career. This is traced through his struggles to enter parliament in the 1830s, his time on the back benches and the years he held parliamentary office from 1852 to 1868, to his first and second premierships from the end of February to December 1868 and 1874 to 1881, respectively. As well as his involvement in parliamentary politics, I examine some of the key themes and messages from his novels. These also provide valuable insights into his worldview. Crucially, Disraeli's Jewish background was significant in his conception of what it means to be English. He was on the receiving end of antisemitism from his political opponents from the very beginning. Disraeli was up-front about both his own colour-coded racism towards Black people in the colonies and his non-colour-coded anti-Irish racism, writing about his fears of 'Anglo-Saxons' mingling with 'negroes and coloured populations' and once declaring Irish people to be members of a 'wild, reckless, indolent, uncertain and superstitious race'.

In the Appendix to chapter 1, address Jonathan Freedland's review of David Cesarani on Disraeli. Cesarani was an historian who specialized in Jewish history. In the review, Cesarani makes the case that in his fiction, Disraeli peddled antisemitic themes. I consider Friedland's interpretation that today Cesarani's critique amounts to assigning Disraeli the status of a 'self-hating Jew'.

I begin chapter 2 of the book by continuing my discussion of scientific racism from Social Darwinism to eugenics, the brief of the latter being to improve the genetic quality of White European 'races'. This was related to the championing of imperialism, the subject matter of the first section of the chapter. This championing of imperialism in turn needs to be understood in the context of the Long Depression of 1873–1896 and the challenge to British imperialism from other burgeoning imperial powers. This led to the 'scramble for Africa'. In the decade bridging the 19th and 20th centuries, Britain was governed by a unionist coalition of Liberals and Conservatives, headed by two Tory Prime Ministers, Robert Gascoyne-Cecil and Arthur Balfour, in power from 1895 to 1905. The country took part in the second Boer War which lasted from 1899 to 1902. That war is infamous for the establishment by the British of 'White concentration camps' in southern Africa that entailed the racialization of White Boers, and of 'Black concentration camps' for Black Africans. I then turn to an analysis of the invocation of imperialism on the campaign trail between 1880 and 1914 with respect to the Liberals and the Tories to determine which was the 'party of imperialism' of the period, and which championed imperialism more in the elections that took place. I conclude that it was the Tories. Section 1 of the chapter ends with a discussion of social imperialism, the Primrose League and the latter's connection to Disraeli.

In the second section of chapter 2 on antisemitism, I begin with the Russian pogroms that led to an increase in Jewish immigration to Britain. The upsurge in antisemitism that occurred was exacerbated by East End Tory MPs and the British Brothers League. The result was the Aliens Act of 1905, passed under the premiership of Balfour who, in the House of Commons asked why the UK should admit immigrants who are most undesirable. Twelve years later, he gave British support in a statement of support for a national home for Jewish people in Palestine (the Balfour Declaration of 1917). In 1921, he gave his reasons, namely Western civilization's inability to expel or absorb their alien and hostile presence. Balfour was not only antisemitic, but a White supremacist, having argued in 1906 against enfranchizing Black people in South Africa since White and Black 'races' are not born equal and education cannot change that.

. Part 1 of the book ends with an Appendix on the two World Wars. I discuss each in turn, giving a brief history of the causes of World War I. With respect to World War II, I look at the rise of Hitler and the development of his visceral hatred for Jewish people. I go on to address the slaughters that occurred in both wars, and conclude with a discussion of the horrors of the Holocaust as a turning point for scientific racism.

Part 2: From Empire and colonies to Powellism

Chapter 3 addresses the imperial and 'racial' politics of Winston Churchill from 1898 to 1955. The first section focuses briefly on the period between his role in the British army from 1898 to the early 1900s, fighting and killing for the Empire, and supporting and setting up concentration camps. The rest of section 1 focuses on Churchill's colonial racist views from 1920s to the end of his first premiership. Like Disraeli, Churchill believed in the superiority of the White 'race'. I give many examples of this. Churchill was also Islamophobic, although his love of Empire transcended this. I also address the issue of whether these views were merely the norm of the time. I go on to show that he was an early admirer of fascism and a late convert to anti-Nazism, though never a supporter of Nazi 'racial' policies. I then discuss Churchill and Ireland, pointing out that he was responsible for the deaths of ill-prepared Irish troops in Gallipoli, and deployed the hated Black and Tans in Ireland. I move on to a consideration of Churchill as a popular war-time leader and national hero when he led a Coalition Government between 1940 and 1945. During this time, one of his primary objectives continued to be the maintenance of the Empire. I argue that his legendary wartime resistance to the Nazis and resolute determination to defeat Hitler, as well as his wartime leadership deserve acknowledgement from anti-fascists and antiracists. However, this does not excuse his essential racism and imperialism. I conclude the first section of chapter 3 with Churchill's loss of the post-war General Election in a Labour landslide in 1945 and give some reasons for this.

In the second section of the chapter on Churchill's second premiership from 1951 to 1955, I begin by considering the Mau Mau uprising in Kenya that began in 1952 and where Churchill held overall responsibility for the forced internment of hundreds of thousands of Kenyans. I go on to look at the forms of racism that flourished during his second premiership. These included both colour-coded and non-colour-coded forms. The former was directed at post-war migrant workers from the colonies, in particular the Caribbean and the Indian sub-continent, while the latter affected both Irish migrants and the Gypsy Roma and Traveller (GRT) communities. The 1948 Nationality Act had created the status of 'Citizen of the United Kingdom and Colonies' and gave the right of all such citizens to come to the UK. For this reason, the Churchill Government was actively involved in trying to restrict immigration from the former Empire to preserve the 'racial character' of English people, with respect to ongoing racialization during this period. In my discussion, I look at employment, at housing and at unproved stereotypes of Black criminality. Turning to non-colour-coded racism, I begin by providing a brief history of the GRT communities in Britain, pointing out that after World War II, work was difficult to find in rural areas, and there was movement to the towns and cities GRT people met hostility and there began a cycle of rapid repeat evictions. I then give a brief account of Churchill's attitudes towards a Romany couple.

I conclude with a look at anti-Irish racism in this period. This consisted of negatively juxtaposing the Irish with colonial immigrants by the Tory Chief Whip. In addition, there were accounts of the appalling living conditions of some Irish people being self-inflicted. At the same time, there were also attempts by the Churchill Government to deracialize Irish people to build its case against Black immigration, by asserting that the 'problems' caused by the former were social whereas those caused by the latter were 'racial'.

The Appendix to this chapter examines the Government of Clement Attlee that presided over the foundation of the Welfare State. While this is something to be celebrated by all on the Left, it can also be seen as a compromise between capital and labour, and as deeply embedded in gender as well as in 'race' nation and Empire. The Attlee Government also witnessed the beginnings of the end of the Empire and of British colonial rule, starting with India, Burma (now Myanmar), Ceylon (now Sri Lanka) and Palestine. After Britain withdrew from Palestine, Israel declared itself an independent state. I conclude the Appendix with a discussion of the 1948 Nationality Act.

Chapter 4 opens with my continuing discussion of scientific racism, focusing here on Reginald Ruggles and his refusal to let go of his attempts to prove that 'race' was a genetic reality. In the first section of the chapter, I consider Tory politics over the period 1955 to 1963, the premierships of Anthony Eden and Harold Macmillan. Eden, who was in office from 1955 to 1957, was confronted in 1956 with the Suez crisis, often described as the 'last fling of the imperial dice', when, after Colonel Nasser nationalized the Suez Canal, Eden mounted a full-scale invasion. The canal had been a symbol of the British Empire since the 1880s. There was growing opposition in the UK and a House of Commons debate nearly erupted into fist-fights. Eventually, the solo imperial adventure came to a halt through lack of sufficient finances. After Suez, a slew of new countries that had been former colonies were created. The racialization of Irish people continued under Eden. In the 1950s and 1960s, concerns raised about pregnant women fleeing Ireland to give birth in England as well as about prostitution and Irish 'good time girls drifting to London. However, in 1955, a report stated that the Irish were not a different 'race'. This was to prioritize the exclusion of Black migrant workers in what the Cabinet Secretary explained to Eden was the 'grave problem' of 'coloured' immigrants with respect to housing shortages in respect of (again) threats to the 'English "racial" character'.

The Eden Government was followed by that of Harold Macmillan. His government oversaw the independence of both Ghana and Malay (now Malaysia). The former was due to the efforts of Marxist revolutionary, Kwame Nkrumah, while the independence of the latter was more complicated, as explained in the chapter. In 1957, Macmillan famously remarked that people 'have never had it so good'. This most definitely did not apply to racialized workers from the former Empire or pregnant women from Ireland as we saw in the chapter's first section. In 1960, Macmillan gave his famous 'Wind of Change' speech in which he said that whether we like it or not, independence of the colonies was inevitable. As a direct result, some members of the Tory Party formed the right-wing racist Conservative Monday Club that is still in existence, aligned with, though no longer endorsed by, the Party. In 1958, there were anti-Black riots in Nottingham and Notting Hill, London, with a racist murder in the latter in 1959. I go on to address non-colour-coded racism in the form of racism directed at pregnant Irish women in the UK. In 1962, the Macmillan Government passed the Commonwealth Immigrants Act that severely restricted immigration from the ex-colonies (now referred to as the Commonwealth).

The second section of chapter 4 is on the premiership of Douglas-Home and the rise of Enoch Powell and Powellism. Of the chapter titles that feature Tory politicians' names, Powell is the only one included who, much to the regret of the hard and far right inside and outside the Tory Party, never became Prime Minister. The reason he merits such a mention is due to the extent to which he wrenched the Tories rightwards in terms of racism. The brief premiership of Alec Douglas-Home lasted only 364 days. The aristocrat, Douglas-Home was described as an 'elegant anachronism'. I refer to the Cold War and to the assassination of US President John F. Kennedy and to conflict in the Commonwealth and to the independence of Northern Rhodesia (now Zambia) and Nyasaland (now Malawi). I then examine Smethwick and the General Election of 1964 where local Tory members were accused of using the slogan, 'If you want a ni**er for a neighbour, vote Liberal or Labour'. Tory candidate, Peter Griffiths refused to disown the slogan, and, bucking the national trend, won Smethwick with a swing to the Tories from Labour of 7.2%. After briefly considering Labour's response, I move on to the rise of Powellism, after Enoch Powell gave his infamous 'rivers of blood' speech. I conclude the section with the General Election of 1970, where the Tories beat the Labour Government and incoming Prime Minister Edward Heath had refused to disown Powell, an important figure in the election campaign.

Part 3: Oppression in Northern Ireland; immigration control and the birth and consolidation of Thatcher's 'racecraft'

The first section of chapter 5 addresses the policies of the Edward Heath Government in Northern Ireland. Heath's premiership coincided with the height of the Troubles in Northern Ireland, the key issue of which was whether it should remain part of the UK. I provide a brief history of 20th century developments in the six counties before discussing the Heath Government's policy of internment without trial and the 'Bloody Sunday' massacre of 1972, when British soldiers shot unarmed civilians during a protest march against internment. I move on to domestic issues, including the Industrial Relations Act of 1971 and the miners' strike of 1974. The 1971 Immigration Act was a major feature of colour-coded racism in Heath's premiership, while the Ugandan Asian crisis gave a major boost to the Conservative Monday Club and the fascist National Front.

Then in the second section of chapter 5, I look at the development of Thatcher's 'racecraft' that attempted to normalize racism, and at Thatcher and Northern Ireland. In 1978, she made her infamous 'swamping' remarks that brought racism to the heart of Tory politics. Following her victory at the 1979 General Election, Thatcher became Britain's first female Prime Minister and 'racecraft' was consolidated. I next discuss the killing of Airey Neave, Thatcher's spokesperson on Northern Ireland; the hunger strikes there, the 'Blanket' and 'Dirty' protests culminating in the death of hunger striker, Bobby Sands in 1981. The Anglo-Irish agreement followed in 1985. The chapter concludes with an exploration of the links between the British Army and the loyalist paramilitaries, a connection with which Thatcher was involved, and with Thatcher's own anti-Irish racism.

In chapter 6, I look at Thatcher, immigration control, various uprisings in the inner cities, at Imperial warfare in the South Atlantic, and at apartheid in

South Africa from 1981 to 1990. I begin with my continuing discussion of scientific racism, here on an active network of 'race scientists' in existence long after the end of World War II, and shadow financing of the pro-eugenics so-called science journal, *Mankind Quarterly*. I then discuss the 1981 British Nationality Act that attempted to promote White British citizenship. The Thatcher Government also changed the 'primary purpose rule' so that the entry clearance officer had to be sure that the primary purpose of an intended marriage of a person seeking to enter the UK was not to get British citizenship. In addition, further visa restrictions were announced for five former colonies. Between 1982 and 1986, released Cabinet Office files reveal that Thatcher was strongly opposed to admitting 'second wives' of men in polygamous marriages. The Thatcher Government also discussed moving queues of people wanting to enter the UK from Heathrow to their countries of origin. In 1980/1981, there were a series of uprisings in Bristol, London, Liverpool and Manchester, the prelude of which was the New Cross house fire, in which 13 young Black people were killed. Following the uprisings, the Scarman Report highlighted 'racial' disadvantage, inner-city decline and heavy-handed police stop-and-search operations and warned of the need for urgent action.

In the second section, I point out that Thatcher objected to the Report's criticism of the police and contemplated arming them if things got much worse. In 1985, Cherry Groce, a Black woman, was shot by the police and left paralyzed, while another Black woman, Cynthia Jarrett, died from a heart attack during a police search of her home. Following her death, there were riots in Broadwater Farm where she had lived, and a police officer, Keith Blakelock, died following massive stab wounds. I go on to discuss Thatcher's policy unit's response to Broadwater Farm. In 1982, Thatcher resurrected imperial warfare in the Falklands/Malvinas to booster her popularity. I next discuss Thatcher and apartheid South Africa, including inviting hard line South African Prime Minister and future President, P. W. Botha to Chequers. I then consider her White ethno-state solution to South Africa before addressing some other instances of Thatcher's racism that include a mix of biological and cultural racism and Germanophobia.

Chapter 6 goes on to address with some revelations of antisemitism among some Tories during Thatcher's Tory Party leadership. I continue the discussion of Thatcher's racism with her ongoing attempts along with Thatcherite academics to relentlessly pursue monocultural education, as opposed to multicultural or antiracist education. I then briefly consider future Tory Prime Minister's 'jolly' in apartheid South Africa, where the rising Tory star enjoyed an all-expenses trip while future Black President Nelson Mandela was still in prison, paid for by a firm that campaigned against the sanctions that had been imposed on that country, before concluding chapter 6 with Thatcher's leadership challenge, resignation and death. Thatcher's popularity had waned throughout 1990, in large part because of her attempt to introduce a poll tax. Her leadership was challenged by John Major who became the next Tory Prime Minister the same year. Thatcher moved to the House of Lords and died in 2013. At the time of her death, it was revealed by Australian Labor Foreign Minister Bob Carr that Thatcher had made an abashedly racist comment to him about Asian immigration.

Chapter 7 addresses John Major, multiculturalism and monoculturalism as well as a grassroots Tory backlash to ethnic diversity in the Party. The first section of the chapter begins with a discussion of Major's 'dual interventionist strategy' combining immigration controls with anti-discriminatory measures. I then pose and attempt to answer the question, was Major a multiculturalist or a monoculturalist? I move on to a discussion of the Tory backlash, when it was revealed in 1990 that 39% of Tory supporters were racist. In the same year, a Black candidate was adopted as a Tory candidate in the forthcoming 1992 General Election, after which local Tories tried unsuccessfully to stop him running. At about the same time, Churchill's grandson's paid a tribute to Enoch Powell. I then address the publication in 1994 of *The Bell Curve*, a watershed moment for 'scientific' racists, before taking a look at the Salman Rushdie controversy and Rushdie's 1988 book, *The Satanic Verses*. Many in the Muslim communities thought it blasphemous, and a number of antiracists outside those communities felt it was unnecessarily insulting and provocative, with the furore reaching its climax after Ayatollah Ruhollah Khomeini of Iran issued a fatwa in 1989, ordering Muslims to kill Rushdie. The Thatcher Government's refusal to ban *The Satanic Verses* had antagonized the Muslim communities even more. Mobilization of large sections of the communities busted the myth of the *seemingly positive* racialized attribute of a model minority that had been foisted on the Muslim communities to juxtapose them with the 'rioting' Black communities. Major's involvement in the controversy, I point out, was minimalist. The 1997 General Election resulted in a Labour landslide and the birth of 'New Labour' under Tony Blair, ending 18 years of Tory rule.

I go on in the second section of chapter 7 to discuss the Tories' opposition from 1997 to 2010. I begin with the ensuing Tory leadership of William Hague who wanted to initiate a rhetorical shift to a Tory narrative that recognized welfare and public services as well as Thatcherite free markets. Thatcher was furious and Hague too afraid to step out of line again. In 2001, Michael Heseltine, formerly Deputy Prime Minister under Major, highlighted the issue of so-called 'bogus asylum seekers'. In the same year, Tory back-bencher John Townend said the purity of Britain's Anglo-Saxon society had been undermined by mass immigration. In the 2001 General Election, the Tories made no headway. There followed a leadership battle that eventually resulted in a win for Iain Duncan Smith. I point out that it was revealed that Duncan Smith had British National Party (BNP) support that he disassociated himself from. Under his leadership, there were further revelations of BNP support for the Tories. In this chapter I also discuss the uprisings in northern England that involved violent confrontations between young British Asians and the police as well as with local fascist groups that occurred in Oldham, Burnley and Bradford in 2001. I provide an historical account of how these Northern British cities had been impacted by colonialism and its aftermath. I conclude chapter 7 with some other instances of racism in the Tory Party in the first decade of the 21st century.

Part 4: The hostile environment: genesis, incorporation and the end of free movement

I begin chapter 8 on Theresa May and the origins, launch and enactment of the 'really hostile environment' by noting that the 2010 General Election resulted in a hung parliament that led to six years of Coalition Government with Tories David Cameron and Theresa May as Prime Minister and Home Secretary, respectively. I then refer to the unleashing of austerity by Tory Chancellor George Osborne. The hostile environment was formalized when Theresa May was Home Secretary and continued up to and including the Boris Johnson Government. The first section of chapter 8 is on May's first major speech on immigration; Cameron's 'muscular liberalism' speech; more uprisings and May's response to them. May's immigration speech focused on what she perceives as the threat of immigration, and also included an offensive against the 'immigrant family'. Cameron's 'muscular liberalism' speech in 2011 was in part an attack on multiculturalism. The 2011 uprisings followed the killing by police of Mark Duggan, a Black man in his twenties. Next, I address May's reaction to the uprisings.

The next section of chapter 8 is on May's naming, creation and consolidation of the hostile environment. I begin with an interview she gave in 2012 when she announced her plan to create a 'really hostile environment' for so-called 'illegal immigrants'. Shortly after, some draconian changes in family migration rules were made. I then refer to Cameron's ridiculous attempt to portray himself as a 'saviour' of the working-class family by forcing families to make sacrifices for their ultimate well-being. The same year witnessed May's infamous 'go home or face arrest' vans sent into parts of London with high minority ethnic populations. Also in 2013, May moved the second reading of the Immigration Bill which was to become the 2014 Immigration Act. The Joint Council for the Welfare of Immigrants described the Act accurately as seeking to turn landlords, health workers and other public sector workers into 'border guards'. I then look at the 2015 General Election, where a racist consensus among the Tory and Labour Parties formed on immigration controls. When the Tories won an outright majority, Cameron said he would not serve a third term as Prime Minister and named May as a possible successor.

I move on to an analysis of May's 2015 speech to the Tory Party Conference, in essence a bid for Conservative Party leadership. In the speech, consistent with her established ideological orientation, May uses rhetoric of hate and threat, in an attempt to win over the Tory faithful, and to scupper the UK Independence Party. I go on to address the 2016 Immigration Act that amounted to 'doubling up' on 'hostile environment' policies. Following the pro-Europe Cameron's resignation in the light of a 'leave' victory in the EU referendum, May's ambition came to fruition and she became Prime Minister.

Chapter 9 deals with May's premiership and the consolidation and impact of the hostile environment, I begin Section 1 with a discussion of Prime Minister May's relationship with Donald Trump and his world view, which has been critiqued by then leading Liberal Democrat Tim Farron. I go on to address her pledge to kick out foreign students. The June 8, 2017 snap General Election was a disastrous and failed attempt to crush all opposition to her. Next, I consider May's pledge to end free movement once and for all, and her 'jump the queue' remark concerning EU nationals. I turn to an evaluation of the 2018 White Paper on Immigration that has been described as the biggest single attack on migrant rights in a generation. Its key message was that post-Brexit, everyone will need the permission of the authorities to come to the UK to work or study. The rest of the first section discusses the hostile environment's general impact with respect to health and education. I then consider its impact on asylum seekers in terms of their accommodation; right to work; detention; their rights to rehabilitation if they have been tortured; its effect on those trying to cross the English Channel; their health; and finally, what happens to asylum seekers if they are granted refugee status.

The second section of chapter 9 addresses the hostile environment's general impact on women; and those from the Windrush generation, known as the Windrush scandal. I start with a description of Yarl's Wood Detention Centre in 2019; then to the hostile environment's negative impact on domestic violence and migrant women (such violence doubling between 2012 and 2016). I then examine the Domestic Violence Bill (now an Act) of 2019 and the response to it from migrant women's advocacy groups. Moving on to the Windrush scandal, I look at the origins of the Windrush generation before considering its appalling impact on Black people resident in the UK for decades. In so doing I provide a case study of Paulette Williams. I then mention Home Secretary Sajid Javid's acknowledgement that the Home Affairs Select Committee accused the Home Office of setting up immigrants to fail. I conclude chapter 9 with the eventual fall of Theresa May.

There follows an Appendix in which I provide details of my own experiences of the hostile environment in the form of a personal testimony which started in 2011 and is ongoing. I cover such aspects as my being seriously ill in hospital in Bangkok, and the British Embassy in Phnom Penh saying they would only allow my future wife to visit me on condition that she started her visa application all over again; leaving our daughter (my stepdaughter) crying at the airport several times because she was not allowed to come with us; having to prove we were not a 'sham family'; becoming a permanent 'Skype family' in relation to our extended family in Cambodia;

the prohibitive costs and length of time for my wife and daughter to gain British citizenship.

The first section of chapter 10, which is on Boris Johnson, racism and the ongoing march of the hostile environment under his premiership, examines instances of his racism from 1999 to the present. I draw my examples mainly from newspaper articles. I go on to consider whether this colour-coded racism is derived from scientific racism, discussing his connections with Taki Theodoracopulos and Andrew Sabisky. I then note how, in February 2020, Number 10 refused to disassociate Johnson from scientific racism. I move on to discuss Johnson's denial of the existence of institutional racism following the Report of the Commission on Race and Ethnic Disparities (CRED) in July 2020. Significantly, Commission members had been recruited by Director of the Number 10 Policy Unit since 2019, Munira Mirza. Mirza used to be one of Johnson's Deputy Mayors and had cast doubt on the existence of institutional racism in the past. I next address Johnson's appointment of Katharine Birbalsingh to the Social Mobility Commission. Birbalsingh, who is critical of 'woke culture', rose to prominence at the 2010 Tory Party conference with a speech in which she claimed that the underachievement by Black pupils was due partly to the accusation of racism against teachers. I follow all this by noting that, following Johnson's General Election victory in 2019, it was revealed that he had the support of the far right in that election and conclude the chapter's first section with a discussion of the rampant Islamophobia, and indeed sexism in the Tory Party under Johnson.

In the second section of the final chapter, I examine the policies of the Johnson Government. These policies serve to exacerbate and escalate the hostile environment. I begin with a look at two new acts introduced by the Johnson Government, the Nationality and Borders Act and the Police, Crime and Courts Act (PSCS). With respect to the former, I focus on what is arguably the most draconian aspect of the Act, the widely condemned proposal to offshore asylum seekers to Rwanda. I consider human rights in Rwanda and conclude the discussion with a look at the issue of safe routes to the UK. In looking at the PSCS, I address both its attempts to criminalize effective protest and at its major project of non-colour-coded racism, directed at the GRT communities. This amounts to no less than an attempt to criminalize GRT cultures. I then look at Tory attempts to curb political topics in English schools by issuing Guidance entitled 'Political impartiality in schools'. Education unions have argued that it is likely to deter teachers from tackling the subject of racism and the legacy of Empire. I move on to discuss the Johnson Government's tardy and typically bureaucratic response to the 2022 Ukrainian refugee crisis. I conclude the book with the Grenfell Tower disaster, an unnecessary tragedy linked to classism, racism and disablism epitomizing the Tory Party's structural location in the UK and address the question, 'Who is responsible for Grenfell?' I also provide updates on the Windrush scandal, where despite promises from Home

Secretary Priti Patel, an independent progress report found that the Home Office had failed to change its culture.

In the conclusion to the book, I look back to the threads of racism, both colour-coded and non-colour-coded, that run throughout the book and provide an update on the Windrush scandal.

Note on nomenclature and use of language

I have tried to make my own language inclusive and to use appropriate contemporary nomenclature. Given that many of those quoted in the book are not of this more enlightened era, it is inevitable that many of the quotes in the book will not be inclusive and will use older forms of nomenclature that are now considered offensive. I have not made reference to these throughout the book. No doubt readers will themselves spot the use of language that is non-inclusive or inappropriate in the second decade of the 21st century.

Notes

1 My thanks to Alpesh Masuria for suggesting this formulation to me.
2 Kovel. 1970.
3 Dovidio et al. 1986.
4 E.g. Cole. 2016; Cole. 2023a.
5 Clark. 2006a, p. 8; Clark. 2006b, p. 12. This section of the chapter draws on Cole. 2018a. I deal with anti-Gypsy, Roma and Traveller racism under the main heading of 'non-colour-*coded* racism' because my focus is the UK. I am aware, of course, that many European Roma people have darker skin and that this will be a component in the racism directed at them.
6 I have previously used British xeno-racism to refer to racism directed at workers and their families from 'eastern Europe'. I have amended this from September 2021 to more accurately reflect current reality (e.g. Jones and Goodwin. 2021; Stevens. 2021). In a world-wide context, xeno-racism can be thought of as any form of racism directed at an individual or groups of people by anyone for the main reason that they are perceived to be 'foreign' and not belonging. Xeno-racism thus defined can be non-colour-coded, colour-coded or hybridist.
7 Home Office. 2021. 'How many people do we grant asylum or protection to?' November 25. https://www.gov.uk/government/statistics/immigration-statis tics-year-ending-september-2021/how-many-people-do-we-grant-asylum-or-protection-to.
8 Zaheer, Mohammad. 2021. 'Defining Islamophobia is the first step toward addressing it'.
9 Sivanandan. 2000, p. ix. For an in-depth analysis of racism in Britain, the US and Australia, see Cole. 2016. For discussions of racism in the UK that are not political party specific, see Cole. 2018a. 'Racism in the UK: continuity and change', in Cole (ed. *Education, Equality and Human Rights*, London: Routledge; and Cole. 2018b. 'Racism and Education: from Empire to May', in Cole (ed) (*ibid*).
10 It is pertinent here to make a few comments about the relationship between 'imperialism' and 'colonialism'. Asad Rehman, Executive Director of War on Want, notes in an interview early in 2021 that the literary definition of imperialism is 'extending power and control and influence – usually through colonization,

military force, or other means'. However, Rehman argues that it is also part of a longer arc of history connecting slavery, colonialism, imperialism, neoliberalism, climate violence and economic inequalities that is 'the underpinning of racialized capitalism, the sacrificing of the Global South, of its people and its resources, for the economic benefit of the Global North' (Rehman. 2021).

11 Ashe, Stephen D. and McGeever, Brendan. 2011. 'Marxism, racism and the construction of "race" as a social and political relation: an interview with Professor Robert Miles', *Ethnic and Racial Studies*, 34 (12).

12 E.g. Miles, Robert. 1982; Ashe and McGeever. 2011.

13 E.g. Cole. 2016, 2018a, 2018b, 2023a.

14 Miles in Ashe and McGeever, p. 2019.

15 Ibid.

16 Ibid. When challenged by Stephen Ashe and Brendan McGeever that, while in his 1988 article (Miles. 1988), Miles makes the point that central to historical materialism is the dialectic between theory, empirical analysis and strategies of political intervention, his definition of racism is rigidly defined in the course of his work, that he applies it to his historical analyses in quite an undialectical manner, and that his definition did not really change after 1982 (see Miles. 1982). He is asked: Shouldn't, however, the concept always 'be provisional and subject to revision in light of the interrogation of new evidence when studying racism?' Miles responds that there was a point when he became much more interested in the notion of 'racisms', but that he remains committed to the essence of his 1982 position of 'racism' singular (pp. 2019–2020). I would agree with Miles in that, while there are many *types* of racism, they all share one or more of the same fundamental features.

17 I use 'neo' – the Latin for 'new'– before 'Marxist' merely to indicate developments in Marxist theory that go beyond the issues on which Marx and Engels had a primary focus, and/or that relate to developments since Marx's and Engels' time.

18 Coates, Ta-Nehisi. 2015. *Between the World and Me*, New York: Spiegel and Grau, p. 7. In citing Coates, I am acknowledging the eloquence and veracity of his quote, not endorsing his work as a whole, nor his overall theoretical orientation. For a critique of Coates, see West. 2017. https://www.theguardian.com/comm entisfree/2017/dec/17/ta-nehisi-coates-neoliberal-black-struggle-cornel-west. For Coates' reply, see Ta-Nehisi Coates on Cornel West's One-Sided War. Coates says he is 'mystified as anybody else' over West's critique. See Sharma. 2018. https:// www.theatlantic.com/entertainment/archive/2018/01/ta-nehisi-coates-cornel-west/550727/.

19 E.g. Liu H., Prugnolle, F., Manica, A., Balloux, F. 2006. 'A geographically explicit genetic model of worldwide human-settlement history', *American Journal of Human Genetics*, 79 (2); McKie, R. 2020. 'The search for Eden: in pursuit of humanity's origins', *The Guardian,* January 5. https://www.theguardian.com/ world/2020/jan/05/the-search-for-eden-in-pursuit-of-humanitys-origins.

20 Rutherford. 2020. https://www.theguardian.com/world/2020/jan/26/fight-ra cism-using-science-race-genetics-bigotry-african-americans-sport-linnaeus.

21 Ibid.

22 Lewontin, R.C. 1972. 'The apportionment of human diversity', *Evol Biol,* 6, pp. 381–398.

23 Rose and Rose. 2005; see also Darder and Torres. 2004, pp. 1–12, 25–34.

24 The potential of genetic research in medicine was given a major boost in 2021 when 64 human genomes became the new reference for global genetic diversity. In information provided to the journal *Science Daily* by Heinrich-Heine University Duesseldorf, it is explained that this new reference data provides 'an important basis for including the full spectrum of genetic variants in so-called genome-wide association studies'. In laypersons' terms its 'aim is to estimate the

individual risk of developing certain diseases such as cancer and to understand the underlying molecular mechanisms. This, in turn, can be used as a basis for more targeted therapies and preventative medicine'; Heinrich-Heine University Dusseldorf. 2021. '64 human genomes as new reference for global genetic diversity', *Science Daily*, February 25. https://www.sciencedaily.com/releases/2021/02/210225143855.htm.

25 Rose and Rose. 2005.

26 Gellner, Ernest. 1987. *Nations and Nationalism*, Ithaca, New York: Cornell Press, p. 7.

27 Gellner, Ernest. 1964. *Thought and Change*, London: Weidenfield and Nicholson, p. 169 (emphasis added).

28 Anderson, Benedict. 1987. *Imagined Communities: Reflections on the Origin and Spread of Nationalism*, London: Verso, p. 15.

29 See, for example, Worsley, p. 1964. *The Third World,* Chicago: Chicago University Press; Hobbsbawm, Eric. 1983. *The Invention of Tradition*, Cambridge: Cambridge University Press; and, from within the postmodern paradigm, Bhabha, Homi (ed.) *Nation and Narration*, London: Routledge.

30 Miles, Robert. 1989. *Racism,* London: Routledge, p. 89.

31 Miles, Robert. 1987. 'Recent Marxist theories of nationalism and the issue of racism', *The British Journal of Sociology,* 38 (1), pp. 26–27.

32 Nairn, Tom. 1981. *The Break-Up of Britain: Crisis and Neonationalism*, London: Verso, p. 347; also Tom Nairn on Sottish independence: https://www.opendemocracy.net/en/scotland-and-europe-iris-murdoch-and-antonio-gramsci-interview/; see also https://socialistworker.co.uk/art/51842/Imperialism+and+national+liberation.

33 Kohn, Hans. 1955. *Nationalism: Its Meaning and History*, Princetown: Van Nostrand, p. 11.

34 Nairn, Tom. p. 347.

35 Miles, Robert. 1987.

36 Miles. 1989, p. 90.

37 Anderson, p. 87.

38 In this book, the colour-coded racism that looms large is that directed at Black and (South) Asian peoples. Anti-Chinese racism is also a significant form of racism: for examples, see chapter 1; see also Cole. 2016, pp. 29–42.

39 Of these, the overwhelming majority of the White population were congregated in a few main centres: approx. 47 million in the British Islands, and the bulk of the remainder in Canada, Australia and South Africa. The greater part of the people of colour were ruled in practice by a few thousand White people who formed part of the official machinery of the British State. Jackson, T. A. 1922. 'The British Empire', The Communist Party of Great Britain. Marxists Internet Archive. 2007. https://www.marxists.org/archive/jackson-ta/pamphlets/british_empire.htm.

40 BBC World Service, undated.

41 Cited in BBC World Service, undated.

42 BBC World Service, undated.

43 Beckles, Hilary. 2017. 'On Barbados, the first Black slave society', *Black Perspectives,* April 8. https://www.aaihs.org/on-barbados-the-first-black-slave-society/.

44 Harlow, V. T. 1926. *The History of Barbados, 1625–1685*, Oxford: Clarendon Press, p. 21, cited in Miles, Robert. 1987. *Capitalism and Unfree Labour: Anomaly or Necessity*, London: Tavistock, p. 76.

45 Miles. 1987, p. 76.

46 Ibid.

47 Ibid., pp. 79–81.

48 Ibid., p. 81; see also Goveia. 1965, pp. 152–202, 320.

49 Miles. 1987, p. 81; see also Patterson. 1967, pp. 80–83; Dunn. 1973, pp. 239–242.
50 Ringrose. 2021.
51 Sherwood, Marika. Undated. 'Murder in Notting Hill', *Our Migration Story*. https://www.ourmigrationstory.org.uk/oms/murder-in-notting-hill.
52 Ibid.
53 Momodu, Samuel. 2021. 'Tacky's War (1760–1761)', *BlackPast*, December 3. https://www.blackpast.org/global-african-history/tackys-war-1760-1761/.
54 KESSE. 2020. 'Takyi, the Ghanaian king who led a slave rebellion in Jamaica', *Ghanaian Museum*, April 6. https://ghanaianmuseum.com/the-story-of-takyi-the-ghanaian-king-who-led-a-slave-rebellion-in-jamaica-in-1760/.
55 Momodu. 2021.
56 Ibid.
57 The Editors of Encyclopaedia Britannica. Undated. 'Slave rebellions'. https://www.britannica.com/topic/slave-rebellions.
58 https://www.britannica.com/topic/Slavery-Abolition-Act.
59 Momudu. 2021.
60 Rehman. 2021.
61 Ringrose. 2021.
62 Rehman. 2021.
63 Manjapra, Kris. 2018. 'When will Britain face up to its crimes against humanity?'.
64 Rehman. 2021.
65 The Editors of Encyclopaedia Britannica. Undated. 'East India Company'. https://www.britannica.com/topic/East-India-Company.
66 Ibid.
67 Cited in Oppenheim. 2017.
68 Rehman. 2021. The case for an ecosocialist world that is antiracist and feminist and fully inclusive is made in Cole. 2021.
69 Chakra, Hayden. 2018. 'Norman invasion of Ireland', May 16, https://about-history.com/norman-invasion-of-ireland/.
70 Campbell, Kenneth L. 2013. *Ireland's History: Prehistory to the Present*, A & C Black, p. 59.
71 History of England. Undated. 'Ireland – the first colony'. https://www.historyofengland.net/british-empire/ireland-the-first-colony.
72 Ibid.
73 Dorney, John. 2015. 'Ireland and the Spanish Armada 1588'. *The Irish Story*, August 19. https://www.theirishstory.com/2015/08/19/ireland-and-the-spanish-armada-1588/#.YK-r9flKhGN.
74 History of England. Undated. 'Ireland – the first colony'. https://www.historyofengland.net/british-empire/ireland-the-first-colony.
75 Ibid.
76 Ibid.
77 Dorney. 2015.
78 Ibid.
79 Lambert, Tim. 2019. 'Ireland in the 18th century', *Local Histories*. http://www.localhistories.org/ireland18th.html.
80 Ibid.
81 Ibid.
82 Braudel, Fernand. 1992. *The Perspective of the World,* vol III of *Civilization and Capitalism*, University of California Press.
83 O'Grada, Cormac. 1995. *Ireland: A New Economic History 1780–1939*; or see: Braudel, F. 1979; see: Plumb, J.H. 1973. *England in the 18th Century*: 'The Irish Empire'.

84 UK Parliament, Erskine. May 2022. 'Peers of Ireland'. https://erskinemay.parliament. uk/section/4515/peers-of-ireland/.
85 Jacobs, Joseph. 1906. 'England'. https://www.jewishencyclopedia.com/articles/ 5764-england.
86 Ibid.
87 Byrne, Philippa. 'Why were the Jews expelled from England in 1290?'. https:// www.history.ox.ac.uk/why-were-the-jews-expelled-from-england-in-1290.
88 Jacobs, Joseph. 1906.
89 Ibid.
90 Vallely, Paul. 2009. 'A short history of Anglo-Jewry: The Jews in Britain, 1656– 2006', *The Independent,* April 1. https://www.independent.co.uk/news/uk/this- britain/short-history-anglo-jewry-jews-britain-1656-2006-6098403.html.
91 Ibid.
92 Ibid.
93 Marx, Karl. 1852. *The Eighteenth Brumaire of Louis Bonaparte.* Marx uses sexist language that is typical of the period in which he wrote (see my 'Note on nomenclature and use of language' at the end of this Introduction).
Marx is often accused of neglecting 'race' and racism. Since, as the reader will have become aware, I draw liberally on Marx and Engels, and on Marxist and neo-Marxist analysis, I feel it is incumbent on me to make some comments on Marx and racism. I acknowledge that in Marx's works there is a minimal presence of racism. However, I want to make the case that Marx was aware of both colour-coded and non-colour-coded racism. With respect to the former, as a leading European abolitionist, he was London correspondent for the radical anti-slavery *New York Daily Tribune* (Laskey, J. 2003. *Marx and Engels on the Civil War.* https://www.acwrt.org.uk/post/marx-engels-on-the-civil-war). During the US Civil War, Marx urged and organized English textile workers to support the blockade against the Confederacy, even though it was not in their immediate economic interests to do so and, as a result of the cut off of imported cotton, led to massive layoffs (Marx. 1862, p. 153; see also Cole. 2017. *Critical Race Theory and Education: A Marxist Response, revised 2nd edition,* New York: Palgrave Macmillan, pp. 129–130). At the same meeting another motion, expressing 'the warmest sympathy with the strivings of the Abolitionists for a final solution to the slave question' was also adopted unanimously. The final motion, also unanimous, was to forward to the US Government a copy of the resolutions 'as an expression of the feelings and opinions of the working class of England'. Marx took this strong abolitionist position because, as he wrote to Engels on the eve of the Civil War, the uprisings of slaves in the US and of serfs in Russia were the 'two most important events' taking place in the world. (Marx. 1860, p. 5). Marx expresses his views on slavery succinctly in *Capital Vol. 1:* 'In the United States of North America, every independent movement of the workers was paralysed as long as slavery disfigured part of the Republic. Labour cannot emancipate itself in the white skin where in the black it is branded' (Marx. 1887 [1965], p. 301).

As far as non-colour-coded racism is concerned, earlier in this Introduction I discussed Marx's writings on Ireland, how he was aware of the manifestations of English rule there, as well as the key importance of Ireland in the British Empire. Marx was also conscious of the racism involved in the 'divide-and-rule tactics' of the British state with respect to English workers in England. Given that, as noted earlier, the word 'racism' was not recognized until 1902, he used terms like 'prejudice', 'hatred' and 'evil' instead. In an 1870 letter, Marx compares anti-Irish racism with one form of anti-Black racism in the United States:

Every industrial and commercial centre in England now possesses a working class divided into two *hostile* camps, English proletarians and Irish proletarians. The ordinary English worker hates the Irish worker as a competitor who lowers his standard of life. In relation to the Irish worker he regards himself as a member of the *ruling* nation and consequently he becomes a tool of the English aristocrats and capitalists against Ireland, thus strengthening their domination *over himself*. He cherishes religious, social, and national prejudices against the Irish worker. His attitude towards him is much the same as that of the 'poor whites' to the Negroes in the former slave states of the U.S.A. (Letters of Karl Marx. 1870). Marx to Sigfrid Meyer and August Vogt in New York. Source: Karl Marx and Friedrich Engels. 1975. *Selected correspondence,* Progress Publishers, pp. 220–224; Written: April 9, 1870. https://www.marxists.org/archive/marx/works/1870/letters/70_04_09.htm.

He goes on to note how the ideological state apparatus (here the media and religion) worked to uphold this hostility: 'This is artificially kept alive and intensified by the press, the pulpit, the comic papers, in short, by all the means at the disposal of the ruling classes' (ibid.). Marx concludes: '*This antagonism* is the secret of the *impotence of the English working class*, despite its organisation. It is the secret by which the capitalist class maintains its power. And the latter is quite aware of this' (ibid.). This is not to deny that Marx held racist views or made racist comments. Diane Paul (1981) has examined a number of Marx's (and Engel's) public and private comments on 'race' from a historian's point of view. Paul Warmington (personal correspondence, 2008, slightly adapted) has summarized some worthwhile points from Diane Paul's paper:

- Marx's common everyday racism, particularly in private correspondence, was precisely that: dull common everyday racism – in the sense that it was unexceptional in a 19th century European context, in which reified bio-cultural understandings of 'race' and belief in racial hierarchies were orthodox, 'everyday' beliefs. Thus, Marx's racism cannot be denied but it can hardly be viewed as an integral element of a thought out 'Marxist' political position (this may be less true of his antisemitic comments), e.g. Marx wrote in common everyday racist terms in private, but not only publicly opposed the south in the US Civil War, as we have seen, but also, at times, took a public pro-Irish standpoint.
- We should not try to transform Marx into 20th/21st century progressivism on every issue.
- Most importantly, the key issue for Marxists is not to deny or to agonize over Marx's 19th century racism but to recognize that Marxism is a 'living philosophy', continually being adapted and adapting itself 'by means of thousands of new efforts' (Sartre. 1960).

I will follow up on Paul Warmington's word-of-warning on Marx about antisemitism. In 1844, Marx's *On the Jewish Question* was published. Here is not the place to enter the fiercely contested debate as to what extent this demonstrates that Marx was antisemitic. Like Disraeli he was of Jewish origin himself (see the Appendix to chapter 1 of this book for similar accusations of Disraeli). Those who wish to follow up this dispute will find a plethora of References on the Internet. Suffice it to say here that, while Marx was clearly in favour of human emancipation, his line of argument reflects the commonplace thinking of his era (Sacks, Jonathan. 1997. *The Politics of Hope*, London: Jonathan Cape, pp. 98–108) where reasoning as represented in the above quote was 'normal'. Moreover, like 'racism', 'antisemitism' had yet to enter the lexicon.

94 Booth, Adam. 2019. 'The individual and the Marxist view of history'.
95 Engels, Friedrich. 1890. 'Engels to J. Bloch in Königsberg'.

Part 1
'Race', nation and Empire

1 One 'race', one nation, one Empire: 19th century racism in the life and times of Benjamin Disraeli (1804–1881)

SECTION 1: HISTORICAL BACKGROUND

Scientific racism: from the 18th to the 19th century

To make sense of the specific manifestations of racism[1] that follow in this chapter, it is necessary to contextualize them within the nature of institutional racism that characterized Disraeli's lifespan. Rutherford[2] has pointed out that the invention of 'race' occurred earlier, in the 18th century in 'the age of empires and plunder' when men (overwhelmingly) of the emerging discipline of science 'classified the people of the world, mostly from their armchairs'. Such classifications were derived from the accounts of travellers from the western world as they encountered multiple populations in various parts of the world and heralded the birth of scientific racism where such differentiations between humankind were based primarily on skin colour, were hierarchical and had White Europeans at the top. The first to create a 'racial taxonomy' in that imperial century was Scandinavian Carolus Linnaeus, who in *Systema Naturae* published in 1735, claimed that different 'races' were actually different species of living things. In addition to biology, Linnaeus ascribed 'moral and intellectual peculiarities'. At one extreme there was Homo Europaeus, 'of fair complexion, sanguine temperament and becoming form... [who was] of gentle manners, acute in judgment... [and] governed by fixed laws'. At the other was Homo Afer deemed to be of 'black complexion, phlegmatic temperament ... crafty, indolent ... governed in their actions by caprice'[3] and cunning, lazy and careless.[4]

The 19th century witnessed the embedding of scientific racism as 'common sense'.[5] According to leading sociologist of 'race relations', the late Michael Banton, 'By 1850 ... a significant section of the English upper class subscribed to a rudimentary racial philosophy of history'.[6]

Colour-coded racism

Whereas Africans were designated 'savages', Hindus were 'soft' and 'effete'.[7] The concept of scientific racism with respect to anti-Black

DOI: 10.4324/9781003198673-3

racism was articulated by President of the Anthropological Society of London James Hunt in the 1863–1864 publication, *On the Negro's place in nature*:

> There is as good a reason for classifying the Negro as a distinct species from the European, as there is for making the ass a distinct species from the zebra and if we take intelligence into consideration there is a far greater difference between the Negro and the European than between the gorilla and the chimpanzee. The analogies are more numerous between the Negro and the ape than between the European and the ape. The Negro is inferior intellectually to the European. The Negro becomes more humanized when in his natural subordination to the European than under any other circumstances. The Negro race can only be humanized and civilized by Europeans. European civilization is not suited to the Negro's requirements and character.[8]

Britain's colonial subjects in India were also considered fundamentally different to Europeans. The 19th century British explorer Richard Burton wrote as follows:

> of all Orientals, the most antipathetical companion to an Englishman is, I believe, an East-Indian. Like the fox in the fable, fulsomely flattering at first, he gradually becomes easily friendly, disagreeably familiar, offensively rude, which ends by rousing the 'spirit of the British lion'... the 'imbelles Indi' [weak Indians] are still, with few exceptions, a cowardly and slavish people, who would raise themselves by depreciating those superior to them in the scale of creation.[9]

The 19th century, historian John Haller informs us, also witnessed the development by Europeans (and Americans) of 'specially designed measuring devices' to determine 'skull shape, language, hair pile, skin color, temperament, and political belief', the 'facial angle', being the most extensively used.[10] A purely statistical and experimental endeavour detached from any concerns with humanitarian issues, this was undertaken to make *a priori* judgments and to 'confirm' that the 'Negro, Indian, Malay, or Mongol' were below the Caucasian in the scale of civilization to rationalize both the colonial policies on which the development of capitalism rested, and the separation of the 'races'. 'It was', Haller concludes, 'a circular proof seeking to justify what nearly everyone already accepted as true'.[11] By the end of the century, as discussed in chapter 2, the ideology of the 'inferiority' of the colonial subjects and the consequent 'superiority' of the British 'race' was available to all as an integral element of popular culture.

Non-colour-coded racism

Anti-Irish racism

The racialization of Irish people and racist stereotypes about them 'conveniently supported British rule in Ireland',[12] part of the United Kingdom of Great Britain and Ireland since 1801 (where it was to remain until 1922). Such processes are reflective of more embedded and pervasive processes of 'othering' in that the experience of Irish people in Britain has been framed by the 'construction of the Irish (Catholic) as a historically significant Other of the English/British (Protestant)'.[13]

Theories of 'race' were being advanced both by the pseudoscientific community and in the popular daily and periodical press, with the 'science' of phrenology purporting to demonstrate that the structure of the skull, in particular the jaw formation and facial angles, disclosed the position of various 'races' on the evolutionary scale.[14] It also claimed to be able to predict traits or intelligence. The Irish were described as an example of a lower evolutionary form, closer to apes than their 'superiors', the Anglo-Saxon 'race'. The cartoons in *Punch,* the British weekly magazine of humour and satire established in 1841, portrayed the Irish as having bestial, ape-like or demonic features, and especially the Irish political radical 'was invariably given a long or prognathous jaw, the stigmata to the phrenologists of a lower evolutionary order, degeneracy, or criminality', closer to Africans than Anglo-Saxons. It was even hinted that the Irish might be the elusive missing link![15]

The 'ape-like' Celt became something of a malevolent cliche of Victorian racism, both in Ireland and in Britain. Thus, prominent Victorian and fervent Anglo-Saxonist[16] Charles Kingsley could write in 1860:

> I am haunted by the human chimpanzees I saw [in Ireland] along that hundred miles of horrible country. If they were black, one would not feel it so much, but their skins, except where tanned by exposure, are as white as ours.[17]

For much of the 19th century, the only factories in Ireland were the textile mills of the north, the Guinness brewery, and the Jacob's biscuit factory. And for much of the period, as before, the Irish economy provided cheap raw materials to the far more industrialized British economy. Ireland underwent major highs and lows economically during the 19th century from economic booms during the Napoleonic Wars (1803–1815), followed by a depression (1815–1821). Wheat and other grain prices fell by half in Ireland, and together with continued population growth, landlords converted cropland into rangeland with tenant famer eviction legislation in 1816, which led to a greater subdivision of remaining land plots and increasingly less efficient and profitable subsistence farms.[18]

Marx described the period in Ireland between 1801 and 1846 as the 'clearing of the estates'[19] by the system of 'rack-renting' (increasing rent to force the tenant to spend more time working to pay the rent and less time on improving standards of living) and 'middlemen' (sub-letting to force the tenant into smaller and smaller plots of land without reductions in rent), thus ensuring absolutely more labour was devoted to supporting the land-lord system.[20]

Between 1815 and 1845, 1.5 million Irish people emigrated, mainly to Britain (c.0.5 million) and to North America (c.1 million).[21] Marx describes how this decline in population in Ireland meant greater profits for the farmers there in volume I of Capital:

> The depopulation of Ireland has thrown much of the land out of cul-tivation, has greatly diminished the produce of the soil, and, in spite of the greater area devoted to cattle breeding, has brought about, in some of its branches, an absolute diminution, in others, an advance scarcely worthy of mention, and constantly interrupted by retrogressions. Nevertheless, with the fall in numbers of the population, rents and farmers' profits rose, although the latter not as steadily as the former. The reason of this is easily comprehensible. On the one hand, with the throwing of small holdings into large ones, and the change of arable into pasture land, a larger part of the whole produce was transformed into surplus-produce. The surplus-produce increased, although the total produce, of which it formed a fraction, decreased. On the other hand, the money value of this surplus-produce increased yet more rapidly than its mass, in consequence of the rise in the English market price of meat, wool, &c., during the last 20, and especially during the last 10, years.[22]

Depopulation continued with the potato blight (1846–1847) (a disease that made the potatoes impossible to eat) that resulted in starvation and a mass exodus. Common estimates are that more than one million people died and almost the same again emigrated to England. Marx argued that 'rack-renting and middlemen', together with the famine and exodus and new British parliamentary enactments, such as the repeal of the Corn Laws (1846)[23] (that abolished the monopoly position held by Ireland of supplying corn to Britain) and the Poor Law and Encumbered Estates Court (1849) (that facilitated the sale of Irish estates where owners were unable to meet their obligations because of the famine), ushered in a new phase in the coloni-zation of Ireland that merged landed-estate and political strategies into one overriding aim.[24] In Marx's words, '*Clearing of the Estates of Ireland* is now the only purpose of English rule in Ireland'.[25]

Marx believed that the Irish struggle for independence was pivotal at the time, not just for 'feelings of humanity', but because he believed that to 'accelerate the social development in Europe' you must attack England via

Ireland, 'her weakest point', because with 'Ireland lost, the British "Empire" is gone', and given that 'England is the metropolis of landlordism and capitalism all over the world', 'the class war in England, till now somnolent and chronic, will assume acute forms'.[26] Some 50 years after Marx wrote this about Irish independence in March 1870, partition (dividing Ireland into two sections – the 26 and Six Counties) was imposed by the British under the Government of Ireland Act of 1920. The consent of the Irish people was never sought nor freely given. Between the years 1916 and 1921, Irish nationalists waged a combined political and military campaign against British occupation.[27] As this book goes to press (May 2022) the Six Counties remain under the control of the British state in Westminster.

Antisemitism

The 19th century witnessed an ongoing and much contested struggle for Jewish emancipation. Until 1830, Jews were not able to legally carry on retail trade in the City of London, and not until 1833 could Jewish men become barristers, nor could they vote until 1835.[28] As late as 1857, the Tory leader in the House of Lords, Lord Derby, stated: 'what the Jews were in Egypt, they are in England ... though among us they are not with us'.[29] The following year, however, the Jews Relief Act of 1858 allowed Jewish men to become MPs. In 1890 all restrictions for every position in the British Empire were removed and open to every British subject without distinction of creed, except for the monarch, the Lord High Chancellor and Lord Lieutenant of Ireland.

All this limited progress did not, of course, halt the ongoing undercurrent of the long-existing tropes and stereotypes dating back to the Middle Ages,[30] nor did the pro-British industrial capitalist stance taken by Jewish capitalists,[31] Disraeli among them, prevent him, as we shall see, from being on the receiving end of antisemitism. It is important to note here that, although not a component of this book, in Disraeli's time which was the high era of Empire, slavery and 'common sense' scientific racism, an antiracist movement, existed in Britain.[32]

Disraeli's worldview

Both colour-coded and non-colour-coded racism, central features of 19th century Britain, were key components of Disraeli's worldview: the former in his steadfast conviction that the 'great Caucasian race' was the superior one; the latter in his contempt for the Irish. For Disraeli, it was the Semitic or 'Arabian' branch of the Caucasian 'race' that was superior to the other branches, and among Semites it was the Jews at the pinnacle of the hierarchy. His response was to write the Jews into the heart of English/British culture by embracing what he conceived of as an oriental lifestyle and an inclusive 'race' categorization – 'Caucasian'. As a result of his father having him converted to Christianity in the Church of England at the age of his bar mitzvah – partly reflecting a hope of his son's social and political advancement in Britain but also the elder Disraeli's rejection of Judaism[33] – Disraeli was portrayed by his opponents as a 'secret Jew', whose 'politics might be dangerous to the English and to Englishness'.[34] It should be pointed out here that Disraeli insisted throughout his life that he was a hybrid character – both English and Jewish.[35] As such, in the words of Benjamin Jaffe, 'Disraeli was not considered by Christians as a Christian; nor by the Jews as a Jew'.[36] Disraeli's explicit colonial colour-coded racism and his equally obvious non-colour-coded anti-Irish racism co-existed with his belief in the superiority of the 'Caucasian race' that had Jews at the top of the pyramid.

Disraeli's early life

Benjamin Disraeli was born on Dec. 21, 1804, in London to a middle-class Jewish family. His mother, Maria Basevi's family had fled from Spain after 1492, settling first in Italy and then at the end of the 17th century in England. Disraeli's maternal grandfather was president of the Jewish Board of Deputies in London. His father, Isaac D'Israeli, was a Sephardic Jew whose own father, also called Benjamin, had come from Cento near Ferrara, Italy. Benjamin Disraeli went first to a Nonconformist (a Protestant who does not 'conform' to the established Church of England) school and then to a Unitarian (centred on a belief that the Christian God is one entity rather than three as in 'father, son and holy ghost') school[37]. Disraeli was baptized into the Anglican faith at 12 at the behest of his father following a dispute with the Bevis Marks synagogue.[38] At 18, he left school and studied for a year at home in his father's library of 25,000 books (Isaac, who was a famous literary figure best known for *The Curiosities of Literature* published in 1791,[39] has been described as a 'free-thinking gentleman-scholar'[40]).

The first years of Disraeli's adult life were anything but uneventful and included being articled to a firm of solicitors; speculating recklessly in shares and getting into serious debt (from which he did not recover until past middle age); launching a failed newspaper; publishing his first novel *Vivian Grey* in four volumes in 1826–1827; and suffering a nervous breakdown.[41] A major influence on his subsequent life was his grand tour of the Holy Land from 1830 to 1831. On arriving in Jerusalem, Disraeli wrote home, 'I was thunderstruck. I saw before me apparently a gorgeous city'.[42] As Tory historian Robert Blake explains:

> It was one of the most memorable of all Disraeli's experiences. His mystical belief in the mysterious heritage of this race, his romantic love of high-sounding historic names, his exotic imagination, all were heightened by the week which he passed in Jerusalem'.[43]

Disraeli's declaration, 'the most delightful in all my travels', and eloquent passages in his novels testify to the permanent impression which it left upon him.[44] Elsewhere, Blake writes, 'It is not fanciful to see in his few days there the origins of his intense interest in what he called "the race" – an interest which had been lacking hitherto in the rather indifferent atmosphere of his upbringing'.[45] Disraeli was 'intrigued by the great mosques and the imperious power of Islam … and he was sympathetically aware of the depressed and poverty stricken condition of the masses of the Jewish community', but, because of 'personal parallels however far-fetched', that which interested him most were 'the successful Jews who mysteriously rose up in this alien world through its interstices and became rich and powerful and grand – the Rothschild equivalents in the Near East'.[46]

'Two Nations' or class divisions and class struggle in the 1830s and 1840s

Simone Beate Borgstede paints a vivid picture of the state of the class divide in Britain in the 1830s and the beginnings of the 1840s. Agricultural workers burnt corn ricks and destroyed machines in the Swing Riots of 1830, a widespread uprising by agricultural workers in southern and eastern England, protesting agricultural mechanization and harsh working conditions.[47] The Reform Act of 1832 gave middle-class men the vote but not women in general or the working class *per se*. The abolition of slavery in 1833 and of the apprenticeship system in 1838 had opponents as well as supporters. After much campaigning, the Factory Act of 1833 limited the work of children from 12 or more hours to 8 in the textile industry.[48] In 1834, however, the Whig Government of Earl Grey, acting on behalf of the newly enfranchised bourgeoisie, and the aristocracy, abolished the Speenhamland system that guaranteed a minimum existence income and established the New Poor Law (the Poor Law Amendment Act) with its workhouses. The intention was to make the experience of being in a workhouse worse than that of the poorest labourers outside the workhouse.[49] It had the effect, in Karl Polyani's words, of reducing working people to labour as a 'free' commodity.[50]

Since 1780, workers had been organizing themselves in unions and taking part in self-help associations (whereby the working class formally or informally provided for their own welfare rather than [or as well as] acting as supplicants to external agencies, whether Poor Law officials or charity committees[51]), mechanics institutes (educational establishments formed to provide adult education, particularly technical to the working class), libraries and savings banks.[52]

Chartism became a strong political and predominantly working-class movement, emerging in 1836, it was most active between 1838 and 1848. Its People's Charter listed demands: a vote for all men over 21; secret ballots; no property qualification to become an MP; payment for MPs; and electoral districts of equal size[53]. Despite extensive support for the Charter, it was not taken seriously, Disraeli notwithstanding, by politicians.[54] On November 4, 1839, 5,000 men marched into Newport, Monmouthshire, and tried to take control of the town. They gathered outside a hotel, where the local authorities were temporarily holding a number of 'potential troublemakers'. Troops protecting the hotel opened fire, killing at least 22 people, and brought the uprising to an abrupt end.[55] In 1842, riots in the countryside were also violently suppressed and Chartists imprisoned as agitators.[56] In 1844, the *Times* warned its readers: 'War to the mansion, peace to the cottage – is a watchword of terror which may yet ring through the land. Let the wealthy beware!'[57]

The condition of the working class in England, particularly working class children, often led to comparisons with slavery, and attentions was drawn to the hypocrisy of certain middle-class abolitionists who opposed factory legislation and supported the New Poor Law.[58] By contrast, as Borgstede points out, following Marcus Wood,[59] the antisemitic radical William Cobbett as 'the most popular journalist between 1800 and 1830' wrote of the abolitionist plot to distract the nation's attention from the horrible living conditions of the poor in England.[60] Finally, it is important to add that fear of working class revolt was compounded by the fact that Chartism was a multicultural movement. During the trial, on a trumped-up charge of planning to plant a bomb, of Chartist leader William Cuffay who was English of African origin, prominent parts of the media including *The Times* deprecated Chartism as the 'black man and his party'. It went on to refer to Cuffay as 'half a ni**er', adding that 'Some of the others are Irishmen. We doubt if there are half-a-dozen Englishmen in the whole lot'.[61]

Disraeli's solution

Disraeli's 'one nation'/'Young England' values come through in some of his novels, particularly in the second of his Young England trilogy, *Sybil or The Two Nations* (1845). As Andrzej Diniejko argues, that book 'reveals not only the distressing view of both urban and rural poverty, but his views on how to eliminate the "two nation" divide and create a "one nation" which would be led by the reformed Conservatives'.[62] The novel concludes with a clarion call to the youth of England to take up the initiative:

> That we may live to see England once more possess a free Monarchy, and a privileged and prosperous People, is my prayer; that these great consequences can only be brought about by the energy and devotion of our Youth is my persuasion. We live in an age when to be young and to be indifferent can be no longer synonymous. We must prepare for the coming hour. The claims of the Future are represented by suffering millions; and the Youth of a Nation are the trustees of Posterity.
>
> (p. 422)[63]

For Disraeli 'one nation' would be best served by the 'formation of a national party' that he declared in an 1840 letter that, since he first entered public life eight years previous, he had 'worked for no other object and no other end'.[64] This, he believed, given that their 'interests are identical' and 'united they form the nation', would help to create a 'union between the Conservative party and the Radical masses' which was 'the only means by which we can preserve the Empire'.[65] Disraeli articulated the connections that were in his mind between the working class (at least the majority were not revolutionary) particularly clearly in a speech some 30 years later that became known as the Crystal Palace speech of 1872. In it, Disraeli reflected on the Reform Acts of 1832 and 1867 (see later in this chapter), the latter of which terminated any remaining dissent and was founded on:

> a confidence that the great body of the people of this country were Conservative' ... in its purest and loftiest sense. I mean that the people of England, and especially the working classes of England, are proud of belonging to a great country, and wish to maintain its greatness – that they are proud of belonging to an Imperial country, and are resolved to maintain, if they can, the empire of England – that they believe, on the whole, that the greatness and the empire of England are to be attributed to the ancient institutions of this country... I say with confidence that the great body of the working class of England utterly repudiate [Jacobinism] ...They are English to the core. They repudiate cosmopolitan principles. They adhere to national principles. They are for maintaining the greatness of the kingdom and the empire, and they are proud of being subjects of our Sovereign and members of such an Empire. Well, then, as regards the political institutions of this country, the maintenance of which is one of the chief tenets of the Tory party, so far as I can read public opinion, the feeling of the nation is in accordance with the Tory party.[66]

As proclaimed in *Tancred* (1847) the third and final of the Young England trilogy, 'All is race; there is no other truth',[67] the exclusive role of the next generation of 'the English', therefore, was to forge the union between the Conservative Party, the working class and the Empire. Disraeli believed that the 'great difference between nationality and race' is that the former 'is the principle of political independence' while the latter 'is the principle of physical analogy'[68] and 'implies difference' and 'difference implies superiority'.

Here we have a concrete illustration of the ways, as discussed in the Introduction to this book, in which 'race', 'nation' and Empire merge, and recalls Miles' enunciation that English nationalism encapsulates racism and how 'race' and 'nation' merge as in a kaleidoscope.[69] It further connects to Empire and the English *right* to possess one.[70] For Disraeli, this has direct links to social class and 'one nation Conservatism': 'the working class ... are English to the core'.

A Marxist alternative

Published in German about the same time as *Sybil* was Friedrich Engels' *Die Lage der arbeitenden Klasse in England* (*The Condition of the Working Class in England*, published in English in 1885). The message could hardly be more different. In direct contrast to any notion of forging an alliance between the landed aristocracy and the working class against the new industrialists, of any pretence of one 'nation' led by the reformed Conservatives, no identical interests to enable unity between a reformed 'one nation' Tory Party and the Radical masses to preserve the Empire. As Engels puts it in that book in the 'Dedication':

> Having, at the same time, ample opportunity to watch the middle-classes, your opponents, I soon came to the conclusion that you are right, perfectly right in expecting no support whatever from them. Their interest is diametrically opposed to yours, though they always will try to maintain the contrary and to make you believe in their most hearty sympathy with your fates. Their doings give them the lie. I hope to have collected more than sufficient evidence of the fact, that – be their words what they please – the middle-classes intend in reality nothing else but to enrich themselves by your labour while they can sell its produce, and to abandon you to starvation as soon as they cannot make a profit by this indirect trade in human flesh.[71]

Engels also addresses the fantasies of the Young England group directly, referring to Disraeli by name, and contrasting them with the Chartists:

> Tories, who have recently constituted themselves 'Young England', among whom ... [is] ... Disraeli... The hope of 'Young England' is a restoration of the old 'merry England' with its brilliant features and its romantic feudalism. This object is of course unattainable and ridiculous, a satire upon all historic development.[72]

Elsewhere Engels spelt out his solution to the contradictions of capitalism, exalting scientific socialism, as opposed to utopian socialism.[73] In stark contrast to nationalism and 'racial superiority' as proposed by Disraeli, and to a union between the Conservative Party, the working class and the Empire, Engels advocated the end of the nation state and the building of international socialism.

This famous passage from *Socialism: Utopian and Scientific* merits quoting at length:

> **Proletarian Revolution** – Solution of the contradictions. The proletariat seizes the public power, and by means of this transforms the socialized means of production, slipping from the hands of the

bourgeoisie, into public property. By this act, the proletariat frees the means of production from the character of capital they have thus far borne, and gives their socialized character complete freedom to work itself out. Socialized production upon a predetermined plan becomes henceforth possible. The development of production makes the existence of different classes of society thenceforth an anachronism. In proportion as anarchy in social production vanishes, the political authority of the State dies out. Man, at last the master of his own form of social organization, becomes at the same time the lord over Nature, his own master – free. To accomplish this act of universal emancipation is the historical mission of the modern proletariat. To thoroughly comprehend the historical conditions and thus the very nature of this act, to impart to the now oppressed proletarian class a full knowledge of the conditions and of the meaning of the momentous act it is called upon to accomplish, this is the task of the theoretical expression of the proletarian movement, scientific Socialism.[74]

SECTION 2: PARLIAMENTARY CAREER

Disraeli struggles to enter Parliament (1831–1837)

Having decided to enter politics in 1831, still in his twenties, Disraeli sought a parliamentary seat in Buckinghamshire, where his family had settled. As an independent radical, he lost High Wycombe twice in 1832 and once in 1835.[75] In between these attempts to enter Parliament, his novel *Alroy* was published in 1833. In it, the hero's attempt to liberate Jews from their Muslim overlords is described by Patrick Brantlinger as 'couched in natio-nalistic terms that foreshadow Zionism'[76]:

> Empires and dynasties flourish and pass away; the proud metropolis becomes a solitude, the conquering kingdom even a desert; but Israel still remains, still a descendant of the most ancient kings breathed amid these royal ruins, and still the eternal sun could never rise without gilding the towers of living Jerusalem. A word, a deed, a single day, a single man, and we might be a nation.[77]

In his 1835 High Wycombe defeat, Disraeli had been supplied with £500 from Tory funds, the first time that Tories had used money is this way. Blake has suggested that this marks the start of the modern Conservative Party. After his defeat, Disraeli concentrated over the next few months on producing Tory propaganda.[78] Realizing that he must attach himself to a political party, also in 1835 he fought a Taunton by-election, this time as the official Conservative candidate and was defeated yet again. In that year, he had a public argument with his old friend, Daniel O'Connell.[79] Disraeli's change in political affiliation had upset the Radicals (a left-wing alliance that included MPs, one of which was O'Connell), and O'Connell launched a bitter attack, calling him 'a vile creature', 'a living lie', 'a miscreant' and 'a reptile'.[80] He declared that he had himself once been asked to support Disraeli and that the latter, by turning his coat and becoming a Conservative, showed that he possessed 'perfidy, selfishness, depravity and want of principle'.[81] He went on:

> His name shows that he is of Jewish origin. I do not use it as a term of reproach; there are many most respectable Jews. But there are as in every other people some of the lowest and most disgusting grade of moral turpitude; and of those I look upon Mr. Disraeli as the worst ... the lineal descendant of the blasphemous robber who ended his career beside the Founder of the Christian Faith.[82]

While O'Connell's addition of 'as in every other people' was an attempt to distance himself from racism and antisemitism (although he would not have had either word in his mind,[83] and to be fair to O'Connell, he had a good record on human rights).[84] He could have made the same point, of course, without reference to 'origins'. Disraeli spoke of O'Connell in terms that unambiguously epitomized non-colour-coded racism from one racialized White person to another, 'Yes, I am a Jew and when the ancestors of the right honourable gentleman were brutal savages in an unknown island, mine were priests in the temple of Solomon'.[85] The following year, he followed this up:

> The Irish hate our order, our civilization, our enterprising industry, our pure religion. This wild, reckless, indolent, uncertain and superstitious race have no sympathy with the English character. Their ideal of human felicity is an alternation of clannish broils and coarse idolatry. Their history describes an unbroken circle of bigotry and blood.[86]

Disraeli responded by sending an offensive open letter to O'Connell, followed up by a second letter to his son that challenged the son to a duel.[87] As a result of this Disraeli was arrested, bound over to keep the peace.[88] This dispute helped to promote Disraeli's political career, and he was offered the safe Tory seat of Maidstone in the 1837 General Election.

Disraeli on the back benches (1837–1851)

In Maidstone, speaking on the hustings as a Tory candidate for the upcoming 1837 General Election, Disraeli was attacked as 'Shylock' and offered ham and bacon on poles, while his family name was ridiculed.

Blake notes that while Disraeli was successful in the election, his first speech in the House of Commons was a failure, with his elaborate metaphors, affected mannerisms, and foppish dress leading to his being shouted down. Refusing to be silenced, he concluded, defiantly and prophetically, 'I will sit down now, but the time will come when you will hear me'.[89] After this unpromising start he kept a low profile and was a loyal supporter of party leader Sir Robert Peel, under the premiership of the Whig Viscount Melbourne.

The 1841 election saw Disraeli nominated for and winning a seat for Shrewsbury. A big swing from the Whigs (a centre-left party later to merge with the Liberal Party) to the Conservatives propelled Peel to the premiership.[90] While Disraeli was disappointed at remining on the back benches, he remained loyal to Peel. However, unlike most Tories, he was antagonistic towards the rising capitalist class, arguing for an alliance between the landed aristocracy and the working class against the burgeoning power of the merchants and the new industrialists in the middle class.[91] In the early 1840s, Disraeli became associated with the Young England group. Louis Cazamian sums up its 'one nation' philosophy:

> There were three principal aspects of Young England: the landed gentry were outraged by the encroachments of industrial radicalism; romantic young men were filled with imaginative enthusiasm for the majestic monarchy and beautiful religion of the past; and there was a feeling of simple, humane sympathy for the poor in town and country.[92]

Disraeli's philo-semitism (in 20th and 21st century usage, in that it went beyond Biblical notions of a 'race' chosen by God, this would more appropriately be termed Jewish supremacism), was 'certainly one of the most consistent, clearly articulated features of his ideas throughout his career' according to Brantlinger.[93] It was revealed clearly in his first of his Young England trilogy, *Coningsby* (1844, p. 242) in which the narrator declares that all Europeans, along with all Semitic 'races' belong to the vast Caucasian 'race' but the Jewish sage in the novel, Sidonia 'could claim a distinction which the Saxon and the Greek, and the rest of the Caucasian nations, have forfeited. The Hebrew is an unmixed race ... the aristocracy of Nature'.[94] Sidonia expands, 'the Jews ... are essentially Tories. Toryism, indeed, is but copied from the mighty prototype which has fashioned Europe', the Bible[95]. He also says:

> The fact is, you cannot destroy a pure race of the Caucasian organisation. It is a physiological fact ... The mixed persecuting races disappear; the pure persecuted race remains ... If the great Caucasian race is superior to all the others, and if the 'Semitic' or 'Arabian' branch of that race is superior to the other branches, and if the Jewish race is the highest and purist of the Semites, then it follows that Jews are the most 'aristocratic race'.[96]

Brantlinger writes, 'Disraeli often insisted that God had chosen to reveal His truths in just one part of the world and just one race: the Arabian race, to which the Hebrews belonged'.[97] Brantlinger goes on to point out that, for Disraeli, Christianity is simply, 'the consummation of Judaism, a fulfillment accomplished by a superior minority of Jews'.

As a new MP in 1837, cognisant of the antisemitism of most of his fellow Tories, 'with the utmost sangfroid',[98] Disraeli had voted against the Jewish Disabilities Bill (a bill proposing an end to the bar on Jewish members of Parliament). However on the way to leadership of the Tory Party in 1847, Disraeli voted for it, not on the grounds of religious liberty, the basis of Jewish claims, but from the standpoint of a Christian.[99] Using the opportunity to expound his well-known views on Judaism, developed in his books over many years, he began by stating that he was not going to make the case for Jewish emancipation by 'urging their particular merits' and then proceeded to list them: 'persons of peaceable and moral character'; 'distinguished for great talent and intellectual capacity'; and for 'their sagacity and their intelligence' in the 'pursuits of literature and science'.[100] He went on to appeal to 'the principles of Christianity', to love and charity, to love thy neighbour, that 'all men are brethren' to the 'family of man' and to 'one universal brotherhood'.[101] He then repeated his belief that, unlike the 'Pagan' and the 'Mahomedan', the Jews are the authors of the Christian religion. Disraeli concluded with references to 'the brilliant annals of past Jewish magnificence' and 'the beautiful and devotional poetry of the Jew' before ending with a declaration that he was not animated by 'political justice, expediency, and truth' but on 'religious principle'.[102]

Disraeli gains parliamentary office (1852–1868)

In 1852 Disraeli gained parliamentary office, becoming Leader of the House and Chancellor of the Exchequer in Lord Derby's minority government. His 'one nation' budget lowering taxes on malt and tea was designed to appeal to the working class and to make the Tories more attractive to them. However, the Derby Government was defeated over the budget, although the real underlying issue was the repeal of the Corn Laws which Parliament had passed in June 1846, and Derby resigned to be replaced by the Earl of Aberdeen. Aberdeen headed a Coalition Government of Peelites (supporters of Peel and free trade who had broken away from the Tory Party over the repeal of the Corn Laws), Whigs, Radicals and the centre-left Irish Independent Party in December 1852 with his political opponent (with whom he also shared a 'mutual loathing'),[103] William Ewart Gladstone as Chancellor.[104] Now on the Opposition benches but remaining Conservative leader in the Commons, Disraeli opposed the government on all major issues.[105] Disraeli was to become Chancellor two further times (1858–1859 and 1866–1868).

In the same year as the new Government, his political biography of Bentinck, *Lord George Bentinck: A Political History,* was published, partly about his and Bentinck's opposition to the Corn Laws. In it Disraeli continued the theme of Jewish superiority and linked this to anti-Black racism in the Empire and to slavery. He stated the 'first preachers of the gospel were Jews, and none else. No one has ever been permitted to write under the inspiration of the Holy Spirit except a Jew'.[106] He also opined that Jews 'are a living and the most striking evidence of the falsity of that pernicious doctrine of modern times, the natural equality of man'.[107]

Disraeli was worried the principle 'would deteriorate the great races and destroy all the genius of the world'.[108] What would be the consequence on the great Anglo-Saxon republic', he continued, 'were its citizens to secede from their sound principle of reserve, and mingle with their negro and coloured populations?'... 'In the course of time', he concluded, 'they would become so deteriorated that their states would probably be reconquered and regained by the aborigines whom they have expelled and who would then be their superiors'.[109] It should be noted that Disraeli did not hold the inhabitants of India in such contempt. In 1874 he castigated his officers thus: 'Nothing is more disgusting, than the habit of our officers speaking always of the inhabitants of India − many of them descended from the great races − as "ni**ers". It is ignorant, & brutal, − & surely most mischievous'.[110]

In *Lord George Bentinck*, he also lamented the abolition of slavery:

> The movement of the middle classes for the abolition of slavery was virtuous, but it was not wise. It was an ignorant movement. It showed a want of knowledge both of the laws of commerce and the stipulations of treaties; and it has alike ruined the colonies and aggravated the slave trade...The history of the abolition of slavery by the English and its consequences, would be a narrative of ignorance, injustice, blundering, waste, and havoc, not easily paralleled in the history of mankind.[111]

Disraeli, of course, grew up in the context of the 'normality' of the slave trade and would have been about four years old in 1808, when, as noted in the Introduction to this book, the number of enslaved Africans transported across the Atlantic by Britain since 1640 reached 3.1 million.

Since the late 16th and the 17th centuries, European trading companies in India had been competing aggressively with each other, but by the last quarter of the 18th century the English ones had outdone the others and established themselves as the dominant power in India.[112] In 1857, north-central India exploded as Hindu, Muslim and Sikh sepoys (Indian soldiers serving under British imperial rule) mutinied against their officers when ordered to violate religious taboos by using cartridges greased with the fat of 'unclean' animals.[113] Disraeli's response was as follows: 'The decline and fall of empires are not affairs of greased cartridges. Such results are occasioned by adequate causes, and by an accumulation of adequate causes'.[114] Albert Pionke explains the 'numerous "adequate causes" already extant before the Enfield rifle ever arrived on the scene', but not presumably what Disraeli had in mind(!) giving a concise snapshot of the nature of British imperialism in India:

> The Bengal Army was overwhelmingly composed of high-caste Brahmins, many of whom felt contempt not just for the Sikhs and Muslims enlisted with them, but also for their British officers. Both groups were viewed as inferior according to India's complex caste system, and the British officers had the added disadvantages of haughty aloofness from their men and relative ignorance of the native languages. In addition, ... British laws had voided the traditional practice of sati (1829) and made it possible to convert from Hinduism to Christianity without losing inheritance rights to ancestral property (1850). Missionary activity was also spreading throughout British India, much of it apparently receiving official support from proselytizing army officers and the new Governor General, Lord Canning's, connection with conversion societies. Finally, the rapid spread of English education, railroads and telegraphs threatened to enforce cultural homogenization, as did the fact that all legal proceedings were conducted in English.[115]

Taking the British by surprise, the 'mutineers' seized control of a large part of northern India and installed a new Mughal emperor in Delhi. The British fought back hard and the rebels were tied 'across the mouths of loaded cannon and executed by being blasting into fragments'.[116] As Marxist historian Neil Faulkner concludes: 'It was an anti-imperialist struggle in which Indians of different ethnic and religious backgrounds fought side-by-side – the antithesis of the divide and rule fostered by the British'.[117]

After this so-called 'Indian Mutiny', the government of India was transferred from the East India Company to the Crown with the position of Governor General upgraded to Viceroy.[118] This marked the beginning of the British raj, the period of direct British rule over the Indian subcontinent from 1858 until the independence of India and Pakistan in 1947. The British government took possession of the company's assets and imposed direct rule.[119]

Disraeli's belief in the superiority of the English 'race' (albeit with the Jews at the top of the Caucasian pyramid) did not only apply to the peoples of the Empire, but also pertained to some of the 'more excitable races' in mainland Europe whose 'excitement' was less worthy than the English. In a speech in 1862, he opined:

> The English people are, without exception, the most enthusiastic people in the world. There are more excitable races. The French, the Italians, are much more excitable; but for deep and fervid feeling, there is no race in the world at all equal to the English. And what is the subject, of all others, upon which the English people have been most enthusiastic? Religion. The notes on the gamut of their feeling are few,

but they are deep. Industry, Liberty, Religion, form the solemn scale. Industry, Liberty, Religion – that *is* the history of England.[120]

The Second Reform Act, passed in 1867, increased the number of men who could vote in elections, expanding upon the First Reform Act of 1832 by extending the vote to all householders and lodgers in boroughs who paid rent of £10 a year or more, thus doubling those eligible to vote from one to two million men. As noted earlier in this chapter, the 1867 legislation was influenced by the campaign of the Chartist movement, who were dissatisfied by the limited enfranchisement granted in the 1832 Act. Driven by the working class, the movement had petitioned for universal male suffrage.[121] The Act was unpopular with the right wing of the Conservative Party, and Disraeli was accused of 'a political betrayal which has no parallel in our Parliamentary annals'.[122] According to Christopher Hibbert, he gained wide acclaim and became a hero to his party for the 'marvellous parliamentary skill' with which he helped get the Act through the Commons.[123] Peter Dorey has added, then Disraeli argued that the party needed to pursue social reforms in order to achieve electoral success, in his belief that one-nation Conservatism would both improve the conditions of the poor and portray the Liberal Party as selfish individualists.[124]

Disraeli's first premiership (February–December 1868)

Becoming incapacitated with gout, Derby asked Disraeli to lead the Tories in the new session of Parliament in February 1868. Although a caretaker in a minority administration that lasted less than a year, he was able to enact quite a few 'one nation' domestic measures. These included ending public executions with the *Capital Punishment Amendment Act* (1868) and the *Election Petitions and Corrupt Practices at Elections Act* of 1868 that did much to end electoral bribery.[125] In addition, Disraeli's first government authorized an early version of nationalization, with *The Telegraph Act* (1868) that gave the Post Office the power to buy up by the telegraph companies.[126]

With respect to foreign policy, there was an exaltation of imperialism. Disraeli sent Sir Robert Napier on a successful expedition to Abyssinia against the forces of Tewodros II of Ethiopia. When the result got back that Napier had defeated Tewodros's forces and released the British envoy and consul from prison,[127] in moving a motion of thanks to Napier in Parliament, Disraeli paid a tribute to the man who led his army with 'the elephants of Asia, bearing the artillery of Europe, over African passes which might have startled the trapper and appalled the hunter of the Alps', thus 'the standard of St. George was hoisted on the mountains of Rasselas'.[128] Later he added, 'It was a noble feat of arms, and highly raised our prestige in the East'.[129]

Disraeli's government lasted until December, at which time a general election returned the Liberals with a majority of 110.[130] Having time to spare he wrote a new novel, *Lothair*, that was published in 1970 and deals with the comparative merits of Catholicism and Anglicanism as heirs of Judaism, and in reflecting the anti-Catholicism that was popular in Britain at the time, it became a best seller.[131]

Disraeli's second premiership (1874–1881)

Social reform

In 1874, Disraeli became Prime Minister for the second time, allowing him to oversee a larger amount of 'one nation' social legislation, than his short first premiership: the 1875 Climbing Boys Act reinforced the ban on employing juvenile chimney sweeps; the 1875 Artisans and Labourers' Dwelling Act allowed local authorities to destroy slums, though this was voluntary, and provided housing for the poor. In a speech the year before, Disraeli proclaimed:

> I have always felt that the best security for civilisation is the dwelling, and that upon properly appointed and becoming dwellings depends more than anything else the improvement of mankind. Such dwellings are the nursery of all domestic virtues, and without a becoming home the exercise of those virtues is impossible.[132]

In 1875 the Public Health Act provided sanitation such as running water and refuse disposal.[133]

Disraeli's government also passed legislation which dealt with labour relations: there was a Factory Act in 1874 that raised the minimum working age to nine; limited the working day for women and young people to 10 hours in the textile industry, to be between 6 am and 6 pm; and reduced the working week to 56½ hours[134]; the Employers and Workmen Act (1875) made breaches of contract by a worker a civil rather than a criminal offence and therefore made workers and employers equal before the law regarding labour contracts;[135] and the Conspiracy and Protection of Property Act (1875) that amended the law of conspiracy in favour of trade unions and legalized peaceful picketing.[136] As if to underline his 'one nation' philosophy, Disraeli wrote to a friend that these Acts 'will gain and retain for the Conservatives the lasting affection of the working classes'.[137] The Trade Union Manual of Labour Laws called these two Acts 'the charter of the social and industrial freedom of the working classes', and in autumn 1875 the Labour Congress and one of the few labour members of Parliament, Alexander Macdonald, formally thanked the government for passing these measures.[138] Macdonald told his constituents in 1879: 'The Conservative party have done more for the working classes in five years than the Liberals have in fifty'.[139]

Foreign policy

The second premiership also gave Disraeli the opportunity to consolidate Britain's imperial portfolio. In 1875, Britain purchased controlling shares in the Suez Canal company, a very popular measure. Historian Richard Atkins has argued that ownership of the canal marked a new policy, that of an extended British commitment in Egypt, together with ensuring the imperial lifeline to India and Australia would not be controlled by France.[140] Disraeli's words in summing up the purchase reflect his mindset when it comes to nation and Empire: 'You have it, Madam'.[141]

Disraeli who, as we shall see at the beginning of the next chapter, had a very close relationship with the Queen and made her Empress of India on May 1, 1876 under the Royal Titles Act. For Disraeli, this had the advantage of letting the world know that Britain would hold onto India: 'It is only by the amplification of titles that you can often touch and satisfy the imagination of nations; and that is an element which Governments must not despise'.[142]

At about the same time, the Ottoman Empire was in military and economic decline, and Disraeli believed that the survival of that Empire was a barrier to Russian advance in the Mediterranean, a move that was feared as a threat to the British Empire in India and was strongly of the opinion that British interests in the East were as important as any other power's, declaring in November 1876 that if war were forced on Britain by Russia, Britain 'would not terminate till right was done'.[143] When Russia advanced into Adrianople (now Edirne), in January 1878, Disraeli ordered the Royal Navy into the Dardanelles enroute for Constantinople, with Parliament approving £6m for military purposes. A week later, Russia granted the Ottomans an armistice.[144] It was rumoured a week after that that the Russians were in Constantinople, part of the fleet was sent there 'for the protection of life and property'.[145] In response the Russians advanced their army and an outbreak of war fever occurred in Britain and a popular music hall song gave rise to the word 'jingoism' to describe belligerent and aggressive patriotism. Russia agreed not to occupy Gallipoli and Britain agreed not to land any soldiers in Turkey.[146]

Dissatisfied with the subsequent Russian Ottoman peace treaty, Disraeli attended the Congress of Berlin that met for a month in 1878, as one of the British envoys. Described as 'the lion of the Congress' and the centre of attention.[147] Russia conceded to Disraeli's demands and the Treaty of Berlin was signed at the Congress. During the Congress Cyprus was ceded to Britain from the Ottoman Empire in return for a defensive alliance (the Cyprus Convention). This was announced at the conference as 'a sensational stroke' for Disraeli to have achieved.[148]

Back in England, a huge crowd gathered from Charing Cross to Downing Street, singing patriotic songs and from the window of 10 Downing Street, Disraeli announced that he had brought 'Peace with Honour'.[149] In a speech to the House of Lords, Disraeli stated that the Congress and the Cyprus Convention had averted the threat to the British Empire was averted the threat to European independence eliminated,[150] by protecting the route to India: 'In taking Cyprus the movement is not Mediterranean, it is Indian'.[151]

In the same year as Berlin, there was a war in Afghanistan, in which the British had an easy victory, leaving a mission in Kabul.[152] Finally, with respect to Disraeli's imperial manoeuvrings, in 1879 a Zulu army ambushed and destroyed a British encampment in South Africa, and over a thousand British and colonial troops were killed. Disraeli sent a force to the region and the Zulus were defeated.[153]

Later that year, Victoria made Disraeli the Earl of Beaconsfield, after which he governed from the House of Lords.[154] The 1880 election was lost to the Liberals who were to remain in power until 1885. Disraeli threw himself into the job of serving in opposition to Gladstone, his long-time enemy, and was active until a month before his death from bronchitis in April 1881.[155]

Appendix

Jonathan Freedlands' review of David Cesarani on Benjamin Disraeli

In this chapter, I have presented Disraeli as believing in the superiority of the Jewish 'race' (as well as being anti-Black and anti-Irish). Some space deserves to be given therefore to the views of David Cesarani, the late British historian who specialized in Jewish history. Referring to historian David Cesarani's 2016 book, *Disraeli: the novel politician* (London: Yale University Press), *The Guardian* columnist Jonathan Freedland argues that in the book, Cesarani's comments about Disraeli would today 'be used to assail Disraeli as a self-hating Jew',[156] in that he 'peddled antisemitic ideas in his fiction'.

According to Freedland, Disraeli's book, *Henrietta Temple,* 'features Levison, a vulgar moneylender, in gaudy clothes and with gold rings on his fingers, armed with' in Cesarani's words, 'every stereotypical characteristic of the Victorian stage Jew, including a lisp'.[157] Disraeli's 'philo-semitism', according to Cesarani, is a 'meretricious' wish 'to ingratiate himself with those Jews, such as the Rothschild family, who might help his career or his constantly perilous finances' that also explains his 'erratic and often muted support for the fiercely contested legislation that finally allowed Jews political rights'.[158] Freedland goes on to point out that 'Disraeli's myth-making about Jews was to have a lasting and toxic legacy'. In *Coningsby,* Disraeli 'introduces a Jewish wise man, Sidonia, who sketches out a philosophy in which a hierarchy of race is the organising principle of human affairs and in which Jews, operating through "subterranean agencies", are the secret power behind world events'.[159] Cesarani writes that 'no one had so far conjured up the image of the Jews as a potent global force'[160] and, according to Cesarani, Disraeli was the first to shape what would become the enduringly poisonous myth of a world Jewish conspiracy.[161] Freedland concludes by pointing out that the 1920 English version of *The Protocols of the Elders of Zion* cited Disraeli's character Sidonia. *The Protocols of the Elders of Zion* has been described by the United States Holocaust Memorial Museum, Washington, DC, as 'the most notorious and widely distributed antisemitic publication of modern times' whose 'lies about Jews, which have been repeatedly discredited, continue to circulate today, especially on the internet. The individuals and groups who have used the *Protocols* are all linked by a common purpose: to spread hatred of Jews'.[162] In 1941, 'as the final solution was under way, Hitler quoted "The British Jew, Lord Disraeli" approvingly'.[163]

Elsewhere Cesarani casts doubt on Disraeli's Jewish authenticity, noting, 'Benjamin Disraeli ... grew up in a typical Jewish milieu. Typical, that is, of Sephardi Jewish immigrants to London and their descendants'.[164] He goes to describe his forebears as 'port Jews who had migrated along trade routes from northern Italy to London' who 'were only loosely attached to Judaism anyway'.[165] Cesarani states that as a young man, 'Disraeli showed little interest in Jews or Judaism' and suggests that his 'trip to Jerusalem [discussed in chapter 1] was an impulsive diversion', while although 'his novel Alroy depicts a Jewish hero leading a revolt against oppression, it ends in defeat'[166]. 'The descriptions of Jewish life', Cesarani asserts, 'are absurd'.[167]

He acknowledges that in some books, 'Disraeli vaunted the role of Jews in history, mocked assimilation, and condemned anti-Jewish prejudice'.[168] This is the reason, Cesarani argues, 'Jews are apt to cite the relevant passages from such works as Coningsby and Lord George Bentinck'.[169] 'Rather less attention', though, 'is given to the fundamental contribution he made to modern literary antisemitism'.[170] Cesarani cites *Henrietta Temple* where there is 'a Jewish money-lender, Mr Levison, who vies with Fagin as a stereotypical Jew': '"Times is very bad", Levison tells his client. "Me and my pardner don't do annuities now". But he knows another financier and is "in with him wery deep."'[171]

Cesarani also quotes 'Sidonia, Coningsby's enigmatic mentor: "He was lord and master of the money-markets of the world, and of course virtually lord and master of everything else."'[172] 'In depicting Sidonia as a denizen of the "subterranean agencies" that "exercise so great an influence on public events"', Cesarani concludes, 'Disraeli sketched the first draft of the Jewish world-conspiracy theory' (see early in chapter 1 in for a brief discussion of *Sidonia*).

Returning to Disraeli's life, Cesarani says, 'He avoided Jewish London and was silent on Jewish issues. In December 1837, soon after his election, Disraeli kept his head down when MPs debated whether Sir Moses Montefiore or any other professing Jew could take office as a sheriff of

London'.[173] According to Cesarani, Disraeli 'said nothing about the blood libel charge against a dozen Syrian Jews, the Damascus Affair, that triggered protests across the Jewish world in 1840'.[174] When he was finally, grudgingly obliged to advocate the right of Jews to sit in Parliament', Cesarani goes on, 'he conceded half the case that their antagonists made'.[175]

Unlike Cesarani, I have not undertaken a 'close reading … [of Disraeli's] prodigious fictional output' of some 15 novels,[176] so I cannot comment authoritatively on the content of Disraeli's novels, nor on Cesarani's thesis, except to say that in my reading of and around Disraeli for this chapter, the thesis of a 'self-hating Jewish antisemite' does not really ring true to me.

Notes

1   According to Gene Demby, the first recorded utterance in the *Oxford English Dictionary* of the word *racism,* however, was by Brigadier Richard Henry Pratt (1840–1924) in 1902 in a speech decrying it. Pratt's rejection of racism, however, did not extend to Native Americans, underlining the restriction of the concept at the time to the Black/White binary. Pratt is best known for coining the phrase, 'Kill the Indian … save the man'; Demby. 2014. 'The ugly, fascinating history of the word "racism"', *Codeswitch,* January 6. https://www.npr.org/sections/codes witch/2014/01/05/260006815/the-ugly-fascinating-history-of-the-word-racism? t=1614602816933.

2   Rutherford, A. 2020. https://www.theguardian.com/world/2020/jan/26/fight-racism-using-science-race-genetics-bigotry-african-americans-sport-linnaeus; see also Rutherford. 2020. *How to argue with a racist,* W&N.

3   Chuhan. http://revealinghistories.org.uk/legacies-stereotypes-racism-and-the-civil-rights-movement/articles/the-development-of-racist-theories-and-ideas. html.

4   Haller, John S. 1970. 'The species problem: nineteenth-century concepts of racial inferiority in the origin of man', *American Anthropologist*, 72 (6), pp. 1319–1329. https://www.jstor.org/stable/672850.

5   'Common sense' is generally used to denote a down-to-earth 'good sense' and is thought to represent the distilled truths of centuries of practical experience, so that to say that an idea or practice is 'only common sense' is to claim precedence over the arguments of Left intellectuals and, in effect, to foreclose discussion (Lawrence. 1982, p. 48). As Diana Coben (2002, p. 285) has noted, Italian neo-Marxist Antonio Gramsci's distinction between good sense and common sense 'has been revealed as multifaceted and complex'. For common sense is not a single unique conception, identical in time and space. It is the 'folklore' of philosophy, and, like folklore, it takes countless different forms. Its most fundamental characteristic is that it is fragmentary, incoherent and inconsequential (Gramsci. 1978, p. 419). Good sense, on the other hand, for Gramsci is exemplified by Marxism. As Coben (1999, p. 206) has argued, good sense, for Gramsci, 'may be created out of common sense through an educative Marxist politics'. Gramsci believed that "everyone" is a philosopher, and that it is not a question of introducing from scratch a scientific form of thought into everyone's individual life, but of renovating and making "critical" an already existing activity' (Gramsci. 1978, pp. 330–331). Gramsci also believed that '[a]ll men are intellectuals … but not all men have in society the

function of intellectuals' (ibid., p. 9). Extending these insights to the whole of humankind (not just men!) is an essential component of Marxism.

6   Banton, Michael. 1977. *The Idea of Race,* London: Tavistock, p. 25.

7   Kiernan, V. G. 1969. *The Lords of Humankind: European Attitudes to the Outside World in the Imperial Age,* London: Weidenfield and Nicolson, p. 218.

8   Hunt, James. 1863–64. 'On the Negro's place in nature', *Memoirs of the Anthropological Society of London 1,* pp. 51–52, cited in Lorimer, Douglas A. 1978. *Colour, Class and the Victorians: English Attitudes to the Negro in the Mid-nineteenth Century.* Leicester University Press, pp. 138–139.

9   Burton, Richard Francis. 1855–56. 'Life works gallery: more personal narrative of a pilgrimage to Al-Madinah and Meccah: The Nile Steamboat – The "Little Asthmatic"'. Burtoniana.org. https://burtoniana.org/books/1855-Narrative%20of%20a%20Pilgrimage%20to%20Mecca%20and%20Medinah/1893-Memorial%20Edition/HTML/chapter3.html.

10 Haller, pp. 42–43.

11 Ibid, pp. 50–51.

12 Wohl. 1990. 'Racism and anti-Irish prejudice in Victorian England'.

13 Garrett. 2002a, p. 483; see also Hickman. 1997, pp. 290–291; and Swift and Gilley. 1999. This is not, however, to suggest that anti-Irish racism has only been directed at Roman Catholic migrants from Ireland (Garrett. 2002a, p. 489; see also Hickman and Walter. 1995; and Walter. 2001, pp. 164–165).

14 Wohl. 1990.

15 Ibid. The term 'missing link' was influenced by 18th century Enlightenment thinkers who thought of humans as links in 'the Great Chain of Being', a hierarchical structure of all matter and life. Influenced by Aristotle's theory of higher and lower animals, the Great Chain of Being was created during the Medieval period in Europe and was strongly influenced by religious thought (Reader. 2011).

16 Frankel, Robert. 2007. *Observing America: The Commentary of British Visitors to the United States, 1890–1950 (Studies in American Thought and Culture),* University of Wisconsin Press, p. 54.

17 Cited in Davis, W. 2007. 'When English eyes are smiling', *New York Times,* March 11. https://www.nytimes.com/2007/03/11/opinion/11davis-sub.html?_r=0.

18 Blessing, Patrick J. 1980. 'Irish'. In Thernstrom, S., Orlov, A., Handlin, O. (eds.). *Harvard Encyclopedia of American Ethnic Groups.* Cambridge, MA: Harvard University Press. p. 529. Jones, Maldwyn A. 1980. 'Scotch-Irish'. In Thernstrom, Orlov, Handlin. *Harvard Encyclopedia of American Ethnic Groups,* p. 904.

19 'Letter from Marx to Engels'. In Manchester. Abstract. London, November 30, 1867. Marx/Engels, *Selected Correspondence,* Moscow: Progress Publishers, 1955; transcribed and HTML markup by Tim Delaney, 1999. https://www.marxists.org/archive/marx/works/1867/letters/67_11_30-abs.htm.

20 Slater, E. and McDonough, T. 1994. 'Bulwark of landlordism and capitalism: the dynamics of feudalism in nineteenth-century Ireland', *Research in Political Economy, 14.*

21 Hearth Tax Rolls, cited in toppr. Undated. 'How many Irish people emigrated between 1815 and 1845?'. Toppr.com. https://www.toppr.com/ask/question/how-many-irish-people-emigrated-between-1815-and-1845/.

22 Marx, Karl. 1887. *Capital Vol. 1.* https://www.marxists.org/archive/marx/works/download/pdf/Capital-Volume-I.pdf.

23 The Corn Laws protected British agriculture by imposing tariffs on imported grain. Tory Prime Minister Robert Peel wanted their repeal on the grounds that they were holding back British commerce. For many backbenchers, however, from the shires, if they were removed not just agriculture but other

traditional conservative institutions, such as the aristocracy and the Church of England would be threatened. As Peel recorded, 'How can those who spend their time in hunting and shooting and eating and drinking know what were the motives of those who … have access to the best information?' (Bates, Stephen. 2013. 'Two sides of the same party', *History Today*, 63, March 3. http s://www.historytoday.com/archive/two-sides-same-party.   The opponents were led in the Commons by Disraeli and George Bentinck, Disraeli voted against their repeal on the grounds, as he later told fellow MP William Miles, a fellow protectionist, that he did it 'because, from my earliest years, my sympathies had been with the landed interest of England' ('Benjamin Disraeli, letter to Sir William Miles', June 11, 1860, cited in Simkin, John. 2020a. 'Benjamin Disraeli', *Spartacus Educational*. January. https://spartacus-educationa l.com/PRdisraeli.htm.) Disraeli's letter to William Miles is consistent with one half of his 'one nation'/ 'young England' ideological stance that naively aims to combine the preservation of the landed gentry and all that goes with it (the monarchy and the traditional church) with sympathy for the poor against the encroachments of industrial capitalism and accompanying worker militancy (see chapter 1 for a discussion and for the Marxist alternative).

24   Slater, Eamonn and McDonough, Terrence. 2008. 'Marx on nineteenth-century colonial Ireland: analysing colonialism as a dynamic social process', *Irish Historical Studies*, 36 (142), p. 168.
25   'Letter from Marx to Engels' in Manchester, Abstract, London, November 30, 1867 in Marx/Engels, *Selected Correspondence*, Moscow: Progress Publishers, 1955; Transcribed and HTML markup by Tim Delaney, 1999. https://www. marxists.org/archive/marx/works/1867/letters/67_11_30-abs.htm.
26   Karl Marx to Paul and Laura Lafargue, March 1870, in Marx and Engels. 1987. *Ireland and the Irish Question*, Moscow: Progress Publishers, p. 404.
27   Sinn Féin. Undated. 'History of the Conflict'. https://www.sinnfein.ie/ history.
28   Finestein, Israel. 1959. 'Anglo-Jewish opinion during the struggle for emancipation (1828–1858)', *Transactions (Jewish Historical Society of England)*, 20, p. 113. https:// www.jstor.org/stable/29777970 .
29   Finestein. 1959, p. 118.
30   Cardaun, Sarah K. 2015. *Antisemitism in England and Britain: A History of Prejudice and Divided Responses Countering Contemporary Antisemitism in Britain*, Leiden: Brill, pp. 37–40; see also Felsenstein. 1990. 'Jews and devils: antisemitic stereotypes of late medieval and renaissance England', *Literature and Theology*, 4 (1), March. https://www.jstor.org/stable/23927203?seq=1.
31   Cardaun. 2015. *Antisemitism in England and Britain*, pp. 39–40.
32   See Lorimer. 2013; see also Holland. 2010.
33   Kavon, Eli. 2022. 'Why did Benjamin Disraeli's father convert his son?', *The Jerusalem Post*, March 5. https://www.jpost.com/opinion/article-700402. According to Eli Kavon, Disraeli's father had a troubled relationship with the Jewish community in London. He was invited to serve as the chief administrative officer of the Bevis Marks Synagogue, but refused. Perhaps, Kavon suggests, 'he was disillusioned with the ignorance of Judaism of the congregants, although he was no genius himself. This further drove Isaac – while not converting himself – to baptize his children in the Church of England' (Kavon. 2022).
34   Borgstede. 2012, p. 9.
35   Brantlinger, p. 92.
36   Jaffe, B. 1978. 'A reassessment of Benjamin Disraeli's Jewish aspects', *Transactions & Miscellanies* (Jewish Historical Society of England), 27, 115–123. http:// www.jstor.org/stable/29778900.

37 Your Dictionary. Undated. 'Benjamin Disraeli'. https://biography.yourdic
  tionary.com/benjamin-disraeli.
38 For further details, see Cesarani, David. 2016. *Disraeli, the Novel Politician*,
  Newhaven, CT: Yale University Press, pp. 13–25.
39 Your Dictionary. Undated.
40 Parry, Jonathan. 2016. 'Benjamin Disraeli, Earl of Beaconsfield', 4 May. https://
  history.blog.gov.uk/2016/05/04/benjamin-disraeli-earl-of-beaconsfield/.
41 Blake, Robert. 2022. 'Benjamin Disraeli, Prime Minister of United Kingdom'.
  Britannica. https://www.britannica.com/biography/Benjamin-Disraeli.
42 'Home letters', pp. 118–119, cited in Robert Blake. 1969. *Disraeli*, London:
  University Paperbacks, p. 67.
43 Blake. 1969, p. 67.
44 Ibid.
45 Blake, 1982. *Disraeli's Grand Tour: Benjamin Disraeli and the Holy Land 1830–1831*,
  New York: Oxford University Press, p. 106.
46 Ibid., pp. 106–107.
47 Harrison, J. F. C. (John Fletcher Clews). 1985. *The Common People of Great
  Britain: A History from the Norman Conquest to the Present* (1st Midland book
  ed.), Bloomington: Indiana University Press, pp. 249–253.
48 Gray, Robert. 1996. *The Factory System and Industrial England 1830–1860*,
  Cambridge: Cambridge University Press, p. 60, cited in Borgstede, p. 69.
49 The Health Foundation: Policy Navigator. 2022. 'Workhouses and the Poor
  Law Amendment Act 1834'. https://navigator. health.org.uk/theme/work-
  houses-and-poor-law-amendment-act-1834.
50 Polyani, Karl. 1944 [2001]. *The Great Transformation*, Boston: Beacon Press,
  especially pp. 113f and 371f, cited in Borgstede, p. 69.
51 Kidd, Alan. 1999. *State, Society and the Poor: In Nineteenth-Century England*
  (Social History in Perspective), Springer, p. 110.
52 Borgstede, p. 69.
53 The National Archives. 2021. 'Power, politics and protest'. https://www.nationa
  larchives.gov.uk/education/politics/g7/#:~:text=Chartism%20was%20a%20work
  ing%20class,main%20aims%20of%20the%20movement.
54 Borgstede, p. 69.
55 The National Archives. 2021. https://www.nationalarchives.gov.uk/educa
  tion/politics/.
56 Royle, Edward and Walvin, James. 1982. *English Radicals and Reformers 1760–
  1848*, Brighton: Harvester, p. 168, cited in Borgstede, p. 70. Although the
  Chartist movement ended without achieving its aims, the fear of civil unrest
  remained and later in the century, many Chartist ideas were included in the
  Reform Acts of 1867 and 1884. The National Archives. 2021. These acts are
  addressed in this chapter.
57 Engels, Freidrich. 1845. 'Condition of the working class in England: the attitude
  of the Bourgeoisie towards the Proletariat'. https://www.marxists.org/archive/ma
  rx/works/1845/condition-working-class/ch13.htm.
58 Borgstede, p. 70.
59 Wood, Marcus. 2002. *Slavery, Empathy, and Pornography*, Oxford: Oxford
  University Press, pp. 152, 164.
60 Borgstede, p. 71.
61 Fryer, Peter. 1984. *Staying Power: The History of Black People in Britain*,
  London: Pluto Press. p. 242; Virdee, Satnam. 2014. *Racism, Class and the
  Racialised Outsider*, London: Red Globe Press.
62 Diniejko, Andrzej. 2018, 'Benjamin Disraeli and the two nation divide', *The
  Victorian Web*. http://www.victorianweb.org/authors/disraeli/diniejko3.html.
63 Cited in Diniejko.

64   Letter to Charles Attwood (June 7, 1840), quoted in Monypenny, William Flavelle, and Buckle, George Earle. 1929. *The Life of Benjamin Disraeli, Earl of Beaconsfield. Volume I. 1804–1859*, London: John Murray, p. 486.

65   Ibid.

66   Speech at banquet of the National Union of Conservative and Constitutional Associations, Crystal Palace, London (June 24, 1872), cited in 'Mr. Disraeli at Sydenham,' *The Times* (25 June 1872), p. 8.

67   *Tancred; or The New Crusade*, London: M. Walter Dunne, 1847, Vol. I, Ch. XX: A Modern Troubadour, p. 191.

68   Speech in the House of Commons (9 August 1848). http://hansard.millbanksystems.com/commons/1848/aug/09/supply-navy-estimates.

69   Miles, Robert. 1987.

70   Miles. 1989, p. 90.

71   Engels, Friedrich. 1845. 'To the working-classes of Great-Britain', 'Dedication' in *The Condition of the Working Class in England*. https://www.marxists.org/archive/marx/works/1845/condition-working-class/ch00.htm.

72   Engels. 1845.

73   Utopian socialism is exemplified by the work of Henri de Saint-Simon, Charles Fourier and Robert Owen, and has a vision of a future ideal societies, with positive ideals projecting societies forward rather than being grounded in material conditions of existence and having the working class as the agent of change, as is the case with scientific socialism. For an analysis, see Cole, M. 2008. *Marxism and Educational: Origins and Issues*, chapter 2.

74   Engels, Friedrich. 1880. *Socialism: Utopian and Scientific* III [Historical Materialism]. https://www.marxists.org/archive/marx/works/1880/soc-utop/ch03.htm.

75   Blake, 2022. 'Benjamin Disraeli'. https://www.britannica.com/biography/Benjamin-Disraeli.

76   Brantlinger, p. 96.

77   Cited in Brantlinger, p. 96.

78   Blake. 1970. *The Conservative Party from Peel to Churchill*, p. 2.

79   Blake. 2020. 'Benjamin Disraeli'. https://www.britannica.com/biography/Benjamin-Disraeli. O'Connell (the first big 19th century Irish nationalist leader), who had taken a seat at Westminster following the Catholic Emancipation of 1829 (this admitted Irish and English Roman Catholics to Parliament) was, according to Peter Hadden, in reality a reformist (Hadden, Peter. 1980. 'Divide and rule'.

80   Cited in Blake. 1969. p. 125.

81   Ibid.

82   Monypenny and Buckle. 1929. *The Life of Benjamin Disraeli, Earl of Beaconsfield: Volume I*, p. 288.

83   As we saw in the Introduction, the word racism was not recorded in the Oxford English Dictionary until 1902 (Demby. 2014). The term '*anti-Semitism*' was coined in 1879 by the German agitator and antisemite Wilhelm Marr to designate the anti-Jewish campaigns under way in central Europe at that time (according to Zimmerman. 1986, p. 9, toward the end of his life, Marr came to renounce antisemitism, arguing that social upheaval in Germany had been the result of the Industrial Revolution and conflict between political movements, and 'openly requested the Jews' pardon for having erred in isolating the problem'). The conventional spelling has a hyphen between 'anti' and 'Semitism' and a capital 'S' – 'anti-Semitism'. I omit the hyphen and the capital 'S' on the grounds that most contemporary commentators use the unhyphenated 'antisemitism'. This more closely reflects Wilhelm Marr's use of the word. Not using a hyphen or a capital 'S' denotes that antisemitism is a form of racism directed at Jewish people per se, and not at those who speak a

Semitic language per se (Semitic languages are spoken by nearly 500 million people across large parts of the Middle East, North Africa and Northeast Africa, the most widely spoken Semitic language being Arabic).

84 He was an abolitionist and opposed slavery in the US; and a champion of the rights and liberties of people throughout the world including those of Jews in Europe, peasants in India, Maori in New Zealand and Aboriginal people in Australia (Kinealy. 2011). O'Connell had also publicly criticized Pope Gregory XVI's treatment of Jews in a series of states then under direct rule of the Pope Bew and Maune. 2020.
85 Bloy. 2016.
86 Fraser. 2015.
87 Blake. 1969. *Disraeli*, p. 125.
88 Bloy. 2016. http://www.historyhome.co.uk/pms/dizzy.htm.
89 Blake. 2022.
90 Blake. 1967, *Disraeli*, p. 164.
91 Bradford. 1983. *Disraeli*, pp. 116–117.
92 Cazamian. 1903. p. 178.
93 Brantlinger. p. 104.
94 *Coningsby* (1844, p. 242), cited in Brantlinger, p. 90.
95 Ibid. p. 91.
96 Ibid.
97 Brantlinger, Patrick. 2011. *Taming Cannibals: Race and the Victorians*, p. 99.
98 In a letter to his sister, cited in Jaffe, p. 119.
99 Jaffe, p. 119.
100 Hansard 1803–2005 → 1840s → 1847 → December 1847 → 16 December 1847 → Commons Sitting Disabilities of the Jews. HC Deb 16 December 1847 vol 95 cc1234–332. https://api.parliament.uk/historic-hansard/commons/1847/dec/16/disabilities-of-the-jews#S3V0095P0_18471216_HOC_26.
101 Ibid.
102 Ibid.
103 Welford, John. April 4, 2017. 'The rivalry between Benjamin Disraeli and William Ewart Gladstone', *Owlcation*. https://owlcation.com/humanities/The-Rivalry-Between-Benjamin-Disraeli-and-William-Ewart-Gladstone#:~:text=Although%20they%20were%20both%20highly%20intelligent%20and%20ambitious%2C,of%20life%2C%20whereas%20Gladstone%20was%20serious-minded%20and%20unimaginative.
104 Blake. 2011.
105 Blake. 1967, pp. 354–357.
106 Cited in Brantlinger, p. 99.
107 Disraeli. 1852. *Lord George Bentinck: A Political Biography*, p. 496.
108 Ibid.
109 Ibid.
110 Letter to Lord Salisbury (13 December 1875), quoted in Bentley, Michael. 2001. *Lord Salisbury's World: Conservative Environments in Late-Victorian Britain*, p. 224, n. 10.
111 1852. *Lord George Bentinck: A Political Biography*, pp. 324–325.
112 'Cultural India: history of India'. https://www.culturalindia.net/indian-history/index.html#:~:text=%20History%20of%20India%20%201%20India%20Timeline.,the%20third%20emperor%20of%20the%20Mughal...%20More%20.
113 Faulkner, Neil. 2012. 'A Marxist history of the world part 56: The Indian mutiny', *Counterfire*. https://www.counterfire.org/articles/a-marxist-history-of-the-world/15384-a-marxist-history-of-the-world-part-56-the-indian-mutiny.
114 Hansard's Parliamentary Debates. 1857. Third series 147 (20 July 1857–28, August 1857). London: Thomas Curson Hansard et al., pp. 440–545.

(Benjamin Disraeli's speech on the Indian Mutiny), cited in Pionke, Albert. 2004. 'Representations of the Indian mutiny in Victorian higher journalism', *The Victorian Web*. http://www.victorianweb.org/history/empire/1857/intro. html.

115 Pionke, Albert. 2007. 'Representations of the Indian mutiny in Victorian higher journalism', *The Victorian Web*, October 29.

116 Faulkner. 2012. 'A Marxist history of the world part 56: The Indian mutiny', *Counterfire*, January 2, 2012 https://www.counterfire.org/articles/a-marxist-history-of-the-world/15384-a-marxist-history-of-the-world-part-56-the-indian-mutiny.

117 Ibid.

118 The Royal Household. 2022. 'Victoria (r. 1837–1901)'. https://web.archive. org/web/20020202023604/http://www.royal.gov.uk/output/Page118.asp.

119 Wolpert, Stanley, A. 'British raj: Indian and Pakistani history', Britannica. https:// www.britannica.com/event/British-raj.

120 Speech in Wycombe (30 October 1862), quoted in Monypenny and Buckle. 1929. *The Life of Benjamin Disraeli, Earl of Beaconsfield*, p. 98.

121 UK Parliament. 1867. 'Second Great Reform Act'. https://www.parliament. uk/about/living-heritage/evolutionofparliament/houseofcommons/reformacts/ from-the-parliamentary-collections/collections-reform-acts/great-reform-act111/.

122 Blake. 1967, p. 473.

123 Hibbert, Christopher. 2004. *Disraeli: A Personal History*, London: HarperCollins, p. 259.

124 Dorey, Peter. 1995. *The Conservative Party and the Trade Unions,* London: Routledge, p. 17.

125 Rix, Kathryn. 2018. 'Tackling electoral corruption: how Victorian Britain reformed the trial of election petitions in 1868', July 31. https://thehistoryofparliam ent.wordpress.com/2018/07/31/tackling-electoral-corruption-how-victorian-britain-reformed-the-trial-of-election-petitions-in-1868/.

126 Blake. 1967, p. 495.

127 Monypenny and Buckle, p. 383.

128 Ibid., p. 384. *The History of Rasselas, Prince of Abissinia*, originally titled *The Prince of Abissinia: A Tale*, though often abbreviated to Rasselas, is a novel by Samuel Johnson, first published in 1759 in England; according to Thomas Keymer. 2009. 'Early readers considered Rasselas to be a work of philoso-phical and practical importance and critics often remark on the difficulty of classifying it as a novel', *Times Literary Supplement*. 25 March.

129 Monypenny and Buckle, p. 385.

130 Blake. 1967, pp. 496–512.

131 Moore, Diana. 2020. 'Romances of no-popery: transnational anti-Catholicism in Giuseppe Garibaldi's The Rule of the Monk and Benjamin Disraeli's Lothair', *Catholic Historical Review,* 106 (3) pp. 399–420, online.

132 Speech at the opening of Shaftesburgh Park Estate (18 July 1874), cited in *Wit and Wisdom of Benjamin Disraeli, Collected from His Writings and Speeches (1881)*, p. 38.

133 Disraeli, Benjamin. 2017. *Wit and Wisdom of Benjamin Disraeli, Collected from His Writings and Speeches (1881)*, Andesite Press. UK Government. Undated. 'Benjamin Disraeli, the Earl of Beaconsfield.' https://www.gov.uk/government/ history/past-prime-ministers/benjamin-disraeli-the-earl-of-beaconsfield.

134 'Key dates in working conditions, Factory Acts Great Britain 1300–1899'. Undated. http://www.thepotteries.org/dates/work.htm#:~:text=1874%20Fa ctory%20Act%20raised%20the,working%20week%20to%2056%C2%BD% 20hours.

135 Monypenny and Buckle, p. 705.

136   Blake. 1867, p. 555.
137   Ibid.
138   Monypenny and Buckle, p. 705.
139   Ibid., p. 709.
140   Atkins, Richard A. 1974. 'The conservatives and Egypt, 1875–1880', *The Journal of Imperial and Commonwealth History*, 2 (2).
141   Cited in Timms, Elizabeth Jane. 2019. 'Primroses for her Prime Minister: Benjamin Disraeli and Queen Victoria', July 11. https://royalcentral.co.uk/features/primroses-for-her-prime-minister-benjamin-disraeli-and-queen-victoria-126648/.
142   Monypenny and Buckle, p. 805.
143   Cited in Ensor. 1936, p. 46.
144   Ibid., p. 48.
145   Ibid.
146   Ibid.
147   Blake, p. 646.
148   Ibid., p. 649.
149   Monypenny and Buckle, pp. 1217–1218.
150   Ibid., p. 1221.
151   Ibid., p. 1226.
152   Blake. 1967, pp. 658–663.
153   Ibid., pp. 671–672.
154   UK Government. Undated.
155   Ibid.
156   Freedland, J. 2016. 'Disraeli by David Cesarani review – the Jewish prime minister and antisemitism', *The Guardian,* June 11. https://www.theguardian.com/books/2016/jun/11/disraeli-the-novel-politician-by-david-cesarani-review.
157   Cited in Freedland.
158   Ibid.
159   Ibid.
160   Ibid.
161   Ibid.
162   Holocaust Encyclopedia. Undated. 'Protocols of the Elders of Zion'. Washington DC: United States Holocaust Memorial Museum. https://encyclopedia.ushmm.org/content/en/article/protocols-of-the-elders-of-zion.
163   Freedland.
164   Cesarani, David. 2013. 'Disraeli the cad, Disraeli the bounder', *The Jewish Chronicle,* November 17. https://www.thejc.com/disraeli-the-cad-disraeli-the-bounder-1.50964.
165   Ibid.
166   Ibid.
167   Ibid.
168   Ibid.
169   Ibid.
170   Ibid.
171   Ibid.
172   Ibid.
173   Ibid.
174   Ibid. Jonathan Frankel describes the Damascus Affair as one of the best-known examples of a 'blood libel' or Jewish 'ritual murder'. After a Christian monk went missing in Damascus, rumours spread that he had been ritually murdered by Jews. Subsequently, four Jewish people were tortured to death by the authorities and others were coerced into making a confession. A dozen or so

executed. (Frankel, J. 1997. '"Ritual murder" in the modern era: the Damascus Affair of 1840', *Jewish Social Studies* 3, Winter.

175   Cesarani. 2013.

176   Freedland. 2016. Disraeli, Benjamin. 2016. *Delphi Complete Works of Benjamin Disraeli* (Illustrated) (Delphi Series Seven Book 4), Delphi Classics. https://tmbukz.ga/read.php?id=F7dKDAAAQBAJ.

2 Championing imperialism and ramping up antisemitism: the Tories at the turn of the century (1880–1914)

Scientific racism: from Social Darwinism to eugenics

At the beginning of chapter 1, I traced the development of scientific racism through the 18th and 19th centuries. In the late 1800s, Social Darwinism, a loose set of ideologies in which Charles Darwin's theory of evolution by natural selection was used to justify certain political, social or economic views, emerged. To convey his scientific ideas to the British public, Darwin borrowed popular concepts, including 'survival of the fittest', from sociologist Herbert Spencer and 'struggle for existence' from economist Thomas Malthus, who had earlier written about how human societies evolve over time.[1] Social Darwinists believe in 'survival of the fittest' – 'the idea that certain people become powerful in society because they are innately better'.[2] For Social Darwinists, Darwin's theory confirmed what they already believed to be true about human society – that 'the fit' inherited qualities such as industriousness and the ability to accumulate wealth, while 'the unfit' were innately lazy and stupid.[3] Spencer applied the idea of 'survival of the fittest' to *laissez faire* or unrestrained capitalism, whereby capitalists operate with little regulation from governments, during the Industrial Revolution.[4] Social Darwinism has been used to justify imperialism, racism and social inequality at various times over the past century and a half (see chapter 1 of this book). It was also the forerunner of eugenics.

The scientifically backed enterprise of eugenics, focusing on improving the genetic quality of White European 'races', arrived in the late 19th century. This project, that garnered massive popular enthusiasm on both sides of the Atlantic, entailed attempts to remove people deemed inferior.[5] The first person to come up with the term eugenics was Francis Galton (a half-cousin of Darwin) in 1883. Obsessed with the breeding of domestic animals, Galton spent a large part of his life studying variations in 'human ability'. He wrote: 'The question was then forced upon me. Could not the race of men be similarly improved? Could not the undesirables be got rid of and the desirables multiplied?[6] Galton's writings played a key role in launching the eugenics movement in the UK and America. Its supporters advocated government policies to improve the biological quality of the human 'race' through selective parenthood. Eugenics

DOI: 10.4324/9781003198673-4

quickly gained many backers, including leading politicians of all political persuasions.[7]

As the end of the 19th century approached, eugenicists were becoming increasingly influential in British politics. Part of the quest for a 'super race' involved segregating and/or eliminating people with disabilities. A Royal Commission on the Blind, Deaf and Dumb concluded in 1889 that intermarriage between these groups was to be strongly discouraged. In 1896 a pressure group entitled the National Association for the Care and Control of the Feeble Minded was set up in Britain to bring about the lifetime segregation of disabled people. Its campaigning reached its peak in the run-up to the 1910 general election.[8]

Giving evidence before the 1908 Royal Commission on the 'Care and Control of the Feeble-Minded', first president of the Eugenics Education Society, Sir James Crichton-Brown, recommended the compulsory sterilization of those with learning disabilities and mental illness, describing them as 'our social rubbish' which should be 'swept up and garnered and utilised as far as possible'.[9] He went on to complain, 'We pay much attention to the breeding of our horses, our cattle, our dogs and poultry, even our flowers and vegetables; surely it's not too much to ask that a little care be bestowed upon the breeding and rearing of our race'.[10] Winston Churchill, at the time a Liberal MP, held similar views. In a memo to the Prime Minister in 1910, Churchill cautioned, 'The multiplication of the feeble-minded is a very terrible danger to the race'.[11] In 1912, then First Lord of the Admiralty, he attended, along with Tory Arthur Balfour, some European ambassadors and about four hundred delegates, attended the first International Eugenics Conference in London. Organized by the British Eugenics Education Society, founded to campaign for sterilization and marriage restrictions for the weak to prevent the degeneration of Britain's population, the Conference was dedicated to Galton who had died the year before.[12]

SECTION 1: IMPERIALISM

The Long Depression (1873–1896)

To better understand the championing of imperialism from 1880 to 1910, it is important to take account of the effect of what has been termed 'the Long Depression of 1873–1896'. In his discussion of that depression, Dominic Alexander begins by reasserting a basic Marxist tenet that 'crisis, whether temporary or extended, is an ineradicable part of the capitalist system', that even 'during the periods of its greatest stability, capitalism has suffered from regular downturns that modern economics refer to as recessions, during which the size of the economy actually contracts'[13] (growth is essential for capitalist businesses to compete and survive). For mainstream economists:

capitalism is a system of equilibrium, where the free market acts to unite buyers and sellers, demand and supply, to harmonious results, despite the odd moment of imbalance which should automatically correct itself. As a result, major downturns have to be seen as 'random events' caused by some shock from outside the system itself, or by mere chance.[14]

'In contrast', as Alexander points out, 'Marx's analysis of capitalism was fully rooted in a historical understanding of its development and its patterns'. 'These regularly recurring great crises, or depressions', in Alexander's words 'vindicate Marx's understanding of capitalism as inherently unstable, and tending towards crisis'.[15] The Long Depression was not a real depression in the sense of stagnant or negative growth. However, prices fell – great for consumers but disastrous for capitalism, and the crisis was global. There followed a realignment of world capitalism (what happens when there are major crises in the system), with the United States replacing Britain as the leading industrial power.[16] Moreover, from 1898 to 1901, the US ceased being a former outpost of the British Empire, as it annexed Hawaii, gained significant control over Cuba and claimed as territories three other islands: Guam, Puerto Rico and the Philippines. This followed the Spanish-American War of 1898 that 'ended Spain's colonial empire in the Western Hemisphere and secured the position of the United States as a Pacific power'.[17]

The British Empire in the late 19th century was also threatened by competition from European countries, and the need to regenerate British capitalism amid fears that British colonies may be overrun by other European 'races'. From the 1880s onwards, amid the global economic crisis, British imperialism acquired a new impetus: other European countries such as Belgium and Germany were beginning to develop the means to vie as imperial powers, building modern navies and targeting the 'unclaimed' areas of Africa.[18] The so-called 'scramble for Africa' in the 1880s and 1890s saw the continent partitioned into European colonies.

The scramble for Africa

The Berlin Conference (1884–1885)

The scramble was facilitated by the Berlin Conference of 1884–1885, opened by the founder and first Chancellor of the newly created German Empire, Otto von Bismarck at his official residence in Berlin on November 15, 1884.[19]

Its purpose was ostensibly to stamp out slavery and discuss the future of Africa, and while the Berlin General Act of 1885 that ended the Conference, signed on February 26th by the leaders of the 14 European countries attending it plus the United States, included a resolution to 'help in suppressing slavery',[20] the strategic and economic objectives of the colonial powers were more centred on capital and profit and their respective interests in exploiting the continent in the interests of protecting old markets and exploiting new ones, of retaining and intensifying accumulation, than moral imperatives. As prominent 20th century Guyanese Marxist, political activist and academic Walter Rodney explains, quoting Lenin, 'Under the old capitalism, when free competition prevailed, the export of *goods* was the most typical feature', whereas 'Under modern capitalism, when monopolies prevail, the export of *capital* has become the typical feature'. Lenin amplifies as follows:

> We now see that it is precisely after ... [the 1860s and 1870s] that the tremendous 'boom' in colonial conquests begins, and that the struggle for the territorial division of the world becomes extraordinarily sharp. It is beyond doubt, therefore, that capitalism's transition to the stage of monopoly capitalism, to finance capital, is connected with the intensification of the struggle for the partitioning of the world.[21]

This, Rodney goes on, greatly affected Black Africa. During the epoch of the slave trade, 'Europeans carried *goods* to Africa and exchanged them for human beings, who were thus transformed into saleable commodities' (see the beginning of chapter 1 of this book for a discussion of slavery). However, when 'Europe became interested in the raw materials of the continent, *capital* was sent to transform Africans into workers and peasants producing for the capitalist market'.[22]

Saul David notes how the Berlin Conference paid no attention to local culture or ethnic groups, and left people from the same tribe on separate sides of European-imposed borders. Britain was very concerned with maintaining its lines of communication with India, hence its interest in Egypt and South Africa. But as soon as these two areas were secure, imperialist adventurers like Cecil Rhodes encouraged the acquisition of further territory with the intention of establishing a Cape-to-Cairo railway. Britain was also interested in the commercial potential of mineral-rich territories like the Transvaal, where gold was discovered in the mid-1880s, and in preventing other European powers, particularly Germany and France, from muscling into areas they considered within their 'sphere of influence'.[23] David concludes, in the last 20 years of the 19th century, Britain occupied or annexed more than 30% of Africa's population. This included Egypt, the Sudan, British East Africa (subsequently Kenya and Uganda), British Somaliland, Southern and Northern Rhodesia (Zimbabwe and Zambia), Bechuanaland (Botswana), Orange Free State and the Transvaal (South Africa), Gambia, Sierra Leone, Nigeria, British Gold Coast (Ghana) and Nyasaland (Malawi). The other chief colonizers were in addition to Germany and France: Belgium, Italy, Portugal and Spain.[24]

During the Conference, the Siege of Khartoum took place between March 13, 1884 and January 26, 1885. In early 1884, Major General

Charles Gordon had arrived to take command of British and Egyptian forces in Khartoum. Though tasked with leaving the area before Mahdist rebels (who backed independence from the Egyptian rulers and an Islamic nation) arrived, he elected to defend the city. The resulting siege saw Gordon's garrison overwhelmed and wiped out shortly before a relief force arrived. The failure to rescue Gordon and his men was blamed on Prime Minister William Gladstone and caused his government to fall.[25] Robert Gascoyne-Cecil briefly became Tory Prime Minister. However, later in 1885, Gladstone's son leaked to the press that his father favoured Home Rule for Ireland. Vowing to maintain the union of Great Britain and Ireland, Gladstone Senior and the Irish Nationalists joined forces to defeat the government, Gascoyne-Cecil resigned and Gladstone became Prime Minister for the third time in 1886 and subsequently introduced a Home Rule Bill for Ireland that was defeated.[26] Gascoyne-Cecil was returned to power where he remained until 1892, to be replaced by two Liberal administrations, the first by Gladstone whose fourth premiership lasted until 1894; the second by Archibald Philip Primrose. From 1895 to 1905, the Conservatives were in coalition government with the Liberal Unionists (the latter had formed as a separate political party after Gladstone's decision in 1886 to pursue a policy of Home Rule for Ireland divided the Liberal Party to the core).[27] The coalition known as 'Unionist' was headed by Conservative Prime Ministers Robert Gascoyne-Cecil from 1895 until 1902 and Arthur Balfour up until 1905.

The Second Boer War (1899–1902)

From 1899 to 1902, Britain was involved in the second Boer War. The culmination of a sustained period of conflict in southern Africa, Britain backed up from forces across the Empire fought against two Boer republics: the South African Republic (Transvaal) and the Orange Free State. Resulting in British victory, the war is infamous for Britain's use of concentration camps that caused great loss of life among the Boer population, both military and civilian.[28]

The White concentration camps

The South African History Online (SAHO) has documented the treatment of Boer women and children in concentration camps during the second Boer War, 1899–1902:[29]

> Boer women, children and men unfit for service were herded together in concentration camps by the British forces ... The first two of these camps (refugee camps) were established to house the families of burghers who had surrendered voluntarily, but very soon, with families of combatant burghers driven forcibly into camps established all over the country, the camps ceased to be refugee camps and became

concentration camps. The abhorrent conditions in these camps caused the death of 4,177 women, 22,074 children under sixteen and 1,676 men, mainly those too old to be on commando.[30]

The Chief of Staff in the war was Lord Horatio Herbert Kitchener. In addition to the concentration camps, Kitchener is notorious for the 'scorched earth' policy, during which the rural economy was destroyed as crops were ravaged and livestock butchered. Referring to a 'scorched earth' raid, a report to Prime Minister Gascoyne-Cecil stated, and I quote at length:

> This removal took place in the most uncivilised and barbarous manner, while such action is … in conflict with all the up to the present acknowledged rules of civilised warfare. The families were put out of their houses under compulsion, and in many instances by means of force … (the houses) were destroyed and burnt with everything in them … and these families among them were many aged ones, pregnant women, and children of very tender years, were removed in open trolleys (exposed) for weeks to rain, severe cold wind and terrible heat, privations to which they were not accustomed, with the result that many of them became very ill, and some of them died shortly after their arrival in the women's camps. The vehicles were also overloaded, accidents happened and they were exposed to being caught in crossfire. They were exposed to insults and ill-treatment by Blacks in service of the troops as well as by soldiers … British mounted troops have not hesitated in driving them for miles before their horses, old women, little children, and mothers with sucklings to their breasts.[31]

In a memorandum to general officers, Lord Kitchener divided the women and children in the White camps into two categories: '1st. Refugees, and the families of Neutrals, non-combatants, and surrendered Burghers. 2nd. Those whose husbands, fathers and sons are on Commando'. 'The preference in accommodation, etc.', it went on, 'should of course be given to the first class. With regard to Natives, it is not intended to clear … locations, but only such and their stock as are on Boer farms'.[32]

SAHO describes 'Pushing panic-stricken groups of old men, women and children, crowded in wagons and preceded by huge flocks of livestock in front of them'; 'the dispatch of people in open coal trucks'; and '25 tents available for 240 people'. It also records that Henry Campbell-Bannerman, leader of the Liberal opposition to the Tory-led Unionist coalition, said the war in South Africa was carried on by methods of barbarism, while another Liberal David Lloyd-George, though not an opponent of the British Empire *per se*, condemned the concentration camps and the horrors inflicted on women and children, warning, 'A barrier of dead children's bodies will rise between the British and Boer races in South Africa'.[33]

SAHO refers to the anti-war campaigner, Emily Hobhouse, who tells the story of the infant Lizzie van Zyl who died in the Bloemfontein concentration camp. She was placed on the lowest rations and ill-treated owing to the refusal of her father to surrender.[34] Hobhouse also writes of people:

> crowded into small tents: some sick, some dying, occasionally a dead one among them; scanty rations dealt out raw; lack of fuel to cook them; lack of water for drinking, for cooking, for washing; lack of soap, brushes and other instruments of personal cleanliness; lack of bedding or of beds to keep the body off the bare earth; lack of clothing for warmth and in many cases for decency.[35]

The racialization of the White-skinned Boers and their placement in con-centration camps is, of course, an example of non–colour-coded racism. This was to recur just over 30 years later with the establishment of the first Nazi concentration camp at Dachau.

The Black concentration camps

Because the inhuman treatment of Black Africans was typical of the colour-coded racism that epitomized the British Empire, the existence of Black concentration camps in this squalid example of British colonial history tend to get overlooked. As SAHO explains, while the two primary forces in the second Boer War were White, at least 15,000 Black people were used as combatants by the British, particularly as scouts to track down Boer com-mandoes and armed block house guards, but also in non-combatant roles such as wagon drivers by both British and Boer forces.[36] They also suffered severely as result of the British 'scorched earth policy', while those Black people who lived on White farms were removed to concentration camps, as were the women and children of their White employers.[37]

SAHO notes how they 'were rounded up by the British forces and forced into the camps' with the ulterior motive of forced labour, either growing crops or digging trenches for the troops, as drivers and as miners once the gold mines became partly operational again.[38] Treated in typical British colonial fashion, they received no rations, hardly any medical support or shelter and were expected to grow their own crops, exchanging labour for food. Separated on 'racial' lines, the inmates of the Black camps were situ-ated along railway lines and on the border, becoming the eyes and ears of the British army. The strategy alienated Whites and Blacks from each other, and was detrimental to 'racial harmony' in South Africa both during and after the war.[39]

The total number of Black deaths, relying on surviving archives, has been calculated at approximately 20,000, although, according to Garth Benneyworth, a senior research associate with the Department of Historical Studies at the University of Johannesburg specializing in the Black concentration camps of that war, owing to incomplete and in many cases non-existent British records, the death toll was certainly higher.[40] SAHO records that 81% of the fatalities were children.[41]

The party of imperialism and imperialism on the campaign trail (1880–1914)

As noted earlier, the Liberal Gladstone was Prime Minister from 1880–1885, and from 1895 to 1905 the Conservatives were in coalition government with the Liberal Unionists (known as the 'Unionists') headed by Conservative Prime Ministers Gascoyne-Cecil from 1895 until 1902 and Arthur Balfour up until 1905. There is a general consensus among historians of the period that the Conservatives were the Imperial Party of the 1880s and 1890s.[42] For H. C. G. Matthew, Disraeli was behind this and it dates back to his Crystal Palace speech of 1872 (see chapter 1 of this book), the moment when Disraeli 'seized the wand of patriotism from the dead Palmerston's hand ... [and] captured the initiative from the Liberal Party on the dominant theme of late Victorian Britain- imperialism'.[43] Disraeli's particular achievement, according to A. Thompson,[44] was to replace the empire's traditional mid-Victorian connotations of authoritarianism and Napoleonic expansionism with a jingoistic celebration of England's superior civilization, God-given destiny and military might.

A succinct summary of why the Conservatives were the Imperial Party of this era is provided by Ewen Henry Harvey Green. He begins by outlining a 'vulgar Marxist analysis [that] would look to the social make-up of the Conservative party, in that a complex lattice of material interests appears to have linked Conservatives to the Empire'.[45]

First, Green explains, in the period between 1880–1914 over half the Parliamentary party had some form of connection with Britain's military establishment. Many Conservative MPs were or had been officers in the regular army, and many others were high-ranking members of local volunteer forces and the county yeomanry. Although military duties, Green goes on, did not necessarily guarantee enthusiasm for the Empire, the obvious connections between military careers and the Empire made it likely.[46]

Second, for the aristocracy and gentry, the Empire provided new investment and employment opportunities to supplement incomes hit by the agricultural depression. The Long Depression, discussed in the first section of this chapter, was accompanied by an agricultural depression,[47] caused by the huge fall in grain prices that followed the opening-up of the American prairies to cultivation in the 1870s and the advent of cheap transportation with the rise of steamships.[48] This meant that a number of landed families diversified their asset holding with colonies being a popular and patriotic alternative.[49]

Third, the expansion of the Empire also saw an expansion of the Imperial Service. New colonies meant new colonial governorships and many other posts, all of which, in addition to the positions already available, offered suitable employment for the descendants of Britain's traditional elite.[50]

Fourth, the Empire and its markets were regarded as important commercial assets in the depressed and highly competitive environment which existed from the mid-1870s on (see the first section of this chapter). Similarly, Britain's burgeoning service which fuelled the development of suburbia – the home of 'Villa Toryism' (a term coined by Gascoyne-Cecil to refer to the processes by which the Conservative Party consolidated its hold over the urban and middle classes)[51] – owed much of its growth, especially in London, to the increasing market for Indian, dominion and colonial loans, as well as stocks and insurance.[52]

Thus, arguing that 'imperialism can be read off from Conservative material interests in the Empire' is an oversimplification.[53] Green concludes:

> The Conservative constituency was highly stratified and there was plenty of room for disagreement: a clerk from Camberwell did not necessarily see imperialism in the same way as an aristocrat, and neither necessarily shared the same vision of Empire as a Birmingham screw manufacturer, whose views could in turn differ from those of a City financier. ... One should ask not simply whether the Conservative party was imperialist because its constituency was imperialist, but whether the constituency was imperialist because it was Conservative. This acknowledges that ideological constructions are as 'real' as any material factor in shaping political behaviour. ... The creation of Conservative imperialism was just that, a creation and not some innate process. Likewise it was only in the 1870s and 1880s that the Conservatives worked hardest to present themselves as the imperial party, which poses the question as to why it was so important for a Conservative to be an imperialist then. The vital clue to establishing why imperialism was so important to the late nineteenth-century Conservative party lies in the transformation of Britain's imperial position. Britain's annexations in the late nineteenth century were essentially defensive, frequently prompted by the fear that rival powers would seize territories and close them to British trade. Furthermore, the extent of Britain's imperial commitment caused concern over whether Britain had the resources to defend its possessions. Unrest within Britain's formal and informal Empire also threatened to disrupt British imperial interests ... In short, the late nineteenth century witnessed a graphic change in the structures of British imperialism.[54]

Given the general agreement that the Tories were the imperial party of the time, and that 'the empire seemed to have strongly permeated the national consciousness of ... [the 1880–1910] era', Luke Blaxill has posed the question: 'how and how far this popular feeling manifested itself in the arena of politics, particularly during election campaigns which routinely brought people and politicians together in mass public meetings where platform speeches would be delivered'.[55] His article provides a wide-ranging analysis of the issue of imperialism in electoral politics during the 30-year period from 1880 to 1910. Blaxill focuses particularly on its presentation by Liberal and Conservative politicians. For the purposes of this chapter, I will refer to his findings as to which party used imperialism more often.[56]

Using a corpus of about five million words of digitized campaign speeches between 1880–1910, Blaxill examined the language of the nine General Elections held in this timescale through 'computerised text-mining'.[57] To measure this, he selected a group of keywords that reliably correlated to occasions where party speakers talked about the Empire: 'imperial', 'empire', 'colony', 'flag' and 'British'.[58]

His findings were that 'the Conservatives were considerably more likely to champion … [imperialism] and connect it to politically charged and emotive appeals than were their Liberal opponents'.[59] Throughout the 1880–1910 period, the Conservatives from the top of the party to the grassroots mentioned the Empire and related vocabulary close to twice as often as the Liberals, and, when they did, spent close to twice as long talking about it. The also 'connected it much more relentlessly to politically charged and emotional values such as integrity, stability and glory'. Liberals, on the other hand, tended to talk about Empire in more neutral and administrative terms[60]. Conservative celebrations of Empire, Blaxill discovered, were grandiose, and 'left no doubt that to be an imperialist was to be a patriot'.[61] He gives the example of W. L. Priorleau (East-Norfolk) who 'pleaded' with his audience 'to vote straight for the Unionist party, for in-so-doing they would be doing their share in upholding the glory of the greatest empire that ever existed in the world'.[62] Blaxill also refers to H. S. Foster (Lowestoft) who said that the purpose of the election of 1900 was to 'decide whether the great British Empire was to be maintained or not … it was a battle between the Little Englander and the Big Englander'[63]. In King's Lynn, Thomas Gibson-Bowles pointed to a Union Jack above his platform and asked his audience to:

> Look at that flag … it has a great and glorious history. There are no standards of Europe … that have not gone down before that flag … do not forget its past. That flag floated at the mainmast of the Victory when Nelson sailed into action at Trafalgar; that flag waved over the British squares at Waterloo … God grant that this flag, which so many times has shaken out its folds and brought freedom to the slave, comfort to the oppressed, may once more honour the name of Victoria.
>
> (cited in Blaxill, 2017, p. 429)

Praising the Empire was not simply limited to abstract jingoism. Conservatives were also prone to celebrating the expansion of imperial territory. Thus Harry Bullard (Norwich) boasted that 'Lord Salisbury [Gascoyne-Cecil] had demonstrated the might of the empire by sending 200,000 men

7,000 miles', a military manoeuvre that, according to Captain Pretyman (Woodbridge), 'no other nation could hope to accomplish'.[64] Meanwhile, Foster declared that more territory had been added to the Empire than in any other five-year period.[65] Blaxill argues that this 'swagger was arguably something new', since, whereas in the 1880s, 'the scale of military operations and territory acquired by Disraeli and Gladstone often represented albatrosses for their parties', in 1900, the mood and spirit of the times had changed to the extent that W. H. B. Ffolkes (Norfolk North-West) was able to rebut Liberal accusations that for the cost of a single gun, five hundred labourers' families could be kept in comfort, by retorting: 'Where would the families be without that gun? ... England would become a province of France ... where would the Union Jack be if not for our guns?'[66]'It seems doubtful', Blaxill concludes, 'that such defence would have been in keeping with the political weather in (for example) 1885, when rural poverty was high on the agenda in East Anglia'.[67] However, in Blaxill's words, 'in the charged climate of 1900 [during the second Boer War] it became much easier to simply articulate love of country as being synonymous with a pride in Britain's military capacity and ability to project force internationally'.[68]

In the first section of this chapter, we saw how the Long Depression of 1873–1893 provides a backdrop to the challenge to Britain's industrial and imperial hegemony and was a contributory factor in the 'scramble for Africa'. The second Boer War of 1899–1902 witnessed the inhuman treatment of racialized 'White-skinned' Boers, alongside similar but routine treatment of Black people during the days of the British Empire. We considered how social imperialism was the way in which the ruling class provided a mass base for its imperialist 'adventures'. Finally, with specific respect to party political use of the language of imperialism, we noted the consensus from historians that the Tories were *the* Imperial Party of the 1880s and 1890s and how political speeches revealed the connections between nation, racism and imperialism as discussed in the Introduction to this book. At its peak, the British Empire was the largest empire in history. By 1913 it covered 35.5 million sq. km. or 13.7 million sq. mi. (24% of the planet's total land area). In 1920, the Empire's population would be over 413 million people (23% of the world population).[69]

Social imperialism

Bernard Semmel has developed the concept of social imperialism to describe the way in which the ruling class attempted to provide a mass base for imperialism. Social imperialism made the links between nation and empire: 'Social-imperialism was designed to draw all classes together in defence of the nation and empire and aimed to prove to the least well-to-do class that its interests were inseparable from those of the nation'.[70]

On the affinity between 'race' and class in the European mind in general, but prescient of the attitudes of the Victorian ruling class in particular, V. G. Kieran writes:

If there were martial races abroad, there were likewise martial classes at home: every man could be drilled to fight, but only the gentleman by birth could lead and command. In innumerable ways his attitude to his own 'lower orders' was identical with that of Europe to the 'lesser breeds'. Discontented native in the colonies, labour agitator in the mills, were the same serpent in alternate disguises. Much of the talk about the barbarians or darkness of the outside world, which it was Europe's mission to rout, was a transmuted fear of the masses at home.[71]

'As the party of empire', as E. H. H. Green puts it, 'the Conservatives had to face up to the apparent decline of Britain's imperial predominance. As the party of property, the Conservatives had to try and defuse the challenge of socialism for the first time'.[72] Over 30 years had elapsed since the demise of Chartism as a movement, and this was the golden age of British capitalism, with free trade and individualism the dominant ideologies.[73] However, the first English edition of the *Manifesto of the Communist Party*[74] had been published in 1848, and the first nominally Marxist organization, the Social Democratic Federation, was founded in 1881. Its co-founder Henry Mayers Hyndman had been converted to Marxism on reading Marx's *Capital*.[75] For its first conference (June 1881) Hyndman wrote *England for All*, the first socialist book published in England since the decline of Robert Owen's reform movement in the 1830s.[76] The Federation was to be instrumental in the revival of British Socialism.[77]

Disraeli's posthumous legacy to social imperialism: the Primrose League

The ideology of social imperialism, as Semmel points out, was presented to the working class by the Unionist Party in many millions of leaflets and in many thousands of street-corner speeches.[78] The Primrose League was one of social imperialism's important vehicles. To understand the League's connection to Disraeli, a brief detour is necessary. Elizabeth Timms explains that a tradition had arisen between Disraeli and the Queen, whereby she sent him flowers. To Disraeli, according to Timms, Queen Victoria was the 'Faery' – his endearing name for the Queen (*Faerie Queene* was the title of a poem by Edmund Spenser). Disraeli told his friend, Lady Bradford, that on his first visit as Prime Minister to one of Victoria's homes, Osborne House on the Isle of Wight, she was 'wreathed with smiles and ... glided about the room like a bird'. Later, flowers, often primroses, would be sent from the Queen's Isle of Wight home.[79] After his wife's death, Disraeli once declared, 'I love the Queen – perhaps the only person in this world left to me that I do love'.[80] The news of Disraeli's death filled the subsequent journal entries of Queen Victoria. So devastated was she, that she wrote to his private secretary and literary executor while she wept: 'I can scarcely see for my fast falling tears' and for once, was unable to write in her usual third person.[81] She wrote: 'Never had I so kind and devoted a Minister, and very few such devoted friends'.[82] Victoria sent a wreath of primroses from Osborne House for Disraeli's grave, to which was tied a card in her own handwriting: 'His favourite flowers, from Osborne, a tribute of affection from Queen Victoria'.[83]

The League was founded two and a half years after Disraeli's death by Randolph Churchill (the father of Winston) at the Carlton Club, London, on November 17, 1883. According to Alistair Cooke, Randolph Churchill 'thought it would be of some limited use to him in his ruthless campaign, begun three years earlier, to secure a position at the forefront of the Conservative Party'.[84] It had an immediate impact. Organized on mediaeval lines, its full members were Knights and Dames and Imperial Knights; members of the working class were enrolled as 'associate members'. By 1891, it was claiming a million members; by 1901, 1.5 million, of which 1.4 million were said to be working class.[85] Its very effective propaganda exploited each of the imperial highlights of the 1880s and 1890s, such as the death of Gordon at Khartoum and the second Boer War. Its leaflets had direct and simple messages, and it dressed up its propaganda in the guise of popular entertainment, often taking the form of 'tableaux vivants', magic lantern displays, lectures and exhibitions.[86]

As far as popular culture in general is concerned, patriotism and Empire were highly marketable products from the late 1800s to 1914. There were a number of reasons for this. First, important social and economic changes had occurred, especially the transformation of Britain into a predominantly urban, industrial nation.[87] Basic state education, available following the 1870 Act, and underpinned by imperial themes[88] and technical developments,[89] facilitated the introduction of cheap popular imperialist fiction.[90] Britain's imperial 'adventures' were justified by institutional racism in popular culture: in music halls,[91] in juvenile fiction,[92] in popular art[93] and in the education system. For example, textbooks attempted to justify the continuance of 'the strong arm and brave spirit [...] of the British Empire.[94] An imperial 'race' was needed to defend the nation and the colonies.[95] Thus, the African subjects of the colonies were racialized, in school textbooks, as 'fierce savages' and 'brutal and stinking',[96] while freed formerly enslaved Caribbean people were described as 'lazy, vicious and incapable of any serious improvement or of work except under compulsion'.[97] At the same time, references were made to 'the barbaric peoples of Asia'[98] and the most frequent impression conveyed about Indians and Afghans was that they were cruel and totally unfit to rule themselves.[99] Missionary work was seen as 'civilizing the natives'. Racism in all its manifestations had become collective 'common sense'.[100]

John Hobson writes of the importance of 'hero-worship and sensational glory, adventure and the sporting spirit: current history/falsified in coarse flaring colours, for the direct stimulation of the combative instincts'.[101] Springhall states:

that the 'little wars' of Empire, which took place in almost every year of Queen Victoria's reign after 1870, provided the most readily available source for magazine and newspaper editors of romantic adventure and heroism set in an exotic and alien environment.[102]

These images, Springhall[103] continues, were also apparent in commercial advertising, school textbook illustrations, postcards, cigarette cards, cheap reproductions and other ephemera which appropriated and mediated the work of popular British artists of the time. Scientific biological racism had thus become institutionalized in popular culture in many ways during the British Imperial era, such that by the end of the 19th century the ideology of the 'inferiority' of Britain's colonial subjects and the consequent 'superiority' of the British 'race' was available to all. That would no doubt have been of great joy to Disraeli, given his views on 'racial hierarchies'.

SECTION 2: ANTISEMITISM

The Russian pogroms and immigration to Britain

While the championing of imperialism dominated the 1880–1910 period, so did antisemitism. This increased significantly from the 1880s. The historical background to this is the Russian pogroms. The word 'pogrom' comes from a Russian word meaning 'to destroy, to wreak havoc, to demolish violently', and was first used to refer to anti-Jewish street violence by non-Jewish mobs from 1881.[104] The Russian Government had forbidden Jewish subjects from settling in Russian territory outside the Pale of Settlement (parts of present-day Lithuania, Belarus, Ukraine, Moldova and Poland). The first violence occurred there in 1881 and spread rapidly throughout Ukraine and southern Russia, with peasant attackers looting stores and homes, destroying property, beating, raping and murdering. According to Hila Ratzabi, official response was often slow, and in some cases the police and military only intervened after days of violence, and sometimes they joined the mobs in perpetrating the violence.[105]

During the 1880s, the Russian government enacted anti-Jewish legislation limiting the number of Jews who could attend secondary schools and universities, and preventing Jewish law school graduates from joining the bar. In 1882 Czar Alexander III authorized the 'May Laws' that restricted where Jews could settle, forbade non-Jews from providing mortgages to Jews and forbade Jews conducting business on Sundays.[106] Jews were driven from the countryside and forced to live in the towns along the Pale of Settlement. Excluded from education and from public service, most Jewish people belonged to the lowest stratum of the unemployed proletariat or worked as artisans and small 'masters'.[107] Some Jewish people found hope in Zionism, others responded by becoming politically active joining left-wing organizations including the Bolsheviks, and forming self-defence leagues.[108]

Between 1880 and 1914, two million Jews made their way to the United States, Canada, the Argentine, France and South Africa. One hundred thousand travelled by weekly steamer from Rotterdam, Libau, Hamburg and Bremen to the English ports of Hull, Grimsby and London, of which 90% settled in London.[109] Many worked from 6 in the morning until 7 or 8 at night without a break in hot stuffy rooms for wages below 16 shillings a week[110] (80 pence sterling; average wage in 1905 was £1.05).[111] Two thirds of them died of tuberculosis.[112]

Having fled the horrors of tsarist Russia, Jewish people faced racism in England. As discussed in chapter 1 of this book, the 19th century witnessed an obsession with the position of the 'Caucasian' in the scale of civilization and to rationalize colonial policies and the inferiority other 'races'. Fears of 'racial degeneration' fuelled hostility against 'foreign Jews' who it was claimed had unhygienic habits and 'either do not know how to use the latrine ... or prefer ... [to] ... use the floor of their rooms and passages to deposit their filth' (*Eastern Post and City Chronicle* 1884)[113] and never assimilate because 'A Jew is always a Jew' (*East London Advertiser* at the close of the century). There was also widespread accusations that Jewish financial interests were a main driving force for the Boer Wars (1880 to 1881 and 1899–1902).[114]

East End Tory MPs, the Aliens Act of 1905 and the 1906 general election

William Evans-Gordon and the British Brothers League

William Evans-Gordon, educated at Cheltenham College and the Sandhurst Military College, joined the army in 1876, was posted to India in 1877, and in 1878 was made a captain in the Madras (new Chennai) staff corps.[115] After 20 odd years in the service of the British Raj, Evans-Gordon retired from the army in 1897, returned to England and in 1898 was selected as Tory candidate for Stepney. During the 1990 General Election campaign, Evans-Gordon attempted to make Jewish immigration a major political issue, attacking Jews for alleged financial involvement in the Boer Wars.[116]

In addition to Evans-Gordon, the election brought into Parliament the following East End Tory MPs, all committed to restricting immigration: Samuel Forde Ridley (Bethnal Green South West), Claude Hay (Hoxton), Walter Guthrie (Bow and Bromley), Spencer Charrington (Mile End), Thomas Dewar (Tower Hamlets, St George) and Harry Samuel (Limehouse).[117] Evans-Gordon began an 'anti-alien campaign', arguing against 'the settlement of large aggregations of Hebrews in a Christian land', that has 'never been successful'[118] and stating that 'east of Aldgate one walks into a foreign town', 'a solid and permanently distinct block – a race apart, as it were, in an enduring island of extraneous thought and custom'.[119]

Evans-Gordon and other Tory MPs in the area galvanized some of the poor working-class population of the East End into angry street marches calling for an end to Jewish immigration. In one of the indoor rallies, one of the speakers stated that 'Englishmen' 'would not have this country made the dumping ground for the scum of Europe. This was England the heart of the Empire not the dustbin of Austria and Russia'.[120]

Together with Forde-Ridley and William Stanley Shaw, Evans-Gordon forged a populist anti-immigrant movement called the British Brothers' League (BBL), which launched itself at a 1,000-strong rally in the East End in May 1901.[121] The *Eastern Post and City Chronicle* enthusiastically reported BBL activities and demanded that the government end this 'foreign flood which has submerged our native population of East London'.[122] Within months, according to David Rosenberg, writing for *The Guardian*, the League claimed 6,000 members, mostly local factory workers and the unemployed, who were convinced by BBL propaganda that their 'precarious work situation, low pay, overcrowded housing and poor sanitation was caused by immigration'.[123] Rosenberg notes that while the BBL 'marched through impoverished East End districts, voicing working class concerns ... wealthier elements ran the organisation from its Gracechurch Street offices nestled comfortably within the City'.[124] Shaw, who became its first president, claimed the membership of the BBL included 40 Tory MPs.[125]

On a tier above the BBL was the Parliamentary Alien Immigration Committee.[126] The Committee was founded in August 1901 and comprised all the East End MPs (except the Liberal Party MP for Whitechapel, Stuart M. Samuel).[127] Based on the same ideas as those of the BBL, Evans-Gordon formed the Committee to work within Parliament.[128] As a parliamentary pressure group, it urged the government to pass restrictive immigration controls.[129]

The BBL held its largest rally on the periphery of the Jewish area, at the People's Palace, Mile End, in January 1902, with four simultaneous marches led by drummers converging on the building. The marchers held Union Jacks and placards proclaiming, 'British Homes for British Workers' while inside the hall, where 4,000 had gathered, an organ played 'There's No Place Like Home'.[130]

When the government launched a Royal Commission on alien immigration, Evans-Gordon chaired it and set the agenda. It investigated the very charges the BBL had made:

> that immigrants arrived impoverished, destitute and dirty; practised insanitary habits; spread infectious diseases; were a burden on the rates; dispossessed native dwellers; caused native tradesmen to suffer a loss of trade; worked for rates below the 'native workman'; included criminals, prostitutes and anarchists; formed a compact, non-assimilating community that didn't intermarry; and interfered with the observance of Christian Sunday.[131]

The commission struggled to back up the BBL's charges in its 1903 report. As Rosenberg concludes, far from dispossessing the local community, the immigrants themselves lived in 'appallingly overcrowded conditions', and mostly worked 'more than 12 hours a day for other Yiddish-speakers'. Moreover, their 'dedication to education and self-improvement contradicted claims that they lowered moral standards'.[132]

The 1905 Aliens Act

Nevertheless, the Tory Government introduced what was to become Britain's first modern immigration law – the 1905 Aliens Act. When the Bill was introduced into Parliament, Tory Prime Minister Balfour made clear that it would herald the biggest change in immigration policy since Elizabethan times – ending financial support for aliens and, at the same time, barring people 'mentally or physically diseased' from entering the country. Having claimed that the Bill 'has nothing whatever to do with what in Continental Europe, and especially in Eastern Europe, is called the Jewish question',[133] he asked:

> Why should we admit into this country people likely to become a public charge? Many countries which exclude immigrants have no Poor Laws they have not those great charities of which we justly boast. The immigrant comes in at his own peril and perishes if he cannot find a living. That is not the case here. From the famous Statute of Elizabeth we have taken on ourselves the obligation of supporting every man, woman, and child in this country and saving them from starvation. Is the Statute of Elizabeth to have European extension? Are we to be bound to support every man, woman, and child incapable of supporting themselves who choose to come to our shores? That argument seems to me to be preposterous. When it is remembered that some of these persons are a most undesirable element in the population, and are not likely to produce the healthy children… but are afflicted with disease either of mind or of body, which makes them intrinsically undesirable citizens, surely the fact that they are likely to become a public charge is a double reason for keeping them out of the country.[134]

Some 12 years later, as Foreign Secretary in the World War I Coalition Government, Balfour made a statement of British support for 'the establishment in Palestine of a national home for the Jewish people'. This became known as the Balfour Declaration of November 2, 1917, and was made to Lionel Walter Rothschild, a leader of the Anglo-Jewish community.[135] Two years later Balfour gave his reason, being that it would 'mitigate the age-long miseries created for Western civilization by the presence in its midst of a Body which it too long regarded as alien and even hostile, but which it was equally unable to expel or to absorb'.[136] As Youssef Munayyer, editorial committee member of the *Journal of Palestine*

Studies, argues, not only was Balfour an antisemite, he was also a White supremacist. He had made this clear in 1906 in a House of Commons debate about Black people in South Africa. While, according to Munayyer, nearly all the members of Parliament agreed that the disenfranchisement of Black people was evil, Balfour argued against giving Black people the vote in South Africa, asserting: 'We have to face the facts. Men are not born equal, the white and black races are not born with equal capacities: they are born with different capacities which education cannot and will not change'.[137]

As Rosenberg points out, free movement of labour was generally unquestioned until 'Conservative politicians stoked up the immigration issue in the 1880s and 90s and sections of the media fanned the flames'.[138] Rosenberg has summed up the short-term effects of the Aliens Act:

> The Aliens Act drastically reduced the numbers of Jews seeking economic betterment in Britain who were permitted to enter; it also prevented greater numbers of asylum-seekers, escaping harrowing persecution, from finding refuge. In 1906, more than 500 Jewish refugees were granted political asylum. In 1908 the figure had fallen to twenty and by 1910, just five. During the same period, 1,378 Jews, who had been permitted to enter as immigrants but were found to be living on the streets without any visible means of support, had been rounded up and deported back to their country of origin.[139]

The 1906 General Election

About six months after the Act gained royal assent, the 1906 General Election was held. In the Election Campaign, Tory MPs attempted to use immigration to win votes. For example, David Hope Kyd, the prospective MP for Whitechapel, told the electorate that Stuart Samuel, the sitting Liberal MP, was pro-alien and it was 'no good sending to Parliament a man who stands up… for the foreign Jews' and what was needed was 'someone who could speak for the English in Whitechapel'.[140] Another Tory, William Joynson-Hicks, mounted a racist campaign appealing to 'the British working man' to vote against 'Pro-Alien Radical Jews' (Samuel was Jewish[141]) and 'push back this intolerable invasion'.[142] He was taking part, in the memorable words of David Cesarani, in the second election in his 'anti-Jewish career'.[143]Joynson-Hicks was competing against Winston Churchill, then a Liberal MP in North Manchester, a constituency with a large Jewish population. Churchill played up his part in wrecking the first Aliens Bill in 1904. He had made his first speech from the opposition benches to oppose the bill, having recently left the Conservative Party,[144] and wrote a letter to the *Manchester Guardian*: 'To judge by the talk there has been, one would have imagined we were being overrun by the swarming invasion and "ousted" from our island' yet 'all the aliens of Great Britain do not amount to a one-hundred-and-fortieth part of the total population'.[145] He also announced his support for Jewish settlement in East Africa, while Joynson-Hicks enthusiastically defended the Aliens Act. In the end, Joynson-Hicks won by 429 votes.[146] Following his victory, he was invited to address a Jewish dining society, in the hope that he would declare his intention to represent his Jewish constituents. Instead, as if to confirm his antisemitism, he announced:

> If they liked he could say smooth things. He could say that they were a delightful people, that the Jews were delightful opponents, that he was very pleased to receive the opposition of the Jewish community, and that, in spite of all, he was their very humble and obedient servant. He could say that if they liked, but it would not be true in the slightest degree. He very strongly deprecated the position taken up by the great bulk of the Jewish community in Manchester. He thought it was an extraordinary fallacy from their point of view. He had beaten them thoroughly and soundly, and he was no longer their servant.[147]

Churchill, however, won the election, as the Liberals got in with a landslide, ending ten years of Unionist rule under Tory prime ministers. The BBL Tory MPs lost their seats. The Liberal Government under Henry Campbell-Bannerman, however, did not repeal the Aliens Act. In a by-election in 1908 (mandatory because Churchill had been promoted to a cabinet post), the 'Jewish Question' again loomed large and Churchill was widely criticized by members of the Jewish community because his Liberal Government far from repealing the Act were enforcing its provisions.[148] He responded by promising to do all he could to lessen the effects of the Act.[149] Joynson-Hicks, on the other hand, announced that he was 'not going to pander for the Jewish vote'. He would 'treat those who were Englishmen as Englishmen, but as to those who put their Jewish or foreign nationality before their English nationality, let them vote for Mr Churchill'.[150] Churchill accused him of antisemitism:

> I do not think that in his anti-semitic views Mr Johnson-Hicks really represents the Conservative party which, after all, once had its great leader Mr Disraeli ... But last week Mr Joynson-Hicks distinguished himself by putting himself altogether adrift from the interests and aspirations of the Jewish community ... He had indicated that the Jews have no right to their own sectional and communal life and that he was prepared to consider their position only if they came to him as good Englishmen.[151]

The *Manchester Guardian* reported another speech in which Joynson-Hicks had disclaimed support for Churchill as 'bogus deputations going to him from a few Jews who were not even on the register'.[152]

Appendix

The two World Wars: inter-imperialist rivalry and mass slaughter

A book about racism in the Tory Party is self-evidently not the place for a detailed discussion about the complexities of the two World Wars. At the same time, it would be disingenuous and inappropriate to ignore these wars that were devastating for vast swathes of humanity, not least since racism (especially antisemitism), imperialism and nationalism, key topics in the book, all loom large. I will briefly sketch out some salient features of each conflict.

The First World War

It is commonly asserted that the First World War was caused by the assassination of the Austrian Crown Prince Franz Ferdinand on June 28, 1914, by Gavrilo Princip in Sarajevo, a city in Austria-Hungary near the Serbian border. Princip was part of a movement of young Slavs of different ethnic and religious persuasions dedicated to overthrowing Austro-Hungarian rule in the cause of Serb national liberation. Austria-Hungary immediately blamed the Serbian government for the attack,[153] and while it is true that this was the spark that ignited the war, the real causes are to be found in historical processes that had been decades in the making.[154]

Among these were first, the economic evolution of German capitalism and its relation to the already established capitalist states of Britain and France. While the concept of *lebensraum* ('living space') is most commonly associated with Hitler and the Nazi era, it proliferated in Germany from the 1890s. Encompassing policies and practices of settler colonialism, it began with the reign of Kaiser Wilhelm II as King of Prussia and Emperor of Germany from 1888 that saw the meteoric rise of Germany as an economic and military power[155] (see chapter 2 for a discussion).

Second, was what Alan Woods refers to as 'the tangled web of inter-imperialist diplomacy in the same period'[156]. Third, there was the struggle for colonies, markets, and respective spheres of influence[157] (these are dealt with in detail in chapter 2). Fourth, we have the ambitions and expansionist tendencies of tsarist Russia; the wars in the Balkans and the contradictions arising from the decay of the Ottoman Empire.[158]

The Balkan Wars refer to two conflicts that took place in 1912 and 1913. In the first, four Balkan states defeated the Ottoman Empire; in the second, Bulgaria fought against all four original combatants of the first war along with facing a surprise attack from Romania from the north. As a result, the Ottoman Empire lost most of its territory in Europe. Austria-Hungary, although not a combatant, became relatively weaker as a much-enlarged Serbia pushed for union of the South Slavic peoples.[159] Woods sums up the wars as follows:

The Balkan Wars were, in essence, proxy wars mainly between tsarist Russia and Austria-Hungary. The Russians played the card of 'pan-Slavism' as a means of expanding their influence in the Balkans at the expense of both the Ottoman Empire and Austria-Hungary. Greatly enlarged by its conquests, the Serbian ruling class aimed at nothing less than the complete domination of the Balkans under the disguise of a union of the South Slavic peoples (Yugoslavia). This inevitably led to an open conflict with the Austro-Hungarian Empire, which saw itself threatened by Serbian and Russian ambitions. These wars appear on the surface as wars of national liberation and self-determination of the peoples of the Balkans. In reality they were no such thing. Behind every one of the national bourgeois cliques stood a 'big brother' in the shape of one or another of the Great Powers of Europe. ... Russia, Germany, France, Britain and Austria-Hungary used the Balkan nations as small change in their intrigues and manoeuvres.[160]

On the afternoon of August 3, 1914, two days after declaring war on Russia, Germany declared war on France, as part of a long-held strategy for a two-front war against France and Russia. Hours later, France declared war on Germany, getting its troops ready to move to the French-German border.[161] To avoid these fortifications, the German troops had to cross Belgium and attack the French Army by the north. The Belgians refused,[162] and on the morning of August 4, 1914, just over a month after Franz Ferdinand's assassination, Germany invaded Belgium. With the support of Liberal Prime Minister H. H. (Herbert) Asquith, King George V declared Britain to be at war with Germany for failing to respond to Britain's ultimatum demanding that Belgian neutrality be respected.[163]

Woods recounts a well-known story about British and French troops in the trenches at Christmas time. He explains how the first trenches were at first merely improvised affairs, 'often just shell-holes in which terrified soldiers would take refuge from the devastating hail of machine-gun bullets'.[164] However soon they became more permanent and complex, especially on the German side, where the soldiers enjoyed far better conditions than their French and British counterparts. Their trenches were deeper, better protected and provided with kitchens and other amenities.[165] He continues, while all wars consist of short bursts of violent activity separated by long periods of boredom, the static nature of trench warfare and its sheer tedium led to a growing curiosity about what was happening on the other side. Moreover, given the close proximity of troops on either side, they could often be heard but not seen.[166] They could smell each other's cooking, and there were occasional shouted conversations between trenches, where they shared similar conditions of wet and cold, and in some cases, an exchange of goods. In this way a mutual respect began to develop.[167] All this began to worry the generals who prohibited all contact with the enemy. Despite this, at Christmas time in 1914, the troops ventured outside their trenches and exchanged gifts and souvenirs. Instinctively, as Woods recounts, 'the workers in uniform realised that the men in the other trenches were workers like themselves, engaged in a senseless slaughter to protect the interests of kings, lords and capitalists'.[168] On Christmas Eve, 1914, both sides declared an unofficial truce and a football match was played. Apparently, in some places the truce lasted a week. It is estimated that as many as 100,000 men took part. The following Christmas, sentries on both sides had orders to shoot any soldiers who put their heads above the parapet.[169]

For the soldiers, the war was a seemingly endless nightmare. For the civilians on the home front, especially the women, hardly less so. In the end, large tracts of Europe lay wasted, millions were dead or wounded. As with all wars, the great majority of casualties were from the working class. 'Survivors lived on with severe mental trauma. The streets of every European city were full of limbless veterans. Nations were bankrupt – not just the losers, but also the victors'.[170] Woods concludes, the aim of the ruling class is always to divide the working class along national, ethnic, linguistic and other lines, being even more necessary during war than in peacetime, and the generals were horrified by the instinctive socializing of 'the workers in uniform', desiring the fomenting of hatred against 'the enemy' at all times.[171] This barbarity, he points out, was finally ended by the Russian Revolution, which immediately broke down the barriers that divided soldier from soldier and worker form worker, 'establishing the basis for the unity of the international proletariat that is the prior condition for the emancipation of the working class and of all humanity'.[172]

The Second World War

The devastation caused by the First World greatly destabilized Europe. In Germany, political and economic instability fuelled the rise of fascism, of Adolf Hitler and the National Socialist German Workers' Party (the Nazi Party) to power in 1933. The stage was set for the Second World War. Ascending to power in an economically and politically volatile Germany, Hitler rearmed the country and signed strategic treaties with Italy and Japan to further his ambitions of *lebensraum*, of world domination. Under Hitler, nearly half a century after Wilhelm II became Emperor (see the previous section of this Appendix), it was used to justify territorial expansion into Central and Eastern Europe. According to Nazi ideology, *lebensraum* was necessary for Germany's survival and so most of the indigenous populations of those parts of Europe needed to be removed by deportation, extermination or enslavement. In addition, as is universally known, the German Nazi Party also formulated the most extreme form of antisemitism to date, and as early as 1923 in Hitler's book *Mein Kamp*, he had predicted a general European war that would result in 'the extermination of the Jewish race in Germany'.[173]

Elisabeth Grünbauer has recalled that, while boarding with her family for over a year before volunteering in August 14 to fight in World War I, Hitler had commented on his dislike of Jews.[174] According to Dina Kraft, writing for *Haaretz*, this contrasts with historians who 'usually date Hitler's becoming a radical hater of Jews to his tumultuous years in Munich following World War I, a period when anti-Semitic sentiment raged in the city', where Jewish people were blamed for the conditions under which Germany agreed to end the war, as well as for the economic ruin and political upheaval that followed.[175] Apparently Hitler told Grünbauer that 'he did not want to serve in the military in Austria because Austria was too swamped with Jews',[176] which was also why he had left the country (he eventually fought World War I for Germany in the Bavarian army).[177] He also said that 'the Jews were exploiters, as they controlled Austria and the stock exchange'.[178] In *Mein Kamp,* Hitler wrote that his political awakening was sparked when he heard in 1918 about the beginning of what was later to be known as 'the German Revolution', inspired by socialist ideas where Jewish people were among its leaders and supporters. It was then, according to Hitler, that he decided to become a politician who could 'save' Germany.[179] His antisemitism was to become increasingly radical, declaring that he did not support uncontrolled 'emotional' pogroms (see chapter 2). Instead, he argued for an 'antisemitism of the mind'[180] that had to be legal and would ultimately lead to the 'removal' of the Jews.[181] In August 1920, Hitler compared Jewish people to germs, stating that diseases cannot be controlled unless you destroy their causes, arguing that the influence of Jewish people would never disappear without removing its cause, Jewish people, from our midst.[182] Historian and Holocaust scholar Robert Jan van Pelt has argued that Hitler's antisemitism:

> evolved into a complex, many-layered phenomenon that contained earlier strata that embraced popular tropes about Jews as having too much influence, etc., to what turned out to be the genocidal version that did not focus on particular Jews, or for that matter the Jewish people, but on 'the Jew'– a nefarious ogre-like pestilence that somehow had acquired some human form.[183]

This evolved around 1920 in an ongoing dialogue with Alfred Rosenberg, a key ideologue of the Nazi Party, whom he met in Munich and who went on to become one of the masterminds of the Holocaust.[184]

On September 1, 1939, Germany invaded Poland. To justify this, Nazi propagandists falsely claimed that Poland, with its allies Britain and France, had been planning to encircle and dismember Germany, and that Poles were persecuting ethnic Germans.[185] Two days later, Tory Prime Minister Neville Chamberlain announced that Britain was at war with Germany. In May, 1940, Winston Leonard Spencer Churchill replaced Chamberlain as Prime Minister following the latter's resignation after losing a confidence vote in the House of Commons. He was to remain Prime Minister and wartime leader for the duration of the war (see chapter 3 for a discussion of Churchill).

World War II was the deadliest conflict in history, involving all the great powers of the world, divided into Allied and Axis powers. It was the only war to have used nuclear weapons, with the United States detonating two atomic bombs on the Japanese cities of Hiroshima and Nagasaki. Marked by the Holocaust, World War II changed world politics forever.

The slaughters in the World Wars

The total number of military and civilian casualties in World War I was around 40 million. There were 20 million deaths and 21 million wounded. The total number of deaths included 9.7 million military personnel and about 10 million civilians.[186] World War II resulted in between 59 and 80 million deaths of which between 22 and 25 million were military deaths and 37 to 55 million civilian deaths.[187] As well as killing some six million Jews, during the era of the Holocaust in the concentration camps that we should never forget, we should also never forget that Nazi authorities also targeted and killed other groups, including at times their children, because of their perceived 'racial' and biological inferiority. These included around seven million Soviet citizens (including 1.3 Soviet Jewish civilians, who are included in the six million figure for Jews). Victims also encompassed some 300,000 Serbs; up to 250,000 people with disabilities; between 250,000 and 500,000 Roma; nearly 2,000 Jehovah's Witnesses; and hundreds, possibly thousands, of gay men plus other so-called 'asocials',[188] including lesbians.[189]

All these needless deaths must be remembered and commemorated. However, as Michael Chessum argues in the *New Statesman*, the idea of coming together to mourn the dead 'above all the politics' as is often the case in memorial commemorations in many countries is a fantasy.[190] As Chessum correctly notes, war 'is deeply political, and the way we commemorate it even more so'.[191] Underling the essential *political* nature of wars, and referring to World War I, he asserts, a 'million British men were slaughtered in, sent to their deaths in a war fought not against fascism, but for the imperial interests of the British ruling class against the German one'.[192]

The dead in all wars must be remembered. However, to take the case of those British political leaders laying wreaths at the cenotaph in London, most of them, especially Tories, have been and are at the same time involved in arms deals with various countries. Apart from the hypocrisy, remembrances should not be about patriotism and glory (the First World War is often referred to as the 'Great War').

The Holocaust: turning point for scientific racism

At the beginning of chapter 2, I briefly addressed eugenics, a field of enquiry that focuses on improving the genetic quality of the White 'race'. Hitler began reading about eugenics and Social Darwinism while he was imprisoned following a failed 1924 coup attempt known as the 'Beer Hall Putsch',[193] an attempt by Hitler and his followers to take over the Bavarian Government. From 1933 to 1945, Nazi Germany carried out a campaign to 'cleanse' German society of individuals viewed as biological threats to the nation's 'health'. Enlisting the help of physicians and medically trained geneticists, psychiatrists and anthropologists, the Nazis developed 'racial' health policies, beginning with the mass sterilization of 'genetically diseased' persons and ending with the near annihilation of European Jewish people. With the veneer of legitimacy provided by 'racial' science experts, the Nazi regime carried out a program of approximately 400,000 forced sterilizations and over 275,000 euthanasia deaths that found its most extreme manifestation, as we have seen, in the death of millions of 'racial' enemies in the Holocaust.[194]

Following the end of World War II, a worldwide network of racist and fascist scientists found it necessary to cloak their unrepentant eugenicist views, quietly founding journals and funding research, providing the shoddy studies that were eventually cited in Richard Herrnstein's and Charles Murray's 1994 book, *The Bell Curve*, a watershed moment for scientific racism[195] (see chapter 7 for further details of this book). The eugenics campaign continued to gain momentum in the interwar years. Membership of the British Eugenics Society reached its peak during the 1930s. The 1934 report of the Departmental Committee on Sterilisation chaired by Lord Brock recommended legislation to ensure the 'voluntary' sterilization of 'mentally defective women'.

As science writer and freelance journalist Ramin Skibba puts it, 'It would take the Holocaust to show the world the logical endpoint of such horrific ideology, discrediting much race-based science and forcing eugenics' most hardline adherents into the shadows'.[196] *The Bell Curve* notwithstanding, instead of using 'races' and 'racial differences', they used 'populations' and 'human variation'.

Angela Saini gives the example of Reginald Ruggles Gates,[197] describing him as 'one of those well-to-do, gentlemanly race scientists who had been the norm in the 19th century ... a colonial type ... and supporter of segregation in the United States'.[198] Gates could not accept the changing public mood about 'race' and UNESCO's 1949/1950 statements that we all belong to one species, *homo sapiens*,[199] so he called time and again for the objective continuing study of 'race', believing this to be *true* science, and that UNESCO was ignoring facts in favour of liberal antiracist politics.[200] While some eugenicists moved into newer fields such as genetics, evolutionary biology and psychology, others, Gates among them, continued to search for 'proof' that 'race' was genetically tangible, that evidence for deep 'racial' differences could be found at the molecular level.[201]

In remembering the Holocaust, while not in any way lessening the need for mourning and commemorating the loss of six million Jewish people, we should also remember the other casualties of Nazism. In addition, we should be mindful of victims of all forms of genocide, and of course be vigilant about the growth of other forms of fascism. Crucially, especially in the light of the rise of a 21st century fascism in many continents of the world, most significantly in the United States, alongside that of antiracism the promotion of anti-fascism is an urgent priority.[202] To reiterate, remembering and commemorating the dead and the casualties should not be about patriotism and glory, but should involve invoking the dangers of imperialism, nationalism, fascism and war in general, and promoting internationalism and peace and, from this writer's perspective, advocating feminist, antiracist fully inclusive ecosocialism as the best solution for ending wars.[203]

Notes

1 History.com Editors. 2018. 'Social Darwinism', *History.com*, August 21. https://www.history.com/topics/early-20th-century-us/social-darwinism#:~:text=Social%20Darwinism%20is%20a%20loose,%2C%20social%2C%20or%20economic%20views.

2 Ibid.

3 Ibid.

4 Ibid.

5 Skibba, Ramin. 2019. 'The disturbing resilience of scientific racism', p. 1. https://www.smithsonianmag.com/science-nature/disturbing-resilience-scientific-racism-180972243/.

6 Brignell, Victoria. 2010. 'The eugenics movement Britain wants to forget'.

7 Ibid.

8 Ibid.

9 Cited in Brignell. 2010.

10 Ibid.

11 Ibid.

12 Walsh, Pat. 2017. 'The Eugenics Congress, London 1912', *History and Politics Analyst*, May 26. https://drpatwalsh.com/2017/05/26/the-eugenics-congress-london-1912/.

13 Alexander, Dominic. 2017. 'The Long Depression: how it happened, why it happened, and what happens next', June 29. https://www.counterfire.org/articles/book-reviews/19065-the-long-depression-how-it-happened-why-it-happened-and-what-happens-next.

14 Roberts. 2016, p. 2.

15 Alexander. 2017.

16 For an explanation of this crisis, see Sassoon. 2012. 'To understand this crisis we can look to the Long Depression too', *The Guardian*, April 29.

17 Office of the Historian, US Department of State. Undated.

18 Fhlathúin. 2008.

19 Gathara. 2019.

20 Ibid.

21 Lenin, Vladimir Ilyich. 1916. *Imperialism, the Highest Stage of Capitalism*.

22 Rodney. 1970.

23 Saul, David. 2011. 'Slavery and the "Scramble for Africa"'. http://www.bbc.co.uk/history/british/abolition/scramble_for_africa_article_01.shtml.

24 Ibid.

25 Hickman. 2019.

26 Bloy. 2003.

27 Liberal History: The website of the Liberal Democrat History Group. Undated 'Liberal Unionists'.

28 Fhlathúin, Máire Ní. 2008.

29 South African History Online (SAHO). 2019.

30 SAHO. 2019.

31 Cited in SAHO. 2019.

32 SAHO. 2019.
33 Ibid.
34 Ibid.
35 Cited in SAHO. 2019.
36 SAHO. 2017. 'Black concentration camps during the Anglo-Boer War 2, 1900–1902'. https://www.sahistory.org.za/article/black-concentration-camps-during-anglo-boer-war-2-1900-1902.
37 Ibid.
38 Ibid.
39 Ibid.
40 Benneyworth, G. C. 2019, p. 6.
41 SAHO. 2017.
42 Blaxill, p. 418. To back this up, Blaxill cites the work of Shannon. 1996; James. 1970; Charmley. 1996; Green. 1995 and Green 1885.
43 Matthew, 'Rhetoric and politics', p. 49, cited in Blaxill, p. 417. Blaxill informs us that McKenzie and Silver, *Angels in Marble*, pp. 49–50 argue on similar lines, viewing Crystal Palace as the moment Disraeli 'picked up the banner of imperialism', cited in Blaxhill, p. 439, Note 9.
44 Thompson, A., pp. 15–16, cited in Blaxill, pp. 417–418.
45 Green, E.E.H. 1996. *The Crisis of Conservatism: The Politics, Economics and Ideology of the British Conservative Party, 1880–1914*, London: Routledge, p. 59.
46 Ibid.
47 Fletcher, T. W. 1973. 'The Great Depression of English agriculture 1873–1896', in P. J. Perry (ed.), *British Agriculture 1875–1914*, London: Methuen, p. 31.
48 Howkins, Alun. 1991. *Reshaping Rural England. A Social History 1850–1925*, London: HarperCollins Academic, p. 138.
49 Cannadine. 1990. *The Decline and Fall of the British Aristocracy*, New Haven, pp. 133–134, 444–445, 588–605; Davis and Huttenback. *Mammon*, pp. 210–12, cited in Green. 1996, p. 59.
50 Cannadine, *British Aristocracy*, p. 588, cited in Green. 1996, p. 59.
51 Roberts, Matthew. 2006. 'Villa Toryism and Popular Conservatism in Leeds, 1885–1902', *The Historical Journal*, 41 (1), p. 217.
52 de Cecco, 'Money and Empire'; Huttenback and Davis. *Mammon*, cited in Green. 1996, pp. 59–60.
53 Green. 1996, p. 60.
54 Ibid.
55 Blaxill, Luke. 'The language of imperialism in British electoral politics, 1880–1910', *The Journal of Imperial and Commonwealth History*, 45 (3), p. 417. For the centrality of public speeches and meetings to electoral life in these years, see Lawrence, *Electing Our Masters*.
56 Blaxill, p. 417.
57 Ibid., p. 416.
58 Ibid., p. 423.
59 Ibid., p. 416.
60 Ibid., p. 438.
61 Ibid., p. 429.
62 Ibid.
63 Ibid.
64 Cited in Blaxill. 2017, pp. 429–430.
65 Blaxill, p. 430.
66 Cited in Blaxill, p. 430.
67 Blaxill, p. 430. This was during the depression in British agriculture; see also Blaxill. 2015.
68 Ibid.

69   Vivid Maps. 2022. 'British Empire at its territorial peak'. https://vividmaps. com/british-empire-at-its-territorial-peak/.
70   Semmel, 1968. *Imperialism and Social Reform*, p. 12.
71   Kiernan, V. G. 1969.
72   Green, E. E. H. 1985. 'Radical conservatism: the electoral genesis of tariff reform', *The Historical Journal*, 28 (3), September, p. 669.
73   Crick, Martin. 1994. *History of the Social-Democratic Federation,* Edinburgh: Edinburgh University Press, pp. 13–14.
74   https://www.marxists.org/archive/marx/works/download/pdf/Manifesto.pdf.
75   This was presumably Volume 1: Marx, Karl. 1887. *Capital: A Critique of Political Economy. Volume I. The Process of Production of Capital.* https://www.marxists. org/archive/marx/works/1867-c1/. Hyndman's views, like many other socialists of his era, were contradictory. A committed anti-imperialist, he opposed the first Boer War, but then supported the First World War, alienating him from most of his fellow socialists. He was an antisemite who blamed 'Jewish bankers' and 'imperialist Judaism' for the second Boer War. McGeever, Brendan, and Satnam Virdee. 2017. 'Antisemitism and socialist strategy in Europe, 1880–1917: an introduction', *Patterns of Prejudice* 51 (3–4), p. 229 (see the second part of this chapter on 'Antisemitism').
76   The Editors of Encyclopaedia Britannica. Undated. 'Henry Mayers Hyndman British Marxist'. https://www.britannica.com/biography/Henry-Mayers-Hyndman. For a discussion of Robert Owen and the early Utopian Socialists, see Cole, M. 2007. *Marxism and Education: Origins and Issues,* London: Routledge.
77   Crick, Martin. 1994. *History of the Social-Democratic Federation,* Edinburgh: Edinburgh University Press, pp. 13–14.
78   Semmel. 1968, p. 24.
79   Timms, Elizabeth Jane. 2019.
80   Longford, Elizabeth. 2019, p. 438.
81   Longford. 2019. *Queen Victoria*, Orion Publishing Group, p. 402, cited in Tims. https://royalcentral.co.uk/features/primroses-for-her-prime-minister-benjam in-disraeli-and-queen-victoria-126648/.
82   Longford. 2019.
83   Timms, Elizabeth Jane. 2019. 'Primroses for her Prime Minister: Benjamin Disraeli and Queen Victoria', *Royal Central*, July 11. https://royalcentral.co. uk/features/primroses-for-her-prime-minister-benjamin-disraeli-and-queen-vic toria-126648/.
84   Cooke. 2011.
85   MacKenzie. 1984, p. 150.
86   MacKenzie. 1984, pp. 150–151.
87   Lorimer. 1978, p. 107.
88   Mangan, J. A. 1986. 'The grit of our forefathers' in MacKenzie (ed.).
89   Williams. 1961, pp. 168–172.
90   Miles. 1982, pp. 110, 119.
91   Summerfield. 1986, p. 42.
92   Bratton. 1986.
93   Springhall. 1986.
94   Pitman. *King Edward History Readers for Juniors*, cited in Chancellor. 1970, pp. 127–128.
95   Miles. 1993, p. 69.
96   Glendenning. 1973, p. 35.
97   Chancellor. 1970, p. 240.
98   *Cassell's Class History of England*, cited in Chancellor. 1970. p. 122.
99   Ibid.

100 For a discussion of education at this time, see Cole. 2018b.
101 Hobson. 1902, cited in Springhall. 1986, p. 49.
102 Springhall. 1986, p. 49.
103 Ibid., p. 50.
104 Ratzabi, Hila. 2022. 'What were pogroms?', *Jewish Learning*. https://www.myje wishlearning.com/article/what-were-pogroms/.
105 Ibid.
106 Ibid.
107 O'Day, Rosemary. Undated. 'The Jews of London: From diaspora to White-chapel'. http://fathom.lse.ac.uk/Features/122537/.
108 Ratzabi.
109 O'Day. 'The Jews of London: From diaspora to Whitechapel'.
110 Elman, Peter. 1951. 'The beginnings of the Jewish trade union movement in England', *Transactions*, JHSE 17, p. 54.
111 Broadberry, Stephen and Burhop, Carsten. 2010. *Real Wages and Labor Productivity in Britain and Germany, 1871–1938: A Unified Approach to the International Comparison of Living Standards*, p. 407. https://core.ac.uk/download/pdf/ 1353371.pdf.
112 Elman, Peter. 1951.
113 Cited in Holmes, Colin. 1979. *Anti-Semitism in British Society 1876–1939*, London: Edward Arnold, p. 17.
114 Cardaun, p. 40.
115 Brodie, Marc. 2004. 'William Evans-Gordon'. *Oxford Dictionary of National Biography*. https://doi.org/10.1093/ref:odnb/58246.
116 Spartacus Educational. 2020a. 'William Evans-Gordon'. https://spartacus-educa tional.com/William_Evans-Gordon.htm.
117 Spartacus Educational. 2020a.
118 Rosenberg, David. 2011. *Battle for the East End: Jewish Responses to Fascism in the 1930s*, Nottingham: Five Leaves Publications, pp. 22–23.
119 Holmes, Colin. 1979. *Anti-Semitism in British Society, 1876–1939*, p. 27, cited in Spartacus Educational. 2020b. https://spartacus-educational.com/U3Ahis tory45.htm.
120 Cohen, Steve. 1985. 'British Brothers' League: birth of British Fascism?', *Jewish Socialist* 3, cited in Rosenberg, David. 2011. *Battle for the East End: Jewish Responses to Fascism in the 1930s*, p. 23. Approximately 20,000 German, Austrian, Dutch, and Rumanian Jews had entered the country after the turn of the century. 'Eastern European Jews arrive', *The Jewish East End*, 2021. https:// www.jack-the-ripper.org/jewish-east-end.htm.
121 Rosenberg, David. 2015. 'Ukip is nothing new: the British Brothers' League was exploiting immigration fears in 1901', *The Guardian*, 4 March. https://www. theguardian.com/uk-news/2015/mar/04/ukip-nigel-farage-immigrants-british-brothers-league.
122 Cited in Rosenberg. 2015.
123 Rosenberg. 2015.
124 Ibid.
125 Ibid.
126 Holmes, Colin. 2016. *Anti-Semitism in British Society, 1876–1939*, London: Routledge.
127 Toczek, Nick. 2016. *Haters, Baiters and Would-Be Dictators: Anti-Semitism and the UK Far Right*, Abingdon: Routledge.
128 Glover, D. 2009. 'Imperial Zion: Israel Zangwill and the English origins of territorialism' in E. Bar-Yosef and N. Valman (eds), *'The Jew' in Late-Victorian and Edwardian Culture: Between the East End and East Africa*, Houndsmill: Palgrave Macmillan.

129 Toczek, Nick. 2016. *Haters, Baiters and Would-Be Dictators: Anti-Semitism and the UK Far Right*, Abingdon: Routledge.

130 Rosenberg. 2015.

131 Ibid.

132 Ibid.

133 According to Geoffrey Alderman. 1998. *Modern British Jewry*, Oxford: Clarendon Press, p. 133, although the word 'Jew' was absent from the legislation, during the committee stage of the Alien Bill, Balfour did argue that Jews should be prevented from arriving in Britain because they were not 'to the advantage of the civilisation of this country' and that should there 'be an immense body of persons who, however patriotic, able and industrious, however much they threw themselves into the national life' in the country 'they are a people apart and not only had a religion differing from the vast majority of their fellow countrymen but only intermarry amongst themselves'.

134 Arthur Balfour, speech in the House of Commons (2nd May 1905). https://api. parliament.uk/historic-hansard/commons/1905/may/02/aliens-bill-1#S4V0145P 0_19050502_HOC_228. The Statute of Elizabeth that Balfour is referring to is the basis of UK charity law. The preamble to the Charitable Uses Act of 1601 (the Statute of Elizabeth 1) guidance as to what purposes are charitable and begins with: 'the relief of aged, impotent, and poor people', Malik, Nuzhat. 2008. 'Europe: overview of public benefit status defining "charity" and "charitable purposes"' in the United Kingdom, *The International Journal of Not-for-Profit Law*, 11 (1). https://www. icnl.org/resources/research/ijnl/defining-charity-and-charitable-purposes-in-the -united-kingdom.

135 The Editors of Encyclopaedia Britannica. Undated. 'Balfour Declaration United Kingdom [1917]'. https://www.britannica.com/event/Balfour-Declara tion. The first President of Israel, Chaim Weizmann understandably regarded William Evans-Gordon as the 'father of the Aliens Act.' (Gainer, Bernard. 1972. *The Alien Invasion: The Origins of the Aliens Act of 1905*, p. 182, cited in Spartacus Educational. 2020c. 'Anti-Semitism in Britain'. https://spartacus-educational. com/U3Ahistory45.htm.

136 Cited in Munayyer, Yousef. 2017. 'It's time to admit that Arthur Balfour was a white supremacist – and an anti-Semite too', *Institute for Palestine Studies*, November 1. https://www.palestine-studies.org/en/node/232119.

137 Ibid.

138 Rosenberg. 2015

139 Rosenberg. 2011. *Battle for the East End: Jewish Responses to Fascism in the 1930s*, p. 114.

140 Holmes, Colin. 1979. *Anti-Semitism in British Society, 1876–1939*, p. 28, cited in Spartacus Educational. 2020b. https://spartacus-educational.com/ U3Ahistory45.htm.

141 Jewish Telegraph Agency. 1926. 'Sir Stuart Samuel dies; brother of Sir Herbert', May 16. https://www.jta.org/archive/sir-stuart-samuel-dies-brother-of-sir-herbert.

142 Thompson, Paul. 1967. *Socialists, Liberals and Labour: the Struggle for London, 1885–1914*, p. 29, cited in Spartacus Educational. 2020b. https://spartacus-educational.com/U3Ahistory45.htm.

143 Cesarani, David. 1989. 'The anti-Jewish career of Sir William Joynson-Hicks, Cabinet Minister', *Journal of Contemporary History*, 24, p. 461.

144 Churchill's Oldham constituency was an important centre of the cotton-spinning industry, and many of his constituents supported the duties on cheap foreign textiles supported by the Tory party at the time. Churchill defected to the Liberals as a supporter of free trade. Lowe, Josh. 2014. 'Tory crisis: the most famous defectors in British politics', *Prospect*, September 29. https://

www.prospectmagazine.co.uk/other/tory-crisis-british-politicss-most-famous-defectors-mark-reckless.

145 Churchill Book Collection. Undated. 'Mr. Winston Churchill on the Aliens Bill'. https://www.churchillbookcollector.com/pages/books/001777/winston-s-churchill/mr-winston-churchill-on-the-aliens-bill.

146 Cited in Cesarani. 1989, p. 463.

147 Cesarani. 1989, p. 464.

148 Ibid., p. 462.

149 Ibid.

150 Cite in Cesarani. 1989, p. 462.

151 Ibid., p. 462.

152 Cited in Cesarani. 1989, p. 463.

153 History.com. 2022a. 'June 28, 1914: Austria's Archduke Ferdinand assassinated'. https://www.history.com/this-day-in-history/archduke-ferdinand-assassinated#:~:text=The%20assassination%20set%20off%20a,France%20and%20possibly%20Great%20Britain.

154 Woods. Alan. 2019. *The First World War: A Marxist Analysis of the Great Slaughter*, London: Wellred.

155 Imperial War Museum. 2022. 'How Kaiser Wilhlem II changed Europe forever'. https://www.iwm.org.uk/history/how-kaiser-wilhelm-ii-changed-europe-forever.

156 Woods. Alan. 2019. 'Assassination in Sarajevo', in *The First World War: A Marxist Analysis of the Great Slaughter*, London: Wellred. https://www.marxist.com/first-world-war-a-marxist-analysis-of-the-great-slaughter/1.-assassination-in-sarajevo.htm.

157 Ibid.

158 Woods. 2019.

159 Clark. 2013, pp. 45, 559.

160 Woods. 2019.

161 History.com. 2022b. '3 August, 1914: Germany and France declare war on each other'. https://www.history.com/this-day-in-history/germany-and-france-declare-war-on-each-other.

162 Borrell-Verdu, Stephanie. 2018. 'Belgium, U.S. involvement in World War I', *USAG Benelux Public Affairs*, February 16. https://www.army.mil/article/200760/belgium_u_s_involvement_in_world_war_i#:~:text=Germany%20declared%20war%20on%20France,4%2C%201914.

163 UK Parliament. 2022. 'King George V'. https://www.parliament.uk/about/living-heritage/transformingsociety/private-lives/yourcountry/collections/the-outbreak-of-the-first-world-war/king-george-v/.

164 Woods. Alan. 2019. 'The great slaughter begins', in *The First World War: A Marxist Analysis of the Great Slaughter*, London: Wellred. https://www.marxist.com/first-world-war-a-marxist-analysis-of-the-great-slaughter/5.-the-great-slaughter-begins.htm.

165 Ibid.

166 Ibid.

167 Ibid.

168 Ibid.

169 Ibid.

170 Woods. 2019.

171 https://www.marxist.com/first-world-war-a-marxist-analysis-of-the-great-slaughter/5.-the-great-slaughter-begins.htm.

172 Ibid.

173 History.com, Editors. 2021. 'World War II.' https://www.history.com/topics/world-war-ii/world-war-ii-history.

174   Kraft, Dina. 2020. 'When did Hitler start hating Jews? New evidence may change what we know', *Haaretz*, February 16. https://www.haaretz.com/amp/jewish/holocaust-remembrance-day/.premium.MAGAZINE-when-did-hitler-start-hating-jews-new-evidence-may-change-what-we-know-1.8529591.

175   Kraft. 2000.

176   Cited in Kraft. 2000.

177   Kraft. 2000.

178   Cited in Kraft. 2000.

179   Kraft. 2000.

180   'Antisemitismus der Vernunft'. In: *Hitler, Adolf*. 1919. Gutachten über den Antisemitismus, erstellt im Auftrag seiner militärischen Vorgesetzten'. Included in: Maser, Werner. 1973. *Hitlers Briefe und Notizen.*

181   Anne Frank House. Undated. 'Antisemitism: Why did Hitler hate the Jews'. https://www.annefrank.org/en/anne-frank/go-in-depth/why-did-hitler-hate-jews/#source-392934.

182   Ibid.

183   Cited in Kraft. 2020.

184   Kraft. 2020.

185   Holocaust Encyclopedia. Undated. 'Invasion of Poland, Fall, 1939'. https://encyclopedia.ushmm.org/content/en/article/invasion-of-poland-fall-1939.

186   For full details of casualties and combatants, including breakdown by respective countries and empires, see Mougel. 2011. http://www.centre-robert-schuman.org/userfiles/files/REPERES%20%E2%80%93%20module%201-2-0%20-%20explanatory%20notes%20%E2%80%93%20World%20War%20II%20casualties%20%E2%80%93%20EN.pdf.

187   Ibid.

188   For full details of deaths, see U.S. Holocaust Memorial Museum, Washington, DC, 2020.

189   Schoppmann. 1996.

190   Chessum. Michael. 2017. 'War is deeply political, and the way we commemorate it even more so', *New Statesman*, November 11. https://www.newstatesman.com/politics/uk/2017/11/war-deeply-political-and-way-we-commemorate-it-even-more-so.

191   Chessum. 2017.

192   Ibid.

193   History.com, Editors. 2018. 'Social Darwinism'.

194   United States Holocaust Memorial Museum. Undated. 'Nazi racial science'. https://www.ushmm.org/collections/bibliography/nazi-racial-science.

195   Skibba. 2019.

196   Ibid., p. 1.

197   Saini, chapter 4.

198   Ibid., p. 86.

199   Ibid., pp. 88–93.

200   Gavin Schaffer, author of *Racial Science and British Society, 1930–1962*, cited in Saini, p. 93.

201   Saini, p. 96.

202   See Cole, Mike. 2019. For a discussion of Trump and the rise of fascism in the US; see also Cole. 2020a.

203   See Cole, Mike. 2021.

Part 2

From Empire and colonies to Powellism

3   The imperial and 'racial' politics of Winston Churchill (1898–1955)

SECTION 1: FROM 21ST LANCER TO WARTIME LEADER (1898–1950)

Winston Leonard Spencer-Churchill: imperialist and colonial racist

In the Introduction to this book, I discussed the colonial and imperial origin of colour-coded racism. Throughout his life, Winston Churchill espoused and defended the very worst excesses of the Empire. In 1898, riding with the 21st Lancers in one of the British Empire's last cavalry charges, known as the Charge at Omdurman, Churchill was part of an Anglo-Egyptian force sent to reconquer the Sudan to end Dervish rule, which threatened British interests in Egypt[1] (see chapter 2). Led by Horatio Kitchener, Churchill was then a lieutenant in the British army. Compared to less than 50 Britons, it left 10,000 Dervishes dead.[2] As a result of the Charge at Omdurman, the 21st Lancers were awarded the title 'Empress of India's' by Queen Victoria.[3] According to historian Nigel Jones, writing for the right-wing *Daily Mail,* before the battle, Churchill had confided to his mother that he had a 'Keen desire to kill several of these odious dervishes… I anticipate enjoying the exercise very much'.[4] It would seem he had his wish. Afterwards, in language typical of colonial racism in the days of Empire, he boasted of killing three 'savages'.[5] Churchill also took part in the 'Relief of Ladysmith' against the Boers during the second Boer War in South Africa in 1900 and supported the setting up of concentration camps in the early 1900s that resulted in the deaths of thousands of innocent men, women, and children[6] (see chapter 2). Churchill advocated against Black or indigenous self-rule in Africa, Australia, the Caribbean, the Americas and India, believing that British imperialism in its colonies was for the good of the 'primitive' and 'subject races'.[7]

Like Disraeli, Winston Churchill believed in the supremacy of the White 'race'. We saw at the beginning of chapter 2 that Churchill thought that disabled people were a danger to 'the race' and that he was a keen eugenicist who attended the first International Eugenics Conference. Not only was

DOI: 10.4324/9781003198673-6

he a White supremacist, there are also indications that he had similar views to Disraeli on Jewish superiority. In a 1920 article, of Jewish people, Churchill wrote, 'no thoughtful man can doubt the fact that they are beyond all question the most formidable and the most remarkable race which has ever appeared in the world'.[8] In the same article, he was approving of Disraeli, 'the Jew Prime Minister of England, and Leader of the Conservative Party, who was always true to his race and proud of his origin'.[9] Again recalling Disraeli, he writes:

> We owe to the Jews in the Christian revelation a system of ethics which, even if it were entirely separated from the supernatural, would be incomparably the most precious possession of mankind, worth in fact the fruits of all other wisdom and learning put together. On that system and by that faith there has been built out of the wreck of the Roman Empire the whole of our existing civilisation.[10]

Like Disraeli, Churchill also foresaw and looked forward to the creation of Israel, that he believed would coincide with British imperial interests:

> if, as may well happen, there should be created in our own lifetime by the banks of the Jordan a Jewish State under the protection of the British Crown, which might comprise three or four millions of Jews, an event would have occurred in the history of the world which would, from every point of view, be beneficial, and would be especially in harmony with the truest interests of the British Empire.[11]

Not surprisingly though, given his overall anti-socialist worldview, Churchill was highly critical of 'international and for the most part atheistical Jews', who preached 'the gospel of Antichrist',[12] and played an important role in the Russian Revolution. His White supremacist views were clearly enunciated in 1937. As a British politician responsible, along with others, for determining the future status of the Jewish National Home on Palestinian soil (this was of course before World War II and the Holocaust, and the establishment of the state of Israel in 1948),[13] he stated that the Jews would make the desert bloom, and a Jewish national home in Palestine is for the good of the world because the Arabs can never cultivate the land.[14] When William Peel, a former Secretary of State for India, suggested that Britain 'might have some compunction if she felt she was downing the Arabs year after year when they wanted to remain in their own country',[15] Churchill replied, comparing Arabic people and the people of the First Nations of America and Australia to animals:

> I do not admit that the dog in a manger has the final right to the manger even though he may have lain there for a long time ... I do not admit for instance, that a great wrong has been done to the Red

Indians of America or the black people of Australia. I do not admit that a wrong has been done to these people by the fact that a stronger race, a higher-grade race, a more worldly wise race to put it that way, has come in and taken their place.[16]

Churchill's contempt for Arabic people was also revealed when he referred to them as 'hordes of Islam' who had 'smashed up' Palestine and left the country desert for 'thousands of years',[17] and also as 'barbaric hordes who ate little but camel dung'.[18] His Islamophobic views were further revealed in a 1899 book *The River War*, an account of the 1896 to 1899 conquest of the Sudan in which he took part as noted at the beginning of this section of the chapter. In it, he wrote: 'How dreadful are the curses which Moham-medanism lays on its votaries! Besides the fanatical frenzy, which is as dan-gerous in a man as hydrophobia [rabies] in a dog, there is this fearful fatalistic apathy'. Churchill also referred to the 'Improvident habits, slovenly systems of agriculture, sluggish methods of commerce and insecurity of property exist wherever the followers of the Prophet rule or live'.[19]

His love of Empire, however, transcended any Islamophobia, allowing Churchill to authorise the building of a mosque in London during World War II. In 1940 George Lloyd, Secretary of State for the Colonies,[20] sent a memo to Churchill, in which he pointed out:

only London contains more [Muslims] than any other European capital but that in our empire which actually contains more Moslems than Christians it was anomalous and inappropriate that there should be no central place of worship for Mussulmans. The gift, moreover, of a site for a mosque would serve as a tribute to the loyalty of the Moslems of the Empire and would have a good effect on Arab countries of the Middle East.[21]

The Churchill War Cabinet then authorised the allocation of £100,000 for a mosque site in London.[22]

Churchill also admitted that he 'did not really think that black people were as capable or as efficient as white people'.[23] He once wrote of his 'irritation that Kaffirs [racist term for Black people, mainly from South Africa] should be allowed to fire on white men'.[24] He also regarded Ken-yans as 'Light-hearted, tractable if brutish children ... capable of being instructed'.[25]

Churchill hated Asian people too. In 1902, he wrote about Chinese people:

I think we shall have to take the Chinese in hand and regulate them. I believe that as civilized nations become more powerful they will get more ruthless, and the time will come when the world will impatiently bear the existence of great barbaric nations who may at any time arm

themselves and menace civilized nations. I believe in the ultimate partition of China – I mean ultimate. I hope we shall not have to do it in
our day. The Aryan stock is bound to triumph.[26]

As Colonial Secretary in the 1920s, Churchill opined that Indians in East
Africa were 'mainly of a very low class of coolies, and the idea that they
should be put on equality with the Europeans is revolting to every white
man throughout British East Africa'.

Archibald Wavell, the last Viceroy of India but one, viewed Churchill at
heart as having a 'cavalry subaltern's idea of India'.[27] This included his idea
that 'democracy is totally unsuited to India' because they were 'humble
primitives'. When the Viceroy of India, Edward Wood, told him that his
opinions were out of date and that he ought to meet some Indians in order
to understand their views, he rejected the suggestion, declaring, 'I am quite
satisfied with my views of India. I don't want them disturbed by any bloody
Indian'.[28]

Sashi Tharoor has said that Churchill should be remembered alongside
the most prominent dictators of the 20th century.[29] He argues that the
blame for the Bengal Famine that occurred during World War II in 1943,
where up to four million Bengalis starved to death when he diverted food
to British soldiers and elsewhere, should rest with Churchill.[30] In Tharoor's
words:

> Not only did the British pursue its own policy of not helping the
> victims of this famine which was created by their policies. Churchill
> persisted in exporting grain to Europe, not to feed actual 'Sturdy
> Tommies', to use his phrase, but add to the buffer stocks that were
> being piled up in the event of a future invasion of Greece and
> Yugoslavia.[31]

'Ships laden with wheat were coming in from Australia docking in Calcutta
and were instructed by Churchill not to disembark their cargo but sail on to
Europe', Tharoor goes on. And when conscience-stricken British officials
wrote to the Prime Minister in London pointing out that his policies were
causing needless loss of life, all he could do was write peevishly in the
report's margin, of the person he described as a 'rascal',[32] 'Why hasn't
Gandhi died yet?'[33]

Churchill had visceral hatred for Mahatma Gandhi, someone he repeatedly mocked. He described him as a 'malignant subversive fanatic' and 'a
seditious Middle Temple lawyer, now posing as a fakir of a type well
known in the East, striding half-naked up the steps of the Viceregal
palace'.[34] He stated that Gandhi 'ought to be lain bound hand and foot at
the gates of Delhi, and then trampled on by an enormous elephant with the
new Viceroy seated on its back'.[35] Churchill also became obsessed with two
false notions about Gandhi when the latter was fasting in prison after he had

been arrested for launching the 'Quit India Movement' in 1942. As someone who always preached and practiced nonviolence, Gandhi was hurt that he was blamed for the violence that followed his arrest. First, Churchill convinced himself that Gandhi was working for Japan, one of the Axis powers in World War II and made enquiries about this. Second, he became fixated to the notion that Gandhi, a highly principled human being, was secretly taking energy supplements while on his fast.[36]

He also said, 'I hate Indians. They are a beastly people with a beastly religion. The famine was their own fault for breeding like rabbits'.[37] Churchill's own Secretary of State for India, Leopold Amery, denounced Churchill's 'Hitler-like attitude' to India that manifested itself most starkly during the famine.[38]

Quoting Churchill, Pankaj Mishra explains that as late as 1940, he hoped that Hindu-Muslim antagonism would remain 'a bulwark of British rule in India'.[39] Churchill was disinclined to recognize the upsurge of nationalism in India, since from his perspective, imperial authority in India rested on the claim that the British, as representatives of a superior civilization, were essentially benign custodians of a fractious country.[40] In 1943, when challenged by US Vice President Henry Wallace about his notion of Anglo-Saxon superiority, Churchill stated, 'why be apologetic about Anglo-Saxon superiority, that we were superior, that we had the common heritage which had been worked out over the centuries in England and had been perfected by our constitution'.[41]

Views not merely the norm of his day

To paraphrase Miles who I cited in the Introduction to this book: it was a common view that the English are an Anglo-Saxon 'race' with an inherent capacity for freedom and a right widely believed to spread democracy to 'uncivilised' parts of the world.[42] That said, large numbers of commentators have made the case that many aspects of Churchill's politics pertaining to 'race' and Empire were excessively retrogressive or reactionary even by the norms of the day, and even with respect to his own Tory Party. As Johann Hari puts it, it is easy to ask: didn't everybody think that way then?[43] Hari then refers to Richard Toye's book, *Churchill's Empire*, and notes that one of the most striking findings of Toye's research is that people really didn't think like Churchill: even at the time. In fact, Churchill was seen as being at the most brutal and brutish end of the British imperialist spectrum.[44] In the National Government in 1931 (formed during the Great Depression that begun in 1929), according to Mike Wood writing for *History Collection*, 'deputy Tory Prime Minister'[45] Stanley Baldwin, under the premiership of the first Labour Prime Minister Ramsey MacDonald was warned by Cabinet colleagues not to appoint him because his views were so antediluvian [of 'the time before the Biblical flood'!].[46] As Otto English wrote in *Politico*, debate about Churchill is long overdue, in that 'he held views that were frequently unacceptable, even by the standards of his own age.[47] Even his personal doctor, Charles Wilson, said of other 'races': 'Winston thinks only of the colour of their skin'.[48]

In the words of Thatcherite historian and author of *Churchill: The End of Glory*, John Charmley:[49] 'Churchill was very much on the far right of British politics over India. Even to most Conservatives, let alone Liberals and Labour, Churchill's views on India between 1929 and 1939 were quite abhorrent'.[50] His stance was very much that of a late Victorian imperialist. Charmley concludes, he 'was terribly alarmed that giving the Indians home rule was going to lead to the downfall of the British Empire and the end of civilization'.[51] Finally, Jones writes, presumably disapprovingly, 'Churchill was, by the standards of our painfully politically correct modern society, a virulent Victorian racist whose views on "lesser breeds" shocked even his own Cabinet colleagues, and would today land him in the dock accused of incitement to racial hatred'.[52]

Toye argues that, as British Prime Minster during World War II, Churchill's resistance to the Nazis should not be used to make the case that beside this, his racism pales into insignificance.[53] In the next section, I look at some of Churchill's early views on fascism and Nazism.

Early admirer of fascism and late convert to anti-Nazism

Great admirer of fascism

John Simkin points out that, from private letters and diary entries as well as speeches and articles produced in the 1920s and 1930s, it can be gleaned that, in fact 'Churchill was a great admirer of fascism', and that he was not an anti-fascist until very late in the day.[54] In a letter to his wife Clementine, Churchill in 1927, following a visit to Italy under Benito Mussolini, fascist dictator from 1925 to 1945, he wrote, 'This country gives the impression of discipline, order, goodwill, smiling faces. A happy strict school... The Fascists have been saluting in their impressive manner all over the place'.[55]

Churchill met Mussolini and, at a press conference in Rome, said he had been 'charmed' by his 'gentle and simple bearing', praising the way 'he thought of nothing but the lasting good... of the Italian people' and adding that it was 'quite absurd to suggest that the Italian Government does not stand upon a popular basis or that it is not upheld by the active and practical assent of the great masses'. Referring to Mussolini's suppression of left-wing political parties, and addressed to the fascist dictator, Churchill asserted, 'If I had been an Italian, I am sure that I should have been whole-heartedly with you from the start to the finish in your triumphant struggle against the bestial appetites and passions of Leninism'.[56] Churchill also supported Mussolini's aggression overseas. In 1935, Mussolini invaded Abyssinia (now Ethiopia), one of the last two surviving independent African countries. When Emperor Haile Selassie fled to exile, Mussolini took over the government. Churchill told the Anti-Socialist Union, that had links to fascist movements, that Mussolini was 'the greatest lawgiver among living men'.[57] He also wrote in *The Sunday Chronicle* that Mussolini was 'a really great man'.[58] Anti-socialism was an ongoing current in Churchill's rhetoric.

Churchill was also a supporter of General Francisco Franco and his fascist forces during the Spanish Civil War, describing the democratically elected Republican government as 'a poverty stricken and backward proletariat demanding the overthrow of Church, State and property and the inauguration of a Communist regime'. He contrasted it with the 'patriotic, religious and bourgeois forces, under the leadership of the army, and sustained by the countryside in many provinces... marching to re-establish order by setting up a military dictatorship'.[59] It is worth noting the classism inherent in this assertion – 'backward proletariat', something that is apparent, as we shall see, in many of Churchill's pronouncements on racism and imperialism.

Churchill's admiration for Mussolini and Franco and Italian and Spanish fascism is in tandem with his dislike of democracy *per se*, relating to his rich, aristocratic ancestry[60] (he was born in Blenheim Palace, one of England's largest houses and a gift from Queen Anne to Churchill's forebear, John Churchill, 1st Duke of Marlborough),[61] and had an elitist education at Harrow, a prominent British 'public' (private) school.[62] Churchill told his son in 1931 that future historians would record the result of any extension of the franchise as follows: 'within a generation of the poor silly people all getting the votes they clamoured for they squandered the treasure which five centuries of wisdom and victory had amassed'.[63]

For most of the time in the 1930s, Churchill was an advocate of appeasement to Hitler. In an article in the *Evening Standard* also in 1936, he praised the French for their restraint: 'instead of retaliating with arms, as the previous generation would have, France has taken the correct course by appealing to the League of Nations'.[64] In a speech in the House of Commons in the same year, he supported the Government's policy on appeasement and called on the League of Nations to invite Germany to state her grievances and her legitimate aspirations so that under the League's auspices 'justice may be done and peace preserved'.[65] Despite his 1934 declarations of ruthless men who preach intolerance and racial pride, unrestrained by law, Parliament or public opinion,[66] Churchill admired Hitler's patriotism. Writing in September 1937, just under two years before Hitler's invasion of Poland, he opined:

> One may dislike Hitler's system and yet admire his patriotic achievement. If our country were defeated I hope we should find a champion as indomitable to restore our courage and lead us back to our place among the nations. I have on more than one occasion made my appeal in public that the Führer of Germany should now become the Hitler of peace.[67]

He went further the following month:

> The story of that struggle (Hitler's rise to power) cannot be read without admiration for the courage, the perseverance, and the vital force which enabled him to challenge, defy, conciliate or overcome, all the authority or resistances which barred his path. Although no subsequent political action can condone wrong deeds, history is replete with examples of men who have risen to power by employing stern, grim and even frightful methods, but who nevertheless, when their life is revealed as a whole, have been regarded as great figures whose lives have enriched the story of mankind. So may it be with Hitler.[68]

On March 12, 1938, the German Army invaded Austria. Churchill found it difficult to decide how to react to what seemed to him to be a highly popular peaceful union of the two countries. During the debate in the House of Commons, he did not advocate the use of force to remove German forces from Austria, but instead called for discussion between diplomats at Geneva, and still continued to support appeasement.[69] As late as July 1938, Churchill was involved in negotiations with representatives of Hitler's Government in Nazi Germany.[70] In a meeting with a regional leader to the Nazi Party, when asked if discriminatory legislation against the Jews would prevent an understanding with Britain, Churchill replied that he thought 'it was a hindrance and an irritation, but probably not a complete obstacle to a working agreement'.[71]

In September of that year, British Tory Prime Minister Neville Chamberlain met Hitler at his home in Berchtesgaden in the German state of Bavaria. Hitler threatened to invade Czechoslovakia unless he got British support for his take-over of Sudetenland that lay between Czechoslovakia and Germany, and Chamberlain refused.[72] There followed, at Mussolini's suggestion, a meeting between Italy, Germany, Britain and France in Munich at the end of the month. With Chamberlain and French Prime Minister Édouard Daladier desperate to avoid war but anxious to avoid an alliance with Joseph Stalin and the Soviet Union, the Munich Agreement transferred Sudetenland to Germany in return for Hitler's promise not to make any further demands for territory in Europe.[73]

Time to ally with the Soviet Union and defeat the Nazis

In October 1938, Churchill finally decided it was then time to ally with his greatest foe, the Soviet Union, against Nazi Germany. After praising Chamberlain's efforts, he declared that, in sacrificing Czechoslovakia, the negotiations had been a failure.[74] Now critical of the policy of appeasement, on October 16, 1938 Churchill broadcast directly to the United States, appealing for greater American involvement in Europe.[75] In it, now asserting a belief in democracy and antipathy towards the anti-democratic fascist state – 'Nazidom', Churchill said:

> I avail myself with relief of the opportunity of speaking to the people of the United States. I do not know how long such liberties will be allowed. The stations of uncensored expression are closing down; the lights are going out; but there is still time for those to whom freedom and parliamentary government mean something, to consult together ... We are confronted with ... racial persecution, religious intolerance, deprivation of free speech, the conception of the citizen as a mere soulless fraction of the State ... Like the Communists, the Nazis tolerate no opinion but their own. Like the Communists, they feed on hatred ... This combination of medieval passion, a party caucus, the weapons of modern science, and the blackmailing power of air-bombing, is the most monstrous menace to peace, order and fertile progress ... The culminating question ... [is should we] ... meet this menace by submission or by resistance ... We shall, no doubt, arm. Britain, casting away the habits of centuries, will decree national service upon her citizens ... People say we ought not to allow ourselves to be drawn into a theoretical antagonism between Nazidom and democracy; but the antagonism is here now ... You see these dictators on their pedestals, surrounded by the bayonets of their soldiers and the truncheons of their police. On all sides they are guarded by masses of armed men, cannons, aeroplanes, fortifications, and the like ... Is this a call to war? Does anyone pretend that preparation for resistance to aggression is unleashing war? I declare it to be the sole guarantee of peace. We need the swift gathering of forces to confront not only military but moral aggression; the resolute and sober acceptance of their duty by the English-speaking peoples and by all the nations, great and small, who wish to walk with them. Their faithful and zealous comradeship would almost between night and morning clear the path of progress and banish from all our lives the fear which already darkens the sunlight to hundreds of millions of men.[76]

On March 15, 1939, proving that he had been lying in Munich and that he was not just interested in a Greater Germany, Hitler invaded and annexed Czechoslovakia. On September 1, Nazi forces invaded Poland. This had been a red line for the UK, and Chamberlain declared war on Nazi Germany. He resigned the following year after a vote of no confidence in the House of Commons, and Churchill became Prime Minister on May 10, 1940 until after the end of the war.

Never a supporter of Nazi 'racial' policies

Before moving on to the next sub-section of this chapter, it is important to point out that there is no suggestion that Churchill supported Nazi 'racial' policies, even before his October 1938 decision to ally with the Soviet

Union against Nazi Germany. In fact, Churchill was against these central aspects of Nazi politics, and, according to Churchill official biographer Martin Gilbert, was also denounced by Nazi newspapers in Germany for this outspoken criticism of Nazi 'racial' policy.[77] This is hardly surprising, given his pro-Jewish views as exemplified earlier in this chapter,[78] although his remark quoted just above about Jewish persecution 'probably not a complete obstacle' needs to be born in mind in the following brief observations.[79]

In November 1932, just before Hitler came to power, an intermediary tried to get Churchill to meet Hitler. Churchill agreed and said to the intermediary: 'There are a few questions you might like to put ... to ... [Hitler] which can be the basis of our discussion when we meet'.[80] Among them was 'What is the sense of being against a man simply because of his birth? How can any man help how he is born?'[81] So surprised, and possibly angered, according to Gilbert, was Hitler by this question that he declined to meet Churchill.[82] The following year, Churchill wrote, 'There is a danger of the odious conditions now ruling in Germany, being extended by conquest to Poland and another persecution and pogrom of Jews being begun in this new area'.[83] Further warnings of the dangers to Jewish people from the Nazis were expressed in 1937,[84] and in September 1942, Churchill referred in the House of Commons to 'the most bestial, the most squalid and the most senseless of all ... [the Nazis'] ... offenses: namely, the mass deportation of Jews from France with the pitiful horrors attendant upon it'.[85] In the same year, Churchill opined that 'The systematic cruelties to which the Jewish people, men, women and children, have been exposed under the Nazi regime are among the most terrible events of history'.[86] He was also in total agreement with Jewish leaders that after the war the Nazis must be hunted down and brought to trial and justice.[87]

Churchill and Ireland

According to J. P. O'Malley, writing for the *Irish Independent*, 'Whenever a list appears depicting historical figures most hated by the Irish, Sir Winston Churchill – alongside people like Oliver Cromwell and Margaret Thatcher – usually features in the top 10'[88] (for Cromwell and Thatcher and Ireland, see the Introduction and chapter 5 of this book, respectively). As First Lord of the Admiralty, in August 1915 during World War I, Churchill was responsible for the deaths of ill-prepared Irish soldiers, first professional then amateur, sent to fight Turkey in Suvla Bay in Gallipoli.[89] In May 1920, as Secretary of State for War, Churchill ordered the recruit-ment and deployment of the Black and Tans and the Auxiliary cadets, two emergency police forces set up to crush the IRA in Ireland. Both treated the law and the Irish civilian population with contempt.[90] Their intent was clear as Niall O'Dowd explains. The commanding officer, Lt. Colonel Gerald Smyth addressed the first recruits as follows:[91]

Should the order 'Hands Up' not be immediately obeyed, shoot and shoot with effect. If the persons approaching a patrol carry their hands in their pockets, or are in any way suspicious looking, shoot them down. You may make mistakes occasionally and innocent persons may be shot, but that cannot be helped, and you are bound to get the right parties some time. The more you shoot, the better I will like you, and I assure you no policeman will get into trouble for shooting any man ... hunger-strikers will be allowed to die in jail, the more the merrier. Some of them have died already and a damn bad job they were not all allowed to die.[92]

In 1921, given his imperialist and racist colonialism, it is not surprising that Churchill said that allowing Ireland to become independent was akin to offering a country up to a miserable gang of human leopards in West Africa.[93] According to Vicky van Bockhaven, in Europe there has been a long tradition of representing non-Christians and non-Europeans as 'being half man, half beast and behaving like animals, including eating their own species'. Such cultural predispositions, she goes on, have masked the real purposes of secret societies like the Anyoto or 'leopard men' which was to maintain local power relations, performing indigenous justice in secret and circumventing colonial government control.[94]

Finally, during World War II, in his victory speech in 1945, Prime Minister Churchill claimed that Éamon de Valera, the President of Ireland, that was neutral during the war, had frolicked with fascists, and insinuated that Britain could have taken Ireland by force during the war, but refrained from doing so out of goodwill, honour and decency.[95]

Wartime leader

Maintaining the Empire

As Tory Prime Minister, Churchill led a Coalition Government between 1940 and 1945. As Neil Redfern argues, the defence of Empire clearly remained a primary objective in Churchill's war leadership. In August 1941, as part of the price for United States support for Britain's war effort, Churchill committed Britain to upholding the principles of the Atlantic Charter, one of which pledged the signatories to 'respect the right of all peoples to choose the form of government under which they will live'.[96] On his return to the House of Commons, Churchill insisted that this principle was to be applied to those currently 'under the Nazi yoke', and thus, implicitly, not to the peoples of the British Empire.[97] Churchill made his views on self-determination within the Empire explicit on at least two further wartime occasions. In 1942, he told the House of Commons that he had not 'become the King's First Minister in order to preside over the liquidation of the British Empire'.[98] During the Yalta Conference of 1945, where he met with Roosevelt and Stalin to discuss the post-war fate of a defeated Nazi Germany and the rest of Europe, the terms of Soviet entry into the ongoing war in the Pacific against Japan and the formation and operation of the new United Nations, Churchill insisted that the self-determination clauses of the Yalta Accords 'did not apply to the British Empire'.[99] Redfern describes the Tory Party at the time as 'ferociously pro-Empire'.[100]

Popular hero

According to political historian of World War II Paul Addison, Churchill was probably the most popular British prime minister of all time: in May 1945 (the war ended on September 2) his approval rating in the opinion polls, which had never fallen below 78%, was 83%.[101] According to Klaus Larres, a Professor of the Curriculum in Peace, War and Defense, the end of World War II in Europe and the defeat of Hitler and Nazi Germany early in May 1945 turned British Prime Minister Winston Churchill into 'the world's most eminent statesman' and he 'was feted and celebrated every-where he went'.[102] Writing in *Politico*, English is perhaps right to point out that Winston Churchill 'remains undoubtedly Britain's best-known, most respected and arguably best-loved Prime Minister, and that he is a 'national hero',[103] albeit I would add, among people of a certain age group and/or political perspective. It is certainly correct to point out, as English does in another article on Churchill, though again importantly with respect to that particular demographic, that to 'dare to criticize Winston Churchill in 21st century Britain is to risk the ire and outrage of the collective power of the media, the public and ministers of state', with any jab at Churchill inevitably leading to an outpouring of furious patriotism.[104] Churchill's understandable reputation as a popular wartime leader and national hero does not com-pensate for his views on fascism and fascists, his earlier view of Hitler and his long-term distaste for democracy. His racism and his views on 'race', nation and Empire are all connected. In my view, Churchill's legendary wartime resistance to the Nazis, his resolute determination to defeat Hitler and his leadership of World War II deserves acknowledgment from anti-fascists and antiracists, but it does not excuse his pro-fascist and earlier pro-Hitler views, nor does his denunciation of Nazi 'racial' policies exonerate him; indeed such condemnation should surely be taken 'as read' except among diehard fascists and some racists. Moreover, none of this negates Churchill's essential racism and unwavering commitment to the British Empire.

Why did Churchill lose the post-war General Election in a Labour landslide?

The General Election was held on July 5, 1945. When the poll closed the ballot boxes were sealed for three weeks to allow time for the votes of service personnel (1.7 million) to be returned for the count on July 26. It was a high turnout with 72.8% of the electorate voting. With almost 12 million votes, Labour had 47.8% of the vote to 39.8% for the Tories. Labour made 179 gains from the Tories, winning 393 seats to 213. The 12.0% national swing from Tory to Labour, remains the largest ever achieved in a British General Election.[105] So, the question arises, why did he lose to the Labour Party in a landslide?

First, voters at home were 'exhausted by six devastating years of war', and 'wanted a view of a bright future', as did soldiers in the field who were fed up with fighting and looked forward to a new age of prosperity and peace. Labour proposed a progressive social reform program that would transform the future of British society. The Conservative programme was much vaguer and focused on Churchill's leadership.[106] As Addison argues, 'the very qualities that had made him a great leader in war were ill-suited to domestic politics in peacetime'.[107] Addison goes on, politicians are often rejected by voters because they have failed in office. However, in Churchill's case, one of the reasons he lost the General Election in 1945 was because 'he had succeeded in completing the almost superhuman task he had taken on in 1940, and in a way, this made him redundant'.[108] Since the conduct of the war was his overriding passion and military victory by far his most important goal, everything else, including party politics, was secondary. As a result, when party politics resumed, Churchill suddenly found himself without a clear sense of purpose or a direction.[109]

Second, and allied to the first reason, Churchill and the Tories conducted a poor election campaign. Symbolic of this was Churchill's first campaign broadcast, in which he accused Attlee of harbouring socialist dictatorial ambitions and even compared him to the Nazis. Outrageously, Churchill declared that Labour 'would have to fall back on some sort of a Gestapo' to push through its reforms.[110] In reality, Labour's platform was the foundation of the Welfare State: government-supported full employment, the introduction of a free national health service and the nationalization of many key industries such as steel, coal and railways[111] (see the Appendix to this chapter).

Third, the Tories had a poor image. Despite the tremendous esteem Churchill was held in, with his elite background, and paternalistic Victorian habits, he was seen by many as out of touch with the modern world.[112] As we have seen, he also had outdated views about 'race' and Empire that for many – even back in 1945 – sounded not quite right for the new post-war era. Canadian Prime Minister MacKenzie King, who knew him well, concluded that maintaining 'the British Empire and Commonwealth is a religion to him'.[113]

Fourth, apart from the years 1924 and 1929–1931, Britain had been led by Tory Governments for more than two decades. They could hardly avoid being seen as responsible for the high unemployment and miserable social and economic conditions of these years (conditions that continued well into the 1950s).[114]

Fifth, the Conservatives were viewed correctly as the party of the appeasers who had, in the run-up to the war, downplayed the Nazi threat, with Prime Minister Neville Chamberlain having given in to Hitler.[115] As noted earlier, in 1938 the Sudetenland was transferred to Germany in return for Hitler's promise not to make any further demands for territory in Europe. Chamberlain described this as 'Peace for our time'.[116]

Simkin suggests one further reason: Churchill's late conversion to anti-fascism. He argues that while the British people had the opportunity to show their gratitude for his role in winning the war, they remembered his pro-fascism before October 1938.[117]

Churchill did not give up, however. In 1950 he narrowly lost the next General Election. Just over a year later, with the Labour government in deep internal crisis and running out of steam, yet another election was called, and in October 1951, Churchill became Prime Minister for the second time.[118]

SECTION 2: CHURCHILL'S SECOND PREMIERSHIP (1951–1955)

By the time of his second premiership, Churchill was, in the words of Roy Jenkins, Labour MP and later Social Democratic Party co-founder, 'gloriously unfit for office'.[119] Ageing and increasingly unwell, he often conducted business from his bedside, and his leadership was less decisive than it was during the war. His second term was most notable for the Tory Party's acceptance of Labour's newly created Welfare State,[120] and most infamous for Churchill's response to the Mau Mau uprising in Kenya; and the racialization of migrant workers, newly arrived from the colonies and the Indian sub-continent, and of some communities already resident in the UK.

The Mau Mau uprising in Kenya

The year after Churchill became Prime Minister for the second time, the Mau Mau rose up against British rule in Kenya. Regarded as one of the most important episodes in the struggle for a Kenya free from British rule,[121] it took place between 1952 and 1960, with Kenya eventually achieving independence in 1963. The Mau Mau fighters were mainly drawn from Kenya's major ethnic group, the Kikuyu, whose land had increasingly been taken away by White settlers. By 1952, White settler farms were being raided and in October of that year, the Churchill Government declared a state of emergency and began moving army reinforcements into Kenya.[122] Churchill held overall responsibility for the forced internment and brutal torture of 150,000 people.[123] As English puts it, 'That disturbing episode, which saw extrajudicial executions, thousands of hangings, men forcibly castrated, women raped and many more die in internment camps, has been largely absent from narratives about Churchill –

and indeed Britain's recent colonial past'.[124] Echoing the camps of the second Boer War, Marc Parry refers to one and half million Kenyans in a network of detention camps and heavily patrolled villages: 'a tale of systematic violence and high-level cover-ups'.[125] English concludes that:

> Most Britons still view the Empire through rose-tinted spectacles. They like their history to be uncomplicated and to believe that Britain and its leaders behaved in a manner beyond reproach. They are ignorant of the extent of the crimes of our colonial past and happier to bask in the reflected glory of their cigar-chomping hero than to delve into the events of his life.[126]

In 2022, these spectacles are losing their tint as more and more people are revealing more and more of the brutal realities of the British Empire.

Colour-coded and non-colour-coded racism in Britain

Colour-coded racism

The Empire came home to roost after World War II. The demands of an expanding post-war economy meant that Britain, like most other European countries, was faced with a major shortage of labour. The overwhelming majority of migrants who came to Britain were from the Caribbean, the Indian subcontinent, and the Republic of Ireland. In 1948, the *Empire Windrush* brought from Kingston, Jamaica, one of the first large groups of post-war Caribbean immigrants comprising 1,029 people on board.[127] Eight hundred and two of these gave their last country of residence as somewhere in the Caribbean.[128] This cohort of Caribbean migrants are generally known as 'the Windrush Generation' (see chapter 10). They had been taught about 'the glories of a Britain where everyone worked for a good wage, received equal treatment, lived in a democracy, had the right to vote, and schools were available for all children'.[129] Unsurprisingly, as Marika Sherwood argues, 'Caribbean arrivals were bewildered and then angered by the many landlords who refused to rent to their families, or crammed several people into one room, charging an exorbitant price'.[130] They were also, she goes on, 'angered and disappointed by the employers who often refused to hire them; and by the "colour bar"[131] in some pubs, dance-halls, and many other places that led to them being refused admittance'.[132] Racism, racist behaviour and campaigns against these migrant workers were increased by fascist organizations like the League of Empire Loyalists, neo-Nazi Colin Jordan's White Defence League, Oswald Mosley's Union Movement (from 1932 to 1940, he had headed the British Union of Fascists; after World War II, it was the Union Movement, 1948–1973), and a branch of the Ku Klux Klan – all present in Britain at this time. White thugs roamed the streets at night, hunting for 'ni★★ers' who, they claimed, were seducing 'their women'.[133] Those industries where the demand for labour was greatest actively recruited Asian, Black and other minority ethnic workers in their home countries.[134] Despite the heterogeneous class structure of the migrating populations,[135] migrant workers came to occupy, overwhelmingly, the semiskilled and unskilled positions in the English labour market.[136] Furthermore, they found themselves disproportionately concentrated in certain types of manual work characterized by a shortage of labour, shift working, unsocial hours, low pay and an unpleasant working environment.[137]

Bob Carter, Clive Harris and Shirley Joshi have written about the 'myth of the "invisible state"' that holds that in the 1950s, the state was either absent or played a minimal role in the emerging discourse about immigration. Other interpretations, they go on, have suggested that the British state openly welcomed and encouraged immigration.[138] In reality, during the early 1950s racism emerged within the political mainstream, championed by Tory backbenchers such as Cyril Osborne, Normal Pannell, Harold Gurden and Martin Lindsay.[139] The recurrent parliamentary questions from them, although couched, as is usually the case, in such terms as employment and housing availability and the character and health of those coming, only thinly disguising skin colour as their true motivation.[140] At the same time, Government documents and records released around the time Carter et al. were writing (1987) reveal that by 1955 the state had developed a clear policy on immigration. It involved direct intervention on some issues and inactivity on others. Thus, for example, while the Churchill Government 'was systematically collecting information' about immigration to support a draft Immigration Bill, it was also opposing certain measures, such as socialist Fenner Brockway's Bill prohibiting racial discrimination and refusing to respond to requests for assistance from local authorities on housing and other matters.[141] Carter et al. refer to 'the construction of an ideological framework in which Black people were seen to be threatening, alien and unassimilable and to the development of policies to discourage and control Black immigration'.[142]

The period between the 1948 Nationality Act, passed under Attlee's Labour Government which defined British Nationality and created the status of 'Citizen of the United Kingdom and Colonies' (see the Appendix to this chapter), and the 1962 Commonwealth Immigration Act that severely restricted immigration and passed under the Macmillan Government (see chapter 4.1), is frequently depicted as one in which the principle of free entry of UK and colonial citizens was only relinquished with great reluctance and after considerable official debate. As Carter et al. point out, this was not the case, since by 1952, many covert and sometimes illegal, administrative measures had been designed to discourage immigration from the colonies. To take three examples: first, in the Caribbean, 'where the difficulty of refusing passports to applicants whose nationality was not in doubt', Governors were asked to tamper with shipping lists and schedules to place migrant workers at the back of the queue;[143] second, ports were cordoned off to prevent passport-holding stowaways from boarding ships and to delay the issue of passports to migrants;[144] third, in India and Pakistan where passports were refused 'if migrants had no firm prospect of establishing themselves'.[145]

By the early 1950s, some Government departments had come to favour restrictive legislation. The Welfare Department of the Colonial Office, for example, argued that 'it would be far better to have an openly avowed policy of restricted immigration than fall back on rather devious little devices'.[146] On February 3, 1954, under the agenda item 'Coloured Workers', Churchill expressed one of the common racist stereotypes relating to migrant workers: 'they come to take advantage of *our* welfare system'. He is quoted (*with abbreviations*) by Cabinet Secretary Sir Norman Brook: 'Problems wh. will arise if many coloured people settle here. Are we to saddle ourselves with colour problems in UK? Attracted by Welfare State. Public opinion in UK won't tolerate it once it gets beyond certain limits'. Florence Horsbrugh, Conservative MP for Manchester Moss Side, added: 'Already becoming serious in Manchr'.[147] Then David Maxwell-Fyfe, the Home Secretary, gave a figure of 40,000 compared to 7,000 before World War II and raised the possibility of immigration control:

> There is a case on merits for excludg. riff-raff. But politically it wd. be represented & discussed on basis of colour limitation. That wd. offend the floating vote viz., the old Liberals. We shd. be reversing age-long trad[ition] tht. B[ritish] S[ubjects] have right of entry to mother-country of Empire. We shd. offend Liberals, also sentimentalists. The col [onial]. pop[ulations] are resented in L[iverpool], Paddington & other areas by those who come into contact with them. But those who don't are apt to take a more Liberal view.[148]

Churchill intervened: 'Ques. is wtr it is politically wise to allow public feeling to develop a little more before takg. action'. He added that it would be 'fatal' to let the situation develop too far. Churchill concluded: 'Wd lke also to study possibility of "quota" – no. not to be exceeded'.[149] Underlining his unrepentant and ongoing White supremacist views, he 'joked' that D. F. Malan, Prime Minister of apartheid South Africa until 1954, should 'Keep on skelping [beating] the kaffirs!' He also apparently walked out of a 1954 version of 'Carmen Jones' because it had an African American cast, citing the reason as he 'didn't like blackamors'.[150]

In April 1954 a confidential meeting of Ministers at the Colonial Office decided that what was needed was information about unemployment and National Assistance (the National Assistance Act, 1948, passed by the Attlee Labour Government abolished the Poor Law and provided a social safety net for those in need), 'numbers', housing, health, criminality, and miscegenation ['mixed marriages'], which it was hoped would confirm that

'Black immigration posed insoluble problems of social, economic and political assimilation'.[151] According to Carter et al., the widespread 'surveillance of Black communities by the police' was supplemented by surveys undertaken by the Ministry of Labour, the National Assistance Board, the Welfare Department of the Colonial Office, the Home Office, the Commonwealth Relations Office, the Departments of Health, Housing and Transport as well as voluntary organisations.[152] In December 1953, a Working Party on 'The Employment of Coloured People in the UK', had been set up by the Cabinet. Its ensuing report formed a central part of Cabinet discussion in 1954–1955 on the need to control Black immigration.[153] Ministers were particularly alarmed that migration from the Caribbean for 1954 was running at the level of 10,000 compared to 2,000 in previous years, although an examination by the Board of Trade found the figure to be exaggerated.[154] Nevertheless, speculation about numbers continued. Whereas the police estimated less than 25,000, the Ministry of Labour put the unofficial estimate of 50,000 to 60,000.[155] Whatever the figures, Robert Gascoyne-Cecil, then Tory Leader of the House of Lords, complained in 1954 that there 'appears to be no recognition of the dangers of the increasing immigration of coloured people into this country'.[156] In the same year Churchill told the Governor-in-Chief of Jamaica, Hugh Foot, that the presence of Jamaicans in the UK would create 'a magpie society', adding 'that would never do'.[157] Carter et al. refer to a coalescing around a fear that the 'gathering momentum' of Black immigration would bring about 'a significant change in the racial character of the English people'. They argue that the 1953 Working Party had failed to appreciate that the real issue for the Cabinet was not the question of 'numbers' but the very presence of Black people in Britain *per se*.[158]

Half a century later, Churchill said that Asian people had to be taken in hand and that Aryans are bound to triumph (see the section on Churchill's imperialism and colonial racism in the first part of chapter 3), his views had not changed. In May 1954, prominent Liberal and close friend of Churchill, Violet Bonham-Carter asked Churchill for his opinion about a Labour Party visit to China. His reply: 'I hate people with slit eyes and pigtails. I don't like the look of them or the smell of them – but I suppose it does no great harm to have a look at them'.[159]

Having failed to build the case around 'numbers', the Cabinet moved the case for the restriction of immigration to employment, housing and crime, a familiar racist trope. The failure of an earlier propaganda campaign to persuade Black workers that it was not 'in their interests' to migrate to the UK, led to efforts 'to show that those who did migrate were unemployable and represented a burden on public funds'.[160] Accordingly a questionnaire was circulated to Labour Exchanges (government premises established to collect and supply information about job vacancies for unemployed workers and prospective employers) in 1954 asking: 'Is it true that coloured people, or certain classes of coloured people, are work shy? ... Is it true that they are poor workmen? ... Is it true that they are unsuited by temperament to the kind of work available?'[161] Carter et al. point out that the responses were contradictory. While recognizing that Black workers were neither workshy nor poor workers, they also reflected the views of some employers that they were a problem on the grounds of 'their relatively low output: their high rate of turnover: their irresponsibility, their quarrelsomeness and lack of discipline and the objections of white employees'.[162] The unsuitability of 'coloured' labour was a common theme in the Working Party's Report:

> The unskilled workers who form the majority, are difficult to place, because they are on the whole physically unsuited for heavy manual work, particularly outdoors in winter or in hot conditions underground and appear to be generally lacking in stamina. There is also some indication that they are more volatile in temperament than white workers and more easily provoked to violence, though the evidence of this is not conclusive.[163]

According to Carter et al., racist ideas grew steadily during the 1950s, and were reflected in the press. For example, on November 9, 1954, *The Times* proclaimed, 'First Signs of a British Colour Problem'.[164]

This racialized fraction of the working class was differentiated ideologically by gender.[165] In contrast to 'coloured men': 'coloured women' were said to be slow mentally, and the speed of work in modern factories was said to be quite beyond their capacity.[166] As Carter et al. note perceptively, these ascribed racist and sexist stereotypes did not prevent the women giving 'reliable service as domestics in hospitals, institutions and private domestic employment'.[167] The Working Party concluded with confidence that, since the jobs for which 'coloured' immigrants

> are suitable for employment are somewhat limited by their physique and the reluctance of some employers, for various reasons, to take them on, the proportion of unemployment tends to be higher than in the case of white workers and coloured people are principally, for that reason, rather more liable than white people to become a charge on National Assistance.[168]

As Carter et al. conclude their section on 'employment', this 'overlooked the fact that recent Black immigrants, like the 60,000 Irish who were also claiming National Assistance, were ineligible for unemployment benefit since they would not have paid the statutory fifty weeks of National Insurance contributions'[169] (see the section later in this chapter on 'Anti-Irish racism').

With respect to housing, in the mid-1950s Britain's stock was still desperately short of the level of demand. Black immigration was claimed to aggravate this by making the shortage more acute and by creating 'conditions described variously as primitive, squalid and deplorable'.[170] The Cabinet even considered making suitable housing accommodation a condition of permanent settlement for Black immigrants.[171] As *The Times* bluntly put it: 'what are likely to be the feelings of more than 50,000 would be white tenants in Birmingham, who have waited years for a decent house, when they see newcomers, no matter what their colour, taking over whole streets of properties?'[172]

Carter et al. give three reasons for the dubiousness of the 'common sense' correlation of housing shortage with the immigration of Black people. First, it assumes that Black people and White people were competing for the same housing, whereas it was the case that the former were not eligible for council housing. Second, if Black people were 'taking over whole streets of properties', this begs the question of why such properties were not attractive or available to White buyers. Third, the housing shortage in Britain in the 1950s (as is usually the case) was a product of Government policies and market forces, not levels of immigration.[173] In 1954, for example, Harold Macmillan, then Minister of Housing, announced a reduction in council housing for 1955 from 235,000 in 1954 to 160,000. At the same time rent controls in the private sector were lifted.[174]

In addition to accommodation shortage, there was another issue that lent itself to Churchill's Government building a strong case for immigration controls. This was the creation of so-called 'new Harlems' in the heartlands of British cities. Their supposed key features were luridly portrayed in *The Problem of Colonial Immigrants*, a pamphlet produced by the Liverpool Group of the Conservative Commonwealth Association, attempting to link housing with 'loose morals' and illegality:

> Liverpool is admittedly one of the chief centres of coloured settlement and a new Harlem is being created in a decayed residential quarter of the City, where rooms in large and dilapidated houses are sublet at high rentals to coloured immigrants who exist in conditions of the utmost squalor. Vice and crime are rampant and social responsibilities are largely ignored. Hundreds of children of negroid or mixed parentage eventually find their way to the various homes to be maintained by the corporation, to be reared to unhappy maturity at great public expense. Large numbers of the adults are in receipt of unemployment benefit or National Assistance and many are engaged in the drug traffic or supplement their incomes by running illicit drinking dens or by prostitution.[175]

According to Carter et al., this document was circulated widely within the Conservative Party. They conclude the section of their article on Housing: 'Landlordism, declining property values, spiralling rents, overcrowding, dilapidation and decay were cited as the inevitable consequences of Black settlement'. 'Black people', according to this Tory ideological construction, 'not only created slums', but the '"new Harlems" had their provenance in the "racial" character of the inhabitants'. Indeed, the racialization of Black migrant workers constructed their very way of life as 'a fundamental threat to social order'.[176]

The third case for restricting the immigration of Black people centres on 'criminality'. In the House of Commons in November 1954, the Secretary of State for the Colonies, Alex Lennox-Boyd, was asked a question by Jocelyn Lucas, who had been the Portsmouth District Officer for Mosley' British Union of Fascists before his election to Parliament as the Tory MP for Portsmouth in 1939[177] (a seat he retained until his retirement in 1966). The question was 'what machinery exists to ascertain the proportion of Jamaican immigrants who have police or criminal records'.[178] This was not the first time that such an issue had been raised in the House of Commons.[179] In its 1952 survey of the Black population in London and the Provinces, the Colonial Office drew heavily on police accounts and reports. These dwelt upon the size of the Black population, the degree to which it had been assimilated and the extent to which it was involved in criminal activity. In Sheffield, for example, the Chief constable had deputed two police officers to 'observe, visit and report on the Black population'.[180] Subsequently, a card index was compiled, listing the names, addresses, nationalities and places of employment of the City's 534 Black inhabitants,[181] raising concerns emphasizing certain types of deviance, pre-eminently drug trafficking and living on immoral earnings, and the ways in which these endangered the social and moral fabric of British society.[182]

In its evidence to the Working Party, the police claimed that there had been 'a marked number of convictions of coloured men for living on the immoral earnings of white women'.[183] The Working Party's own Report hinted that 'this practice is far more widespread than the few prosecutions indicate'.[184] Such alleged criminality merged into a general condemnation of 'the associations formed between coloured men and white women of the lowest type' that was considered to undermine the sanctity of White British womanhood (and, of course, the White patriarchal structure on which it rested). The picture of an alien wedge with 'exotic features' was graphically presented by Sheffield's Chief Constable, who merged racism with sexism and classism:

> the West Africans are all out for a good time, spending money on quaint suits and flashy ornaments and visiting dance halls at every opportunity. The Jamaicans are somewhat similar, but they have a more sensible outlook and rarely get into trouble. They take great pains with their appearance and use face cream, perfume etc. to make themselves attractive to the females they meet at dances, cafes etc. One feels, however, that they only attract a certain type of female by reason of the fact that they have more money to spend than the average young Englishman.[185]

Stereotypes of Black criminality were never supported by any evidence that Black people were involved in disproportionate amounts of crime. In his report to the Working Party, the Chief Constable of Middlesbrough noted that 'on the whole the coloured population are as well behaved as many local citizens'.[186] Underlining the ongoing racialization of Irish people (see the next section of this chapter), *The Times* similarly observed: 'Everywhere they have appeared the police and magistrates are ready to say that the West Indians make no trouble, which is more than some are ready to say of Irish workers'.[187]

The failure of the Tory Cabinet to obtain evidence of links between Black people and social problems to legitimate a 'strong case' for immigration control did not deflect them from the conviction that Black immigration needed to be curtailed by legislation. As Carter et al. put it, 'a different kind of case had to be made which conveyed to the public the deep anxieties felt by the Cabinet about the threat to the "racial character of the English."'[188] The Home Secretary, Gwilym Lloyd-George, proposed a Committee of Enquiry in November 1954.

In January 1955, Churchill made another personal intervention on immigration in one of his cabinet meetings. With a General Election likely to happen within the year, he tried to persuade his colleagues to adopt the campaign slogan 'Keep England White' (a demand that prefigures the rallying cries of the far right in the decades that followed); he suggested it would be a good message.[189] Churchill was adamant that restricting Caribbean migration was 'the most important subject facing this country'.[190]

Non-colour-coded racism

Anti-Gypsy, Roma and Traveller racism

During Churchill's second premiership, non-colour-coded racism affected both the Gypsy, Roma and Traveller communities and the Irish communities.

By the late 19th century, despite increased statutory controls, such as the 1822 General Turnpike Road Act that levied a fine for camping on the side of a turnpike road[191] (a law that was still in place until 1980),[192] traditional stopping places were reasonably freely available,[193] and, as Duffy and Tomlinson argue,[194] always surviving on the margins of society, Gypsy people became a useful source of cheap labour seasonally in the fields, as blacksmiths and as entertainers.

A pattern of travelling on specific circuits continued until World War II when, with the need for intensive labour, members of the Gypsy Roma and Traveller communities were recruited into semi-permanent work on the land, in the mining industries, in the army, and in factory and munitions work.[195]

After World War II, with the mechanization of farming, the lifestyle of Gypsies changed drastically.[196] This mechanization of traditional rural work started in the 1950s, and previous sources of livelihood in the rural areas were no longer sufficient. With industrialization, began the migration from rural areas. The changes in society were also reflected in the Romany Gypsy population. No longer wanted for hop or strawberry picking and other traditional trades, they found that they had to adapt. Work was difficult to find for some families, and the motorization of families also changed the travel patterns. Many Gypsies moved from the rural areas to the cities and towns,[197] often meeting hostile reactions from the local population and from the authorities.[198] Where caravans were visible to non-Gypsy Roma and Traveller people, for example next to a roadside, this attracted the attention of the authorities, and thus began a cycle of rapid repeat evictions.[199] Many families reluctantly sought to be rehoused into local authority (Council) accommodation.[200]

Churchill and a Romany couple

While I can find no indications that Churchill was anti-Gypsy, Richard M. Langworth has provided a telling anecdote, and I have thought carefully about whether to include it, and realize that some may think I am stretching the point. According to Langworth, Churchill 'did frequent kindnesses for common folk, privately and without fanfare'.[201] Langworth is writing for the Churchill Project, which is based at Hillsdale College, Michigan, USA, and is an institution for whom the 'study of statesmanship' is central to its teaching mission. This includes 'cultivating the moral and intellectual virtues'.[202] 'Winston Churchill's career', according to the Project's website, 'presents an unsurpassed opportunity for such study because it was so long, because the facts of it are so well recorded, and because its quality was so very high'.[203] In light of this appraisal, what is to follow is somewhat predictable:

> Take for example the Romany couple, 'Mr. & Mrs. Donkey Jack', who frequented his home town of Westerham, Kent. Churchill thought gypsy life romantic, and allowed them to camp in his wood. Said Churchill's former secretary, Grace Hamblin: 'Sir Winston allowed her to live in his wood, in a little gazebo which had been there for years, full of earwigs and that sort of thing, but she loved it. It would have been stupid to offer her a house because she wouldn't have understood it. He knew just what would give her pleasure.' Later, when Mrs. Donkey Jack fractured an ankle, Churchill saw to her medical care, paid the bills, and took care of her two dogs in her absence.

A different perspective to Langworth's would be that viewing gypsy life as 'romantic', allowing a gypsy to live in a gazebo 'full of earwigs' because she wouldn't have 'understood' a house could be that it is condescending and (maybe unintentionally) racist. Overall, it seems to be consistent with some aspects of Churchill's racism that are patronizing (see the section earlier in this chapter on 'Churchill's imperialism' where he is quoted as stating that British imperialism in its colonies was for the good of the 'primitive' and 'subject races'). Even if we stretch the point and see 'having a romantic life' as a positive attribute, as I argued in the Introduction 'seemingly positive' attributes will probably ultimately have racist implications. In this case, having such a life entails 'a love for living with lots of insects, not understanding what houses are for' and goodness knows what else in Churchill's mindset.

Anti-Irish racism

In the Introduction, I traced the development of anti-Irish racism from the colonization of Ireland by the English in the 12th century up to the Act of Union in 1801. I also refer a number of times to anti-Irish racism in chapters 1 and 2 on Disraeli. With reference to this section of the chapter, Carter et al. note several instances of such racism in their article. Two of them involve negatively juxtaposing the Irish with colonial immigrants (since some found it difficult to reconcile Britain's position as Head of the Commonwealth and Empire with the anti-Black racism that was being fostered by the state, and, of course, anti-Irish racism in Britain was well-established). Thus, they cite a summary for Churchill by the Tory Chief Whip, Patrick Buchan-Hepburn, of a Commonwealth Affairs Committee meeting on January 27, 1955: 'Why should mainly loyal and hard-working Jamaicans be discriminated against when ten times that quantity of disloyal [sic] Southern Irish (some of them Sinn Feiners)[204] come and go as they please?' (according to Carter et al., there were some 60,000 recent Irish immigrants at the time).[205] There is also the afore-mentioned quote from *The Times* that law enforcers think that, unlike 'West Indians', Irish workers cause trouble. They also point out that, like recent Black migrants, recent Irish immigrants, as noted earlier, were not able to claim National Assistance.[206]

In the 1950s many families of the urban poor were characterized as 'problem families' who were indolent, feckless, dirty and a drain on the resources of the post-war welfare state.[207] Paul Michael Garrett argues that '"problem families" can be understood as part of a matrix of ideas historically preoccupied with Irish people in Britain'.[208] In the early 1950s, for example, B. M. Spinley gave an account of 'one of the worst slums in London', going on to describe a district that was 'notorious ... for vice and delinquency ... a major prostitution area' and the 'blackest spot in the city for juvenile delinquency'.[209] In this part of London, she stated, 'a large proportion of the inhabitants are Irish; social workers say: "The Irish land here, and while the respectable soon move away, the ignorant and the shiftless stay."'[210] The author, in Nancy Fraser's words, with the 'stigmatising gaze of a culturally dominant other',[211] then painted a picture of a typical house in the locality:

The most noticeable characteristic of the house is the smell, indeed on a first visit the middle-class stomach may find it impossible to stay longer than five minutes. These strong odours are partly due to the fact windows are not opened and so no current of air can carry away the smells of cooking, lavatory bucket, mattress wet in the night, and the baby's vomit hurriedly wiped up.[212]

As Garrett points out, descriptions like this are 'recursive in that similar descriptions of the living conditions of Irish people were produced in the nineteenth century'.[213] Carter et al. conclude their brief references to anti-Irish racism by arguing that the Churchill Government of 1951–1955, in building its case against Black immigration on the grounds that it 'would create problems which were insoluble precisely because their provenance was "racial" and not social, simultaneously involved the deracialization of the Irish'.[214] (I return to this in the next chapter).

Churchill resigns

Churchill's second premiership came to an end when poor health forced him to resign on April 5, 1955, aged 80, making way for his Foreign Secretary and Deputy Prime Minister, Anthony Eden to become Prime Minster. Churchill died ten years later.

Appendix

The Government of Clement Attlee: the foundation of the Welfare State and the beginnings of the end of British colonial rule (1945–1951)

Nationalization of Industry and foundation of the Welfare State

Labour's promise to take over the commanding heights of the economy via nationalization were, of course, anathema to committed Tories, but, after almost six years of wartime state direction of the economy, more generally it did not seem nearly so radical as it had before the war[215] – or indeed as it seems now. On the first day of the new Parliament, the massed ranks of Labour members sang the socialist anthem, the Red Flag. Tories everywhere were scandalized.[216] The large number of new Labour MPs who entered the Commons in 1945 included the then radical Denis Healey (who made an impassioned first speech urging world socialist revolution), as well as future Labour Prime Ministers Harold Wilson and James Callaghan.

Despite the 'Red Flag', Healy's pleas for revolution, and 'The Labour Party is a Socialist Party, and proud of it' buried in the party's 1945 election manifesto,[217] the Attlee Government was not, as noted earlier, socialist, but radically social democratic.[218] Despite Britain having been made bankrupt by World War II,[219] one by one the key industries of the post-war economy became nationalized. For the most part the takeovers were highly popular; none more so than the nationalization of the coalmines in 1946.[220] As Derek Brown points out, pit owners still employed a million men, many of them in dire and dangerous conditions, with the National Coal Board, seen as much as a humanitarian institution as an economic one.[221] Also in 1946, the Bank of England was nationalized. All this took place, despite recurring currency crises and shortages of food and resources so severe that rationing had to be maintained long after the war.[222]

As Brown puts it, the 1942 Beveridge Report that 'spelled out a system of social insurance, covering every citizen regardless of income … offered nothing less than a cradle-to-grave welfare state'.[223] The National Health Service (NHS) made medical services free of charge and brought major improvements in the health of working-class people, with deaths from diphtheria, pneumonia, and tuberculosis significantly reduced.[224] According to Terry McCarthy, the NHS treated some 8.5 million dental patients and dispensed more than 5 million pairs of spectacles during its first year of operation.[225] Other major measures included the National Insurance Act 1946 that created flat-rate pension, sickness benefit, unemployment benefit and child benefit,[226] while a large house-building programme was carried out with the intention of providing millions of people with high-quality homes.[227] In 1947, the Electricity Act brought into public ownership the electricity supply industry. The railways were also brought under state control. Area gas boards were created under the provisions of the Gas Act of 1848.[228]

A capital/labour comprise, not a benign gift from the state

Notable as these achievements are and something to be celebrated by all, from a Marxist perspective, they are viewed as a compromise between capital and labour after decades of struggle rather than a gift from the state. Gail Lewis summarizes the long accepted interpretation among all sections of the Left that the creation and administration of the Beveridge Welfare State was a 'settlement' between capital, organized labour and the state – reform not revolution.[229] Confrontations between capitalists and their supporters and labour intensified in the late 19th and early 20th centuries and, as trade unions, that were legalized in 1871, grew stronger and gradually gained ground, they increasingly represented a potential threat to capital's interests. As Asbjørn Wahl argues, this process 'was solidified when a big part of the movement turned politically toward socialism, breaking its old alliances with liberalism, with the aim of ending capitalist exploitation'.[230] Demands for more systemic changes grew accordingly and prepared the ground for a class compromise.[231]

An important feature in the wider political landscape was the existence of a competing economic system in the Soviet Union and Eastern Europe, since the 1917 Bolshevik revolution. Capitalists in the West realized that prevent social revolution, there was a need to come to terms with labour. It is important to note that the Welfare State was never an expressed aim for the labour movement before it was created. Ruling class fear of socialism reached its height in the inter-war period between the world wars, as socialists and communists took prominent roles in the fight against fascism, and as a consensus in favour of social change developed among the working class. It was 'a particular balance of social forces, not the spirit of compromise itself', which made the Welfare State possible.[232]

In the Appendix to chapter 2, I noted how the devastation caused by the World War I (1914–1918) greatly destabilized Europe. In Britain the 1920s were a time of mass unemployment, industrial unrest and capitalist crisis.[233] In that Appendix, I also noted how, following the slaughter of World War, Liberal Prime Minister David Lloyd George promised 'a fit country for heroes to live in',[234] but, as Scott Jones points out in *The Socialist,* by Spring 1921, millions were unemployed, some 23.4% of Britain's workforce.[235]

The Communist Party of Great Britain, which had been formed in 1920, set about organizing the country's unemployed with the formation of the National Unemployed Workers' Movement (NUWM) in 1921 into a mass organized body, adopting the principle of 'work or full maintenance at trade union rates of wages'.[236] As well as fighting for demands for real help for the unemployed and an end to the variation in the inadequate relief that was available, the NUWM also recognized what Marx and Engels described as capitalism's need for a 'reserve army of labour', arguing that the unemployed were being used by the ruling class to drive down wages and conditions of those in employment.[237] As Jones explains, massive strikes took place in 1919, 1921 and 1925, culminating in the mighty 1926 General Strike, 'when workers tasted their own power, and revolution was on the cards in Britain'[238] (for an interesting and informative account of the General Strike, including the role of Churchill in trying to suppress it, see the article by John Simkin).[239]

The 1920s and 1930s were also a time of extensive poverty. Mass hunger marches organized by the NUWM took place in 1922 and 1927 and continued in 1930, 1932 and 1934,[240] in addition to the famous Jarrow crusade in 1936, during the Great Depression. Paula Bartley, author of a biography of Ellen Wilknson, the Labour MP who played a prominent role in the march,[241] has chronicled the story of Wilkinson and the people who marched with her. As Malcolm Pearce and Geoffrey Stewart put it, the march shaped 'the post-war perceptions of the 1930s and ensured the attachment of the word "Hungry" to the 1930s in the popular mind'.[242] More importantly, as Bartley puts it, 'Jarrow became a by-word for resistance against heartless and unjust governments'.[243] A hated 'means test' was introduced in 1931 by the National Government, headed by Labour MP Ramsay MacDonald, requiring unemployed workers to sell possessions before receiving any benefit, Moreover, if there was a working member of the household, that also disqualified the applicant.[244]

'Race', nation, gender and Empire

As well as being a capital/labour compromise, deeply embedded in the conceptualization and practice of the Beveridge welfare reforms, we see the links between 'race', nation and Empire (the ways in which racism articulate with 'nation' and imperialism is discussed in the Introduction to this book). Another key component of the settlement was a normative family form of male breadwinner, dependent 'housewife' and their children. In the Beveridge Report, the link between 'race', nation, Empire and gender is made explicit. For example, the argument deployed in favour of introducing child allowances was that 'with its present rate of reproduction the British race cannot continue, means of reversing the recent course of the birth rate must be found'.[245] Women were assigned the role of baby-machines in the service of the Empire and were told, 'In the next thirty years housewives as Mothers have vital work to do in ensuring the adequate continuance of the British Race and British Ideals in the world'.[246] The clearest example of 'race' and nation inherent in the Beveridge Report can be seen in Beveridge's essay, 'Children's Allowances and the Race'. In it, he stated:

> Pride of race is a reality for the British as for other peoples ... as in Britain today we look back with pride and gratitude to our ancestors, look back as a nation or as individuals two hundred years and more to the generations illuminated by Marlborough or Cromwell, or Drake, are we not bound also to look forward, to plan society now, so that there may be no lack of men or women of the quality of those earlier days, of the best of our breed, two hundred and three hundred years hence?[247]

The Bretton Woods System

As we saw in the Appendix to chapter 2, the 1940s saw mass slaughter tear societies apart for the second time in the century. In their wake, politics came to be shaped by popular demands for peace, social security, full employment, and political control of the economy.[248] This was the backdrop to the Bretton Woods Conference in 1944. The resulting Bretton Woods System was largely the product of Anglo-American negotiations, with Britain represented by John Maynard Keynes[249] (it was under the Keynesian model of regulated capitalism – a mixed economy of state ownership and spending on economic infrastructure, utilities and welfare alongside private capitalist businesses) with a commitment to full (male) employment that the social and economic foundation for the Welfare State was created. As Wahl summarizes the reasons for this post-war economic order: 'unregulated, crisis-stricken capitalism had to come to an end because, if it didn't, the balance of forces meant that capitalism itself might fall'.[250] Wahl sums up the nature of the agreement for both sides:

For the trade union movement, the compromise meant the acceptance of the capitalist mode of production, an economy still governed by private ownership and employers' right to lead the labor process. In exchange for the gains in terms of welfare and working conditions, unions were expected to guarantee industrial peace and restraint in wage negotiations. Simplistically, the welfare state and the gradual improvement of living conditions were what dominant parts of the labor movement achieved in exchange for giving up its greater socialist ambitions.[251]

As Wahl concludes, in retrospect, it is clear that capitalists saw the pact as a truce between warring factions rather than a partnership that could be sustained indefinitely, using it to bide time, embed new consumer ideologies, and dampen socialist sentiments in the labour movement.[252] It led directly to the latter's depoliticization and the bureaucratization of its leadership and staff. It became the historic role of unions and social democratic parties to administer this policy of class compromise. Over time, 'each atrophied – transitioning from mass organizations for the working class into bureaucratic mediators between labor and capital', heralding the end of social democracy's heyday.[253]

The beginnings of the end of British colonial rule

India

India is a country with a long period of imperialist rule about which I have dealt elsewhere in this book. Tharoor describes that country's eventual break from the British Empire on August 15, 1947, as 'a moment of birth that was also an abortion, since freedom came with the horrors of the partition, when East and West Pakistan were hacked off the stooped shoulders of India by the departing British'.[254] He goes to refer to the rioting, rape and murder that took place as millions were uprooted from their homes. Within months, Tharoor points out, India and Pakistan were embroiled in a war over Kashmir, the consequences of which remain with us.[255] He goes on, there 'was an intangible partition, too', as 'Friendships were destroyed, families ruined, geography hacked, history misread, tradition denied, minds and hearts torn apart':

> The creation and perpetuation of Hindu-Muslim antagonism was the most significant accomplishment of British imperial policy: the colonial project of "divide et impera" (divide and rule) fomented religious antagonisms to facilitate continued imperial rule and reached its tragic culmination in 1947.[256]

Burma

Burma (now Myanmar) had been made a province of India in 1886. As Dinyar Godrej explains, divide-and-rule was also a tactic of the British there as Indians were brought in to fill civil-service jobs and the business interests of Indians and Chinese in Burma were encouraged, breeding resentment among Burmese people.[257] In addition, agriculture was geared towards export and Burma became the world's largest exporter of rice. Following resistance to British rule, in 1890 whole villages were destroyed to stop guerrilla activity. In 1920, protests by university students were followed by strikes and anti-tax protests with Buddhist monks playing a prominent role, including armed rebellion. A Rangoon University law student Aung Sang gained increasing prominence in the movement for national autonomy.[258]

The start of World War II saw the administration of Burma separated from India, with nationalists viewing this as an opportunity to gain concessions towards autonomy in return for Burmese support in the hostilities, but not Aung Sang who rejected participating in the war and founded the Communist Party of Burma, drawing inspiration not just from Marx, but from Sinn Féin.[259]

Aung Sang was offered a deal by Japan – military training in exchange for support for a national uprising against the British colonialists. But with the Japanese invasion of Burma in 1942 came the growing realization that one set of colonialists had been exchanged for another. Consequently, Aung San quickly changed sides and negotiated with the British to drive out the Japanese. Having experienced the imperial ambitions of Japan, he became one of the founders of the Anti-Fascist People's Freedom League (AFPFL). The Japanese were successfully banished from Burma in May 1945, leaving a British-run military administration. That administration was pragmatic about the popular support for Aung San, who eventually managed to negotiate Burma's independence from Britain in January 1947.[260]

Aung San concluded an agreement with the country's different 'ethnic groups' for a unified Burma. An interim government was elected with Aung San's AFPFL winning by a landslide. However, on July 19, 1947, at the instigation of an opposition politician, Aung San and several members of his cabinet were gunned down. His colleague, U Nu, took over the reins and Burma finally became independent on January 4, 1948. Godrej concludes, 'anti-British sentiment was so strong that Burma decided not to join the British Commonwealth, unlike other colonies that had also gained independence'.[261]

Ceylon

Sri Lanka was known as Ceylon from Portuguese colonization in 1505 until 1972 when it became independent from the UK and a republic, having left the British Empire in 1948[262] (between 1948 and 1972, it had 'Dominion' status). Prominent antiracist socialist activist and academic and former Director of the Institute of Race Relations, the late Ambalavaner Siva-nandan, was based in Britain up to his death in 2018 following his departure from the then Dominion of Ceylon after the anti-Tamil pogrom and unrest the first island-wide to target that minority known as the '58 riots'. On his arrival in London, he found himself in the middle of the anti-Black riots in

Notting Hill (see chapter 4). In 1990, he wrote this of the British departure from Ceylon:

> When the British left Ceylon in 1948, the lines of communal conflict had already been drawn. One hundred and fifty years of British rule had brought together three different social formations under one central administration for purposes of economic exploitation; but for purposes of political control, the colonial government had reinforced the communal divisions that ran like a seam around those social formations. It divided in order to rule what it integrated in order to exploit.[263]

In the late colonial period, the first stirrings of Sinhala–Buddhist nationalism, popularly known in Sinhala as 'Jathika Chinthanaya',[264] became politically influential, largely as a response to this familiar colonial divide-and-rule policy, a strategy that was also denounced by the Sinhala majority elites who were aspiring for political and economic power and felt that the colonial administration was unjustly favouring minorities.[265]

Kanishka Goonewardena explains how the anti-colonialist struggle was compromised at the outset by Jathika Chinthanaya on the one hand and the Tamil ethno-nationalists on the other. These 'strategically accentuated ethnic divisions within the Crown Colony of Ceylon' tended to view the other more as rivals than allies capable of uniting as one political force, a position that also had 'disastrous post-colonial consequences that are still unfolding'.[266] Socialist anticolonial politics came mainly from mobilizations with the single exception to such ethno-nationalist anti-colonial politics came principally from socialist mobilizations led by the internationalist Marxist Lanka Sama Samaja Party (LSSP) and the Communist Party, a pro-Moscow breakaway from the LSSP. According to Goonewardena, both were at the forefront of anti-imperialist struggles in Ceylon.[267]

During World War II, the island served as an important front-line British base against the Japanese, with a large segment of the British and American fleet deployed there. There was considerable opposition to the war, and the LSSP leaders were arrested by the Colonial authorities. In April, 1942, the Japanese Navy bombed Colombo and LSSP leaders were able to escape. Following the war, popular pressure for independence intensified. On February 4, 1948 the country won its independence as the Commonwealth of Ceylon, with Don Stephen Senanayake of the centre-right United National Party (UNP) who had won the country's first General Election in 1947, becoming its first Prime Minister.[268]

Palestine

Near the end of World War II, after over two decades of British rule in Palestine that started in 1920, the Jewish settler community there embarked on a campaign to push the British out of Palestine.[269] A wave of attacks took place against British forces and Palestinian Arabs, in response to which the British declared martial law, enacted draconian emergency regulations and undertook brutal collective punishments on local Jewish communities.[270]

The Attlee government decided to hand the problem over to the recently formed United Nations. According to Mark Curtis, Attlee regarded Palestine as 'an economic and military liability' and Britain began to promote the partition of Palestine into Jewish and Arab states. This was supported by the Jewish leadership, who made up one-third of the population, but not, understandably, the two-thirds Palestinians. In November 1947, the UN imposed General Assembly Resolution 181 partitioning Palestine and awarding the Jews a state that comprised over half the country.[271] Arab groups began to form volunteer armies throughout Palestine.

In May 1948, less than a year after the Partition Plan was introduced, Britain withdrew from Palestine and Israel declared itself an independent state. Almost immediately, neighbouring Arab armies moved in to try to prevent this. The ensuing 1948 Arab Israeli War was between Israel and five Arab nations: Jordan, Iraq, Syria, Egypt and Lebanon. By the end of the war in July 1949, Israel controlled more than two-thirds of the former British Mandate, while Jordan took control of the West Bank, Egypt and the Gaza Strip.[272]

As the History.com editors conclude, the '1948 conflict opened a new chapter in the struggle between Jews and Palestinian Arabs, which now became a regional contest involving nation-states and a tangle of diplomatic, political and economic interests'.[273]

The 1948 Nationality Act

As Michael Wood points out, in July 1948 at the same time as the formation of the NHS, which Attlee hoped would make us 'not only a healthier, but a happier nation', there was also an attempt to redefine what it meant to be British. Specifically, the issue was what would be the relation of the peoples of the Empire to the 'motherland' – what would be the status of its former subjects who in no small measure, Wood reminds us, had helped in the war effort, particularly troops from India, Africa and the Caribbean?[274] At the time of the death of Queen Victoria in 1901, if you could prove you were born within the British Empire you could claim full nationality rights in Britain. In practice, though, immigration was small-scale – there were still only 7,000 people from the Indian subcontinent in the UK in the 1930s. But all that would change with the British Nationality Act of 1948.[275]

The Act conferred the status of 'British citizen' on all Commonwealth subjects and recognized their right to work and settle in the UK – and to bring their families with them. It gave citizenship to over a quarter of the planet, some 600–700 million people.[276] Importantly, it marked the first time that married British women gained independent nationality, regardless of the citizenship of their spouses.[277]

In reality, the Act, which created the new status of 'citizen of the United Kingdom and Colonies' (CUKC) for people born or naturalized either in the UK or one of its colonies, was never intended to facilitate mass migration but to encourage skilled and unskilled workers from the colonies to come to Britain to assist with post-war reconstruction and industry, and to help in public services like the NHS, railways and transport (in the 1950s, London Transport lent migrants money for boat tickets from the Caribbean).[278] Without the Act, Wood concludes, 'a battered postwar Britain and its new welfare state would simply have ground to a halt'.[279]

Notes

1 Jones, Nigel. 2012. 'Cameron, Churchill, race… and a historical howler', *Daily Mail*, March 15. https://www.dailymail.co.uk/debate/article-2114950/amp/Cameron-Churchill-Race--historical-howler.html.
2 Ibid.
3 Ibid.
4 Cited in Jones. 2012.
5 Cited in Tharoor, Ishaan. 2015. 'The dark side of Winston Churchill's legacy no one should forget', *The Washington Post*, February 3. https://www.washingtonpost.com/news/worldviews/wp/2015/02/03/the-dark-side-of-winston-churchills-legacy-no-one-should-forget/.
6 English, Otto. 2020.
7 Duffield, Charlie. 2020. 'Was Winston Churchill racist?'
8 Churchill, Winston. 1920. 'Zionism versus Bolshevism: A struggle for the soul of the Jewish People', p. 5. https://en.wikisource.org/wiki/Zionism_versus_Bolshevism.
9 Ibid.
10 Ibid.
11 Ibid.
12 Ibid.
13 See the Appendix to chapter 2.
14 Attar, pp. 8–9.
15 Attar, p. 9.
16 Cited in Attar, p. 9.
17 Gilbert, Martin. 1977. *Winston S. Churchill, 1922–1939, Vol. 5,* Boston: Houghton and Mifflin, pp. 847–848.
18 MacDonald, Malcolm. 1972. *Titans & Others,* London: Collins, pp. 91–92.
19 Cited in Heyden, Tom. 2015. 'The 10 greatest controversies of Winston Churchill's career'.
20 Lloyd was very strongly opposed to Indian independence or even bringing a measure of democracy to the Raj, writing of what he called 'the fundamental unsuitability of modern western democratic methods of government to any Oriental people' (cited in Charmley, John. 1988. *Lord Lloyd and the Decline of the British Empire,* New York: St Martin's Press, p. 170). He was thus a fervent believer in what he regarded as the greatness of the British empire. According to historian, Louise Atherton Lloyd was 'Idealistically, almost mystically, devoted to the British Empire, he advocated the use of force, if necessary, to maintain British control'; Atherton, Louise. 1994. 'Lord Lloyd at the British Council and the Balkan Front, 1937–1940', *The International History Review,* 16, (1) February, p. 26.
21 Cited in Alibhai-Brown, Yasmin. 2015. *Exotic England, The Making of a Curious Nation,* p. 194.

22   War Cabinet, 276 (40). National Archives, 24 October 1940. https://discovery.nationalarchives.gov.uk/details/r/C9110640. See also Report WP (G) (40) 268 of 18 October 1940.
23   Cited in Toye. 2020.
24   Wood, Mike. 2018. 'His darkest hour'.
25   Jones, Nigel. 2012.
26   Ohlinger, 'WSC: A midnight interview, 1902'
27   Cited in Toye. 2020.
28   Ponting, Clive. 1994. *Winston Churchill,* p. 338, cited in Simkin.
29   Oppenheim. 2017. 'Winston Churchill is no better than Adolf Hitler'.
30   Ibid.
31   Cited in Oppenheim. 2017.
32   Mishra, Pankaj. 2007. 'Exit wounds: The legacy of Indian partition', *The New Yorker,* August 6. https://www.newyorker.com/magazine/2007/08/13/exit-wounds.
33   Cited in Oppenheim. 2017.
34   Ramachandra, Guha. 2019. 'Churchill, the greatest Briton, hated Gandhi, the greatest Indian', *The Atlantic,* April 6. https://www.theatlantic.com/international/archive/2019/04/churchill-gandhi-briton-indian-greatest/584170/.
35   *The Week Staff.* 2020. 'Winston Churchill: antifascist hero or racist war-monger – or both?'
36   Ramachandra. 2019.
37   Cited in Oppenheim. 2017.
38   Mishra, 'Exit wounds'.
39   Cited in Mishra, 'Exit wounds'.
40   Mishra, 'Exit wounds'.
41   Cited in Toye. 2020.
42   Miles. 1989, p. 90.
43   Hari. 2020.
44   Ibid.
45   According to Eccleshall and Walker. 2002, p. 273 and Stanton. 2000, p. 26; Baldwin was the effective deputy prime minister in the Conservative-dominated Cabinet, serving as Lord President of the Council.
46   Wood, Mike. 2018. 'His darkest hour'.
47   English. 2020.
48   Cited in Hari. 2020.
49   Cathcart, 'History gets a handbagging'.
50   Cited in Haq, 'Post-truth partition narrative delegitimizes Pakistan'.
51   Ibid.
52   Jones. 2012.
53   Toye, Richard. 2020.
54   Simkin, John. 2020.
55   Winston Churchill, letter to Clementine Churchill (6th January, 1927), cited in Simkin. 2020.
56   Gilbert. 1991, p. 480.
57   Winston Churchill, speech (17th February, 1933), cited in Simkin. 2020.
58   Winston Churchill, *The Sunday Chronicle* (26th May, 1935), cited in Simkin. 2020.
59   Winston Churchill, *The Evening Standard* (10th August, 1936), cited in Simkin. 2020.
60   UK Government. Undated. 'Past Prime Ministers: 21st century, Winston Churchill'. https://www.gov.uk/government/history/past-prime-ministers/winston-churchill.

61 Dawson. Sarah. 2017. 'A brief history of Blenheim Palace', *The Culture Trip*, August 22. https://theculturetrip.com/europe/united-kingdom/england/arti cles/a-brief-history-of-blenheim-palace/.

62 Simkin, John. 2020b.

63 Simkin. 2020b. Winston Churchill, letter to Randolph Churchill (8th January, 1931) cited in Spartacus Educational. Undated. 'Second World War political figures: Winston *Churchill*'. https://spartacus-educational.com/PRchurchill.htm.

64 Winston Churchill, *The Evening Standard* (13th March, 1936), cited in Simkin. 2020.

65 Winston Churchill, speech in the House of Commons (6th April, 1936), cited in Simkin. 2020.

66 https://www.parliament.uk/globalassets/documents/parliamentary-archives/ Churchill-for-web-Mar-2014.pdf.

67 Winston Churchill, *The Evening Standard* (17th September, 1937), cited in Simkin. 2020.

68 Winston Churchill, *The Evening Standard* (14th October, 1937), cited in Simkin. 2020.

69 Winston Churchill, speech in the House of Commons (12th March, 1938), cited in Simkin. 2020.

70 Simkin, John. 2021. 'Was Winston Churchill a supporter or an opponent of fascism?'

71 Ponting, Clive, p. 394.

72 Simkin. 2020.

73 Darby, Graham. 1999. *Hitler, Appeasement and the Road to War*, p. 56.

74 Simkin. 2020.

75 The Library of Congress. Undated.

76 Churchill, Winston. 1938. 'The defence of freedom and peace (The lights are going out)', *International Churchill Society*, October 16. https://winstonchurchill. org/resources/speeches/1930-1938-the-wilderness/the-defence-of-freedom- and-peace/.

77 Gilbert, Martin. 2007.

78 Tory Prime Minister Chamberlain's views were anything but similar. At the time of the infamous Kristallnacht, or 'Night of Broken Glass', a Nazi pogrom throughout Germany in 1938, in which Jewish synagogues and property were smashed and lives lost, Chamberlain wrote in a private letter to his sister, 'Jews aren't lovable people, I don't care for them myself' (Gilbert. 1993).

79 For a full account, see Gilbert. 1993.

80 Cited in Gilbert, Martin. 1993. 'Churchill and the Holocaust', Speech at the International Churchill Society Conference.

81 Ibid.

82 Gilbert. 1993.

83 Cited in Gilbert. 1993.

84 Gilbert. 1993.

85 Cited in Gilbert. 1993

86 Ibid.

87 Gilbert. 1993.

88 O'Malley. J.P. 2016. 'Churchill and his uneasy Irish legacy', *Irish Independent*, May 9. https://m.independent.ie/entertainment/books/churchill-and-his-uneasy- irish-legacy-34691865.html.

89 Davin-Power, David. 2015. 'Gallipoli: Churchill's folly must be remembered 100 years on', *The Irish Times*. April 20. https://www.irishtimes.com/culture/herita ge/gallipoli-churchill-s-folly-must-be-remembered-100-years-on-1.2182702.

90 O'Malley. 2016.

91   O'Dowd. Niall. 2020. 'Winston Churchill ordered Black and Tans into Ireland in 1920', *Irish Central,* June 16. https://www.irishcentral.com/roots/history/winston-churchill-black-tans-ireland.amp.

92   Cited in O'Dowd. 2020. For an account of the more recent hunger strikes during the premiership of Margaret Thatcher, see Chapter 5.2.

93   O'Mally. 2016.

94   van Bockhaven, Vicky. 2009. 'Leopard-men of the Congo in literature and popular imagination', *Tydskr. letterkd,* 46 (1) January. http://www.scielo.org.za/scielo.php?script=sci_arttext&pid=S0041-476X2009000100006.

95   O'Mally. 2016.

96   Redfern, Neil.

97   Roberts. 2009, p. 130, cited in Redfern, p. 178.

98   Louis. 1977, p. 200, cited in Redfern, p. 178.

99   Kolko. 1969, p. 249, cited in Redfern, p. 178.

100   Redfern, p. 179.

101   Addison. 2011. http://www.bbc.co.uk/history/worldwars/wwtwo/election_01.shtml.

102   Larres, Klaus W. 2020. 'When a winner becomes a loser'.

103   English, Otto. 2020. 'The Churchill factor'.

104   English, Otto. 2019. 'A Churchill history lesson for Brexit Britain'.

105   1945 General Election. https://spartacus-educational.com/GE1945.htm.

106   Larres. 2020.

107   Addison, Paul. 2011. 'Why Churchill lost in 1945'.

108   Ibid.

109   Ibid.

110   Larres. 2020.

111   Ibid.

112   Ibid.

113   Cited in Jones, Dan. 2010. 'Becoming a Victorian', *The Spectator*, March 20. https://www.spectator.co.uk/article/becoming-a-victorian. Throughout the rest of the book, there will be a number of references to 'Commonwealth'. It may be useful at this point to provide some clarification on the difference between the early Commonwealth and the modern Commonwealth. In 1926, Britain and the Dominions agreed that they were all equal members of a community within the British Empire. They all owed allegiance to the British King or Queen, but the United Kingdom did not rule over them. This community was called the 'British Commonwealth of Nations or just the Commonwealth'. The 'modern Commonwealth' dates from 1949, with independent countries from Africa, the Americas, Asia, Europe and the Pacific, being members. Membership 'is based on free and equal voluntary co-operation', The Commonwealth. 2021. 'Our history'. https://thecommonwealth.org/about-us/history.

114   Larres. 2020.

115   Ibid.

116   The National Archives. Undated. 'Chamberlain and Hitler 1938'. https://www.nationalarchives.gov.uk/education/resources/chamberlain-and-hitler/#:~:text=At%20Munich%2C%20Chamberlain%20got%20an,demands%20to%20make%20in%20Europe.

117   Simkin. 2020.

118   Larres. 2020.

119   Cited in Gov.uk. https://www.gov.uk/government/history/past-prime-ministers/winston-churchill.

120   Ibid.

121   BBC News. 2011. 'Mau Mau uprising: Bloody history of Kenya conflict', April 7. https://www.bbc.co.uk/news/uk-12997138.
122   Ibid.
123   English, Otto. 2020; see Elkins, Caroline. Britain's Gulag: The Brutal End of Empire in Kenya, Jonathan Cape.
124   Ibid.
125   Parry, Marc. 2016. 'Uncovering the brutal truth about the British empire', The Guardian, August 18. https://www.theguardian.com/news/2016/aug/18/uncovering-truth-british-empire-caroline-elkins-mau-mau.
126   English. 2020.
127   Rodgers, Lucy and Maryam Ahmed. 2018. 'Windrush: Who exactly was on board?', BBC News. (27 April 2018).
128   Ibid.
129   Sherwood. Undated.
130   Ibid.
131   'Colour bar' simply means refusing someone anything, including a job or a service on account of the colour of their skin (example, in my terminology, of 'colour-coded racism').
132   Sherwood. Undated.
133   Ibid.
134   Fryer. 1984; Ramdin. 1987.
135   See Heath and Ridge. 1983.
136   Daniel. 1968: Smith. 1977.
137   Smith. 1977.
138   Carter, Bob; Harris, Clive; and Joshi, Shirley. 1987. 'The 1951–55 conservative government and the racialisation of Black immigration', Policy Papers in Ethnic Relations, 11, Centre for Research in Ethnic Relations, University of Warwick. https://web.warwick.ac.uk/fac/soc/CRER_RC/publications/pdfs/Policy%20Papers%20in%20Ethnic%20Relations/PolicyP%20No.11.pdf.
139   Van Hartesveldt. 1983. 'Race and political parties in Britain, 1954–1965', p. 127.
140   See, for example, Hansard's Parliamentary Debates, 538 (March 10, 1955), p. 125.
141   Carter et al. 1987.
142   Ibid. Because of the date this article was written, it is likely that Carter et al. are using 'Black' to encompass all people of colour. Nomenclature changes constantly. Trying to keep up-to-date is about respect for people's wishes, not about 'political correctness'. Indeed 'political correctness' or 'PC' is a pernicious concept invented by the Radical Right, which, unfortunately, has become common currency. The term was coined to imply that there exist (Left) political demagogues who seek to impose their views on equality issues, in particular appropriate terminology, on the majority. In reality, nomenclature changes over time. Using current and acceptable nomenclature is about fostering a caring and inclusive society, not about 'political correctness'.
143   Carter et al. 1987.
144   Ibid.
145   Ibid.
146   Cited in Carter et al. 1987.
147   Smith, David. 2007. 'What Churchill said about Britain's immigrants'.
148   Cited in Smith.
149   Ibid.
150   Jones, Nigel. 2012.
151   Carter et al. 1987.
152   Ibid.
153   Ibid.
154   Ibid.

155 Ibid.
156 Cited in Carter et al. 1987. This remark is attributed to Robert Arthur James Gascoyne-Cecil, the 5th Marquess of Salisbury, not to be confused with Prime Minister Robert Gascoyne-Cecil referred to earlier in this chapter who was the 3rd Marquess of Salisbury.
157 Goodfellow, Maya. 2019.
158 Carter et al. 1987.
159 Addison, Paul. 2006. *Churchill: The Unexpected Hero*, p. 233.
160 Carter et al. 1987.
161 Original endnote 16, https://discovery.nationalarchives.gov.uk/details/r/C337545> C.O.1028/22, STU 91/143/01, CWP (53) 15, 28 September 1953, cited in Carter et al. 1987.
162 Ibid., Draft Report of the Working Party on Coloured People Seeking Employment in the United Kingdom, 17 December 1953.
163 Ibid.
164 Cited in Carter et al. 1987.
165 Cole, Mike. 1989. '"Race" and class or "race", class, gender and community?: A critical appraisal of the racialised fraction of the working-class thesis', *The British Journal of Sociology*, 40 (1) March.
166 Draft Report of the Working Party on Coloured People Seeking Employment in the United Kingdom, 17 December 1953.
167 Carter et al. 1987.
168 Ibid.
169 Carter et al. 1987.
170 Ibid.
171 Ibid.
172 *The Times*, November 8, 1954, cited in Carter et al. 1987.
173 Carter et al. 1987.
174 Ibid.
175 CAB 124/1191, Conservative Commonwealth Association, Liverpool Group, *The Problem of Colonial Immigrants*, January 1954, cited in Carter et al. 1987.
176 Carter et al. 1987.
177 Bartlett, Roger. 2017. 'When Mosley men won elections'. http://britishguardian.blogspot.com/2017/05/when-mosley-men-won-elections.html.
178 Hansard, vol. 532, 3 November 1954.
179 Carter et al. 1987.
180 C.O.1028/25, Police Report upon the Coloured Population in Sheffield, 3 October 1952, enclosed in Town Clerk (Sheffield), John Heys to V.Harris, 8 October 1952.
181 C.O.1028/22, STU 91/143/01, CWP (53) 10, 11 July 1953.
182 Ibid.
183 Ibid.
184 C.O.1028/22, Draft Report of Working Party on Coloured People Seeking Employment in the United Kingdom, 17 December 1953.
185 C.O.1028/25, Police Report upon the Coloured Population in Sheffield, 3 October 1952, enclosed in Town Clerk (Sheffield), John Heys to V.Harris, 8 October 1952.
186 C.O.1028/25, Town Clerk (Middlesborough), E.Parr to V.Harris, 14 October 1952.
187 *The Times*, November 9, 1954.
188 Carter et al. 1987.
189 Goodfellow, Maya. 2019. 'Keeping Britain White'.
190 Ibid.
191 Greenfields. 2006, pp. 60–61.

192   Diverse Herts. 2009.
193   Greenfields. 2006, p. 62.
194   Duffy and Tomlinson. 2009, p. 2.
195   Greenfields. 2006, p. 63.
196   Duffy, R. and Tomlinson, Andy. 2009, 'Education on the hoof', Lincoln: Bishop Grosseteste University, p. 2. https://s3.eu-west-1.amazonaws.com/bishopg.ac. uk/documents/Centre-for-Education-for-Social-Justice.pdf.
197   Ibid., p. 2.
198   Greenfields. 2006, p. 65.
199   Ibid., p. 66.
200   Ibid., p. 71.
201   Langworth, Richard M. 2018. 'Churchill and common folk: a case of misconception', The Churchill Project, January 18. https://winstonchurchill. hillsdale.edu/churchill-common/.
202   The Churchill Project. 2016. 'Hillsdale & statesmanship'. https://winstonchurchill. hillsdale.edu/about-the-churchill-project/.
203   Ibid.
204   Buchan-Hepburn is referring to Sinn Féin, a political party founded in 1905, whose core political objective is a united Ireland, and who, since first elected in 1918, refuses to send its MPs to Westminster, believing that British political institutions should play no part in governing the people of Ireland, and that they as MPs should not make decisions on behalf of British people.
205   Carter et al. 1987.
206   Ibid.
207   Garrett. 2002a, p. 482; see also Philp and Timms. 1957; Hall. 1960, ch. 10; and Starkey, P. 2000. 'The feckless mother: women, poverty and social workers in wartime and post-war England', Women's History Review, 9 (3).
208   Garrett. 2002a, p. 483.
209   Spinley, B. M. 1953. The Deprived and the Privileged, London, Routledge & Kegan Paul, p. 40.
210   Ibid.
211   Fraser, Nancy. 2000. 'Rethinking recognition', New Left Review, May/June, p. 109.
212   Spinley. 1953, p. 40, cited in Garrett. 2002, p. 483.
213   Garrett. 2002a, p. 483.
214   Carter et al. 1987.
215   Brown. 2001b.
216   Ibid.
217   Ibid.
218   Katzarov, Konstantin. 2012. 'The theory of nationalisation', Springer Science & Business Media, (6 December), p. 213.
219   https://www.gov.uk/government/history/past-prime-ministers/clement-attlee.
220   Brown, 2001b.
221   Ibid.
222   https://www.gov.uk/government/history/past-prime-ministers/clement-attlee.
223   Brown, Derek. 2001b. '1945–51: Labour and the creation of the welfare state', The Guardian, March 14. https://www.theguardian.com/politics/2001/mar/ 14/past.education.
224   Lowe, Norman. Mastering Modern World History.
225   McCarthy, Terry. 2017. A Short History of the British Labour Movement, Labour History Movement Publications, pp. 48–50.
226   Thorpe, Andrew. 2001. A History of the British Labour Party, London: Palgrave.
227   Jeffries. 2014.
228   Brady, Crisis in Britain, pp. 132–138.

229   Lewis, Gail. 1996. 'Welfare settlements and racialising practices', *Soundings* 4 (Autumn), p. 110. http://banmarchive.org.uk/collections/soundings/04_109. pdf.

230   Wahl, Asbjørn. 2021. 'Class struggle built the welfare state', *Jacobin,* May 2. https://jacobinmag.com/2021/05/welfare-state-class-struggle-confrontation-compromise-labor-union-movement.

231   Wahl. 2021.

232   Ibid.

233   Jones, Scott. 2021. 'Lessons from history: 1920s–30s Britain: A working-class movement fighting unemployment and capitalism', *The Socialist,* April 14. https://m.socialistparty.org.uk/articles/32371/14-04-2021/1920s-30s-britain-a-working-class-movement-fighting-unemployment-and-capitalism.

234   Madeley, Peter. 2018. 'A fit country for heroes: 100 years since Lloyd George made legendary speech in Wolverhampton', *Express and Star,* November 23. https://www.expressandstar.com/news/politics/2018/11/23/a-fit-country-for-heroes-100-years-since-lloyd-georges-legendary-wolverhampton-speech/.

235   Jones. 2021.

236   Ibid.

237   Ibid.

238   Ibid.

239   Simkin, John. 2020c. 'The General Strike', https://spartacus-educational.com/TUgeneral.htm.

240   Jones, 2021.

241   Bartley, Paula. 2014. *Ellen Wilkinson: From Red Suffragist to Government Minister,* London: Pluto Press.

242   Pearce, Malcolm and Stewart, Geoffrey. 1992. *British Political History, 1867–2001,* Routledge, p. 359.

243   Bartley, Paula. 2016. 'Ellen Wilkinson and the Jarrow Crusade October 1936'. https://www.plutobooks.com/blog/ellen-wilkinson-and-the-jarrow-crusade-october-1936/.

244   Jones. 2021.

245   Beveridge, William. 1942. *Social Insurance and Allied Services,* Cmd 6404, London: HMSO, para 413.

246   Ibid., para 117.

247   Cited in Cohen, Steve. 1985. 'Anti-semitism, immigration controls and the welfare state', *Critical Social Policy,* 13 (Summer), pp. 88–89.

248   Wahl. 2021.

249   The National Archives: The Cabinet Papers. Undated. 'The IMF and Bretton Woods Conference'. https://www.nationalarchives.gov.uk/cabinetpapers/themes/bretton-woods-conference.htm.

250   Wahl. 2021.

251   Ibid.

252   Ibid.

253   Ibid.

254   Tharoor, Shashi. 2017. 'The Partition: The British game of "divide and rule"'.

255   Ibid.

256   Ibid.

257   Godrej, Dinyar. 2008. 'A short history of Burma', *New Internationalist,* April 18. https://newint.org/features/2008/04/18/history.

258   Ibid.

259   Ibid.

260   Ibid.

261   Ibid.

262   Goonewardena, Kanishka. 2020. 'Populism, nationalism and Marxism in Sri Lanka: from anti-colonial struggle to authoritarian neoliberalism', *Human Geography,* 102 (3), p. 290.

263   Sivanandan, A. 1990. 'Sri Lanka: A case study', *Communities of Resistance: Writings on Black Struggles for Socialism,* London: Verso, p. 199.

264   Goonewardena, p. 292.

265   Ibid., pp. 299–300.

266   Ibid.

267   Ibid., p. 300.

268   New World Encyclopedia contributors. 2021. 'Sri Lanka', *New World Encyclopedia,* January 2. https://www.newworldencyclopedia.org/p/index.php?title=Sri_Lanka&oldid=1030045.

269   Curtis, Mark. 2017. 'Britain's role in the war in Palestine, 1948', British foreign policy declassified, March 16. http://markcurtis.info/2017/03/16/britains-role-in-the-war-in-palestine-1948/.

270   Ibid.

271   Ibid.

272   History.com editors. 2017. 'Palestine', History.com, August 11, 2017. https://www.history.com/.amp/topics/middle-east/palestine.

273   Ibid. The role of Jordan in this is, of course, related to British imperialism. A series of treaties between Britain and Jordan (then known as Transjordan) between 1928 and 1945 had led to almost full independence for Transjordan (following World War 1, the newly-founded League of Nations had awarded Britain mandates over Transjordan and Iraq as well as Palestine). In March 1946, the Emir Abdullah negotiated a new Anglo-Transjordanian treaty, ending the British mandate and gaining full independence for Transjordan. In exchange for providing military facilities in Transjordan, Britain continued to pay a financial subsidy and supported the Arab Legion (a British-run mobile police force). In May 1946, the Transjordanian Parliament proclaimed Abdullah King, while officially changing the name of the country from the Emirate of Transjordan to the Hashemite Kingdom of Jordan; The Making of Transjordan. http://www.kinghussein.gov.jo/his_transjordan.html.

274   Wood. Michael. 2018. 'It was a visionary idea born out of postwar optimism and fairness', *BBC History Magazine,* January 25. https://www.pressreader.com/uk/bbc-history-magazine/20180125/281981787997579.

275   Wood. 2018.

276   Ibid.

277   Baldwin, M. 2001. 'Subject to empire: Married women and the British Nationality and Status of Aliens Act', *Journal of British Studies,* 40 (4), pp. 553–554.

278   Wood. 2018.

279   Ibid. The fact that this Act was passed under the Attlee Labour Government does not mean that it met with its full approval. According to historian David Olusoga even before the Empire Windrush had left Jamaica, Attlee 'had examined the possibility of preventing its embarkation or diverting the ship and the migrants on board to East Africa'. Moreover, again according to Olusoga, after the ship had arrived at Tilbury, Colonial Secretary Arthur Creech Jones is said to have reassured his cabinet colleagues that, although 'these people have British passports and must be allowed to land there's nothing to worry about because they won't last one winter in England'; Olusoga, David. 2018. 'The Windrush story was not a rosy one even before the ship arrived', *The Guardian,* April 22. https://amp.theguardian.com/commentisfree/2018/apr/22/windrush-story-not-a-rosy-one-even-before-ship-arrived.

4 'Last fling of the imperial dice' to 'rivers of blood': Tory politics from Anthony Eden to Enoch Powell (1955–1969)

Scientific racism: Gates never gives up

At the end of the Appendix to chapter 2, I wrote about Reginald Ruggles Gates who, even after the Holocaust would not let go of his attempts to prove that 'race' was a genetic reality. Gavin Schaffer, author of *Racial Science and British Society 1930–1962*,[1] points out that Gates sincerely believed that his own research was objective and that those challenging him were the ones driven by ideology, seeing himself as the bearer of truth, held back by an anti-science political agenda mistakenly trying to impose racial equality on the world.[2] According to Schaffer, Gates continued to believe this even while receiving funding from segregationists in the United States.[3]

In the final years before his death in 1962, he and a handful of others, including former Nazi scientist Otmar von Verschuer, founded the journal *Mankind Quarterly*, in the words of William Tucker, author of the 2002 book, *The Funding of Scientific Racism*, 'a publication frankly written *by* racists *for* racists'.[4]

SECTION 1: THE PREMIERSHIPS OF EDEN AND MACMILLAN (1955–1963)

Robert Anthony Eden (1955–1957)

The Suez crisis

The Suez crisis that confronted Eden the year after he took office in 1956 has often been described as Britain's 'last fling of the imperial dice'.[5] Derek Brown describes the background. At the time of crisis, the globe was still circled with British possessions and dependencies, from the Caribbean in the west to Singapore, Malaya and Hong Kong in the east. Much of the African map was still imperial pink.[6] The reality, however, was that the sun had long since begun to sink over the British Empire. As we have seen, the 'greatest possession of them all, the Indian subcontinent, had taken its freedom'.[7] If Churchill had become totally unfit for premiership, Eden was, in

DOI: 10.4324/9781003198673-7

Brown's words, 'a curiously inadequate man', who, after a lifetime at the cutting edge of British statesmanship, had never absorbed the simple post-war truth, 'that the world had changed forever'.[8]

In 1953, a group of army officers, members of the left nationalist 'Free Officers Movement', formally took over the Egyptian Government (King Farouk had been forced into exile in mid-1952).[9] The power behind the 1952 coup was Gamal Abdel Nasser, 'an ambitious and visionary young colonel who dreamed of reasserting the dignity and freedom of the Arab nation, with Egypt at the heart of the renaissance.[10] Nasser wanted the British out of the canal zone, where the military presence, a symbol of the British Empire since the 1880s, was a source of bitter resentment in Egypt. In July 1956, the last British soldiers left the canal zone, and Nasser announced the nationalization of the Suez Canal Company that operated the canal. Eden was scandalized and, riding a wave of popular indignation, prepared for full scale invasion,[11] along with France and Israel.

The British invasion began in November of the same year. From a military perspective, the invasion was successful with considerable advances for relatively little loss of British lives. The same could not be said of Egyptian casualties.[12] At home, huge opposition to the invasion was growing, with the opposition Labour Party leadership was coming under huge pressure to break with Eden, and this they reluctantly did, having originally supported the Tory Government. Apparently, a House of Commons debate nearly erupted into fistfights.[13] Opinion polls were showing growing opposition to the invasion and a massive anti-war protest was held in London on November 4, the day before British troops landed in Egypt. Eden even wanted to take direct control of the BBC to direct propaganda in support of the invasion but was resisted.[14]

The Americans were worried because the Soviet Union was starting to use the imperialist adventure to curry support in the Arab world, at America's expense. Something had to be done, and quickly. The United Nations had met on November 2, passing a US motion calling for peace. Britain, France, Israel and some other countries allied to them either voted against or abstained. The US continued pressure on France and Britain to call off the invasion and withdraw, noting that Russia had made threats to use nuclear bombs to back Nasser. At the same time, Israel was now looking to build on this at the Arab world's expense, and was considering a complete redrawing of the political map.[15] The US could no longer wait, and an oil embargo was started by Saudi Arabia, under its direction. Neither Britain nor France had the financial resources, still depleted from World War II, to withstand this.

Though Eden scarcely seemed to appreciate it, Britain was simply no longer capable of mounting a solo imperial adventure. The whole episode was, in fact, viewed with distaste as a nakedly imperial exercise in a post-imperial age. An expert in self-delusion, Eden thought he had received a nod and wink of approval for the invasion from the US. The last straw for

Eden came when the Treasury told the government that sterling, under sustained attack over the crisis, needed urgent US support to the tune of a billion dollars. President Eisenhower told him: no ceasefire, no loan. The invaders were ordered to halt and await the arrival of a UN intervention force. Brown concludes:

> The years immediately following Suez saw a slew of new countries on the world stage which had formerly been colonies and dependencies. There is little doubt that the end of the imperial era was greatly accelerated by the squalid little war in Egypt.[16]

Non-colour-coded racism: racialization of Irish people continues under Eden's premiership

In the 1950s and 1960s, Irish women were subject to racialization, when women temporarily fled Ireland to give birth to 'illegitimate' children (this was disgracefully how children born out of wedlock were labelled in both Britain and Ireland at the time). This pre-natal emigration was prompted as much by social intolerance in Ireland as it was by a belief that the solution was to come to England. In contrast to Ireland where an unmarried mother might spend two years or more in a Mother and Baby Home, in England the stay was only four months.[17] Abortion was not made legal until 1967 (coming into effect in 1968) in the UK (but not Northern Ireland)[18] and until 2018 (coming into effect in 2019) in Ireland.[19] The women were given the initials PFI or 'pregnant from Ireland' as part of the everyday language of the social workers who dealt with them.[20] According to Paul Michael Garrett, in the mid-1950s, 'it appears that all recent arrivals from Ireland were looked on as *potentially* suitable for repatriation' and '61 per cent of the almost eight hundred expectant mothers referred to the ... [English Catholic Rescue Society (ECRS)] originated in the Irish Republic'.[21] Minutes of the Liverpool Vigilance Association show that 'several letters had been received from probation officers in the London area asking for ... assistance with deporting Irish girls'.[22] In addition, fears were also expressed concerning the involvement of 'Irish girls' in prostitution with the BBC, for example, screening a documentary about 'good time girls', including Irish immigrants, who 'drifted' to London.[23]

In the last part of chapter 3, I referred to Carter et al.'s contention that the Churchill Government's racialization of Black immigrants meant deracializing Irish people. This was less to do with combatting anti-Irish racism and more because, to avoid political criticism, it had to exclude Irish people from the draft 1955 Bill (this also entailed 'playing down the significance of Irish neutrality during World War II and erasing the Black contribution to the Allied war effort').[24] As Carter et al. put it, this meant 'nothing less than a political project in which notions of "belonging" and "community" were reconstructed in terms of "racial" attachments and national identity organised around skin colour'.[25] Accordingly, the 'Report of the Committee on the Social and Economic Problems Arising from the Growing Influx into the United Kingdom of Coloured Workers from Other Commonwealth countries' on August 3, 1955, stated that the Irish 'are not – whether they like it or not – a different race from the ordinary inhabitants of Great Britain'.[26]

Anti-Black racism

The purpose the Committee of Enquiry proposed in November 1954 concerning the threat to the perceived 'racial' character of the English referred to in the second part of chapter 3, as explained to Anthony Eden by Cabinet Secretary, Norman Brook in a briefing note in June 1955 was to find a sufficient body of public support for legislation.[27] In the event due to a number of complex inter-related factors, it was not until the beginning of the next Parliamentary Session in October 1955 that this draft was presented to the Cabinet. A statement prepared by the Cabinet for publication in 1955 asserted that:

> The most serious problem arising at present from coloured immigration is undoubtedly in the field of housing. The bulk of the coloured immigrants have congregated in relatively few areas, mainly in London and the Midlands, where there is already an acute housing shortage.[28]

The document then expanded on the 'grave problem' this constituency posed for local authorities:

> Their resources are quite insufficient to enable them to undertake rehousing on the scale required and they would in any case be seriously embarrassed by having to give priority on the basis of need to these newcomers over long term residents who have had their names on the housing list for many years.[29]

It noted that the 'problem of colonial immigration has not yet aroused public anxiety, although there was some concern, mainly due to the housing difficulties in a few localities where most of the immigrants were concentrated'. 'On the other hand', it went on, 'if immigration from the colonies, and, for that matter, from India and Pakistan, were allowed to continue unchecked, there was a real danger that over the years there would be a significant change in the racial character of the English people'.[30]

On the other hand, for the first time in Cabinet discussions according to Carter et al., arguments were made about the economic benefits of Colonial immigration: 'On economic grounds immigration, including Colonial immigration, was a welcome means of augmenting our labour resources'.[31] As Carter et al. put it, 'this seems to sit uneasily with the conviction that

Britain faced a general labour shortage in the post war period'. 'However', they explain, 'although it was recognized by the Cabinet that full employment generated demands for labour in specific branches of production, including those run by the state, it was also felt that Black labour, by its "racial" nature, would be unsuitable to meet these demands'.[32] Some Ministers too were of the opinion that full employment would not last and grave problems would be created by the presence of an 'unassimilable' Black unemployed and unemployable population. This provided a sharp contrast with the efforts that were in the late 1940s to demonstrate the invaluable contribution that European Volunteer Workers could make to the British economy.

Also in 1955, Cyril Osborne attempted to limit immigration with a Ten Minute Rule Bill, but opposition from the party committee helped to ensure the measure got no Government support.[33] Moreover, many MPs of both parties, as well as the TUC, believed that immigration to the UK would end only if jobs were created in the colonies. Such a solution also had the advantage of not jeopardizing the interests of the British business community in Commonwealth and Colonial territories.[34] Nor would it undermine the post-war reconstruction of the Empire as a trading bloc, which was the basis of Britain's claim to superpower status.[35] 'Unsurprisingly, Carter et al. conclude their discussion of the proposed legislation, 'the Cabinet decided to "reserve judgment" on the Bill.'[36]

With the passing of the 1948 Nationality Act, they conclude the paper, and it merits quoting at length:

> a contradictory process was set in motion. The Act had proposed a formal definition of 'Britishness' which embraced Black British subjects abroad, granting them full rights of citizenship. Yet, even as it entered the statute books, the Act had been qualified by a series of 'devious little devices', designed to 'hold the tide' of Black immigration. When these proved insufficient, legislative control increasingly became a favoured option amongst Ministers and senior Civil Servants. For public consent to be won for legislation, however, a 'strong case' had to be built. A consequence of this was an extension of the control and surveillance of the Black population in the UK. Integral to the policy and these measures was the development of a racialised construction of 'Britishness' which excluded and included people on the grounds of 'race' defined by colour. Black immigration, it was alleged, would create problems which were insoluble precisely because their provenance was 'racial' and not social. Black people were unemployed not because of discrimination, but because of their 'irresponsibility, quarrelsomeness and lack of discipline'. Black people lived in slums not because of discrimination, but because they knew no better. Indeed, their very nature was held to predispose them towards criminality. All of these stereotypes were evoked vividly in the concept of 'new

Harlem', an alien wedge posing an unprecedented threat to the 'British way of life'. So powerful was this racialised construction that anti-discrimination legislation was seen as irrelevant to the 'social problems' of housing and employment. This was evident from the consistent opposition to Fenner Brockway's Bill seeking to proscribe racial discrimination and from the rejection of appeals for assistance from local authorities such as Birmingham and Lambeth. In building its strong case, the state undertook nothing less than a political project in which notions of 'belonging' and 'community' were reconstructed in terms of 'racial' attachments and national identity organised around skin colour.[37]

As the Commonwealth Office had put it in August 1953 in the middle of Churchill's second premiership, 'a large coloured community as a noticeable feature of our social life … is certainly no part of the concept of England or Britain to which people of British stock throughout the Commonwealth are attached'.[38] In Carter et al.'s views, while 'wishing to prevent Black British subjects from entering the UK, the Cabinet was concerned to preserve the right of white "kith and kin" in the Dominions and to free entry [to the UK]'.[39]

Eden had become shattered by Suez, politically, physically and emotionally. On November 19, 1956, just three days before the last of the British invaders finally left the canal zone, he abruptly took himself off to Jamaica to recover. Just under two months later, on January 9, 1957, Eden resigned, and Harold Macmillan moved in to Downing Street.[40]

Harold Macmillan – loss of Empire and the racialization of migrant workers (1957–1963)

Independence of Ghana

The British Empire that had spanned a quarter of the world in 1921, was becoming financially unsustainable. Macmillan also differed from his two immediate predecessors with respect to his attitude to the maintenance of the British Empire. Spurred by increasing nationalism in both Africa and Asia, his government realized the Empire's various colonies were moving towards independence.[41]

In his first premiership (1957–1959) Macmillan oversaw the independence of the Gold Coast. It had been a British colony since 1821 and became Ghana in 1957. Decolonization was far from a benign gesture on the part of Britain, however, and had more to do with the efforts of Marxist revolutionary and advocate of Pan-Africanism (the political union of all the indigenous peoples of Africa), Kwame Nkrumah.

Nkrumah was a founding member of the Organisation of African Unity, some of whose key aims were to encourage political and economic integration among member states, and to eradicate colonialism and neo-colonialism from the African continent. In May 1956, Nkrumah's Gold Coast Government issued a White Paper with proposals for the colony's freedom from colonial rule, subsequently adopted by the Gold Coast Assembly who demanded independence from Britain. Macmillan's Government stated it would agree to a firm date for independence if a reasonable majority in favour were obtained in the Gold Coast Legislative Assembly after a General Election.[42] The 1956 election returned the Convention People's Party to power with such a majority, Britain ceded its control, and Ghana became the first African country to gain independence,[43] with Nkrumah as its first Prime Minister and President. Nkrumah was the author in 1965 of *Neo-Colonialism, the last stage of imperialism*,[44] the title obviously inspired by Lenin's *Imperialism, the highest stage of capitalism*.[45] In it, he defined the essence of neo-colonialism for the State that is subject to it, as 'in theory, independent' with 'all the outward trappings of international sovereignty', but in reality 'its economic system and thus its political policy ... directed from outside'.[46]

Independence of the Federation of Malaya (now Malaysia)

The Federation of Malaya also became independent in 1957, but in very different circumstances. Malaya had been captured by Japan during World War II. Like Britain, Japan was a racist imperial power and regarded the Chinese population there as enemies (Chinese people had been in the region for centuries as traders).[47] The Malayan Communist Party (MCP), mainly Chinese in composition, organized the Malayan People's Anti-Japanese Army (MPAJA), which became the most effective resistance force in the occupied Asian countries. As Bruce Boon explains, 'With it began the real struggle for national liberation'.[48]

In 1951 and 1952, an Alliance of the right-wing nationalist United Malays National Organisation (UMNO) and the Malayan Chinese Association (MCA) (a body with wealth behind it, whose formation had been encouraged by the British as an alternative to the MCP), won several local elections.[49] With the support of Chinese capital, and the MCP isolated in the jungle (after the British 'Malayan Emergency' gave police the power to imprison Communists without trial), the Alliance felt safe to ask for self-government, and Britain now felt safe to grant them independence.[50]

In 1955, the Alliance, joined by the Malayan Indian Congress (MIC) won the first Federal General Election with a massive majority of 51 out of 52 seats. UMNO president Tunku Abdul Rahman became Chief Minister, but ruled under the guidance of Britain. He therefore made a trip to London to negotiate Malayan independence, and August 31, 1957 was decided as the date. Like in other colonies though, while formal independence had been achieved, imperialism continued to exploit Malaya through the world market.[51] This was achieved via a compromise between Britain and the Alliance that preserved the position of domiciled Chinese capital and control of the state apparatus by the Malay aristocrats that led

UMNO.[52] Malaysia was established in 1963, comprising Malaya, but also Singapore, Sarawak and Sabah (formerly under British rule as well). Singapore seceded in 1965 to become an independent republic.[53]

'Wind of change' tour and speech 1960

Macmillan was returned to power in the General Election in October 1959, marking the third consecutive win for the Tories.[54] The following year during the months of January and February, he made a tour of Africa. In the previous year, in Nyasaland (now Malawi), a state of emergency had been declared, under which over 1,300 members or supporters of the Nyasaland African Congress were detained without trial, and most of the party's leaders including its president, Hastings Banda, were imprisoned in Southern Rhodesia (now Zimbabwe). In the week before the Emergency and during its first month, over 50 Africans were killed and many more wounded by the colonial security forces.[55] In Kenya, 11 prisoners had been killed. The end of the states of emergency were not in sight in either country, something that concerned not only the Opposition Labour Party, under Hugh Gaitskell, but also many members of the Tory Party itself.[56] Macmillan was very worried about the future of Africa and its potential alignment with 'the Communist bloc', and with the way African states would interact with White supremacist apartheid South Africa, and more generally about his Party's policy towards the continent.[57]

In January he made his famous 'Wind of Change' speech, so named from a quotation embedded in it, 'The wind of change is blowing through this continent. Whether we like it or not, this growth of national consciousness is a political fact',[58] in Ghana, but with little reaction. In Cape Town in February, however, he got a strong reaction from Prime Minister Hendrik Verwoerd, architect of apartheid and member of the fascist Afrikaner Broederbond (Brotherhood). After referring to 'our earnest desire to give South Africa our support and encouragement', Macmillan stated, 'I hope you won't mind my saying frankly that there are some aspects of your policies which make it impossible for us to do this without being false to our own deep convictions'.[59] Verwoerd responded that the 'tendency in Africa for nations to become independent, and at the same time to do justice to all, does not only mean being just to the black man of Africa, but also to be just to the white man of Africa'.[60] He went on, 'We call ourselves European, but actually we represent the white men of Africa', claiming that they 'are the people' who 'through major portions of Africa ... brought civilisation here'.[61] He continued, 'we believe in balance, we believe in allowing exactly those same full opportunities to remain within the grasp of the white man who has made all this possible'.[62]

While apartheid remained intact until Nelson Mandela became its first President in 1994, soon after MacMillan's speech, British Colonial Secretary Iain Macleod decreased the original timetable for independence in East Africa by a decade. It was granted to Somaliland in 1960, Tanganyika in 1961,

Uganda in 1962 and Kenya in 1963.[63] This started a decade in which the dismantling of the British Empire reached its climax, with at least 27 former colonies in Asia, Africa and the Caribbean became independent nations.[64]

Colour-coded racism at home

Racist reaction to the 'Wind of Change' speech: the formation of the Monday Club

As a direct result of Macmillan's 'Wind of Change' intervention, some Tory MPs formed the Conservative Monday Club on January 1, 1961, to debate party policy change and prevent decolonization. The afore-mentioned Cyril Osborne and Harold Gurden were early members, as was Jonathan Guinness. Director of Guinness plc., Jonathan is the son of Diana Mitford, who married Oswald Mosley in 1936, when Guinness was six years old, at the home of Nazi propaganda minister, Joseph Goebbels, with Hitler as guest of honour.[65] Guinness twice failed to obtain a parliamentary seat for the Tories.

The Club was concerned that during Macmillan's premierships 'the left wing of the Party [had] gained a predominant influence over policy', the result of which was a leftward shift in the Conservative Party to such an extent that 'the floating voter could not detect, as he should, major differences between it and the Socialists' and, moreover, 'loyal Conservatives had become disillusioned and dispirited'.[66]

The Monday Club, that brought together supporters of White supremacist Rhodesia and South Africa, is infamous for its policy of voluntary or assisted repatriation for 'non-White immigrants'. The 5th Marquess of Salisbury was its first president. A hard-line imperialist, he resigned from Macmillan's Cabinet in opposition to the Government's release of Archbishop Makarios of Cyprus from detention (Cyprus became independent in August 1960, with Makarios its first president), stating, 'there was never a greater need for true conservatism than there is today'.[67] Robert Copping notes that the Club was courted by many Conservative politicians, including Alec Douglas-Home (see the next section of this chapter) who was guest-of-honour at the Club's annual dinners in 1964 and 1969, and Enoch Powell (see chapter 3) who, in a speech in 1968, said that 'it was due to the Monday Club that many are brought within the Conservative Party who might otherwise be estranged from it'.[68]

Anti-Black riots in Nottingham and Notting Hill (1958)

Harold Macmillan presided over a time of national prosperity for some. At a Tory rally in 1957, he famously remarked, 'most of our people have never had it so good'.[69] It is interesting that he said 'most of our people', since, although there was at the time a trend towards some post-war recovery and levelling up of income,[70] as we shall shortly see, there was hardship in the industrial cities, and this could hardly be said of the racialized workers from the colonies.

We saw in chapter 2, in particular drawing on the work of Carter et al., how the common interpretation of the 'absent state' in the 1950s does not align with the facts and how at the Cabinet, parliamentary and Civil Service level the issues raised by a Black presence were extensively discussed. We have further seen how a policy of preserving the homogeneous 'racial character' of British society led to specific measures to discourage and restrict Black immigration. This included miscegenation, which along with other issues such as 'housing, health and criminality', from the state's ideological stance posed 'insoluble problems of social, economic and political assimilation'.[71]

The issue of immigration was raised by Norman Pannell in 1958, in a couple of his habitual racist interventions. In April, coinciding with the rise in Indian and Pakistani entrants, in an EDM (Early Day Motion),[72] he complained of impoverished immigrants who 'immediately sought national assistance', and urged reciprocity and deportation powers.[73] In July at the Commonwealth Affairs committee, Pannell argued for reciprocal legislation with the Commonwealth, which had seen other member states take unilateral steps to restrict immigration. In support of this, he gave figures for immoral earning convictions in London.[74]

In August 1958, there were anti-Black riots in Nottingham, where 2,500 Caribbean and 600 Asians had moved. Like many contemporary industrial cities, the post-war economic boom there was coming to an end, and some migrant workers were denied work in Nottingham's factories.[75] An incident in a pub 'acted as the catalyst to previously suppressed brutality'.[76] As Emily Cousins explains:

> A West Indian man, boyfriend, suitor, or potential partner, was seen enjoying a drink with a blonde British woman. This symbolized the belief many held that the immigrant community was seizing the opportunities that should be reserved only for the country's domestic citizens. The young man was assaulted and soon a crowd of over 1,000 had gathered in the area.[77]

Violence between White and Black male communities lasted for many hours, with the *Nottingham Evening Post* describing the scene as 'like a slaughterhouse'.[78] A week later crowds gathered again, but with very few Black people present and the predominantly White mob turned on itself.[79]

Sociologist, Lisa McKenzie who moved to St Ann's, aged 18 and lived in the area for 25 years, told the BBC in 2018 about the explosive mixture of generalized poverty, racism and male rivalry: 'the economic hardships harboured suspicion and hardened attitudes towards the Windrush arrivals, which, mixed with the "overt racism" of the times and "male competition" for female affection, fed resentments that eventually exploded into violence'. She added that there 'were thousands of people living cheek by jowl, very close to each other, often in very unsanitary conditions', and that everyone 'was struggling, whether they had just come from the West Indies or had been there for generations'.[80]

A week later, riots broke out in Notting Hill, London, lasting for five nights. 'Hundreds of young [White] men rampaged around the area at the end of August, smashing the windows of houses West Indians lived in and anything owned by them, and attacking many on the streets'.[81]

Senior Metropolitan police officers tried to dismiss events as the work of 'ruffians, both coloured and white'. However, files released in 2002 from police eyewitness reports confirm that they were 'overwhelmingly the work of a white working class mob out to get the "ni★★ers,"'[82] that the disturbances were overwhelmingly triggered by 300- to 400-strong 'Keep Britain White' mobs, armed with iron bars, butcher's knives and weighted leather belts, who went 'ni★★er-hunting' among residents of Notting Hill and Notting Dale. Mosley infamously distributed a pamphlet there saying 'Take action now. Protect your jobs. Stop coloured immigration. Houses for white people – not coloured immigrants'.[83] The first night left five Black men lying unconscious on the pavements of Notting Hill.[84] Recalling the earlier riots in Nottingham, Majbritt Morrison, a young White Swedish bride of a Jamaican was pelted with stones, glass and wood, and struck in the back with an iron bar as she tried to get home.[85] In October 1958, Osborne claimed there would be six million 'coloured people' in Britain by 1974.[86] As Fred Van Hartesveldt puts it, even though no systematic statistics were kept until after July 1, 1962, with Osborne and his supporters kept citing figures about supposedly massive immigration, terrible increases in serious diseases and hospital waiting lists and criminal activity disproportionate to numbers.[87]

Death in Notting Hill: the murder of Kelso Cochrane

On May 17, 1959, just after midnight, less than a year after the riots, Kelso Cochrane, from the British colony Antigua in the Caribbean, was walking home, having been to the local hospital. Cochrane had been in the UK for five years. Like almost everywhere else in the Caribbean, Antigua had a plantation economy that relied on the labour of enslaved Africans (see the Introduction to this book). Conditions had deteriorated after World War II, and he had come to Britain for work.[88]

A gang of White youths surrounded him: they 'called him many insulting names, punched, pushed, thumped and then stabbed him. When he collapsed they ran away'.[89] Two Black men walking nearby rushed over. A taxi stopped and Cochrane was picked up and put in the cab. By the time they reached the hospital he had stopped breathing. Someone called a *Sunday Express* reporter and said 'three white youths have stabbed a darkie named Cochrane'.[90] Witnesses did give the names of the perpetrators to the police. Two men were arrested, held overnight and then released without any charges.[91] Despite evidence to the contrary, the police claimed it was an attempted robbery, not a 'racial murder'.[92]

The response of the Macmillan Government

Claudia Jones, the Trinidad-born editor of the *West Indian Gazette*, directed her attention to the need for a campaign against the treatment of all non-White people in Britain. With the Coloured People's Progressive Association (CPPA) and other groups she formed the Inter-Racial Friendship Co-ordinating Council, whose Central Executive Committee was all women. A letter was sent to Macmillan asking for a law to make incitement to racial violence illegal and emphasizing that Black citizens of the UK had lost confidence in the ability of the law enforcing agencies to protect them.[93] According to Sherwood, instead of agreeing to this, 'the government gave permission for the White Defence League to hold a meeting in Trafalgar Square'.[94] After the rally on May 24, a letter from the League and the National Labour Party (a neo-Nazi party founded in 1957 by John Bean, who had formerly been briefly associated with the Barnes Tory Party)[95] was handed in to 10 Downing Street, urging the Tory Government to stop further Black immigration, stating that 'it would aggravate the housing shortage and put British-born workers in unjust competition with newly arrived immigrants'.[96]

There were a number of responses to this escalation of racism in Britain, including the Council who met with the Home Office and held a vigil outside 10 Downing Street, to 'express a lack of confidence in arrangements for the security of coloured people'.[97] In the House of Commons on June 4, 1959, Macmillan was non-committal when asked about a letter from the Committee for African Organisations 'concerning the colour question' stating that he had received such a letter about the murder of Cochrane and 'racial discrimination' in general, and that 'the police are prosecuting their inquiries into the murder with all possible vigour and that the maintenance of public order in London is the responsibility of the Metropolitan Police, which they will discharge without fear or favour'.[98]

When asked about the need to make 'racial discrimination' illegal, Home Secretary Rab Butler rejected it, replying:

> that it was not known in our law, and perhaps deliberately to take action against it might not be so effective as the hon. Member might think. That is why I do not want to step into that part without a great deal more consideration.[99]

Questioned about the role of the Press in fostering racism, he stalled:

> It is, naturally, possible to fan a particular incident, or to treat the matter wrongly. My contacts with the Press indicate that it is willing to take a responsible view of this matter. I have studied the position in Liverpool as well as that in other large cities where there is a colour problem and I shall study all the evidence that can be brought to me and maintain my contact with the Press.[100]

In the General Election in October 1959, Macmillan was returned to power with an overall increased majority. Among the new Tories in the House of Commons were Leslie Seymour, Leonard Cleaver and John Hollingworth, all representing Birmingham constituencies. All were keen to get involved in the campaign to control immigration that rapidly gained momentum,[101] with Tory back-benchers piling on the pressure.[102] Van Hartesveldt refers to 'the use of vans with loudspeakers blaring racist slogans'.[103] In January 1961, Gurden organized a private meeting of these back-benchers from London, Birmingham, Liverpool and Manchester to co-ordinate efforts to increase control.

Non-colour-coded racism at home

As discussed earlier, in the 1950s and 1960s, women running away from Ireland to give birth in England were labelled in the UK, PFI or 'pregnant from Ireland'. According to Garrett, the London County Council (LCC) was reported to be so concerned about the apparent 'influx' of pregnant Irish women that it sent children's officers to Ireland to try to find adoptive homes for Irish babies.[104] Thousands of Irish unmarried mothers were, however, also repatriated to Ireland – arrangements had been made between the voluntary and statutory services in Britain and 'rescue societies' in Ireland.[105] In some instances this occurred after the babies had been born, sometimes before. Importantly, the impetus for repatriation appears to have originated with English agencies, although the Dublin-based Child Protection and Rescue Society of Ireland (CPRSI) did co-operate in assisting in the return of many women, often with their new-born babies, being afraid that these women and their children may have been 'lost to the Faith' in England.[106] Although the repatriations were not underpinned by force of law, they can be seen as an exclusionary process bound up with a range of discourses and practices preoccupied with the 'otherness' of Irish women.[107]

To investigate the 'PFI' and repatriation in more detail, Garrett examined case records in a Roman Catholic 'rescue society' in England in 1958, which he suggests 'are perhaps revealing about more pervasive and embedded exclusionary processes historically directed at Irish people in Britain'.[108] Furthermore, he points out, the records of the CPRSI make it clear that a number of English agencies were involved in repatriation schemes.[109]

Case papers show that the possibility of returning to Ireland was addressed during a woman's initial interview with one of the case workers in the agency.[110] It was also revealed that some women felt pressurized when moves were made to have them repatriated.[111] This would be substantiated by a study conducted in Ireland in the late-1960s.[112] Creegan interviewed one hundred unmarried mothers in a large Mother and Baby Home in Ireland and found out that just over a quarter had been repatriated from England. Sixteen of the women reported that they had returned to Ireland because the English welfare agencies that they approached for help 'offered them no alternative' but repatriation.[113] Even more alarmingly, it was not only unmarried mothers who had migrated on a temporary basis who were repatriated. One woman had in fact left Ireland when she was eight years old and 'brought up' by her sister in Britain. She did not even know anyone in Ireland when she became pregnant and was repatriated years later.[114]

The 1958 case files suggest that once the agency had decided to repatriate, there was little the women could do, being in a foreign country, often alone and probably hiding a pregnancy from an employer and landlord in England and family in Ireland.[115] Three of the Mother and Baby Homes in the survey had blanket 'No RCs [Roman Catholics] policies', while the matron of another expressed a 'common attitude',[116] when she said: 'We find RCs a bit spiky because we can't help them very much, so we don't encourage them unless they're lapsed'.[117] One can only imagine how these women felt, as Garrett puts it, 'initially having planned to give birth and have the child adopted in England, but then compelled to travel, often with the new baby, back home to Ireland'.[118] While it is true that unmarried mothers *per se* did not at the time have the 'motherhood mandate' of more recent times,[119] given the anti-Irish racism discussed in this and other chapters of this book, it is clear that such racism was a key element in the treatment of unmarried pregnant Irish women, and that not only were these Irish people racialized, they were also gendered. Moreover, as Garrett points out, the criminalization of (young) Irish women in Britain is reflected in the proportion they comprised of the prison population.[120]

Finally, in the early 1960s, a member of the House of Lords set up a 'social offences group', with one of the group's concerns 'Irish girls' working as prostitutes.[121] As Garrett puts it, 'this inchoate moral panic about "Irish girls" who were, it was claimed, turning to prostitution, continued throughout the early 1960s and, on occasions, the issues of illegitimacy and prostitution were inter twined'.[122]

The 1962 Commonwealth Immigrants Act

As explained in the Appendix to chapter 3, under the 1948 Nationality Act, British citizens were designated 'Citizens of the UK & Colonies', and that this continued until 1983. However, as James McKay argues, by July 1961 Tory determination to restrict immigration had hardened, as Butler discovered when he addressed a joint meeting of the Home Office Affairs and Commonwealth Affairs committees.[123] The minutes of that meeting record that 'Mr Norman Pannell, Mr John Hall and the majority of members considered that action to control immigration should be taken urgently', and that immigrants should be 'easily assimilated',[124] presumably a code for 'not people of colour from the Commonwealth'. According to McKay, at the same time, concerns were also increasing over Irish immigration.[125]

In February 1961, Osborne put forward a motion requiring that anyone from the Commonwealth wishing to live in Britain should be required to have a guaranteed job and place to live, a certificate of good health, and no criminal record, on grounds of housing shortages, growth of slums, lack of employment, and costs to welfare services.[126] In response to a comment from the Liberal Jeremy Thorpe, Osborne said that 'coloured immigrants' were the major problem because 'they have altogether a different standard of civilization'.[127] According to Van Hartesveldt, Pannell's 'comments added to the open racism of the debates',[128] while David Renton, Joint Under-Secretary of State for the Home Office, denied or minimized every 'problem' mentioned, assuring the House that the Government held no brief for discrimination, and went on to assert that immigration would become a worse and worse problem if it continued (!), and that although the Government was not ready to act, it was seriously considering possible solutions.[129] Earlier in the month, Osborne had said: 'This is a white man's country and I want it to remain so'.[130] Six months later, he cited the conversion of a Smethwick church into a Sikh temple as evidence of the danger of Britain ceasing to be a Christian country, while Pannell drew on gonorrhoea infection figures to persuade members of the need to control UK borders.[131]

Public comment on immigration and 'race', Van Hartesveldt points out, continued to increase and the press, respectable and sensationalist. Within the foreseeable future, for example, it was suggested, 'Birmingham would have a population in which one person in ten was an immigrant or the child of an immigrant'.[132] A judicial comment deploring the tendency of 'blacks' to carry and use knives and razors was overplayed.[133]

It was Home Secretary Rab Butler who had in 1960 pressed for legislation. The Cabinet appointed a committee and Butler oversaw the production of the Bill.[134] Butler said the Irish would be included in the Government's Bill, but crucially the powers to restrict Irish people would not be used, provided that Ireland closed its doors to the Commonwealth as well.[135] There then followed a series of confusing, contradictory and convoluted attempts to avoid accusations of colour-coded racism (the 'colour bar' in the language of the time). Many MPs favoured a system similar to the Northern Ireland 'Safeguarding of Employment Act', which controlled immigration by restricting job opportunities for people from the Republic. When, at a meeting of the 1922 Committee,[136] attended by 110 members, Macleod doubted that such a method to keep people out could be adopted in the rest of the UK, cries of 'why not?' were hurled back at him.[137] By the time he left the meeting, Macleod was in no doubt that they wanted the Irish to be covered by controls, even if it was a case of making the best of a flawed system.[138]

There were thus two elements at play: a pro-Commonwealth and an anti-Irish stance. These streams of opinion had opposing views on the desirability of immigration into the UK, and therefore were incapable of making common cause.[139] As we have seen throughout this book, anti-Irish racism, along with colour-coded racism of course, was a key component of Tory thinking.

For example, at the 1922 committee meeting that took place during the debate on the second reading of the Bill, it was stressed that 'we must try and find a solution to the Irish problem', and that in Birmingham there were '40,000 coloured and 80,000 Irish'.[140] Interestingly, as McKay points out, of those within the party that held the hardest restrictionist beliefs, opinion was divided over what should be done. Thus, Osborne at this meeting was in favour of a system along the lines of the 'Safeguarding of Employment Act' so the Irish could be 'kept out'.[141] On the other hand, Pannell saw a danger that arguments over the White Irish might derail the legislative action to keep out Blacks and Asians that he and Osborne had long sought.[142] On December 4, Pannell said that 'the Irish were not the real problem and begged members not to lose sight of the main issue'.[143]

McKay sums up the tensions among the Tory racists (although he does not describe them as such) as follows:

> the restrictionists were generally against any immigration, but valued the 'prize' of restricting black and Asian inflow at the cost of a continuing Irish stream. Part of the pro-Commonwealth lobby felt a snub to the Old Dominions that Republicans were being given preferential treatment, but they too were unsure of the levels of non-white immigration and the problems of integration and race relations. Those with an anti-Irish bias may not have been keen to press this publicly, given the large Irish presence in the electorate, whilst those who felt that the situation amounted to a colour bar did not have the party as a whole on their side. The Conservatives had already decided that non-white immigration had to be controlled at the very least, and would therefore not be open to the proposition that the legislation was operating on colour lines. They knew that it would, as that had been the unspoken aim all along. This had been recognised by Butler when he made his 'gaffe' that June, saying that legislation would not be based on colour prejudice *alone*.[144] All that united these disparate groups was an anger felt towards the Irish exclusion, but this was not anger that was capable of being effectively channelled.

Butler did not want to restrict the Irish, reasoning that they were 'seasonal' rather than 'permanent' migrants, who tended to work in the building trade.[145] (As McKay remarks astutely, following Spencer,[146] this analysis is rather ironic since one of the effects of the 1962 Act was to change the nature of Black and Asian immigration from temporary migration into permanent settlement.) With this in mind, Butler developed a system of merely monitoring immigration, and making the Act subject to annual renewal.[147] As McKay explains, at the price of collecting some statistics, the Government managed to defer a decision on the question of Irish immigration.[148]

The 1962 Commonwealth Immigrants Act, passed on July 1, ended the automatic *legal* right of people of the British Commonwealth and Colonies to settle in the UK (as we have seen numerous covert, and sometimes illegal, administrative measures had been designed to discourage immigration from the colonies). The Act entailed stringent restrictions on the entry of Commonwealth citizens into Britain.[149] Only those with work permits (which were typically only for high-skilled workers, such as doctors) were permitted entry. However, many Commonwealth nurses and doctors could not work as such, because their qualifications were deemed invalid in England.[150]

For the first time, free movement was curtailed for citizens of the United Kingdom and Colonies (CUKCs). As Ros Taylor explains, 'CUKCs all had the same title, whether born in Swindon or Swahililand, but some had more rights than others'.[151] Those who retained the right to live and work in the UK were:

1   CUKCs born in the UK.
2   CUKCs with a CUKC passport issued by the UK.

Those who were subject to control were everyone else:

1   CUKCs born in the colonies or independent Commonwealth countries or with CUKC passports issued by the colonial governments.
2   Commonwealth citizens.[152]

Exemptions also applied to Commonwealth citizens who were ordinarily resident in the UK at any point from 1960 to 1962, as well as wives and children under 16 accompanying a family member resident in the UK.[153]

A significant group exempted under 'CUKCs with a CUKC passport issued by the UK' were 'East African Asians', as they became known.[154] They were residents of Kenya, Uganda and Tanzania whose families were originally of Indian origin and who had used their rights of free movement as British subjects within the Empire to relocate, encouraged by the British and colonial governments[155] (see chapter 5).

Whenever a country became independent, its citizens would lose the citizenship of the old country and gain citizenship of the new, losing CUKC status in the process and being subject to controls under the 1962 Act.[156]

However, some new countries excluded a whole swathe of East African Asian residents from their new citizenships. If CUKC status was removed from them, they would literally be stateless. If they were allowed to retain it, they might well move to the UK, as was their right, particularly given that the fact they were being excluded from citizenship in the new countries was a sign of worse to come (see chapter 5).[157]

McKay[158] cites Stephen Brooke who said of the 1962 Act, it marked and symbolized the 'unbridgeable dichotomy' that had emerged between the defence of Empire and the defence of Nation, and the final opting for the latter over the former.[159] The leader of the Labour opposition, Hugh Gaitskell, had called the draft 'cruel and brutal anti-colour legislation'.[160]

Twelve days after the Act was passed, Macmillan reshuffled his Cabinet, dismissing seven members, one-third of the total. The reshuffle took place against a backdrop of declining Conservative popularity in Britain. Tax cuts he had introduced in 1959 had been reversed in the 1960 budget,[161] pay had been frozen and Tories were losing by-elections. A pay-pause and rising prices, together with discontent at high taxation that was demonstrably inequitable, drove voters to protest against government policies by switching their votes to the Liberals, or by abstaining from voting Conservative.[162] While the damage was short-lived and Macmillan's position improved,[163] the Tories were rocked by further problems, not least the 'Profumo affair'.[164] By the summer of 1963, 84% of the population felt that too many immigrants had been admitted to their country.[165]

In October 1963, Macmillan developed a prostate problem and resigned soon after. According to Alistair Cooke, official historian to the Conservative Party, replying in a letter to the *Daily Telegraph's* medical correspondent, this benign condition was not the result of his resignation. Rather, he used his illness, as recorded by his surgeon, 'as a vehicle for resignation to extricate himself from an increasingly difficult political position'.[166]

SECTION 2: THE PREMIERSHIP OF DOUGLAS-HOME AND THE RISE OF POWELLISM (1963–1969)

Alexander (Alec) Frederick Douglas-Home (1963–1964): a brief 'elegant anachronism'

Following Macmillan's resignation, Alec Douglas-Home became Prime Minister on October 19, 1963, his only premiership and lasting just short of a year. Douglas-Home was described by the then leader of the Opposition Labour Party Harold Wilson as 'an elegant anachronism'. Wilson wondered how 'a scion of an effete establishment' could lead a 'new Britain' that would need to be forged in what he described as the 'white heat' of a 'scientific revolution'.[167] Wilson also referred to the ascendancy of Douglas-Home as a 'counter-revolution', adding that after 'half a century of democratic advance, of social revolution, the whole process has ground to a halt with a fourteenth earl!'[168] In a typical aristocratic retort, Douglas-Home called Wilson 'this slick salesman of synthetic science' and from the stance of a pre-eminently privileged upper class male, the Labour party 'the only relic of class consciousness in the country'.[169]

The Cold War

The world was approaching the mid-point of the Cold War and Anglo-American relations appeared increasingly one-sided, and worse was to come when President John F. Kennedy was assassinated in November 1963 by Lee Harvey Oswald. According to Andrew Holt, the new president Lyndon B. Johnson, 'was temperamentally and politically far-removed from Douglas-Home, and would prove less predisposed towards Britain than his Anglophile predecessor'.[170] There was particular antagonism over continued British trade with Fidel Castro's Cuba, with a deal to supply Leyland buses, the cause of much anger in the White House that dominated the February 1964 Anglo-American summit.[171]

The Commonwealth

Douglas-Home's premiership began just two months before there were violent events in Nicosia, Cyprus, in December 1963 between Greek and Turkish speakers. His response was the creation of the United Nations Peacekeeping Force in Cyprus (UNFICYP) in March 1964.[172] At the time the Tories faced international criticism for its relationship with apartheid South Africa and there was also overt dominative racism in Southern Rhodesia (now Zimbabwe). In Aden, Britain's only Crown Colony in the Middle East, there was an assassination attempt against the British high commissioner, Kennedy Trevaskis, in December 1963.[173] In South-East Asia, Britain looked to defend the newly created federation of Malaysia against incursions sponsored by Sukarno's Indonesia,[174] a former Dutch colony. Finally, under Home's spell as Prime Minister, the colonies of Northern Rhodesia (now Zambia) and Nyasaland (now Malawi) gained independence, though this had been negotiated under the previous Macmillan Government.[175]

Smethwick and the General Election of 1964

In the 1964 General Election, Douglas-Home faced Labour leader Harold Wilson. During the election campaign, the politicization of Black immigration intensified.[176] In election speeches in Bradford and Birmingham, Douglas-Home claimed credit for the Tory Government for excluding nearly a million people as a result of the 1962 Commonwealth Immigrants Act and promised rigorous reassessment, while Wilson accused the Tories of using immigration as an excuse for their neglect of slums and inadequate schools and poor education.[177] Thus in Bradford, one of Britain's main immigration centres, on October 6, 1964, Douglas-Home, who in 1958 as Minister for Commonwealth Relations had said in a speech in Vancouver that some restriction on West Indian immigration into Britain was needed',[178] stated:

> What had been a trickle of immigrants from the Commonwealth was developing into a flood. We saw that if it was not brought under control it would create very serious social and economic problems – problems of employment, housing and education, for instance. So we

brought in legislation. The Socialists – aided by the Liberals – opposed it all along the line ... Most people will agree that it is necessary to keep the conditions and the number of permits under the strictest review, and to strengthen the safeguards against evasion.[179]

On the same day in Birmingham, Wilson retorted:

There is a very real problem of overcrowding which the Government has neglected ... We're not having the immigration question used as an alibi for the total Tory failure to handle the problems of housing, slums, schools and education in this country.[180]

Meanwhile, in nearby Smethwick, less than four miles from Birmingham, an overtly racist storm had been brewing. At the time, Smethwick Tory Party members had been accused of using the slogan, 'If you want a ni**er for a neighbour, vote Liberal or Labour'.[181] While Colin Jordan claimed that fellow neo-Nazis had produced the initial slogan as well as spread the poster and sticker campaign, Tory candidate Peter Griffiths refused to disown it. Although he himself did not approve its use,[182] when asked to disown it, he replied, 'I would not condemn any man who said that. I regard it as a manifestation of popular feeling', adding that the quote represented 'exasperation, not fascism'.[183]

In an article in *The People,* a Sunday national newspaper in 1962, Griffiths had written:

I feel that we should keep the white/coloured ratio in true proportion. We must avoid setting up a coloured quarter. We want to see the whites in these roads where coloured people are living so that they can set an example to the coloureds, and live free from racial troubles.[184]

The following year in the local newspaper *Smethwick Telephone,* he wrote that 'Neither the immigrants nor the white people want integration. I would have thought the word is meaningless'.[185] In the run-up to the General Election, in June 1964, Griffiths gave his complete support to a Bradford petition calling for a complete ban on immigration for at least five years, and commented on the 6,000 signatures from Smethwick, 'This is stronger action than the Parliamentary Party has taken, but it is what Smethwick Tories want'.[186] The following month, confident of an a Tory victory in Smethwick, he declared ominously, 'There will be much to do in the years ahead. Smethwick rejects the idea of being a multi-racial society. The Government must be told this'.[187] The same month, following months of arguments by the Labour candidate Shadow Foreign Secretary Patrick Gordon Walker that the real immigration problem was lack of accommodation,[188] Griffiths delivered what socialist Paul Foot describes as 'perhaps the most nauseating of all his utterances on this subject' a response to his opponent:

> Will more houses end the nuisance and the filth ... Would more houses end the knife fights? Would more houses make the streets safe for women and girls? There are 300,000 immigrants in India and Pakistan waiting to come here if restrictions are lifted. Would Labour house all these too?[189]

According to Foot, Griffiths only held three meetings during the campaign. At one, on October 2, following a half-hour speech on conventional Tory policy, Dorrie Crow, a member of the fascist British National Party (BNP) with violent views on immigrants, interrupted half-way through, 'What about immigration? That's what we've come to hear about'.[190] At question time, she insisted, 'To bring in a lot of people when there is not enough room is wicked and breeds hatred. I want immigration stopped at once, otherwise in twenty years' time we shall be ruled by them'. According to Foot, 'Griffiths leapt to his feet' and shouted back: 'This lady has put over the kind of thing that for years I have heard on hundreds of thousands of doorsteps. Without fear of favour, I will forward what I hear because I believe it is the duty of an M.P.'[191] When asked, 'Do you personally accept the idea of a multi-racial society?', he replied that if he were to be elected on October 15, 'what more do you want that I should go supporting [a complete ban on immigration]?'[192]

Foot concludes, 'It was the final seal ... Griffiths had pledged himself to fight in Parliament on *the* issue ... to speak out against a multi-racial society, and for a complete and immediate ban on immigration'.[193] Foot goes on to recall the many lies that were circulating in Smethwick: 'Gordon Walker had sold his house in Smethwick to the blacks'; 'Gordon Walker's wife was a black. So was Gordon Walker'; 'many immigrants were lepers ... and ... two leper hospitals were being built, secretly in the town' and so on.[194] Foot writes:

> That such slander gained wide credence is hardly surprising in view of the invasion of Smethwick during the final campaign by every known extremist right-wing organization. The British National Party threw its meagre resources into the campaign. Even Colin Jordan sent as many of his storm-troopers as he could muster ... to work ... on the doorsteps and in the streets ... Tom Jones, a well-known Birmingham admirer of ... Oswald Mosley who [believed] ... Jews [were] ... responsible for coloured immigration, rang Griffiths personally and asked if he could come and help ... Griffiths assented willingly.[195]

Bucking the national trend, Griffiths won with a swing to the Tories from Labour of 7.2%; nationally it was a swing the other way round of 3.5%.[196] As Gordon Walker left the count, Foot concludes, he was followed to his car 'by a crowd of dancing gleeful, blue-rosetted [Tory] fanatics'.[197] Their chants were stereotyped and consistent: 'Where are your Ni**ers now,

Walker?'; 'Take your Ni**ers away!'; 'Up the Tories!'[198] Griffiths' defeat of
Gordon Walker resulted in Harold Wilson turning the tables on the racist
stereotypes of Black people, by claiming in the House of Commons that
Griffiths should 'serve his term here as a parliamentary leper'.[199]

Although, he went on, on a number of occasions to distance himself from
racism, and to stress in the House of Commons that he personally was 'in
favour of complete equality as between the different races',[200] Griffiths both
'supported and arranged for Smethwick Council to purchase a row of
houses with the intention of letting them exclusively to white families'[201]
(this was blocked by Labour's Housing Minister, Richard Crossman).[202]

According to Zig Layton-Henry, writing in 1992, Griffiths was never
repudiated by the Tory Party leadership[203], it would appear quite the contrary. Just before the 1964 General Election, Griffiths wrote in the *Birmingham
Post,* 'I have had no adverse comments from any of the Conservative leaders
either on my campaign or on my politics'.[204] Just after the Election, in the
same newspaper, he declared, 'I am in receipt of the Conservative Party whip
and have been more than welcomed by members of the Conservative
Party'.[205] Not only that, as Foot points out, the Whips actually urged 'the
backbenchers not to boycott Griffiths and to afford him "every courtesy."'[206]
In a speech to the London Young Conservatives, Griffiths predicted that, 'At
least twenty seats in London, the West Midlands and elsewhere can be won if
the Conservatives take a firm line on immigration'.[207]

Adding credence to Griffiths's claims that he had the support of the Tory
Party leadership, Douglas-Home, now Leader of the Opposition, remained
silent in the Commons when challenged to comment on Griffiths's campaign.
As Foot comments, Douglas-Home 'knew too much about it for any public
comment. He knew only too well what kind of consequences a full-scale
debate on the Griffiths affair might have for him'.[208] However, in a speech to
the Conservative Association at Cambridge University, he said of a by-election
at Leyton that Gordon Walker lost after his Smethwick defeat, 'I wish I was an
elector at Leyton. I would do exactly the same as the electors did at Smethwick'.[209] Foot points out that, in fact the Tories sent two special agents to
Leyton to make sure the Smethwick campaign was not repeated. As Foot
conclude, 'Sir Alec could boast about Smethwick – but he knew too much
about it to let his boasting get out of hand'.[210]

In his book, *A Question of Colour,*[211] published in 1966, Griffiths asserted
that he had 'no colour prejudice',[212] while at the same time stating that he
considered South Africa to be 'a model of Parliamentary democracy' and
that 'Apartheid, if it could be separated from racialism, could well be an
alternative to integration'.[213]

Labour responds

Having won a narrow victory at the polls in 1964, Labour had its chance to
act on the questions raised by immigration, the result being a shift to new

ground with the Race Relations Act of 1965, the first piece of legislation in the UK to address the prohibition of racial discrimination and followed previously unsuccessful bills. The Act banned 'racial discrimination in public places and made the promotion of hatred on the grounds of "colour, race, or ethnic or national origins" an offence'.[214] It was criticized for failing to address vital areas where discrimination was most prevalent, namely employment and wider aspects of acquiring accommodation. This led to the passing of the 1968 Race Relations Act, which made unlawful 'acts of discrimination within employment, housing and advertising'.[215] Prior to that, signs in shop windows proclaiming 'No blacks, no dogs, no Irish' or similar were commonplace (and seen often by the author).

As Van Hartesveldt concludes, the debate moved from 'control' to the question of how all people might live together, irrespective of colour, ethnicity or national origins. In this way, 'Labour sought to protect its liberal tradition while tacitly accepting a policy which it had only recently opposed as illiberal.[216] The Irish, however, were again excluded, with the Wilson Government, claiming this was 'religious' and a matter for the Stormont (Northern Ireland) Parliament.[217]

As Layton-Henry points out, at the same time tough immigration laws were imposed clearly designed to curb 'New Commonwealth' (i.e. non-White) immigration.[218] Sometimes it is necessary to spell out the obvious, as does Gareth Jenkins. With great clarity and force, he debunks one of Labour's 'most enduring myths' – that restricting numbers is good for 'race relations':

> 'Without integration, limitation is inexcusable. Without limitation, integration is impossible'. This was neat but untrue. Implementing controls reinforces the notion that it is immigrants, rather than the defects of capitalist society, which cause the problems ordinary people face. That makes integration more, rather than less difficult to achieve. It also flies in the face of logic to assume that discrimination to keep immigrants out eradicates discrimination at home.[219]

He goes on, equally, experience shows that, far from calming anti-immigrant feeling, controls only provoke demands for greater restrictions.[220]

In the summer of 1967, the press gave a lot of publicity to small numbers of 'illegal' Asian immigrants landing on beaches in the south-east of England. British Asians had been arriving from Kenya, having lost their jobs, following that Government's labour market policies prioritizing Kenyan nationals at the expense of Asians who had retained their British citizenship following independence in 1963.[221] Tory MPs Duncan Sandys, son-in-law of Winston Churchill and active member of the Monday Club, and Enoch Powell, Member for Wolverhampton South West, started a campaign to control this new source of immigration.[222] The second Commonwealth Immigrants Act became law in 1968. This further reduced the rights of entry to those born there or who had at least one parent or grandparent born, adopted or naturalized in the UK.[223]

The rise of Powellism

Despite the 1965 Race Relations Act, by the mid-1960s racism was a fact of British political life and Powell become the populist leader and spokesperson for the anti-non-White immigration lobby. He began to demand a net immigration of nil and advocated a programme of voluntary repatriation of non-White people already in the UK.[224]

'Rivers of blood'

On April 20, 1968, two days before the second Race Relations Bill was introduced by the Wilson Government, he made his infamous 'Rivers of blood' speech (though he never actually used that precise phrase) that made him a national figure. In Layton-Henry's words, Powell very much became:

> the focal expression of anti-immigrant resentment and a challenger for the leadership of the Conservative Party ... [the speech's] reception in the media made it a cataclysmic event in the remorseless process by which the 'race' issue [had] been politicized in Britain.[225]

Powell began by referring to immigration as a 'preventable evil'.[226] He went on to recall a conversation with a constituent, 'a middle-aged, quite ordinary working man' ... 'who suddenly said, 'If I had the money to go, I wouldn't stay in this country ... In this country in 15 or 20 years' time the black man will have the whip hand over the white man'.[227] Quite obviously intending to stir up trouble, since earlier in the week, Powell had said to his friend Clement (Clem) Jones, editor at the *Wolverhampton Express and Star,* 'I'm going to make a speech at the weekend and it's going to go up "fizz" like a rocket; but whereas all rockets fall to the earth, this one is going to stay up'.[228] He went on to claim that the motive behind the speech was his duty'. What the 'decent, ordinary fellow Englishman' is saying, 'thousands and hundreds of thousands are saying and thinking'.[229] For Powell, the solution was 'simple and rational' ... 'stopping, or virtually stopping, further inflow, and by promoting the maximum outflow':

> Those whom the gods wish to destroy, they first make mad. We must be mad, literally mad, as a nation to be permitting the annual inflow of some 50,000 dependants, who are for the most part the material of the future growth of the immigrant-descended population. It is like watching a nation busily engaged in heaping up its own funeral pyre.[230]

'Hence the urgency', he stressed, of 'implementing now … the Conservative Party's policy: the encouragement of re-emigration'.[231] He then castigated those who advocate legislation 'against discrimination', claiming that the 'legislation of the kind before parliament at this moment is to risk throwing a match on to gunpowder'.[232] 'Whatever drawbacks attended the immigrants', he stated, 'arose not from the law or from public policy or from administration, but from those personal circumstances and accidents which cause, and always will cause, the fortunes and experience of one man to be different from another's'.[233] The 'existing population' for 'reasons which they could not comprehend' and for 'which they were never consulted', 'found themselves made strangers in their own country'.[234] Raising the stakes still higher to include 'their wives', he warned that they are:

> unable to obtain hospital beds in childbirth, their children unable to obtain school places, their homes and neighbourhoods changed beyond recognition, their plans and prospects for the future defeated; at work they found that employers hesitated to apply to the immigrant worker the standards of discipline and competence required of the native-born worker.[235]

In addition, 'they began to hear, as time went by, more and more voices which told them that they were now the unwanted'. To cap it all, they

> now learn that a one-way privilege is to be established by act of parliament; a law which cannot, and is not intended to, operate to protect them or redress their grievances is to be enacted to give the stranger, the disgruntled and the agent-provocateur the power to pillory them for their private actions.[236]

Powell then mentioned the 'hundreds upon hundreds of letters' he 'received when … [he] … last spoke on this subject two or three months ago'. There was, 'one striking feature' – 'the high proportion of ordinary, decent, sensible people, writing a rational and often well-educated letter, who believed that they had to omit their address because it was dangerous to have committed themselves to paper to a Member of Parliament agreeing with the views' he had expressed.[237] He proceeded to reveal the content of one of them. It was, as expected, full of emotive contrasts between 'us' and 'them': 'a respectable street' and 'a house sold to a negro'; an old White woman with growing fear as the immigrants moved in; 'taken over' a street became 'a place of noise and confusion'; 'afraid to go out'; 'windows broken'; 'excreta through the letter box' and 'wide-grinning piccaninnies' chanting 'racialist', their only word of English.[238] Powell concludes this little cameo with the following: 'When the new Race Relations Bill is passed, this woman is convinced she will go to prison. And is she so wrong? I begin to wonder'.[239]

He moved on to attack 'integration', complaining that immigrants want to keep their culture and religion which in his racist rant Powell refers to as 'racial and religious differences, with a view to the exercise of actual domination'.[240] He once again had a dig at the Race Relations Bill before concluding with the most widely cited part of the speech:

> As I look ahead, I am filled with foreboding; like the Roman, I seem to see 'the River Tiber foaming with much blood'. That tragic and intractable phenomenon which we watch with horror on the other side of the Atlantic but which there is interwoven with the history and existence of the States itself, is coming upon us here by our own volition and our own neglect ... Only resolute and urgent action will avert it even now. Whether there will be the public will to demand and obtain that action, I do not know. All I know is that to see, and not to speak, would be the great betrayal.[241]

The public did indeed speak, gaining Powell massive publicity and popular support. Overnight, he became the best-known and popular Tory politician. Four opinion polls showed support ranging from 67 to 82%.[242] The speech also let to 80 Tory Party constituency resolutions on immigration for the annual Conference, where Powell received a standing ovation.[243] There was also public support, notably by east London dockers and Smithfield market porters who marched for Powell and against the Race Relations legislation. However, according to Richard Norton-Taylor and Seumas Milne, citing secret MI5 intelligence briefings to Prime Minister Harold Wilson, this was organized by extreme right-wing activists.[244] MI5 refers to Harry Pearman, a supporter of the anti-communist fundamentalist group Moral Rearmament. Pearman had been 'at some pains to conceal his identity'.[245] MI5 also notes that porters on a separate demonstration had been got up by a fascist, Dennis Harmston, who stood for Oswald Mosley's party in the 1966 general election.[246] The MI5 reports also describes the anti-Powellite counter-campaign led by Jack Dash and other Communist Party dockers' leaders.[247]

The Eastbourne speech

Just over six months later in November, Powell delivered another speech in Eastbourne. In it, he warned of the dangerous gap between the vast majority of the population and a small group in charge of communications who refuse to face the facts and will not acknowledge reality. He went on to advocate a Ministry of Repatriation:

> The resettlement of a substantial proportion of the Commonwealth immigrants in Britain is not beyond the resources and abilities of this country, if it is undertaken as a national duty, in the successful discharge

of which the interests both of the immigrants themselves and of the countries from which they came are engaged. It ought to be, and it could be, organized now on the scale which the urgency of the situation demands, preferably under a special Ministry for Repatriation or other authority charged with concentrating on this task.[248]

Powell then stated, 'The West Indian or Indian does not, by being born in England, become an Englishman. In law, he becomes a United Kingdom citizen by birth; in fact he is a West Indian or Asian still'.[249] As in the 'Rivers of blood' speech, he ended on a note of urgency: 'we must be told the truth and shown the danger, if we are to meet it. Rightly or wrongly, I for my part believe that the time for that has come'.[250]

In December 1968, the Conservative Political Centre did a survey of its 412 constituency groups and discovered that 327 wanted all immigration stopped indefinitely, with another 55 wanting strictly limited immigration of dependents and a five-year ban on new immigration.[251] Recalling Griffiths' admiration of South Africa some suggested special housing complexes on an apartheid system, and, reminiscent of Nazi Germany, one even talked of 'permanent camps'.[252]

The years 1969 to 1970 saw 'Paki-bashing' (hate-fuelled physical attacks targeted at South Asians that continued through the 1970s to the 2000s)[253] reach a peak, in the aftermath of Powell's racist interventions. The magazine *Race Today* gives numerous examples during that year of 'racial' attacks and fights in widely dispersed locations, some resulting in death.[254]

The General Election of 1970

The 1968 Conservative Political Centre survey contributed to the decision by the Tory Party leadership to include in the 1970 Election Manifesto the promise of a new Immigration Act and assistance for voluntary repatriation,[255] although the document avoided use of this term. It did, however, promise 'no further large scale permanent immigration' twice.[256] According to Layton-Henry, the most extraordinary feature of the election was the role of Enoch Powell who 'acted as a political force in his own right'.[257] For example, in June 1970, he once again raised the temperature of racism when he returned to an old theme of his, the state misleading the public about the scale of immigration to the extent that 'one begins to wonder if the Foreign Office was the only Department of State into which enemies of this country were infiltrated'.[258] The Tory Party's choice for Prime Minister Edward Heath refused to disown Powell as a Tory candidate.[259] The Tories, including the Ulster Unionist Party (UUP) who at the time sat with the Tories at Westminster and voted with them, secured a majority of 30 seats over Wilson's Labour Party. One of the incoming Tory MPs was Harold Soref, staunch colonialist, founding member of the Conservative Commonwealth Council[260] and ex-member of Mosley's British Union of Fascists and a B.U.F. standard bearer at the fascist Olympia Rally in 1934, who was to become a leading member of the Monday Club.[261]

Notes

1   Schaffer, Gavin. 2008. *Racial Science and British Society*, Basingstoke: Palgrave Macmillan, pp. 1930–1962.
2   Schaffer cited in Saini, pp. 96–97.
3   Cited in Saini, p. 97.
4   Ibid., p. 102.
5   Brown, Derek. 2001a. 'Suez and the end of empire'.
6   Ibid.
7   Ibid.
8   Ibid.
9   Jones, Steve. '1956 Suez Crisis: the death of an empire', *Socialist Appeal*, November 7. https://www.socialist.net/1956-suez-crisis-the-death-of-an-empire.htm.
10 Brown. 2001a.
11 Ibid.
12 Jones. 2016.
13 Ibid.
14 Ibid.
15 Ibid.
16 Brown. 2001a.
17 Garrett, Paul Michael. 2010. 'The hidden history of the PFIs: The repatriation of unmarried mothers and their children from England to Ireland in the 1950s and 1960s', *Immigrants & Minorities*, 19 (3), p. 29.
18 https://www.msichoices.org.uk/abortion-services/abortion-and-your-rights/.
19 https://www.abortionrightscampaign.ie/abortion-law-in-ireland/.
20 Garrett. 2002a, p. 485; see also Viney. 1966; and Wallace. 1995.
21 Garrett, Paul Michael. 2010.
22 Minutes of meeting taking place on March 11, 1957. The Merseyside Record Office, Liverpool, holds minutes of the Liverpool Vigilance Association committee meetings and other related papers (1908–1976). (Reference 326VIG), cited in Garrett, Paul Michael. 2010.
23 The programme was entitled *Special Enquiry* and the BBC screened it on October 24, 1956.
24 Carter et al. 1987.
25 Ibid.
26 Ibid.
27 Ibid., p. 33.
28 Ibid., p. 21.
29 Ibid., p. 22 [cabinet meeting November 3, 1955 Eden PM CAB 128/29, C. M.39(55), minute 7, Cabinet Meeting, November 3, 1955.
30 Endnote 1 cabinet meeting November 3, 1955.
31 Carter et al. November 3, 1955, 40.
32 Ibid.
33 Lamb, Richard. 1987. *The Failure of the Eden Government*, London, pp. 18–19.
34 Carter et al.
35 Ibid.
36 Ibid.
37 Ibid.
38 Ibid., p. 42.
39 Ibid.
40 Brown. 2001a.
41 Watts, Carl Peter. 2011. 'The "Wind of Change": British decolonisation in Africa, 1957–1965', *History Review* (71).

42   South African History Online (SAHO). 1956. 'Ghana demands independence from Britain', August 3. https://www.sahistory.org.za/dated-event/ghana-demands-independence-britain.

43   Ibid.

44   Nkrumah, Kwame. 1965. 'Neo-Colonialism, the last stage of imperialism: Introduction'. https://www.marxists.org/subject/africa/nkrumah/neo-colonia lism/introduction.htm.

45   Lenin, Vladimir. 1916. 'Imperialism, the highest stage of capitalism'. https://www.marxists.org/archive/lenin/works/1916/imp-hsc/.

46   Nkrumah. 1965.

47   Boon, Bruce. 2007. 'Malaysia: 50 years of independence'.

48   Ibid.

49   Ibid.

50   Ibid.

51   Ibid.

52   Khoo Boo Teik, cited in *The Political Economy of South-East Asia*, edited by Rodan, Hewison and Robison, pp. 181–182.

53   https://www.britannica.com/place/Malaysia.

54   *BBC News*. 2005. '1959: Macmillan wins Tory hat trick'. http://news.bbc.co.uk/1/hi/uk_politics/vote_2005/basics/4393287.stm.

55   McCracken. 2012. *A History of Malawi, 1859–1966*, pp. 352–359.

56   Baker, Colin. 1998. 'Macmillan's "Wind of Change" Tour, 1960', *South African History Journal*, May, 38 (1), p. 171.

57   Ibid.

58   http://www.africanrhetoric.org/pdf/J%20%20%20Macmillan%20-%20%20the%20wind%20of%20change.pdf.

59   Harold Macmillan. 1960. 'The Wind of Change Speech', 3 Feb. https://web-archives.univ-pau.fr/english/TD2doc1.pdf.

60   South African History Online. 2020. 'Hendrik Verwoerd's response to the "Winds of Change" speech'. https://www.sahistory.org.za/archive/hendrik-verwoerds-response-winds-change-speech.

61   Ibid.

62   Ibid.

63   Watts, Carl Peter. 2011. "The 'Wind of Change': British decolonisation in Africa, 1957–1965', *History Review* (71).

64   'How Britain said farewell to its Empire', *BBC News*, July 23, 2010. https://www.bbc.co.uk/news/magazine-10740852.

65   Robinson, Abby. 27 August 2019. 'Peaky blinders, Oswald Mosley – the real story behind Tommy Shelby's new foe', *Digital Spy*. Hearst UK Entertainment.

66   *The Aims of the Monday Club*, Executive Council publication, Monday Club, 1970, p. 1.

67   Copping. 1972, p. 5.

68   Ibid., p. 26.

69   BBC. 2005. '1957: Britons "have never had it so good"'. http://news.bbc.co.uk/onthisday/hi/dates/stories/july/20/newsid_3728000/3728225.stm.

70   Hennessy, Peter. 2007. *Having It So Good: Britain and the Fifties*, London: Penguin.

71   Carter et al.

72   Early day motions (EDMs) are motions submitted for debate in the House of Commons for which no specific day has been fixed; hence, very few are debated. EDMs are used to put on record individual MPs' views or to draw attention to specific events or campaigns. By attracting the signatures of other MPs, they can be used to demonstrate the level of parliamentary support for a particular cause or point of view. They tend to attract a great deal of public

interest and media coverage. UK Parliament, 2021a. 'What are early day motions?' https://www.parliament.uk/about/how/business/edms/.

73　McKay, James. 2008. 'The passage of the 1962 Commonwealth Immigrants Act, a case-study of backbench power'.

74　CPA: Commonwealth Affairs committee minutes, July 17, 1958, CCO 507/1/1, cited in McKay. 2008.

75　Cousins, Emily. 2010. 'Nottingham Riots (1958)', *Blackpast*, August 30. https://www.blackpast.org/global-african-history/nottingham-riots-1958/.

76　Ibid.

77　Ibid.

78　Ibid.

79　Ibid.

80　https://www.bbc.co.uk/news/uk-england-nottinghamshire-45207246.

81　Sherwood.

82　After 44 years, secret papers reveal truth about five nights of violence in Notting Hill. 'Senior officers tried to play down reports of race riots but police on street witnessed attacks by White mobs', Alan Travis, home affairs editor, August 24, 2002. https://www.theguardian.com/uk/2002/aug/24/artsandhumanities.nottinghillcarnival2002.

83　Sherwood, Marika. Undated. 'Murder in Notting Hill', *Our Migration Story*. https://www.ourmigrationstory.org.uk/oms/murder-in-notting-hill.

84　Travis. 2002.

85　Ibid.

86　Hansard, 594, October 29, 1958, p. 196, cited in Van Hartesveldt. 1983, pp. 127–128.

87　Van Hartesveldt. 1983, p. 128.

88　Sherwood, Marika. Undated. *Our Migration Story.* https://www.ourmigrationstory.org.uk/oms/murder-in-notting-hill.

89　Ibid.

90　Cited in Sherwood.

91　Sherwood.

92　Ibid.

93　Ibid.

94　Ibid.

95　Bean, *Many Shades of Black*, p. 93.

96　*The Times,* May 25, 1959, p. 6.

97　Cited in Sherwood.

98　Hansard. vol 606 c37W, Written Answers, 47.

99　House of Commons Debate, June 4, 1959, Hansard. vol. 606 cc368–72.

100　Ibid.

101　Foot. 1965, p. 133. Foot incorrectly recorded two of their names.

102　Van Hartesveldt. 1983, p. 129.

103　Ibid., p. 130.

104　Garrett. 2002a, p. 485; see also CPRSI. 1955, p. 2; and Viney. 1966, p. 40.

105　Garrett. 2002a, p. 485; see also Garrett. 2000b.

106　Ibid.

107　Walter. 2001.

108　Garrett. 2002a, p. 486.

109　Ibid.

110　Ibid.; see also Garrett. 2000c.

111　Garrett. 2002a, p. 486.

112　Creegan, M. F. 1967.

113　Creegan. 1967, para 6.20.

114　Ibid., para 6.21.

115   Garrett. 2002a, p. 486.
116   Nicolson. 1968, p. 47.
117   Cited in Garrett. 2002a, p. 487.
118   Garrett. 2002a, p. 488.
119   See Wheeler. 1998, p. 120.
120   Garrett. 2002a, p. 488; see Russell. 1964, p. 144.
121   'MPs probe call girl racket in Liverpool', *Liverpool Daily Post*, December 7, 1961.
122   Garrett. 2002a, p. 488; see, for example, Russell. 1964, p. 114. Based on the work of sociologist Stanley Cohen (Cohen. 1972), 'moral panic' has been succinctly defined by Mia Belle Frothingham: Moral panic is a situation in which media reporting has created a folk devil of a particular social group, and the public demand of the authorities that something is done about it. This expression of concern is described as a moral panic because it is based on an outraged sense of offense to public standards of behavior, though the information which prompts it is often limited and inaccurate (Frothingham. 2021).
123   McKay. 2008.
124   Ibid.
125   Ibid.
126   Van Hartesveldt. 1983, p. 130.
127   Cited in Van Hartesveldt, p. 130.
128   Van Hartesveldt, p. 130.
129   Ibid.
130   Cited in Van Hartesveldt, p. 130.
131   McKay, James. 2008, citing *Commons Debates*: vol. 645, Col. 1319–27, August 1, 1961.
132   Van Hartesveldt, p. 131.
133   Ibid.
134   https://www.nationalarchives.gov.uk/cabinetpapers/themes/commonwealth-immigration-control-legislation.htm.
135   McKay. 2008. https://journals.openedition.org/osb/433.
136   The 1922 Committee, actually set up in 1923, is defined on the UK Parliament website as a committee of all backbench Conservative MPs that meets weekly when the Commons is sitting. Its chair, usually a senior MP, is elected by committee members and has considerable influence within the Parliamentary Party. (UK Parliament. 2021). In actuality, it often acts as a pressure group, often in conflict with the leadership, tending to uphold traditional Tory values.
137   McKay. 2008.
138   Macmillan Mss: Knox Cunningham minute to the Prime Minister, November 17, 1961, Macmillan Mss dep c 354, cited in McKay. 2008.
139   McKay, 2008.
140   Macmillan Mss: Knox Cunningham minute to the Prime Minister, November 14, 1961, Macmillan Mss dep c 354.
141   Ibid.
142   Ibid.
143   Ibid.
144   McKay. 2008.
145   CPA: Home Office Affairs committee minutes, December 4, 1961, CRD 2/44/2, cited in McKay. 2008.
146   Spencer, Ian R.G. 1997. *British Immigration Policy since 1939: The making of multi-racial Britain*, London: Routledge, pp. 132–133.
147   McKay. 2008.
148   Ibid.

149   BBC History. 2014. 'Family history research timeline: Migration'. http://www.bbc.co.uk/history/familyhistory/bloodlines/migration.shtml.

150   Ibid.

151   Taylor, Ros. 2017.

152   Ibid.

153   Watson, James L. 2004. 'Presidential address: Virtual kinship, real estate, and diaspora formation: The Man Lineage revisited', *The Journal of Asian Studies*, 63 (4).

154   Taylor. 2017.

155   Ibid.

156   Ibid.

157   Ibid.

158   McKay. 2008.

159   Brooke, Stephen. 1996. 'The Conservative Party, immigration and national identity, 1948–1968', in Francis, Martin and Zweiniger-Bargielowska, Ina (eds.), *The Conservatives and British Society 1880–1990*, Cardiff: University of Wales Press.

160   Younge, Gary. 10 January 2020. 'In these bleak times, imagine a world where you can thrive', *The Guardian*.

161   Lamb, Richard. 1995. *The Macmillan years 1957–1963: The emerging truth*, London: John Murray, p. 443.

162   Ibid., p. 444.

163   Ibid., p. 447.

164   For an analysis of this scandal from the viewpoint of the women, rather than the men involved, see https://www.independent.co.uk/life-style/christine-keeler-trial-profumo-affair-bbc-true-story-real-yevgeny-ivanov-a8095576.html.

165   Butler, David and Stokes, Donald. 1969. *Political change in Britain: Forces shaping electoral choice*, New York: St Martin's Press, p. 350, cited in Van Hartesveldt.

166   Cited in https://www.alistairlexden.org.uk/news/harold-macmillans-resignation.

167   https://www.theguardian.com/science/political-science/2013/sep/19/harold-wilson-white-heat-technology-speech.

168   Pike, E. Royston. 1968. *Britain's Prime Ministers*, London: Odhams, p. 463. Wilson is referring to the fact that Douglas-Home was the fourteenth Earl of Home, a centuries-old Peerage of Scotland.

169   'Fighting Reply from Prime Minister', January 21, 1964, *The Times*, p. 10.

170   Holt. 2014.

171   Ibid.

172   Ibid. As noted in the first chapter of this book, during the 1878 Congress of Berlin, adding to Disraeli's imperialist credentials, Cyprus was ceded to Britain from the Ottoman Empire. This was on the understanding that once the Ottomans got their territories back, the island was to be handed back to the Ottoman Empire. However, when the Ottoman Empire backed Germany in World War I, that epitome of inter-imperialist rivalry (see the Appendix to chapter 2), Britain announced that it had annexed the island. The Treaty of Lausanne in 1923 confirmed the annexation of Cyprus and the island officially became a colony of Britain in 1925. As Zeynep Günes explains, at that time the majority of Cyprus's population consisted of Greeks with a minority of Turks. In 1931, the island's Greek-speaking population burnt down the British Imperial Governor's palace during a revolt against British imperialism. Britain subsequently formed a police force from among the Turkish speaking population who had not taken part in the revolt, but had opposed it, and thus started 'the familiar British policy of Divide and Rule, playing off the Greeks and Turks against one another' (Günes. 2005. 'A Marxist approach to the problem of Cyprus').

173   Holt. 2014.
174   Ibid.
175   Newsom, David. 2001. *The Imperial Mantle*, Bloomington: Indiana University Press, p. 114.
176   Layton-Henry, Zig. 1992. *The Politics of Immigration,* Oxford: Blackwell Publishers, p. 77.
177   Ibid., p. 77.
178   Foot. 1965. pp. 130–131.
179   Cited in Foot. 1965, p. 148.
180   Ibid., p. 180.
181   Geddes, Andrew. 2003. *The Politics of Migration and Immigration in Europe*, London: Sage Publications, p. 34.
182   Foot, Paul. 1995. 'Tearing up the race card', *London Review of Books,* 17 (23), November 30.
183   *The Times,* 'Labour accusation of exploitation', March 9, 1964, p. 6, cited in Jeffries, Stuart. 2014. 'Britain's most racist election: the story of Smethwick, 50 years on', *The Guardian*, October 15. https://www.theguardian.com/world/2014/oct/15/britains-most-racist-election-smethwick-50-years-on.
184   Cited in Foot. 1965, p. 25.
185   Ibid.
186   Ibid., p. 46.
187   Ibid.
188   Ibid., p. 47.
189   Ibid.
190   Ibid., pp. 47–48.
191   Ibid., p. 48.
192   Ibid.
193   Ibid.
194   Ibid., p. 49.
195   Ibid.
196   Ibid., p. 50.
197   Ibid.
198   Cited in Foot. 1965, p. 50.
199   'Peter Griffiths', *The Times*, December 11, 2014. https://www.thetimes.co.uk/article/peter-griffiths-qdlkzggcbbq.
200   Cited in Foot. 1965, p. 51.
201   Stanley, Tim. 2013. 'Peter Griffiths and the ugly Tory racism of the 1960s killed rational debate about immigration', *The Telegraph*. https://web.archive.org/web/20131201001553/http:/blogs.telegraph.co.uk/news/timstanley/100248091/peter-griffiths-and-the-tory-racism-of-the-1960s-killed-rational-debate-about-immigration/.
202   'Peter Griffiths – obituary', *The Daily Telegraph*, November 27, 2013. https://www.telegraph.co.uk/news/obituaries/10479104/Peter-Griffiths-obituary.html.
203   Layton-Henry, Zig. 1992. *The Politics of Immigration,* Oxford: Blackwell Publishers, p. 78.
204   *Birmingham Post,* October 5, 1964, cited in Foot. 1965, p. 63.
205   Ibid.
206   Foot. 1965, p. 74.
207   Cited in Foot. 1965, p. 63.
208   Foot. 1965, p. 72.
209   Cited in Foot. 1965, p. 72.
210   Foot. 1965, p. 72.
211   Griffiths, Peter. 1966. *A Question of Colour*, London: Leslie Frewin.
212   *The Times.* 2014.

213   *The Daily Telegraph*. 2013.
214   UK Parliament. 2021b. 'Race Relations Act 1965'. https://www.parliament.
      uk/about/living-heritage/transformingsociety/private-lives/relationships/col
      lections1/race-relations-act-1965/race-relations-act-1965/.
215   Ibid.
216   Van Hartesveldt. 1983.
217   Hindell, Keith. 1965. 'The genesis of the Race Relations Bill', *Political Quarterly*,
      34 (October-December) pp. 392, 398.
218   Layton-Henry. 1992, p. 78. I should point out here that the term 'New Com-
      monwealth' has been used in the UK (especially in the 1960s and 1970s) in debates
      about immigration to refer to recently decolonized countries, predominantly non-
      White and developing (Hennessy. 2014) while Britain and the pre-1945 domin-
      ions became informally known as the 'Old Commonwealth' or more pointedly as
      the 'White Commonwealth' (Miles, Robert. 1990). 'The racialization of British
      politics', *Political Studies*, 38 (2).
219   Jenkins, Gareth. 1999. 'The badge of prejudice', *Socialist Review*, 234. http://
      pubs.socialistreviewindex.org.uk/sr234/jenkins.htm.
220   Ibid.
221   Layton-Henry. 1992, p. 51.
222   Ibid.
223   Ibid., p. 79.
224   Ibid., p. 80.
225   Ibid.
226   Powell, Enoch. 1968. 'Rivers of Blood speech', delivered to a Conservative
      Association Meeting in Birmingham, April 20. https://anth1001.files.wordpress.
      com/2014/04/enoch-powell_speech.pdf.
227   https://anth1001.files.wordpress.com/2014/04/enoch-powell_speech.pdf.
228   Jones, Nicholas. October 8, 2016. 'My father and Enoch Powell', Weekend
      supplement. *Shropshire Star*, p. 3. (Clem Jones's son, condensed from the book
      Mair, John, Keeble, Richard and Fowler, Neil. 2013. *What Do We Mean By
      Local? The Rise, Fall - and Possible Rise Again – of Local Journalism*. Bury St
      Edmunds: Arima.) Clem Jones's grandson Rupert Jones comments, 'like many
      people that day, my grandparents were shocked and upset by the racist and
      inflammatory nature of the speech, which was filmed by a television crew and
      was immediately all over the TV and on radio bulletins. In fact, that very after-
      noon, my grandmother told my grandfather that she never wanted to see Powell
      again'. (Jones, Rupert. 2016. 'My grandparents, Enoch Powell and the day they
      fell out over his "rivers of blood" speech', *The Guardian*, October 26. https://
      amp.theguardian.com/lifeandstyle/2016/oct/22/my-grandparents-enoch-powell-
      andthe-day-they-fell-out-over-his-rivers-of-blood-speech.)
229   'Enoch Powell's "Rivers of Blood" speech'.
230   Ibid.
231   Ibid.
232   Ibid.
233   Ibid.
234   Ibid.
235   Ibid.
236   Ibid.
237   Ibid.
238   Ibid.
239   Ibid.
240   Ibid.
241   Ibid.
242   Layton-Henry. 1992, p. 81.

243 Ibid., pp. 81–82.
244 Norton-Taylor, Richard and Milne, Seumas. 1999. 'Racism: Extremists led Powell marches', *The Guardian*, January 1. https://www.theguardian.com/uk/1999/jan/01/richardnortontaylor2.
245 Norton-Taylor and Milne. 1999.
246 Ibid.
247 Ibid.
248 'Speech to London Rotary Club, Eastbourne November 16, 1968'. https://www.enochpowell.net/fr-83.html.
249 'Speech to London Rotary Club, Eastbourne'.
250 Ibid.
251 Walker, Martin. 1977. *The National Front,* p. 111.
252 Ibid.
253 Bhalwani, Saarah and Zia Ud Din, Muhammed. 2021. 'The history of Paki-bashing: Educating on British BAME experiences', part of the Oxford Brookes University series of talks on 'Conversations on race, racism and anti-racism', April 13. https://bxtra.brookes.ac.uk/the-history-of-paki-bashing-educating-on-british-bame-experiences/.
254 Layton-Henry, p. 126.
255 Walker. 1977, p. 111.
256 PoliticalNews.co.uk. 2001. '1970 Conservative Party general election manifesto'. http://www.conservativemanifesto.com/1970/1970-conservative-manifesto.shtml.
257 Layton-Henry, p. 83.
258 Schoen, Douglas, E. 1977. *Enoch Powell and the Powellites,* London: Palgrave Macmillan, pp. 51–52.
259 Layton-Henry, p. 84.
260 Pottins, Charlie. 2007. 'Book review: The Man Who Might Have Been', *Jewish Socialist,* 53, Spring. https://www.jewishsocialist.org.uk/reviews/item/the-man-who-might-have-been.
261 Bartlett, Roger. 2017. *When Mosley Men Won Elections.* http://britishguardian.blogspot.com/2017/05/when-mosley-men-won-elections.html.

Part 3

Oppression in Northern Ireland; Immigration Control and the birth and consolidation of Thatcher's 'Racecraft'

5 Edward Heath and Margaret Thatcher (1970–1990)

SECTION 1: HEATH, NORTHERN IRELAND AND IMMIGRATION CONTROL (1970–1974)

Northern Ireland: ongoing colonial and racist legacy

Over eight and a half centuries since the English colonization of Ireland, the racist and imperialist legacy remains. Heath's time as Prime Minister coincided with the height of the Troubles that lasted from the 1960s until 1998. This was the culmination of an ongoing conflict, the key issue that was during Heath's premiership and is now[1] whether Northern Ireland should remain part of the UK.

'Remain' is the demand of the Unionists and loyalists (mostly Ulster Protestants) as opposed to the insistence by Irish nationalists and republicans, predominantly Irish Catholics, that the six counties of Antrim, Armagh, Derry, Down, Fermanagh and Tyrone in the north should be part of a united Ireland. Despite the terms 'Protestant' or 'Catholic' to describe the two sides, the conflict was and is primarily political, with the Irish nationalists and republicans on the left, predominantly favouring social justice and equality, though with some regressive or reactionary elements within its ranks; and the Unionists and loyalists on the right favouring conservatism and the status quo. While both sides are nationalists, Irish nationalists and republicans may be seen as engaging in a healthy nationalism, as described by Nairn (see the Introduction), also containing degrees of reaction, centred on a post-colonial free and united Ireland, the unionists and loyalists embrace a nationalism embedded in racism based on religion and 'Britishness', and all that this entails. In the Introduction and first four chapters, I examine centuries of British colonialism and imperialism, including Ireland's colonization by England in the 12th century up to the Act of Union in 1801; and anti-Irish in Britain in the 19th century and the 'clearing of the estates' in Ireland between 1801 and 1846, as described by Marx.

In the 20th century, pressure for the British occupying forces to leave Ireland intensified after the 1916 Easter Rising that took place in Dublin, and a few other places across the country, during which revolutionaries led

DOI: 10.4324/9781003198673-9

by socialist, republican and trade union leader, James Connolly, declared independence from British rule.[2] Lasting just under a week, the revolution was ruthlessly crushed in a swift British military response,[3] and the leaders, including Connolly, were executed by firing squad.[4] As a military campaign, the 'Rising' was ultimately a failure but it had an important legacy in that the British response to the event turned the majority of the Irish public away from the idea of Home Rule and towards the concept of a fully independent Irish Republic.[5]

There then followed the Irish War of Independence, a guerrilla conflict between the British state and its forces in Ireland and Irish republican guerrillas in the Irish Volunteers or Irish Republican Army (IRA). The war is usually said to have run between 1919 and 1921, but violence both preceded these dates and continued afterwards.[6] In 1920, the British Government, struggling to cope with a war that was making Ireland increasingly ungovernable, introduced a bill to create two devolved governments: one for the six counties (northern Ireland) (the ruling elite was keen to hold on to the profitable industries in the Protestant-majority north-east)[7] and one for the rest of the island. The Government of Ireland Act came into force in May 1921 as a *fait accompli*. Following the 1921 elections, later the same month, Ulster Unionists formed a Northern Ireland Government, Stormont.

In 1922, 'Northern Ireland' began functioning as a self-governing region of the UK. Two-thirds of its population (roughly one million people) was Protestant and about one-third (about half a million) was Catholic. The best jobs went to Protestants.[8] The long-existing dominance of politics by the Ulster Unionist Party (UUP) was enhanced and ensured by gerrymandering (drawing the boundaries of electoral districts to give that party electoral advantage).[9] Moreover, by restricting the vote to ratepayers and their spouses, representation was further limited for Catholic households, which tended to be extended families and include unemployed adult offspring. In addition, ratepayers with more than one residence (more likely to be Protestants) were granted an additional vote for each ward in which they held property (up to six votes).[10] Catholics maintained they were discriminated against when it came to the allocation of public housing, appointments to public sector jobs, and government investment in neighbourhoods. Racism extended to the repressive apparatuses of the state in the sense that Catholics were also more likely to be the subjects of police harassment by the almost exclusively Protestant Royal Ulster Constabulary and the infamous Ulster Special Constabulary (B Specials),[11] the latter seen by many Catholics as a 'Protestant army'.[12] The abolition of proportional representation in 1929 meant that the structure of party politics gave the UUP a continual sizeable majority in the Parliament of Northern Ireland, effectively leading to decades of one-party rule.

In the 1960s, however, at a time when political activism was on the rise in Europe, notably the events of May 1968 in France and the US civil rights movement, Catholic activists in Northern Ireland came together to form the Northern Ireland Civil Rights Association (NICRA).[13] A turning point was in October 1968, when the RUC violently suppressed NICRA marchers who had been protesting against discrimination and gerrymandering with batons and water cannon. In 1969, the Provisional IRA (Provos) emerged from the IRA prepared to use force to bring about unification, becoming the champion of Northern Ireland's nationalists and the dominant faction of the IRA in the 1970s. For the Provos, their fight was a continuation of the Irish War of Independence, and they adopted guerrilla warfare, financed partly by members of the Irish diaspora in the US, and later supplied with arms and munitions by the government of Libya, then led by Muammar al-Qaddafi. Unionists also took up arms, swelling the numbers of loyalist paramilitary organizations, most notably the Ulster Volunteer Force (UVF) and the Ulster Defence Association (UDA).[14]

Heath and internment

At a meeting between Edward Heath and Brian Faulkner, leader of the Stormont Government, on August 5, 1971, it was agreed to introduce internment without trial. The goal was to weaken the IRA and reduce their attacks, but it was also hoped that tougher measures against the IRA would prevent a loyalist backlash and the collapse of Faulkner's government.[15] On August 9–10, 1971, approved by the Heath Government, the British Army carried out 'Operation Demetrius', involving the mass arrest and imprisonment without trial of those suspected of being involved with the IRA. Dawn raids resulted in the arrest of 342 people, sparking four days of violence in which 20 civilians, two IRA members and two British soldiers were killed.[16] Internment entailed torture, the 'so-called five techniques': wall-standing; hooding; subjection to white noise; sleep deprivation and deprivation of food and drink.[17] It was further alleged, according to Gerry Moriarty writing for *The Irish Times,* that some were made to believe they were being ejected from helicopters from hundreds of feet, when in fact they were thrown to the ground from a relatively short distance.[18]

In 2014, it was revealed in *The Irish Times,* in the form of a letter that former Labour Home Secretary Merlyn Rees had written to Prime Minister Jim Callaghan in 1977, that British ministers sanctioned this torture in the early 1970s.[19] The letter was discovered in the British National Archives in Kew by the Investigation Unit of Raidió Teilifís Éireann (RTÉ), Ireland's National Public Service Media. In June 2014, the channel broadcast *The Torture Files,*[20] a *Prime Time* television documentary into the treatment of some of those interned without trial.[21] As Mark Hennessy points out, Rees's letter emerged on the back of earlier research by that suggested the Irish Government and the European Court of Human Rights were deliberately misled by London about the treatment of people interned in 1971.[22] Moreover, in 2019 also reported in *The Irish Times,* the Court of Appeal in

Belfast ruled that, if implemented today, what happened during internment 'would be torture'.[23] According to Rees, ministers in the Heath Government were involved in the decision for it to go ahead. In his letter, he states it was his view that 'the decision to use methods of torture in Northern Ireland in 1971/72 was taken by ministers – in particular Lord Carrington, then Secretary of State for Defence'.[24]

At the time of writing (August 2021), 50 years since the British Army started arresting people in nationalist areas, Martin Hannan, reporting for *The National,* a newspaper that supports Scottish independence, informs us that the head of the British Army in Northern Ireland and the Chief Constable of the RUC had both warned Faulkner against internment, but he flew to London to see Heath and came back with an agreement, allowing internment without trial to proceed under the Special Powers Act.[25] Hannan also notes that in the first three days in one area of Belfast alone, Ballymurphy, ten people were shot dead by soldiers, while another died of a heart attack. The families of those who died in the Ballymurphy Massacre, he tells us, have yet to receive justice, despite a coroner's verdict earlier in 2021 that the ten people, including Catholic priest Father Hugh Mullan, were 'entirely innocent'.[26]

Heath and 'Bloody Sunday'

Heath was further involved in 'Bloody Sunday', when, in January 1972, British soldiers shot 26 unarmed civilians in Derry during a protest march against internment. Fourteen people died, with 13 killed outright, while the death of another man four months later was attributed to his injuries.[27] A further 14 were wounded.[28] According to Maggie O'Kane and David Pallister, reporting in *The Guardian* in 2000 on the Saville Inquiry into the killings, it was a deliberate plan approved by Heath and Falkner, as well as their most senior military advisers, following demands by local and powerful Protestant businessmen to get the 'hooligans' under control.[29] Heath denied that his Government planned the events of Bloody Sunday, describing the suggestion as 'absurd'.[30] Speaking at the public inquiry in London, he recalled that Quintin Hogg, then Lord Chancellor, had told a ministerial meeting that anyone obstructing the army could be shot as enemies of the Queen, but added, 'I did not take his comment seriously, nor, so far as I am aware did anyone else'.[31] Lord Gifford, representing the family of one of the dead, Jim Wray, said the 'turkey shoot' was not the actions of undisciplined troops, but 'rather a group of soldiers who had been authorised by their superiors to shoot'.[32] According to O'Kane and Pallister, it led to hundreds of young Catholics joining the IRA.[33]

The Saville Inquiry first sat in London in 2000 to hear evidence from soldiers, because they said they could not come to Derry because of fear for their safety.[34] One of them, known only as 'Soldier F', admitted killing four civilians.[35] Heath further denied pressuring Lord Widgery, who presided over the Widgery Tribunal on Bloody Sunday, into exonerating the soldiers who fired the fatal shots.[36] However, documents released under the 30-year-rule revealed that Heath had been warned days before the events that soldiers sent to the city had already 'over-reacted' at civil rights protests, and in a conversation with Widgery, Heath had warned him not to forget that Britain was fighting a propaganda war as well as a military one. When questioned about this, he said there had been 'nothing sinister' in his comments.[37] When a barrister asked him whether innocent people were murdered, Heath refused to answer, saying he had not made a statement at the time and would not do so now. He also refused to apologize to the families of those killed on the grounds that he had already expressed intense regret at the time.[38]

The Inquiry itself did not hold the British government at the time 'directly responsible for the atrocity', finding that there was 'no evidence' that either the British government or the unionist-dominated Northern Ireland administration encouraged the use of lethal force against the demonstrators. It also exonerated the army's then commander of land forces, Major General Robert Ford, of any blame. Ford was in Derry on the day of the military operation. He had agreed to deploy the parachute regiment in the city. The report concludes that 'he neither knew nor had reason to know at any stage that his decision would or was likely to result in soldiers firing unjustifiably on that day'. Most of the damning criticism against the military was directed at the soldiers on the ground who fired on the civilians.[39]

Ten years after the Saville Inquiry first sat, on June 15, 2010 Prime Minister David Cameron made a statement to the House of Commons on 'Bloody Sunday'.[40] In so doing, he risked the wrath of fellow Tory MPs (some on his own benches had served as soldiers in Northern Ireland when younger men).[41] Stating that, although he was 'deeply patriotic' and never wanted to believe 'anything bad about our country', or 'the behaviour of our soldiers and our army', the conclusions of the Saville Report are absolutely clear. 'What happened on Bloody Sunday was both unjustified and unjustifiable. It was wrong'.[42] Cameron was unambiguous in his belief that 'on balance' British troops fired the first shots during the 'tragic events' in Derry in January 1972 without issuing a warning.[43] He went on, 'Some members of our armed forces acted wrongly. The Government is ultimately responsible for the conduct of our armed forces and for that, on behalf of the Government – and indeed our country – I am deeply sorry'.[44] Cameron added, 'what happened should never, ever have happened. The families of those who died should not have had to live with the pain and the hurt of that day and with a lifetime of loss'.[45] Moreover, he pointed out that the Report showed that soldiers lied about their involvement in the killings and that all of those who died were innocent.[46] In the words of the Report, 'None of the firing by the Support Company [Paratroopers] was aimed at people posing a threat or causing death or serious injury'.[47] A former Derry priest, who narrowly escaped being shot on the day, said he was 'amazed' at how damning the findings were against the soldiers: 'This city has been vindicated, this city has been telling the truth all along'.[48]

Heath and domestic issues

Heath's most prominent moment with respect to domestic issues came in 1973 when he led the UK on January 1, 1973 into membership of the European Communities (EC) (later European Union or EU). This was to become a bone of contention within the Tory Party, until Britain officially exited the EU on January 31, 2020, under the Tory Government of Boris Johnson (see chapter 10). According to his biographer John Campbell, Heath regarded this as his personal 'finest hour'.[49]

Heath was also responsible for the Industrial Relations Act of 1971 that was an attempt to legally shackle the workers' movement, specifically the power of shop stewards who were directly answerable to the mass of organized workers, rather than union officials.[50] As Bill Mullins, former senior shop steward puts it:

> The UK ruling class was desperate to make the economy competitive with its foreign rivals, but since the capitalists had refused to reinvest sufficiently the enormous profits they had made from empire and the sweat of the British working class, they only had one option: that was to super-exploit the labour of the working class in the factories and industry in general. But to do that they had to remove their greatest obstacle, the power of the organised workers on the shop floor manifested in the power of the shop stewards.[51]

As Mullins explains, the Tory manifesto had promised 'to stabilise industrial relations by forcing concentration of bargaining power and responsibility in the formal union leadership, using the courts'.[52] Despite action from a number of trade unionists, the Act was passed early in 1971. However, it was made inoperable from the start by the continuing action of the unions. It was eventually repealed by the 1974 Labour Government.[53] As Mullins concludes:

> The battle against the Industrial Relations Act was won by the organised working class, and it would take the political defeat on the electoral plane in the 1979 general election, which brought to power Maggie Thatcher, for the capitalist class to get their revenge ... The early 1970s witnessed the organised British working class flexing their muscles and defeating by direct strike action all attempts by the new Tory government of Ted Heath to bring them to heel.[54]

A miners' strike at the start of 1974 further damaged the Government, causing the implementation of the Three-Day week, implemented to conserve energy. In an attempt to repair the damage to his government, Heath called a General Election for February 1974. This resulted in a hung Parliament, and, failing to form a Coalition with the Liberal Party, Heath resigned as Prime Minister and was replaced by Labour Prime Minister Harold Wilson. After losing a second General Election, as party leader in October 1974, Margaret Thatcher challenged him in a leadership contest in January 1975. After she won the first round. Heath resigned as leader and returned to the backbenches, where he would remained until 2001. He died four years later.

Colour-coded racism

The 1971 Immigration Act

There is no doubt that the role of Enoch Powell had played a significant part in Labour's defeat and Heath's victory. In his memoirs, published in 1998,[55] Heath noted, 'Between 1968 and 1970, my mailbag had contained many letters, largely from Conservative supporters, in support of Enoch Powell ... frequently abusive, towards me as much as towards black people'.[56] He also acknowledged that there 'were certainly those in the party, even on the front bench, who wanted to harness racist support'.[57] Heath was generally considered a moderate on immigration.[58] However, I think that what follows will demonstrate that this is not the case. The most charitable interpretation of Heath's racism might be to describe it as aversive (we don't want too many of them, 'them' being the racialized 'immigrant')[59] as opposed to direct and oppressive like Powell (see the Introduction for a discussion on types of racism). Thus, in his memoirs, he notes how, when he came to power, 'race was already a major source of conflict in Britain'.[60] He then refers to 'Labour's 1948 British Nationality Act ... [that] ... had granted British citizenship to all people in Commonwealth countries past and present'.[61] While he admits the existence of 'racial prejudice' that 'culminated in the Notting Hill race riots in 1958', he then states that it was 'inter-racial friction' (not racism) that 'eventually prompted Rab Butler to bring in the Commonwealth Immigration [sic] Act in 1962 *to limit the numbers of non-white immigrants*'[62] (my emphasis) (see chapter 4). He acknowledges that the Act was 'discriminatory in practice', 'the principle behind it was to give white Britons time to adjust to new arrivals and thereby, to give existing immigrants and their descendants more of a chance to integrate'.[63] So for Heath, like so many British politicians past and present, the problem is, to repeat, *numbers*, there are too many of 'them'. Accordingly, Heath lost no time in implementing the 1971 Immigration Act. He had been elected on June 19, 1970, and the Bill passed its second reading in March 1971. The Act replaced employment vouchers with work permits granted only to those whose skill was in short supply in Britain,[64] and did not give rights to permanent residents or the right of entry for dependents. Arguably the most racist aspect of the Act was that patrials – people with close connections with the UK through birth or descent (in other words largely White people) would be exempt from all controls. Provisions were also made to strengthen powers to prevent 'illegal immigration' and some modest financial assistance was given for voluntary repatriation.[65] The overall intention and effect was to give the UK Government control over the immigration of 'non-partials' and end the right of 'non-White' Commonwealth citizens to migrate to and settle in the UK. Powell had helped get the partiality clause incorporated at committee stage of the Bill, predicting in February 1971 that there would be 'an explosion' unless there was a massive repatriation scheme for immigrants.[66] As Layton-Henry concludes, the legislation did not end the controversy over non-White immigration, but it was 'another major milestone in the process of erecting racist immigration controls',[67] a process that is ongoing and continues to this day, as will be demonstrated in the rest of this book.

Alan Travis points out that the Heath Government knew it would face charges of racism.[68] However, Home Secretary Reginald Maudling, whose racism appears to be more hard-line that Heath's, said such racism could be defended on the grounds that Britain had a special relationship with Australia, Canada and New Zealand and 'from Gallipoli to Inchon there are enduring monuments to its reality'.[69] He told the Cabinet that tougher restrictions on the inflow of Asian immigrants were 'necessary and defensible given their propensity in contrast to aliens to settle permanently and bring in their dependants'.[70]

State papers released in January 2002 by the Public Record Office show that Maudling told Heath secretly, 'The number of aliens who want to settle here is relatively few, and for this reason – because they come from a cultural background generally fairly akin to our own – it is not difficult to assimilate them'.[71] He went on to reveal his overt colour-coded racism:

> But of those wishing to come here to work from the Commonwealth, particularly the new Commonwealth, the vast majority would want to settle permanently and by reason both of this factor and of the fact that they come generally from a different cultural background, the task of assimilation – as experience so bitterly shows – is all but impossible. If we put the Commonwealth citizen on the same basis as what at present is the practice for aliens, and abolish the quota which presently applies only to Commonwealth citizens, the result would be a great increase in coloured immigration[72]

The Cabinet Secretary Burke Trend had made clear that the main motive behind the Act was 'to avoid the risk of renewed "swamping" by immigrants from the new Commonwealth'; and that such a 'resurgence would inflame community relations in Britain'.[73]

Powell, of course, was still not satisfied and continued his rants on immigration, again accusing the state of fraud in the presentation of statistics and warning of 'racial' civil war.[74]

The Ugandan Asian crisis

In August 1972, General Idi Amin, President of Uganda, announced the expulsion of all the Asians (known as 'East African Asians'; see chapter 4) from the country, giving them just 90 days to leave. According to Amin, God appeared in person in a dream and instructed him to banish all 50,000 Asian residents, most of them third generation. Exemplifying the point made in the Introduction that *anyone* can be racist towards anyone, the Asians, Amin charged, had been sabotaging Uganda's economy, deliberately retarding economic progress, fostering widespread corruption and treacherously refraining from integrating in the Ugandan way of life.[75] The previous year, unsurprisingly for a Tory Government, it had supported a coup led by Amin that toppled Milton Obote's increasingly socialist administration whose egalitarian domestic politics was posing more and more of a threat to the privileges of the armed forces. The coup has been described as 'class action by the military'.[76] Obote had also pursued a policy of African Nationalism, supporting independence in southern Africa and opposing British arms sales to apartheid South Africa.

The Heath Government was unruffled by Amin's announcement.[77] As Yasmin Alibhai-Brown explains, although things had soured between the UK and Amin, he 'was felt to be a man the British could manipulate, trained by our soldiers, a chap who loved the Queen'.[78] However, she points out, they were wrong: Amin was ruthless, a clever populist who intended to carry out the expulsions.[79] Most of the 50,000 Asians were British passport-holders, so it was clear that Britain would have primary responsibility for receiving them.[80] This was greeted with shock and horror, most noticeably by Powell, who claimed that Britain was not obliged to take them, and said they should be returned to India or Pakistan.[81] Strenuous diplomatic efforts followed to try to get other countries to admit some, and a substantial number were accepted by India, Canada and other countries. The British Government ultimately permitted 27,000 Ugandan Asians to move to the UK, providing a major boost to anti-immigration organizations such as the Conservative Monday Club and the fascist National Front (NF).[82]

The former began a 'Halt Immigration Now!' campaign. In September 1972, it held a public meeting in Central Hall, opposite Parliament, at which the speakers Ronald Bell, John Biggs-Davison, Harold Soref and John Heydon Stokes, all Tory MPs and Monday Club members, called on the government to halt all immigration, repeal the Race Relations Act and initiate a full repatriation scheme. According to Martin Walker, author of *The National Front*,[83] out of the 2,000 people at the rally, at least 400 were

NF members.[84] A resolution was delivered to Heath who refused to repeal the Act.[85] As Layton-Henry concludes, when Powell's motion at the Tory Annual Conference condemning the Government was successfully amended, some Tories left the party and joined the NF, the major beneficiary of the 'Ugandan Asian crisis'. The NF began a period of growth and electoral advance that was not decisively rebutted until Margaret Thatcher's General Election victory in 1979[86] (see the last section of this chapter).

SECTION 2: THATCHER, THE BIRTH OF 'RACECRAFT;' AND NORTHERN IRELAND (1975–1990)

Thatcher became leader of the Tory Party in February 1975. As Layton-Henry affirms, on immigration she sympathized with Powell and those on the hard right of the party, favouring 'the most stringent controls of New Commonwealth immigration'.[87] Heath had sacked Powell from the Tory shadow cabinet in 1968 following the latter's 'rivers of blood speech'. Later Thatcher recalled, 'I told Ted then that I thought it best just to let things cool down and that it would be unwise to dismiss someone like Enoch. Looking back, I can see that it was not just unwise, it was disastrous'. She also wrote that, having fallen out with Powell, she was glad that during her last period in office and afterwards they became closer again, and that 'Powellism' helped create 'Thatcherism'.[88] Thatcherism, as we shall now see, was a major turning point in Tory racism, in terms of what Layton-Henry refers to as Thatcher's 'racecraft', an obvious reference to her book, *Statecraft*.[89] He defines it as 'the strategy and policies of Mrs Thatcher and her administration in the areas of immigration and race relations'[90] The strategy and associated policies involve nothing less than the normalization of racism, as one of the key components of the Tories' mainstream agenda, a component, as we shall see in the rest of this book, that saturates the Party to this day. Another major turning point, the one for which Thatcher is most famous, is her adoption of neoliberal capitalism, and helping to move the UK (and the world) down its tortuous path.[91]

In May 1976, a media panic over small numbers of Asians coming to Britain from Malawi resulted in an upsurge of support for the NF in local elections in the same month and 140 resolutions at the Tory Annual Conference in October. Thatcher wanted even tighter controls. Her Shadow Home Secretary, Deputy Leader of the Party and close confidant Willie Whitelaw (after becoming Britain's first female Prime Minister in 1979 she famously said, 'every Prime Minister needs a Willie')[92] promised the conference that the party would develop a policy that was clearly designed to move towards an end to 'immigration as we have seen it in the postwar years'.[93]

Thatcher expanded on this in her interview on British television in a popular programme at the time, *World in Action*. A General Election was pending the following year, and opinion polls pointed to a recovery in support for Labour. In the last two polls before the programme was aired on January 27, 1978, the Labour share of the vote had gone up two points, while that of the Tories had gone up by half a point and was behind Labour.[94] When asked by interviewer Gordon Burns, 'If you do get to power, how severely would you cut the numbers?',[95] Thatcher replied with what became one of her most quoted television interview quotes:[96]

> Well now, look, let us try and start with a few figures as far as we know them, and I am the first to admit it is not easy to get clear figures from the Home Office about immigration, but there was a committee which looked at it and said that if we went on as we are then by the end of the century there would be four million people of the new Commonwealth or Pakistan here. Now, that is an awful lot and I think it means that *people are really rather afraid that this country might be rather swamped by people with a different culture* [emphasis added] and, you know, the British character has done so much for democracy, for law and done so much throughout the world that if there is any fear that it might be swamped people are going to react and be rather hostile to those coming in.[97]

She added, 'we do have to hold out the prospect of an end to immigration',[98] and went on to argue that, although she would not make immigration a major issue in the General Election (which she didn't) but 'never be afraid to tackle something which people are worried about. We are not in politics to ignore peoples' worries: we are in politics to deal with them'.[99] Thatcher's intervention had an immediate short-term effect on public opinion. From being one and half points behind Labour before, in a poll held immediately after the interview, the Tories jumped into a nine-point lead.[100]

Thatcher's 'swamping' remarks was significant in that it brought racist discourse to the heart of normal (Tory) politics. As Daniel Trilling put it:

> Thatcher brought Powell's ideas back into the heart of Conservative politics, as part of a wider nationalist project that grasped the narrative of imperial decline – the 'postcolonial melancholia' identified by Paul Gilroy – and turned it around, promising voters that she would make Britain 'great' again.[101]

Culture and ethnicity were conflated with 'nation'; the unspoken assumption about the fearful 'people' that Thatcher referred to was that they were White, while the 'people of a different culture' were not.[102] Moreover as Alfred Sherman, one of Thatcher's closest advisors, wrote in the *Telegraph* that same year, 'It is from a recognition of racial difference that a desire develops in most groups to be among their own kind; and this leads to distrust and hostility when newcomers come in'.[103] At the Ilford North by-election the following month, the Tories easily captured the seat from Labour, and Thatcher's 'swamping remarks' seem to have been an important factor.[104]

Hostility to immigrants was to become official Tory policy 34 years later, when Theresa May initiated 'the hostile environment' in 2012, heralding another era of Tory racist politics that continues to this day (see chapters 9 and 10).

The 1979 General Election

Sixteenth months after her 'swamping remarks', Thatcher won the General Election on May 4, 1979, with an 8% swing to the Tories from Labour, while the NF, which stood a record number of candidates, failed to win a single seat, and collapsed amid bitter recriminations.[105] One of the main reasons is seen as the so-called 'Winter of Discontent' that took place during 1978–79. It was characterized by widespread strikes by private, and later public, sector unions demanding pay rises greater than the limits Labour Party Prime Minister James Callaghan had imposed against TUC (Trades Union Congress) opposition in an attempt to control inflation. The Tory campaign was most memorably captured in the poster, designed by Saatchi and Saatchi, depicting a queue outside an employment office with the words: 'Labour isn't working'.

However, just as with Heath's victory in 1970, racism also played a key role. As a result of Thatcher's public identification of her party with a hard line on immigration, there were massive swings to the Tories, averaging over 14%, throughout the East End of London, where the NF had achieved some of its highest support in the past.[106]

Margaret Hilda Thatcher became the first female Prime Minister of Britain on May 4, 1979. A precursor to her unique theatrical rhetorical style (she had voice lessons in the 1970s to make her voice seem firmer and more powerful),[107] on arriving at 10 Downing Street she paraphrased the Prayer of St. Francis of Assisi: 'Where there is discord, may we bring harmony. Where there is error, may we bring truth. Where there is doubt, may we bring faith. And where there is despair, may we bring hope'. In November, she started introducing her monetarist economic ideas[108] by raising the base interest rated to 17% in an attempt to curb inflation, despite which it peaked at 20% in the middle of 1980. Also in 1980, Thatcher implemented her manifesto promise of the 'right to buy' for council tenants, giving millions the opportunity to purchase their homes at discounted rates as part of her vision of creating a so-called 'property-owning democracy'.[109] Her first ministry was to last until 1983, she had two more: from 1983 to 1987 and 1987 to 1990.

Northern Ireland

The killing of Airey Neave

Writing for the Irish publication, *The Journal,* Hugh O'Connell recalls the afternoon of March 30, 1979, just over a month before Thatcher became

Prime Minister, the former campaign manager in her successful 1975 leadership challenge, Airey Neave, at the time spokesperson on Northern Ireland, was assassinated in a car bomb attack in the car park at Westminster. The (Irish National Liberation Army (INLA) later claimed responsibility.[110] Neave had been born into a wealthy family who had gained their prominence as merchants in the 18th century, importing goods from the Caribbean,[111] then the British West Indies and part of the British Empire (see the Introduction). A 'military man', he had been widely expected to instigate a tough crack down on Republican paramilitaries, much more so than the previous Labour government had he become Secretary of State for Northern Ireland.[112]

Paul Routledge expands on why he became a target. A World War II hero, he had been promoted in rank and into MI9 (military intelligence). Once firmly inside 'intelligence', he never really left.[113] Neary remained an officer in the Territorial Army/SAS (volunteer army/Special Air Services) until the early 1950s, when he realized his ambition by becoming a Tory MP in 1952. As Routledge notes, 'He maintained close links with the security services, in dining groups in London clubs, and secretive groups of businessmen and old sweats who thought Britain was going to the dogs, or communism, which was worse'.[114] When Thatcher made him head of her private office following her leadership win, it was an easy move to his coveted job, Northern Ireland.[115] In Routledge's words, 'this was his chosen battlefield ... he could achieve his longstanding ambition to take on an enemy and win, through a combination of arms and military intelligence'.[116] The Provisional IRA and INLA feared him because Neave had been a prisoner of war, 'like their "men behind the wire" in Long Kesh [H–Block], who played a key role in the war against British troops'. Routledge concludes, '[Neave] understood their weaknesses, their way of thinking. He had to go'. 'The soldier-politician', he went on, 'knew he was in mortal danger, and almost how the hit would come'.[117] Though devastated by the death of this key Thatcherite, Thatcher was also angered and undeterred and became even more concerned with ensuring security forces cracked down on dissent in the North rather than focus immediately on achieving a lasting peace.[118]

The hunger strikes

In October 1980, the first modern hunger strike organized by Provisional IRA and INLA prisoners ended after 53 days, when a 'compromise' was agreed through a top-secret back-channel, facilitated by MI6 officer Michael Oatley.[119] In the words of Peter Taylor, who has been reporting on Northern Ireland since 1972, 'Remarkably the compromise was sanctioned by Thatcher'. Taylor asked Oatley if the formula allowed prisoners to wear their own clothes. This was extremely important for the prisoners because they thought of themselves as 'political prisoners', under the Geneva Convention, fighting to achieve the IRA's historic goal of a united Ireland; prison uniforms criminalized them, they argued.[120]

Oatley replied, 'I think it left that sort of question rather open. It did suggest some concessions'.[121] As Taylor stresses, 'The prisoners certainly ended their hunger strike in the belief that they were getting their own clothes – families brought them into the prison in readiness – but the government had other plans'.[122] Taylor recalls a Northern Ireland Office official in Belfast 'opening his desk drawer and producing a shirt still crisp in its Marks and Spencer's wrapper'. 'But they'll never wear it', Taylor responded. 'And they didn't'.[123]

Today Oatley describes the strike as 'a searing tragedy that could have been avoided'.[124] When Taylor heard that the IRA's commanding officer in the Maze, Bobby Sands,[125] was to lead a second hunger strike, starting on March 1, 1981 – the fifth anniversary of the abolition of special category status – he knew that this time, failing any compromise, it would be to the death. He was right (Sands did not have long to go).[126] On April 9, Sands was elected to the UK Parliament as Anti-H-Block/Armagh Political Prisoner candidate (Armagh was the women's prison). It was the first electoral victory for militant Irish republicanism and was caused by the death of the sitting MP, Frank Maguire, who was an Independent but a nationalist.[127]

On April 21, even though Sands was now an MP, Thatcher reiterated her total refusal to consider 'political prisoner status': 'Crime is crime is crime. It is not political. It is crime. There can be no question of political status'.[128]

That Sands and the others were convinced that their struggle was not only political but humanitarian, is clearly revealed in his prison diary, in the entry on the first day of the second hunger strike:

> I am standing on the threshold of another trembling world. May God have mercy on my soul. My heart is very sore because I know that I have broken my poor mother's heart, and my home is struck with unbearable anxiety. But I have considered all the arguments and tried every means to avoid what has become the unavoidable: it has been forced upon me and my comrades by four-and-a-half years of stark inhumanity. I am a political prisoner. I am a political prisoner because I am a casualty of a perennial war that is being fought between the oppressed Irish people and an alien, oppressive, unwanted regime that refuses to withdraw from our land. I believe and stand by the God-given right of the Irish nation to sovereign independence, and the right of any Irishman or woman to assert this right in armed revolution. That is why I am incarcerated, naked and tortured. Foremost in my tortured mind is the thought that there can never be peace in Ireland until the foreign, oppressive British presence is removed, leaving all the Irish people as a unit to control their own affairs and determine their own destinies as a sovereign people, free in mind and body, separate and distinct physically, culturally and economically.[129]

The Blanket Protest and the Dirty Protest

To clarify Sands's reference to 'naked', the hunger strikes were preceded by the 'blanket protest' and the 'dirty protest'. In September 1976, newly convicted prisoner Kieran Nugent began the blanket protest, in which IRA and the INLA prisoners refusing to wear prison uniform either went naked or fashioned garments from prison blankets.[130] The 'Bobby Sands Tribute' website has provided a graphic insight into life in H-Block.[131] In March 1978, some prisoners refused to leave their cells to shower or use the lavatory on account of attacks by prison officers, and were subsequently provided with wash-hand basins in their cells. They requested showers to be also installed in their cells, and when this was turned down they refused to use the basins. The following month, a fight occurred between a prisoner and a prison officer in H-Block 6. The prisoner was taken to solitary confinement, and news spread across the wing that he had been badly beaten.[132] The prisoners' response was to smash the furniture in their cells, and the prison authorities' response was to remove the remaining furniture from the cells, leaving the prisoners with just blankets and mattresses. The prisoners then refused to leave their cells, and as a result the prison officers were unable to clear them. This led to the 'blanket protest' escalating into the 'dirty protest', as the prisoners were unable to 'slop out' (empty their chamber pots) so resorted to smearing excrement on the walls of their cells. Prisoner Pat McGeown described the conditions inside the prison:

> There were times when you would vomit. There were times when you were so run down that you would lie for days and not do anything with the maggots crawling all over you. The rain would be coming in the window and you would be lying there with the maggots all over the place.[133]

The prison authorities tried to keep the cells clean by breaking the cell windows and spraying in disinfectant, then temporarily removing the prisoners and sending in rubber-suited prison officers with steam hoses to clean the walls. However, as soon as the prisoners were returned to their cells they resumed their protest. By the middle of 1978 there were between 250 and 300 protesting prisoners, and the protest was attracting media attention from around the world. Tomás Ó Fiaich, the Roman Catholic Cardinal Archbishop of Armagh, visited the prison on July 31, 1978 and condemned the conditions there:

> Having spent the whole of Sunday in the prison, I was shocked at the inhuman conditions prevailing in H-Blocks, three, four and five, where over 300 prisoners were incarcerated. One would hardly allow an animal to remain in such conditions, let alone a human being. The nearest approach to it that I have seen was the spectacle of hundreds of

homeless people living in the sewer pipes in the slums of Calcutta. The stench and filth in some of the cells, with the remains of rotten food and human excreta scattered around the walls was almost unbearable. In two of them I was unable to speak for fear of vomiting.[134]

Despite the conditions, Ó Fiaich reported the morale of the prisoners to be high:

From talking to them it is evident that they intend to continue their protest indefinitely and it seems they prefer to face death rather than to submit to being classed as criminals. Anyone with the least knowledge of Irish history knows how deeply this attitude is in our country's past. In isolation and perpetual boredom they maintain their sanity by studying Irish. It was an indication of the triumph of the human spirit over adverse material conditions to notice Irish words, phrases and songs being shouted from cell to cell and then written on each cell wall with the remnants of toothpaste tubes.[135]

The protest continued with no sign of compromise from the Thatcher Government, and by late 1979, 90% of newly arriving prisoners were choosing to join the protest. In January 1980 the prisoners issued a statement outlining what were known as the 'Five Demands':

1   The right not to wear a prison uniform;
2   The right not to do prison work;
3   The right of free association with other prisoners, and to organize educational and recreational pursuits;
4   The right to one visit, one letter and one parcel per week;
5   Full restoration of remission lost through the protest.[136]

In February 1980, Mairéad Farrell and over 30 other prisoners in Armagh Women's Prison joined the 'dirty protest' following a series of disputes with the prison governor, including allegations they had been ill-treated by male prison officers. They did not conduct a blanket protest, since women prisoners in Northern Ireland already had the right to wear their own clothes, but this did include smearing their menstrual blood on the cell walls.

In June 1980 the Thatcher Government's intransigent position was strengthened when the European Commission of Human Rights rejected a case by four prisoners, including Kieran Nugent, that conditions inside the prison were 'inhuman', ruling that the conditions were self-inflicted and 'designed to enlist sympathy for the [prisoners'] political aims'.[137]

In March 1981, in a speech in Belfast, Thatcher stated that while, 'Of course those convicted of serious crimes and sentenced to long terms of imprisonment should serve their sentences in humane conditions. We will continue to maintain and, if we can, to improve the high standards which Northern Ireland prisons already provide'.[138]

The death of Bobby Sands

It was only after all the prisoner protests failed to bring any change from the Thatcher Government that they resorted to a hunger-strike, and ultimately deaths. After 66 days on hunger strike, Bobby Sands MP died on May 5, 1981.[139] Here are the last recorded words in his prison diary:

> An official was in with me and gave me some lip. He said, 'I see you're reading a short book. It's a good thing it isn't a long one for you won't finish it'. That's the sort of people they are ... If they aren't able to destroy the desire for freedom, they won't break you. They won't break me because the desire for freedom, and the freedom of the Irish people, is in my heart. The day will dawn when all the people of Ireland will have the desire for freedom to show. It is then we'll see the rising of the moon.[140]

Nine volunteers followed Sands, making a total of ten deaths in 1981. Unlike the first strike, the prisoners has joined it one at a time and at staggered intervals, which they believed would arouse maximum public support and exert maximum pressure on Thatcher.[141]

According to Peter Taylor, around 100,000 mourners came to Bobby Sands's funeral on May 7, 1981, confounding the expectations of the Government, which believed the hunger strike had limited support. To those who marched behind his coffin, Sands was a martyr.[142] For Thatcher, 'Mr Sands was a convicted criminal. He chose to take his own life. It was a choice that his organisation did not allow to many of their victims'.[143] In July 1981, Bernie Sanders, then Mayor of Vermont in the US, wrote the following letter to Margaret Thatcher:

> We are deeply disturbed by your government's unwillingness to stop the abuse, humiliation and degrading treatment of Irish prisoners now on hunger strikes in Northern Ireland. We ask you to end your intransigent policy towards the prisoners before the reputation of the English people for fair play and simple decency is further damaged in the eyes of the people of Vermont and the United States.[144]

A month after the end of the hunger strike, at Sinn Féin's Annual Conference in December 1981, the party's director of publicity, Danny Morrison gave birth to the slogan, 'The Armalite and Ballot Box'. As Taylor explains, this phrase reflected 'the fusion of violence and politics that was to define IRA/Sinn Fein strategy for the next 15 years'.[145]

The following year, Taylor goes on, Martin McGuinness, who in 1973 had told an Irish court he was proud to be a member of the Provisional IRA, was elected to the Northern Ireland Assembly and in 1983 Gerry Adams was elected to Westminster. That was the 'Ballot Box'. The

'Armalite' followed in 1984 when the IRA bombed the Grand Hotel in Brighton, where the Tories were holding their annual conference. Five members of the party were killed, and Thatcher narrowly survived. For the IRA leadership and rank and file, it was seen as revenge for the hunger strike.[146]

The Anglo-Irish agreement and unionist dissent

According to Campbell, British military intelligence told Thatcher that she could not take the IRA head on and the likelihood of never-ending violence persuaded her to seek a political solution to the Troubles.[147] On November 15, 1985, Thatcher and Garret FitzGerald the Irish Taoiseach (Prime Minister) signed the Anglo-Irish Agreement (AIA) that gave the Irish Government an official consultative role in the affairs of Northern Ireland. It outlined cooperation in four areas: political matters; security and related issues; legal matters, including the administration of justice; and the promotion of cross-border cooperation.[148]

The rest of Thatcher's premiership witnessed unionist protest and dissent. In the same month as the signing, Tom King, then Thatcher's Secretary of State for Northern Ireland, was physically attacked by Loyalist protesters as he arrived for a function at Belfast City Hall. George Seawright, then a Loyalist councillor, was jailed for nine months for his part in this protest. There was then a huge Unionist rally, estimated at over 100,000 people, at Belfast City Hall to protest against the AIA, the slogan adopted was 'Ulster Says NO', that was to appear throughout the region, remaining for a considerable number of years. Towards the end of the month, the House of Commons approved the AIA by 473 votes to 47, with Thatcher pledging that the Government would not give way to threats or violence.[149]

The following month, the Alliance Party of Northern Ireland (APNI) took the decision to withdraw from the Northern Ireland Assembly, the first meeting of the new Inter-Governmental Conference established under the Anglo-Irish Agreement AIA was held, Protestant workers from a number of firms in Belfast staged walk-outs and there were violent clashes between the demonstrators and the RUC. Also, in December 1985, all 15 Unionist MPs resigned their seats in protest at the AIA.[150]

In February 1986, James Molyneaux, then leader of the Ulster Unionist Party (UUP), and Ian Paisley, then leader of the Democratic Unionist Party (DUP), met Thatcher in London to discuss the AIA. Following the meeting the two Unionist leaders said that they welcomed Thatcher's promise to consider their proposals for talks on devolution for Northern Ireland. When they returned there, in consultation with the leaders of workers in the power stations and the shipyard, they decided that they would hold no further discussions with Thatcher until the AIA was overturned. Belfast City Council and 17 other councils voted to refuse to set a 'rate' (local government tax) in protest at the AIA.[151]

On March 3, there was a widespread general strike, or 'Day of Action', in Northern Ireland in support of Unionist demands for the ending of the Anglo-Irish Agreement AIA, with most aspects of life across the region disrupted. While many Protestants supported the strike, there was also a high level of intimidation with masked Loyalists setting up barricades. There were riots in Loyalist areas and shots were fired at the RUC. Later RUC figures showed that there had been 237 reported cases of intimidation, 57 people arrested, and 47 RUC officers injured. The Government and the security forces were later criticized for not keeping the main roads open and for not trying to end the intimidation. Ten days after the strike, it was announced that additional British soldiers would be sent to Northern Ireland to support the RUC, and on March 24, Thatcher wrote a letter to Unionist leaders in which she rejected a demand for a suspension of the AIA to allow talks on devolution to begin.[152]

In April 1986, Molyneux and Paisley announced a 12-point plan of civil disobedience in protest at the AIA, and the UUP Executive voted to end the special relationship with the Tory Party, while in May, there were a series of protests and demonstrations to mark the six-month anniversary of the imposition of the AIA. Gerry Adams, then President of Sinn Féin, also criticized the AIA, saying it secured the partition of the six counties of northern Ireland.[153] Later in May, King informed the House of Commons of the decision to dissolve the Northern Ireland Assembly, and in June, it was officially dissolved. A group of 200 Loyalist protesters gathered outside Stormont, and when trouble erupted the RUC baton-charged the crowd. Inside the debating chamber, 22 Unionist politicians refused to leave the building, including Paisley. Early the next day the RUC removed him. Paisley declared that Northern Ireland was on the verge of civil war. In July, his deputy, Peter Robinson, along with 4,000 Loyalists, staged an early morning protest in which they 'took over' and 'occupied' Hillsborough, County Down, where the AIA was signed.[154]

In October, Charles Haughey, then leader of Fianna Fáil (FF), said that since the signing of the AIA, the position of Nationalists in Northern Ireland had 'seriously worsened' and that when FF returned to government, his party would seek to renegotiate the Agreement, while in November, at a closed meeting where Paisley and Robinson were the main speakers, a new organization, 'Ulster Resistance' was formed to 'take direct action as and when required' to end the AIA. There were further clashes between Loyalists and the RUC the same month. Just before Christmas, Thatcher paid a visit to Northern Ireland, during which she reiterated her Government's commitment to the AIA. In January 1987, the Democratic Unionist Party (DUP) and the Ulster Unionist Party (UUP) organized a petition against the AIA and 400,000 signatures were collected and the petition handed into Buckingham Palace in February. In November, Molyneaux and Paisley led a protest march against the AIA in London, followed by one in Hillsborough.[155]

Links between the British Army and loyalist paramilitaries

The year 1988 was much less eventful. However, in 1989 an event occurred that 'ignited a political furore and led to the progressive exposure of links between security forces and loyalist paramilitaries'.[156] On the afternoon of February 12, two loyalist gunmen used a sledgehammer to smash their way into the north Belfast home of Pat Finucane, a solicitor who was sitting down to Sunday dinner with his wife and their three children. He was first shot twice in front of his children and then 12 times in his face and head as they hid under the table.[157] Three weeks before, the then Junior Home Office minister Douglas Hogg had told the House of Commons there were a number of lawyers in Northern Ireland 'unduly sympathetic to the IRA',[158] subsequently maintaining, when interviewed by the British police, that the timing of the statement was unfortunate, nothing else.[159] It emerged that the loyalist paramilitary intelligence officer responsible for directing the UDA attacks, Brian Nelson was an agent controlled by the British army's euphemistically-named Force Research Unit (FRU), whose job it was to identify potential victims.[160] Ken Barrett, one of Finucane's killers, later fled to Britain where a BBC Panorama team recorded him claiming a police officer had told him Finucane was a senior IRA man: 'The peelers[161] wanted him whacked. We whacked him and that is the end of the story'.[162]

Nelson was a fanatical and sectarian Protestant from Belfast's Shankill Road, who had been recruited in 1985 by British military intelligence to act as an army agent in the UDA, which he had joined a decade earlier. According to Foot, he 'performed his delicate and dangerous new task with great enthusiasm', being provided with a house, a car and £200 per week expenses, all paid for by the British Army (the British taxpayer).[163] In 1987, Nelson went to South Africa to shop for arms for the UDA and supervised the shipment of two huge batches of arms, at least one of which ended up in the hands of the paramilitaries. As Foot points out, throughout Nelson's time in the UDA, he worked closely with army intelligence, whose policy at the time was shamelessly on the side of the Protestant paramilitaries, who were seen as pro-British; and against the IRA who were seen as the enemy, drawing British military intelligence into a gang war. Nelson would pass on the names and addresses of known IRA activists to the UDA, whose gunmen would promptly go out and 'execute' the suspects.[164]

The success of Nelson's work impressed the UDA hierarchy, who appointed him 'head of intelligence'. His role in sectarian murders was eventually discovered by John Stevens, a deputy chief constable who was conducting an inquiry into the relationship between British Army and Protestant paramilitaries such as the UDA. Stevens insisted on Nelson's prosecution, and Nelson was arrested. This caused dismay in the British army and the undercover FRU, but Stevens was adamant and frantic negotiations followed. For nearly two years, Foot informs us, Nelson was held in the relatively comfortable police 'supergrass suite' in Belfast.[165]

When a deal was finally struck in January 1992, Nelson agreed to plead guilty to five conspiracies to murder, and at least four sectarian murder charges against him were dropped, including that of Finucane. In a court case that lasted less than a day, Nelson's real role was effectively covered up, and after a moving tribute to his sterling work for the British army from a then anonymous colonel, Nelson got 10 years. He was released after serving less than half of that and spent the rest of his life under a false identity.[166]

Thatcher's involvement

Stephen Kelly, whose 2021 book, *Margaret Thatcher, the Conservative Party and Northern Ireland, 1975–1990*[167] reveals the extent of collusion between elements of the state and Loyalist paramilitaries throughout Thatcher's premiership, points out that Finucane's murder was only one of several incidents during her Downing Street years in which the state was involved in widespread collusion between Loyalist paramilitary 'death squads' and agencies of the British state.[168] For example, Raymond White, a former head of the RUC special branch, admitted that in 1986 he raised the subject of collusion with Thatcher, seeking legal clarification for the handling of British undercover agents who had penetrated paramilitary groups. After a meeting with Thatcher, he was told, to 'carry on, but don't get caught'.[169] Moreover, in a 2015 interview, Michael Mates, a former Minister at the Northern Ireland Office from 1992 to 1993 during Tory John Major's premiership that followed Thatcher's conceded that the scale of the collusion between the British state and Loyalist paramilitaries during the 1980s was much greater than he had believed it to be at the time.[170]

There were three official British Government inquiries, led by Stevens, concerning alleged collusion in Northern Ireland. In the first published in 1990, Stevens found that collusion was 'neither wide-spread nor institutionalised', but the third and final one published in 2003 found 'collusion in the killing of Finucane between members of the security forces, especially the FRU and Loyalists'.[171] In 2012, the British Government commenced an official review into Finucane's murder. Chairing the review, Desmond De Silva found that employees of the state 'actively facilitated' Finucane's murder, 'through a dark web of collusion between elements of the British security forces and Loyalist paramilitaries' and claimed that successive British governments knew but 'did nothing about it'.[172]

In January 2015, Cameron, publicly placed on the record that 'employees of the state actively furthered and facilitated Patrick Finucane's murder'.[173] In apologizing publicly to the family, he referred to 'shocking levels of state collusion' in the killing of Patrick Finucane.[174] He refused, however, to order a public inquiry. Earlier in 2020, the Boris Johnson Government was urged to have such and inquiry by a wide constituency of people, including four Northern Ireland political parties, the SDLP, the Greens, the Liberal Alliance and Sinn Féin; Finucane's family[175] (his son John is Sinn Féin MP for North Belfast); Taoiseach Micheál Martin;[176] the Labour Party;[177] and both Democrats and Republicans in the US Congress.[178] But in November 2020, the Government refused, a decision that Amnesty International UK described as 'shameful', adding: 'Mr Finucane's family had to live through the horror of witnessing his death, a killing organised in partnership with the State, and they continue to suffer at the Government's hands in being denied the truth'.[179]

Kelly concludes:

> Finucane's assassination at the hands of UFF,[180] together with similar controversial murders by Loyalist paramilitaries during the 1980s, continues to cast a dark shadow over Thatcher's legacy on Northern Ireland. Indeed, Thatcher's association with Northern Ireland during her premiership is further complicated by accusations – which she strenuously denied – that she knowingly supported the British security forces' 'shoot-to-kill' policy, in which many Republican paramilitaries were found in 'compromising situations' and were duly 'executed'.[181]

Frustratingly, Kelly goes on, no one will never know the true extent of Thatcher's involvement. However, the murder of Pat Finucane, together with broader accusations of collusion, 'confirms the argument that throughout her premiership, Thatcher was obsessed with security-related matters in relation to Northern Ireland, channelling much of her energy and thinking into how to tackle paramilitary, chiefly Irish Republican violence'.[182]

In January 1990, the *Belfast Telegraph* published the results of an opinion poll of people in Northern Ireland showing that 68% of Protestants and 62% of Catholics felt that the AIA had made no difference to the political situation in Northern Ireland, while in May 1990, Peter Brooke, then Secretary of State for Northern Ireland, told Unionist leaders that proposed political talks would consider an alternative to the AIA, and agreed to a gap in the meetings of the Anglo-Irish Intergovernmental Conference (AIIC) to allow talks to begin. The AIIC meeting in September 1990 was to be the last before Thatcher's resignation.[183]

Thatcher's anti-Irish racism

Mary Lou McDonald, who has served as President of Sinn Féin since 2018, and Leader of the Opposition in Ireland since 2020, said of Thatcher, at the time of the hunger strikes she was the 'quintessential hate figure', hated 'almost universally by people who would describe themselves as nationalist or republican, not simply Sinn Féiners'.[184] In a reference to Thatcher's refusal to grant the prisoners any privileges, McDonald notes the 'malice with which she approached a situation that was hugely politically fraught, but was also hugely human, and to see the men die, one after the other'.[185] Later, she also said of Sands, 'he stands forever as an enduring symbol of resistance to British imperialism, to British rule'. Referring to Sands's remark that our revenge would be, that it would be the laughter of our children, McDonald concludes, 'In other words, it's not about revenge at all, but it is actually about a society which, to quote the Proclamation, cherishes all of the children equally'.[186]

Lest we are tempted to deduce that Thatcher's contempt for the prisoners was merely 'political', it is instructive to look at several of the anti-Irish racist remarks she made during her premiership and after. First in 1984 during a trip to the United States to meet her political and ideological soulmate, Ronald Reagan, she spoke at a press conference, attended by Niall O'Dowd, an Irish American journalist and the founder and publisher of IrishCentral.com. At that time, O'Dowd points out, there was huge controversy about American weapons being supplied to the RUC that was conducting a shoot-to-kill policy in many parts of Northern Ireland and clearly colluding with Loyalist killers,[187] as the 1989 Patrick Finucane murder was to demonstrate. O'Dowd asked her about the RUC and its reputation and whether she condoned shoot-to-kill:

> There was a moment of quiet. Then suddenly I heard her stentorian tones. 'Stand up!' she demanded. 'Stand up and explain what you mean'. Suddenly every one in the room was staring at me, and I felt the full power of the Iron Lady's piercing stare.[188]

O'Dowd explains the reason for her reaction. She was upset that the 'trivial matter of police collusion and American weapons for the RUC' coming from 'an Irish ingrate' being brought up at a press conference on world matters (I would add she was obviously also uncomfortable about the second part of the question). Her response therefore was to ridicule the question and to ridicule O'Dowd.[189] The media were fawning over her, he informs us, 'even when she praised South Africa, supported the Chilean junta and the Khmer Rouge'. 'She clearly disliked the Irish', he goes on, 'and especially the whole notion of Northern Ireland being less British than Finchley'. Finchley was Thatcher's constituency.[190]

Second, State papers released in 2018 revealed that in June 1988 in an exchange between Thatcher and former Taoiseach Charles Haughey, she said to Haughey (note her use of 'your people' juxtaposed with 'us', and the racist stereotype, concerning why people move to England):

> Your people come over to us. I wish they wouldn't. They come looking for housing and services. It's the same in Northern Ireland. If there was a vote tomorrow they would vote to stay with us. They have better conditions in Northern Ireland and in England.[191]

Third, former Labour Northern Ireland Secretary Peter Mandelson recalled how the only time she spoke to him was on the day he was appointed to the post in 1999. She unambiguously revealed her anti-Irish racism. As he puts it:

> She came up to me and she said, 'I've got one thing to say to you, my boy ... you can't trust the Irish, they are all liars, liars, and that's what you have to remember, so just don't forget it'. With that she waltzed off and that was my only personal exposure to her.[192]

Notes

1   More than half of voters in Northern Ireland want a referendum on a united Ireland in the next five years, according to a series of polls commissioned by *The Sunday Times* in 2021. Scotland and Wales also face escalating calls for independence. As *The Irish Times* points out, 'the findings highlight some of the difficulties facing British prime minister Boris Johnson as he struggles to keep his country together following its departure from the European Union' (see chapter 10). 'More than half in North want vote on a united Ireland, poll finds', *The Irish Times,* January 24. https://www.irishtimes.com/news/politics/more-than-half-in-north-want-vote-on-a-united-ireland-poll-finds-1.4466547.

2   Gilmore. 2016. Connolly, who was born in Edinburgh, deserted from the British Army in 1889, having served in Ireland. He became a socialist, and in 1896 moved to Dublin as an organizer of the Dublin Socialist Society, founding the Irish Socialist Republican Party in the same year. Simkin. 2022.

3   RTÉ (Raidió Teilifis Éireann). 2022.

4   *Morning Star.* 2021.

5   https://www.rte.ie/centuryireland/index.php/articles/what-was-the-easter-rising.

6   Dorney, John. 2012a. 'The Irish War of Independence – a brief overview', *The Irish Story.* September 18. https://www.theirishstory.com/2012/09/18/the-irish-war-of-independence-a-brief-overview/#.YRYG7IhKgUU.

7   RTÉ. 2022.

8   Wallenfeldt, Jeff and Lotha, Gloria. 2020. 'The Troubles: Northern Ireland history', *Britannica,* August 21. https://www.britannica.com/event/The-Troubles-Northern-Ireland-history.

9   Ibid.

10 Ibid.

11 Ibid.

12 *BBC News.* 1969. '1969: Ulster's B Specials to be disbanded', October 10. http://news.bbc.co.uk/onthisday/hi/dates/stories/october/10/newsid_3146000/3146929.stm.

13 Wallenfeldt and Lotha. 2020.

14 Ibid.

15 Dorney, John. 2012b. '9 August 1971, Internment is introduced in Northern Ireland', *The Irish Story.* https://www.theirishstory.com/2012/08/10/today-in-irish-history-9-august-1971-internment-is-introduced-in-northern-ireland/#.YRTixIhKgUU.

16 CAIN Web Service. 2021a. 'Internment – Summary of Main Events'. https://cain.ulster.ac.uk/events/intern/sum.htm.

17 Moriarty, Gerry. 2019. 'Internment explained: When was it introduced and why?', *The Irish Times,* August 9. Operation Demetrius began at the height of

the Troubles, Friday, August 9, 2019. https://www.irishtimes.com/news/poli
tics/internment-explained-when-was-it-introduced-and-why-1.3981598.

18 Ibid.

19 Hennessy, Mark. 2014. 'British ministers sanctioned torture of NI internees',
The Irish Times, June 5. https://www.irishtimes.com/news/politics/british-m
inisters-sanctioned-torture-of-ni-internees-1.1820882.

20 Video RTÉ Investigations Unit: The Torture Files, broadcast June 4, 2014.
https://www.rte.ie/news/player/prime-time-web/2014/0604/.

21 Hennessy. 2014.

22 Ibid.

23 Erwin, Alan. 2019. '"Hooded men": court rules treatment of men would be
torture if deployed today', *The Irish Times,* September 20. https://www.irish
times.com/news/crime-and-law/hooded-men-court-rules-treatment-of-men-
would-be-torture-if-deployed-today-1.4024773.

24 Ibid.

25 Hannan, Martin. 2021. 'Northern Ireland: Impact of internment still felt by
many 50 years on', *The National,* August 14. https://www.thenational.scot/
news/19513550.northern-ireland-impact-internment-still-felt-many-50-years/.

26 Ibid.

27 CAIN Web Service. 1972, compiled by Martin Melaugh, '"Bloody Sunday",
Derry, 30 January 1972 - Circumstances in which people were killed'. https://
cain.ulster.ac.uk/events/bsunday/circum.htm.

28 McDonald, Henry, Bowcott, Owen and Mulholland, Hélène. 2010. 'Bloody
Sunday report: David Cameron apologises for "unjustifiable" shootings', *The
Guardian,* June 15. https://www.theguardian.com/uk/2010/jun/15/blood
y-sunday-report-saville-inquiry.

29 O'Kane, Maggie and Pallister, David. 2000. 'Heath "approved Londonderry
massacre"', *The Guardian,* November 23. https://amp.theguardian.com/poli
tics/2000/nov/23/uk.bloodysunday.

30 Happold, Tom. 2003. 'Heath gives Bloody Sunday evidence', *The Guardian,*
January 14. https://www.theguardian.com/politics/2003/jan/14/northernirela
nd.devolution1.

31 Cited in Happold. 2003.

32 O'Kane and Pallister. 2000.

33 Ibid.

34 *BBC News.* 2010. 'The Saville Inquiry 2003', *BBC News,* June 11. https://
www.bbc.co.uk/news/10181619.

35 Ibid.

36 Foy, Henry. 2010. 'Bloody Sunday: Saville report v Widgery report'. https://
www.theguardian.com/uk/2010/jun/15/bloody-sunday-saville-report-widgery.

37 *BBC News.* 2010.

38 Ibid.

39 McDonald, Henry, Bowcott, Owen and Mulholland, Hélène. 2010.

40 Stratton. 2010.

41 Stratton, Allegra. 2010. https://www.theguardian.com/commentisfree/2010/
jun/15/david-cameron-bloody-sunday-apology.

42 *BBC News.* 2010. 'Bloody Sunday: PM David Cameron's full statement', June
15. https://www.bbc.co.uk/news/10322295.

43 Stratton. 2010.

44 Cited in Stratton. 2010.

45 McDonald, Henry, Bowcott, Owen and Mulholland, Hélène. 2010.

46 Ibid.

47 Cited in McDonald, Henry, Bowcott, Owen and Mulholland, Hélène. 2010.

48 Ibid.

49   Campbell, John. 1993. *Edward Heath*, pp. 404–405.
50   Mullins, Bill. 2021. 'How militant trade unionism defeated the 1971 Indus-
      trial Relations Act', *The Socialist,* February, 24. https://www.socialistparty.
      org.uk/issue/1122/32086/24-02-2021/how-militant-trade-unionism-defea
      ted-the-1971-industrial-relations-act.
51   Mullins. 2021.
52   Cited in Mullins. 2021.
53   Mullins. 2021.
54   Ibid. See chapter 6 for an examination of the Thatcher Government.
55   Heath, Edward. 1998. *The course of my life: the autobiography of Edward Heath*,
      London: Hodder and Stoughton.
56   Ibid., p. 455.
57   Ibid.
58   e.g. Latour, Vincent. 2017. 'Between consensus, consolidation and crisis:
      Immigration and integration in 1970s Britain', p. 2.
59   The use of 'racialised' here is crucial. As noted in the Introduction and as
      developed later in the book while for Heath, like Thatcher (see later in this
      chapter and chapter 6) it was too many 'non-White immigrants' (colour-
      coded racism); for others, such as Theresa May and Boris Johnson (see chapters
      9 and 10) it was, in general, too many central and eastern Europeans (non-
      colour-coded xeno-racism) and asylum-seekers (hybridist racism), although it
      is crucial to stress that the effects of May's 'really hostile environment' was
      colour-coded too, as we shall see, impacting on a wide constituency of
      people, including notoriously, 'the Windrush generation'.
60   Heath. 1998, p. 456.
61   Ibid.
62   Ibid.
63   Ibid.
64   Latour. 2017. p. 3.
65   Home Office. *Immigration Act 1971.* https://www.legislation.gov.uk/ukpga/
      1971/77/contents.
66   Cited in Travis, Alan. 2002. 'Ministers saw law's 'racism' as defensible', *The Guar-
      dian*, January 1. https://www.theguardian.com/politics/2002/jan/01/uk.race.
67   Layton-Henry, p. 85.
68   Travis. 2002.
69   Cited in Travis. 2002.
70   Ibid.
71   Ibid.
72   Ibid.
73   Ibid. The verb 'to swamp' is common in racist discourse.
74   Layton-Henry, p. 85.
75   Munnion, Christopher. 1972. 'The African who kicked out the Asians, who said
      Hitler was right, who has made his country a state sinister', *The New York Times*,
      November 12. https://www.nytimes.com/1972/11/12/archives/if-idi-amin-
      of-uganda-is-a-madman-hes-a-ruthless-and-cunning-one.html. Travel writer
      Paul Theroux once wrote, 'the reaction of most Africans and Europeans in
      East Africa to the Asian presence was flagrantly racist' (cited in Alibhai-Brown.
      2014). Further underlining the point made in the Introduction that anyone
      can be racist, Alibhai-Brown, herself a British Asian, originally from Uganda,
      refers to 'hideous black and white prejudices' there. She also notes that some
      older people 'have been unable to talk about the humiliation they went
      through'. At the same time, according to Alibhai-Brown, most Asians there
      'were deeply racist, unable to imagine marrying Africans and living with them
      as equals'. 'Like all racists', she goes on, 'we fantasised that Africans wanted to

possess our women. So rumours spread that hundreds of "our" girls were raped by black Ugandans', adding that these were 'unsubstantiated wild allegations' (Alibhai-Brown. 2014).

76 Lofchie, Michael F. 1972. 'The Uganda coup – class action by the military', *The Journal of Modern African Studies*, 10 (1) May.

77 Alibhai-Brown, Yasmin. 2014. 'Racism and the truth about the Ugandan Asians'.

78 Ibid.

79 Ibid.

80 Layton-Henry, p. 86.

81 Ibid.

82 Ibid.

83 Walker, Martin. 1977. *The National Front,* Fontana.

84 Ibid., p. 127.

85 Copping. 1972, pp. 6–7.

86 Layton-Henry. 1992, pp. 86–87.

87 Ibid., p. 181.

88 Cited in *The Irish Times,* 'Powell right – Thatcher', November 23, 1998. https://www.irishtimes.com/news/powell-right-thatcher-1.217653?mode=amp.

89 Thatcher, Margaret. 2002. *Statecraft.*

90 Layton-Henry, p. 212, Note 44.

91 Neoliberalism or neoliberal capitalism has had an enormous impact on the world. George Monbiot has described it as a conscious attempt to reshape human life and shift the locus of power. It views competition as the defining characteristic of human relations, recatagorizing citizens as consumers, 'whose democratic choices are best exercised by buying and selling, a process that rewards merit and punishes inefficiency'. It maintains that '"the market" delivers benefits that could never be achieved by planning' (Monbiot. 2016. 'Neoliberalism – the ideology at the root of all our problems'). Given the central focus of this book, neoliberal capitalism will not be dealt with here, although I will allude briefly to some of its key manifestations under the Thatcher regime. Much has been written critiquing neoliberal capitalism. For a Marxist and Keynesian critique, see Saad-Filho, Alfredo. 2008. 'Marxian and Keynesian critiques of neoliberalism'. In Panitch, Leo and Leys, Colin Leys, *Socialist Register.* https://www.researchgate.net/publication/282184624_MARXIAN_AND_KEYNESIAN_CRITIQUES_OF_NEO LIBERALISM. For some recent texts, see for example, Maisuria, Alpesh. 2022. 'Introduction to Marxism for critical educators', in Maisuria, Alpesh (ed.) *Encyclopaedia of Marxism and Education*, The Netherlands: Brill Publishing; and Maisuria, Alpesh. 2021. 'Antonio Gramsci – hegemony'. In Themelis, Spyros (ed.) *Critical Reflections on the Language of Neoliberalism in Education Dangerous Words and Discourses of Possibility*, London: Routledge.

92 *BBC News*. 2004. 'Thatcher's Class of '79'. http://news.bbc.co.uk/1/shared/spl/hi/uk_politics/04/thatchers_government/html/whitelaw.stm.

93 Layton-Henry. 1992, p. 94.

94 UK Polling Report 1974–1979. http://ukpollingreport.co.uk/voting-intention-1974-1979.

95 Thatcher, Margaret. 1978. 'TV interview for Granada *World in Action* ("rather swamped")', January 27. Margaret Thatcher Foundation. https://www.margaretthatcher.org/document/103485.

96 Trilling, Daniel. 2013. 'Thatcher: the PM who brought racism in from the cold', Verso Blog, April 10. https://www.versobooks.com/blogs/1282-thatcher-the-pm-who-brought-racism-in-from-the-cold.

97 Thatcher, Margaret. 1978.

98 Ibid.

99   Ibid.
100 UK Polling Report 1974–1979.
101 Trilling, Daniel. 2013.
102 Ibid.
103 Cited in Trilling. 2013.
104 Layton-Henry, p. 95.
105 Trilling, Daniel. 2013.
106 Layton-Henry, p. 96.
107 Gardner, Bill. 2014. 'From "shrill" housewife to Downing Street: the changing voice of Margaret Thatcher'. Gardner describes her new voice as powerful and persuasive, but at the same time soft and cajoling. Her distinctive voice, he suggests, was one of Thatcher's 'most potent political weapons'.
108 Monetarism is mainly associated with the work of Milton Friedman who criti-cised Keynesian economics (after John Maynard Keynes) – fighting economic downturns with government spending, and advocated slowing the growth rate of the money supply instead. With more cash held in bank accounts, it is believed, and less being spent, money supply tightens and demand for goods drops. Lower demand for goods should make them cheaper, lowering inflation.
109 *The Independent*. 2013. 'Margaret Thatcher's timeline: From Grantham to the House of Lords, via Arthur Scargill and the Falklands War'. For a critique of this concept, see Moore, Rowan. 2014. 'Margaret Thatcher began Britain's obsession with property. It's time to end it', *The Guardian*, April 6. https://amp.theguardian.com/society/2014/apr/06/margaret-thatcher-britains-obsession-property-right-to-buy.
110 O'Connell, Hugh. 2013. '6 key moments that defined Margaret Thatcher's relationship with Ireland', *The Journal,* April 9. https://www.thejournal.ie/margaret-thatcher-ireland-haughey-north-861575-Apr2013/.
111 Thoburn, Ethan. 2020. 'Airey Neave: The man who helped make Margaret Thatcher', The Bruges Group, April 3. https://www.brugesgroup.com/blog/airey-neave-the-man-who-helped-make-margaret-thatcher.
112 O'Connell, Hugh. 2013.
113 Routledge, Paul. 2019. 'Why Margaret Thatcher's advisor Airey Neave became an INLA target 40 years ago', *The Mirror*, March 29. https://www.mirror.co.uk/news/uk-news/margaret-thatchers-advisor-airey-neave-14205986.
114 Routledge, 2019.
115 Ibid.
116 Ibid.
117 Ibid.
118 O'Connell, Hugh. 2013.
119 Taylor, Peter. 2021. 'Bobby Sands: The hunger strike that changed the course of N Ireland's conflict', *BBC News*, May 1. https://www.bbc.co.uk/news/stories-56937259.
120 Taylor. 2021.
121 Cited in Taylor. 2021.
122 Taylor. 2021.
123 Ibid.
124 Cited in Taylor. 2021.
125 Sands was born in 1954 in Rathcoole, a predominantly loyalist district of north Belfast. The sectarian realities of ghetto life materialized early in Bobby's life when in 1962, his family were forced to move home owing to loyalist intimidation. He was later to write, 'I was only a working-class boy from a Nationalist ghetto, but it is repression that creates the revolutionary spirit of freedom. I shall not settle until I achieve liberation of my country, until Ire-land becomes a sovereign, independent socialist republic' (cited in Bobby Sands Trust. 2019a. 'Bobby Sands MP'). His first job was as an apprentice

coach builder. He worked there for less than a year, enduring constant harassment from his Protestant co-workers, which according to several co-workers he ignored completely, as he wished to learn a meaningful trade (O'Hearn. *Bobby Sands: Nothing but an Unfinished Song*). He was eventually confronted after leaving his shift in January 1971 by a number of his co-workers wearing the armbands of the local Ulster loyalist tartan gang, held at gunpoint and told that the factory was off-limits to 'Fenian scum' and to never come back if he valued his life. He later said that this event was the point at which he decided that militancy was the only solution. In June 1972, the family were intimidated out of their home in Doon-beg Drive, Rathcoole, and moved into the newly built Twinbrook estate on the fringe of nationalist West Belfast. Bernadette again recalled: 'We had suffered intimidation for about eighteen months before we were actually put out. We had always been used to having Protestant friends. Bobby had gone around with Catholics and Protestants, but it ended up when everything erupted, that the friends he went about with for years were the same ones who helped to put his family out of their home. In December 1971, when the Shankill Road was packed with Saturday shoppers, a green car pulled up outside the Balmoral Fur-niture Company at the corner of Carlow Street and Shankill Road. One of the occupants got out and left a box containing a bomb on the step outside the front door. The person got back into the car and it sped away. The bomb exploded moments later, bringing down most of the building on top of those inside the shop and on passers by outside (*The Troubles: A Chronology of the Northern Ireland Conflict* magazine, Glenravel publications, Issue #8. pp. 36–37, 51). Four people were killed. The bombing was followed by a gun-battle in which two men were wounded. Sands was in a car near the scene with three other young men. The RUC captured them and found a revolver in the car. The men were arrested and subjected to brutal interrogations for six days. Sands refused to answer any ques-tions during his interrogation, except his name, age, and address. (Bobby Sands Trust. 2019). Sands was convicted in April 1973, sentenced to five years impri-sonment, and released in April 1976 (Hanke, Philip. 2011. *Bobby Sands – An Irish Martyr?* GRIN Verlag. p. 20). Peter Taylor argues that the Provisional IRA bombed Balmoral in retaliation for the McGurk's Bar bombing a week before that had killed 15 Catholic civilians. (Taylor, Peter. 1999. *Loyalists*, London: Bloomsbury Publishing Plc. p. 90). Upon his release, he returned to his family home in West Belfast, and resumed his active role in the Provisional IRA. Bobby set himself to work tackling the social issues which affected the area. Immediately after his sentencing, Sands was implicated in a fight and sent to the punishment block in Crumlin Road Prison. The cells contained a bed, a mattress, a chamber pot, and a water container. Books, radios, and other personal items were not permitted, although a Bible and some Catholic pamphlets were provided. Sands refused to wear a prison uniform, so was kept naked in his cell for twenty-two days without access to bedding from 7:30 am to 8:30 pm each day. https://en. wikipedia.org/wiki/Bobby_Sands.

126 Taylor. 2021.
127 'Fermanagh and South Tyrone 1973–1982'. https://www.ark.ac.uk/elections/cfst.htm.
128 Cited in Taylor. 2021.
129 Bobby Sands Trust. 2019b. 'Prison diary'. https://www.bobbysandstrust.com/writings/prison-diary/.
130 'The Troubles: A Chronology of the Conflict – 1976'.
131 Bobby Sands Tribute. Undated. 'Dirty protest'. http://bobbysandstribute.weebly.com/maze—dirty.html.
132 Ibid.
133 Cited in The Bobby Sands Tribute. Undated.

134   Ibid.
135   Ibid.
136   Ibid.
137   Ibid.
138   Margaret Thatcher Foundation. 2021. '1981. March 5. Margaret Thatcher. Speech in Belfast'. https://www.margaretthatcher.org/document/104589.
139   Taylor. 2021.
140   Bobby Sands Trust. 2019a. 'Prison diary'.
141   Taylor. 1997, p. 237.
142   Taylor. 2021.
143   Cited in Taylor. 2021.
144   Tharoor, Ishaan. 2016. 'The angry letter Bernie Sanders wrote to Margaret Thatcher', *The Washington Post,* February 19. https://www.washingtonpost.com/news/worldviews/wp/2016/02/19/the-angry-letter-bernie-sanders-wrote-to-margaret-thatcher/.
145   Taylor. 2021.
146   Ibid.
147   Campbell, p. 427.
148   The Editors of Encyclopaedia Britannica. 2021. https://www.britannica.com/event/Anglo-Irish-Agreement.
149   CAIN. 2021b. 'Anglo-Irish Agreement – Chronology of events'. https://cain.ulster.ac.uk/events/aia/chron.htm.
150   Ibid.
151   Ibid.
152   Ibid.
153   Ibid.
154   Ibid.
155   Ibid.
156   Carroll, Rory. 2020. 'Pat Finucane's murder: a pitiless act and a political storm', *The Guardian,* November 30. https://www.theguardian.com/uk-news/2020/nov/30/pat-finucane-murder-a-pitiless-act-and-a-political-storm.
157   Carroll. 2020.
158   Ibid.
159   Hopkins, Nick and Norton-Taylor, Richard. 2001. 'Police talk to ex-minister Hogg about Ulster killing', *The Guardian,* June 13. https://www.theguardian.com/uk/2001/jun/13/northernireland.richardnortontaylor.
160   Carroll. 2020.
161   'Peeler' is Irish and British slang for police officer.
162   Bowcott, Owen. 2006. 'Loyalist gunman who killed Pat Finucane goes free after three years under early release pact', *The Guardian,* May 24. https://www.theguardian.com/uk/2006/may/24/northernireland.northernireland.
163   Foot, Paul. 2003. 'Brian Nelson', *The Guardian,* April 17. https://www.theguardian.com/news/2003/apr/17/guardianobituaries.northernireland.
164   Foot. 2003.
165   Ibid.
166   Ibid.
167   Kelly, Stephen. 2021a. *Margaret Thatcher, the Conservative Party and the Northern Ireland Conflict, 1975–1990,* London: Bloomsbury Publishing.
168   Kelly, Stephen. 2021b. 'Margaret Thatcher, state collusion, and the murder of Pat Finucane', *LSE British Politics and Policy,* March 3. https://blogs.lse.ac.uk/politicsandpolicy/margaret-thatcher-state-collusion-and-the-murder-of-pat-finucane/.
169   Cited in Kelly. 2021b.
170   Kelly. 2021b.
171   Cited in Kelly. 2021b.

172 Kelly. 2021b.

173 Cited in Kelly. 2021b.

174 Amnesty International UK. 2020. 'Northern Ireland: "Shameful" refusal to agree public inquiry in Finucane murder will undermine confidence in rule of law', November 30. https://www.amnesty.org.uk/press-releases/northern-ireland-shameful-refusal-agree-public-inquiry-finucane-murder-will.

175 Finucane, John. 2020. 'The British government is still hiding the truth about my father's murder', *The Guardian*, December 4. https://www.theguardian.com/commentisfree/2020/dec/04/british-government-father-murder-bor is-johnson-pat-finucane-loyalist-northern-ireland.

176 The Newsroom. 2020. 'Taoiseach Micheal Martin wants Boris Johnson to hold full public inquiry into at Finucane murder, family say', *News Letter*. https://www.newsletter.co.uk/news/crime/taoiseach-micheal-martin-wants-boris-johnson-hold-full-public-inquiry-pat-finucane-murder-family-say-3048470.

177 *BBC News*. 2020. 'Pat Finucane: Labour urges Boris Johnson to order inquiry', October 27. https://www.bbc.co.uk/news/uk-northern-ireland-54698006.

178 Forrest, Adam. 2020. 'US politicians urge Boris Johnson to set up public inquiry into murder of human rights lawyer,' *The Independent*, 26 November. https://www.independent.co.uk/news/uk/politics/boris-johnson-finucane-murder-us-congress-b1762173.html.

179 Amnesty International UK. 2020.

180 The UFF (Ulster Freedom Fighters) was a group within the UDA tasked with launching paramilitary attacks. The UDA used the cover name UFF so that the UDA would not be outlawed. The UDA finally became proscribed as a 'terrorist group' in August 1992. Home Office. 2013. 'Proscribed terrorist groups or organisations', July 12. https://web.archive.org/web/20100118084213/http://security.homeoffice.gov.uk/legislation/current-legislation/terrorism-act-2000/proscribed-groups.html.

181 Kelly. 2021b.

182 Ibid.

183 CAIN. 2021b.

184 *BBC News*. 2018. 'Margaret Thatcher was the "quintessential hate figure", says Mary Lou McDonald', December 28. https://www.bbc.com/news/uk-nor thern-ireland-46611049.amp.

185 Cited in *BBC News*, 2018.

186 Cited in McClements, Freya. 2021. 'What Bobby Sands means to me: "The hunger strikers chose to die. Daddy didn't"', *The Irish Times*, April 3. https://www.irishtimes.com/culture/heritage/what-bobby-sands-means-to-me-the-hunger-strikers-chose-to-die-daddy-didn-t-1.4525223. McClements is refer-ring to the 'Proclamation of the Irish Republic, 24 April 1916'. https://cain.ulster.ac.uk/issues/politics/docs/pir24416.htm.

187 O'Dowd, Niall. 2013. 'Margaret Thatcher was anti-Irish – my encounter with the British PM in Texas', *Irish Central*, April 13. https://www.irishcentral.com/opinion/niallodowd/margaret-thatcher-was-anti-irish-my-encounter-with-the-british-pm-in-texas-202833091-238178111.

188 Ibid.

189 Ibid.

190 Ibid.

191 Donaghy, Gerard. 2018. 'Thatcher "wished the Irish wouldn't come to Britain", State papers reveal', *Irish Post*. https://www.irishpost.com/news/thatcher-wished-irish-wouldnt-come-britain-state-papers-reveal-162970.

192 *The Irish Times*. 2013. 'Thatcher believed the Irish were "all liars"', April 18. https://www.irishtimes.com/news/thatcher-believed-the-irish-were-all-liars-1.1363098.

6 Thatcher, immigration control, uprisings; imperialism resurrected; apartheid; and promoting British culture (1981–1990)

'Race realists' promoting scientific racism in 1980s

In chapter 3, I began by suggesting the Holocaust was a turning point for scientific racism in that racist and fascist scientists had to hide their unrepentant opinions. In that chapter, I referred to Angela Saini's book *Superior: The Return of Race Science*.[1] In a chapter entitled 'Race realists', Saini paints a vivid picture of the palpable fear that Barry Mehler, a Jewish historian of eugenics and genocide, felt in the 1980s on discovering an active network of 'race scientists' working long after the end of World War II. She points to shadow financing by the extremist US non-profit Pioneer Fund, which supports studies on eugenics, race and intelligence, and outlets such as the pro-eugenics so-called science journal *Mankind Quarterly*. She also notes that in the 1980s, the academic Ralph Scott, a contributor to that outlet, was appointed by the administration of US President Ronald Reagan to serve on the Iowa Advisory Commission on Civil Rights.[2]

SECTION 1: COLOUR-CODED RACISM AND THE UPRISINGS

Immigration control

The 1981 British Nationality Act

As noted at the end of the last chapter, like Heath's 1979 victory in 1970, racism played a key role because of Thatcher's public identification of the Tory Party with a harsh stance on immigration. In 1981, her administration passed the British Nationality Act. It received Royal Assent on October 30, 1981, and came into force on January 1, 1983. The legislation made significant changes to the requirements for British citizenship, with citizenship reclassified into three categories: British citizenship, British Dependent Territories citizenship and British Overseas citizenship.[3]

Before the Act, any person born in Britain was entitled to British citizenship. However, after the Act, at least one parent of a child born in the

DOI: 10.4324/9781003198673-10

UK had to be a British citizen or a permanent resident to claim citizenship. The legislation therefore left a generation of effectively 'stateless' children, whose citizenship was demoted to Overseas Citizen status, despite their having been born and raised in the UK.[4] As the Runnymede Trust points out, British Overseas Citizenship was more symbolic than functional, since it was not recognized for immigration control in other countries. Canada, for example, viewed Overseas Citizens passports as 'not a passport at all' unless it included a stamp confirming the right of readmission to Britain.[5] As a result, nearly 21,000 people of Indian ancestry were left stateless, while White South Africans, on the other hand, continued as citizens because of direct ancestry.[6] Wives of British men could no longer acquire British nationality purely by marriage.

As Radhika Natarajan argues, by discarding the social and cultural ties of the Empire, Thatcher did away with old ideas of 'Britishness' based on 'allegiance, desire, history and character'. From the passing of the Act onwards, it was 'blood' that mattered.[7] This helps us to understand why, in the early 1980s, as we shall see, the blood to be protected was that of the Britons in the Malvinas, and not the blood spilled in New Cross, Brixton, Southall, Toxteth and Moss Side.[8] Thatcher's brand of Britishness, she goes on, allowed White Britons to see themselves as the aggrieved party in the face of what they perceived to be migrants' innate cultural differences and refusal to integrate.[9] It celebrated what the 'British character' had done in the world, which for Thatcher, as we saw in the last chapter in her 'swamping remarks' was the creation of 'democracy' and 'law' in Britain and then taking both to the world (read 'Empire and colonies'). What else could White British people do other than be 'hostile' to Black and Brown people 'coming in' and refusing to adopt 'British values?' 'Hostile', as we have seen and will continue to see, is a commonplace adjective in Tory discourse and policy towards those wishing to live in the UK.

The Thatcher Government's British Nationality Act defined British Citizenship for the first time in law and was a culmination of the rhetoric concerning who counted as 'British'. Moreover, as Natarajan points out, 'the exclusionary implications of the British Nationality Act were fully understood at the time by Commonwealth Citizens who equated immigration laws with their standing in Britain'.[10] Summing up, she writes, 'They argued for their right to belong in terms of Britishness, which they understood to be broad and based in a shared history of empire'. Natarajan then cites Sivanandan's (originally from Sri Lanka as discussed in the Appendix to chapter 3), namely his deservedly oft-quoted aphorism, 'we are here because you were there'.[11]

Change in the 'primary purpose rule'

Prior to the Thatcher Government changes, the primary purpose rule stated that entry clearance to the UK would be refused if a person seeking admission for marriage to a person already present and settled or who is on the same occasion being admitted for settlement unless the entry clearance officer (ECO) is satisfied that it is not the primary purpose of the intended marriage to obtain admission to the UK, and that it is intended that they will live together permanently as husband and wife and that they had met.[12] In 1980, it was changed as follows:

1   An applicant had to satisfy the ECO *both* that they intended to live together as man and wife *and* that the primary purpose of the marriage was not to obtain admission to the UK. In other words the two elements of a 'marriage of convenience' were separated for the first time as two separate tests.
2   A husband could only be admitted if the woman was a British citizen either born in the UK or had a parent born there.
3   If the applicant failed to meet either of these qualifications, refusal was mandatory. There was no discretion either at the time of decision or on appeal.[13]

In 1982, faced with a challenge from the European Court of Human Rights, the Government proposed amending the rule by removing '2'. This was defeated in January 1983, so in February 1983, it added a new rule: the burden of proof was on *the applicant* to prove that the primary purpose of the marriage was not to obtain admission to the UK. Entry could thereafter be refused if the ECO was not satisfied that this was the case. In 1985, following a European Court of Human Rights ruling that the UK violated the prohibition of sex discrimination, the rules were changed to wives as well as husbands.[14]

New visa restrictions

In 1985, new racist visa restrictions were announced by the Thatcher Government for India, Pakistan, Bangladesh, Nigeria and Ghana,[15] citing increasing numbers of refusals of admission as a reason. The Home Secretary Douglas Hurd gave figures of a rise from 18,000 in 1985 to 22,000 in the year ended June 1986.[16] Speaking in a House of Commons debate in October 1986, Labour MP Gerald Kaufman noted that, despite 'that increase – and the rise is offered on a very dubious statistical basis – the increase of 4,000 does not seem large against the figure of 8.5 million arrivals in Britain from non-EEC countries during 1985'.[17] Kaufman pointed out that in 1985 the number coming to the UK from the five countries as a proportion of the 8 million arrivals, those arriving from non-EEC countries was just 0.07%, and that there was a disproportion between refusals of people coming from the five. Figures show that in the year ended May 1986, a Bangladeshi had one chance in 20 of being refused entry; for a Canadian it was one in 7,857, while a Bangladeshi was 393 times more likely than a Canadian to be refused admission.[18] He went on to tell MPs how when he visited Heathrow to see the results of people trying to get to the UK before the change in rules, he saw how some were made to wait in a series of ante-chambers (small rooms where one waits before an interview) until the hard-pressed immigration staff were able to conduct the interview, while others were held in large numbers in the gate rooms, where passengers await the call for departure.[19] He described conditions of gross overcrowding, with some having to sleep on the floor, and 'when wanting to go to the lavatory' being 'sent in batches of 10 under escort as if they were prisoners'.[20] Kaufman continued:

> At night many were held in a detention centre. Others were held in a youth custody centre. One group was sent as far afield as Canterbury prison. All of these people sent to penal institutions, whether admitted to this country or sent home, were citizens of friendly countries innocent of any crime. They were not even charged with any crime. The treatment of these people was shameful. We all know that they would not have been treated like that if their skins had been white.[21]

He later made the cutting point that the Home Secretary needs a visa to go to India, an Indian now needs a visa to come here, Hurd also needs a visa to go to South Africa, but a White South African does not need a visa to come to this country. Thus the 'measure is specifically aimed at black people alone'[22] (Kaufman is using 'black', as was common at the time, in an inclusive way to refer to all people of colour, as is Nellist in the indented quote just below).

In the same debate, Jeremy Corbyn made the point that the immigration panic created by the Government 'was essentially the product of a series of subjective and racist decisions by immigration officers over the past year to create just the atmosphere in which visas could be introduced and to create a racist hype for further restrictive immigration legislation later?',[23] while fellow socialist MP and Marxist Dave Nellist stated that, whereas in the past the Tories:

> had encouraged immigration to provide cheap labour for employers and industrialists ... the British capitalist economy has declined from the illusion of the booms of the 1950s and 1960s to the realities of the recessions and slumps of the 1970s and 1980s ... [now], together with the gutter press of this country, they are carrying out a relentless campaign, especially among the unemployed, the elderly and those in receipt of supplementary benefits, to portray black people as the cause of the increase in social problems through talk of floods of immigrants ... Chief among them has been the Prime Minister.[24]

Growing pressures on immigration detention accommodation resulted in additional capacity being provided in a floating detention centre. In 1987,

The Earl William, a former cross-channel ferry was refitted as a static 'secure' holding facility moored at Harwich, and contracted into service under the management of private company Securicor, who had been running immigration detention facilities since 1970. In October of the same year, the strongest gale to hit England in 200 years broke the vessel free of its moorings and it ran aground on a sandbank. Although none of its 78 detainees was injured,[25] they had to be rescued.[26] Also in 1987, the Carriers Liability Act imposed fines on carriers of £1,000 for each 'illegal' entrant brought to the UK (the fine was doubled under the John Major Government in August 1991 and two years later extended to cover passengers without transit visas where these were required).[27] Daniel Trilling points out that the Tories' hard line on immigration policy under Thatcher also extended to refugees, giving rise to the modern stereotype of the 'bogus asylum-seeker'.[28]

Thatcher, polygamy and repatriation

Cabinet Office files released in 2016, covering immigration policy from 1982 to 1986, reveal that Thatcher was strongly opposed to admitting women to the UK who were the 'second wives' of men in polygamous marriages. However, the Government was concerned about how Commonwealth countries, the European Court of Human Rights and its own MPs would react to changes in policy.[29] Nevertheless, in March 1986 Home Secretary Douglas Hurd even contemplated breaking the law over the issue of 'second wives' in polygamous marriages. He wrote, 'There is no way in which the issue of entry clearance applications by polygamous wives can be made acceptable to public – or Parliamentary – opinion', saying until the law was changed, he was prepared to 'postpone compliance with his legal obligation' to admit 'second wives'.[30] The Attorney-General Michael Havers responded that, 'Such unlawful action by the government cannot be contemplated'. Thatcher was on Hurd's side over the matter which he referred to as 'a mischief'. A note from one of her advisers stated that she 'strongly shares the Home Secretary's view that an early change in the law is required'. Indeed when Hurd suggested making future polygamous marriages invalid but recognizing existing ones, she wrote in the margin, 'We do not recognise polygamy at all'.[31] Lastly, on a memo from Foreign Secretary Geoffrey Howe outlining the difficulties involved in changing the law, Thatcher wrote, with multiple underlinings, 'The country would be with us on this. We are crazy to discriminate in favour of the coloured Commonwealth against the UK'.[32]

The Thatcher Government also discussed moving the queues of people wanting to enter the UK from Heathrow to their countries of origin,[33] and the scheme to pay immigrants who wanted to return to their country of origin – used by 100 or 200 people a year – was rebranded 'assisted return' because 'voluntary repatriation', its original designation, sounded too much like the kind of repatriation that was advocated by Powell.[34]

Prelude to the uprisings

The New Cross house fire and Thatcher's response

On January 18, 1981 in the early hours of the morning, a fire occurred in the house where a party was taking place in New Cross, south-east London. It killed 13 young Black people aged between 14 and 22, and one survivor died two years later.[35] Many believe Anthony Berbeck took his own life because of the trauma of that night. Wayne Hayes, who was 17 at the time, recalled in an interview for the *Huffington Post* in 2020 the horrors of the night. He described dozens of teenagers and young people trapped upstairs in the house after the stairs had collapsed jumping out of second-floor windows. It was so hot 'people's skin was peeling back'. Hayes had 140 skin grafts, shattered 163 bones and has been disabled ever since.[36] He has received no compensation, and in 2020 was struggling to get back his disability card which was taken away from him.[37] More than 50 were injured that night.[38] Despite reports that a white car was spotted driving away from the scene on New Cross Road, two inquests, one three months after the fire and another in 2004, both returned an open verdict. At the second, the coroner said it was 'probable' the fire was started on purpose and two key witnesses had held back vital information at the time.[39]

In the immediate aftermath of the fire, a New Cross Massacre Action Committee (NCMAC) was set up that organized a 'Black People's Day of Action' in March 1981 when 15,000 to 20,000 people marched for eight hours through London.[40]

In 2017, the '13 Dead, Nothing Said' exhibition was hosted at Goldsmiths, University of London in New Cross. The exhibition presents a body of photographs documenting the Black People's Day of Action, taken by scholar/activist Vron Ware, who had attended the 1981 march.[41] Forty years later, no one has ever been charged.

As film-maker Menelik Shabazz, who was 26 at the time, explains 'it was a racist attack' and it is a widely held assumption in Black communities that the fire was started by fascists, most likely using a petrol bomb.[42] Local history also supports the view that it was a racist attack. Ten years before, a Caribbean house party had been attacked by firebomb in Sunderland Road, in nearby Forest Hill, leaving 22 injured; and just three years before in 1978, Deptford's Albany Empire community theatre was burned down. The National Front claiming responsibility.[43] As we saw in chapter 5, this was the era of far-right extremism. The fact that the case remains unsolved, Andrews points out, has led 'to a complete lack of faith in the official investigations'.[44]

Andrews describes the context. There was already a lack of trust among Black communities. Abuse of the so-called 'sus laws' (from 'suspected person') was a 'stop and search' law that permitted a police officer to stop, search and potentially arrest people on suspicion of their being in breach of section 4 of the Vagrancy Act of 1824, for example, allowed police to not only stop and search but actually take people into custody on mere suspicion. 'Stop and search' was and continues to be directed primarily at young Black men. Police raids on parties and accusations of brutality were a constant issue.[45] David Michael, the first Black police officer to serve in Lewisham in the 1970s (of which New Cross is part), described the force as behaving like an 'occupying army'.[46] This is the approach, Kehinde Andrews Professor of Black Studies at Birmingham City University argues, many felt they took in the investigation of the New Cross fire. For example, the line of inquiry into a firebombing was quickly dropped in favour of a theory that a fight had broken out and that 'the unruly black youth' had caused their own deaths.[47] Cecil Gutzmore, an academic and activist who was active in the mobilizations after the fire, explained to Andrews that 'almost immediately victims became suspects'.[48]

Andrews goes on to explain Thatcher's indifference. It took her five weeks to reply to Sybil Phoenix, who had written on behalf of the New Cross families and community, condemning 'the failure of... government to reflect the outrage... of the black community'. Her disrespect was summed up in her request to Phoenix to pass on her sympathies rather than making any effort to contact the families herself.[49] As Andrews sums up, the 'lack of an official response to New Cross demonstrated the value placed on black lives in Britain'.[50] In contrast, a month later, when 45 people were killed at a Dublin disco. Thatcher immediately sent their condolences.[51] Given what we saw about Thatcher's views on Ireland and Irish people as discussed in the last section of this chapter, it is possible that her main reason for doing this was as protocol (the Queen also sent condolences). Aggrey Burke, a retired psychiatrist and academic who provided psychotherapeutic support to bereaved families, summed up his views: 'Mrs Thatcher didn't provide any leadership', while Velvetina Francis, whose 17-year-old son, Gerry, died in the fire, said in a BBC interview aired in 1981: 'Had it been white kids, she would have been on the television, on the radio, and sent her sympathy'.[52]

As the Fire Brigades Union, representing the firefighters who dealt with the blaze, explains:

> It is customary for Prime Ministers and the Crown to acknowledge a mass loss of life by the way of sending a message of condolence. Yet Margaret Thatcher, after nearly two years in office at that time, failed to reach out to the community. Thatcher fostered a hostile environment for the black and minority ethnic community, and was widely considered to be courting supporters of the far-right National Front group through the use of anti-immigrant rhetoric. This was taken further by her minister Jill Knight, who appeared to condone direct action against parties with sound systems, a staple of the Black British culture at the time. The Prime Minister's silence propelled the wave of black activism that had

been sparked by the fire, as protestors rallied to the words 'thirteen dead and nothing said'. The parallels were all too familiar when, in 2017, Theresa May failed to meet the community when visiting the site of the Grenfell Tower fire[53] (for an update on Grenfell, see chapter 10).

Andrews concludes, 'The National Black People's Day of Action was the crest of a substantial wave of black power mobilisation, with ripple effects across the decade that crashed into the rocks of Thatcherism, individualism and the myth of equal opportunities'.[54]

The1980s uprisings

St Pauls Bristol

If the National Black People's Day of Action was a jolt for Thatcher and Thatcherism, it was to be followed by a number of further major challenges in the 1980s: the urban uprisings (commonly referred to as 'race riots'). The first occurred in St Pauls in 1980. In the 1970s it had seen an increase in unemployment (in Bristol at the time, according to Laurie O'Garro, it was 5.5% and in St. Pauls, 15% at the time of the rebellion).[55] As O'Garro explains, these high levels of unemployment were caused in part by the Thatcher Government's move away from manufacturing towards service-based industries, that resulted in fewer apprenticeship opportunities.[56] There were also upsurges of racism as the NF campaigned in local and national elections. St Pauls was also affected by the development of the M32 motorway that split the area from the neighbouring district of Easton. Much of the housing in the area was in a poor state, and local education services failed to cater adequately for the needs of minority ethnic communities as well as many working-class White communities.[57] In addition, increasing use by the police of 'sus laws' raised tension. There was also a rise in racist harassment on local council housing estates, which was largely ignored by the Housing Department.[58]

In O'Garro's words, those who took to the streets were responding 'to years of systemic injustice that their parents, immigrants from the Caribbean, had endured since their arrival to the UK at the end of the 1940s'.[59] Events started when, on April 2, 1980 police officers were sent to the 'Black and White Café' (named such because of the couple that owned it, one was Black and the other White) to remove alcohol. Their arrival was viewed as yet another example of police harassment, and they were eventually driven out of the area by a large crowd no longer prepared to put up and shut up.[60] Later in the day, shops were looted and burned, and the following day, more officers drafted in to restore law and order. Of the 140 people arrested, 16 were charged with rioting offences. All, however, were acquitted.[61]

In the opinion of Paul Stephenson, who had been at the forefront of the Bristol bus boycott of 1963 (after the refusal of the Bristol Omnibus

Company to employ Black or Asian bus crews in the city), the uprising 'was about young blacks who were born in this country saying that they weren't prepared to be treated as second-class citizens any longer'.[62]

For Black Bristolians, St Pauls was a safe haven. There were parts of the city that Black people avoided, areas made unsafe by far-right groups and by the White inhabitants in general. And with concerns about the racist attitudes held by the police, any prospect of being protected in the event of an attack was unrealistic. The raid on the Black and White Café was the last straw.[63] Bristol is my home city, and I can vouch for the fact that a local myth was that St Pauls was too dangerous for White people to visit, rather than areas outside St Pauls being too dangerous for Black people to go to. I remember being unable to get a taxi from a pub in a White working-class district of Bristol to the Inkerman pub in St Pauls and being told by the taxi company that no taxi would take me into St Pauls. In the end I had to get a driver from St Pauls to come and pick me up. The reaction of the locals to the arrival of this young Rastafarian taxi driver was a sight to behold.

The Thatcher Government's response to the St Pauls uprising was to send MPs, along with local politicians, 'on a fact-finding tour to discover what had gone wrong'.[64] The Government, O'Garro concludes 'learned little, if anything, from its Bristol walkabout' (in 1986, police 'intervention' was to occur again at the Black and White Café, resulting in violence).[65]

O'Garro quotes Frederick Douglass, who after escaping from slavery in the United States, became a national leader of the abolitionist movement who was also famous for his oratory:[66]

> Power concedes nothing without a demand. It never did and it never will. Find out just what any people will quietly submit to and you have found out the exact measure of injustice and wrong which will be imposed upon them, and these will continue till they are resisted with either words or blows, or with both. The limits of tyrants are prescribed by the endurance of those whom they oppress.[67]

Brixton London

In the words of the late Chris Harman, socialist journalist and Marxist theoretician, 'Bristol was the shape of things to come'[68] Nevertheless, he goes on, it was 12 months before the 'next great riot', in Brixton south-west London, on April 10–12. The scale of the disturbances was even greater than in Bristol: petrol bombs were used on a wide scale, a bus was hijacked and driven at the police, and scores of shops were looted.[69] Once again, this resulted from police racism and increased use of stop and search, in particular *Operation Swamp 81* (obviously and provocatively named after Thatcher's 'swamping remarks'). According to Layton-Henry, between April 6 and April 11, 112 police officers made 943 stops, 118 people were arrested and 75 charged.[70] During the uprising that followed it, 226 people were injured of which 150 were police officers, and 200 arrests were made. Twenty-six buildings and 20 vehicles were burnt.[71] Writing for *The Guardian*, Lindsay Mackie and Mike Phillips refer to estimates of 5,000 people being involved.[72]

Commenting on the events in Brixton in an interview from Number 10, Thatcher declared, 'Nothing, but nothing, justifies what happened... And I cannot condemn it too strongly'.[73] They were described by Thatcher as 'frightening' and 'reminiscent of riots in the United States during the 1960s and '70s', and she accepted Whitelaw's suggestion that Lord Scarman should conduct an inquiry into the causes and make recommendations.[74] Scarman was to describe *Operation Swamp 81* as a serious mistake.[75] In the wake of Brixton, there were a number of minor disturbances, especially with crowds of young people attending fun fairs in the London area (Finsbury Park, Wanstead, Ealing, Peckham), fighting the police, and in Sheffield a demonstration of skinheads against police violence ending with a rampage through the streets to chants of 'Brixton, Brixton'.[76]

Southall London

However, it was on July 3–4 that anything on the scale of Bristol or Brixton took place. On Friday, July 3, a group of Nazi skinheads got off a coach in Southall to go to a gig at the *Hambrough* pub. On the way there, they stormed into an Asian-owned shop and beat up a woman. Crowds of British Asians soon began to gather to take over the street near the pub.[77] Harman describes the scene:

> Police arrived to protect the skinheads, and later the Asians barricaded the road, and threw bricks and petrol bombs at the police. The battle raged for a couple of hours, with the police eventually evacuating the pub. But they were not able to prevent the Asian youth breaking through their lines and burning it to the ground.[78]

Toxteth Liverpool

Harman continues, a week of rioting had begun which was to involve 'full-blooded riots' in a number of major inner-city areas, to less serious disturbances in dozens of places and to 'panic boarding up of shops in wide areas of many cities'.[79] The biggest confrontation was in Toxteth, Liverpool. It began with a relatively small disturbance the same night as Southall (July 3, 1981). Police officers tried to arrest a young Black man who, they wrongly claimed, had stolen a motor bike he was riding; a crowd rescued him, but another Black person, whose family had been subject to a campaign of police harassment, was seized. The following evening an uprising erupted on a massive scale. Barricades were built with overturned cars and a builders' compressor, with scores of petrol bombs thrown at police. Masks were worn to avoid identification.[80] According to Harman, the police could not cope, and *The Guardian* reported a local academic, Ilene Melish, as stating 'the police produced a show of force sufficient to enrage the black population, but not enough to quell the riots'. The streets were barricaded again the next night. 'By then as many whites as blacks' had joined in against the police.[81] A fleet of milk floats and a concrete mixer were seized to drive at the police lines, forcing the 800-strong force to retreat. Several buildings were burnt down, including the National Westminster Bank and the local *Racquets* 'businessmen's club'. With the area clear of police, 'there was an assumption that anyone who was not police would help themselves' in the wholesale looting of shops.[82] Reports told of middle-aged women, White and Black, queuing with shopping trolleys to loot supermarkets. Of the rioters, 'fewer than 40% were black'.[83] The Deputy Chief Constable Peter Wright made it clear that 'at the savage climax of the trouble, the rioters were mostly white'. There were smaller, 'imitation' disturbances in White areas like Kirkby, Scotland Road, Walton, Woodchurch and Birkenhead.

Moss Side Manchester

About 3 a.m. on July 8, a brick was thrown through the window of a clothes shop in Moss Side. Apparently some police had shouted insults at a group of young people, mainly Black, who were leaving a club.[84] They responded by breaking windows and setting fire to shops, while holding the police at bay with petrol bombs. There were about seven arrests that night. The arrests fuelled further unrest. Throughout the day, groups began to gather on street corners, wondering what was going to happen. They coalesced into a 1,500 strong crowd of Black and White young people who attacked the police station that evening, shattering its windows and trying to break in. Failing to do so, they turned their attention to burning out and looting shops.[85] Hundreds were involved in building barricades and throwing petrol bombs. Yet in the lulls between fighting, there was a carnival atmosphere. There were only 47 arrests.[86] The following night the police took their revenge: 'Police swamped the Moss Side area. Vans swept about carrying teams of the Tactical Action Group (Manchester SPG) ... police swooped on any potential gathering of people, white or black – and made any necessary arrests'.[87] There were three times as many arrests on this night of very low level rioting as on the previous two nights combined. Virtually anyone who was foolish enough to be seen on the streets of the area could be picked up. The savagery of the police that stopped the disturbance provoked bitter complaints from all sections of the local population.[88]

Solidarity uprisings

After Moss Side came what the press referred to disparagingly as 'copycat riots',[89] or might be better described as 'solidarity riots'. These occurred in a large number of places, including Handsworth Birmingham, Chapeltown

Leeds, Bolton, Luton (including an attack on the Tory Party HQ), Leicester, Nottingham, Brixton, Hackney London, High Wycombe, Cirencester, Wood Green London, Walthamstow, Sheffield, Coventry, Portsmouth, Bristol, Edinburgh and dozens of other places. What started the disturbances varied enormously from location to location.[90]

Finally, there were a whole series of disturbances provoked by rumours that something was going to happen, rumours often encouraged by the police themselves.[91]

The Scarman Report (November 25, 1981)

According to the Scarman report, the riots were a spontaneous outburst of built-up resentment sparked by specific incidents. Scarman added that 'complex political, social and economic factors' created a 'disposition towards violent protest'. Report highlighted problems of 'racial' disadvantage and inner-city decline and warned that 'urgent action' was needed to prevent such disadvantage becoming an 'endemic, ineradicable disease threatening the very survival of our society'.[92]

The Report concluded that the 1981 Brixton riots were essentially an outburst of anger over a heavy-handed stop-and-search operation (*Swamp 81*) which had a disproportionate impact on Black residents and lacked local support.[93] Liaison arrangements between police, community and local authority had collapsed before the riots, and according to the Scarman report, the local community mistrusted the police and their methods of policing. Scarman recommended changes in training and law enforcement, and the recruitment of more officers from minority ethnic minorities. Disappointingly, Scarman reported that 'institutional racism' did not exist, pointing instead to 'racial disadvantage' and 'racial discrimination'.[94]

But the Commission for Racial Equality argued that the wider social and economic reforms were 'seriously out of key' with the political tempo of the times.[95] Scarman later acknowledged he could have been 'more outspoken about the necessity of affirmative action to overcome racial disadvantage',[96] the Joint Council for the Welfare of Immigrants (JCWI) linked the civil unrest of 1981 to the Nationality Act, pointing to the negative effects of such laws on the security of and discrimination against the Black community.[97]

SECTION 2: STATE RESPONSES TO THE UPRISINGS, IMPERIAL WARFARE, ANTISEMITISM, APARTHEID, AND THE PROMOTION OF BRITISH CULTURE IN SCHOOLS

Thatcher's response to Scarman

While the Scarman Report was positively received by a cross-section of MPs from different parties, Thatcher's reaction, in contrast, is indicated by a handwritten note on a summary of the report that reads: 'I'm afraid the report seems highly critical of the police'.[98] Whitelaw, on the other hand, described Scarman's recommendations as 'a statement of philosophy and direction for the future', adding, 'I accept and endorse this statement of philosophy'.[99] Whitelaw paid particular attention to, in his words, 'the need to develop formal arrangements in every police force area for consultation between police and community'.[100] In June 1982, Thatcher received a briefing telling her of the Home Secretary's intention to introduce a statutory duty on police to consult the community. The briefing stated, this would have the advantage of 'increasing the flow of information between the Police and the community which Scarman felt to be essential'.[101] Her response was, 'I confess to being very worried about this. It will soon be said that the police cannot prosecute or search without consultation. I cannot see what they are going to be compelled to consult about'.[102]

In 1984, the Thatcher Government passed the 'Police and Criminal Evidence Act'. While the Act, passed after Willie Whitelaw had been replaced by Leon Brittan as Home Secretary, did require that arrangements be made in each police area for obtaining the views of the people in that area about matters concerning policing and for obtaining their cooperation with the police in preventing crime,[103] it also extended the right to stop and search. Before 1984, not all local authorities gave the police the right to stop and search, but with the passing of the Act, police throughout the country could stop and search persons and vehicles believed to be carrying stolen goods. It also established a new type of stop and search power, that of stopping and searching for 'offensive weapons' that were made or could be adapted for burglaries or thefts. Finally, the Act enabled the police to set up road-blocks if they reasonably suspected that a person had 'committed a serious arrestable offence' or 'having regard to a pattern of crime in that area, a serious arrestable offence is likely to be committed in that area within the period for which the road check would be setup'.[104]

Thatcher contemplated arming the police if things got much worse at the time of the Brixton uprising, while National Archives files released in 2011 revealed that she and Whitelaw also considered sending in troops to Brixton and the other areas across England later that year. Instead, they decided to focus on getting better equipment for officers, including water cannons, CS gas, rubber bullets and surveillance helicopters.[105]

Some police responses

Brixton Commander Brian Fairbairn, who enforced *Swamp 81*, remarked:

> If you knew clearly that blacks were responsible for the greater number of muggings than whites you would be foolish, you don't have to be a trained officer to know, that you would be foolish to go chase whites rather than blacks.[106]

In October 1982 Basil Griffiths, a police inspector and Deputy Chairman of the Police Federation told a fringe meeting of the Tory Party organized by the Monday Club:

> There is in our inner cities a very large minority of people who are not fit to salvage ... the only way in which the police can protect society is quite simply by harassing these people and frightening them so they are afraid to commit crimes.[107]

On the other hand, Brian Paddick currently a Liberal Democratic life peer in the House of Lords, was serving as a sergeant in Brixton at the time of the uprising, going on to become Deputy Assistant Commissioner in the Metropolitan Police. He said: 'We were the occupying army'. And of Operation Swamp 81, he admitted: 'It was simply stopping and searching any young black man that happened to move'.[108]

Tragedies at the hands of the police

Cherry Groce Brixton shooting (1985)

At 7 a.m. on September 28, 1985, when he was 11, Lee Lawrence was at home in Brixton in bed in a bedroom he shared with his mother Cherry, father Leo and sister Sharon. Suddenly there was an almighty crash, his mother jumped out of bed to see what was happening, and the next thing Lawrence heard was a gunshot.[109] The bedroom door had been smashed down and his mother was lying on the floor with a man still pointing a gun at her. She had been shot in the spine, and she said she could not feel her legs, she couldn't breathe and she was going to die. Lawrence screamed at the officer that he'd kill him if he touched his mother again. According to Lawrence, the officer then pointed his gun at him and said, 'Somebody had better shut this fucking kid up'.[110]

Lawrence explains how it gradually dawned on the family that the man with the gun was not an armed burglar but a police officer. Thirty armed men emerged from nowhere, yelling incoherently, dogs straining on their leashes. In this horrifically botched dawn raid, the police had been looking for Lawrence's 21-year-old brother Michael, who had allegedly threatened officers with a sawn-off shotgun a few days earlier.[111] An ambulance arrived, and his father went to hospital with his mother leaving Lawrence and his sister with two police officers – colleagues of the man who had shot their mother.[112]

Rumours circulated that Cherry Groce had died and there followed a two-day uprising in Brixton. Mild scuffles had developed into larger battles. Two cars were set on fire, and large crowds dispersed by 50 or more police officers banging their truncheons on their riot shields. They re-formed and further confrontations took place.[113] Several people were injured; a photographer said he had been bitten by a police dog and an 18-year-old young man was hit by a truncheon as he walked his girlfriend home. He lay unconscious and bleeding for several minutes, a police sergeant chasing away those who tried to help. Forty-three civilians and 10 police officers were hurt, one seriously.[114]

Richard Wells, the Metropolitan Police Deputy Commissioner, told a Scotland Yard press conference:

> Following our tragic shooting of Mrs Groce yesterday, feelings began to run understandably high in Brixton, with marked hostility towards the police. These genuine feelings, particularly those of the relatives and friends of Mrs Groce, were taken up by others, who apparently knew sadly little of the true facts or background.[115]

Michael Groce, the man police were looking for when they raided his mother's home and shot her, gave himself up. He was later charged with illegal possession of a sawn-off shotgun.[116] Cherry Groce, who was 37 when she was shot, was left paralysed below the chest.[117] She had moved to England when she was 15 and was proud of her Maroon lineage: the Maroons had fought against the British, escaped slavery and established free communities in the mountains of Jamaica.[118] Sixteen months after the shooting and having faced criminal charges, the officer who fired the shot, Inspector Douglas Lovelock, was acquitted at the Old Bailey of maliciously wounding Groce.[119] Lawrence was 13 or 14 when he next came into contact with the police. He was riding pillion on a friend's moped, which turned out to be stolen. The arresting officer called him a monkey.[120]

As the teenage Lawrence became more politicized, he started to wonder why nobody seemed interested in his mother's story: 'In Black History Month, there would be programmes on telly about the 1981 uprisings, but when it came to 1985, and a woman shot in her home in front of her children, it was skimmed over'.[121]

On July 10, 2014, 29 years after Mrs Groce had been shot, the inquest jury at Southwark coroner's court found that 'Dorothy Groce was shot by police during a planned, forced entry raid at her home, and her subsequent death was contributed to by failures in the planning and implementation of the raid'.[122] The Metropolitan Police Commissioner Bernard Hogan-Howe apologized 'unreservedly' for the shooting and the time it had taken to say sorry.[123]

The death of Cynthia Jarrett, Broadwater Farm (1985)

A week after Groce was shot, Cynthia Jarrett died of heart failure during a police search of her home in Tottenham, London.[124] On October 5, 1985, four police officers burst into the home of Cynthia Jarrett on the Broadwater Farm estate looking for stolen property that they believed wrongly her son Floyd might have there. They failed to find any, but Cynthia Jarrett during the search became distressed and suffered a massive heart attack and died.[125] The local council leader, Bernie Grant (who in 1987 was to be elected as MP for Tottenham, one of the UK's first Black British MPs) later condemned the search and urged the local police chiefs to resign immediately as their behaviour had been 'out of control'.[126]

Later that day police were pelted with bricks, bottles and petrol bombs. Cars were overturned and set alight, as were shops and other buildings.[127] Up to 500 police officers were drafted in. Police Constable Keith Blakelock, who was trying to protect firefighters tackling a blaze, was repeatedly stabbed. Of the 40 wounds counted on his body, eight had been to his head which led those who saw him afterwards to believe his assailants had tried to decapitate him.[128] He died later in hospital. Police in riot gear occupied the estate for two months after the disturbance, using police dogs, helicopters and surveillance equipment. The residents of the estate complained of feeling under siege. Hundreds of people were arrested in the search for Blakelock's killers. Of the first wave of arrests, over half were young people. Complaints were also made by residents that 'juveniles were deliberately targeted, held incommunicado, given no access to solicitors or their families and those families that were notified, were often given misinformation as to where their children were'.[129]

Thatcher's policy unit responds

At the time, Oliver Letwin and Hartley Booth both members of Thatcher's policy unit (Booth was to succeed Thatcher as Tory MP for Finchley from 1992 to 1997) co-authored a memo in response to Broadwater Farm, urging her 'to ignore reports that rioting in mainly black urban areas was the result of social deprivation and racism', arguing that poor White people were not prone to public disorder, that the riots had been caused not by poverty or racism but by 'bad moral attitudes' in Black neighbourhoods, and that efforts to foster Black entrepreneurs would prompt them to create businesses 'in the disco and drug trade'.[130]

The memo also poured scorn on suggestions by Senior Cabinet Ministers that helping Black people start businesses, refurbishing public housing and establishing training programs for low-income young people would have an ameliorating effect and would do little more than 'subsidise Rastafarian arts and crafts workshops'.[131] In Letwin and Booth's words:

> The root of social malaise is not poor housing, or youth 'alienation', or the lack of a middle class. Lower-class, unemployed white people lived for years in appalling slums without a breakdown of public order on anything like the present scale; in the midst of the depression, people in Brixton went out, leaving their grocery money in a bag at the front door, and expecting to see groceries there when they got back. Riots,

criminality and social disintegration are caused solely by individual characters and attitudes. So long as bad moral attitudes remain, all efforts to improve the inner cities will founder.[132]

Citing the proposals of Ministers in the Thatcher Government, they wrote, 'David Young's new entrepreneurs will set up in the disco and drug trade; Kenneth Baker's refurbished council blocks will decay through vandalism combined with neglect; and people will graduate from temporary training or employment programs into unemployment or crime'.[133]

Letwin and Booth concluded that the Government should place 'young delinquents' in 'good' foster homes and should create a 'youth corps' to promote 'moral values' and encourage 'personal responsibility, basic honesty' and respect for the law from an early age.[134]

When the document was released in 2015, Letwin, then running Prime Minister David Cameron's Cabinet Office as Chancellor of the Duchy of Lancaster, apologized 'unreservedly' for the comments, adding 'I want to make clear that some parts of a private memo I wrote nearly 30 years ago were both badly worded and wrong' and no offense had been intended. To this I would comment, either of course he knew it would offend, or he was and is so convinced of his superiority as a White Eton-educated man that he thought he was doing Black people a favour in trying to make them more like how he perceived himself.

When asked by a journalist if she would like to express her concern for Blakelock, Thatcher replied, who died in Tottenham? 'Concern? We are all *horrified*. This is a new depth of terrorism. And, as the Home Secretary said, we have to fight it with all the means at our disposal and everything else'.[135] I can find no comments from Thatcher on either Cherry Groce or Cynthia Jarrett.

Eventually in 1987, Winston Silcott, Engin Raghip and Mark Braithwaite were convicted of PC Blakelock's murder. However, four years later in 1991 their convictions were quashed by the Court of Appeal, after questions were raised about the way police interviews were carried out.[136] All three convictions were overturned when scientific tests showed Silcott's confession had been fabricated.[137] Two police interrogators were also charged with perverting the course of justice but were acquitted.[138] A second investigation between 1992 and 1994 did not result in prosecutions. At the time of writing (2021) no one has ever been charged with the murder.

Thatcher resurrects imperial warfare to stay in power

On March 19, 1982, the Argentine military junta seized control of the Falkland Islands – also known as the Malvinas – 8,000 miles from Britain and a relic of the British Empire, plunging Thatcher's Government into crisis.[139] The reason for the seizure was that the Argentine military regime was facing widespread internal opposition and decided to retake the islands to boost its prestige and its claim to control large parts of Latin America.[140] At the same time, Thatcher saw a chance to reverse her own declining fortunes.

As Simon Jenkins explains, at the last Tory Party conference there was much dissent. The so-called 'wets' (those who opposed many of Thatcher's hard-line policies) were openly conspiring against her. Well behind in the polls and with the new Social Democratic Party challenging both Labour and Conservatives, few believed Thatcher would ever lead her party to another election win. Thatcher appeared a weak, broken leader with little support even within her party. The ruling obsession was reducing double-digit inflation and cutting public spending. Nothing else seemed to concern the Government.[141] Defence and foreign affairs were in the frontline, and according to John Newsinger, author of *The Blood Never Dried – A People's History of the British Empire*,[142] the Government had been scaling back Britain's already minimal military commitment in the South Atlantic.[143]

Nobody in Britain, according to Newsinger, 'was remotely interested in the Falklands before the war'.[144] Moreover, the Government had offered to hand over sovereignty of the islands at a clandestine meeting with a senior Argentinian official less than two years before the British invasion.[145] The secrecy of the meeting is underlined by the fact that colleagues of arch-Thatcherite Nicholas Ridley, the Foreign Office Minister involved, set up a diversionary cover story to explain his absence, saying he was off to Switzerland to do a little watercolour painting with his wife.[146] This was revealed by Lawrence Freedman, Professor of War Studies at King's College, London, in 2005. In June 1980, the Foreign Office drew up a proposal, approved by the cabinet's defence committee, whereby Britain would hand Argentina titular sovereignty over the islands, which would then be leased back by Britain for 99 years.[147] In Jenkins' words, 'a tiny colony of islands in the south Atlantic was being negotiated for "sale and leaseback" to neighbouring Argentina by Thatcher's trusted junior foreign minister'.[148]

Ridley had already agreed to the sale of helicopters and naval missiles to Argentina, and he and the Argentinian official seemed to enjoy a mutually warm relationship. However, the plan was wrecked after Ridley, whose mission was not helped by a rather off-hand and patronizing manner, according to Newsinger, made an ill-fated trip to the Falklands/Malvinas where he tried to sell a deal to the islanders. Suspicion about the government's long-term intentions grew, fuelling opposition among both Tory and Labour MPs to any such deal:[149]

> Thatcher faced a choice between a humiliating acceptance of the Argentine occupation – followed by her resignation and the collapse of her government – or risking a military expedition to an area of no strategic importance to Britain simply to save herself and her government.[150]

The decision was never in doubt, and a task force was sent to supposedly 'liberate' the British settlers in the Falklands.[151]

To justify the war the Tories suddenly started raging about human rights and 'despicable Latin American juntas'. These same MPs had done nothing when Argentine leader General Leopoldo Galtieri launched a military coup in 1976, while the 'disappearance' of some 30,000 people provoked not a whimper. Moreover, Thatcher was a staunch ally of Augusto Pinochet, with whom she shared a faith in neoliberal economics, who in 1973 had launched a violent military coup against the Chile's elected Socialist President, Salvador Allende. Pinochet's soldiers rounded up thousands in Santiago's sports stadiums and, then and there, suspects were marched into the locker rooms, corridors and bleachers, and tortured and shot dead. Hundreds died in such a fashion. They also burned the books of authors the regime did not like.[152] Britain regarded Pinochet's killing spree as unseemly and sanctioned his regime by refusing to supply it with weapons. However, in 1980 Thatcher had lifted the arms embargo against Pinochet and he was soon buying arms from the UK.[153] Thatcher also ended the regime's diplomatic isolation by restoring a British ambassador to Santiago and authorizing the first visits by British ministers to Chile since Pinochet's coup in 1973.[154] UK diplomats worked behind the scenes at the United Nations to water down international condemnation of Pinochet. According to Grace Livingstone, when confronted with an outcry in the UK about the torture and disappearance of a British-Chilean citizen, the Foreign and Commonwealth Office (FCO) knowingly withheld information from parliamentarians who enquired about his fate.[155]

By the time the Argentinians surrendered on June 14, over 250 members of the British armed forces had died to keep Thatcher in power, along with over 1,000 Argentinians. Pinochet helped Thatcher's Government with intelligence on Argentina.[156] While the Falklands/Malvinas war was only a small-scale war, it had a disproportionate impact. The conflict was amplified by a jingoistic media, led by Rupert Murdoch's hard right-wing Thatcherite newspaper, the *Sun*.[157] The *Sun* remained loyal to Thatcher right up to her resignation in 1990. As Newsinger argues, the war certainly played a part, if only a part, in the Tory election victory the following year. It also 'made Thatcher's personal position within the Conservative Party unassailable'.[158]

Many, including Thatcher, made the case that the Falklands war had at last laid to rest the 'Suez syndrome', thereby removing the inhibitions that had supposedly paralysed British Governments since Britain's disastrous invasion of Egypt in 1956.[159] Many Tories felt humiliated by this 'last fling of the imperial dice' (see chapter 4) and still fantasized about Britain reasserting its imperial destiny against United States hegemony.[160]

The reality, as Newsinger concludes, was very different:

> After Suez, British governments, both Conservative and Labour, willingly subordinated themselves to the US. This so-called 'special

relationship' became the touchstone of British foreign policy. The reason for this is quite clear. British capitalism had global interests, but now that the empire was gone, it no longer possessed the military power or political influence to protect them. Instead the British ruling class looked to the US to protect its interests.[161]

Thatcher and apartheid South Africa

On September 10, 1985, the EEC denounced South Africa's apartheid system and nine of its 10 members agreed a package of mildly punitive measures against the South African government. Thatcherite Britain's opposition prevented a unanimous agreement on the deal the nine plus representatives of Spain and Portugal said they will implement.[162] This included a ban on oil exports, a halt to all trade that could aid the South African military and police and a ban on new agreements on nuclear cooperation.

The following month, Commonwealth leaders agreed to impose limited economic sanctions against South Africa and to set up a group to try to persuade the Pretoria Government to negotiate with Black leaders on ending apartheid, giving South Africa six months to 'bring about concrete progress' or face tougher sanctions, including a ban on airline flights.[163]

Bhota's Chequers meeting

Thatcher's non-compliance strategy was to attempt to preserve trade with South Africa, while persuading the government there to abandon apartheid. This was because she clearly realized the inevitability of its demise and wanted to maintain her friendship and business ties with White suprema-cists, such as the country's hard-line apartheid Prime Minister and subsequently President P. W. Botha (he only just avoided being detained as a 'Nazi sympathizer' during World War II[164] and was later found by South Africa's Truth and Reconciliation Commission to be complicit in 'gross violations of human rights').[165] Thus Thatcher invited Botha to the UK Prime Ministers' country retreat of Chequers in June 1984 at a time when he was facing global isolation, the first time a British Prime Minister had received a South African leader since Hendrik Verwoerd's visit in 1961, when he led the country out of the Commonwealth.[166] Thatcher began by stating, 'Many people in Britain had relatives in South Africa. So that was a natural reservoir of goodwill'.[167]

What are the other reasons that Thatcher decided to meet Botha? She would obviously have been aware of the inevitable demonstrations against apartheid that were to ensue and was prepared to take the consequences. At least 50,000 people marched through London to tell Botha he was not welcome in Britain. London's Black and Asian community were at the forefront of opposition to Botha's visit. The demonstration was the beginning of an upsurge of anti-apartheid action which gathered pace for the rest of the decade (London had not, at first, been on the Botha itinerary).[168] The main reason, as History Workshop explains, was that this was the height of the apartheid government's 'rampage across southern Africa' – its troops had attacked targets all across the region and Pretoria had just forced Mozambique to sign the Nkomati accord expelling ANC (African National Congress) fighters from its soil.[169] The West fully supported the South African Government's aim of halting Soviet and Cuban influence in Africa. The US Secretary of State for African Affairs, Chester Crocker, had described the withdrawal of Cuban troops from Angola as 'of vital importance'.[170] The anti-communist, anti-Thatcher was of course in agreement. There were other matters for discussion such as security issues for both governments.[171] Thatcher was later to report that she did not particularly 'warm' to Botha.[172] However, given what has been revealed about her in this book, this is more likely to do with his 'great crocodile' persona,[173] rather than anything else.

When the visit was over, the Foreign Office was able to report from South Africa that Mr Botha had been 'delighted with the courtesy and respect with which he was everywhere received, even though European leaders were careful to maintain a certain reserve in their public welcoming'.[174] As History Workshop concludes, 'In reality the visit marked something of a high-watermark for the apartheid government – a breach in the wall of international isolation that increasingly surrounded the regime'.

Nevertheless, apartheid was on its way out. In January 1984, ANC President Oliver Tambo called on residents to 'make townships ungovernable' by destroying the Black Local Authorities. Councillors and police were asked to resign their positions. Municipal buildings and homes of African Councillors and collaborators were attacked. As the state's administrative system broke down, people established their own democratic structures, street committees and people's courts to administer their communities. Troops and police who had moved into the townships at the end of 1984 engaged in running battles with young people in an effort to re-establish control. An atmosphere of mass insurrection prevailed in many townships and rural towns across the country during 1985 and 1986 as mass struggles and the armed struggle began to support one another. In the 1980s community, civic, student, youth, cultural, sports and women's organizations were established all over South Africa.[175]

Nevertheless, as late as 1987, Thatcher declared, 'The ANC is a typical terrorist organisation ... Anyone who thinks it is going to run the government in South Africa is living in cloud-cuckoo land'.[176] History would prove her wrong. Less than six years after Thatcher's friendly meeting with Botha, in February 1990 his successor, F. W. de Klerk released future President Dr Nelson Mandela (who unsurprisingly the Thatcher Government had tried to stop the University of Lancaster giving an honorary doctorate in 1982)[177] finally signalling the end of apartheid.[178]

Thatcher's White ethno-state solution

In the run-up to the 1986 Commonwealth Games held in Edinburgh, Thatcher was warned by Foreign Secretary Howe that she would be viewed as a 'friend of apartheid' because of her Government's refusal to impose sanctions on South Africa. With South Africa under a state of emergency amid increasing repression and violence, and after the withdrawal of Malaysia and the Bahamas from the Games, it was conveyed in a letter to Downing Street in early July that Howe was 'seriously concerned'.[179] The letter said:

> As the Prime Minister knows, in Sir Geoffrey's view the problem is that, because of our vigorous and persistent public opposition to comprehensive economic sanctions, many Commonwealth leaders now see us as the main defender of the South African government and of apartheid. In order to start putting that right, the Foreign Secretary included a strong attack on apartheid in his Commons speech this afternoon. But he believes it would also be extremely helpful if the Prime Minister could reinforce the message... If she took that opportunity herself to deliver a strong attack on apartheid the addition of her authority would greatly help our efforts to stem the tide of withdrawals.[180]

Howe's suggestions as to what Thatcher could say included a statement that would 'reiterate my total rejection of apartheid and all it stands for'.[181] However this was not to happen. Notes written on top of the Foreign Office letter suggest that officials did not want Thatcher to be able to give too much consideration to the proposals. One instruction read: 'Please bury deep' while a further note added: 'CDP [Charles Powell, her Private Secretary] to bury'.[182] The Games were being boycotted by 32 of the 59 eligible countries. A large number of the boycotting countries were African, Asian and Caribbean countries meaning that the Games were reduced to almost a Whites-only affair.[183]

Attempts were also made unsuccessfully to persuade Thatcher to reverse her decision not to offer any public money to fund the Games. Her response was 'if the Government were to go back now they would never be believed on other matters'.[184] Eventually the deficit was resolved with the help of a £1.3 million donation from billionaire Japanese Ryoichi Sasakawa. After Thatcher agreed to write a letter of thanks to the 'businessman', the Foreign Office revealed that this person who had come to Thatcher's aid had been arrested as a suspected war criminal after World War II, held extreme right-wing views and was a possible gangster. The letter was still sent.[185]

In his memoirs, Howe commented that 'Margaret would quite rightly denounce the violence of ANC terrorism, but without ever acknowledging, even by the tone of voice, that the whole white-controlled repressive structure of the apartheid legal system was bound itself to provoke inter-racial conflict'.[186]

At her meeting with Botha in 1984, Thatcher had said to him, 'our political attitude was affected by one enormous problem':

> we felt strongly that peoples' rights should not be determined by the colour of their skin. Particular repugnance was felt at the forced removal of blacks to new areas. We appreciate the great strategic importance of South Africa. Nor did we wish Communism to spread in Africa or elsewhere because to us Communism represented denial of human dignity.[187]

So, having conveyed the views of most British people, what did she personally think should be the future of South Africa? Thatcher's White supremacist views on the country are damningly and clearly revealed by Patrick Wright, the most senior civil servant in the Foreign Office for the final four years of Margaret Thatcher's premiership.[188] On June 20, 1986, Wright was invited to lunch with Thatcher. She opened the conversation, he explains:

> by thrusting a newspaper cutting about Oliver Tambo in front of us [also present was Antony Acland, from whom Wright was about to take over as Permanent Under-Secretary] saying that it proved that we should not be talking to him ...She continued to express her views about a return to pre-1910 South Africa, with a white mini-state partitioned from their neighbouring black states.[189]

When he argued that this would be seen as an extension of apartheid, Thatcher barked: 'Do you have no concern for our strategic interests?'[190]

Four days later, Wright visited Geoffrey Howe who was having 'a very difficult time with her, particularly on South Africa, where their views were poles apart'.[191] Just to underline the fact that her White-supremacist remark on June 20 was no aberration, on August 3 at a meeting in the PM's study in Number 10 Thatcher again started talking about 'partition as a solution to South Africa'. All her and husband Dennis Thatcher's 'instincts are in favour of the South African Whites', Wright concluded.[192]

Comments on South Africa by other Torty politicians include Teddy Taylor who in the mid-eighties, said: 'Nelson Mandela should be shot', later claiming in 1994, it was meant jokingly: 'Unfortunately, I do still regard him as an ex-terrorist'.[193] According to Labour MP Brian Wilson speaking in 1996 said Federation of Conservative Students (FCS) conferences had been littered with slogans like 'Hang Nelson Mandela'.[194]

In 1990, when Mandela declined to meet Thatcher on a trip to London, Tory MP Terry Dicks asked: 'How much longer will the Prime Minister allow herself to be kicked in the face by this black terrorist?[195] Dicks died in 2020. In his obituary in *The Guardian,* Julia Langdon wrote:

> He won early notoriety as chairman of housing [in Hillingdon Council in west London] in 1978 by refusing to provide council accommodation for a family of homeless Kenyan Asians, instead calling them a minicab and instructing the driver to 'dump them on the Foreign Office steps' … He … described the [black] Labour MP Bernie Grant wearing traditional dress as looking 'like a Nigerian washerwoman'.[196]

In the same year, Tory MP for Luton North John Carlisle was furious at the BBC's screening of the 1990 Mandela concert in London: 'The BBC have just gone bananas over this and seem to be joining those who are making Mandela out to be a Christ-like figure'.[197] He went on, 'Many will remember his record and the record of his wife as they take the podium. This hero worship is misplaced'.[198] In 1983 he had called on the Marylebone Cricket Club (MCC) to tour South Africa as a means of establishing if contemporary opinion polls approving of reviving sporting links were correct. The suggestion was rejected by MCC members.[199]

Also in 1990, another Tory MP Andrew Hunter called for an investigation into alleged secret links between the ANC and the IRA. Hunter was to leave the Tory Party in 2002 after becoming increasingly at odds with its then leader Iain Duncan Smith because of the former's hard right views. He went on to run unsuccessfully as a DUP candidate in the 2003 Northern Ireland Assembly elections.[200] He stated, 'The DUP has a consistent approach of opposition to the Belfast agreement – to its implementation – and that, I think, is the way forward. My political home is with the mindset of the DUP and I very much hope I can play a part in their affairs'.[201]

Some other instances of Thatcher's racism

A mix of biological and cultural racism

In this and the previous chapter we have seen many aspects of Thatcher's racism. In a classic combination of biological and cultural racism ('they are an island race' and 'their way of life is British'), at the time of the Falklands Malvinas war in 1982, Thatcher had said:

> The people of the Falkland Islands, like the people of the United Kingdom, are an island race. They are few in number but they have the right to live in peace, to choose their own way of life and to determine their own allegiance. Their way of life is British; their allegiance is to the Crown. It is the wish of the British people and the duty of Her Majesty's Government to do everything that we can to uphold

that right. That will be our hope and our endeavour, and, I believe, the resolve, of every Member of this House.[202]

As if to underline the genetic component of her racism, when US Secretary of State Alexander Haig proposed a ceasefire, she refused, stating 'We have lost a lot of blood, and it's the best blood'.[203]

Keep White countries White

During an official visit to Switzerland in 1984, according to the published memoirs[204] of former Swiss Foreign Minister Edouard Brunner, the then Swiss President Jean-Pascal Delamuraz asked Thatcher how to cope with immigration from outside Europe. Brunner, a fluent English speaker, records that 'Mrs Thatcher cleverly passed the buck, leaving her husband to reply, and I remember exactly what he said':[205] 'The only advice I can give you, *and I am sure that the prime minister agrees with it,* is: keep Switzerland white' (emphasis added).[206]

Thatcher had contempt for the 'Vietnamese boat people'.[207] After a discussion of the issue in June 1989, according to Howe, at which she refused to listen to any arguments she disagreed with, was 'moving towards a policy of "pushing off" [refusing to allow them to land] – apparently oblivious of the appalling implications, with photographs reminiscent of Palestinians and Jews in 1947 in sinking boats'.[208] Wright says she was 'at her worst' during this crisis.[209]

Germanophobia

Thatcher also held (non-colour-coded) racist views about Germans and Germany. In 1989, a series of rebellions against the leadership of countries in the Eastern Bloc (those ideologically aligned to the Soviet Union) caused a chain reaction that was eventually to lead to the fall of the Berlin Wall in November 1989. The wall had divided west Berlin physically and ideologically from the German Democratic Republic (GDR), including east Berlin since 1961. Its fall marked the end of the Cold War. From the perspective of west Berlin, aligned to the capitalist west, the wall had been part of the 'iron curtain' that separated the 'free' west from the 'communist' east. From the point of view of the GDR, it was an anti-fascist construction (*Antifaschistischer Schutzwall*) that aimed to undermine the construction of socialism in the GDR.

The GDR had an unlikely ally in the first part of this formulation, but clearly not the 'construction of socialism' as a positive development. Writing for the *Daily Mail,* Stephanie Linning points out that, according to Government papers released in 2016, Margaret Thatcher 'feared the fall of the Berlin Wall could lead to a return of the Nazis'.[210] Apparently, concerns over how 'a cultured and cultivated nation had allowed itself to be brainwashed into barbarism' were raised during a meeting at Chequers in March 1989, months before formal reunification of Germany. Some asked: 'If it happened once, could it not happen again?'[211] The 'national character' of the German people was also discussed at the meeting. According to a confidential minute prepared by Powell, Thatcher's Private Secretary, the meeting examined questions such as 'Who are the Germans?', 'Have the Germans changed?' and 'What will be the consequences of reunification?'[212]

Powell's notes also reveal that:

> Apprehension about Germany did not relate just to the Nazi period, but to the whole post-Bismarckian era, and inevitably caused deep distrust. The way in which the Germans currently used their elbows and threw their weight about in the European community suggested that a lot had still not changed.

However, Powell concluded, 'In sum, no-one had serious misgivings about the present leaders or political elite of Germany. But what about ten, fifteen or twenty years from now? Could some of the unhappy characteristics of the past re-emerge with just as destructive consequences?'[213]

In a letter to the *Financial Times,* published on January 3, 2017, Oxford historian Timothy Garton Ash, who was present at the meeting, described how Powell also listed alleged German qualities as 'angst [underlined], aggressiveness, assertiveness, bullying, egotism, inferiority complex, senti-mentality' but made it clear that this 'in no way reflected the spirit of the meeting'.[214] Garton Ash went on to point out that:

> In fact, all the historians present urged the prime minister to recognise that the opportunity of having a peacefully united, democratic Ger-many, firmly anchored in the west, was one we should seize with both hands. Of course there would be risks, and power would shift towards a united Germany at the centre of Europe, but the potential benefits far outweighed the risks.[215]

'[Thatcher] recognised this overwhelming view', he concludes, 'in her summing up, memorably saying that she would henceforth be "very nice to the Germans."' On a final note, Garton Ash said he doubted whether 'Thatcher became much nicer to the Germans'.[216] His doubts were well-founded. Some six months after the Chequers meeting and just before the fall of the Berlin Fall, as Wright put it in an entry dated September 29, 1989, 'Margaret Thatcher has been showing signs of her Germanophobia over the past few weeks... she seems to be obsessed by a feeling that German-speakers are going to dominate the community. Any talk of German reunification is anathema to her'.[217] Earlier that year in February, Wright had written that his talks with his Austrian opposite number were mainly about Austria's application to join the European Community 'on which Mrs Thatcher was already showing her dislike of the thought of "another German" joining the club'.[218] In February 1990, following 'a tempestuous Cabinet meeting', Foreign Secretary Hurd remarked, 'Cabinet now consists of three items: parliamentary affairs; home affairs; and xenophobia'.[219]

Further instances of Thatcher's anti-German racism are recounted by Wright in that year, namely referring to Munich, she said she could never bring herself to visit 'that place',[220] and 'an extraordinary meeting between the PM and a Treasury', where her 'loathing of the Germans and the European Commission is such that she apparently started to refer to the Commission as being in Bonn'. 'When corrected', Wright points out, 'she said: "No. I meant Bonn. After all, the Germans are going to take it all over."'[221] The fall of the Berlin Wall on November 9, 1989 paved the way for the reunification of Germany, while the relaxation of travel restrictions between eastern and central and western Europe also allowed movement of labour that heralded the birth of xeno-racism in the UK, particularly from the early 20th century on, as discussed throughout this book.

Antisemitism from some Tories (1979–1990)

Alan Clark

In 1981, Alan Clark, a Minister in Thatcher's first term, told Tory journalist Frank Johnson that he, Clark, was a Nazi. He wrote in his diary: 'I really believed it to be the ideal system, and that it was a disaster for the Anglo-Saxon races and for the world that it was extinguished'.[222] The following year, well-known as a diarist, Clark made the following diary entry:

> Today I asked an offensive question about Jews. It is always thought to be rude to refer to 'Jews', isn't it? I remember that slightly triste occasion, watched from the gallery, of my father being inaugurated into the Lords and my rage at Sidney Bernstein, who was being ennobled on the same afternoon and would not take the Christian oath. As loudly as I could I muttered and mumbled about 'Jews' in order to discomfit his relations who were also clustered in the gallery.[223]

He continued, 'I had hung it around the Foreign Secretary's visit to Israel ... It is always fun to see how far you can go with taboo subjects'.[224] Five years later in December 1986 while Minister of State for Trade, Clark described in his diary the colour of someone's gold Rolls-Royce as 'Jewish racing yellow', adding that apparently that is what 'the colour is termed in the [Officers'] Mess at Knightsbridge'.[225]

Alan Clark, a member of the Monday Club since 1968, in 1971 was barred from the Tory Party for being too right-wing but was subsequently allowed back in.[226] Clark was a supporter of Enoch Powell to whom he referred to as 'the Prophet'. He once declared, 'It is natural to be proud of your race and your country', and described Africa as 'Bongo Bongo Land'.[227] He once told left-wing Labour MP Dennis Skinner, 'I'd rather live in a socialist Britain than one ruled by a lot of foreigners'.[228]

Clark argued that the media and the government failed to pick out the racism towards White people and ignored any racist attacks on White people. When Clark was Minister for Trade between 1986 and 1989, responsible for overseeing arms sales, he was interviewed by socialist journalist John Pilger:

JP: Did it bother you personally that this British equipment was causing such mayhem and human suffering (by supplying arms for Indonesia's war in East Timor)?

AC: No, not in the slightest, it never entered my head. You tell me that this was happening, I didn't hear about it or know about it.

JP: Well, even if I hadn't told you it was happening, the fact that we supply highly effective equipment to a regime like that is not a consideration, as far as you're concerned. It's not a personal consideration. I ask the question because I read you are a vegetarian and you are quite seriously concerned about the way animals are killed.

AC: Yeah.

JP: Doesn't that concern extend to the way humans, albeit foreigners, are killed?

AC: Curiously not. No.[229]

Neil Hamilton

As Jamie Wilson explains, 'the buffoonish image cultivated by Neil Hamilton in public has managed to gloss over his extreme views, was a leading light in the Federation of Conservative Students and the ultra-right at the university of Aberystwyth', while a '1979 election flyer in Bradford, where Mr Hamilton was standing as Conservative candidate, espoused "coloured" repatriation, as did a speech to the Tory selection committee at the same time'.[230] On an August 1983 parliamentary trip to Berlin, then a Tory MP, Neil Hamilton (currently acting leader of the right-wing UK Independence Party (UKIP) since 2020) made a Nazi salute 'with two fingers to his nose to give the impression of a toothbrush moustache' when outside the Reichstag.[231] The salute was reported on January 30, 1984 in a BBCV *Panorama* programme. Hamilton sued the BBC for libel, claiming that he had no recollection of making the salute.[232] The BBC pulled out of the case and Hamilton was awarded £20,000 in damages.[233] However, after the case collapsed, Hamilton admitted in a *Sunday Times* article to having done this.[234]

Antisemitism towards Jewish people in Thatcher's premiership

There were a number of Jewish MPs in Thatcher's Cabinet, all of whom experienced antisemitism from their colleagues. Harold Macmillan commented that the Cabinet 'was more old Estonian than old Etonian', which in MacShane's words was 'a none-too-subtle way of putting Nigel Lawson, Leon Brittan or Michael Howard in their place'.[235]

Jonathan Aitken wrote of Brittan's resignation as Trade and Industry Secretary in 1986 over a Government scandal, 'Soon after a poisonous meeting of [the Tory] ... 1922 Committee he fell on his sword. It was a combination of a witch hunt and a search for a scapegoat – tainted by an undercurrent of anti-Semitism ... to deflect the fire that ... [Margaret Thatcher] had started and inflamed'.[236] In the discussion that followed over who should replace Brittan after he was removed from the cabinet, Tory MP John Stokes, Monday Club member and speaker at the Club's *Halt Immigration Now!* meeting in 1972, calling for a halt to all immigration, the repeal of the Race Relations Act and the start of a full repatriation scheme (see chapter 5), commented that the 'replacement should at least be a "proper red-faced, red-blooded Englishman"'.[237]

Tory MP Anna McCurley described Edwina Currie as a 'pushy Jewess',[238] while an advisor to Tory Secretary of State for Social Security from 1988 to 1989, John Moore, commented that the Tory backbenches were 'riddled with prejudice of every kind', with 'anti-Semitism [being] secondary to the male chauvinism' in the case of Currie.[239] Finally, in 1982 Michael Howard finally became a Tory election candidate for Folkestone after having been rejected by about 40 constituency parties because of antisemitism within those parties.[240]

Promoting 'British culture' in education

Finally, Thatcher and a number of Thatcherite academics and politicians were infamous in education circles for the relentless pursuit of mono-culturalism (promoting 'British culture'), their hatred of multiculturalism and their strident opposition to antiracism, particularly in the context of teacher education. One (personal) example will suffice. In her memoirs, *The Downing Street Years*,[241] Thatcher writes:

> There was the need radically to improve teacher training. Unusually, I had sent a personal minute to [Education Secretary] Ken Baker in November 1988 expressing my concerns. I said we must go further in this area and asked him to bring forward proposals.

She goes on to explain the context: the Council for the Accreditation of Teacher Education (CATE) that had been set up in 1984, but 'the position had barely improved'.[242] Thatcher complains of 'too much stress on the sociological and psychological aspects', and proceeds to cite one of my courses as an example:[243]

> I could barely believe the contents of one of the B.Ed. courses – duly approved by CATE – at Brighton Polytechnic about which one concerned Tory supporter sent in details. Entitled 'Contexts for learning', this course claimed to be enabling teachers to come to terms with such challenging questions as 'To what extent do schools reinforce gender stereotypes?' It continued: 'students are then introduced to the debate between protagonists [sic] of education [there was a missing word in the course document and it should have been 'multicultural education', not 'education][244] and those who advocate anti-racist education. I felt that the 'protagonists' of education had a better case.[245]

Prominent in the promotion of monocultural education were the Radical Right Hillgate Group, launched in 1986. With Dave Hill in 1989 I co-founded the Hillcole Group of Radical Left Educators.[246]

Cameron's sanctions–busting jolly to apartheid South Africa

In 1989, near the end of Thatcher's premiership future Tory Prime Minister David Cameron accepted an all-expenses paid trip to apartheid South Africa while Nelson Mandela was still in prison. The sanctions-busting holiday was when Cameron was a rising star of the Conservative Research Department, seen as a training ground for leading Tory politicians. It was a chance for him to 'see for himself' and was funded by a firm that lobbied against the imposition of sanctions on the apartheid regime.[247] As Mary Dejevsky explains it an article written in April 2009 when details of the trip were revealed in a then newly updated edition of Cameron's biography,[248] it 'raised questions about the character of the man who, after a week when the Government's credibility on the economy hit a new low, is now on course to be prime minister in a little more than a year's time'.[249] Cameron's office replied feebly that the visit by the 23-year-old future leader was a 'fact-finding mission' that took place 20 years ago, and the Thatcher government was opposed to sanctions against South Africa at the time.[250]

A spokesperson for Cameron said he met union leaders and Black opposition politicians, including the head of the Pan Africanist Congress (PAC) during the trip that was organized and funded by Strategy Network International (SNI), created in 1985 specifically to lobby against the imposition of sanctions on South Africa. When asked by the authors of the biography if Mr Cameron wrote a memo or had to report back to the office about his trip, Alistair Cooke – in 1989 his boss at Central Office, and at the time of writing a Tory life Peer – said it was 'simply a jolly', adding: 'It was all terribly relaxed, just a little treat, a perk of the job. The Botha regime was attempting to make itself look less horrible, but I don't regard it as having been of the faintest political consequence'.[251]

The trip was offered to the Conservative Research Department by Derek Laud, then a leading light in the Monday Club and probably its only Black member (now a Liberal Democrat), who was employed by SNI.

Peter Hain, the former Labour Cabinet Minister and prominent anti-apartheid campaigner, said in April 2009:

> David Cameron asks us to judge a leader's character – well, Gordon Brown at this time was active in the anti-apartheid movement, while Cameron was enjoying a sanctions-busting jolly. That is a measure of character. This just exposes his hypocrisy because he has tried to present himself as a progressive Conservative, but just on the eve of the apartheid downfall, and Nelson Mandela's release from prison, when negotiations were taking place about a transfer of power, here he was being wined and dined on a sanctions-busting visit. This is the real Conservative Party, shown by the fact that his colleagues who used to wear 'Hang Nelson Mandela' badges at university are now sitting on the benches around him. Their leader at the time Margaret Thatcher described Mandela as a terrorist.[252]

Conclusion

Thatcher's leadership challenge, resignation and death

Throughout 1990 the popularity both of Thatcher and her Conservative government waned considerably, particularly because of Thatcher's attempt to introduce the so-called 'poll tax', aimed at changing local taxes from the rating system based on the theoretical rental value of properties, dependent on, for example, the length of the front of the property and the number of bedrooms and bathrooms, to the number of adults living in a property rather than its size. This meant that richer people living in large houses would be paying less than before and poorer people and extended families in smaller houses more than before. Cabinet papers for 1989 and 1990, released in December 2016, reveal how involved Thatcher herself was in trying to implement it.[253] They show a succession of crisis meetings with ministers 'desperately tried to find a way out of their predicament, including the perceived unfairness of a system in which "Dukes and dustmen" both paid the same'.[254]

In 2016, Michael Portillo, in 1990 Minister of State for Local Government, said that he and Environment Secretary Chris Patten wanted to find a way to effectively abolish the poll tax: 'We wanted to take the guts out of it, take the bits that were hurting out of it... but we recognised for ... [Thatcher's] sensitivity that it would still have to be called the poll tax'.[255] But nothing worked and Mrs Thatcher's career was foundering. In March

1990, there was an uprising in Trafalgar Square, the most serious in central London for a century.[256] Oliver King, a student at the time, describes what he saw:

> For no discernible reason a riot squad van drove from Charing Cross Road straight into the Trafalgar Square crowd and knocked a young woman yards across the road. It was an incendiary moment. The air then filled with bottles and missiles and mayhem ensued. Thousands of non-rioters were trapped in the square and before my girlfriend and I could escape, we saw a photographer's arm broken by a policeman's truncheon, people viciously trampled and a scaffolding pole that nearly killed a police officer. There were almost surreal moments of levity too. Huge cheers erupted when a failed attempt was made to torch the apartheid South African embassy.[257]

In November 1990, Michael Heseltine, an outspoken critic of the poll tax, triggered a leadership contest from which John Major emerged the winner, becoming the new Tory Prime Minister in November 1990. Major appointed Heseltine as Environment Secretary, increased VAT to generate extra cash for councils and announced the abolition of the poll tax and its replacement by council tax in March 1991.[258]

In June 1992, Thatcher took her seat in the House of Lords. She continued to be active in politics, until advised by her doctors to give up making public speeches in March 2002 after a series of strokes.[259]

Margaret Thatcher died in 2013.[260] At the time of her death, the then Australian Labor Foreign Minister Bob Carr, like Black South Africans and other antiracists the world over, distanced himself from the chorus of overseas politicians eulogizing Thatcher, and while saying he respected her for the 'boldness of her political leadership', he recalled an 'unabashedly racist' comment she made in relation to Asian immigration. During a conversation with Thatcher after she had retired, and with his Malaysian-born wife Helena nearby, but not able to hear their conversation, she warned him 'against Asian immigration, saying that if we allowed too much of it, we'd see the natives of the land, the European settlers [sic], overtaken by migrants'.[261]

Notes

1   Saini. 2019.
2   Saini. 2019, pp. 111–117.
3   Runnymede Trust. 2019. 'The struggle for race equality: British Nationality Act 1981'. https://www.runnymedetrust.org/histories/race-equality/61/brit ish-nationality-act-1981.html.
4   Ibid.
5   Ibid.
6   Ibid.

7   Natarajan, Radhika. 2013. 'Ties of blood: how Thatcher altered "British"', *Open Democracy*, April 17. https://www.opendemocracy.net/en/opendemocra cyuk/ties-of-blood-how-thatcher-altered-british/.

8   Ibid.

9   Ibid.

10   Ibid.

11   Ibid.

12   Pannick, David. 1993. *The Primary Purpose Rule: A Rule With No Purpose*, London: Young Justice, p. 3. The rule was, of course, before civil partnerships came into effect in 2005, and same sex marriages in 2017. https://files.justice. org.uk/wp-content/uploads/2015/01/06171917/PrimaryPurposeRuleRule WithNoPurpose.pdf.

13   Ibid., pp. 5–6.

14   Ibid., p. 6.

15   Hansard, 1803–2005 → 1980s → 1986 → October 1986 → 24 October 1986 → Written Answers (Commons) → Home Department. Visitors HC Deb, 24 October 1986, vol 102 cc1013–21W. https://api.parliament.uk/historic-hansa rd/written-answers/1986/oct/24/visitors#S6CV0102P0_19861024_CWA_125.

16   Cited by Kaufman Hansard 1803–2005, cc77–138. https://api.parliament.uk/ historic-hansard/commons/1986/oct/27/immigration.

17   Ibid.

18   Ibid.

19   Ibid.

20   Ibid.

21   Ibid.

22   Ibid.

23   Ibid.

24   Ibid.

25   Historic Hansard. 1987. 'Prison ships', *Written-Answers*. https://api.parliament. uk/historic-hansard/written-answers/1987/oct/21/prison-ships# S6CV0120P0_19871021_CWA_309.

26   Ames, Jonathan, Legal Editor. 2020. 'Would floating detention centres for asylum seekers work?', *The Times*, October 1. https://www.thetimes.co.uk/a rticle/would-floating-detention-centres-for-asylum-seekers-work-bkldrv2zn.

27   Nicholson, Frances. 1997. 'Implementation of the Immigration (Carriers' Liability) Act 1987: Privatising immigration functions at the expense of international obliga- tions?', *The International and Comparative Law Quarterly*, 46 (3), p. 586. https://www. jstor.org/stable/pdf/761276.pdf?refreqid=excelsior%3A1a 7b79c510813005f87c87e84c9dfa82.

28   Trilling, Daniel. 2013. 'Thatcher: the PM who brought racism in from the cold'.

29   Higham, Nick. 2016. 'Margaret Thatcher concerned over "second wives"', *BBC News*, July 21. https://www.bbc.co.uk/news/uk-36838760.

30   Cited in Higham. 2016.

31   Ibid.

32   Ibid.

33   Higham. 2016.

34   Ibid. To end this section of the chapter with a final note on immigration control, this was to take on a new dimension following the fall of the Berlin Wall on November 9, 1989. The fall of the Wall changed the political land- scape opening up new travel routes and also new sources of cheap labour power, with the re-emergence of 'nation states' which had been part of or ideologically assigned to the Soviet Union (see the Introduction for a discus- sion of 'nations' as imagined communities). At the same time, this New Labour source exemplified the respective needs of capitalists and the state, and

provided a xeno-racist rationale for future immigration legislation (xeno-racism is addressed throughout the book).

35 Boycott. 'Inquest begins into 14 victims of 1981 fire'.

36 Cited in Andrews, Kehinde. 2021. 'Forty years on from the New Cross fire, what has changed for black Britons?', *The Guardian,* January 17. https://www.theguardian.com/world/2021/jan/17/forty-years-on-from-the-new-cross-fire-what-has-changed-for-black-britons.

37 Operation Black Vote (OBV). 2021. 'Remembering the New Cross fire', January 21. https://www.obv.org.uk/news-blogs/remembering-new-cross-fire.

38 Andrews. 2021.

39 Adkins, Frankie. 2021. '"13 dead, nothing said" – remembering the New Cross Fire', *News Shopper,* January 18. https://www.newsshopper.co.uk/news/19019348.13-dead-nothing-said—remembering-new-cross-tragedy/.

40 The George Padmore Institute. Undated. 'New Cross Massacre Campaign, 1980–1985'. https://catalogue.georgepadmoreinstitute.org/records/NCM.

41 '13 Dead, Nothing Said | 16 May 2017–27 May 2017 – Exhibition notes by Professor Les Back'; '13 Dead, Nothing Said" Exhibition at Goldsmiths – Exhibition video, 10 March 2017.

42 Cited in Andrews. 2021.

43 Andrews. 2021.

44 Ibid.

45 Ibid.

46 *The Economist.* 2008. 'Race and the police. No quick fix', September 18. https://www.economist.com/britain/2008/09/18/no-quick-fix.

47 Andrews. 2021.

48 Cited in Andrews. 2021.

49 Andrews. 2021.

50 Ibid.

51 Ibid.

52 Mohdin, Aamna. 2021. 'How the New Cross fire became a rallying cry for political action', *The Guardian,* January 15. https://www.theguardian.com/uk-news/2021/jan/15/how-the-new-cross-fire-became-a-rallying-cry-for-political-action.

53 Fire Brigades Union. 2021, January 18. '40th anniversary of the New Cross fire tragedy'. https://www.fbu.org.uk/blog/40th-anniversary-new-cross-fire-tragedy. For a discussion of Theresa May and the *official* creation of the hostile environment, including her response to Grenfell Tower, see chapter 9.

54 Andrews. 2021.

55 O'Garro, Laurie. Undated. 'The 1980 St Paul's "Riots"', *Everyday Magazine.* https://theeverydaymagazine.co.uk/opinion/the-bristol-riots.

56 Ibid.

57 Dresser, Madge and Fleming, Peter. 2007. *Bristol: Ethnic Minorities and the City 1000–2001.* Victoria County History. Chichester: Phillimore and Company, pp. 146–149.

58 Ibid.

59 O'Garro, Laurie. Undated. 'The 1980 St Paul's "Riots"', *Everyday Magazine.* https://theeverydaymagazine.co.uk/opinion/the-bristol-riots.

60 Ibid.

61 Ibid.

62 Cited in Jones, Elizabeth. 2018. 'The Bristol Bus Boycott of 1963', *Black History Month 2021,* October 7. https://www.blackhistorymonth.org.uk/article/section/bhm-heroes/the-bristol-bus-boycott-of-1963/.

63 O'Garro. Undated.

64 Ibid.

65   Ibid.
66   Gatewood Jr., Willard B. 1981. 'Frederick Douglass and the building of a "Wall of Anti-Slavery Fire" 1845–1846. An essay review', *The Florida Historical Quarterly*, 59 (3).
67   Cited in O'Garro. Undated.
68   Harman, Chris. 1981. 'The Summer of 1981: a post-riot analysis (Autumn 1981)', *International Socialism*, 2 (14), Autumn. https://www.marxists.org/archive/harman/1981/xx/riots.html.
69   Harman, 1981.
70   Layton-Henry, p. 129.
71   Ibid.
72   Mackie, Lindsay and Phillips, Mike. 1981. 'How smouldering tension erupted to set Brixton aflame – archive', *The Guardian*, April 13. https://www.theguardian.com/theguardian/1981/apr/13/fromthearchive.
73   We must acknowledge the legacy of the Brixton Riots Siddy Shivdasani, Saturday 10 April 2021. Shivdasani. Siddy. 2021. 'We must acknowledge the legacy of the Brixton Riots', *Metro*, April 10. https://metro.co.uk/2021/04/10/40-years-later-we-must-acknowledge-the-legacy-of-the-brixton-riots-14353854/.
74   Thatcher, Margaret. 1993. *The Downing Street Years*, London: HarperCollins, p. 143.
75   Lord Scarman. 1981. *The Brixton Disorders 10–12 April 1981,* report of an inquiry, Cmnd 8427, HMSO, pp. 56–59.
76   Harman. 1981.
77   Ibid.
78   Ibid.
79   Ibid.
80   Ibid.
81   *The Guardian*, 31 July 1981, cited in Harman. 1981.
82   Ibid.
83   Ibid.
84   Harman. 1981.
85   Ibid.
86   Ibid.
87   *Financial Times*, 10 July 1981, cited in Harman. 1981.
88   Harman. 1981.
89   Ibid.
90   Ibid.
91   Ibid.
92   *BBC News*. 2004. 'Q&A: The Scarman Report', April 27. http://news.bbc.co.uk/1/hi/programmes/bbc_parliament/3631579.stm.
93   Shiner, Michael. 2015. 'Stop and search: the police must not revive this discredited tactic', *The Guardian,* October 19. https://www.theguardian.com/commentisfree/2015/oct/19/stop-and-search-riots-2011-section-60-knife-crime-police-chiefs.
94   *BBC News*. 2004.
95   Ibid.
96   Ibid.
97   https://www.runnymedetrust.org/histories/race-equality/61/british-nationality-act-1981.html.
98   *BBC News*. 2014. 'Margaret Thatcher's criticism of Brixton riot response revealed', December 30. https://www.bbc.co.uk/news/uk-30600064#:~:text=Prime%20Minister%20Margaret%20Thatcher's%20concerns,public%20for%20the

%20first%20time.&text=A%20handwritten%20note%20by%20Mrs,highly%20cri
tical%20of%20the%20police.%22.

99 Cited in *BBC News*. 2014.
100 Ibid.
101 Ibid.
102 Ibid.
103 Morgan, R. 1985. 'Setting the PACE (Police and Criminal Evidence Act 1984) Police Community Consultation Arrangements in England and Wales', NCJ Number, US Department of Justice: Office of Justice Programs. https://www.ojp.gov/ncjrs/virtual-library/abstracts/setting-pace-police-and-criminal-evidence-act-1984-police-community.
104 Terrill, Richard J. 1989. 'Margaret Thatcher's law and order agenda', *The American Journal of Comparative Law*, 37 (3) Summer, 1989, p. 443. https://www.jstor.org/stable/pdf/840088.pdf?refreqid=excelsior%3A04e01cfffafce6cb813bd899793ae74e.
105 Shivdasani. 2021.
106 Cited in Shivdasani. 2021.
107 *The Times,* October 7, 1982, cite in Layton-Henry, p. 128.
108 Cited in Shivdasani. 2021.
109 Hattenstone, Simon. 2020. 'The man who shot my mum is still living his life'.
110 Cited in Hattenstone. 2020.
111 Hattenstone. 2020.
112 Ibid.
113 Parry. Gareth, Tirbutt. Susan and Rose. David. 2009. 'From the archive: Riots in Brixton after police shooting'.
114 Ibid.
115 Cited in Parry, Tirbutt, and Rose. 2009.
116 Parry, Tirbutt, and Rose. 2009.
117 Hattenstone. 2020.
118 Ibid.
119 Ibid.
120 Ibid.
121 Ibid.
122 Ibid.
123 https://www.bbc.co.uk/news/uk-england-london-28248588.
124 Hattenstone. 2020.
125 Smith, Natalie. 2018. 'The Tottenham 3: the legacy of the Broadwater Farm riot', *The Justice Gap,* July 13. https://www.thejusticegap.com/the-tottenham-3-the-legacy-of-the-broadwater-farm-riot/.
126 Parry, Gareth; Rawnsley, Andrew; Ezard, John. 1985. 'Policeman killed in riot', *The Guardian*, 7 October. https://www.theguardian.com/uk/1985/oct/07/ukcrime.garethparry.
127 *BBC News*. 2015. 'Broadwater Farm riots: PC Keith Blakelock's 1985 murder recalled'. https://www.bbc.co.uk/news/uk-england-london-34433752.
128 Smith, Natalie. 2018.
129 Ibid.
130 Erlanger, Steven. 2015. 'Release of 1985 race riots memo prompts apology from Cameron aide', *New York Times*, 30 December. https://www.nytimes.com/2015/12/31/world/europe/oliver-letwin-riots.html?_r=0.
131 Travis, Alan. 2015. 'Oliver Letwin blocked help for black youth after 1985 riots: Cameron's policy chief makes apology over advice to Thatcher that assistance would benefit "disco and drug trade" and Rastafarian crafts', *The Guardian*, 30 December. https://www.theguardian.com/politics/2015/dec/30/oliver-letwin-blocked-help-for-black-youth-after-1985-riots.

132   Cited in Erlanger. 2015.

133   Ibid.

134   Ibid.

135   Margaret Thatcher. 1985. 'Remarks on murder of PC Keith Blakelock (Broadwater Farm riot)', Margaret Thatcher Foundation, October 8. https://www.margaretthatcher.org/document/106143.

136   *BBC News*. 2015.

137   Hattenstone. 2020.

138   *BBC News*. 2015.

139   Newsinger, John. 2007. 17 March 2007, Issue No. 2042. Falklands/malvinas, 19 March 1982. https://socialistworker.co.uk/art/10711/Falklands:%20war%20and%20lies#:~:text=It%20is%2025%20years%20since%20Thatcher%20launched%20the,Malvinas%20%E2%80%93%20plunging%20Britain%E2%80%99s%20Tory%20government%20into%20crisis.

140   Ibid.

141   Jenkins. 2013. 'How Margaret Thatcher's Falklands gamble paid off'.

142   Newsinger, John. 2006. *The Blood Never Dried – A People's History of the British Empire*.

143   Newsinger. 2007.

144   Lawrence Freedman (cited in Norton-Taylor and Evans. 2005) refers to the islands' ambiguous imperial status. Britain relied, not on prior discovery, but on a small settlements established in 1766 but abandoned in 1774. When Britain recognized Argentinian independence in 1825, it did so without any claim to the Falklands, which were then under an Argentinian governor living there.

145   Newsinger. 2007.

146   Ibid.

147   Ibid.

148   Jenkins. 2013.

149   Newsinger. 2007.

150   Ibid.

151   Ibid.

152   Anderson, Jon Lee. 2013. 'Neruda, Pinochet, and the Iron Lady', *New Yorker*, April 9. https://www.newyorker.com/news/daily-comment/neruda-pinochet-and-the-iron-lady.

153   Ibid.

154   Ibid.

155   Livingston, Grace. 2020. 'Torture "for your amusement": How Thatcher's government misled MPs and public about its dealings with the Pinochet regime', *Daily Maverick*, April 21. https://www.dailymaverick.co.za/article/2020-04-21-torture-for-your-amusement-how-thatchers-government-misled-mps-and-public-about-its-dealings-with-the-pinochet-regime/.

156   Anderson. 2013. As Jon Lee Anderson puts it, 'Thereafter, the relationship became downright cozy, so much so that the Pinochets and his family began making an annual private pilgrimage to London. During those visits, they and the Thatchers got together for meals and drams of whiskey'. Writing for *The Daily Maverick,* Grace Livingstone informs us that 17 years after the Falklands/Malvinas war, Thatcher was to express 'outrage at the callous and unjust treatment of Senator Pinochet' at the 1999 Tory Party Conference (Livingstone. 2020). Pinochet had been arrested in London the previous year, and Thatcher was to become 'his most high-profile defender' (Livingstone. 2020).

157   Newsinger, 2007.

158   Ibid.

159   Ibid.

160   Ibid.

161 Ibid.
162 *LA Times* Archives. 1985. 'European Community Approves Sanctions on S. Africa', September 11. https://www.latimes.com/archives/la-xpm-1985-09-11-mn-7171-story.html.
163 *The New York Times.* 1985. 'Commonwealth leaders agree on sanctions against South Africa', October 21. https://www.nytimes.com/1985/10/21/world/commonwealth-leaders-agree-on-sanctions-against-south-africa.html.
164 History Workshop. 2014. 'The Thatcher-Botha Papers', January 5. https://www.historyworkshop.org.uk/the-thatcher-botha-papers/.
165 Beatty, Andrew. 2013. 'Thatcher's apartheid legacy still stirs anger in S. Africa', *Modern Ghana.*
166 History Workshop. 2014. 'The Thatcher-Botha Papers'.
167 Cited in History Workshop. 2014.
168 'Demonstration against PW Botha, 2 June 1984', *Forward to Freedom.* https://www.aamarchives.org/archive/history/1980s/pic8433-demonstration-against-pw-botha-2-june-1984.html.
169 History Workshop. 2014.
170 Cited in History Workshop. 2014.
171 See History Workshop. 2014 for full details.
172 Thatcher. 1993, p. 515.
173 Beresford, David. 2006. '"Great crocodile" of apartheid dies at 90', *The Guardian,* November 1. https://amp.theguardian.com/world/2006/nov/01/southafrica.davidberesford. Beresford sums up his legacy: 'He will be remembered as South Africa's "securocrat" – a man with a legendary temper who tried to bring a "total strategy" to bear on his perceived enemies, the black people of South Africa, whom he believed were waging a "total onslaught" against the state. As part of this strategy he created a hidden form of government, the "national management system", made up of the military, which shadowed their civilian counterparts. Beresford continues, he is widely believed to have been responsible for the setting up of "hit squads" that conducted a murderous campaign against anti-apartheid activists. The number of deaths for which Botha was responsible will never be known. But under his government the security forces killed more than 2,000 people, and an estimated 25,000 people were detained without trial and often tortured' (Beresford. 2006). In Botha's own words: 'Where in the whole wide world today can you find a more just society than South Africa has?' (1976); 'The separation of races happened long before the nationalist government. God separated the races' (1984); 'I'll keep order in South Africa and nobody in the world is going to stop me' (1985); 'I switch off the lights and sleep within a few minutes. I never take a guilty conscience with me to bed' (1987) (Dirk-Uys, Pieter. 1987. *P.W. Botha: In His Own Words,* Harmondsworth: Penguin, cited in Beresford. 2006).
174 Cited in History Workshop. 2014.
175 South African History Online (SAHO). Undated. 'The people armed, 1984–1990'. https://www.sahistory.org.za/article/people-armed-1984-1990.
176 Cited in Bevins, Anthony. 1996. 'Nelson Mandela: From "terrorist" to tea with the Queen', *The Independent,* July 8. https://www.independent.co.uk/news/world/from-terrorist-to-tea-with-the-queen-1327902.html.
177 Cowburn, Ashley. 2016. 'Margaret Thatcher's government tried to prevent Nelson Mandela being honoured by British university, documents reveal', *The Independent,* January 25. https://www.independent.co.uk/news/uk/politics/margaret-thatcher-s-government-tried-prevent-nelson-mandela-being-honouredbritish-university-documents-reveal-a6831986.html.
178 History Workshop. 2014.

179   Milmo, Cahal. 2016. 'Margaret Thatcher's aides stopped her from condemning apartheid', *The Independent*, February 19. https://www.independent.co.uk/news/uk/politics/margaret-thatcher-aides-buried-plan-make-her-condemn-apartheid-a6882706.html.
180   Ibid.
181   Ibid.
182   Ibid.
183   Inside the Games. 2021. '1986 – Edinburgh'. https://www.insidethegames.biz/articles/5285/1986-edinburgh.
184   Cited in Milmo. 2016.
185   Milmo. 2016.
186   Williams, Elizabeth M. 2015. *The Politics of Race in Britain and South Africa: Black British Solidarity and the Anti-apartheid Struggle*, I. B. Tauris.
187   Cited in History Workshop. 2014.
188   Walters, Simon. 2018. 'Margaret Thatcher "wanted a whites-only South Africa": Diaries of one of the Iron Lady's top diplomats also reveal she wanted to "push" Vietnamese 'boat people' into the sea and "loathed" Germans', *MailOnline,* January 21. https://www.dailymail.co.uk/news/article-5292859/Margaret-Thatcher-wanted-whites-South-Africa.html. This is an article about Patrick R. H. Wright's book, *Behind Diplomatic Lines: Relations With Ministers*.
189   Cited in Walters. 2018.
190   Ibid.
191   Ibid.
192   Ibid.
193   Cited in Bevins, Anthony. 1996.
194   Ibid.
195   Ibid.
196   Langdon, Julia. 2020. 'Terry Dicks obituary', *The Guardian,* June 22. https://www.theguardian.com/politics/2020/jun/22/terry-dicks-obituary.
197   Cited in Bevins. 1996.
198   Ibid.
199   Williams, Jack. 2001. *Cricket and Race*, Oxford: Berg, pp. 112–113.
200   *The Guardian*. 2004. 'Basingstoke's ex-Tory MP Hunter joins DUP', December 10. https://www.theguardian.com/politics/2004/dec/10/northernireland.devolution.
201   Cited in *The Guardian*. 2014.
202   https://www.margaretthatcher.org/document/104910. Part of this speech was to be quoted in a tweet by arch-Thatcherite Priti Patel, nearly 40 years later (see chapter 10).
203   Cited in Norton-Taylor and Evans. 2005.
204   Brunner, Edouard. 2001. *Lambris dorés et coulisses Broché [Gilded Panels and Corridors]*, Georg.
205   Maguire, Kevin. 2002. 'Switzerland? Keep it white – a classic case of the DT's', *The Guardian,* March 14. https://amp.theguardian.com/uk/2002/mar/14/conservatives.politics.
206   Cited in Maguire. 2002. Denis Thatcher's racism was well known. He once referred to 'fuzzy wuzzies in Brixton', complained that India was 'high on the buggeration factor', and finding himself seated next to the wife of a foreign diplomat, he asked if she 'likey soupy?' after realizing her English was poor. At a Commonwealth Conference, he asked delegates, 'Who do you think is worse, Sonny bloody Ramphal or Ma sodding Gandhi?' (Commonwealth Secretary-General and Prime Minister of India, respectively). Finally, for Denis Thatcher, the national lottery was 'just another of those disgusting continental habits' (cited in Maguire. 2002).

207 This is a term that refers to the refugees who fled Vietnam by boat and ship after the end of the American war in Vietnam in 1975. It created a humanitarian crisis that continued until the early 1990s.

208 Cited in Walters. 2018.

209 Ibid.

210 Linning, Stephanie. 2016. 'Margaret Thatcher feared the fall of the Berlin Wall could herald return of Nazis as aides told her Germans were aggressive, egotistical and bullying', *DailyMail*, 30 December. https://www.dailymail.co.uk/news/article-4074992/Margaret-Thatcher-feared-fall-Berlin-Wall-herald-return-Nazis-aides-told-Germans-aggressive-egotistical-bullying.html.

211 Linning. 2016.

212 Cited in Hope, Christopher and Willgress, Lydia. 2016. 'Margaret Thatcher had deep misgivings over reunification of Germany, National Archives reveal', *Telegraph*, December 30. https://www.telegraph.co.uk/news/2016/12/30/margaret-thatcher-had-deep-misgivings-reunification-germany/.

213 Ibid.

214 Letter from Prof. Timothy Gordon Ash St Antony's College, Oxford, 'UK PM's private secretary composed the "little list" of alleged German qualities', *Financial Times,* January 3, 2017. https://www.ft.com/content/222d2562-cec2-11e6-864f-20dcb35cede2.

215 Ibid.

216 Ibid.

217 Cited in Walters. 2018.

218 Ibid.

219 Ibid.

220 Ibid.

221 Ibid.

222 Lawson, Dominic. 2014. 'Alan Clark was not "wonderful". He was sleazy and cruel', *The Independent,* July 8. https://www.independent.co.uk/voices/commentators/dominic-lawson/alan-clark-was-not-wonderful-he-was-sleazy-and-cruel-1787343.html.

223 Cited in MacShane, Denis. 2008a. 'Fear and loathing in Westminster', *Total Politics,* October 27. https://www.totalpolitics.com/articles/culture/fear-and-loathing-westminster; see also MacShane, Denis. 2008b. *Globalising Hatred: The New Antisemitism,* London: Weidenfeld and Nicolson.

224 Ibid.

225 Clark, Alan. 2011. *Diaries: In Power 1983–1992,* London: Hachette.

226 Trewin, Ion. 2009. *Alan Clark – The Biography*, London: Orion, pp. 230, 246–247.

227 *Financial Times.* 1985. 'Tory minister faces row over race remark', February 7.

228 Trewin, pp. 250–251.

229 Pilger, John. 1994. Documentary: *Death of a Nation: The Timor Conspiracy.* https://johnpilger.com/videos/death-of-a-nation-the-timor-conspiracy [Video].

230 Wilson, Jamie. 1999. 'Who will listen to his story now?', *The Guardian,* December 22. https://www.theguardian.com/uk/1999/dec/22/hamiltonvalfayed.jamiewilson3.

231 Ibid.

232 Ibid.

233 Ibid.

234 Ibid.

235 MacShane. 2008b.

236 Aitken, Jonathan. 2013. *Margaret Thatcher: Power and Personality*. London: Bloomsbury, p. 514.

237   Johnson, R.W. 1989. 'Is this successful management?', *London Review of Books*, 11 (8) (April 20). https://www.lrb.co.uk/the-paper/v11/n08/r.w.-johnson/is-this-successful-management.

238   Jewish Telegraphic Agency. 1989. 'British TV show explores government anti-semitism: the Jewish Chronicle', November 3. https://www.jta.org/archive/brit ish-tv-show-explores-government-anti-semitism-the-jewish-chronicle.

239   Ibid.

240   Freedland, J. 2003. 'The trailblazer', *The Guardian*, October 31. https://www.theguardian.com/politics/2003/oct/31/conservatives.politicalcolumnists.

241   Thatcher, Margaret. 1993. *The Downing Street Years,* London: Harper Collins.

242   Ibid., pp. 597–598.

243   Ibid., pp. 598.

244   This course was written before the days when all staff had (access to) computers and had been typed on an old-fashioned manual typewriter.

245   Thatcher. 1993, pp. 598.

246   For details of the Hillcole Group and the Hillgate Group, see Hill, Dave. Undated. 'The Hillcole group of radical left educators'. http://www.ieps.org. uk/media/1043/hillcole_group_chapter.pdf.

247   Dejevsky, Mary. 2009. 'Cameron's freebie to apartheid South Africa', *The Independent,* April 26. https://www.independent.co.uk/news/uk/politics/cam eron-s-freebie-to-apartheid-south-africa-1674367.html.

248   This in a then newly updated edition of Hanning, James and Elliott, Francis. 2009. *Cameron: The Rise of the New Conservative,* New York: Harper Perennial; Updated edition.

249   Dejevsky, Mary. 2009.

250   Ibid.

251   Cited in Dejevsky. 2009.

252   Ibid.

253   Higham, Nick. 2016. 'National Archives: Thatcher's poll tax miscalculation', *BBC News*, December 30. https://www.bbc.co.uk/news/uk-38382416.

254   Ibid.

255   Cited in Higham. 2016.

256   King, Oliver. 2015. 'The poll tax riot 25 years ago was the day I woke up poli-tically', *The Guardian,* March 31. https://www.theguardian.com/commentisfree/2015/mar/31/poll-tax-riots-25-years-ago-political-awakening-carnage-trafalgar-square.

257   Ibid.

258   Higham. 2016.

259   Owen, Paul. 2013. 'The life of Margaret Thatcher – timeline', *The Guardian*, April 8. https://www.theguardian.com/politics/2013/apr/08/life-of-margaret-thatcher-timeline.

260   *The Independent.* 2013. 'Margaret Thatcher's timeline: From Grantham to the House of Lords, via Arthur Scargill and the Falklands War', April 9. https://www. independent.co.uk/news/uk/politics/margaret-thatcher-s-timeline-grantham-house-lords-arthur-scargill-and-falklands-war-8564555.html.

261   Cited in Marks, Kathy. 2013. 'Margaret Thatcher an "unabashedly racist": The view of the Australian Foreign Minister', *The Independent,* April 10. https://www.independent.co.uk/news/world/australasia/margaret-thatcher-unabashedly-racist-view-australian-foreign-minister-8567946.html?amp.

7 John Major, multiculturalism and monoculturalism; grassroots Tory backlash to ethnic diversity in the Party (1990–2010)

SECTION 1: THE MAJOR GOVERNMENT (1990–1997)

Dual interventionism

Major's ministry was marked by a 'dual interventionist strategy' of combining immigration controls with anti-discrimination measures.[1] With respect to the former, the Major governments especially targeted what Tories perceived as the hitherto over-generous political asylum legislation.[2] According to Didier Lassalle, numbers of asylum applicants had risen from an average of 4,000 a year in the 1985–1988 period to 48,800 in 1991 alone.[3] The Asylum and Immigration Appeals Act of 1993, therefore, incorporated a number of deterrents and restrictions. The Act defined a claim for asylum in terms of the UK's obligations under the United Nations Convention 1951 and the 1967 Protocol relating to the Status of Refugees, under which a person must have a well-founded fear of persecution for reasons of race, religion, nationality, social group or political opinion. These obligations also gave the right of appeal before a special adjudicator for all unsuccessful asylum applications before removal from the UK. However, it gave the power to fingerprint all asylum applicants (and their dependants) as a means of detecting and deterring 'multiple applications'; reduced the obligation of housing authorities under the homelessness legislation towards asylum seekers; introduced accelerated and fast track appeals procedures; and stipulated time limits within which the Immigration Appellate Authorities must determine appeals.[4] As a result, between June 1994 and June 1996, 19,500 'illegal immigrants' [or, more accurately 'illegalized immigrants'] were identified, 6,300 of whom were repatriated.[5] Three years after the 1993 Act, the 1996 Asylum and Immigration Act was passed, which came into effect on January 1 1997. This set out the law on the prevention of 'illegal working' making it a criminal offence for employers to employ someone aged 16 or over, who has 'no right to work in the UK'.[6]

As regards anti-discriminatory measures, the Race Relations legislation framed by the Harold Wilson Labour Governments (notably the 1976 Race Relations Act and its main provision, the Commission for Racial Equality

DOI: 10.4324/9781003198673-11

was kept intact by the Major Government). Indeed, not only was the existing framework upheld, but it was expanded along what would be *described* as 'multiculturalist' lines.[7] As Vincent Latour points out, the 1991 census was partly inspired by the 1990 US census, which featured four 'ethno-racial categories.[8] That census, he goes on, was in fact the first to feature a question on ethnicity. The eight categories were 'Black', 'Black-Caribbean', 'Black-African', 'Black-Other', 'Indian', 'Pakistani', 'Bangladeshi' and 'Chinese', with people who did not fit specifically in those categories, being able to combine several of them, thus recognizing the 'ethnic' diversity of Britain in the late 19th century. In April 1996, the Home Office made it compulsory for all police forces to monitor the 'ethnic origin' of suspects and offenders, arguing that the reason for this was that the criminal justice system had been alleged to discriminate against minority ethnic communities and that Black people were supposedly disproportionately involved in crime.[9]

John Major: multiculturalist or monoculturalist?

According to Latour, on many occasions during his seven years in office, 'John Major recognised Britain's multicultural dimension and the positive contribution of immigrant communities'. Having already left No. 10, in 1999, he alleged that a speech he made in 1993[10] on the possibility of capitalism being fashioned into a meritocratic 'classless society'[11] targeted 'racial' as well as class barriers:

> When I talked of a classless society I wanted to say that the people who pushed wheelbarrows when I mixed cement for a living[12] were human beings worthy of respect. Class distinction is to me ... the same as racial discrimination.[13]

If we delve a little deeper, we can see that Major's *alleged* belief in 'multiculturalism' is a sham. While he may genuinely have been opposed to the traditional Tory values of keeping 'them' all out as much as possible, his ideological position was focussed on what he perceived to be the 'distinctive and unique contribution' Britain makes to Europe and his wish for the country to be remain part of the European Community.[14] This is best summed up in his own words:

> Fifty years from now Britain will still be the country of long shadows on county grounds, warm beer, invincible green suburbs, dog lovers and pools fillers and – as George Orwell said – 'old maids bicycling to Holy Communion through the morning mist' and if we get our way – Shakespeare still read even in school. Britain will survive unamendable in all essentials.[15]

It is not immediately clear how multiculturalism fits into this scenario. However, it is instructive to turn back to the ongoing debate of the time, as outlined in chapter 6, amongst educationists as to the relative merits of monocultural (the teaching in educational institutions of so-called 'British values and culture') multiculturalism (the celebration of diversity) and antiracism (a focus on education's role in undermining the institutional racism in British society). Stephen Ball argued that once Major had replaced Thatcher as Prime Minister, the influences of 'New Right' monoculturalists had already become 'more evident than before in government education policy'.[16] Ball cites Brian Cox, 'one time doyen of the traditionalist critique of educational modernisation',[17] as referring in *The Guardian* to 'a persistent rumour ... going round in education that the Prime Minister has agreed to do a deal with right wing Conservatives', namely that they would keep quiet about their opposition to Maastricht (the Maastricht Treaty signed on February 7, 1992, created the European Union) if Major will allow them to take control of education.[18] Whether this rumour had substance or not, by mid-1992 monoculturalists (or 'cultural restorationists' in Ball's terminology) were entrenched as the 'new' 'educational establishment' under what Ball refers to as 'Majorism'.[19]

Two of the examples of three National Curriculum subjects under Majorism that Ball gives to highlight different aspects of monoculturalism are Music and History. Classical music was viewed by the 'organic intellectuals of the New Right' (e.g. Anthony O'Hear and Roger Scruton) as 'the highest achievement of European culture'.[20] Ball points out that steel bands were often juxtaposed with Beethoven as a form of Eurocentric, cultural racism that informed their aesthetic judgements.[21] At the same time, History courses concentrated on key events in British History, including in Baker's words, 'the spread of Britain's influence for good in the world'. Baker's view was that 'we should not be ashamed of our history, our pride in the past gives us our confidence to stand tall in the world today'.[22] Ball concludes, the 'modernist project of comprehensive education is damned and rejected root and branch' and 'the attempt to recognise the pluralism and multi-culturalism of late twentieth century Britain is derided and replaced by a regressive "little Englandism."'[23]

It would seem, therefore that despite Latour's depiction of Major as a multiculturalist, he presided over and promoted an entrenched monoculturalism.

Tory backlash to ethnic diversity in the Party

Forty percent of Tory supporters racist and attempt to block non-White Tory candidate

In December 1990, a poll showed that 39% of Tory supporters were 'racially prejudiced', as against 29% of Labour supporters.[24] Also, in December 1990, just a few days after Major's arrival at No. 10, Black candidate John Taylor, a barrister and the son of Jamaican immigrants,[25] was adopted as Tory candidate for Cheltenham, an almost totally White, heavily middle-class town[26] for the 1992 General Election. In the same month, the Cheltenham Conservative Association tried to deselect him,[27] with Tory Party member Bill Galbraith expressing on national television his dissatisfaction over the adoption of a 'bloody ni**er'. On the day the vote was due to take place on expelling him from the local Tory Party, Galbraith issued an apology, following condemnation by Major and other local and national Tory leaders.[28] Major subsequently got involved in Taylor's General Election campaign, making a personal appearance on his upturned soapbox in the run up to the 1992 Election.[29] Galbraith was expelled, as well as banned from two local pubs.[30]

In similar developments, the Wallsend Conservatives adopted Hugh Neil, a Black candidate in November 1990, but unexpectedly replaced him in August 1991 with Neil suggesting he had been treated in a manner 'incompatible with normal decency'.[31] Likewise, hostility to a non-White Labour candidate was felt when Labour candidate Ashok Kumar won the marginal Langbaurgh seat at a by-election held in November 1991, despite the very small-sized Black and minority ethnic (BME) population in the constituency. Labour accused the local Tory Party of playing the 'race' card, by unnecessarily referring to his place of birth (Hardwar, India) and frequently his name in their own literature. Labour Shadow Home Secretary Roy Hattersley called the Langbaurgh campaign on 'race', 'the dirtiest campaign I have known since the Tories did very similar things in Smethwick, 27 years ago'.[32] For a discussion of Smethwick, see chapter 4 of this book.

Although no Black or Asian Conservative MP was elected in 1992, the Tories had adopted eight minority ethnic candidates, almost as many as Labour's nine non-White candidates and more than the Liberal-Democrats' six.[33]

Churchill's grandson pays tribute to Enoch Powell

In 1993, Winston Spencer-Churchill, the grandson of the former Prime Minister Winston Leonard Spencer-Churchill paid a tribute to Enoch Powell's 'Rivers of Blood' speech (see chapter 4) and insisted that Muslims would outnumber Christians in a matter of few decades.[34] Major immediately responded by asserting that Christianity would still be significant, to which Churchill's grandson replied, 'More likely the muezzin will be calling Allah's faithful to the High Main Street Mosque'.[35]

The Bell Curve published

In 1994, Richard Herrnstein and Charles Murray's book, *The Bell Curve*, was published. It was widely regarded by 'scientific' racists as a watershed moment, since it attempted to assign lower 'intelligence' to African Americans. Following universal condemnation of the book from the genuine scientific community based on its reasoning, its sources or the authors' associations with the more notorious sources, Eric Siegel, writing for the

Scientific American, argues that those points should actually take a secondary position, and that the real problem with the book is that 'it purports to investigate "racial" differences in IQ – without being honest about the authors' motives'.[36] It is racist (in Siegel's words, it 'endorses prejudice') 'by virtue of what it does not say'. Nowhere, Siegel points out, does the book address *why* it investigates 'racial' differences in IQ. 'By never spelling out a reason for reporting on these differences', he goes on, the authors transmit an unspoken yet unequivocal conclusion: 'race' is helpful in deciding whether a given individual or group has certain capabilities, the net effect being to tacitly condone the prejudgment of individuals based on 'race'.[37] As he puts it, this:

> curtails the individual's opportunities and livelihood, and contributes to what is often a self-fulfilling, systematic cycle of disadvantage for an entire group. It also curtails the prejudger's potential to wholly evaluate a person as an individual by his or her prior behavior, choices, and character. This is why the term 'civil rights' has a nice ring to it and 'bigotry' does not.[38]

In the final chapter of *The Bell Curve* (chapter 22), the suggested policy implications include:

> simpler tax codes, decreasing government benefits that could incentivize childbearing among the low-income, and increasing competency-based immigration ...Did the authors mean to imply that immigration screening could be based in part on race?...Much to the book's disgrace...that's at least a reasonable interpretation ... More so since, earlier in the book... they say, "Latino and black immigrants are, at least in the short run, putting some downward pressure on the distribution of intelligence."[39]

Herrnstein and Murray suggest you ask yourself, 'If it were known that the black/white difference is genetic, would I treat individual blacks differently from the way I would treat them if the differences were environmental?' This clearly implies that one may already be treating individual Black people differently in the first place.[40] Siegel concludes:

> With a certain eerie silence on the matter, 'The Bell Curve' spurs readers to prejudge by race. Astonishingly, this tome's hundreds of pages never actually specify what one is meant to do with the information about racial differences, and never attempt to steer readers clear of racial prejudgment. That's an egregious, reckless oversight, considering this is a pop science bestseller that comprehensively covers great numbers of subtopics and caveats, maintaining a genuinely proficient and clear writing style throughout. So we must call this book what it is: racist.[41]

In the same year as the book was published, in a Christmas Day message to the people of Britain in Channel 4, African American civil rights activist Jesse Jackson commented on the Tory Party, stating:

> We must no longer allow the clock to be turned back on human rights or put up with political systems which are content to maintain the status quo. In South Africa the status quo was called racism. We rebelled against it. In Germany it was called fascism. Now in Britain and the US, it is called conservatism.[42]

Jackson continued by saying that 'the oppressed must take responsibility for their own condition'. He concluded that while the enslaved and the exploited are not 'responsible for slavery or exploitation ... they must be responsible for taking the initiative to end it ... The oppressed must ... engage in sane, sober, sensitive and disciplined resistance to end their oppression'[43]

The Salman Rushdie controversy

Salman Rushdie's book *The Satanic Verses* was published in 1988. Many in the Muslim communities thought it blasphemous, and a number of antiracists outside those communities felt it was unnecessarily insulting and provocative.[44] The furore over its publication reached its climax after Ayatollah Ruhollah Khomeini of Iran issued a fatwa in February 1989 ordering Muslims to kill Rushdie. As Latour argues, its residual impact could still be felt throughout Major's time in office.[45] The Thatcher Government's refusal to ban *The Satanic Verses* had antagonized the Muslim communities even more, the vast majority of whom accepted Khomeini's fatwa. In December 1991, Rushdie's suggestion that there should be a paperback version of the *Satanic Verses* twisted the knife in the wound[46] and the further mobilization of large sections of the communities busted the myth of the *seemingly positive* racialized attribute of a model minority that had been foisted on the Muslim communities to juxtapose them with the 'rioting' Black communities.

On April 30, 1994, in Birmingham, UKACIA-affiliated organizations decided to create a National Interim Committee on Muslim Unity (NICMU) so as to provide the adequate and efficient representation which British Muslims had lacked during their unsuccessful campaign to have Rushdie's book banned.[47] In May 1996, NICMU delegates decided to create the Muslim Council of Britain, Britain's leading Muslim umbrella organization.

Latour argues that the involvement of Major's government was minimalist, with Michael Howard, Home Secretary from 1993 to 1997, merely offering encouragement and pledges of support and recognition.[48] The launch of the UK-supported US-led invasion of Iraq in 1991, followed by ethnic cleansing in Bosnia, of course, further alienated British Muslims.

The 1997 General Election

The 1997 General Election, held on May 1, 1997, resulted in a Labour Party landslide and heralded the birth of 'New Labour' under Tony Blair. A taste of what this was to mean for the Labour Party was provided Thatcher who, when before his victory has described Blair as: "probably the most formidable" Labour leader since Hugh Gaitskell, adding correctly 'I see a lot of socialism behind [Labour's] front bench, but not in Mr Blair. I think he genuinely has moved'.[49] Gaitskell had tried to change Labour's socialist Clause 4.

Major had unsuccessfully sought to rebuild public trust in the Tories following a series of scandals. *BBC News* commented that his 'tenure as prime minister was littered with fallen politicians'.[50] They included Tory National Heritage Secretary David Mellor who resigned from the Government in September 1992 after battling for almost two months to remain in the Cabinet against a background of unremitting publicity about his private life;[51] Michael Mates, Minister of State for Northern Ireland, who handed in his resignation in June 1993 after it was revealed he had lobbied Parliament on behalf of fugitive tycoon Asil Nadir;[52] while in January of the next year a tabloid revealed that Environment Minister Tim Yeo was the father of a child born to Conservative Councillor Julia Stent, when they weren't married to each other a sacrifice to Tory 'family values'.[53] This was followed by a number of other 'scandals' in 1994 and 1995.[54] In the run-up to the Election, opinion polls showed strong support for Labour due to Blair's personal popularity,[55] and Blair received a personal public endorsement from *The Sun* two months before the vote.[56] The election of 120 women, including 101 to the Labour benches, came to be seen as a watershed moment in female political representation in the UK.[57] The 1997 General Election ended 18 years of Tory Government. The future Prime Minister, Theresa May, who was to initiate the 'really hostile environment' (see the remaining chapters) was one of the Tory newcomers in Parliament.

SECTION 2: THE TORIES IN OPPOSITION (1997–2010)

Richard Hayton has argued that the leadership strategy provided by William Hague, Ian Duncan Smith and Michael Howard between 1997 and 2005 was characterized by uncertainty and inconsistency.[58] Between these years, the Tories changed their leader four times (Hague: June 1997 – June 2001; Smith: September 2001 – November 2003; Howard: November 2003-December 2005; after this David Cameron became leader until July 2016).

The leadership of William Jefferson Hague

Rather than a radical reassessment of Tory Party policy, following the big defeat in the election, Hague tried more to change the language, tone and emphasis of the Tory message in an attempt to distance himself from the

Thatcher-Major era.[59] In 1999, he cleared a speech by deputy Tory leader Peter Lilley that was meant to elucidate the philosophy of 'Kitchen Table Conservatism', to create a rhetorical shift to a Tory narrative that recognized the value of welfare and public services as well as Thatcherite free markets.[60] In the event, Lilley's speech was derided by Thatcher, whose aides apparently told Hague that she had 'gone ballistic' over the speech which, according to Simon Walters, had coincided with the 20th-anniversary celebrations of Thatcher's first election victory in 1979.[61] Following outrage from the Tory Shadow Cabinet, parliamentary party and local activists, Lilley was sacked. According to Walters, Hague was 'seared' by the experience: 'Having tried, tentatively, to take one-step out of the towering shadow of Margaret Thatcher, he had been forced to go running back to mummy. He was too scared to step out of line again'.[62]

Hague accordingly decided to align himself with traditional reactionary or regressive Tory politics. Thus, campaigning in the June 1999 elections to the European Parliament on the Eurosceptic Manifesto, *In Europe, not run by Europe,* and despite a resurgence by UKIP, Hague secured a dramatic victory in this first nationwide test of the Government's popularity since the 1997 General Elections, thus securing his position as leader and consolidating the hold of the right on the Tory Party.[63] The campaign had stressed, for example, that the Tories were 'a proudly British party' that would 'resist any attempt to develop a common immigration policy for the EU'.[64]

In a January 2001 article for the *Daily Mail*, which had been highlighting cases of so-called 'bogus asylum seekers' almost daily for two months, Heseltine summed up his position on the issue on the basis of 'three stark conclusions'.[65] First he said that 'a very large number are cheats deliberately making bogus claims and false allegations to get into this country'; second, he claimed that British citizens were being pushed to the back of the queue for housing and hospital treatment by 'dubious asylum seekers'; third, the problem of 'phoney asylum seekers was likely to grow as the impression spread that this country was a soft touch'.[66] As Alan Travis explains, Heseltine's real and hostile agenda lay 'deep in the detail of the article' where he made clear that his solution was to persuade the rest of the European Union, and the United Nations if necessary, 'to tear up the 1951 Geneva Convention which guarantees the right of an individual fleeing persecution to seek asylum'.[67] Heseltine said he wanted to 'redefine it for the new millennium', code for ensuring that it is even harder for those fleeing tyrannies, such as Iraq or Iran, to clamber over the walls of Fortress Europe.[68] According to Travis, the Tory's general election campaign strategist Andrew Lansley had pointed out that 'bogus asylum seekers' is an issue that plays particularly well in the tabloids and has the power to hurt Labour.[69]

Travis goes on to address Heseltine's three claims. With respect to 'asylum cheats', he pointed out while in the previous three months the Home Office had turned down 88% of the cases it had considered in the past three months, this masks the fact that only 48% of those cases were refused after full consideration was given to whether their claim to be suffering from persecution was genuine or unfounded. Over 50% were either given full refugee status or allowed to stay on exceptional grounds or were refused without proper consideration of their case.[70]

As to the second claim that 'dubious' asylum seekers were pushing British citizens to the back of the queue for housing and hospital treatment, the Home Office's response was: 'Council taxpayers' money is not being used to house asylum seekers and therefore local people are not being disadvantaged. We are using properties that do not have a waiting list'.[71] The reality, therefore, as Travis points out, is that this means slum housing and bed and breakfast hostels. As for hospital waiting lists, the number of asylum seekers is not a major factor: the NHS treats millions of people each week.[72]

Finally, is Britain a soft touch compared with the rest of Europe? In fact, Britain lay quite a way down the European league table of benefits for asylum seekers. 'Perhaps a more convincing explanation of why people come here', Travis concludes, 'rests on their historic links through Britain's colonial past and the fact that English is the global language',[73] itself also a product of colonialism and imperialism.

A Tory backbencher continued the same theme in March 2001, but this time directly relating asylum seekers to scientific racism.[74] Claiming he was a victim of 'political correctness', John Townend said he had been right to say in a speech earlier that month that the purity of Britain's 'homogeneous Anglo-Saxon society' had been 'seriously undermined' by mass immigration. He also said immigrants were partly to blame for rising crime rates in some areas.[75] In the speech that included a tribute to Enoch Powell, he also said that immigration 'did change the character of Britain; nobody can deny that; it is a fact'.[76]

Later in an interview on BBC Radio 4, he further claimed:

> Having absorbed that wave of immigration that basically was legal – and then we stopped it by the Immigration Act – we now face another wave and the vast majority of people in this country, including my constituency, are very worried. There is no doubt in this country there is a great political correctness which tries to push many of these things under the table.[77]

He also said:

> If people had been aware that by the new Millennium, London, our capital, would have over 25 per cent of its population from ethnic minorities and that forecasts expect that by 2014 over half of the city will be non Anglo-Saxon, that Leicester and Birmingham would be vying as to which city would have a black majority first, Enoch Powell would have been prime minister.[78]

In a statement, Hague said that Mr Townend's comments were 'totally unacceptable' and that they were in conflict with the compact on race relations. The main party leaders had signed an agreement with the Commission for Racial Equality not to allow election candidates to issue material 'likely to generate hostility or division between people of different racial, national or religious groups'. However the agreement covered only election candidates, and Tory sources said there was no need to take action against Mr Townend because he was standing down.[79]

The 2001 General Election

The twin issues of Europe and immigration dominated the 2001 Tory General Election campaign. The dominant theme of Hague's speeches and campaigning was the 'Common Sense Revolution' that was open to 'all Britons' and implicitly, according to Hayton, excluded minority ethnic groups.[80]

The Tories made no headway, Tony Blair remained in power and Hague resigned as Party leader on June 8, 2001,[81] plunging the Tory Party into what Michael White describes as 'one of the sharpest crises of self-confidence in its history as MPs recoiled from a succession battle few of them really want'.[82] Hague allies such as Ann Widdecombe (later to join the Brexit Party)[83] and Iain Duncan Smith were both potential contenders on the 'social authoritarian', wing of the Party, while the favourite, Michael Portillo, represented the 'inclusive' wing. Portillo launched his bid on June 13 and Duncan Smith launched his six days later. On June 21, Michael Ancram joined the race and on June 26, Kenneth Clarke, a pro-Europe contender, finally decided to enter the contest to lead the Tory Party.[84]

Uprisings in northern England

From April to July 2001, the northern English towns of Oldham, Burnley and Bradford saw violent confrontations between young British Asians and the police, culminating in the clashes of July 7–9 in Bradford in which 200 police officers were injured.[85] As Arun Kundnani explains, the clashes were prompted by racist gangs attacking Asian communities and the failure of the police to provide protection from this threat. In Kundnani's words:

> The fires that burned across Lancashire and Yorkshire through the summer of 2001 signalled the rage of young Pakistanis and Bangladeshis of the second and third generations, deprived of futures, hemmed in on all sides by racism, failed by their own leaders and representatives and unwilling to stand by as, first fascists, and then police officers, invaded their streets.[86]

'It was the violence', Kundnani argues, 'of communities fragmented by colour lines, class lines and police lines. It was the violence of hopelessness.

It was the violence of the violated'.[87] Colonialism, he explains, has been interwoven with the history of the northern mill towns since the beginning of the (first) Industrial Revolution. Specifically, cotton-spinning – on which the towns' early success was based – was a technology, borrowed from India, which became central to the emergence of northern England as the 'factory of the world'. Cotton grown in the plantations of the Caribbean, the US deep South or the fields of Bengal was brought to Lancashire and Yorkshire to be spun into cloth and sold back at profit to the Empire.[88]

By the 1960s, the mills were investing in new technologies which were operated 24 hours a day to maximize profit. The night shifts, which were unpopular with the existing workforce, soon became the domain of the Pakistani and Bangladeshi workers who were now settling in the mill towns.[89] But as technology advanced and replaced labour, the work once done cheaply by Bangladeshi workers in the north of England could now be done even more cheaply by Bangladeshi workers in Bangladesh.[90]

As the mills declined, entire towns were devastated, and White and Asian workers became unemployed. The only future now for the latter communities was in the local service economy. Relatives would pool their savings and set up a shop, a restaurant or a take-away. There was also mini-cabbing, with long hours and the risk of violence, often racially motivated. With the end of the textile industry, the largest employers were now the public services, but racism kept most of these jobs for White people.[91]

By the end of the 20th century, a whole generation had lived with soaring rates of unemployment, reaching around 50%, for example, among young Asians in Oldham. In Burnley, Accrington, Blackburn, Preston, Bradford and Leeds, Pakistani and Bangladeshi communities were among Britain's poorest 1%.[92]

As a result of racist council housing policies, there was segregation in the allocation of accommodation which in turn contributed to segregated schooling. Moreover, despite the commonplace racist perception that 'Asians keep to themselves', the reality was that the fear of racial harassment meant that most Asians sought the safety of their own areas, in spite of the overcrowding, the damp and dingy houses and the claustrophobia of a community penned in.[93]

Some school catchment areas contained nearly 100% populations of just one ethnic group. In others, where catchment areas ought to have produced mixed intakes, the mechanism of parental choice allowed White parents to send their children to majority-White schools a little further away. The result was Asian ghetto schools in which expectations of failure were common: poor results could be explained away by 'cultural problems:' e.g. Asian girls would be married off anyway, so why bother? The minority of teachers willing to tackle these issues found themselves struggling against a mass of institutionalized preconceptions. With mainstream schooling mired in a culture of failure, some Asian parents looked to 'faith schools' – which would offer education within an Islamic framework – as a way of raising standards for their children's education.[94]

Lack of social interaction and racist local media fostered mutual distrust, with the media promoting the idea that young Asians were thugs hellbent on attacking Whites at random. The regular racist violence against Asians was marginalized, while Asian crime on White people was sensationalized and misinterpreted as racially motivated:

> The segregation of communities, the roots of which lay in institutional racism, came to be perceived as 'self-segregation' — the attempt by Asians to create their own exclusive areas or 'no-go areas' because they did not want to mix with whites. It was a self-fulfilling prophecy.[95]

As Anila Baig explains, on July 7, 2001, Bradford was a powder keg waiting to explode into what was to become the worst outbreak of violence in mainland Britain, the repercussions are still being felt 20 years later.[96] Fascist groups such as the British National Party and the National Front had sparked trouble in other northern towns and cities, including Oldham and Burnley, and announced plans to march through Bradford. The Labour Home Secretary at the time David Blunkett banned the march and, instead, a rally was held by the Anti-Nazi League which was peaceful and well-attended by almost 500 people.[97]

Late in the afternoon, however, trouble erupted outside a pub in the centre of the city when Far Right supporters started shouting racist abuse. A fight ensued and an Asian man was stabbed. In Baig's words: 'The spark had been lit. Young Asians, who believed the authorities were protecting the neo-Nazis rather than them, clashed with police'. One of the organizers of the rally, then a youth worker, now a Labour Councillor Mohammed Amran points out that there was also a rumour circulating that the BNP was attacking mosques.[98] About one thousand were involved and it went on long into the night, with cars, shops, businesses and the city's main BMW garage targeted and destroyed. The Manningham Labour Club, with 23 people inside, was firebombed. The following evening young mainly White people began attacking Asian-owned businesses, and violence lasted until the Monday night. About 300 police officers were injured, and nearly the same number of people sentenced for their part in the violence.[99]

One of them was an Asian man jailed for two-and-a-half years for throwing a stone. A youth worker, he had originally gone on the first night of violence:

> I was trying to disperse the crowds and get them to go home. I even saved a TV reporter from being attacked. She was taking pictures of the rioters and they were getting aggressive so I intervened and took her to safety. I also got a white family out of a pub to safety. I was there as a helper.[100]

As time went on he says he wanted to 'fit in'. 'I threw a small stone but it was like throwing a bomb at my own life, everything exploded'.[101] On pleading guilty to riot, he was jailed:

> Going to prison was a horrible experience, it changes you as a person. I don't think anyone who was involved in the riots was unaffected. We were given the harshest sentences, never before had anyone been sent to jail for throwing a stone. We were punished severely for what happened and taught a very hard lesson.[102]

A Report into the cause of 'the riots' concluded people in Bradford were living 'a series of parallel lives' and 'deeply polarised'. According to Amran, speaking in 2021, the city is recovering, and the young people are its greatest asset. 'We have the youngest city in Europe. We have great talent here and need to harness that and turn them into our greatest asset'.[103] Elizabeth Hellmich, who the day after the events of July 7, 2001 formed a 'Mums' Army' to help the community feel safer, commented, 'The big issues instrumental in contributing to the riots are still here – inequality, racism, and poverty and also the cuts to youth services which means there are no activities for young people in the area. But at grassroots level there are so many people working together'.[104]

The Tory leadership contest concludes with BNP support for Duncan Smith

Meanwhile back in the Westminster bubble, the Tory leadership continued apace. On July 10, 2001, in the first round of the leadership contest, Portillo won 49 votes – less than a third of the parliamentary party,[105] and, two days later, in the second round, he increased his share of the vote by just one.[106] On July 14, Portillo's faltering campaign was dealt a serious blow when Thatcher turned against her former acolyte, telling friends that she personally blamed him for falsely claiming her support. *The Sunday Telegraph* had just reported that she privately supported him. Thatcher said, 'This story is plain wrong. I do not hold the views which it attributes to me and I am not backing Michael Portillo against Iain Duncan Smith'.[107]

Edgar Griffin campaigns for Duncan Smith

In August 2001, Edgar Griffin, father of Nick Griffin, Chairman of the BNP, had been sacked from the Tory Party because of his support for his son's party. Edgar Griffin's views were that 'If coloured people wish to go home, we would be crazy not to make the money available to them'.[108] As Angelique Chrisafis comments, 'It was not clear if he meant that all non-whites born and living in Britain should consider going "home."'[109] She points out that Mr Griffin had attended NF rallies and had taken along his then young son Nick. The BNP position that multiculturalism in Britain was eroding society, he described as 'common sense':

> Some of the BNP's policies are very sensible and the Conservative party would do well to listen to them, in the same way that Tony Blair listened to the Conservative party's economic policy. I understand the bad press the BNP have had in the same way that the Conservative party have. For the BNP to have such bad press is not a democracy. It is distorting things above all belief.[110]

He also said that 'If they [Black people] wish to be repatriated then they should be assisted, of course', claiming it 'is Tory grass-roots opinion'. He went on, 'My views are ordinary Tory views – there is nothing startling or extraordinary about my views. They are simply in line with frankly the ordinary common or garden worker in the party'.[111]

Referring to his sacking from the Tory Party, Griffin, a vice chairman of Montgomeryshire Conservatives Association, said it was a 'ridiculous' blip in his 53-year career as a Conservative activist. He had raised money for the party through Christmas fairs and had chaired workshops designed to inform members of Tory party policy. He said he felt he would remain a party member, despite news of his expulsion.[112] Apparently, he had been forced out of the Tory Party when he answered a call to the BNP helpline on a phone that was installed in his living room, since he was expecting a long-distance BNP-related call for his wife, Jean, who had popped out to post a letter.[113] According to Nicholas Watt, she had stood as a BNP candidate against Duncan Smith in his Chingford and Wood Green constituency.[114]

It was further revealed that Edgar Griffin's name appeared on Duncan Smith's campaign letterhead. According to Nicholas Watt, Duncan Smith immediately distanced himself from the BNP. 'The views of the BNP are abhorrent to me', he said. 'I have fought racism all my life'.[115] David Davies, a member of the Welsh assembly, commented:

> We are greatly disturbed that someone who holds office has this connection. He became involved in the Iain Duncan Smith campaign [after] we telephoned him along with other association officers who we felt might be sympathetic to Iain Duncan Smith to ask for his backing. It is embarrassing.[116]

This happened in August 2001 after Heseltine had warned that the Party would be 'out to lunch' for a generation if it elected Duncan Smith as its new leader, describing him as an extreme Europhobe. This was echoed by Clarke, who clashed bitterly with Duncan Smith over Europe during a head-to-head encounter: 'The idea we should go further to the right and become even more Eurosceptic is, I think, a suggestion that will put us in opposition for a generation'.[117]

Further BNP support for the Tories

Following these revelations about far-right support and connections among Tory rank-and-file, the BNP claimed between 150 and 200 Tories were BNP activists, but would give no further details: 'There are a large number of activists from the Conservatives. We are not prepared to divulge names. They are just ordinary people and we don't want their houses to be firebombed', according to a BNP spokesperson, while Edgar Griffin made a further claim that the BNP is 'nowhere near as right-wing as the Tory party'.[118]

Further revelations were forthcoming. A second Tory with links to the BNP was uncovered. Cresswell Rice from Somerset said he had been a member of the Tory party for 15 years but had also joined the BNP a year ago.[119] In yet another case, Chris Green, who stood for the Tories in elections for Peterborough City Council, in 2001 was a BNP officer, having first joined the BNP in 1997 then left to join the Tories in 1999 only to rejoin the BNP soon after.[120] The local Labour MP Helen Clarke wrote to Michael Ancram, then the Tory party chairman asking him to investigate the Peterborough Conservative Association. However, nothing was done, and Ancram's reply included a suggestion that she looked to the problems Labour had with Militant [a socialist grouping within the Labour Party] instead of troubling herself with Conservative Party politics.[121]

Finally, *The Independent on Sunday* also learned that Stephen Newman, forced to resign as a school governor in May 2001, was a Conservative Party member but had been an organizer for the National Front in Wales in his youth.[122] The BNP said Tory members would find the 'common-sense' policies of the BNP 'largely in line with their own views':

> The BNP is becoming home to large numbers of activists and members from the Conservative Party and we welcome it. A large number of BNP organisers … are themselves ex-Tory and ex-Labour activists and left those organisations in disgust at their craven sell-out to the forces of political correctness.[123]

The final ballot saw Clarke and Duncan Smith come out on top, and Portillo, abandoned his ambitions.[124] After much bickering, Duncan Smith was eventually elected leader on September 14, 2001.[125] Although he had been initially viewed as an outsider, his campaign was bolstered by Thatcher's public endorsement of him, and also helped by the fact that he had Clarke as his opponent in the final vote of party members whose strong support for the European Union conflicted with the views of much of the Tory Party.

The brief leadership of George Iain Duncan Smith

Duncan Smith's first performance as Leader of the Opposition in the House of Commons was the September 14, when Parliament was recalled to discuss the 9/11 (September 11, 2001) terrorist attacks in America, and in November 2001, he was one of the first politicians to call for an invasion of Iraq, subsequently holding talks in Washington, DC, with senior US officials.[126]

In the 2002 local elections, the Tories gained extra seats,[127] and at the 2002 Tory Party Conference in October, he told the audience, we are on the road back to power and his opponents that they should not underestimate 'the determination of the quiet man',[128] while in February 2003, following efforts to undermine him, he warned the party to 'unite or die'.[129] In the same month, *The Independent on Sunday* newspaper published an article claiming that 14 MPs were prepared to sign a petition for a vote of 'no confidence' in him (25 signatories were then needed) for a vote on his removal as leader.[130] At the 2003 Tory Party Conference in October, he tried to assure the party, 'The quiet man is here to stay, and he's turning up the volume'.[131] The 2003 local elections saw further gains,[132] but soon after Shadow Secretary of State for Trade and Industry Crispin Blunt resigned, calling Duncan Smith's leadership a 'handicap'.[133]

Things got worse when dubious payment claims Duncan Smith made to his wife Betsy out of public funds were revealed. The ensuing scandal became known as 'Betsygate'. Following a parliamentary commissioner's inquiry, according to Duncan Smith's solicitor David Hooper, it was found in 2004 that Betsy Duncan Smith should have been made out of 'short money' funds rather than MPs normal staffing allowance, that the parliamentary committee on standards and privileges seemed to think was very much a technical matter.[134]

However, the damage had been done, and following months of speculation over a leadership challenge, Duncan Smith called upon critics within his party to either gather enough support to trigger a no-confidence motion or support him. A no-confidence vote was called on Wednesday October 29, 2003, which Duncan Smith lost by 90 votes to 75,[135] and Michael Howard became the new Tory Party leader.[136]

Other instances of Tory racism in the first decade of the 21st century

In 2002, Anthony Browne, a former policy director to Boris Johnson when he was Mayor of London, published *Do we need mass immigration?: The economic, demographic, environmental, social and developmental arguments against large-scale net immigration to Britain*.[137] This book accused British Muslims of having divided loyalties and attributed a catalogue of social ills and health problems to immigration.[138] He wrote:

> The fact that African immigration has overtaken gay sex as the main cause of HIV in Britain is a sign that Europe can no longer ignore the entirely preventable AIDS holocaust consuming the continent next

door. But the solution is to treat the majority where they live, rather than the small number who can make it to Britain to access HIV treatment on the NHS.[139]

In a passage about Muslim leaders warning the Iraq war could cause social unrest, he wrote: 'Whatever the merits or demerits of war on Iraq, it is hardly a national strength to have a large minority with such divided loyalties during war'.[140] In addition, in articles in *The Spectator,* Browne also accused immigrants of spreading hepatitis and HIV/AIDS in the UK. In one of them, Browne wrote: 'It is not through letting in terrorists that the government's policy of mass migration – especially from the third world – will claim the most lives. It is through letting in too many germs'.[141] He also suggested that 'curbing the influx of HIV immigrants' would be a better public health approach to tackling HIV than telling people to wear condoms.[142] Browne was elected as a Tory MP at the 2019 General Election when Johnson won a landslide victory (see chapter 10).

In 2004, ten new countries joined the EU, mainly from eastern Europe and in 2007, two more, Bulgaria and Romania (see the remaining chapters of this book for discussions of the xenoracism that this engendered).

In 2008, Tory frontbencher Robert William Dixon-Smith used a racist phrase, 'ni★★er in the woodpile' during a House of Lords debate, apologizing later and saying the phrase was common when he was younger.[143] A spokesperson for David Cameron, then Tory leader, said the phrase was not appropriate, that it was right that he apologized, but that he would not be sacked from the front bench.[144] Finally, in 2009, Tory Councillor Bob Allen was suspended by the Party after he posted a picture of a gorilla next to a story about Asian Labour Councillor Ebrahim Adia on this personal blog.[145]

Notes

1   Solomos, John. 1993. *Race and Racism in Britain,* 2nd edition, London: Macmillan.
2   Latour, Vincent. 2009. 'Multiculturalism upheld? Immigration, "race relations" and diversity management under John Major (1990–1997)', *Observatoire de la Société Britannique* (7), https://journals.openedition.org/osb/804.
3   Lassalle, Didier. 1997. *Les minorités ethniques en Grande-Bretagne: Aspects démographiques et sociologiques contemporains,* Paris: L'Harmattan, p. 41.
4   UK Government. 1993. 'Asylum and Immigration Appeals Act 1993'. https://www.legislation.gov.uk/ukpga/1993/23/contents.
5   Lassalle. 1997, p. 41.
6   https://www.legislation.gov.uk/ukpga/1996/49/introduction.
7   Latour. 2009.
8   Ibid.
9   Ibid.
10 This was ten months after his only election victory. As we saw in the last chapter, Major had succeeded Thatcher following her resignation in 1990.
11 John Major Archive. 1993. 'Mr Major's speech to the Carlton Club', February 3. https://johnmajorarchive.org.uk/1993/02/03/mr-majors-speech-to-the-carlton-club-3-february-1993/. From a Marxist perspective, a classless capitalist

society is an oxymoron since, according to Marxist theory, capitalism is dependent for its very existence on the exploitation of the working class by the capitalist class.

12 According to Whitney R. Craig, Major grew up in a two-bedroom apartment in working class Brixton and left school at 16, working for a while as a labourer. It was at this time that he mixed cement for the London Electricity Board Whitney (Whitney, Craig. 1990).

13 Wragg, Ted. 2016. 'Education policy and class inequality', *Sociology Review*. https://www.longroad.ac.uk/wp-content/uploads/2016/06/Sociology-Education-policy-and-class.pdf.

14 Mr Major's Speech to Conservative Group for Europe – 22 April 1993. https://johnmajorarchive.org.uk/1993/04/22/mr-majors-speech-to-conservative-group-for-europe-22-april-1993/

15 Ibid.

16 Stephen J. Ball. 1993. 'Education, Majorism and the "Curriculum of the Dead."' Ball does not use the term 'monocultural', but instead describes this ideological faction as 'cultural restorationists' or the 'hard line, old humanists of the New Right … within the British Conservative Party' (p. 195).

17 Ibid., p. 198.

18 Cited in Ball. 1993, p. 198. *The Guardian* article appeared on p. 22 on September 15, 1992.

19 Ball. 1993, p. 199. He notes how the 'reform process' (the re-assertion of traditional forms of education and curriculum) had been set in train by the Education Reform Act of 1988, enacted by Education Secretary Kenneth Baker under the Thatcher Government (p. 197).

20 Ibid., p. 200.

21 Ibid., p. 201.

22 Cited in Ball. 1993, p. 203.

23 Ball. 1993, p. 205.

24 *The Independent*, December 14, 1990.

25 *BBC News*. 2011. 'Profile: Lord Taylor of Warwick (Updated)', January 25. https://www.bbc.co.uk/news/uk-politics-12175980.

26 AP. 1990. 'Conservative Party member apologizes for racist remark', December 11. https://apnews.com/article/fb84d210671f045606397e6e54261f86.

27 *The Guardian*. 1990.

28 AP. 1990.

29 Travis, Alan. 1992. 'Major raises horror spectre', *The Guardian*, March 31.

30 Latour, Vincent. 2009. 'Multiculturalism upheld? Immigration, "race relations" and diversity management under John Major (1990–1997)'. https://journals.openedition.org/osb/804?lang=en.

31 *The Journal* [Newcastle] August 23, 1991, quoted in *The Political Quarterly*, 'Ethnic minority candidates in general elections', January-March 1993.

32 'Racism charge clouds result', *The Guardian*, November 9, 1991, cited in Latour, 2009.

33 'Ethnic minority candidates in general elections', *The Political Quarterly*, January-March 1993, p. 107.

34 Feder, Don. 'Enoch Powell spoke the truth on immigration', *Jewish World Review*. http://www.jewishworldreview.com/cols/feder021698.html. I should point out that Feder's article is very pro-Powell.

35 Ibid.

36 Siegel, Eric. 2017. 'The real problem with Charles Murray and "The Bell Curve"', *Scientific America*, April 12. https://blogs.scientificamerican.com/voices/the-real-problem-with-charles-murray-and-the-bell-curve/.

37 Ibid.

38 Ibid.
39 Cited in Siegel. 2017.
40 Siegel. 2017.
41 Ibid.
42 Cited in Associated Press. 2016. 'Jackson blasts the status quo in US, Britain', *DeseretNews*, December 26. https://www.deseret.com/1994/12/26/19150027/jackson-blasts-the-status-quo-in-u-s-britain.
43 Ibid.
44 See, for example, Wilkins, Chris. 1992. 'Freedom of speech in the multicultural society', in James Lynch, Celia Modgil and Sohan Modgil (eds.) *Cultural Diversity and the Schools. Vol. 3 Equity or Excellence? Education and Cultural Reproduction*, London: The Falmer Press.
45 Latour. Vincent. 2009. 'Multiculturalism upheld?'.
46 Ibid.
47 Ibid.
48 Ibid.
49 Cited in Castle, Blair Stephen. 1995. 'Thatcher praises "formidable" Blair', *The Independent*, May 28. https://www.independent.co.uk/news/thatcher-praises-formidable-blair-1621354.html.
50 *BBC News*. 1998. 'UK Politics: The Major scandal sheet', October 27. http://news.bbc.co.uk/1/hi/uk_politics/202525.stm.
51 Kareem, Abdul. 2017. 'September 24, 1992: Mellor resigns amid scandals', *Gulf News*, September 23. https://gulfnews.com/today-history/september-241992-mellor-resigns-amid-scandals-1.2094643.
52 *BBC News*. 2008a. '1993: Minister resigns over business links', June 24. http://news.bbc.co.uk/onthisday/hi/dates/stories/june/24/newsid_2519000/2519201.stm.
53 Bates, Stephen and Chaudhary, Vivek. 1994. 'Tim Yeo sacrificed to family values', *The Guardian*, January 6. https://www.theguardian.com/politics/2010/jan/06/tim-yeo-sacrificed-family-values.
54 Ibid.
55 *BBC News*. 2001. 'Blair ahead in leadership ratings', May 3. http://news.bbc.co.uk/news/vote2001/hi/english/opinion_polls/newsid_1306000/1306664.stm.
56 Greenslade, Roy. 1997. 'It's the Sun wot's switched sides to back Blair', *The Guardian*, 18 March. https://www.theguardian.com/politics/1997/mar/18/past.roygreenslade.
57 Harman, Harriet. 2017. 'Labour's 1997 victory was a watershed for women but our gains are at risk', *The Guardian*, April 10. https://www.theguardian.com/commentisfree/2017/apr/10/labour-1997-victory-women-101-female-mps.
58 Hayton, Richard. 2012. *Reconstructing Conservatism? The Conservative Party in opposition, 1997–2010*, Manchester: Manchester University Press, pp. 40–41.
59 Ibid., p. 43.
60 Ibid., p. 46.
61 Walters, Simon. 2001. *Tory Wars: Conservatives in Crisis*, London: Politicos, p. 117, cited in Hayton. 2012, p. 47.
62 Ibid.
63 Hayton, pp. 47–48.
64 Conservative Party European Elections Manifesto, 1999, cited in Hayton, p. 48.
65 Travis, Alan. 2001. 'Asylum issue takes election centre stage', *The Guardian*, January 5. https://www.theguardian.com/society/2001/jan/05/asylum.socialcare.
66 Ibid.
67 Ibid.
68 Ibid.
69 Ibid.

70   Ibid.
71   Cited in Travis. 2001.
72   Travis. 2001.
73   Ibid.
74   Sparrow, Andrew. 2001. '"I refuse to keep quiet on race", says rebel MP', *The Telegraph*, March 29. https://www.telegraph.co.uk/news/uknews/1328295/I-refuse-to-keep-quiet-on-race-says-rebel-MP.html.
75   Ibid.
76   Cited in Sparrow. 2001.
77   Ibid.
78   Ibid.
79   Sparrow. 2001.
80   Hayton. p. 49.
81   *The Guardian*. 2021. 'Tory leadership timeline', September 14. https://www.theguardian.com/politics/2001/sep/14/conservatives.uk.
82   White, Michael. 2001. 'Demoralised Tories face lengthy leadership battle', *The Guardian*, June 9. https://www.theguardian.com/politics/2001/jun/09/uk.conservatives1.
83   Brexit simply means the departure of the UK from the European Union. The Brexit Party was formed in 2019, initially on a platform of getting the UK out of the European Union as quickly as possible.
84   'Tory leadership timeline'. 2021. *The Guardian*.
85   Kundnani, Arun. 2001. 'From Oldham to Bradford: the violence of the violated', Institute of Race Relations, October 1. https://irr.org.uk/article/from-oldham-to-bradford-the-violence-of-the-violated/.
86   Ibid.
87   Ibid.
88   Ibid.
89   Ibid.
90   Ibid.
91   Ibid.
92   Ibid.
93   Ibid.
94   Ibid.
95   Ibid.
96   Baig, Anila. 2021. 'Bradford race riots 20 years on as man recalls throwing stone "like bomb at my own life"', *The Mirror*, July 7. https://www.mirror.co.uk/news/uk-news/bradford-race-riots-20-years-24474030.
97   Ibid.
98   Ibid.
99   Ibid.
100 Cited in Baig. 2021.
101 Ibid.
102 Ibid.
103 Ibid.
104 Ibid.
105 Watt, Nicholas and Ward, Lucy. 2001. 'Portillo falters in chaotic vote', *The Guardian*, July 11. https://www.theguardian.com/politics/2001/jul/11/uk.conservatives2.
106 Watt, Nicholas. 2001a. 'Stalled Portillo hustles for votes', *The Guardian*, July 13. https://www.theguardian.com/politics/2001/jul/13/uk.conservatives2.
107 Watt, Nicholas. 2001b. 'Furious Thatcher rounds on Portillo', *The Guardian*, July 16. https://www.theguardian.com/politics/2001/jul/16/uk.conservatives1.

108   Cited in Chrisafis, Angelique. 2001. 'I'm a normal Conservative with perfectly normal views'. *The Guardian*, August 25. https://www.theguardian.com/politics/2001/aug/25/uk.conservatives.
109   Ibid.
110   Cited in Chrisafis. 2001.
111   Ibid.
112   Chrisafis. 2001.
113   Ibid.
114   Watt, Nicholas. 2001c. 'Duncan Smith sacks backer with BNP link', *The Guardian*, August 24. https://www.theguardian.com/politics/2001/aug/24/uk.conservatives.
115   Cited in Watt. 2001c.
116   Ibid.
117   Watt. 2001c.
118   Goodchild, Sophie and Dillon, Jo. 2001. '"Hundreds" of Conservatives are in the BNP', *The Independent*, August 26. https://www.independent.co.uk/news/uk/politics/hundreds-of-conservatives-are-in-the-bnp-9134986.html?amp.
119   Ibid.
120   Ibid.
121   Ibid.
122   Ibid.
123   Cited in Goodchild and Dillon. 2001.
124   White, Michael and Watt, Nicholas. 2001. 'Clarke takes pole position as shocked Portillo quits the race', *The Guardian*, July 18. https://www.theguardian.com/politics/2001/jul/18/uk.conservatives7.
125   'Tory leadership timeline'. 2021. *The Guardian*, September 14. https://www.theguardian.com/politics/2001/sep/14/conservatives.uk.
126   Tempest, Matthew. 2001. 'Duncan Smith backs action against Iraq', *The Guardian*, November 29. https://www.theguardian.com/politics/2001/nov/29/conservatives.uk.
127   *BBC News*. 2002. 'Local Elections 2002'. http://news.bbc.co.uk/hi/english/static/vote2002/local_elections/atoz.stm.
128   Davies, Mark. 2002. 'Duncan Smith: The Tories are back,' *BBC News*, October 11. http://news.bbc.co.uk/1/hi/uk_politics/2314149.stm.
129   *BBC News*. 2003a. '"Unite or die' warns Tory leader', 21 February. http://news.bbc.co.uk/1/hi/uk_politics/2403923.stm.
130   McSmith, Andy and Dillon, Jo. 2003. 'Tory MPs line up to deal death blow to IDS', *The Independent*, February 23. https://www.independent.co.uk/news/uk/politics/tory-mps-line-up-to-deal-death-blow-to-ids-120094.html.
131   *BBC News*. 2003b. 'Tory leader: 'Back me or get out', October 9. http://news.bbc.co.uk/1/hi/uk_politics/3175680.stm.
132   *BBC News*. 2003c. 'Local elections: A-Z of results'. http://news.bbc.co.uk/1/shared/bsp/hi/vote2003/locals/html/atoz.stm.
133   Peoplepill. Undated. 'British Politician: Crispin Blunt'. https://peoplepill.com/people/crispin-blunt.
134   Hooper, David. 2004. 'The injustice of Betsygate', *The Guardian*, March 31. https://www.theguardian.com/politics/2004/mar/31/conservatives.uk1.
135   *BBC News*. 2003d. 'Tory leader ousted', October 29. http://news.bbc.co.uk/1/hi/uk_politics/3225127.stm.
136   *BBC News*. 2003e. 'Howard crowned Tory leader', November 6. http://news.bbc.co.uk/1/hi/uk_politics/3245561.stm.
137   Browne, Anthony. 2002. *Do we need mass immigration?: The economic, demographic, environmental, social and developmental arguments against large-scale net immigration to Britain*. London: Civitas.

138   Mason, Rowena. 2019. 'Tory candidate faces calls to quit over "disgusting racism"', *The Guardian*, November 11. https://www.theguardian.com/politics/2019/nov/11/tory-candidate-anthony-browne-faces-calls-quit-over-disgusting-racism.

139   Ibid.

140   Ibid.

141   Mason. 2019.

142   Cited in Mason. 2019.

143   *BBC News*. 2008b. 'Peer's apology over racist phrase', July 9. http://news.bbc.co.uk/1/hi/uk_politics/7497097.stm.

144   Ibid.

145   Greaves, Andrew. 2009. 'Gorilla picture Tory suspended', *The Bolton News*, February 26. https://www.theboltonnews.co.uk/news/4155201.gorilla-picture-tory-suspended/.

Part 4

The hostile environment: genesis, incorporation and the end of free movement

8   Theresa May and the 'really hostile environment': origins, official launch and enactment (2010–2016)

The 2010 General Election

Despite a large swing to the Tories, the 2010 General Election in May resulted in a hung Parliament. Discussion about forming a Coalition Government between the Tories and the Liberal Democrats went on for five days. When the outgoing Labour Prime Minister Gordon Brown realized that a deal between the other two parties was imminent, he resigned ending 13 years of Labour government.[1] There then began six years of ConDem Coalition Government, under the premiership of Tory David Cameron. Cameron appointed Tory Theresa May as his Home Secretary in the first ConDem Cabinet.

Austerity is unleashed

On October 20, 2010, Tory Chancellor of the Exchequer, George Osborne had unleashed what the *Financial Times* referred to as 'the most drastic budget cuts in living memory, outstripping measures taken by other advanced economies which are also under pressure to sharply reduce public spending'.[2] This ushering in of a 'new age of austerity' had been promised by Cameron some 18 months before the ConDem October 2010 announcement.[3] The sweeping cuts in spending and entitlements amounted to £81 billion over four years – the equivalent of 4.5% of projected 2014–2015 gross domestic product.[4] Declaring that 'today is the day where Britain steps back from the brink', Osborne promised a £7 billion fall in welfare support and 490,000 public sector job cuts by 2014–2015. Reflecting Tory TINA (There Is No Alternative) used by Thatcher to justify neoliberal capitalism) ideology, Osborne insisted that there is no alternative to making the working class pay for the bankers' crisis[5]: 'Tackling the budget deficit is unavoidable. To back down now and abandon our plans would be the road to economic ruin'.[6]

It is the degree of austerity that condemned the working class as a whole to varying degrees of poverty and desperation and misery[7] that prompted me to abbreviate this emerging alliance of Tories and Liberal Democrats appropriately to ConDem.[8]

DOI: 10.4324/9781003198673-13

SECTION 1: MAY WADES IN; CAMERON'S 'MUSCULAR LIBERALISM'; MORE UPRISINGS AND MAY'S RESPONSE

Home Secretary May wades in on immigration[9]

In her first major speech on immigration on November 5, 2010, May described it as 'one of the most important issues facing our country'.[10] She began with the usual softener – 'managed well, immigration is something that can bring great benefits' – then launched into an offensive against (prospective) migrants by continuing: '[but] managed poorly, it is something that can cause great economic and social pressure', and the 'government is committed to reducing the number of non-EU migrants'. 'Net inward migration in the last year', May went on, 'was nearly 200,000'. Upping the alarmist rhetoric, she stated, 'Between 1997 and 2009, net migration to Britain totalled more than 2.2 million people. That is more than twice the population of Birmingham'.[11] May then mentioned 'stories of abuse of the system', before referring to 'serious social impacts in some areas, with pressure being placed on key public services such as schools, the health service, transport, housing and welfare'.[12]

As we have seen, it is a convenient convention for (right-wing) governments to falsely blame immigrants for putting pressure on public services, rather than privatization and lack of government funding, both part of ongoing neoliberalization. Moreover, crucially May was, as a Cabinet Minister, complicit in the ideological *choice* to impose austerity on the working class and making them pay for the bailout of the banks, following the 2007/2008 financial crisis.

Directly and assertively, May then alluded to 'the segregation we see in too many of our communities' that 'created community tensions and helped contribute to a society that is not as integrated as we would like', before pledging: 'The public should know that I will take action. I am determined to get the immigration system back under control'.[13]

This callous rhetoric of hate, blame and threat – 'immigrants create segregation and community tension and we will take action to control them' – belies the fact that an alternative to denouncing immigrants and trying to make them pay psychologically and financially to earn the right to be in the UK, is to welcome them in various ways into our communities and to value the various contributions that they make.

Comparing controlling immigration using the 'points-based system alone' (where applicants must reach a points score above a minimum threshold to be successful) to 'squeezing a balloon', she spewed further scaremongering, emotive and hostile rhetoric:

> *Push down* work visas and the number of student visas will *shoot up*. *Clamp down* on student visas and family visas will *spring up*. *Bear down* on family visas and work visas will *explode*. With unskilled labour set to

zero, all that happened was student visas *rocketed by thirty per cent to a record 304,000 in just one year*, as some applicants used it as an alternative work route.[14]

Making a direct pitch for immigration from capitalists and highly qualified scientists – 'the brightest and the best' – and the need to keep out impoverished workers, May proclaimed: 'We can increase the number of high value migrants: the entrepreneurs, the investors, the research scientists – at the same time as we reduce the total number of people coming to Britain through the economic routes'.[15]

After revealing measures for the economic route, with further reference to 'cracking down', May moved on to the education route, promising a 'more robust system ... to ensure [students'] departure at the end of their legitimate stay'; she proclaimed:

> People might imagine that by students we mean people who come here for a few years to study at university and then go home – but that's not always the case. We estimate that nearly half of all students coming here from abroad are coming to study a course below degree level. We have to question whether these are the brightest and the best that Britain wants to attract – they may be, or they may not.[16]

She then compared the education route to the economic, using further hostile hateful rhetoric:

> We will follow exactly the same principle as in the skilled work route – a more selective approach, which attracts the highly skilled, the talented and the genuinely needed, but reduces numbers overall by *weeding out those who do not deserve to be allowed in*. The *sheer number* of students coming in, and the large proportion of total inward migration this represents, means we cannot delay in taking this *necessary and decisive action*.[17]

While this makes party political 'sense', given government intentions to pander to popular racism, within the confines of the 'logic' of capitalism there is a contradiction. Capitalism values entrepreneurs because they create the conditions for the extraction of surplus value from workers by setting up capitalist enterprise, but it also aims to drive down wages to increase surplus value, and immigrants historically are a source of cheap labour.[18] Hence, there are often competing demands between politicians playing 'the "race" card' and capitalists hungry for low-paid workers. Thus, in an interview on the *BBC News* Channel on November 19, 2018, Josh Hardie, Confederation of British Industry (CBI) Deputy Director-General stressed the need for lower-skilled workers as well as entrepreneurs.

Widening the net of her targeted scapegoats, May used alarmist and hostile rhetoric when she blamed immigration once again for the decline in 'public services', which she obviously knew was about to increase dramatically with the onset of austerity:

> uncontrolled immigration is bad for our economy and it is bad for our society. It puts pressure on the public services that people rely on and creates unnecessary tension and discord. I want a more selective approach which prioritises our universities, attracts the brightest and best workers and minimises abuse in the study and family routes ... I want to bear down on all the routes into Britain and to crack down on abuse of the system. We will cap the number of economic migrants from outside the EU and ensure only those workers who are genuinely needed for our economy are allowed in. We will reduce the numbers of bogus students coming here to study. And we will strengthen controls on family visas.[19]

May concluded by repeating Cameron's unrealistic pledge to drastically reduce the immigration of *workers* into the UK to the tens of thousands, by claiming that only the rich deserve to migrate to the UK:

> For all these routes, I want a clear way to control who can settle in Britain — that is a historic privilege that we should not fritter away lightly. I want the message to go out loud and clear that Britain will remain open for business. Our economy will remain accessible to the best and the brightest in the world, that's why, as the Prime Minister said yesterday, entrepreneurs will be welcome; scientists will be welcome; wealth creators will be welcome. But we must make sure that migration is properly controlled. We will reduce net migration from the hundreds of thousands to the tens of thousands. It will not be easy. It will take hard work and a great deal of political courage. But the British people want us to do it and it is the right thing to do. So we will do it.[20]

May's offensive against the 'immigrant family'

A central plank of May's offensive was directed at the family, as constituted of a British and foreign spouse/civil partner; engaged (with plans to marry within six months) or who have been living together in a relationship for two years. 'An area where we have already taken action', she asserted: 'is the family visa route. Unsurprisingly perhaps, over two-thirds of the 63,000 people who entered the UK in 2004 to join family here, were still in Britain five years later. And last year, some 40,000 marriage visas were issued'.[21] 'We estimate', May went on, 'that the family route accounted for nearly 20 per cent of non EU migration last year'. Heralding what was later to crystallize into that part of the 'really hostile environment' that was to divide families, this clergy's daughter, singling out an imprisoned cleric, threatened and warned:

This summer, we ordered the UK Border Agency to clamp down on sham marriages. They have had significant success, conducting 53 operations and making 118 arrests. Shockingly, this included the arrest of a vicar who was subsequently jailed for staging over 300 sham marriages. As well as tackling abuse of the marriage route we need to ensure that those who come here can integrate successfully into society and play a part in their local community. So from 29 November, those applying for marriage visas will have to demonstrate a minimum standard of English. This is only right. People coming to this country must be able to interact with the rest of the population.[22]

May added: 'And we need to go further. We must look at measures to tighten this route, for example by introducing processes to allow us to check that the UK sponsor is able to maintain and accommodate the foreign spouse'.[23] Referring to 'temporary versus permanent migration', she promised that 'No one is suggesting that those who come here to marry legitimately should not be able to make the UK their permanent home'.[24] The reality is that she went on to make this as difficult as she possibly could.

Just over two weeks later (November 23, 2010), May's resolve to play 'the "race" card' was repeated to the House of Commons[25] and reiterated by Cameron in April 2011, when he said that he had: 'made a clear commitment to the British people that we would aim to reduce net migration to the levels we saw in the 1980s and 1990s. Now we are in government, we are on track to meet that aim'.[26]

Cameron's 'muscular liberalism' speech

In February 2011, Cameron made his infamous 'muscular liberalism' speech on radicalization and the causes of terrorism, but that was also an attack on multiculturalism. 'Muscular liberalism' was contrasted with the supposedly 'passive tolerance' associated with multiculturalism:

Frankly, we need a lot less of the passive tolerance of recent years and a much more active, muscular liberalism. A passively tolerant society says to its citizens, as long as you obey the law we will just leave you alone [...] But I believe a genuinely liberal country does much more; it believes in certain values and actively promotes them. Freedom of speech, freedom of worship, democracy, the rule of law, equal rights regardless of race, sex or sexuality.[27]

Cameron argued that the UK needed a stronger national identity to prevent people turning to all kinds of extremism.[28] The Labour MP for Luton South, Gavin Shuker, asked if it was wise for Mr Cameron to make the speech on the same day the far-right English Defence League (EDL) staged a major protest in his constituency, while Labour Shadow Justice Secretary,

Sadiq Khan was reported as saying Cameron was 'writing propaganda material for the EDL'.[29]

A genuine liberal country, he said 'says to its citizens: This is what defines us as a society. To belong here is to believe these things'.[30] Under the 'doctrine of state multiculturalism', he went on, different cultures have been encouraged to live separate lives: 'We have failed to provide a vision of society to which they feel they want to belong. We have even tolerated these segregated communities behaving in ways that run counter to our values'.[31]

The 2011 uprisings

As Andy Southwark argues, similar conditions create similar results and thus with a Tory-led Government carrying out brutal attacks on the British working class 'it was inevitable that sooner or later we'd see a return to the social unrest that characterised the 80s'.[32] The catalyst, he points out, is the all too familiar story of police violence. On August 4, 2011, Mark Duggan, a 29-year-old Black man, was shot dead by police in Tottenham, North London. An inquest jury in 2014 found the shooting to be lawful. However, it concluded that Duggan did not have a weapon in his hands when confronted by police but had thrown it from the cab he was travelling in. In 2015, the Independent Police Complaints Commission (IPCC) found no case to answer for any officer involved. Its investigation reported that Duggan was most likely shot while holding a gun that he was probably 'in the process of throwing' away. But this was challenged in 2020 by Forensic Architecture (FA), a human rights research organization based at Goldsmiths, University of London.[33]

Ten years after his death, Mark Duggan's cousin, Marsha Farmer, told ITV News how the five days of unrest in the summer of 2011 was traumatic for the family and exposed deep wounds within society.[34] Two days after his death, she explains, members of his family were still waiting for answers: 'We didn't know much about what had happened to Mark: 'We were watching it unfold through the media like everyone else'.[35] 'The first reports that came out about Mark's death', she went on, 'was that Mark had shot at a police officer. So for us as a family, we're stunned, we're shocked because we're like "that's not something Mark's going to do."'[36] Since nobody 'came ... officially to say what had happened to Mark ... the following day, my family peacefully went down to Tottenham police station to find out'.[37] She concluded, 'They were treated with contempt, and that's when it all just kicked off'.[38]

Two hundred protesters, consisting of local residents, community leaders and some of Duggan's relatives gathered outside Tottenham police station to demand answers. Reports indicate that the protesters were initially peaceful and good natured but the mood became increasingly angry as the police failed to engage with them.[39] Those present said the spark for the rioting was a specific incident involving a 16-year-old young woman, who stepped forward to confront police demanding answers, but was attacked with shields and batons.[40] According to Anthony Johnson: 'They beat her with a baton, and then the crowd started shouting "run, run", and there was a hail of missiles. She had been saying: "We want answers, come and speak to us."'[41] As news of the attack spread, violence throughout the area quickly escalated. A double-decker bus and several shops were set alight as police fought running battles with protestors along Tottenham High Street.[42] Southwark explains that both the media and the ConDem Government inevitably focused on the incidents of looting and violence 'while excusing the police's actions and failing to even consider the deep seated resentment that lies behind the incident' being 'unanimous in both their support for the police and their condemnation of the people of Tottenham'.[43] He goes on:

> regardless of its tactical effectiveness as a means of protest property damage is not real violence. Smashing a few windows or nicking some trainers from footlocker doesn't actually physically hurt anyone and in most cases is a perfectly understandable response, however desperate, to the violence of the police and the state.[44]

'Capitalism on the other hand', he correctly points out, 'wreaks violence upon society on a daily basis: from dire poverty and famine through to the very police brutality that sparked this whole incident'.[45] 'The reality is of course that the people on the streets of Tottenham were not "violent" criminals looking to line their pockets with stolen goods', they were poor people, 'simply a community that has been pushed to the edge by the economic system they live under and the police violence that supports it'.[46]

Neo-Marxist Louis Althusser viewed the police, along with the armed forces, the courts and the prisons, as part of the Repressive State Apparatus. As he put it, in Marxist theory:

> the State is explicitly conceived as a repressive apparatus. The State is a 'machine' of repression, which enables the ruling classes ... to ensure their domination over the working class, thus enabling the former to subject the latter to the process of surplus-value extortion.
> (i.e. to capitalist exploitation)[47]

As we have seen, Cameron's ConDem Government implemented an austerity programme after being formed, and was expecting a response to it, with the police given free rein to control the growing discontent accordingly. The police were ready in 2011, just as they had been for the student demonstrations in November and December 2010 in opposition to planned spending cuts to further education and an increase of the cap on tuition fees. They had also prepared for the vicious clampdown on dissent around the Royal wedding of William and Kate Middleton, after which 'exemplary' sentences were handed out for minor protest offenses – all part of the same programme to discourage resistance and demonstrate to capitalism that the Government is capable of maintaining control in the face of further resistance.[48] Tottenham must therefore be seen, as agued by Southwark, 'in context of a deep economic crisis and historically large cuts to public welfare'.[49] Tottenham is located in Harringey which was already in a bad state in 2007 prior to the recession when it was ranked the 18th most deprived local authority in England out of 326. In 2010, its ranking dropped to 13th with one out of two children living in poverty, 'demonstrating the devastating effect of the recession on a community already struggling under the weight of the capitalist system'.[50] Left Labour MP John McDonnell illustrated the depth of the cuts there:

> In March [2011] Haringey Council approved cuts of £84 million from a total budget of £273 million. There was a savage 75% cut to the Youth Service budget, including: closing the youth centres; connexions careers advice service for young people reduced by 75%; and the children's centre service reduced.[51]

Theresa May's reaction to the uprisings

What was the reaction of Home Secretary May? While a report from the charity, the Children's Society, which surveyed 13- to 17-year-olds and adults, found that young people across the UK believed poverty was one of the key reasons behind the August uprisings, and while 66% of adults and 57% of young people believed people had taken part 'to get goods and possessions they couldn't afford to buy', May described those involved as an 'unruly mob' who were 'thieving, pure and simple'.[52] For her, the events were not about 'protest, unemployment or cuts. They weren't about the future, about tomorrow and a person's place in the world', they were about working-class inability to defer satisfaction of their needs, 'They were about today, about now. They were about instant gratification'.[53] Stating that, 'On average each rioter charged had committed 11 previous offences', she opined, underlining her contempt for the working class, that:

> they were career criminals. Naturally, they don't like the police and I'm glad they feel upset by them. One rioter … said the police are always 'causing us hell'. In my role as home secretary, I can only say: 'Good'.[54]

Cameron echoed May's comments, calling the actions 'common or garden thieving, robbing and looting'.[55]

SECTION 2: MAY NAMES, CREATES AND CONSOLIDATES THE 'REALLY HOSTILE ENVIRONMENT'

The rhetoric of 'real hostility' becomes enshrined in government policy

The rhetoric of hostility was heralded and enshrined in government policy in an interview with the *Telegraph* on May 25, 2012, when Theresa May, having been Home Secretary and Minister for Women and Equality for just over two years, announced, 'The aim is to create here in Britain a really hostile environment for illegal migration'.[56] As a prelude to the plan to turn landlords, health workers and other public sector workers into border guards, she explained: 'What we don't want is a situation where people think that they can come here and overstay because they're able to access everything they need'.[57] Although May referred to so-called '*illegal immigration*', irrespective of her intentions, the hostile environment has served to encourage people in the UK to be both hostile towards and to fear (prospective) immigrants *in general*, and to instil fear and terror in the hearts and minds of those migrants in the UK and those wishing to come to the UK.

As *The Guardian* Home Affairs correspondent, Jamie Grierson argues, only May knew at the time whether the 'hostile environment' strategy – 'essentially empowering figures across society to become immigration enforcement officers – would evolve into a catch-all brand for her approach to migrants, illegal or otherwise' because '"the hostile environment" came to encapsulate not just her approach to illegal immigration but to reflect a broader rancour towards migrants in the UK'.[58]

Official figures at the time of the interview showed that net immigration was running at about 250,000 a year, well above the 'tens of thousands' that the Tories (but not the Lib Dems) promised that the ConDem government would deliver.[59]

With respect to that part of the 'really hostile environment' that was used to create divided families (see the Appendix to chapter 9 of this book),[60] in a diatribe against 'sham marriages and sham civil partnerships' in her speech on the second reading of the Immigration Bill in October 2013, Theresa May stated that the Home Office estimated that between 4,000 and 10,000 applications to stay in the UK are made on the basis of unions 'undertaken by a fraudulent couple for their own immigration advantage'. May pointed out that registration officials already had a duty to report 'suspected sham marriages and sham civil partnerships to the Home Office', and the number of reported cases had risen in recent years, with 1,891 reports received in 2012. She continued with a rhetoric of threat and cruelty, so cold-hearted that it is difficult to believe that May is talking about fellow human beings:

At the moment we have the ridiculous situation where we cannot always stop a marriage or civil partnership that a registrar believes to be a sham. The current 15-day notice period provides very little time for the Home Office to act before the ceremony takes place. This Bill will increase the marriage and civil partnership notice period to 28 days in England and Wales. It also allows for it to be extended to 70 days where we have reasonable grounds to suspect that a marriage or civil partnership is a sham. The Home Office will investigate the genuineness of the couple's relationship and consider taking immigration enforcement action where we believe it to be a sham. *If the couple do not comply with the investigation, we will stop a marriage from taking place. Should a sham marriage or civil partnership go ahead, couples will not gain an immigration advantage. They will be removed or prosecuted.*[61]

Contra May's contempt for immigrants and a lack of consideration and concern that a couple in love may object to being 'investigated', there is, of course, a *moral* case that marriages based not on love, but on compassion, where one partner provides economic, emotional or other forms of security, or sanctuary from mental or physical harm out of genuine human decency, could be lauded as exemplary acts of authentic human kindness.

Draconian changes in family migration rules; then Cameron champions the working–class family

In July 2012, key changes to family migration rules came into force. These draconian, vicious and callous assaults on (working-class) family life[62] were summarized by Richmond Chambers Immigration Barristers and included[63]:

Spouses and partners

- Spouses, civil partners, unmarried partners and same sex partners of people who are British or settled in the UK now have to complete five years of limited leave to remain in this category before they are eligible for indefinite leave to remain. The five years will be made up of two periods of two and a half years each;
- Since October 2013, spouses and partners applying for indefinite leave to remain will need to pass both the Life in the UK Test and an English test at level B1;
- Spouses or partners who have been married to or living with the British or settled person outside the UK for four years are no longer able to get indefinite leave to enter or remain immediately. They need to wait for five years;
- There must be at least £18,600 per year available to the couple. This can be made up of savings, pension or gross income from employment/self-employment (prior to 2012, there was only a requirement that the couple had enough to live on);

- If the spouse or partner is not already in the UK with an entitlement to work at the date of the application, they are not able to rely on their own predicted income from employment in the UK;
- If the couple are relying on income from employment, then they need to have had the job for at least six months before the date of application;
- The couple can only rely on savings if they have at least £16,000 and have held this for at least six months;
- It will not be possible to rely on offers of financial support from family and/or friends;
- There is a new list of factors that the UK Border Agency (UKBA) will take into account when assessing whether a relationship is genuine.[64]

Children

- Children who are eligible for indefinite leave to enter will continue to have to meet the current requirements of the Immigration Rules;
- Children who are being granted limited leave only (because only one parent is settled in the UK and they are applying with the other parent) have to show that there is an extra £3,800 per year for the first child and £2,400 per year for each additional child.

Adult dependant relatives

- The only dependant relatives over 18 who can apply will be parents, grandparents, children and siblings;
- The dependant relative has to show that because of age, illness or disability they require long-term personal care;
- The required care must be unavailable in the relative's home country even with the UK sponsor's financial assistance, because it is not affordable or there is no one to provide it;
- It is not possible to apply under this category from inside the UK.

Human rights and discretionary leave to remain

- People granted leave to remain on human rights grounds will not have recourse to public funds;
- Limited leave to remain on human rights grounds will be granted for two and a half years at once;
- A person will have to complete ten years of human rights-based leave before they are eligible for indefinite leave to remain;
- Leave to remain based on private life in the UK will usually only be granted after a person has lived in the UK for 20 years' residence (for adults), seven years (for children), more than half their life (if they are aged 18 to 25). It may be granted earlier if the person has no ties with their home country;

- The Immigration Rules will set out what the United Kingdom UKBA believes to be in the 'public interest' in Article 8 claims based on private and/or family life in the UK;
- The '14-year rule', whereby people can get indefinite leave to remain after living in the UK for 14 years, is abolished.[65]

As 'saviour' of the working-class family, Cameron invokes TINA

Early the following the year (March 7, 2013) Cameron, like Thatcher, invoked TINA, in a bid to champion austerity as the saviour of the working-class family: 'If there was another way I would take it. But there is no alternative [TINA]'.[66] Also reminiscent of Thatcher, Cameron drew on the familial interpellation[67] to impress on the working class that their sacrifices will ultimately reap benefits:

> I know things are tough right now. Families are struggling with the bills at the end of the month. Some are just a pay-cheque away from going into the red. Parents are worried about what the future holds for their children. Whole towns are wondering where their economic future lies. And I know that is especially true for people here in Yorkshire and in many parts of the north of our country who didn't benefit properly from the so-called boom years and worry they won't do so again. But I'm here to say that's not going to happen. Because we have a plan to get through these difficulties – and to get through them together.[68]

May toughens up the message on the vans: 'go home or face arrest'

Between July 22 and August 22, 2013, vans were sent by Theresa May's Home Office into six London boroughs with high minority ethnic populations. As Simon Hattenstone explains, the pilot operation was to test the hypothesis that people without leave to remain would depart voluntarily if they were made aware of 'a near and present' danger of being arrested. He goes on, the pilot is best remembered for the message, 'In the UK illegally? Go home or face arrest'.[69] Underneath the threatening question was a picture of a handcuff, and to the right the purported number of arrests in that particular area. Under the main message was the invitation to 'Text HOME to 78070 for free advice, and help with travel documents', and underneath that, 'We can help you to return home voluntarily without fear of arrest or detention'.

Hattenstone points out that other Home Office operations over the years were often given simple neutral names taken from nature, rather than being related to the case in question. This particular one, however, was named

Operation Vaken. According to Sally Tomlinson, it was named after a poem promoting fascism in 1930s Germany. Posters were also placed in minority ethnic newspapers, and in mosques and temples urging people to 'Go Home'. Detention of immigrants increased, although four in ten appeals against detention were successful.[70]

According to political reporter Thomas Colson and political editor Adam Bienkov of *Business Insider*, May and her special advisers were sent plans and publicity images for the vans as early as March 2013. Not only did she approve the proposals, but also requested that the language of the slogans was 'toughened up' before the vans were rolled out.[71] As Hattenstone concludes (underlining the fact that May was determined to make UK Independence Party (UKIP)-style hatred central to her hostile discourse):

> Like much Home Office policy, it appeared to be a response to the then growing popularity of Ukip. If the Con-Dem coalition was to keep Ukip at bay, it believed it would have to convince voters it was not a soft touch: that it was equally determined to reduce the number of immigrants ... Theresa May was almost obsessively determined to get the figure down to tens of thousands ... and had a zero tolerance policy to those who had no right to be in the country.[72]

Even UKIP Leader Nigel Farage described the tone of the billboards as 'nasty' and 'unpleasant',[73] while Shadow Home Secretary at the time Yvette Cooper accused the Tories of 'borrowing the language of the 1970s National Front'.[74] Robert Kerslake, head of the civil service between 2012 and 2014, went further, stating that the whole 'hostile immigration environment Theresa May set out to create when she was at the Home Office was regarded by some ministers as "almost reminiscent of Nazi Germany" in the way it worked'.[75] Writing more recently in *The Guardian* in the context of a review of Sonita Gale's 2022 documentary *Hostile* about the 'hostile environment' that he describes as 'powerful ... interesting and highly pertinent', the newspaper's film critic Peter Bradshaw describes 'the go home vans' as 'one of the ugliest and most fatuous chapters in Home Office history'.[76] In his own words:

> Of course, this ridiculous piece of toxic bossiness was not really addressed to illegal immigrants: Home Office officials were well aware that they themselves[77] would be unable or unwilling to respond. It was a piece of taxpayer-funded party-political posturing, dogwhistling or humanwhistling to the bigots and intended as part of a charmless new policy of 'hostile environment' – making things unpleasant in the country generally, a way of trying to pressure people to leave of their own free will.[78]

Following the theme of Gale's documentary, Bradshaw suggests that the policy 'is coming to a crisis now that Brexit has brought it home to the governing classes just how reliant our service industry is on casual labour, and how reliant the NHS is on immigrants'.[79]

The second reading of the Immigration Bill (2013)

On October 22, 2013, May moved the second reading of the Immigration Bill, and in so doing pledged again to reduce immigration to the tens of thousands. She began by reaffirming the creation of the hostile and aggressive-sounding Border Force (Border Force, itself, being a brief sobriquet of the discourse inherent in the 'really hostile environment').[80] At this point in the chapter, it will not be a surprise that the standard rhetoric of hostility with respect to the 'significant problem' of immigration was deployed in abundance. Again, while 'illegal' figures prominently, it would have been received by many as legitimating and encouraging hostility to all migrants and to 'foreigners' in general. Thus May ended her stark, cruel and callous diatribe of venom, her rhetoric of 'real hostility' as follows:

> It is frankly ridiculous that the Government has to operate such a complex system to deal with *foreigners* who fail to abide by *our laws*. It is ridiculous that the odds are stacked in favour of illegal migrants. It is unacceptable that hard working taxpayers have to compete with people who have no right to be here. This Bill will begin to address these absurdities and restore the balance.[81]

The speech contained more talk of 'abuse' (twice in its first paragraph), along with 'clamping down', 'cracking down', 'taking advantage', 'removals', 'not fair to the public' who are 'fed up'. In May's words: 'This is not just about making the UK a more hostile place for illegal migrants – it is about fairness'. Having made three references to 'foreign criminals', May then coupled them with immigration lawyers: 'Under the current system the winners are foreign criminals and immigration lawyers and the losers are the victims of those crimes and the law-abiding public'.[82]

The 2014 Immigration Act

The ConDem government's Immigration Act of 2014 came into effect in May of that year. Key aspects of the Act included:

- Limiting appeals against Home Office decisions from 17 to 4;
- The right to deport first and hear appeals later in certain circumstances; the right to 'respect for family and private life' should not always take precedence over public interest, which should be 'at the heart of [the court's] decisions' in immigration control[83] and deporting foreign criminals;
- Clamping down on those who live and work in the UK illegally and take advantage of our public services; ensuring that only legal migrants

have access to the labour market, health services, housing, bank accounts and driving licences;

- Penalties for employers who do not ensure that Non-EEA (European Economic Area) nationals only work as legally permitted;
- Restricting access to free NHS care to those non-EEA nationals with 'indefinite leave to remain' and those granted refugee status or humanitarian protection, thus bringing the NHS into line with government policy on access to benefits and social housing;
- Temporary migrants seeking to stay in the UK for more than six months to pay an immigration health surcharge on top of their visa fee;
- Landlords required to check the immigration status of their prospective tenants; powers to deal with 'rogue landlords' who rent homes to 'illegal immigrants';
- With respect to 'removals', create a system where only one decision is made, informing the individual that they cannot stay in the UK, and enabling Immigration Enforcement to remove them if they do not leave voluntarily;
- For illegal migrants held in immigration detention, no bail when the detainee is booked onto a flight in the next few days and there are no exceptional circumstances; no multiple repeated bail applications;
- Full rights equivalent to the police for entry clearance officers to take fingerprints before entry to the UK, and to take enforcement action;
- Simplifying the appeals procedure so that instead of appealing to an immigration judge, applicants can contact the Home Office and ask for a simple administrative review to remedy case working errors, thus resolving errors in decisions cheaply and quickly.[84]

The last point meant that an 'independent' judge was replaced by the 'hostile' Home Office. The Immigration Act of 2014 also provided for the removal of citizenship from naturalized citizens, if their conduct is 'seriously prejudicial to the vital interests of the United Kingdom'. This could include cases involving 'national security, terrorism, espionage or taking up arms against British or allied forces' even if removing citizenship could result in their being made stateless.[85]

Significantly, as part of the Act, the government quietly removed a key protection from the statute books for some British residents of the Windrush generation. The Home Office *claimed* that the clause was not included because adequate protections were already in place for people who were initially granted temporary rights to remain in the UK and have stayed for decades.[86] Four years later, these particular British people would face detention, the denial of legal rights, and would be threatened with deportation, with some actually wrongly deported (see chapters 9 and 10).

With respect to the provisions of the Act, Saira Grant of the Joint Council for the Welfare of Immigrants (JCWI) has argued that the Act sought to turn landlords, health workers and other public sector workers into border guards.[87]

Racism and the run–up to the May 7, 2015 General Election

Mindful of the threat from UKIP and the need to keep the Eurosceptics in the Tory Party in line, in January 2013 in a speech six months in the planning, Cameron pledged to renegotiate the UK's relationship with the EU, followed by a simple in/out referendum. This was promised by the end of 2017 at the latest – if the Tories were to win the next general election on May 7, 2015. During Prime Minister's Questions, Labour Leader Ed Miliband said Mr Cameron was 'running scared' of the UK Independence Party, whose poll ratings had been rising. Cameron declared that if he managed to secure a new relationship he was happy with, he would campaign 'heart and soul' to stay within the EU.[88]

In November 2013, Cameron announced a raft of anti-immigrant measures ahead of new EU rules that came into effect on January 1, 2014, ending restrictions on Bulgarians and Romanians entering the United Kingdom. While Eastern Europeans in general were on the receiving end of xeno-racism (that form of non-colour-coded racism directed at central and eastern European workers and their families), the prime scapegoats were originally the Poles.

Sivanandan has defined xeno-racism as follows:

> It is a racism that is not just directed at those with darker skins, from the former colonial territories, but at the newer categories of the displaced, the dispossessed and the uprooted, who are beating at western Europe's doors, the Europe that helped to displace them in the first place. It is a racism, that is, that cannot be colour-coded, directed as it is at poor whites as well, and is therefore passed off as xenophobia, a 'natural' fear of strangers. But in the way it denigrates and reifies people before segregating and/or expelling them, it is a xenophobia that bears all the marks of the old racism. It is racism in substance, but 'xeno' in form. It is a racism that is meted out to impoverished strangers even if they are white. It is xeno-racism.[89]

The new rules meant the additional (xeno-) racialization of Bulgarians and Romanians. Cameron's measures included no unemployment benefits for new migrants for the first three months of their stay; out-of-work welfare payments to end after six months, unless the claimant can prove they have a 'genuine prospect' of a job; new migrants not allowed to claim housing benefits immediately; and any migrant caught begging or sleeping rough to be deported and not allowed to return to the UK for a year. In addition, migrants wishing to claim benefits were subject to more restrictions. This included a new minimum earnings threshold. Failure to meet the requirements led to the removal of welfare benefits, including Income Support.[90]

A racist consensus forms

In the light of the defection of several Tories to UKIP, including one on the eve of the September 2014 Tory Party Conference, as well as the switching of a major donation by one ex-Tory from the Conservatives to UKIP, and in the context of a concerted campaign of interpellation by the right-wing tabloids to demonize and criminalize Eastern Europeans, the main parties tried desperately to outbid each other to establish their anti-immigrant credentials.

Yvette Cooper, at the 2014 Labour Party Conference, stated that Labour 'got things wrong on immigration – on transitional controls for Eastern Europe, on the impact on jobs'. Castigating the Tories for not reducing net immigration and interpolating that 'people are more worried than ever' because things have got worse, Cooper pledged that 'a Labour Government will bring in stronger border controls to tackle illegal immigration', with proper 'entry and exit checks, so visas can be enforced and criminals stopped'. She went on:

> And we need radical reform when it comes to Europe. To stop the growing crisis at Calais, strengthen restrictions on new countries, change benefit rules so people can't claim when they first arrive, change deportation rules to make it easier to send home EU citizens who commit crimes and to change employment rules to stop employers exploiting cheap migrant labour to undercut wages and jobs. Not free movement, but fair movement.[91]

She insisted that 'it is not racist to be worried about immigration or to want stronger controls', and in an unconvincing attempt to restrict racism to its colour-coded dimension, concluded that 'when a UKIP candidate says [Black entertainer] Lenny Henry should leave the country because of the colour of his skin,[92] that is racist. We will never let racism go unchallenged'.[93] In the toxic climate of racism created in part by the 'really hostile environment' and associated practices, policies and legislation, Farage stated at the 2014 UKIP Conference in September of that year that the issue that would dominate the next election was open door immigration. He added, to a huge cheer of agreement, that we are 'borderless Britain'.[94] Racism, particularly xeno-racism, was indeed to loom large.[95]

In his speech to the Tory Party Conference on October 2, 2014, Cameron's mantra was 'A Britain that everyone is proud to call home'. Relating this to controlling immigration, he referred to 'getting our own people fit to work ... controlled borders and an immigration system that puts the British people first'. He went on to interpolate his audience: 'But we know the bigger issue today is migration from within the EU'. Cameron continued with a number of xeno-racist sound bites:

Immediate access to our welfare system. Paying benefits to families back home. Employment agencies signing people up from overseas and not recruiting here. Numbers that have increased faster than we in this country wanted ... at a level that was too much for our communities, for our labour markets.[96]

Following on from his promise the previous year for a relationship negotiation before a referendum, he declared: 'All of this has to change – and it will be at the very heart of my renegotiation strategy for Europe'. The interpellation continued: 'Britain, I know you want this sorted so I will go to Brussels, I will not take no for an answer and when it comes to free movement – I will get what Britain needs'. He concluded with a reiteration of his referendum pledge, together with a promise to abolish the UK Human Rights Act enacted by the Labour Party in 1998, and its replacement with a new British Bill of Rights 'rooted in our values'.[97]

As Jonathan Freedland argued, with respect to the days leading up to the forthcoming general election:

> From now until May, the Tories will seek daily to blunt Ukip's bayonets .... Ukip wants out of the EU, so Cameron promises a referendum. And Ukip slams 'human rights', damned as the co-conspirator of 'political correctness' in sending the country to the dogs, so the Tories promise to crack down on them too – and forget the pesky details.[98]

Freedland concluded that this is 'the pool of fury Ukip drinks from and which the Tories want to channel their way'. It is not about constitutional reform and legal jurisdictions, but an outlet 'for a much more visceral rage, the furious sense that the world is not as it should be – and that someone faraway must be to blame'. Freedland referred to the real problem, not Brussels or the European courts, but the 'borderless forces of globalisation that have upended economic life everywhere'.[99] These forces he failed to name are those of local, regional and international global neoliberal capital, and he did not point out that if for the xeno-racists Brussels and Strasbourg comprise the distant threat, the (xeno-) racialized 'enemies' on British streets emanate from Sofia and Bucharest.

In late October 2014, the then Defence Secretary Michael Fallon apologized for saying that British towns were being 'swamped' and 'under siege [with] large numbers of migrant workers and people claiming benefits'.[100] These comments were correctly likened by freelance writer Stuart Jeffries in *The Guardian* to the rhetoric of Thatcher and Enoch Powell.[101] Presumably Fallon felt he was only getting into the spirit of the times.

The 2015 General Election Campaign began officially on December 19, 2014. In addition to the racist consensus that had been forged, the Cameron factor was important in the eventual result of the election. As Deputy Political Editor of *The Telegraph*, Steven Swinford put it, the Tories had always been acutely aware that Cameron was 'significantly more popular than his own party', whereas the Labour leader was 'afflicted by the opposite problem – Ed Miliband [was] significantly less popular than his party', a factor that was exacerbated by Tories questioning Miliband's fitness to lead Britain. The Tories were also remorseless in their attacks on the Liberal Democrats, their Coalition partners of five years, with Cameron repeatedly visiting Liberal Democrat target seats. Finally, while Labour was riven by infighting, Eurosceptic Tory backbenchers were placated by the promise of an EU Referendum.[102]

Prime Minister Cameron names May as a possible successor

On May 7, 2015, the Tories won an outright majority in the General Election. In March of that year, David Cameron had said he would not serve a third term as Prime Minister if the Tories were to remain in power after the election, amid growing speculation among Conservative MPs that he might, in fact, quit after the EU Referendum,[103] before the end of the 2020 third term. As he put it:

> There definitely comes a time where a fresh pair of eyes and fresh leadership would be good, and the Conservative Party has got some great people coming up – the *Theresa Mays*, and the George Osbornes, and the Boris Johnsons. There's plenty of talent there. I'm surrounded by very good people.[104]

As Andrew Grice has argued, speaking about possible departure dates is a minefield that impacted on both Margaret Thatcher, who had stated that she intended to 'go on and on', and was subsequently ousted by her party, and Tony Blair, who ruled out a fourth term, and came under intense (successful) pressure to stand down a year earlier than he had intended.[105]

May's bid for the Tory Party leadership

No doubt cognisant of this potential opportunity for self-advancement on October 6, May made a speech to the 2015 Tory Party Conference, widely viewed as a bid for Tory leadership. Thus, the then Shadow Secretary of State for International Development Diane Abbott tweeted: 'Theresa May gets down in the gutter with UKIP chasing votes for her leadership bid',[106] while Steven Woolfe, at the time an MEP and UKIP Immigration Spokesman, declared on Twitter: 'Theresa May's speech on migration today is simply posturing to the Tory faithful, to prop herself up for a leadership bid in 2020'.[107]

A leadership bid was also transparent for the then Executive Editor, Politics James Kirkup at the Tory-supporting online 'broadsheet', *The Telegraph*. As he stated, 'It's hard to know where to start with Theresa May's awful, ugly, misleading, cynical and irresponsible speech to the Conservative Party conference today': 'If you haven't seen reports of it, allow me to summarise: "Immigrants are stealing your job, making you poorer and ruining your country. Never mind the facts, just feel angry at foreigners. And make me Conservative leader"'.[108]

Kirkup analysed two of May's key sentences as follows:

1)   *And we know that for people in low-paid jobs, wages are forced down even further while some people are forced out of work altogether.*

He pointed out that a review of the evidence by May's own officials concluded: 'There is relatively little evidence that migration has caused statistically significant displacement of UK natives from the labour market in periods when the economy is strong'.[109]

2)   *Immigration makes it impossible to build a cohesive society.*

As Kirkup rightly replied, this is more of a subjective issue. However, he reminded his readers that there is (considerable) 'evidence [...] that the less personal acquaintance with migrants a person has, the more worried they are about immigration'. As he went on, *if* immigration makes UK society less cohesive, that may be partly the result of 'politicians pandering to ignorance and prejudice and wilfully distorting the evidence to persuade people to be angry and afraid'.[110] Kirkup concluded his comments on the rhetoric of hate in her speech:

> The Home Secretary says she's worried about immigration social cohesion. If she really wants to help, she could start by abandoning this cheap and nasty speech and the politics behind it. [...] But then [...] political ambition is more important than talking responsibly and honestly about immigration, isn't it? What a curious form of leadership.[111]

In her speech, May yet again blamed immigrants for pressures on public services: 'It's difficult for schools and hospitals and core infrastructure like housing and transport to cope',[112] whereas the real blame should be attributed to Tory governments that refuse to properly fund the NHS, which they continue to privatize by the back door or by stealth;[113] and prioritized at the time new grammar schools over more schools for all (schools nationwide were set to lose £3 billion a year in real terms by 2020);[114] and refused to build affordable housing.

Referring specifically to asylum seekers, May suggested that they should not even be allowed into Britain before their claims were assessed:

> At the moment, the main way people claim asylum here is when they're already in Britain. That fails on three counts ... I want to offer

asylum and refuge to people in parts of the world affected by conflict and oppression, rather than to those who have made it to Britain.[115]

Refugee Council chief executive Maurice Wren responded to May's disturbing rhetoric of threat as follows:

> The Home Secretary's clear intention to close Britain's border to refugees fleeing for their lives is thoroughly chilling, as is her bitter attack on the fundamental principle enshrined in international law that people fleeing persecution should be able to claim asylum in Britain.[116]

In addition, May reinforced her rhetoric of hate, this time labelling those seeking sanctuary as lawbreakers who contribute nothing to the economy, claiming that a significant number of asylum seekers are 'foreign criminals', and contrary to the vast majority of economists' analyses, summed up her view that 'the net economic and fiscal effect of high immigration is close to zero'.[117]

Britain is and has always been a multicultural society (Cole, 2018b, 99–100; see also Fryer, 1984; Visram, 1986; Walvin, 1973). May, however, dismissed the idea that Britain was a 'country of immigrants', claiming that 'we have until recently always been a country of remarkable population stability'.[118]

The 2016 Immigration Act

On May 12, 2016, the Immigration Act that focuses on 'illegal migration' and accompanying punitive measures, came into force. Like other facets of the 'really hostile environment', the Act will impact on all migrants. Its key changes were:

- Employers who hire illegal migrants and the workers themselves face criminal sanctions.
- Migrants who do not have permission to be in the UK can have certain privileges revoked, such as the seizure of their driving licence and the freezing of their bank accounts.
- It becomes a criminal offence for a landlord to knowingly rent premises to an illegal migrant, with up to five years in prison for offenders.
- The 'deport first, appeal later' scheme becomes extended to all migrants.
- Pregnant women can now only be detained by immigration authorities for up to 72 hours (or one week with special permission).
- Arrangements are now to be made to relocate unaccompanied refugee children from other countries in Europe to the UK.[119]

The Joint Council for the Welfare of Immigrants (JCWI) welcomed the 72 hour limit for pregnant women, the relocation of child refugees and another feature of the Act – immigration detainees not facing deportation after a criminal conviction are now entitled to an automatic bail hearing after four months of detention. These were all achieved, it points out, through months of hard work by campaigners, NGOs and a number of parliamentarians. With respect to other features of the Act, it offered the following overall critique:

> these concessions do little to ameliorate the full force of the measures brought in by this Act which will make the UK a more hostile and unwelcoming place. The ... Act ... introduces a vast number of draconian, unaccountable and poorly thought out powers and offences that will have a huge impact on the lives of both migrants and British citizens, particularly those in black and minority ethnic communities. It sets back the progress of integration, and many of the measures that the Government claims are to protect migrants from exploitation, actually increase the risk of this.[120]

'This doubling down on "hostile environment" policies', it continues, can be seen in the following changes brought in by the Act. Here are some of the main problems, as identified by the JCWI:

Labour market exploitation

- Given that prosecutors can confiscate anything acquired through 'illegal working', this can lead to further exploitation since unscrupulous employers can threaten to report people for this new 'crime'.

Driving licences, bank accounts and powers of immigration officials

- The Act introduces new stop and search powers where police have 'reasonable grounds' for believing that someone is not lawfully resident in the UK and is in possession of a driving licence. Given the history of discrimination in the use of 'stop and search' in the UK it is very hard to see how this power will not result in black and minority ethnic drivers being targeted by immigration officials or the police.
- With respect to freezing bank accounts, given the long record of poor decision-making by the Home Office, this is likely to impact on many people who have every right to be here. It also increases the risk of exploitation of undocumented migrants, as they will be driven to use cash, lodge money with others and use black market financial services.
- More generally, the Act gives immigration officials new powers to search property and seize documents, as well as to perform strip searches of individuals in order to search for documents.

Landlord immigration checks

- As far as these checks are concerned, the JCWI has found that this scheme is unworkable; that it causes discrimination against those who aren't British; and it has a disproportionate effect on members of minority ethnic communities. Landlords faced with a potential fine or prison may take the safe option and rent to those with a British passport where possible. Furthermore, the Home Secretary is granted the power to require a landlord to evict tenants who do not have a 'right to rent' from their property, by issuing a written notice, for which there is no judicial oversight.

Finally, out-of-country appeals, up to the passing of the Act, were restricted to foreign national offenders, but now apply across the board. It is far more difficult to appeal from abroad for a number of reasons, including the cost and the difficulty of gathering evidence and presenting a case when not physically present.[121]

'Leave' side wins the referendum and May replaces Cameron as Prime Minister

The Referendum to decide whether the UK should stay in or leave the European Union was held on June 23, 2016, following a four-month campaign, with Theresa May and David Cameron joining the Remain camp. Satnam Virdee and Brendan McGeever identify the two distinct organizational formations behind the Leave campaign: the official Leave campaign, Vote Leave, composed of right-wing Conservatives, notably Boris Johnson, as well as lone UKIP MP, Douglas Carswell, a couple of Labour MPs and Independent Frank Field; and the UKIP-led project, Leave.EU, funded by multi-millionaires Aaron Banks and Richard Tice, and fronted by Nigel Farage.[122]

When pro-EU membership leaflets costing £9m of public money were sent to 27 million UK homes in early April, Farage declared it 'outrageous' to spend taxpayers' money 'to tell us how we should think and how we should vote'. Cameron stressed the government was 'not neutral' in the referendum and the cost was 'money well spent'.[123]

From the Leave side, there were racist scare stories about how soon Turkey might be able to join the EU, while one of the most surreal scenes in the campaign witnessed Farage and Bob Geldof, co-founder of Band Aid, throw insults at each other in a mock 'nautical battle', as Farage led a flotilla of fishing boats up the Thames to urge Parliament to take back control of British waters. As Esther Webber puts it, 'His Brexit armada was greeted by a rival Remain fleet carrying Mr Geldof, who yelled that the UKIP leader was "no fisherman's friend,"' while Farage 'accused Mr Geldof of "mocking" impoverished fishermen'. Shortly afterwards, Farage released an infamous poster bearing the words 'breaking point', depicting a line of migrants at the Slovenia border.[124]

Significantly, coverage of immigration more than tripled over the course of the campaign, rising faster than any other political issue.[125] Martin Moore and Gordon Ramsay summarize the results of their survey of the coverage in all articles published about the 2016 EU referendum by the leading UK national news outlets online, including national press, digital-only news services and the online news services of the leading broadcasters for the period of the official referendum campaign:

- Immigration was the most prominent referendum issue, based on the number of times it led newspaper print front pages (there were 99 front pages about immigration, 82 about the economy).
- Coverage of the effects of immigration was overwhelmingly negative. Migrants were blamed for many of Britain's economic and social problems – most notably for putting unsustainable pressure on public services.
- Specific nationalities were singled out for particularly negative coverage – especially Turks and Albanians, but also Romanians and Poles.
- The majority of negative coverage of specific foreign nationals was published by three news sites: the *Express*, the *Daily Mail*, and the *Sun*.[126]

These findings serve to underline the racist, Islamophobic and xeno-racist nature of the reporting, and serve to detract from Jeremy Corbyn's (then the Labour Party leader) state of inequality in the UK agenda.

The result of the Referendum was an unexpected win by Leave of 51.9% to Remain's 48.1%. With respect to social class and age, while exit polls showed that around two-thirds of those who voted in social classes D and E chose Leave,[127] it should also be pointed out that the proportion of Leave voters who were of the lowest two social classes was just 24%.[128] As Virdee and McGeever point out, Leave voters among the elite and middle classes were crucial to the final outcome,[129] with almost three in five votes coming from those in social classes A, B and C1.[130] Additionally, age seems to have been central to the Brexit vote since, while 62% of 25–34-year-olds chose to Remain, 60% of those aged 65 and over voted to Leave.[131] 'In sum', they conclude:

> it is too simplistic to suggest that Brexit constituted the revolt of the 'left behind'; rather, what needs to be understood is how the campaign to Leave managed to successfully cohere a significant cross-class coalition of middle-aged and older men and women.[132]

The 'left behind' that they are referring to are those of pension age, low-skilled and less-educated blue-collar workers, and others pushed to the margins by neoliberalism, the same constituency that had voted UKIP in the 2014 European Parliamentary elections.[133]

The day after the Brexit result, Cameron, having staked his position on a Remain vote, announced that he would resign, admitting that the country now needed 'fresh leadership', that is 'strong, determined and committed'.[134]

After receiving the overwhelming support of Tory MPs in the ensuing Tory Leadership contest, Theresa May stated:

> I am pleased with this result, and very grateful to my colleagues for their support. There is a big job before us: to unite our party and the country, to negotiate the best possible deal as we leave the EU, and to make Britain work for everyone. I am the only candidate capable of delivering these three things as prime minister, and … it is clear that I am also the only one capable of drawing support from the whole of the Conservative Party.[135]

The vacuous nature of these claims would come back to haunt her as she quickly began to preside over a totally disunited party, a divided country and a deal that she was unable to get through Parliament.

When the last remaining candidate withdrew from the leadership race on July 11, precluding the need for a vote by Tory Party members, May was confirmed as Tory Party leader. Cameron resigned as Prime Minister two days later, and May became Britain's second female Prime Minister. In her Prime Ministerial statement, focusing on 'fighting against burning injustice', she said she wanted to address the 'ordinary working-class family' and that her government would be driven by their interests, not those of the privileged few,[136] an oxymoron for a party whose raison d'être is to protect and further the interests of the ruling class. Moreover, despite mentioning Black people in this pledge (shallow words in light of the Windrush scandal [see chapters 9 and 10 of this book]), her failure to mention (potential) immigrants and asylum seekers, given how May's 'hostile environment' was directed at them, was no doubt an intentional omission. Unsurprisingly, given her *real* position on the political spectrum, her first appointments tilted the cabinet to the right.[137]

Notes

1   *BBC News.* 2010. 'Gordon Brown resigns as UK prime minister', May 11. http://news.bbc.co.uk/1/hi/uk_politics/election_2010/8675913.stm.
2   Pimlott et al. 2010.
3   Summers, Deborah. 2009. 'David Cameron warns of "new age of austerity"', *The Guardian*, April 26. https://www.theguardian.com/politics/2009/apr/26/david-cameron-conservative-economic-policy.
4   Pimlott et al. 2010.
5   For a discussion of this crisis, see Cole. 2020, pp. 11–13.
6   Pimlott et al. 2010.
7   E.g. Portes, Jonathan. 2018. 'Austerity really has hit poor people hardest – the figures prove it', *The Guardian,* March 14. https://www.theguardian.com/commentisfree/2018/mar/14/austerity-poor-disability-george-osborne-tories; Booth, Robert and Butler, Patrick. 2018. 'UK austerity has inflicted "great misery" on citizens, UN says', *The Guardian*, November 16. https://www.theguardian.com/society/2018/nov/16/uk-austerity-has-inflictedgreat-misery-on-citizens-un-says.
8   Cole. 2012, p. 5.

9   This chapter is an amended and updated version of Cole, Mike. 2020b, chapter 1.
10   GOV.UK. 2010.
11   Ibid.
12   Ibid.
13   Ibid.
14   Ibid.; emphases added.
15   GOV.UK, 2010.
16   Ibid.
17   Ibid.; emphases added.
18   From a Marxist perspective, capitalism relies for its very existence on the extraction of surplus value from workers who have to sell their labour power to survive: capitalists pay them less than the value they produce, with the value added by workers' labour appropriated as profit by and for the capitalist when goods are sold. For an elucidation of Marx's value theory, see Marx. 1887, especially chapter 1. For a brief summary and a numerical example of how this works, see Cole. 2011, pp, 42–44.
19   GOV.UK. 2010.
20   Ibid.
21   Ibid.
22   Cited in GOV. UK, 2010.
23   GOV.UK. 2010.
24   Ibid.
25   UK Parliament. 2014. 'The work of the Immigration Directorates (January – June 2014) – Home Affairs Committee Contents'. https://publications.parliament.uk/pa/cm201415/cmselect/cmhaff/712/71204.htm.
26   Ibid.
27   Cited in Latour, Vincent. 2012. 'Muscular liberalism: surviving multiculturalism? A historical and political contextualisation of David Cameron's Munich speech', *La nouvelle donne politique en Grande-Bretagne (2010–2012)*, 12. https://journals.openedition.org/osb/1355.
28   *BBC News*. 2011. 'State multiculturalism has failed, says David Cameron', February 5. https://www.bbc.co.uk/news/uk-politics-12371994.
29   Cited in *BBC News*. 2011.
30   Ibid.
31   Ibid.
32   Southwark, Andy. 2011. 'Tottenham Riots: A community on the edge', *Socialist Appeal,* August 8. https://www.socialist.net/tottenham-riots-a-community-on-the-edge.htm.
33   See Siddique, Haroon. 2020. 'Mark Duggan police shooting: can forensic tech cast doubt on official report?', *The Guardian,* June 10. https://www.theguardian.com/uk-news/ng-interactive/2020/jun/10/mark-duggan-shooting-can-forensic-tech-cast-doubt-on-official-report; for an examination of the evidence.
34   Taylor, Pablo. 2021. 'We need to ask why: Cousin of Mark Duggan speaks out 10 years after riots', *ITV News,* October 28. https://www.itv.com/news/central/2021-10-28/cousin-of-mark-duggan-speaks-out-10-years-after-riots.
35   Cited in Taylor. 2021.
36   Ibid.
37   Ibid.
38   Ibid.
39   Southwark. 2011.
40   Lewis, Paul. 2011. 'Tottenham riots: a peaceful protest, then suddenly all hell broke loose', *The Guardian,* August 7. https://www.theguardian.com/uk/2011/aug/07/tottenham-riots-peaceful-protest.
41   Cited in Lewis. 2011.

42 Southwark. 2011.
43 Ibid.
44 Ibid.
45 Ibid.
46 Ibid.
47 Althusser, Louis. 1970. 'Ideology and ideological state apparatuses (Notes towards an Investigation)', in *"Lenin and Philosophy" and Other Essays*, transcribed: by Andy Blunden. https://www.marxists.org/reference/archive/althusser/1970/ideology.htm.
48 Southwark. 2011.
49 Ibid.
50 Ibid.
51 Cited in Southwark. 2011.
52 Cited in Topping, Alexandra. 2011. 'Rioters were "unruly mob" claims Theresa May'. https://www.theguardian.com/uk/2011/dec/18/london-riots-theresamay.
53 Ibid.
54 Ibid.
55 Ibid.
56 Cited in Kirkup and Winnett. 2012. According to Alan Travis, writing for *The Guardian,* in May 2007, Liam Byrne, who was the Labour Immigration Minister at the time, had referred to a 'hostile environment' in an announcement of a consultation document: 'We are trying to create a much more hostile environment in this country if you are here illegally' (Travis, Alan. 2007. 'Officials launch drive to seek out illegal migrants at work'). For an interesting discussion of the origins of the term, 'hostile environment', see Hansard. 2018. 'Immigration: Hostile environment', Volume 791: debated on Thursday 14 June 2018.
57 Cited in Kirkup and Winnett. 2012.
58 Grierson, Jamie. 2018. 'Hostile environment: anatomy of a policy disaster', *The Guardian,* August 27. https://www.theguardian.com/uk-news/2018/aug/27/hostile-environment-anatomy-of-a-policy-disaster.
59 Kirkup and Winnett. 2012.
60 See also Cole. 2020b.
61 GOV.UK. 2013. 'Speech by Home Secretary on second reading of Immigration Bill'. https://www.gov.uk/government/speeches/speech-by-home-secretary-on-second-reading-of-immigration-bill; emphasis added.
62 I put 'working class' in brackets because, although the measures pertain to all affected families, the financial requirements clearly discriminate against workers most. From a Marxist perspective, as opposed to a sociological one, the overwhelming majority will be working class because they have to sell their labour power in order to live, irrespective of whether they are middle or working class in its everyday (sociological) sense (see note 18, above (From a Marxist perspective, capitalism relies…).
63 Richard Chambers Immigration Barristers. 2012. 'Summary of key changes in family Immigration Rules on 9 July 2012'. https://immigrationbarrister.co.uk/summary-of-key-changes-to-immigration-rules-on-9-july-2012/.
64 Ibid.
65 These are the rules as formulated by May's Home Office; for the most recent updates, see GOV.UK, 'Immigration rules: updates' (ongoing).
66 Cited in Robinson, Nick. 2013. 'Economy: there is no alternative (TINA) is back', *BBC News*, March 7.
67 Interpellation is the *process* by which the legitimation, values, and attitudes required by capitalism are instilled in the populace. Interpellation is the concept neo-Marxist, Louis Althusser. 1970, used to describe the way in which

ruling class ideology is upheld and the class consciousness of the working class – that class's awareness of its structural location in capitalist society – undermined. Interpellation makes us think that ruling class capitalist values are actually congruent with our values as *individuals*. Thus a right-wing newspaper might say, for example, 'the British people are fed up with these immigrants taking our jobs' in an attempt to instil these values whether people hold them or not, the response might be 'That's obvious! That's right! That's true!' (Althusser. 1970).

68   Cited in Robinson. 2013.
69   Hattenstone, Simon. 2018. 'Why was the scheme begind May's "Go Home" vans called Operation Vaken?', *The Guardian*, April 26. https://www.theguardian.com/commentisfree/2018/apr/26/theresa-may-go-home-vans-operation-vaken-ukip.
70   Tomlinson. 2019, p. 189.
71   Colson and Bienkov. 2018.
72   Hattenstone. 2018.
73   *BBC News*. 2013. 'Farage attacks "nasty" immigration posters', July 25. https://www.bbc.co.uk/news/uk-politics-23450438.
74   Cited in Travis, Alan. 2013. 'Tory immigration language "like National Front of 1970s"', *The Guardian*, September 25. https://www.theguardian.com/uk-news/2013/sep/25/tory-immigration-language-national-front-yvette-cooper.
75   Perkins, Anne and Quinn, Ben. 2018. 'May's immigration policy seen as "almost reminiscent of Nazi Germany"', *The Guardian*, April 19. https://www.theguardian.com/uk-news/2018/apr/19/theresa-may-immigration-policy-seen-as-almost-reminiscent-of-nazi-germany.
76   Bradshaw, Peter. 2022. 'Hostile review – documentary highlights nastiness of UK immigration policy', *The Guardian,* January 19. https://www.theguardian.com/film/2022/jan/19/hostile-review-documentary-highlights-nastiness-of-uk-immigration-policy.
77   Bradshaw, 2022.
78   Ibid.
79   Ibid.
80   *UK Border Force* is a documentary about the Border Force, broadcast on British TV. Here one can see public rhetoric of hatred, contempt, and brutality on the front line. One can only surmise what went on when the cameras were not rolling.
81   GOV.UK. 2013; emphases added.
82   Ibid.
83   See the Appendix to chapter 9 and Cole. 2020, on how families came to be and continue to be divided as a result of the hostile environment.
84   GOV.UK. 2013; for ongoing updates to UK immigration legislation, see GOV.UK, 'Immigration rules: updates'.
85   Salmon, Rachel. 2014. 'The 2014 Immigration Act 2 June 2014', LGiU Policy Briefing. www.lgiu.org.uk/wp-content/uploads/2014/06/The-2014-Immigration-Act.pdf.
86   Taylor, Diane. 2018. 'UK removed legal protection for Windrush immigrants in 2014', *The Guardian*, April 16. https://www.theguardian.com/uk-news/2018/apr/16/immigration-law-key-clause-protecting-windrush-immigrants-removed-in-2014.
87   Electronic Immigration Network (EIN). 2014a.
88   *BBC News*. 2013.
89   Cited in Fekete. 2001.
90   Stevens. 2013; for ongoing updates to UK immigration legislation, see GOV.UK, 'Immigration rules: updates'.
91   Cited in EIN. 2014b.

92 See BBC News. 2014. 'Lenny Henry racism row candidate quits UKIP', April 29. www.bbc.co.uk/news/uk-politics-27202753.

93 Cited in EIN. 2014b.

94 Cited in *BBC News*. 2014.

95 Cole. 2016, pp. 70–83, includes a timeline of anti-immigrant and racist announcements and events in the seven months leading up the election on May 7, 2015. Two interpolative devices *that continue to this day* were particularly noticeable in the speeches of all the mainstream Westminster politicians prior to that election. They were a constant referral to 'our country', rather than 'the country', and a persistent reference to 'working people'. The former worked to reinforce a sense of verified and demonstrated patriotism as well as a stress on 'us' and 'them' thus excluding 'foreigners', while the latter was useful to the ruling class on at least two levels. First, it served to render social class obsolete (since the term was working people, not the working class); second, it conveyed the message that there are just two groups of people: those who work and those who do not, thus denigrating those unable to find work and people receiving welfare. It also reinforced the myth of the Eastern European worker, who was just in the United Kingdom for benefits and free health and education. If anything was slightly more prominent than racism in the election run-up, it was fears over the demise of the NHS.

96 UKPOL.CO.UK. 2015. 'David Cameron – 2014 Speech to Conservative Party Conference'. https://www.ukpol.co.uk/david-cameron-2014-speech-to-conservative-party-conference/.

97 Ibid.

98 Freedland, Jonathan. 2014. 'Scrapping Human Rights Law is an act of displaced fury', *The Guardian*, October 3. www.theguardian.com/commentis free/2014/oct/03/scrapping-human-rights-law-european-court-ukip.

99 Ibid.

100 Cited in Jeffries, Stuart. 2014. 'Swamped' and 'riddled': the toxic words that wreck public discourse', *The Guardian*, October 27. https://www.theguardian.com/uk-news/2014/oct/27/swamped-and-riddled-toxic-phrases-wreck-politics-immigration-michael-fallon.

101 Ibid.

102 Swinford, Steven. 2015. 'Election 2015: How David Cameron's Conservatives won', *Telegraph*, May 8. www.telegraph.co.uk/news/general-election-2015/11592230/Election-2015-How-David-Camerons-conservatives-won.html.

103 Grice, Andrew. 2015. 'David Cameron rules out third term as PM and reveals favourites for next Tory leader', *The Independent*, March 23. www.independent.co.uk/news/uk/politics/david-cameron-admits-he-wont-serve-beyond-2020-10128858.html.

104 Cited in Grice. 2015; emphasis added.

105 Grice. 2015.

106 Cited in *The Week*. 2016. 'Theresa May rejects calls to increase Indian visa quota', November 7. https://www.theweek.co.uk/60665/theresa-may-rejects-calls-to-increase-indian-visa-quota/page/0/4.

107 Cited in Dearden. 2015.

108 Kirkup, James. 2015. 'Theresa May's immigration speech is dangerous and factuwrong', *Telegraph*, October 6. www.telegraph.co.uk/news/uknews/immigration/11913927/Theresa-Mays-immigration-speech-is-dangerous-and-factually-wrong.html.

109 See Devlin et al. 2014.

110 Kirkup. 2015.

111 Ibid.

112   Stone, Jon. 2016. 'What Theresa May said about immigration in her infamous speech to Tory conference', *Independent*, August 25. www.independent.co.uk/news/uk/politics/theresa-may-immigration-policies-speech-conference-2015-tory-conservative-party-views-a7209931.html.

113   Harvey, Fiona. 2021. 'Tories accused of corruption and NHS privatisation by former chief scientist', *The Guardian*, April 13. https://www.theguardian.com/politics/2021/apr/13/tories-accused-of-corruption-and-nhs-privatisation-by-former-chief-scientist. Campbell, Denis and Kollewe, Julia. 2022. 'Javid tells NHS England to give private hospitals up to £270m in case of Omicron surge', *The Guardian*, January 13. https://www.theguardian.com/society/2022/jan/13/sajid-javid-nhs-england-private-hospitals-omicron.

114   See Pearce, Tom. 2017. 'UK budget steps up attacks on education', World Socialist Web Site (WSWS), March 21. www.wsws.org/en/articles/2017/03/21/educ-m21.html.

115   Cited in Stone. 2016.

116   Ibid.

117   Ibid.

118   Ibid.

119   Lea, Sian. 2016. 'The Immigration Act 2016 in plain English', *Human Rights News, Views & Info*, May 31. https://rightsinfo.org/immigration-act-2016-plain-english/.

120   JCWI (Joint Council for the Welfare of Immigrants). 2016. 'What's next for the Hostile Environment: The Immigration Act 2016 and the Queen's Speech', May 23. https://jcwi.org.uk/blog/2016/05/23/what%E2%80%99s-next-hostile-environment-immigration-act-2016-and-queen%E2%80%99s-speech.

121   Ibid.; for updates to UK immigration, see GOV.UK, 'Immigration rules: updates' (ongoing).

122   Virdee, Satnam and McGeever, Brendan. 2017. 'Racism, crisis, Brexit', *Ethnic and Racial Studies*, 41 (10). https://doi.org/10.1080/01419870.2017.1361544.

123   Webber. 2016.

124   Ibid.

125   Moore, Michael and Ramsay, Gordon. 2017. 'UK media coverage of the 2016 EU Referendum campaign', London: Centre for the Study of Media, Communicaand Power. The Policy Institute, King's College London, May. www.kcl.ac.uk/sspp/policy-institute/CMCP/UK-media-coverage-of-the-2016-EU-Referendum-campaign.pdf.

126   Ibid. 'UK media coverage of the 2016 EU Referendum campaign', pp. 8–9. https://www.kcl.ac.uk/policy-institute/assets/cmcp/uk-media-coverage-of-the-2016-eu-referendum-campaign.pdf.

127   Ashcroft, Michael. 2016. 'How the United Kingdom voted on Thursday... and why', Lord Ashcroft Polls, June 24. https://lordashcroftpolls.com/2016/06/how-the-united-kingdom-voted-and-why/.

128   Dorling. 2016.

129   Virdee, and McGeever. 2017.

130   Dorling, Danny. 2016. 'Brexit: the decision of a divided country', *British Medical Journal (BMJ)*, 354:i3697, July 6. www.bmj.com/content/354/bmj.i3697.

131   Virdee and McGeever. 2017.

132   Ibid.

133   Ibid.

134   Wright, Oliver. 2016. 'David Cameron resigns: Prime Minister announces resignation after vote for Brexit', *The Independent*, June 24. www.independent.co.uk/news/uk/politics/david-cameron-resigns-resignation-brexit-eu-referendum-result-live-latest-prime-minister-general-a7099936.html.

135   Cited in Boyle, Danny, et al. 2016. 'Conservative leadership election: Theresa May wins more than half of MPs' votes as Stephen Crabb pulls out and Liam Fox is eliminated', *Telegraph*, July 5. www.telegraph.co.uk/news/2016/07/05/boris-johnson-backs-andrea-leadsom-tory-mps-vote-leadership-race/.

136   GOV.UK. 2016. 'Statement from the new Prime Minister Theresa May'. www.gov.uk/government/speeches/statement-from-the-new-prime-minister-theresa-may.

137   Stewart, Heather. 2016. 'Theresa May appeals to centre ground but cabinet tilts to the right', *The Guardian*, July 14. www.theguardian.com/politics/2016/jul/13/theresa-may-becomes-britains-prime-minister.

9 The May premiership: hostile environment – consolidation and impact (2016–2019)

SECTION 1: REFUSAL TO ROLL BACK THE HOSTILE ENVIRONMENT AND ITS GENERAL IMPACT

May refuses to roll back 'hostile environment' policy

Farron lays into May

In late January 2017, Theresa May visited the new US President Donald J. Trump in Washington. Criticizing this visit a few months later at his Liberal Democratic Party's Conference, Tim Farron laid into Theresa May who he noted 'took office claiming she would be a social justice crusader. And here she is today, to the right of Thatcher, holding hands with Donald Trump'.[1]

May's government, he went on, is 'a government that is as anti-refugees as Nigel Farage'. 'One of the most despicable things this Government has done', he suggested, 'happened quietly, in a ministerial written statement on the day that Article 50 passed the House of Commons', when the 'Home Office quietly confirmed that Britain would stop taking in desperate, unaccompanied child refugees'. This was not

> because the crisis was at an end or because we had rescued the thousands of children that the Government had promised, under duress, to help… Of the tens of thousands of unaccompanied children fleeing war and destitution, in the end we will take just 350… because they calculated that they could get away with it… But just to make sure, they sneaked out the news on the same day that Tory and Labour MPs voted Article 50 through. A despicable act, done in a despicable way.[2]

Kick out international students

Shortly after May became Prime Minister in July, 2016, she returned to her familiar theme of reducing net migration to the tens of thousands. As it was reported in the *Independent*, May believed that further tough regulation on universities by scrutinizing foreign students' visas was a way of doing this,

DOI: 10.4324/9781003198673-14

since she believed that higher education institutions had become an easy route into Britain for economic migrants. In a confidential letter to other ministers, she also argued that universities should 'develop sustainable funding models that are not so dependent on international students'.[3]

Peter Yeung also reported that Theresa May could have wrongly deported tens of thousands of international students, with the Upper Tribunal (Asylum and Immigration) ruling that the then Home Secretary's evidence suffered from 'multiple frailties and shortcomings'.[4] The students were accused of cheating in English language tests in 2014, with May acting swiftly to cancel, cut short or refuse the visas of 35,870 students who had taken the test.[5] In February 2019, it was revealed that some of these students were still being detained and are living in 'terror', with some in poverty or having mental health problems.[6] Labour MP Stephen Timms said ministers should allow the students to sit a fresh test, grant visas to those who pass and allow them 'time to complete their studies and to clear their names'.[7]

The June 8 snap General Election

On April 18, 2017, May announced a snap General Election to take place on June 8, giving as her reason that the opposition parties were jeopardizing her Government's preparations for Brexit.[8] It was a drastic miscalculation for May that changed parliamentary arithmetic from a Tory working majority of 17 to a hung Parliament, forcing May to enter a 'confidence and supply' agreement with the Democratic Unionist Party (DUP) (the DUP agreed to back the Conservatives on key votes in return for political favours).

The election was described by Scottish National Party (SNP) leader Nicola Sturgeon as a naked power grab and a bid to crush all opposition.[9] The catastrophic changes in May's fortunes can be viewed as the result of a number of factors. These include actually calling the election when she had previously ruled it out; constantly repeating 'strong and stable;' underestimating and not taking seriously Opposition leader Jeremy Corbyn and his anti-austerity message.[10] For insiders, according to Alex Hunt and Brian Wheeler, the turning point in the campaign was May's U-turn on social care. Team May had apparently been so confident of victory that it felt bold enough to cost-cut. Thus there were proposals for a 'dementia tax' that would lead to more people having to sell their homes to pay for care; for means testing the winter fuel allowance (an annual tax-free payment for those in receipt of state pension) and for ending the 'triple lock' that guarantees a minimum 2.5% annual increase in state pension. Finally, May was an introvert by Westminster standards and ran a negative and uninspiring presidential-type campaign when she did not like media interviews and dodged TV debates and big rallies (towards the end of the campaign, she had to rely on Boris Johnson to whip up the crowds).[11]

Tens of thousands and the end of free movement

On Friday, June 2, 2017, political journalist Ashley Cowburn reported that May had stated at a campaign rally the day before that she 'would be working' to achieve the 'tens of thousands' target, pledged ad finitum and ad nauseum, and repeated in the Conservative Manifesto, published in May 2017 by 2022.[12] According to an editorial run by the former Tory Chancellor George Osborne, then Editor of the London *Evening Standard*, none of the senior members of the Cabinet supported the pledge privately and said retaining it was 'economically illiterate'.[13]

May's claims as to the negative effects of immigration were subsequently repeated again in Prime Minister's Questions in September 2017,[14] while in that same month, Liberal Democratic Leader, Vince Cable claimed that while he was Business Secretary in the ConDem Government and May was Home Secretary, she suppressed up to nine reports showing no immigration impact on jobs and (contrary to the imperatives of capitalism) on wages because the findings were 'inconvenient' to the government, a claim denied by a spokesperson for the Prime Minister.[15]

On his BBC1 programme on the eve of the 2018 Tory Party Conference on September 30, Andrew Marr interviewed Theresa May on a number of issues that included her 'hostile environment' and the Immigration Act of 2014. She apologized for their combined effects on the Windrush genera-tion (see later in this chapter and chapter 10 for update on the Windrush scandal) that Marr described as a 'burning injustice' (a reference to her 2016 prime ministerial victory statement). However, after being asked repeatedly by Marr to apologize for the 'hostile environment' policy itself and the accompanying Act, May refused to apologize for either, and managed to slip in: 'we maintain the compliant environment policy' (changing 'really hos-tile' to 'compliant' was announced by Sajid Javid when he became Home Secretary in March 2018).

At the conference itself, May reiterated her 'end of free movement' pledge and her promise to reduce net migration, but without a mention of actual numbers:

> And with control of our borders, we can do something that no British government has been able to do in decades – restore full and complete control of who comes into this country to the democratically elected representatives of the British people… The free movement of people will end, once and for all… Those with the skills we need, who want to come here and work hard, will find a welcome. But we will be able to reduce the numbers, as we promised.[16]

However, asked during Prime Minister's Questions on December 9, 2018 if the government still wanted to keep immigration in the tens of thousands, May simply said 'yes'.

EU nationals 'jump the queue': May plays the (xeno-) 'race' card

In November 2018, May faced a backlash[17] over remarks made in a speech to business leaders, in which she again vowed to end EU free movement once and for all after Brexit. May stated in a bid possibly aimed at promoting xeno-racism Europe-wide, rather than being Eastern-Europe specific:

> It will no longer be the case that EU nationals, regardless of the skills or experience they have to offer, can jump the queue ahead of engineers from Sydney or software developers from Delhi.[18]

The European Parliament's Brexit co-ordinator Guy Verhofstadt responded, 'EU citizens living, working, contributing to UK communities, didn't "jump the queue" and neither did UK nationals in Europe', since they 'were exercising rights which provided freedom and opportunities'. He went on to say: 'We will fight to ensure these continue in the future, especially after any transition'.[19] Meanwhile, EU citizens living in the UK took to social media to accuse the Prime Minister of using them as scape-goats to shore up support for her Brexit agreement.[20]

Writing for the *Huffington Post*, Tanja Bueltmann, pro-vice-chancellor and a history professor at Northumbria University, underlined the effects of May's ongoing rhetoric of hate:

> May's words ... are not only insulting, but also directly harmful. They continue to invoke the lies that EU citizens here have not contributed. It is in such rhetoric that we can find the roots of hate against us. This hate can manifest in verbal abuse – from telling us to 'f*** off back to the s***hole' we came from to labelling us 'enemy aliens'.[21]

She went on,

> Home Office figures clearly show a rise in hate crimes against EU citizens, and police already predict another rise as Brexit day comes closer. The EU referendum, and everything May and her government have done since then, directly enabled this.[22]

Bueltmann concluded by accusing May of 'pinning people against people, casting one group as better than another', adding:

> That is despicable. And it is one of the hallmarks of xenophobia [I would say, 'xeno-racism']. As a result, there can now be no doubt that EU citizens need to brace themselves for yet more hate over the coming months.[23]

May was challenged by SNP MP Philippa Whitford in the House of Commons over the comment, who asked if she would apologize for managing 'to insult and upset over 3 million European citizens who live and work in this country'. May replied, 'I should not have used that language in that speech'.[24]

The 2018 White Paper on immigration

'Free Movement' has provided a useful summary and critique of the 2018 White Paper on immigration that it describes as a 'charter for the wealthy'.[25] The organization, which offers updates, commentary and advice on immigration and asylum law, argues that there is one overwhelming message in the document: 'prioritise and facilitate movement for those with access to large sums of capital; and the ongoing importance of a migrant's country of origin in line with political expediency'. 'In short', while it claims that its aim is to 'attract the brightest and best to a United Kingdom that is open for business', the reality is that it will 'attract the richest migrants, highest earners and create parallel rules for numerous types of migrants, dependent upon the trade deals struck in a post-Brexit world'.[26] It notes that the White Paper does not propose any immigration rule changes, but that these will be published following a year of 'extensive engagement'.

The White Paper's key message is that, post-Brexit 'Everyone will be required to obtain a permission if they want to come to the UK and to work or study here', but that until the end of the implementation period, EU free movement rules will continue to apply. From January 1, 2021, EU citizens and their family members must apply under the EU Settlement Scheme, and will have until June 2021 to do so.[27]

The White Paper allows low-skilled migrants to come to the UK to work for up to a year in, for example, skill gap areas such as 'sectors like construction and social care'. This route will contain a 12-month cooling-off period to prevent further applications for leave from such migrants. Most importantly, the Immigration Law Practitioners Association (ILPA), a group of leading immigration law practitioners that promotes and improves the advising and representation of immigrants, notes that 'the visa … will not carry entitlements to access public funds or rights to extend a stay, switch to other routes, bring dependants or lead to permanent settlement'.[28] As Free Movement argues, this 'is particularly perverse, as it is assumed that low-skilled migrants do not pay taxation'. In fact, migrants on work-based visas all pay tax on their UK earnings. It is therefore unclear as to the policy reason for denying people who pay for public services through general taxation the right to then access those self-same public services that are paid for through general taxation.[29]

There is also a salary requirement of £30,000 (or the 25% earnings threshold of that occupation, whichever is higher) for skilled migrants seeking five-year visas. Free Movement points out that the current 25%

salary threshold qualified teachers in primary and secondary schools is £22,022, and for nurses, the minimum salary does not reach £30,000 until they are at band 7: typically a specialist nurse in a particular area of medicine, or a ward manager with budgetary control and responsibility for management of the ward's nursing staff. The £30,000 threshold will, therefore, mean an incapability of responding to shortages in primary and secondary teaching and nursing at the junior end.[30]

This means that 'the government has chosen to completely ignore the contributions that key public sector employees, such as nurses and teachers, make to the UK economy'.[31]

The White Paper refers to 'low-risk' countries from which migrants can apply for a visa-free Electronic Travel Authority that will allow them to apply to enter the country without the need for documentary leave to enter/remain for six months. This serves political expediency and reinforces detrimental structural stereotypes about certain cohorts of migrants. The ILPA notes that it is unclear why some countries are classified as 'low-risk' while others are not.

Commenting on the White Paper, Ed Lewis, migration campaigner at Global Justice Now, reminds us that 'The Brexit result did not require an end to free movement – this is a political choice by the most anti-migrant prime minister in living memory'.[32] As he puts it:

> The white paper is the biggest single attack on rights we've seen in a generation. It will create 'Fortress Britain' where migrants come and go at the behest of big business but lack many of the rights which EU migrants have enjoyed to date. It is a recipe for a race to the bottom in terms of worker pay and conditions. As a country that pillaged and exploited the world to gain its wealth – and still does today – it is unconscionable to further close our doors to human beings.[33]

Lewis goes on, 'If people are worried about having their wages undercut by migrants, the white paper makes this more likely. You can only avoid this when you give migrants real rights. The white paper is all about removing rights'.[34] 'Perhaps the most shocking aspect of the White Paper', he argues, 'is that it wants Britain to sign up to dodgy deals with repressive regimes like Turkey or Egypt in the hope those countries will keep refugees and migrants out of Britain'.[35] Such a policy has resulted in thousands of deaths in the Mediterranean and 'slave camps in Libya'. 'On top of this', Lewis points out, 'the government wants to sign up to a version of the Dublin Convention which leaves migrants in already struggling countries like Italy and Greece… This is truly a charter for making our human rights responsibilities "someone else's problem."'[36] He then makes links to the source of migrants' needs to migrate:

> Britain is a country that continues to derive much wealth off the backs of other countries around the world. Too often, people are here

because of the effects of wars, arms sales, trade deals, tax avoidance and corporate behaviour sanctioned by Britain. It is outrageous to drain other countries of wealth and then refuse to give a place to those who lose out from these policies.[37]

'The freedom to move', Lewis concludes, 'shouldn't just be confined to the rich or middle classes'.[38]

The hostile environment: general impact under May's watch

Health

According to former head of NHS Digital Kingsley Manning, he repeatedly clashed with Theresa May's Home Office over requests to hand over confidential patient data to help trace 'immigration offenders'.[39] He said he was 'under immense pressure' to share patient data despite concerns about the legal basis and fears it would undermine claims that NHS Digital was 'a safe haven' for personal data.[40] According to Alan Travis, then Home Affairs editor for *The Guardian*, writing in early 2017, 'the non-clinical personal details including last known address, GP's details and date registered with their doctor, of more than 8,100 people ... [over the previous year were] ... passed to Home Office immigration enforcement'. When Manning first got the job in 2013, the year after May had named the 'really hostile environment', he asked the Home Office what the legal basis was for handing over such data, and was told that the 'Home Office view was that tracing illegal immigrants was a manifesto commitment'. If he didn't 'agree to cooperate [with the sharing of patient data] they would simply take the issue to Downing Street'.[41] Also writing for *The Guardian*, this is how freelance feature writer, Simon Usborne begins his survey of how the hostile environment has crept into everyday life in the UK:

> For a doctor in Birmingham, it was the pregnant patient eating less to save money to cover an NHS bill. For a primary school teacher in an inner-city school, it was the moment he sat down with new parents for an uncomfortable conversation about their child's nationality. For a London lecturer, it was the worry that A-level students were being put off university for fear of being deported. In banks, hospitals, lettings agencies, schools and lecture theatres, the government's current immigration policy has effectively erected a border within, along which people delivering vital services are coming to terms with unwanted new powers.[42]

NHS doctor Neal Russell refers to a political agenda that 'has been allowed to stand in the way of patients accessing healthcare'.[43] He goes on to explain that the effects of the government's 'really hostile environment' towards migrants in the NHS became clear to him when, as a children's doctor, he saw a new-born baby girl become one of its victims. Her mother, he points out, was an undocumented migrant living in the UK, who had attended an appointment during pregnancy, but was deterred from coming back for further care because of the cost, which for maternity care for migrants starts at £4,000 (apparently a mark-up of 150% of the actual cost) and can rise to tens of thousands for more complex care.[44] Many women, Russell points out, have been sent intimidating letters, while pregnant, 'threatening Home Office intervention if bills were unpaid'.[45] After delivery, moreover, they are even subjected to court proceedings.[46] Understandably, he continues, the woman I treated avoided antenatal care after that first encounter, but at the last minute, as she started her contractions, fear for her baby meant that she did go to hospital. She gave birth to a baby who had complications with permanent implications.[47]

Episodes like this, Russell points out, 'are recorded as involving women with "social issues", who have "poor engagement with antenatal care,"' with those who cannot pay being referred to the Home Office for potential detention and deportation. Given that the NHS 'has abandoned its founding principles in service of a political agenda', Russell and his colleagues are handing back medals given to them by the UK Government for humanitarian work on Ebola in West Africa.[48]

Writing for *The Guardian,* Chaminda Jayanetti tells a similar story, with hundreds of patients being denied treatment for serious health problems including cancer, arrhythmia and cardiac chest pains. In one case, a patient with advanced stage cancer died after she went a year without treatment because an NHS hospital demanded £30,000 upfront to provide chemotherapy.[49]

Data obtained by *The Guardian* under the Freedom of Information (FOI) Act showed that across 84 of England's 148 acute hospital trusts, 2,279 patients were charged upfront between October 2017 and June 2018. Of these, 341 patients in 61 trusts did not proceed with their intended treatments or appointments after being told to pay.[50] As Jayanetti points out, the true figure is certain to be higher, since 64 trusts did not provide figures.[51]

Labour's Shadow Health Secretary Jon Ashworth called for upfront charging to be suspended:

> Patients feeling they have no option but to deny themselves treatment because of Theresa May's obnoxious 'hostile environment' agenda is not only leaving people who are ill without help but could potentially have wider public health implication as well.[52]

The FOI data revealed that across 80 hospital trusts, the total amount charged upfront to patients – including most of those who did not proceed with treatment – was about £4 million for the first eight months of the upfront charging regimen that came into effect in October 2017.[53]

Education

With respect to the education system, Sally Weale, education correspondent for *The Guardian*, has pointed out how headteachers and campaigners have expressed outrage at the fact that pupils who are among the poorest in society are missing out on free school meals because their parents/carers have no access to benefits as a part of the rule introduced in 2012 known as 'no recourse to public funds' (NRPF).[54] As Weale explains, all children in reception, year 1 and year 2 automatically get free meals, irrespective of immigration status, and refugees are entitled to free meals. However, older children whose parents'/carers' access to benefits is limited by the NRPF condition are being denied free meals, though many say they lack the means to pay.[55]

According to The Children's Society (2016), over a two-year period more than 50,000 individuals with dependents had the 'no recourse to public funds' condition applied to their leave to remain. Its Chief Executive Matthew Reed commented:

> It is shocking to think of any child going hungry at school, but the reality is that there are thousands of children in the UK living in families who are facing destitution but being denied vital benefits like free school meals – all because of their immigration status.[56]

Usborne cites academic Francesca Zanatta, a lecturer in children's rights at the University of East London, a university that along with all other UK universities is legally required to perform immigration checks on behalf of the government. Zanatta argues that the 'really hostile environment' of which she is now a part, 'is like a disease, a virus' that she sees 'as an infringement of the universal declaration of human rights which says everyone has a right to education'.[57] As we have seen, international students have been targeted by May to drive down net migration. Many such students have to take 'credibility interviews' to make sure they are 'genuine students'.

Zanatta points out that, while lecturers do not perform the checks themselves, staff feel uncomfortable with the environment created by them. She also fears the effects on some UK students:

> Recently, I was approached by a secondary school student whose friend didn't really have ID because they had arrived here aged three. They asked what would I recommend. And I didn't have an answer.... People are very fearful of exposing themselves to the possibility of being deported.[58]

Moreover, students from some countries staying longer than six months must register with the police within a week of arriving. In 2019, this comprised some 40 countries, of which over 60% were predominantly Muslim countries. Universities must also subject international students to more rigorous attendance rules and periodic document checks.[59] Failure to comply[60] can result in the loss of the licence that allows institutions to admit international students, whose fees they increasingly rely on to balance their books.[61]

Impact on asylum seekers

On March 1, 2017 a *Guardian* investigation reported that 'Britain is one of the worst destinations for people seeking asylum in western Europe', taking fewer refugees; offering less generous financial support; providing housing that is often sub-standard; and not giving asylum seekers the right to work.[62] Reflecting the hostile environment, Alex Fraser, director of refugee support at the British Red Cross, stated: 'I don't think we will see a reduction ... by making the experience tougher. All it will do is make the experience of people in the system more difficult'.[63]

Accommodation

With respect to accommodation for asylum seekers, on January 31, Travis described a House of Commons Home Affairs Select Committee report that exposed how some destitute asylum seekers are housed in accommodation infested with mice, rats and bedbugs, with one woman complaining of a kitchen 'full of mice' that 'ran across the dining room table' while they were eating, and a torture survivor for whom the presence and noise of rats triggered flashbacks to the rat-infested cell where he had been detained and tortured.[64] Moreover, asylum seeker housing tends to be concentrated in the most deprived areas: the report noted that while there were 1,042 asylum seekers housed in Bolton and 1,029 in Rochdale, there were only 88 housed in the then Home Secretary Amber Rudd's[65] Hastings and Rye constituency and none at all in Theresa May's Maidenhead constituency.[66] Committee chair Yvette Cooper said that the state of accommodation was a 'disgrace', with 'lack of healthcare for pregnant women, or inadequate support for victims of rape and torture'.[67]

The right to work

As far as the right to work is concerned, in a parliamentary debate, Sarah Newton, a parliamentary undersecretary of state at the Home Office, stated in a distinctive Tory callous fashion, typical of the 'really hostile environment', that the Government opposed giving asylum seekers the right to work in order to ensure 'that access to jobs is prioritised for British citizens and those with leave to remain' and to avoid a 'pull factor' for asylum seekers.[68]

Detention

As Niamh McIntyre and Diane Taylor explain, immigrants can be detained at any time and those who do not speak English and who are newly arrived in the UK are least able to challenge a Home Office decision to detain them. The most recent figures available in October 2018 indicated that more than 27,000 people were detained in 2017. Some people were detained as soon as they arrived by Home Office officials at airports and ports, while others were detained after living in Britain for many years when they tried to renew work, family or study visas. A *Guardian* survey found 15% were detained at a Home Office reporting centre, where immigrants had to attend regular appointments while their applications were processed, and where they could find themselves starting the day queuing to see a bureaucrat and ending the day in a small cell with a stranger. Others were apprehended during dawn raids at their homes, after rough sleeping, when found working illegally or while making applications for leave to remain.[69]

Lyons et al. point out that Britain was the only country out of the five European countries (the others being Germany, France, Spain and Italy) in *The Guardian* investigation that did not set a maximum time limit for holding asylum seekers in detention facilities, and the only country that did not allow unaccompanied children who arrived and claimed asylum the right to apply to be reunited with their parents. While the Government announced it would end indefinite detention of immigrant families with children in 2010 and detaining unaccompanied children for more than a day was banned in 2014, unaccompanied children could still be detained during criminal cases and escorted during returns. In addition, families were still detained together in 'exceptional circumstances'.[70] *The Guardian* survey uncovered 'multiple examples of children being detained in adult facilities'.[71]

In February 2019, annual government figures revealed that just 364 of 6,300 individuals who were identified by doctors and social workers as at particular risk of harm were subsequently allowed out of detention, representing just 6% of detainees classified as 'vulnerable and at risk' after abuse including torture, sexual violence or trafficking.

Lack of refugee protection

Sile Reynolds, Senior Policy Advisor at Freedom from Torture, points out that the

> hostile environment ... has undoubtedly made it harder for asylum caseworkers to perform their functions to a standard that reflects the principle of refugee protection, the right to rehabilitation for torture survivors and respect for the rule of law... It has driven policy and

legislative measures ... that have redirected resources away from strained asylum casework teams and towards enforcement, indefinite detention and removal.[72]

Accordingly, the majority of Freedom from Torture's clients describe applying for asylum, in the UK as 'harrowing', since the determination of Home Office caseworkers to 'find the lie' in the applicant's account of past torture means that an individual's testimony is virtually worthless unless corroborated by a level of documentary evidence that is not available to all applicants and that, even when such evidence of torture is available, it is mishandled and dismissed by asylum caseworkers preoccupied with under-mining the credibility of the applicant.[73] Sajid Javid, then Home Secretary, Reynolds (2018) concludes: 'could start with the most pronounced moral concern: Protecting torture survivors and asylum seekers from the "hostile environment" and asking Home Office case workers to go in with a will-ingness to believe their stories'.[74]

In an interview, after pledging that would-be migrants crossing the English Channel in small boats 'would see their asylum request processed "in the normal way,"'[75] Javid added that the journey across the world's busiest shipping lane was highly perilous and being undertaken by children as young as nine: 'It's incredibly dangerous, please do not do that, you are taking your life into your own hands'.[76] He then issued this threat to would-be migrants, immediately contradicting his 'normal processing' pledge by warning that it would be harder for such migrants to gain asylum:

> Also, if you do somehow make it to the UK, we will do everything we can to make sure that you are often not successful because we need to break that link, and to break that link means we can save more lives.[77]

Colin Yeo, a leading immigration and asylum barrister pointed out that the Home Secretary's apparent threat was illegal: 'Sending genuine refugees to face persecution in order to dissuade others from seeking to come here is plainly illegal'.[78] Yeo continued:

> I imagine the home secretary knows this, but if so it is depressing that he is still saying it as a way of trying to make himself sound tough. The latest asylum statistics show that around three-quarters of Iranian asylum claims succeed, so we are talking here about genuine refugees.[79]

Labour backbencher Stella Creasy, who has visited migrant camps in Calais, accused Javid of normalizing 'anti-refugee rhetoric online' and that 'People will continue to die and be at the mercy of traffickers all the time politicians pretend to play tough for votes rather than recognise why people flee'.[80]

Lisa Doyle, director of advocacy at the Refugee Council, agreed about the illegality of Javid's threat: 'The 1951 refugee convention acknowledges that refugees may enter countries through irregular routes and should not be penalised for this'.[81]

Doyle pointed out: 'The outcome of an asylum application cannot be pre-judged before it has been made and must be processed on its individual merit, irrespective of how that person reached the country'. 'Let us not forget', she went on, 'that we are talking about people who are in desperate need of protection, having fled countries with prolific human rights abuses'.[82]

'It's a shame', she concluded, 'that the Home Secretary seems to need reminding that seeking asylum is a right and the UK has an obligation to assess claims fairly and grant protection to those who need it'.[83]

Jon Date, Oxfam's head of government relations, also criticized Mr Javid's comments. He said:

> Anyone who arrives in this country seeking safety from war or perse-cution should have their asylum claim considered. To reject it because we don't like the manner in which they arrive would be illegal and is an affront to fairness and decency. If the Home Secretary is serious about protecting lives, he should provide more safe options for people seeking asylum. This includes changing the restrictive rules on family reunion so that people with relatives in the UK can apply to live with them.[84]

Javid had abandoned a luxury safari holiday to 'get a grip' on what he described as 'a major incident'.[85] This largely successful attempt (it hit the headlines) to play 'the "race" card' came a couple of weeks before May's crucial Commons vote on her widely criticized Brexit deal. Writing in *The Independent*, Richard Godwin wonders:

> perhaps the general cynicism of 2018 has infected my cheerful little heart, but I can't help wondering if the reason Javid cancelled his holiday was to create headlines about Javid cancelling his holiday, in order to open the 2019 news cycle with fresh new headlines about some sort of terrifying migrant flotilla that requires tough new measures from our safari-spurning home secretary?[86]

As Godwin succinctly concludes, 'a little anti-migrant hysteria is hardly going to hinder Theresa May's anti-movement agenda, is it?' Godwin rightly argues that it is not that we shouldn't be concerned with human traffickers operating in the English Channel, but he doesn't 'remember any Tory ever cancelling a luxury sojourn to deal with, say, the uni-versal credit catastrophe; or indeed Brexit', and, underlining the real intent of the Conservative Party stunt, Godwin describes it as 'a pro-duction written, directed and orchestrated by the Tory party, starring you and everyone you know'.[87]

Javid also queried whether the migrants were genuine asylum seekers:

> if you are a genuine asylum seeker why have you not sought asylum in the first safe country you arrived in? Because France is not a country where anyone would argue it is not safe in any way whatsoever, and if you are genuine then why not seek asylum in your first safe country?[88]

In an interview on *Sky News* in 2019,[89] around about the same time as Javid's query, Clare Moseley, CEO of CARE4CALAIS, which provides direct care for refugees in Calais, including food, clothing and camping equipment, offered an answer, when asked why they are trying to get to the UK. Their immediate problem, she explained is that they want to get out because conditions in Calais are very bad, with people sleeping rough with no shelter from the elements. They have come from the most dangerous places in the world and are looking for somewhere safe to live and rebuild their lives. Asked why they are trying to get to the UK in particular, Moseley pointed out that the majority of refugees who come to Europe do claim asylum in other countries: there are 1 million in Germany; half a million in Italy, and France processes 100,000 applications a year, a lot more applications than the UK:

> The specific thing about the refugees who come to Calais is they are the few who have a really strong reason for wanting to get to the UK, and the most common reason that we hear is family ties. Because the people who might have lost their families, lost everything in conflicts *do* have a remaining family member in the UK, they will do a lot to get to that family member.[90]

This is, of course, directly related to Britain's imperial past. With respect to the dismantling of the so-called 'jungle' in Calais in 2016, Moseley explained that the French authorities are determined not to let the camps form, so if people have a tent, they get to sleep in it for two or three days before it is taken away from them: 'It's actually a lot worse than it was when the jungle camp was there, and God knows, that was bad enough'.[91] Estimating that there was about a thousand refugees across Calais and Dunkirk, so closing the camp did not work, nowadays Moseley states, people do not get to change their clothes, there is no sanitation and a lot of fungal disease.[92]

Asked if by handing out care, food and tents, she is not encouraging people to come and take the perilous journey, Moseley replied, 'I very much doubt that anyone would come to Calais and live in the mud and the squalor and the rain just for the second-hand clothes or the small bit of food that we give them'.[93] Moreover, she points out there is no academic evidence that pull factors exist. She stresses that we do know that there are massive push factors, and that it is these strong push factors that make people leave, such as persecution and terror, rather than economic reasons. Most of the people in Calais at the time, she concludes, came from Syria, Afghanistan, Sudan, Eritrea and Iran (all ranked very low for peace and high for tensions, conflicts and crises),[94] so the Government needs to provide a safe and legal route to claim asylum. To press home the point, Moseley states that when the refugees were taken out of the Calais camp in 2016, in a fairly tough process, 86% were granted asylum in France, and were therefore genuine refugees, and not 'economic migrants'.[95]

Finally, in February 2019, it was revealed that, since Robert Mugabe was forced from power in November 2017, the Home Office had pushed ahead with a removals process for refused asylum seekers, many of whom had been in the UK for over a decade.[96] Despite high-profile human rights abuses in the country, it had been working with the Zimbabwean government to accelerate the deportation process to such an extent that, over the previous few months, Zimbabweans across the UK had been asked to attend interviews at Home Office centres. When they attended, they found Zimbabwean government officials waiting to interview them. One woman, who had been in the UK for six years, said she attended one such interview and was told by a man speaking her native language, Shona, that she was 'one of thousands of Zimbabweans that the UK government wanted to remove from the country'.[97] Having relatives who were politicians in the opposition Movement for Democratic Change, the official had a file on her with her photo and biographical details. Understandably, she commented: 'I am so anxious and I am so petrified. If the Home Office now is sharing my details with the Zimbabweans, then they are selling my life to them'.[98]

As if to back up the woman's claim, Andrew Nyamayaro, principal solicitor at Tann Law Solicitors, pointed out: 'Civilians are being tortured by members of the armed forces and the ruling party. Enforcing removals of Zimbabweans from the UK at this juncture is tantamount to sending someone to a death chamber', while Nyamayaro's colleague, Rumbi Bvunzawabaya, added: 'We have clients who are suicidal, who have been sectioned, since the news [about the interviews] came out. People are afraid'.[99] The then Shadow Home Secretary, Diane Abbott responded: 'The government's resumption of deportations to Zimbabwe is in line with their hostile environment policy. The Home Office appear to have little regard for potential human rights abuses and are deporting people who may be at risk'.[100]

It would seem that, far from being over, the 'really hostile environment', routinely levelled at innocent people, was actually intensifying. Indeed, this has continued up to and including the Johnson Government (see chapter 10).

Health

A report by the Equality and Human Rights Commission (EHRC) conducted by Doctors of the World and Imperial College London, in collaboration with the Equality and Human Rights Commission and published on November 29,

2018, revealed that 'cost and fears about how they will be treated, or consequences for their immigration status, are preventing people seeking or refused asylum from using health services'.[101] This particularly affected pregnant women and disabled people.[102] Rebecca Hilsenrath, Chief Executive of the EHRC, commented:

> Everyone should have access to good quality healthcare, regardless of who they are and where they come from. People seeking and refused asylum are likely to have particular health needs because of past distressing experiences and the traumatic effects of fleeing to a different country. It's therefore crucial that they are able to fully and easily access healthcare and that their rights are protected by keeping healthcare separate from immigration enforcement. This is just about common humanity. We encourage the UK Government and healthcare providers to review this new research and take action on our recommendations to ensure health services are culturally appropriate, accessible to everyone and that staff are trained to recognise and respond to the specific needs of marginalised patients.[103]

Consistent barriers to healthcare included: associated costs such as travel and prescriptions; the NHS charging policy in England, that does not apply in Scotland and Wales, being unaffordable; data sharing with the Home Office that meant asylum seekers were concerned that they may be arrested, detained or deported; no choice dispersal when accommodation is changed that disrupts healthcare and social networks; lack of knowledge of entitlements and eligibility.[104] In addition, some were worried that their health conditions, in particular those considered stigmatizing such as HIV and mental health conditions, would be taken into account in the asylum process. Moreover, people who had traumatic pre-migratory experiences found it difficult to build trust in health professionals, with one stating that she avoids health services after being refused registration for an urgent appointment by a receptionist who said: 'Why do you worry? The Home Office gave you a house, and money for eating'.[105] Finally, information provided to asylum seekers was not always accurate or in a language or format they understood, and often interpreters were not provided. This meant that many were unaware of their rights or how to assert them.

Katherine Taylor, a GP and health advisor for Doctors of the World, concluded:

> People seeking asylum have fled war, conflict or persecution. Many will have experienced loss of or separation from family and loved ones, and some have gone for long periods without any healthcare. When they arrive in the UK looking for protection, it's essential that they are able to get the healthcare they need.[106]

If granted refugee status

From the onset of May's 'hostile environment' policies, once granted refugee status, asylum seeker support ceases, and refugees must apply for mainstream benefits and have 28 days to leave the accommodation provided to them by the Home Office. Because of the difficulties involved in applying for these benefits, very few refugees are able to register in this 28-day period, and are forced to go to food banks and charities for food and many also become homeless.[107] As Policy Manager for the Refugee Council Judith Dennis put it:

> What we do is force [refugees] into homelessness and destitution almost routinely. It's hard to see how someone without an advocate or a special need that makes them a priority for council housing will be able to move on within 28 days. We would expect the majority of those who have to source private sector housing will become homeless.[108]

SECTION 2: THE HOSTILE ENVIRONMENT AND WOMEN; AND THE WINDRUSH SCANDAL

The following two examples show that the hostile environment impacts negatively on women, and the ways in which women are struggling against racism and patriarchy, sexism and misogyny.

Yarl's Wood Detention Centre

In 2019, the official Yarl's Wood Immigration Removal Centre (this official description perhaps a more sinister sobriquet than the 'detention centre' of common parlance) website[109] featured a text box at the top of the page with the words, 'Respect, Support, Commitment. That's Our Promise' to the left and a picture of six happy, smiling Asian women to the right. Below the text box under the heading 'Welcome to Yarl's Wood' was the following description:

> Yarl's Wood IRC is a fully contained residential centre housing adult women and adult family groups awaiting immigration clearance. We focus on decency and respect in all aspects of care for our residents and use continuous innovation to further improve and develop our service.[110]

Beneath that was an equally beaming White man, Centre Manager Steve Hewer who states:

> Our role is to provide a caring, yet safe and secure environment for all our residents at Yarl's Wood IRC. We do this by promoting Trust, Care, Innovation and Pride within the centre, and this is at the forefront of all our policies and procedures.

In his letter he assures readers that Yarl's Wood is unique in providing specialist and innovative services including:

- healthcare
- faith and cultural provision
- educational and recreational activities
- work opportunities aimed at supporting residents throughout their period of detention and preparing them for release and resettlement.[111]

In August 2017, in a mixed report, HM Chief Inspector of Prisons Peter Clarke concluded after inspections in June of that year:

> The leadership and staff could and should take much of the credit for the improvements, but it was clearly a frustration for them that the centre was not able to gain higher assessments in some areas of this inspection because of failings that were outside their control. For instance, weaknesses in immigration casework and health care provision, which had a significant negative impact on the experiences of detainees, were the responsibility of the Home Office and the commissioned health care provider respectively. If I had invested the energy and commitment to making improvements at Yarl's Wood that the current management team clearly have, I too would be frustrated.[112]

May Bulman explains that the 400 plus held at the centre were there not because they had committed criminal offences, but because they needed to establish their identities or facilitate immigration claims. As a visitor, not as a journalist, Bulman was there to meet Opelo Kgari, 27, who had been in Yarl's Wood for five weeks, and was one of the 120 detainees on hunger strike. 'It is quickly clear from the way she speaks and her ease of communication that she is very much British', Bulman explained. 'It's not a surprise. She came to the UK from Botswana with her mother when she was just 13 years old'.[113]

However, despite going through the British education system and achieving good A-level results, she was rejected when applying for an undergraduate degree at the University of the West of England due to her immigration status. Opelo had been thrown into Yarl's Wood twice in the year prior to Bulman's visit. The first time she had been on her way back from a short weekend in Belfast with friends when she was placed in a holding cell for two days – 'a memory that brings tears to her eyes – before being driven to the centre'.[114] The second time, after reporting to the Home Office as required every two weeks, she was picked up on her way to yoga and again locked in a holding cell for more than 12 hours with her mother, and then taken straight to Yarl's Wood at about 3 a.m., with only what she had on her back and no change of clothes.[115]

Bulman explains the background to the case. Opelo and her mother had been fighting for their right to stay since 2010. Having been refused asylum, they were arguing that, after living in the UK for 14 years, throughout Opelo's formative years, they had a human right to remain, yet 'despite ongoing legal proceedings, they find themselves locked in Yarl's Wood'.[116] However Opelo's main concern was fellow detainees, more vulnerable than herself, who were not having their health needs met:

> There's one woman who spends all day walking around the centre with a packed handbag, claiming she had everything she needs in there. She's clearly not well. And there's an Iranian woman who's on suicide watch. Officers just sit outside her cell with the door open. She clearly shouldn't be in here at all. It's inhumane.[117]

Opelo concludes, 'There are days when it's really hard and I feel like I have no future. I struggle to sleep'. 'The idea of going back to Botswana is unfathomable', she points out. 'I was never close to my family there and I don't even speak the language … I couldn't recognise myself as a non-Brit now'.[118]

Towards the end of February 2018, nine months after Chief Inspector Clarke's castigation of the Home Office, Deputy Leader of the Green Party Amelia Womack described her personal experience of a visit to Yarl's Wood:

> I'll never forget my first visit to Yarl's Wood – one of our Government's brutal and inhumane detention centres. I had joined one of the many protests that gather in front of the building, making fleeting moments of contact with the incarcerated women. I saw handmade signs, waved through cracks in their open windows. I heard their voices call out to us, defiant in the face of their detention. And while we were separated by bricks and barbed wire, we were united in solidarity. Together, we would bring these walls down, and set these women free.[119]

She continued:

> As I write these words, over 100 women in Yarl's Wood are on hunger strike … today marks eight days of action against the injustices our Government is inflicting on them. They won't eat. They won't work. They won't participate in any way until the Government meets their demands.

Womack describes how, the day before, she had joined others outside the Home Office, demanding that the Theresa May Government listen to these women and recognize their humanity. Womack went on, 'I have heard first-hand accounts of how some of these women are being treated, and the descriptions of their lives were heart-breaking':

Living under fear of their guards. Being separated from their families. Feeling powerless in a system, and never knowing when their hell would be over. Because, unlike every other country in Europe, we lock people up indefinitely, just because of their immigration status.[120]

The woman I spoke to, Womack points out, called this purgatory. 'She didn't know how long she'd be there, if she'd be reunited with her partner in London'. She did not know 'if she'd be forcibly removed and deported from the country on one of the charter flights that sporadically take women from the centre with no warning. And this was just the tip of the iceberg'. The women's demands were clear:

- a 28-day limit to detention
- adequate healthcare and mental health provision for detainees
- a fair bail process
- recognition by the Home Office that rape is torture[121] (rape victims are detained despite a policy stating that victims of torture must not be detained for immigration reasons).[122]

Womack rightly notes: 'These are hardly radical demands and women shouldn't be forced to go on hunger strike to receive these basic rights'. However, the Home Office will not even meet with the women in Yarl's Wood. 'It is time', she concludes, for the Government to recognize 'that detention centres like Yarl's Wood are inhumane, costly and utterly unnecessary. Everyone deserves to be treated with humanity and dignity'.[123]

Domestic violence

May's 'really hostile environment' had an alarmingly negative impact on migrant women (and presumably some men) experiencing domestic violence. The refusal rate for migrants applying to stay in the UK after suffering domestic violence more than doubled between 2012 (the year Theresa May initiated her rhetoric of hostility) and 2016.[124] A new rule had been introduced in 2002 that gave people who entered the UK on a spouse visa and then suffered domestic abuse the right to apply for leave to remain.[125] This was enacted, following representations from campaigners, who argued that women were being forced to choose between deportation and continued abuse or domestic violence.[126]

However, as data journalist Niamh McIntyre and news reporter Alexandra Topping, both at *The Guardian*, pointed out, a Freedom of Information (FOI) request by that newspaper revealed that the refusal rate for applications under the domestic violence rule rose from 12% in 2012 to 30% in 2016, the last year for which full-year data was available, with figures showing that 1,325 people were refused out of a total of 5,820 applications made between 2012 and 2016.[127] Radhika Handa, legal policy and campaigns officer at Southall

Black Sisters – a group of Black and minority women with years of experience of struggling for women's human rights in the UK – commented on the effect of May's hostile environment since 2014, in dramatically exacerbating domestic violence:

> We have this really hostile state climate where migrant women suffering domestic violence are being sacrificed at the altar of an immigration policy obsessed with limiting rights. That is not the hallmark of a civilised democratic society. We've been horrified by it.[128]

Specifically, campaigners 'accuse the Home Office of using the testimony of violent husbands to deny victims of domestic violence the right to remain in the UK after they have escaped abusive relationships'.[129]

In a key case in November 2017, the Home Office deported a woman who said she had been abused by her husband and his family, with a judge ruling that the Home Office had accepted his account 'without evaluation and then relied on it as the main reason for rejecting [the claimant]'s account'.[130] Lucy Mair, a barrister from the law firm Garden Court Chambers who represented the claimant in the November case, pointed out that since 2015, people making applications under the domestic violence rule only have a right to an administrative review rather than an appeal. Thus, up until 2015, appeals had a very high rate of success. Since then, however, there is effectively no recourse to challenge a decision.[131]

A FOI request, reported by McIntyre and Topping, revealed that just 2% of administrative reviews from 2015 to May 2018 resulted in an initial Home Office decision being overturned, just 15 out of 630 requests. By contrast, between January and March 2011, 82% of appeals made under the old system successfully overturned a Home Office decision, according to evidence submitted to Parliament by 'Rights of Women', a charity that 'specialises in supporting women who are experiencing or are at risk of experiencing, gender-based violence'.[132]

Labour MP for Bristol West Thangam Debbonaire, who before becoming an MP worked for Women's Aid and is a specialist in domestic violence, told McIntyre and Topping she was dealing with several cases where constituents were being forced to stay in abusive relationships because vital documents were kept by their partners. She went on, 'We have domestic violence laws which give out good signals – but what we are doing in these cases is saying we care about tackling domestic violence, except if you have insecure immigration status, and then we don't'.[133] Southall Black Sisters officer Handa also points out that, 'Women who have been taken back to their home country and abandoned often have any documentation taken away from them'.[134]

As with all aspects of the 'really hostile environment', costs are prohibitively expensive (see the Appendix to this chapter). If the victims could not prove they were destitute in order to apply to remain in the UK under the domestic violence rule, costs more than doubled between 2014 and 2018, from £1,093 to £2,389, plus an additional £2,389 for each dependent child,[135] thus reinforcing the anti-working-class as well as anti-immigrant rationale of the Theresa May Government.

In February 2018, May issued a new policy document for Home Office staff that made it incumbent on officials to take into account the length of the couple's relationship and stated that police evidence against both parties should be considered. Handa summarizes its effects:

> We find that when the police are faced with cross-allegations from the perpetrator, if he says things like 'she attacked me/my mum/all of us and I was restraining her', police may arrest the woman or treat both perpetrator and victim the same, and caution or warn them both.[136]

After a report by Claire Waxman, a victims' commissioner appointed by Sadiq Khan, Mayor of London, highlighting how people can be forced to remain in abusive relationships due to their immigration status, the Mayor and the Victims' Commissioner jointly called for:

- The reinstatement of legal aid for immigration cases to ensure those with insecure status can access independent advice and support.
- Victims of violence to be entitled to financial support and safe accommodation in order to leave an abusive relationship, irrespective of their immigrations status.
- Operational guidelines on how to respond to victims with insecure immigration status, including prioritizing safety and support over immigration offences.[137]

Khan laid the blame squarely on Theresa May: 'The government's hostile environment policies are leading to vulnerable people being denied access to much-needed services and facing significant risk of being unlawfully detained'.[138]

The Domestic Abuse Bill

On January 21, 2019, the first draft of the Domestic Abuse Bill was published. Under it, types of *economic* abuse (such as restricting a partner's access to bank accounts or employment) were to be recognized as a form of domestic abuse in England and Wales. Economic abuse also includes an abuser taking control of their victim's food, transportation (such as not allowing use of a car or housing) or deliberately damaging their credit ratings.[139] Sian Hawkins, head of campaigns and public affairs at the charity Women's Aid, commented:

> We know that economic abuse has not been very widely understood or treated as seriously, so it's really important that this new legal definition recognizes economic abuse as a key part of domestic abuse. It

makes victims incredibly financially dependent on the perpetrators, and makes it difficult for them to leave an abusive relationship.[140]

In addition to economic abuse, the bill also: encompasses 'controlling and manipulative non-physical abuse'; prevents abusers from cross-examining their victims in court; introduces new protection orders; and establishes a national domestic abuse commissioner. Finally, it may force offenders to take mandatory lie-detector tests on release from prison.[141]

With respect to migrant women, Amnesty International (2019) points out that, while under human rights law, the Government has a duty to protect every woman in the UK from violence, irrespective of immigration status, and while the Bill recognizes the need to overcome barriers to reporting for women with insecure immigration status, it offers little more than current provisions aimed at addressing the problem. The organization explains that guidance is already in place for police to support victims, but in reality police forces often share data with the Home Office and 'domestic violence victims are treated as suspects by immigration enforcement'. The Bill, it points out, introduces nothing on a statutory footing to prevent this from happening.[142] Moreover, according to Amnesty International, instead of ensuring migrant women can access vital support services such as refuges, the Government suggests that some victims of domestic abuse 'may be best served by returning to their country of origin and, where it is available, to the support of their family and friends'.[143]

The draft Bill included the provision of £300,000 funding for BAME (Black, Asian and minority ethnic) organizations that are supporting survivors of abuse. While Amnesty International welcomed the fact that the Government recognized the need to support BAME organizations, such funding, it concluded, will go only a little way to support a sector that is hugely underfunded.[144]

Step Up Migrant Women (SUMW), which comprises more than 30 organizations, including the Latin American Women's Rights Service (LAWRS), Southall Black Sisters, Amnesty International UK, Sisters For Change and the End Violence Against Women Coalition, also welcomed the Bill since the Government puts survivors at the heart of its plans. But it has urged the Government to 'ensure equal protection for migrant, refugee and BAME women survivors of domestic abuse who often slip through the gaps because of their particular experiences of violence'.[145] As Lucila Granada, Director of the Latin American Women's Rights Service, pointed out:

> The draft Bill offers little hope for migrant victims to access safety and support. This is particularly alarming, as the Bill itself recognises the 'significant vulnerability' of migrant victims who fear deportation as a result of coming forward. Every day we support women who are unable to trust that the police and the law will prioritise their lives and their safety simply because they are migrants. Deterring migrant

women from reporting crimes gives impunity to perpetrators. We need a Bill that doesn't leave migrant women behind. We need safe reporting pathways, appropriate support, and a fair chance for migrant women to be able to break free from violence.[146]

In the view of Kate Allen, Director of Amnesty UK, while in some ways the Bill is ambitious, many of the protections it provides will remain out of reach for some of society's most vulnerable women:

> Migrant women in abusive relationships are currently trapped and further victimised by their immigration status – excluded from financial support which often makes them reliant on their abuser and threatened with deportation should they seek support from the police. In its current form, the Bill barely tinkers at the edges of what is necessary to ensure migrant women are treated fairly. To truly be ground-breaking, the Bill must ensure all women can access housing and welfare support and report abuse without fear of immigration enforcement. Otherwise perpetrators will continue to use the immigration status of their victims as a weapon to control and abuse their victims.[147]

Finally, Andrea Simon, Public Affairs Manager at the End Violence Against Women Coalition, commented on the need to abandon May's 'really hostile environment':

> The Government recognises that they must do more to protect domestic abuse victims with no recourse to public funds, but proposals announced today do not address or reverse the hostile environment policies created by successive immigration bills, which create barriers to women seeking help and support and can be weaponised by abusers.[148]

Her conclusion underlines the cruel implications of Theresa May's obsession with cutting net migration:

> A truly victim-centred Bill would recognise that *all* women who've experienced domestic violence should have access to protection and justice regardless of their immigration status. This is currently not the case, because only some women can access the limited safety net offered by the government in the Destitution and Domestic Violence Concession. This shames us as a society – when we clearly put immigration enforcement over women's and children's lives.[149]

The SUMW Coalition lists the following prerequisites for the Domestic Violence Abuse Bill. It should:

- offer a system of full confidentiality, protection and support for all migrant women who report their abuse, regardless of their immigration status. This policy must apply to all statutory services, including the police and GPs;
- make specialist organizations led by and for migrant and Black and minority ethnic women – which have had their services decimated by funding cuts – a central part of tackling domestic abuse and violence;
- recognize the gender inequality underlying domestic abuse and the disproportionate impact on women and girls;
- ensure refuge provision becomes a statutory obligation backed by national ring-fenced funding;
- ensure all migrant women at risk of experiencing abuse have access to public funds and routes to regularize their immigration status independent of their perpetrator.[150]

The Domestic Abuse Act received Royal assent on April 29, 2021 and its provisions come into force through 2022 and the Government has provided an ongoing update.[151]

The Windrush Scandal[152]

It was confirmed on BBC *Newsnight* in 2019 by Norman Baker, who was a Minister in the Home Office from 2013 to 2014 during May's tenure as Home Secretary (2010–2016), what many people already suspected or knew that there was 'a conflation of people who were asylum seekers with people who were economic migrants, with people who were here with "leave to remain,"' since May 'wanted to exclude as many people as possible from the country, and, those who were here, she wanted to deport if she possibly could'.[153] Baker, a Liberal Democrat in the Coalition Government, described being the only Liberal Democrat in the Home Office as 'walking through mud', and as like being 'the only hippy at an Iron Maiden concert'.[154] Unsurprisingly, he resigned from the Home Office on November 3, 2014, citing conflicts with May.[155] Among her excludees are members of the Windrush Generation. An extraordinary event came to light in 2018 and became known as the Windrush scandal. British subjects, mainly from the Caribbean, who had arrived in the UK before 1973, were detained, denied legal rights, threatened with deportation and some actually wrongly deported.

Commonwealth citizens who arrived in the UK after World War II and before 1973 are commonly known as the 'Windrush Generation', after the ship (as noted in chapter 3 of this book) the *Empire Windrush* on which citizens from the Caribbean first arrived in 1948. The ship arrived at Tilbury, a town on the north bank of the River Thames, on June 22, carrying 492 passengers from Jamaica, the first large group of African-Caribbean migrants to arrive in the UK after World War II.[156] At the time, there were no immigration restrictions on people from Commonwealth countries entering the UK, who were known as the 'freely landed', and who were allowed to live and work anywhere within the territories of the 'United Kingdom and Colonies'.[157] Commonwealth migration continued throughout the 1950s and 1960s, with the Immigration Act 1971 confirming that those who were already present and settled in the UK when the Act came into force on January 1, 1973, and without any restriction on their leave, were entitled to stay indefinitely in the UK. The Act also recognized the right of wives (husbands were not allowed entry until changes made in 1974) and children to join them, a right that was retained until the Immigration Act 1988.[158]

Until the onset of the 'hostile environment', no Government had set out comprehensive policies to ensure that the Windrush generation had their legal status fully documented. However, the subsequent introduction of policies requiring people to 'prove their right to be in the UK' in order to access essential services led to 'thousands of people being placed in a precarious position through no fault of their own'.[159] As the Home Affairs Select Committee[160] points out:

> People have lost their homes and their jobs and been refused health-care, pensions and access to social security. Not only did they not have documentation which proved their legal status in the UK but ... it was made very difficult for them to gain it.

During its inquiry, the Committee heard how

> vulnerable people did not understand why they were told they did not have the necessary documentation – since they considered themselves British – or what they should do about it... Many more tried unsuccessfully to prove their rights only to come up against the barrier of Home Office bureaucracy and poor decision making.

Moreover, some could simply not afford the fees.[161] The Committee also expressed a concern that:

> a target-led approach may have led immigration enforcement officers to focus on people like the Windrush generation, who may have been easier to detain and remove than those less vulnerable, for example by detaining individuals such as Paulette Wilson and Anthony Bryan who clearly presented no risk of absconding.[162]

Paulette Wilson

To give just one example, on November 28, 2017, Paulette Wilson, who had lived in the UK for more than half a century and had been paying national insurance contributions for 34 years, with a long history of working and paying taxes in the UK, spoke to *The Guardian*. Although she had indefinite leave to remain in the UK because she arrived before 1973, she received a letter from the Home Office in 2015 informing her that she was an 'illegal immigrant' and had six months before she would be sent to Jamaica, the country she left when she was ten and had never visited since. 'I was panicking. I was too scared to tell my daughter', she told *The Guardian*.[163] Her housing benefit was stopped immediately, leaving her homeless, as were her sickness benefits. Her daughter Natalie started to support her financially and a friend let her stay in his flat. She was told to report monthly to the Home Office.[164]

Wilson's mother had put her on a plane to the UK decades ago, to live with her grandfather, a factory worker, and her grandmother, a care worker. Her mother, who she never saw again, sent her to the UK for a better life and, on the whole, Wilson has been happy there. She never applied for a passport and never gave a thought about her immigration status.[165]

Wilson spent a week at Yarl's Wood detention centre,[166] before being sent to the immigration centre at Heathrow, where detainees are taken before removal from the UK. A last-minute intervention by her MP and a local charity prevented a forced removal. She was then allowed to return home.[167] Amelia Gentleman (2017) gives us a glimpse of Wilson's life in the UK:

> Paulette ... arrived in the UK in 1968, went to primary and secondary school in Britain, raised her daughter ... here and has helped to bring up her granddaughter. For a while, she worked in the House of Commons restaurant overlooking the Thames, serving meals to MPs and parliamentary security staff. More recently, she has volunteered at her local church, making weekly meals for homeless people... The week of detention in Yarl's Wood was the worst experience of her life: 'I felt like I didn't exist. I wondered what was going to happen to me. All I did was cry, thinking of my daughter and granddaughter; thinking that I wasn't going to see them again'. She was taken from the Home Office reporting centre in Solihull, Birmingham, in a secure van and told she was going to be sent out of the country: 'I couldn't eat or sleep; still now I can't eat and sleep properly'.[168]

When staff at Yarl's Wood told her she was being taken to the removal centre, she was allowed to call her daughter. She remembers screaming in terror down the phone: 'I was panicking because that evening they took away a lady. I watched her crying and being taken away. It was very scary'.[169]

Natalie described the devastating effect the near destitution over a two-year period had on her mother: 'They have deprived her of everything ... I am surprised we didn't lose her from the stress. She is normally so bubbly and sociable. Since she came out of Yarl's Wood she has withdrawn'.[170] A few times in the last month, Natalie explained that her mother, who lives nearby, had come to her flat in the middle of night, waking her to tell her she was scared that Home Office workers were going to come to take her away, and that she couldn't sleep until she got into Natalie's bed.[171]

Wilson's caseworker, who has dealt with as many as 40 similar cases of people who have lived here for decades but do not have British citizenship, spoke about the difficulties of dealing with the Home Office: 'It's very hard to communicate with anyone in the Home Office. It's hard to get through on the phone and you never speak to the person making the decision because those numbers aren't provided. You're always talking to an intermediary.'[172]

In a response to Wilson's MP, a member of the Home Office 'account management team' wrote: 'It may help to explain that Ms Wilson currently has no legal basis of stay within the UK and is liable to detention or removal'.[173] She despaired at the pressure to prove that she was British, while the application to process leave to remain documents cost more than £240, money she did not have (legal aid being no longer available for cases such as hers). She was terrified that she could be separated from her family: 'I don't know anyone in Jamaica. I had no passport so I couldn't go'.[174] Understandably, she does not like to be asked if she feels British:

> I don't feel British. I am British. I've been raised here, all I know is Britain. What the hell can I call myself except British? I'm still angry that I have to prove it. I feel angry that I have to go through this.[175]

On January 11, 2018, the Government finally relented and gave Paulette Wilson official leave to remain in the UK. In July 2020, it was reported that:

> Paulette Wilson, a prominent Windrush campaigner ... has died unexpectedly at the age of 64, a month after delivering a petition to Downing Street calling on the government to deliver justice to those affected by the scandal ... daughter ... Natalie ... said she had found her mother on Thursday morning; she appeared to have died in her sleep. 'My mum was a fighter and she was ready to fight for anyone. She was an inspiration to many people. She was my heart and my soul and I loved her to pieces'.[176]

The mother and daughter had dedicated much of the past two-and-a-half years of Wilson's life to raising awareness of the difficulties experienced by thousands of people who had arrived in the UK legally in the 1950s and '60s, before wrongly being categorized as immigration offenders. When she visited Downing Street to deliver a petition calling for compensation to be speeded up, she said she was disappointed that she was still having to campaign for justice. She had hoped two years before that there would be a swifter resolution of everyone's difficulties and faster payment of compensation to all victims.[177] 'The word "sorry" can roll off anyone's tongue easily, but we don't want more apologies', she said.[178]

Home Office setting up immigrants to fail

In May 2018, the then Home Secretary Sajid Javid admitted in May 2018: 'there is no question … that a number of people from that generation have been mistreated', they 'have been seriously let down by the immigration system'.[179] After examining the case files of Ms Wilson and another similar case of Anthony Bryan,[180] the Home Affairs Select Committee accused the Home Office, saying it has 'set immigrants up to fail', and that unless the system is overhauled the scandal 'will happen again, for another group of people'.[181] The committee pointed out that 'Thousands of people have been affected and denied their rights – with 8,000 referrals to the taskforce, and over 2,000 documents confirming status issued so far'.[182]

The previous month, Dawn Butler, then Shadow Equalities Secretary, was asked by *Sky News* whether Theresa May could personally be accused of racism. She replied:

> Yes. She is the leader that's presiding over legislation that's discriminating against a whole group of people who came from the Commonwealth, who suffered racism when they came over, the 'no blacks, no Irish, no dogs'. And now they're having to relive that trauma all over again because of Theresa May.[183]

As noted in chapter 4, in the 1960s such notices or similarly racist variations on them were common when property was advertised for letting. Abbott commented at the time with respect to recompense for those affected by the Windrush scandal:

> It is an absolute disgrace that the government has still not come forward with a clear plan for compensation, and is refusing a hardship fund, even for people who have been made homeless or unemployed by their policies. The government should act immediately on these recommendations, including restoring immigration appeals and legal aid, and removing the net migration target. But this scandal will continue as long as the 'hostile environment' policy is in place, which treats people who are legally entitled to be here as if they are here illegally. This policy must go.[184]

In chapter 10, I provide an update on the effects of the ongoing hostile environment under the Boris Johnson Government.

End game: the fall of Theresa May

May's first *stated* goal on entering Downing Street in 2016, as noted earlier, was to be driven not by the interests of the privileged few, but by 'ordinary working-class families'. Her second goal was to deliver Brexit to the British people. Toby Helm succinctly summarizes what this was to entail, it 'was to consume almost all her time and energy and, in the end, bring her leadership of the country to its disastrous finale'.[185]

In the words of one ally, a Tory Minister, 'Over time she became defined not by her achievements but by her ability to hang on and survive everything that went wrong'.[186] From the point of view of her survival, less than a year into her time at Number 10, as Helm observes, May had made 'arguably her worst of decision of all, to call a snap election in the hope of winning her own mandate to deliver Brexit – only to lose the Tories their majority and leave her dependent on the Democratic Unionist party to get legislation through the Commons'.[187] But somehow, he goes on, 'she staggered on, setting new standards for defiance with every month that passed'.[188]

In the end, she was forced into opening talks with her arch-rival, Corbyn. At the same time, the prospect of EU elections left her party in open revolt, and Nigel Farage and his new Brexit party stood ready to exploit the Tories' and May's woes. Then Labour pulled the plug on the cross-party negotiations, and the last hope of a Brexit deal passing through Parliament disappeared. In typical stubborn fashion, she tried one last ploy, offering Corbyn a vote on whether to hold a second referendum. That was a non-runner. As one Government Minister said, 'She is dead now. It is just a case of when the life support machine is switched off'.[189]

May delayed making an announcement of her resignation until after the EU elections. But once she did, Boris Johnson, the early favourite to enter Number 10, set out his stall without delay, insisting that under his leadership Brexit would happen in Autumn 2019, no matter what:

> Playing to the hard-Brexit wing of the Tory party at Westminster and the 100,000-plus Tory members who …[would] … ultimately choose the new leader, Johnson said at a meeting in Switzerland: 'We will leave the EU on 31 October, deal or no deal'.[190]

Appendix

The hostile environment: a personal testimony (2011–?)

I have provided this Appendix to give a further example of the effect of Theresa May's callous and cruel 'really hostile environment' has had on families. Basing it on my wife, my stepdaughter and my extended family has been cathartic.[191] When I was writing my book on Theresa May,[192] on November 28, 2017 the most popular website for supporting families divided my May's legislation and subsequent policies, I LOVE MY FOREIGN SPOUSE had 11,830 members on Facebook. As a demonstration of the hostile environment's ongoing disastrous impact, as at January 29, 2022, it had 19,988, meaning that membership has been increasing at an average of four per day.

Setting the scene

After just six months of marriage, in June 2010, my wife at the time left me without prior notice, having seized the opportunity while I was on my way to work. Meanwhile, a few months earlier, over 6,000 miles away, the partner of a woman named Lyka and biological father of her daughter Meoun (not her real name) walked out on them.

Fast forward a year, just as I was getting over a very acrimonious and traumatic divorce, I got a phone call from my elder daughter telling me that my only son Dave had died in tragic circumstances in Bangkok. On the day of his funeral, one of his closest friends, Tom, and I vowed to take the trip that Dave had been unable to complete. (Dave had been waiting for Tom in Bangkok to travel to Laos and Cambodia.)

It was in Phnom Penh, travelling with Tom in August 2011, that I met Lyka and entered into a romantic relationship with her. Lyka had worked very long hours on pittance wages in garment factories for most of her working life to provide care for Meoun.[193] Shortly after meeting Lyka, I went back to the UK with Tom, but returned to Phnom Penh in September 2011. That was when I met Meoun, age three. Lyka and I lived together and got married in the UK in 2012. It was not until May 2018, however, that Lyka and Meoun obtained UK citizenship, even though Lyka and I were married and I have supported Meoun financially and in every other way, since. The length of time it took to get citizenship, and the inconveniences, financial and personal hardships in the account that follows are direct results of Theresa May's 'really hostile environment'.

Our struggle[194]

In October 2011, we applied in Phnom Penh for a visitor's visa for Lyka to come to the UK at my expense (maximum stay six months) and were turned down on the grounds that, in the words of the entry clearance officer: 'I am not satisfied on a balance of probabilities that … you intend to leave the United Kingdom on completion of your visit'. Having more than enough money to finance the visit and having provided full details of my financial and professional status, I was surprised that we were both being accused of lying to the British Embassy in Phnom Penh, and potentially also being accused of being complicit in an attempt to break UK immigration law. Not only had such a thing never crossed my mind, I felt personally slighted because, given that I was sponsoring Lyka because I knew her well enough to trust her, my integrity was being undermined as well as hers. Nothing like this had ever happened to me before, but it was just the beginning of a long process of our having to prove that we were not lying, rather than the Home Office having to prove that we were. In effect, we were guilty unless we could satisfy UK immigration that we were innocent. We applied again for a visitor's visa in January 2012.

Shortly afterwards, I was air-ambulanced, courtesy of my travel insurance policy, with (symptoms of) heart failure from Phnom Penh to Bangkok, where I was told the facilities I needed were available. I can only surmise that my poor health was, in part, the result of my divorce and the unexpected death of my son. Lyka asked the British Embassy in Phnom Penh if she could have her passport back to visit me in hospital, and was told: 'You can have your passport back to visit him in hospital, but you'll have to start your visa application all over again'.[195] Could it be that the Embassy was already on alert for the imminent implementation of the hostile environment? (Jeremy Corbyn made a similar point in 1986, with respect to decisions being made by immigration officers to create the right atmosphere for further restrictions during Thatcher's premiership; see chapter 6 of this book.) I was in hospital in bed for a week while they brought my heart rate down. Not recovering as fast as the cardiologist had hoped, on release from hospital my only hope was that I would be with Lyka at least until the following Christmas.

The second application for a visitor's visa was successful and valid for six months. Lyka came to the UK with me in February 2012 for about five months, after which time we wanted to go back to Phnom Penh to apply for a spouse visa, so that after we got married, which we had already decided to do, we could live together in the UK (marriage does not allow this without the spouse visa) and because it could not be applied for in the UK. Not being aware of the *details* of Theresa May's forthcoming changes in family immigration rules that were to come into effect on July 9, 2012, we decided to get married urgently on July 8, 2012.

Lyka had, of course, not seen her daughter for the duration of her first visit to the UK, and we had become a 'Skype family'. This is a term used to describe families who can only have contact remotely.[196] As Robert Wright explains, the thousands of families the Home Office was refusing to grant the right to remain in the UK each year were being told by the Home Office that, although they would be separated, the existence of phones, messaging apps, Facebook, and other Internet modes of communication made the distance immaterial.[197] According to the Joint Council for the Welfare of Immigrants (JCWI) at the time, the Home Office used the Skype argument in nearly every case involving the splitting-up of families or other close relationships.[198] This was, of course, a ridiculous and laughable tactic by the Home Office.

After getting married, we returned to Phnom Penh, spending about three months there, waiting for the spouse visa, obtaining it in October 2012. This was just as well, since we had not envisaged waiting so long for the visa and were literally running out of money to the extent that, out of desperation, I was contemplating flying to Bangkok and back to withdraw money there on the only card on which I still had credit (that card was not accepted in Cambodia). We returned to the UK once again in October 2012 without Meoun, with vivid memories of the heartbreak of being in a divided family, as Meoun was crying all the way to the airport.

We returned to Phnom Penh in March 2013 to apply for an initial visa for Meoun to come to the UK. We obtained this in early May, and we all returned to the UK where we stayed for about a month before taking Meoun back to Phnom Penh, on the advice of our solicitor, in June 2013, so that she could return to school in Phnom Penh, having taken a month off to come to the UK. We stayed for about a week, and once again had the trauma of leaving Meoun at the airport in Phnom Penh to remain with our extended family. Although, six months older than the last time we had to leave her at the airport, at age five Meoun was not fully cognizant as to what was happening to her life, and we said our goodbyes with her sobbing and clinging onto her mother before boarding the plane.

We resorted to being a Skype family again from June 2013 until late October when we returned to Phnom Penh once again to apply for a 'to join mother' visa which we obtained in December 2013. From then on, Theresa May's new family visa rules allowed us to apply for subsequent visas in the UK, but we had to wait until July 2015, two and a half years before applying for and obtaining 'leave to remain' for both Lyka and Meoun in July 2015. There followed another two-and-a-half-year wait to obtain 'indefinite leave to remain', and after that UK citizenship and UK passports. All along the way, we had to *prove* with documentation (including photographs of us together) that we were not, to use Theresa May's terminology, in a 'sham marriage' or a sham family.

At least we did not suffer the humiliation, as did other couples, of having our wedding ceremony interrupted so we could be questioned about our 'sex lives', or a dawn raid to check if we were sharing a bed or told that our relationship was not genuine because we were wearing pyjamas in bed. Nor did we have our number of toothbrushes checked. Finally, our marriage was not delayed for up to 70 days, nor was my wife 'detained for months' on suspicion of being in a 'sham marriage'.[199]

Information obtained by *The Guardian* through a Freedom of Information request shows registrars sent 2,868 section 24 reports (which alert the authorities to a potential sham marriage) in 2018, a 40% rise from 2,038 in 2014. Lawyers said registrars had become 'infected with the culture of the hostile environment'.[200] For further indications that the 'really hostile environment' is currently being cranked up, see chapter 10. Prior to 2012, officials just needed to be satisfied that the marriage was genuine.

The six and a half years of anxiety about whether Lyka and Meoun would eventually get UK citizenship were tempered by the certainty that, were they to be refused, I would go to live with them in Cambodia, not an option open to the vast majority of divided families.

Our costs

Following is an approximate breakdown of what all this cost us financially from 2011 until the end of 2025. We were able to pay this exorbitant amount, solely because my financial status *at the time* was such that I was able to get into considerable debt – the final loan payments for which are due at the end of 2025.

Total visa costs, Lyka and Meoun: £9,000
Total solicitor' fees: £2,800
Flights: £9,000 (11 returns)
Hotels in Phnom Penh: £11,000 (10 months)
Subsistence in Phnom Penh: £15,000 (10 months)
Total: nearly £47,000

The adult dependent relative rules

Since Theresa May's July 2012 immigration rules, it has been virtually impossible, in practice for adult dependent relatives to get leave to remain in the UK. If a dependent relative does, or relatives do, get leave to remain on human rights grounds (initial cost £2,622), the granting of indefinite leave to remain takes a phenomenal ten years, and UK citizenship a further year after that. The ensuing costs for a couple were nearly £20,000 at 2019 levels to obtain UK citizenship after being granted leave to remain, amounting 'to ten years of indentured servitude to the Home Office'.[201]

The rules give no weight 'to any emotional ties that might exist between older people and their adult children and grandchildren'.[202] Thus, though in our case the ties with our Cambodian extended family are very strong – Lyka's mother and father had looked after Meoun for the many years that she worked in the factories, and I have a very close relationship with the whole extended family, for whom I have been the main financial supporter since 2012 – having her mother and father come and live with us (even though we wanted to) was ruled out. Instead, we applied for a visitor's visa for Lyka's mother, my mother-in-law. This was met in March 2016 with the familiar response:

> I am not satisfied on the balance of probabilities that you are genuinely seeking entry as a visitor for a limited period or that you intend to leave the United Kingdom at the end of the visit … there is no right of appeal or right of administrative review.

After four years of successfully 'proving' to the authorities that our intentions were honest, we were once again, along with Lyka's mother, being accused of lying and colluding in so-called 'illegal immigration'. Such is the nature of the 'really hostile environment'. Notwithstanding occasional visits to Cambodia, until a radically different non-Tory government we have resigned ourselves to not even contemplating anything beyond remaining an extended family via Skype for the foreseeable future. For this reason, unlike the rest of the chapters and appendices, no end-date has been given to this final Appendix.

Notes

1   Cited in Lindsay. 2017. To be fair, it should be pointed out that the gesture was apparently nothing to do with close affection between the pair – but instead Trump was leaning on May while suffering a phobic episode. He is said to be scared of germs – but his fear of stairs and ramps is even worse, and is known as 'bathmophobia'. A White House spokesperson stated: 'He hates heights where you can see the ground or sharp inclines even more than germs. He particularly dislikes stairs and his biggest nightmare of all is a dirty stair rail' (cited in Campbell. 2017). If this is the case, one would have thought he could have held May's arm rather than her hand.

2   It should be pointed out that Farron's speech, though it makes some good anti-racist points, was very much pro-capitalist and patriotic, arguing for capitalism and against socialism.

3   Yeung. 2016.

4   Cited in Yeung. 2016.

5   Merrick. 2019.

6   Ibid.

7   Cited in Merrick. 2019.

8   Asthana et al. 2017.

9   Hunt and Wheeler. 2017.

10   Ibid.

11   Ibid.

12   Cowburn. 2017.

13   Cited in Cowburn. 2017.

14   Hughes. 2017,

15   Casalicchio. 2017.

16   Cited in Whitfield. 2018.

17   *BBC News*. 2018a.

18   Cited in *BBC News*. 2018a.

19   Ibid.

20   *BBC News*. 2018a.

21   Cited in Kentish. 2018.

22   Ibid.

23   Ibid.

24   Holton and Smout. 2018.

25   Free Movement. 2018.

26   Ibid.

27   Ibid.

28   Cited in Free Movement. 2018.

29   Free Movement. 2018.

30   Ibid.

31   Ibid.

32   Global Justice Now. 2018.

33   Cited in Global Justice Now. 2018.

34   Ibid.

35   Ibid.

36   Ibid.

37   Ibid.

38   Ibid.

39   Travis. 2017a.

40   Ibid.

41   Ibid.

42   Usborne, Simon. 2018.

43 Russell. 2018
44 Ibid.
45 Ibid.
46 Ibid.
47 Ibid.
48 Ibid.
49 Jayanetti, Chaminda. 2018.
50 Ibid.
51 Ibid.
52 Cited in Jayanetti. 2018.
53 Jayanetti. 2018.
54 Weale, Sally. 2018.
55 Ibid.
56 Cited in Weale, Sally. 2018. 'Children "denied free school meals because of parents' immigration status."', *The Guardian*, May 9. https://www.theguardian.com/education/2018/may/09/children-denied-free-school-meals-because-of-parents-immigration-status.
57 Cited in Usborne. 2018.
58 Ibid.
59 Ibid.
60 Maisuria and Cole. 2017.
61 Usborne. 2018.
62 Lyons et al. 2017.
63 Cited in Lyons et al. 2017.
64 Travis. 2017b.
65 Theresa May was Home Secretary up until July 13, 2016; thereafter Amber Rudd. Rudd carried on in much the same vein as May. Some, like Jeremy Corbyn, consider that, having inherited a 'failing policy', she actually made it 'worse' (cited in Grierson. 2018).
66 Travis. 2017b.
67 Cited in Travis. 2017b.
68 Cited in Lyons et al. 2017.
69 McIntyre and Taylor. 2018.
70 Lyons et al. 2017.
71 McIntyre and Taylor. 2018.
72 Reynolds, Sile. 2018.
73 Ibid.
74 Ibid.
75 Press Association. 2019.
76 Cited in Press Association. 2019.
77 Cited in Elgot and Walker. 2019.
78 Ibid.
79 Ibid.
80 Cited in Press Association. 2019.
81 Cited in Elgot and Walker. 2019.
82 Cited in Press Association. 2019.
83 Ibid.
84 Cited in Press Association, 2009.
85 Godwin, Richard. 2018.
86 Ibid.
87 Ibid.
88 Cited in Elgot and Walker. 2019.
89 *Sky News*. 2019a. 'Interview with Clare Moseley', January 31. Watched live by the author.

90   Cited in *Sky News*, 2019a.
91   Ibid.
92   Ibid.
93   Ibid.
94   The Global Peace Index, which lists countries for levels of peace, had the following ranks for 2018. Syria was the least peaceful at 163 out of 163, and Afghanistan next at 162. Sudan was at 153; Eritrea at 138; and Iran at 131 (Institute for Economics & Peace. 2018).
95   *Sky News*. 2019a.
96   Perraudin. 2019.
97   Ibid.
98   Cited in Perraudin. 2019.
99   Ibid.
100 Ibid.
101 EHRC. 2018.
102 Ibid.
103 Cited in EHRC. 2018.
104 EHRC. 2018.
105 Cited in EHRC. 2018.
106 Ibid.
107 Lyons et al. 2017.
108 Cited in Lyons et al. 2017.
109 Yarl's Wood. 2019.
110 Ibid.
111 Ibid.
112 HM Inspectorate of Prisons. 2017.
113 Bulman. 2018.
114 Ibid.
115 Ibid.
116 Ibid.
117 Cited in Bulman. 2018.
118 Ibid.
119 Womack. 2018.
120 Ibid.
121 Ibid.
122 Sharma. 2018.
123 Womack. 2018.
124 McIntyre and Topping. 2018.
125 UN WOMEN. 2016.
126 McIntyre and Topping. 2018.
127 Ibid.
128 Cited in McIntyre and Topping. 2018.
129 McIntyre and Topping. 2018.
130 Garden Court North Chambers, 2017, cited in McIntyre and Topping. 2018.
131 McIntyre and Topping. 2018.
132 www.parliament. 2013, cited in McIntyre and Topping. 2018.
133 Cited in McIntyre and Topping. 2018.
134 Ibid.
135 Debbonaire, cited in McIntyre and Topping. 2018.
136 Cited in McIntyre and Topping. 2018.
137 Mayor of London. 2018.
138 Cited in Mayor of London. 2018.
139 CNN. 2019.
140 Cited in CNN. 2019.

141 CNN. 2019.
142 Amnesty International. 2019.
143 HM Government. 2019, p. 25, cited in Amnesty International. 2019.
144 Amnesty International. 2019.
145 Cited in Amnesty International. 2019.
146 Ibid.
147 Ibid.
148 Ibid.
149 Ibid.
150 Ibid.
151 https://www.gov.uk/government/publications/domestic-abuse-bill-2020-fa
   ctsheets/domestic-abuse-bill-2020-overarching-factsheet.
152 This section of the chapter is adapted from Cole. 2020, pp. 76–82.
153 Cited on *BBC Newsnight*. 2019. February 28.
154 Watt, Nicholas. 2014. 'Norman Baker resigns as Home Office minister with
   parting shot at May', *The Guardian,* November 3. https://www.theguardian.
   com/politics/2014/nov/03/norman-baker-resigns-home-office-minister.
155 *BBC News.* 2014. 'Norman Baker quits as Home Office minister', November
   4. https://www.bbc.co.uk/news/uk-politics-29891132.
156 Mead. 2007, p. 112.
157 Home Affairs Select Committee. 2018, p. 5.
158 Ibid.
159 Ibid.
160 Ibid.
161 Ibid.
162 Ibid., p. 23.
163 Cited in Gentleman. 2017.
164 Gentleman. 2017.
165 Ibid.
166 See chapter 9 for a discussion of Yarl's Wood.
167 Gentleman. 2017.
168 Cited in Gentleman. 2017.
169 Ibid.
170 Ibid.
171 Gentleman. 2017.
172 Ibid.
173 Ibid.
174 Ibid.
175 Ibid.
176 Gentleman, Amelia. and Campbell, Lucy. 2020. 'Windrush campaigner Paulette
   Wilson dies aged 64', *The Guardian,* July 23. https://amp.theguardian.com/
   uk-news/2020/jul/23/windrush-campaigner-paulette-wilson-dies-aged-64.
177 Ibid.
178 Cited in Gentleman and Campbell. 2020.
179 Home Affairs Select Committee. 2018, p. 5.
180 See Cole. 2020, pp. 80–81.
181 Cited in Agerholm. 2018.
182 Ibid.
183 Ibid.
184 Cited in Allegretti. 2018.
185 Helm, Toby. 2019. 'End game: the fall of Theresa May', *The Guardian,* May 26.
   https://www.theguardian.com/politics/2019/may/26/end-game-fall-of-theresa
   -may.
186 Cited in Helm. 2019.

187   Helm, 2019.
188   Ibid.
189   Cited in Helm. 2019.
190   Helm. 2019.
191   This is an amended and updated version of Cole. 2020, pp. 91–95.
192   Cole. 2020.
193   For Lyka's account of factory life, see Thorn. 2013.
194   While reading this section, the reader may like to refer back to the heading, 'Spouses and partners' in chapter 8.
195   Communication from the British Embassy, Phnom Penh, early 2012.
196   Wright, Robert. 2018. 'Home Office tells couple it divided to stay together on Skype', *Financial Times*, May 15. https://www.ft.com/content/38dfc2bc-575e-11e8-bdb7-f6677d2e1ce8.
197   Ibid.
198   Cited in Wright. 2018.
199   Taylor, Diane, and Perraudin, Francis. 2019. 'Couples face "insulting" checks in sham marriage crackdown', *The Guardian*, April 14. https://www.theguardian.com/uk-news/2019/apr/14/couples-sham-marriage-crackdown-hostile-enviroment.
200   Cited in Taylor and Perraudin. 2019.
201   Vassiliou. 2019. John Vassiliou provides an example and breakdown of costs.
202   Ibid.

10 Boris Johnson and racism and the ongoing march of the hostile environment (1999–2022)

SECTION 1: THE COLOUR-CODED RACISM OF BORIS JOHNSON

Boris Johnson's colour-coded racism dates back over 20 years. In a diary piece for the *Independent on Sunday* in October 1999, he wrote that Tony Blair had made people feel good about getting rich, and added: 'All the young people I know – i.e. those under 30 – are just as avaricious as we flinty Thatcherite yuppies of the 1980s, in fact, they have an almost Nigerian interest in money and gadgets of all kinds'.[1]

The following year, in an article written for *The Guardian*, Johnson said that seeing a 'bunch of black kids' out and about set off alarm bells in his head. He started off the article with the familiar denial used by racists to claim immunity from racism, namely that because his forebears were from 'India, Turkey, France, Germany, Russia, international Jewry, Wales and England, how could he be?'[2] Instead he preferred to admit to 'spasms of incorrectitude, soon over, soon regretted'.[3] Back to the 'black kids, shrieking in the spooky corner by the disused gents', Johnson 'cannot rule out that I have suffered from a tiny fit of prejudice'.[4] He also attacked antiracism reforms undertaken in response to the murder of Stephen Lawrence and said Britain should 'axe large chunks of the anti-racism industry'.[5] He then levelled an attack on the author of the Stephen Lawrence Inquiry Report (see the Introduction):

> Heaven knows why Macpherson made his weird recommendation, that the law might be changed so as to allow prosecution for racist language or behaviour 'other than in a public place'. I can't understand how this sober old buzzard was prevailed upon to say that a racist incident might be so defined in the view of the victim 'or any other person'.[6]

David Lammy, an antiracist campaigner and now a Labour MP, commented: 'Stephen Lawrence's horrific murder and the institutional racism evidenced by the Macpherson report showed beyond doubt the desperate need for anti-racism reforms'.[7] Lammy concluded, 'The fact Boris Johnson

DOI: 10.4324/9781003198673-15

used his well-paid, privileged platform to oppose those reforms and to normalize prejudice shows beyond doubt that he is unfit to be our prime minister'[8] Michael Mansfield, the barrister who represented the Lawrence family at the Macpherson inquiry, told the *Daily Mirror*: 'This is a man who is deeply prejudiced and obviously I'm horrified about the possibility that he may remain prime minister. He is fundamentally sexist and racist'.[9]

In January 2008, during a debate for the London mayoral contest sponsored by the (London) *Evening Standard*, Johnson responded to Michael Eboda, former editor of *New Nation*, in its day Britain's number 1-selling Black newspaper, who had said that some of Johnson's writings had been offensive: 'These things are an extremely big obstacle to being able to work with what is 12% of London's population.'[10] Johnson said he was 'sad' that people had been offended, and apologized for something he had written, at the same time insisting that the words had been taken out of context.[11] He was referring to the following published column in the *Daily Telegraph* six years earlier, when Johnson was the relatively newly elected Tory MP for Henley. Johnson was mocking the then Labour Prime Minister Tony Blair's globetrotting:

> What a relief it must be for Blair to get out of England. It is said that the Queen has come to love the Commonwealth, partly because it supplies her with regular cheering crowds of flag-waving piccaninnies; and one can imagine that Blair ... is similarly seduced by foreign politeness. They say he is shortly off to the Congo. No doubt the AK47s will fall silent, and the pangas will stop their hacking of human flesh, and the tribal warriors will all break out in watermelon smiles to see the big white chief touch down in his big white British taxpayer-funded bird.[12]

According to Unite the Union, no disciplinary action was taken.

Herman Ouseley, the former Chair of the Commission for Racial Equality had also expressed concerns about Johnson as Mayor of London, writing to David Cameron, then Tory leader, saying: 'I personally recognise that you have to move on, but there are other people who he will have to convince'.[13] Johnson was nevertheless elected Mayor of London on May 3, 2008 and remained in the post until May 7, 2016.

Underlining Mansfield's comments about Johnson being 'fundamentally sexist and racist', in response to Malaysian Prime Minister Najib Razak saying at the 2013 World Islamic Economic Forum that 68% of women were going to be attending university, Johnson replied that the reason female students go to university is because they have got to find men to marry.[14] Writing in *Quartz Africa*, Lily Kuo picked up on the *Daily Telegraph* quote when Johnson was appointed Foreign Secretary on Theresa May first becoming Prime Minister in July 2016 and added further racist comments from Johnson. In Kuo's words, 'An unlikely diplomat, Johnson "jokingly" compared the Tory party with "Papua New Guinea-style orgies of cannibalism and chief-killing'",[15] drawing criticism from the country's High Commission.

At the height of the Brexit referendum in 2016, when US President Barack Obama urged 'citizens of the United Kingdom take stock of their relationship with the EU' and 'be proud that the EU has helped spread British values and practices – democracy, the rule of law, open markets – across the continent and to its periphery', Johnson, the most prominent Leave campaigner, wrongly claimed that Obama had removed a bust of Winston Churchill from the Oval Office, following his inauguration, because of his 'ancestral dislike of the British empire'. Writing in the *Sun*, Johnson said: 'Some said it was a snub to Britain. Some said it was a symbol of the part-Kenyan president's ancestral dislike of the British empire – of which Churchill had been such a fervent defender'[16] (see chapter 3 for a discussion of Churchill's racism and imperialism). Obama responded by calling Johnson the British version of Donald Trump and was 'taken aback' by the perceived racial connotations of Johnson's remarks.[17]

In a 2018 column, again for *The Daily Telegraph,* relating to a burqa ban, Johnson wrote that it was 'absolutely ridiculous' that 'people should choose to go around looking like letter boxes'. He continued:

> If a constituent came to my MP's surgery with her face obscured, I should feel fully entitled… to ask her to remove it so that I could talk to her properly. If a female student turned up at school or at a university lecture looking like a bank robber then ditto: those in authority should be allowed to converse openly with those that they are being asked to instruct.[18]

Is Johnson's colour-coded racism derived from scientific racism?

Johnson and Taki Theodoracopulos

In the Introduction, I wrote that racism can be unintentional as well as intentional, although the former can sometimes cause as much distress as the latter. I also made the case that you do not have to be a racist (intentional) to be racist (which can be unintentional). So, is Johnson's racism unintentional and/or taken out of context, as he claims? Or is it intentional? I also wrote that racism can be based on genetics – biological racism, or culture – cultural racism, or it can be a combination of both. So what informs Boris Johnson's very obvious racism? The likelihood of his believing in scientific racism become apparent as early as 2003, when as editor of the right-wing *Spectator,* he allowed an article entitled 'Thoughts on thuggery' by Taki Theodoracopulos to be published in the January 11 edition of the magazine.[19] In the article Theodoracopulos displayed unequivocal biological racism based on 'scientific racism' when he wrote, 'oh boy, oh boy, was Enoch – God rest his soul – ever right!'[20] He went on:

> Britain is being mugged by black hoodlums, people are being cut down in the streets. It doesn't take an extremely high IQ to figure out that the two girls who were shot in Birmingham were killed because a member of their family belonged to a rival gang. Nor does it take a genius to conclude that turf wars between mostly black gangs are fought over the control of drugs, mainly crack cocaine. Finally, only a moron would not surmise that what politically correct newspapers refer to as 'disaffected young people' are black thugs, sons of black thugs and grandsons of black thugs, in it for the money.[21]

Now in his stride Theodoracopulos opined, 'West Indians were allowed to immigrate after the war, multiply like flies, and then the great state apparatus took over the care of their multiplications'.[22] Returning to Powell, he states, 'The Rivers of Blood speech by Enoch was prophetic as well as true' (Powell's hate-filled racist rant and its aftermath is discussed in chapter 4). Theodoracopulos's column 'High Life' (from a wealthy Greek shipping-magnate family, he is famous for his lifestyle which involves a large consumption of alcohol and a great deal of gambling)[23] continues to appear in *The Spectator*, where it has been a regular feature of the British weekly since 1977.

Theodoracopulos has made a number of other racist comments: 'I'm white (although always sun-tanned) ... I inherited from my old man'; New York Puerto Ricans are a 'bunch of semi-savages ... fat, squat, ugly, dusky, dirty and unbelievably loud. They turned Manhattan into Palermo [he is alluding to the Sicilian mafia] faster than you can say "Latino"'; 'Democracy is as likely to come to bongo-bongo land [Africa] as I am to send a Concorde ticket to my children'.[24] He has also made sexist comments: 'Not that I'm calling Cherie Blair a whore. She couldn't be one even if she wanted to; not good-looking enough'; Hilary Clinton 'too, could not make a living from the world's oldest profession because of ugly looks and terrible ankles'.[25]

In 2002, Theodoracopulos co-founded *The American Conservative* magazine (TAC). It promotes a form of conservatism that opposes unchecked power in both government and business; encourages the flourishing of families and communities through vibrant markets and free people; and embraces realism and restraint in foreign affairs based on America's national interests, or paleoconservatism (traditional Republican values combined with right-wing populism).[26] Unsurprisingly in April 2020, according to Caleb Ecarma, under senior writer for *The American Conservative* Curt Mills, TAC was poised to be Donald Trump's 'in-house, in-flight magazine'.[27]

Theodoracopulos was also the publisher of the British magazine *Right Now* that had connections with the Monday Club and the fascist National Front. In 2013 he wrote in *The Spectator* in support of the Greek fascist party, Golden Dawn, describing them as 'good old-fashioned patriotic

Greeks' in an editorial. The editor of *The Spectator* at the time, Fraser Nelson, defended Theodoracopulos by tweeting that 'Our readers like diversity and well-written pieces that they disagree with. We have no party line'.[28] Theodoracopulos currently publishes and writes for the far-right *Taki's Magazine* that in 2016 launched the fascist Proud Boys,[29] and in 2018, he wrote an article commemorating D-Day in which he praised the Nazi defence forces and asked readers to sympathize with them.[30] Consistent with his political orientation, Theodoracopulos sent a letter to the satirical magazine *Private Eye* threatening legal action against being labelled a 'cocaine dealer' (it had habitually described him as 'Taki Takealotofcokeupthenos'), the *Eye* was happy to issue a disclaimer, stating 'Taki is not a cocaine dealer, merely a convicted cocaine smuggler, a liar, and fascist sympathiser'. No legal action ensued.[31]

In 2008, during the aforementioned London Mayoral contest when he was challenging the incumbent Labour Mayor Ken Livingston, Johnson came under fire from Livingstone and a leading Black lawyer over a number of pieces published in the *Spectator* magazine under his editorship. In one, Theodoracopulos had written that 'Orientals ... have larger brains and higher IQ scores. Blacks are at the other pole'.[32] In another, he had described Black American basketball players as having 'arms hanging below their knees and tongues sticking out'.[33] When asked if he had condoned the articles, unearthed by *New Nation*, Johnson replied rather unconvincingly, telling the *Standard*: 'I am sorry for what was previously written as it does not reflect what is in my heart'.[34] He then launched into an attack on Livingstone, claiming he:

> has nothing positive to say about the future of London, or the wave of criminal violence that has cost the lives of 11 young people killed on our streets this year, or yet another strike on our Tube which will disrupt millions of commuters next week, so he has again resorted to negative personal attacks.[35]

But despite Johnson's apology for his reference to 'piccaninnies' and 'watermelon smiles', and his insistence that he 'loathed and despised' racism and his claim that his words, written more than five years before, had been taken out of context (he also told *New Nation* that he had been on holiday when Theodoracopulos's January 2003 article was published), Livingstone rightly viewed the articles as further proof of Johnson's lack of commitment to an ethnically diverse city like London:

> Such statements are completely unacceptable and Boris Johnson as editor of the *Spectator* should never have let them appear. It shows that Boris Johnson has no adequate understanding of what it means to lead a great multicultural and multi-ethnic city. Taki is basically an unpleasant racist-bigot. You just don't give anyone like that a job. If you're happy

for that sort of crap to come out in a magazine you're editing, you can't really claim to be fit to represent the most culturally and racially diverse city on earth.[36]

Prominent Black Barrister Courtenay Griffiths commented: 'It is surprising that a columnist in the UK could be displaying such Neanderthal attitudes, and you have to call into question Boris Johnson's judgment as editor of the *Spectator*'.[37]

Johnson becomes Tory Party Leader and Prime Minister

On July 24, 2019 Johnson became Tory Party leader, following the resignation of Theresa May, after winning a convincing victory over Jeremy Hunt.[38] Significantly, Johnson's victory was almost immediately welcomed by Donald Trump, who tweeted: 'He will be great!'[39] As Heather Stewart points out, 'Johnson had been the runaway favourite to become leader after securing support from both wings of the bitterly divided Tory party', with the backing of both the Health secretary, Matt Hancock, and the Chair of the European Research Group, Jacob Rees-Mogg.[40] He was seen, she goes on, as the best person to beat the 'formidable electoral challenge' from Nigel Farage's Brexit Party.[41] Johnson re-opened Brexit negotiations, and in September prorogued Parliament, giving anti-no-deal MPs less chance to stop a no-deal Brexit.[42] After agreeing to a revised Brexit withdrawal agreement with the EU that replaced the Irish backstop (a device designed by the Theresa May Government to try to prevent a border with customs controls between the Republic of Ireland and Northern Ireland)[43] with a new Northern Ireland Protocol.[44] However, this failed to get support from Parliament and Johnson called a snap General Election for December 2019.

This resulted in a Tory landslide, with Johnson winning 43.6% of the popular vote – the highest percentage for any party since Thatcher's first election victory in 1979 and giving him a majority of 80.[45] He said he would work 'flat out' and lead a 'people's government', while Jeremy Corbyn, who, out of the two, I would describe as the real people's contender, said he would not fight another election as Labour leader. He was replaced by someone very much to the right of Corbyn, Keir Starmer.

Many of the Tory gains were in long-held Labour seats, described as the 'red wall'[46] that had registered a strong Leave vote in the 2016 EU Referendum. Although a wide manual working-class support for Brexit is well known, this is still somewhat surprising in that Johnson, even more than most other Tories, epitomizes the class arrogance and social privilege of Britain's upper-middle class.[47] In the words of Julie Hyland, writing on the World Socialist Website (WSWS), 'This is a man whose experience with the "lower classes" extends only to giving orders'.[48]

Johnson now had the mandate he wanted to formally implement the withdrawal from the European Union. He formed a Cabinet that he described as a 'Cabinet for modern Britain',[49] but which was more accurately viewed as an 'ethnically diverse but ideologically homogeneous statement of intent'.[50]

Johnson lost his working majority on September 3, 2019, when Phillip Lee crossed the floor of the House of Commons to join the Liberal Democrats.[51] On the same day 21 Tory MPs voted against the Government in order to enable Parliament to take control of the order paper and to debate a back bench bill designed to prevent a no-deal Brexit.[52] For this, they were expelled from the Party. Two days later, Johnson's brother and fellow Tory announced his intention to resign, because he had 'been torn between family loyalty and the national interest', adding 'it's an unresolvable tension and time for others to take on my roles as MP and Minister'.[53] On September 7, Amber Rudd announced she was resigning as Secretary of State for Work and Pensions and Minister for Women and Equalities, and leaving the Conservative Party.[54] As a result of these defections, Johnson called for a General Election on December 12 that he won with a majority, thus forming his second ministry on December 16, 2019. On January 31, 2020, Britain left the European Union (EU), heralding the beginning of the end of free movement to Britain from the EU and the EEA (European Economic Area – Iceland, Liechtenstein and Norway) (it actually ended on December 31, 2020 after a transition period).

Johnson and Andrew Sabisky

Johnson, now Prime Minister, had hired as an adviser Andrew Sabisky, who was appointed after chief aide Dominic Cummings put out a job description in early January 2020 just before Brexit for 'weirdos and misfits with odd skills' to join him in trying to shake up the Tory Government and break up the civil service's alleged stranglehold over policy.[55] In 2014, Sabisky had written on Cummings' website that to get around unplanned pregnancies in the UK, there should be the legal enforcement of long-term contraception: 'One way to get around the problems of unplanned pregnancies, creating a permanent underclass would be to legally enforce universal uptake of long-term contraception at the onset of puberty. Vaccination laws give it a precedent, I would argue'.[56] In another post circulated on Twitter, Sabisky claimed that Black Americans had a lower average IQ than White people and were more likely to have an 'intellectual disability'. It was reported by *BBC News* on February 18, 2020 that Sabisky had resigned (according to *BBC News*, Number 10 never officially confirmed his appointment or any role he may have had)[57] as a result of these views becoming public.[58] Lammy gave a warning that needs to be taken very seriously in light of the contents of this book: 'Andrew Sabisky has some very ugly views, but depressingly he's not alone. There is a resurgent belief in Eugenics across fringes of the right. It's dangerous claptrap. Skin colour has no more relevance to an individual's intelligence than their hair colour'.[59]

Johnson refuses to disassociate himself from scientific racism

In February 2020, Number 10 refused to say whether Johnson thinks Black people have lower IQs on average, or agrees with eugenics.[60] As Rowena Mason explains, in a tense briefing with the media, Johnson's deputy official spokesperson declined several times to distance Johnson from the views of Sabisky, refusing to comment on Sabisky, his controversial views, or whether the prime minister agreed with them.[61] The Prime Minister's 'views are well publicised and well documented', the spokesperson repeated more than 10 times.[62]

Ian Lavery, then Labour Party Chair, commented:

> It is disgusting that not only has No 10 failed to condemn Andrew Sabisky's appalling comments but also seems to have endorsed the idea that white people are more intelligent than black people. Boris Johnson should have the backbone to make a statement in his own words on why he has made this appointment, whether he stands by it, and his own views on the subject of eugenics.[63]

The geneticist Adam Rutherford (see the Introduction and chapter 1) also criticized Sabisky, tweeting 'Like Cummings, he appears to be bewitched by science, without having made the effort to understand the areas he is invoking, nor its history'.[64] Rutherford went on, saying that the 'moral repugnance' of the remarks was 'overwhelming', adding that Sabisky and indeed Cummings look bewitched by science without doing the legwork: 'Instead this resembles the marshalling of misunderstood or specious science into a political ideology. The history here is important, because this process is exactly what happened at the birth of scientific racism and the birth of eugenics'.

Then Tory Transport Secretary Grant Shapps claimed that Sabisky's comments were 'not my views and those are not the views of the government'. Tellingly, the deputy official spokesman said Shapps was speaking only for himself when he made that statement.[65] This would seem to confirm the worst about Johnson's own views on 'race' and eugenics.

Johnson denies the existence of institutional racism

So, given these many obvious instances of his own colour-coded racism firmly in the public domain; and in the face of his association with known racists, a fascist sympathizer and eugenicists; and notwithstanding his refusal to disassociate himself from scientific racism, not to mention centuries of institutional racism in the UK, both inside and outside the Tory Party, Johnson found himself in the position of having to investigate racism (in Government-speak, 'race and ethnic disparities') in the UK. He could have chosen to start from a fresh slate, he could have chosen to admit to some mistakes in the past. This was in the light of the murder of George Floyd in America and the ensuing Black Lives Matter protests. Johnson's solution, however, was to seize upon a trusted ally, Tony Sewell, who had led Johnson's Mayor's Education Inquiry into London schools in 2012. Sewell, a long-term commentator on 'race' and education, had been criticized in the past for claiming and that 'the mantra "institutional racism" [is] a hurdle',[66] that boys were being failed by schools because lessons have become too 'feminized' in recent years, and calling for more nurturing of traditional 'male' traits, such as competitiveness and leadership.[67] In 2010, he claimed that 'much of the supposed evidence of institutional racism is flimsy'.[68]

Sewell was accordingly appointed Chair of the Commission on Race and Ethnic Disparities (CRED) in July 2020. Commission members were recruited by Director of the Number 10 Policy Unit since 2019, Munira Mirza, who used to be one of Johnson's Deputy Mayors. According to Rajeev Syal, Rowena Mason and Lisa O'Carroll, writing for *The Guardian,* Mirza was a prominent critic of Theresa May's 'racial disparities audit for public services', apparently commenting that the 'scene was being set for another bout of political self-flagellation regarding the subject of race in Britain'.[69] Mirza has also 'cast doubt on the existence of institutional racism and condemned previous inquiries for fostering a "culture of grievance."'[70] In 2017, she condemned an audit of racial inequalities in public services commissioned by Theresa May, writing that it showed how 'anti-racism is becoming weaponised across the political spectrum'.[71]

Totally unsurprisingly, therefore, the CRED report, published in March 2021, concluded that the claim that 'the country is still institutionally racist is not borne out by the evidence'.[72] For his part, Sewell said that although the report did not deny that racism exists in Britain, but there was no evidence 'of actual institutional racism'.[73]

With the whitewash complete and the conclusions of the Stephen Lawrence Inquiry Report undermined, Downing Street's official response to the social justice movements connected to Black Lives Matter remains that the UK should be seen as an international exemplar of racial equality, and that the impact of structural factors in ethnic disparities is not significant, and that as in the preview summarizing the report, which is described as a 'major shift in the race debate', notes that while overt racism does still exist in the UK, achievements elsewhere should make the country 'a model for other white-majority countries'.[74]

In contrast, Halima Begum, the chief executive of the Runnymede Trust, said:

> As we saw in the early days of the pandemic, 60% of the first NHS doctors and nurses to die were from our BAME [Black, Asian and minority ethnic] communities. For Boris Johnson to look the grieving families of those brave dead in the eye and say there is no evidence of

institutional racism in the UK is nothing short of a gross offence. The facts about institutional racism do not lie, and we note with some surprise that, no matter how much spin the commission puts on its findings, it does in fact concede that we do not live in a post-racist society.[75]

Campaigners for the rights of those affected by the Windrush scandal (see later in this chapter) expressed concern that the issue was raised just twice in the 258-page report: first alongside Grenfell – also discussed later in this chapter – in its Foreword as an instance 'where ethnic minority communities have rightly felt let down', but continued: 'Outcomes such as these do not come about by design, and are certainly not deliberately targeted', and second in the Conclusion, when Windrush is mentioned in passing as an exceptional example of things going wrong.[76] As Amelia Gentleman puts it, despite the scandal providing one of the clearest examples in recent history where government decisions caused catastrophic racist outcomes, the report claims that Britain is no longer a place where 'the system is deliberately rigged against ethnic minorities.[77]

Patrick Vernon, whose campaigning helped force the government to take action on Windrush, commented: 'I can see why they haven't included it. If they had focused on the scandal they would have had to admit that there was a systematic, structural failure in how the Home Office targeted the Windrush generation'.[78] He describes the narrative of the report as:

> it is up to the individual to succeed: if you work hard, keep your head down, you will achieve and be successful in Britain, and if you don't then, that's your fault. The policies of the hostile environment took away people's rights, but the report tries to say: actually you have all the rights you need.[79]

Echoing my own personal experience of the 'hostile environment' and being presumed to be lying until you prove you are being honest (see the Appendix to chapter 9), community activist Desmond Jaddoo, who helps run the Windrush National Organisation to secure justice for the thousands of people who were wrongly classified as immigration offenders, added, 'There was a culture of not believing members of the Windrush generation, who had to jump through hoops to prove that they were telling the truth'.[80] Elwaldo Romeo, who was told he was in the UK illegally and faced detention after being 59 years in the country, said he was disappointed: 'There's no compassion and no understanding of what we have gone through. Of course they want to sweep it under the carpet. Is there racism within the government and the Home Office? Yes'.[81] Finally, Halima Begum, the chief executive of the Runnymede Trust, said the report tried to reference racism as a historical matter, despite the recent evidence, concluding: 'The hostile environment still operates and victims of the Windrush scandal still do not have justice'.[82]

If all that was not enough, officials at Downing Street have been accused of rewriting much of the report.[83] Moreover, it was not made available to be read in full or signed off by the Commission members, nor were they made aware of its 24 final recommendations. Instead, the finished report was produced by Number 10.[84] One of the members, Kunle Olulode, an antiracist activist and director of the charity Voice4Change England, condemned the Government publicly, and the charity was scathing of the way evidence was cherrypicked, distorted and denied in the final document:

> The report does not give enough to show its understanding of institutional or structural discrimination ... evidence in sections, that assertive conclusions are based on, is selective [and]...gives no clear direction on what expectations of the role of public institutions and political leadership should be in tackling race and ethnic disparities. What is the role of the state in this?[85]

Another commissioner, who spoke out on condition of remaining anonymous, accused the government of 'bending' the work of its commission to fit 'a more palatable' political narrative and denying the working group the autonomy it was promised:[86]

> We did not read Tony's [Sewell] foreword. We did not deny institutional racism or play that down as the final document did. The idea that this report was all our own work is full of holes. You can see that in the inconsistency of the ideas and data it presents and the conclusions it makes. That end product is the work of very different views.[87]

The person revealed that they had been privy only to the section of the report they were assigned, and that it had soon become apparent the exercise was not being taken sufficiently seriously by Number 10, and concluded: 'Something of this magnitude takes proper time – we were only given five months to do this work, on a voluntary basis'.[88] In contrast to the landmark 1999 Stephen Lawrence Inquiry Report (see the Introduction to this book) which, as Nosheen Iqbal points out, took 18 months to conclude, the report by the Commission on Race and Ethnic Disparities was not peer-reviewed and was published just seven months after the group first met on a videocall.[89] To cap it all, Samuel Kasumu, Number 10's most senior Black special adviser, who set up the group to write the report, resigned from his post on the day the report was published, aghast at its final findings.[90] The response to the report from Simon Woolley, an independent member of the House of Lords who had appointed Kasumu to Number 10's Race Disparity Unit during Theresa May's premiership, was unequivocal:

> The only black special adviser in No 10 has felt that his only recourse to this grubby, divisive Sewell report is to resign. I appointed Samuel to

the race disparity advisory group when we first launched. He is a decent man whose energy has been hellbent on serving his country and tackling systemic racism. This is going to be a real moment for the PM and his aides at No 10 Downing Street. Black people around the country are incandescent with rage that their lived experience of persistent race inequality is being denied and belittled.[91]

The Social Mobility Commission appoints Katharine Birbalsingh

In June 2020, the Social Mobility Commission (SMC) whose remit is to monitor the effectiveness of the Government's Child Poverty Strategy[92] said, according to May Bulman, that progress on social mobility in the UK had been 'disappointing', after only one in four of its recommendations were delivered. It referred to the pledges by Theresa May as she entered Number 10 in 2016 to tackle 'burning injustice' (see chapter 9) and by Boris Johnson to 'level up' Britain in his prime ministerial campaign[93] (the latter was an attempt to appeal to Labour's 'red wall'). As will have become clear, from the perspective from which this book is written, such promises made by Tory Prime Ministers, whose remit is the promotion of (neoliberal) capitalism, are farcical and absurd.

The figures speak for themselves. The SMC found that 600,000 more children are now living in relative poverty than in 2012, that just one in four disadvantaged GCSE pupils get a good pass in English and maths compared with half of their better-off peers, and that life expectancy is falling for women in the most deprived areas.[94] Moreover, children from Black and minority ethnic groups, it reported, are also more likely to be poor, with a rate of 45% compared with 26% for children in White British families. Half of all adults from the poorest backgrounds receive no training at all after leaving school.[95] Of the 52 proposals it made between 2013 and 2020, only one-quarter (23%) had seen strong progress made, or the proposal delivered.[96]

The following year, SMC painted a depressing picture of life in the UK:

> Across the UK there are already signs that attainment gaps between advantaged and disadvantaged children are getting wider. Every critical measure of low social mobility – child poverty, income inequality, access to stable housing, unemployment for young people and gaps in school attainment – was poor in 2019. The impact of COVID-19 is threatening to make each of these factors worse.[97]

Late in 2021, Katharine Birbalsingh, the headteacher of Boris Johnson's favourite school (he praises the rote learning),[98] Michaela Community School in North London, was appointed the Social Mobility Commissioner. The school appears to be run on the lines of a cross between the factory floor during a 1960s time-and-motion inspection where workers were timed for every task they performed during a given period, and an army camp. In the words of Flora Carr who has visited the school, at lunchtime, 'less than 10 minutes since the school first sat down to eat … adult visitors scramble to finish their meals in the face of outstretched hands trying to take their plates, as teachers time the students' progress'. The pupils 'study in an atmosphere of rigid austerity' and 'demerits' are given out 'for the slightest errors: forgetting a pen, slouching, turning to look out of a window during a lesson' and 'two demerits' in one class 'equals a detention'.[99] Carr cites an English teacher telling one girl who's struggled to find her textbook in the allocated ten seconds: 'That's another demerit… you're too disorganized'.[100] A black line, she explains, 'runs down the center of the corridor carpets, and children are expected to silently proceed either side to their next classes' as eagle-eyed 'teachers stand ready to reprimand those who walk too slowly'. 'In the student bathrooms', she explains, 'there are no mirrors, lest they distract the students'.[101]

Birbalsingh, who founded the school in 2014 and describes herself as its 'headmistress', says with satisfaction that she has had 'ex-servicemen' visit and tell her Michaela reminds them of the British Army.[102] Just like the military:

> the school has established its own vernacular. 'SLANT!' a teacher will shout, and students are expected to sit bolt upright, arms crossed, face turned to the front. Children are also expected to 'track' the teacher with their eyes. Such is the range of commands to learn, new pupils joining the school at 11 years old are expected to attend a seven-day bootcamp before term starts.[103]

The school's students are drawn from the local neighbourhood, which, according to Carr, is among the least privileged in London. Wembley Park is a district of London borough Brent, where one-third of households are in poverty, and that has the second-highest eviction rate in London.[104] One boy tells Carr, 'Sometimes, when visitors come… they write a little message saying, "Ah, this school's like a *prison* nearly". Like, it's really really good'.[105]

Birbalsingh rose to prominence at the 2010 Tory Party conference in 2010 with a speech about Britain's 'broken' education system and was applauded for claiming that underachievement by Black pupils was due partly to 'the chaos of our classrooms, and, in part, to the accusation of racism [against teachers]'.[106] Her response to the Sewell Report is predictable. She tweeted:

> It is always acceptable in our woke culture[107] of 2021 to mercilessly attack black conservatives. They have 'betrayed' their leftist masters by daring to think for themselves, when they should be grateful. THAT is institutionalised/cultural racism. And it is everywhere.[108]

Foreign Secretary Liz Truss has also attacked 'woke culture', urging the nation to 'dump the baggage holding us back' and calling for an end to culture wars and 'woke' attacks on the UK's history. We should not be 'ashamed of our history', warning that internal rows about the past only help the UK's enemies. The UK should, she went on, embrace its history and insisted it is 'time to be proud of who we are and what we stand for'. The free world, she concluded, must 'wake up' and end its 'age of intro-spection' as she called for NATO allies to boost defence spending to counter Russian aggression: 'Our history, warts and all, makes us what we are today. Britain is the greatest country on earth, whoever you are, wherever you come from, you can achieve your dreams'.[109]

Birbalsingh said she was looking forward to taking up her role when 'improving social mobility is more vital than ever', adding:

> On the one hand, I want to inspire real action that will encourage people to seize the opportunities available to them and, on the other, I want to ensure that the government and other public bodies are deli-vering on their commitments to providing such opportunities, so that we really can "level up" every region of the UK.[110]

Truss's message to Birbalsingh is to focus on 'education, enterprise and employment'. Our equality work, she stressed, will address the worries that keep people up at night – like having a good job and getting their child a good education – not tokenistic issues divorced from their everyday concerns.[111]

Johnson's lacklustre response to Black Lives Matter and his refusal to condemn Trump

In June 2020, as people across the world protested against police brutality after the murder of George Floyd by police officer Derek Chauvin in America (Chauvin was subsequently sentenced to 22 1/2 years in prison), 'many people wearily tuned in to Prime Minister's Questions to see whe-ther Boris Johnson would address the unrest'.[112] As Sirena Bergman explains, in Johnson's opening statement, he made no mention of it. But leader of the opposition Keir Starmer immediately brought it up. 'Johnson's response', Bergman goes on, 'was lacklustre, and SNP MP Ian Blackford used his time to call him out on it'. Blackford asked him why in the seven days since George Floyd's death the British Government had failed to directly speak on the unrest, specifically, 'what representations he's made to his ally [President] Donald Trump', and asked him to 'at the very least say it now: black lives matter'.[113]

Johnson stated: 'Of course black lives matter, and I totally understand the anger, the grief that is felt not just in America but around the world, and in our country as well. And I totally understand that and I get that.'[114] John-son went on to say that he 'supports the right to protest', but immediately followed up with a metaphorical 'but', saying (for the second time in 20 minutes) that 'protests should be carried out lawfully'[115] (see later in this chapter for a discussion of the Police, Crime, Sentencing and Courts Bill). He also refused to condemn Trump, which was clearly what Blackford was hoping for, and 'what many British voters – especially black people and people of colour – were hoping to hear'.[116]

This is hardly surprising. As Matt Mathers points out, prior to the attempted coup at the Capitol on January 6, 2021, Johnson generally avoided criticizing the Trump administration.[117] While Theresa May's Foreign Secretary in 2018, he suggested that if Trump could 'fix' North Korea and restore the Iran nuclear deal, then he could be considered for one of the world's most prestigious honours. In Johnson's words, 'I don't see why he's any less of a candidate for the Nobel Peace Prize than Barack Obama', adding that Obama received the honour 'before doing anything'.[118] Johnson defended that statement in January 2021, brushing it off as nothing more than diplomacy and telling a Commons committee: 'I'm in favour … of the UK having the best possible relationship with the President of the United States'.[119]

Johnson's pro-British Empire views

In an article, again written when he was a Tory MP and editor of *The Spectator*, Johnson said that colonialism in Africa should never have ended and downplayed Britain's role in the slave trade. In the piece, published in 2002, he also argued that Africans would not have grown the right crops for export without British direction.[120] In his words, 'The continent may be a blot, but it is not a blot upon our conscience. The problem is not that we were once in charge, but that we are not in charge any more'.[121] Around the time of the Black Lives Matter protests in the UK, Johnson argued for the retention of statues of slavers and British colonialists in UK cities, on the spurious grounds that they 'teach us about our past with all its faults'.[122] I say 'spurious' because in *The Spectator* article he reveals an active admiration for colonialists, and I quote Johnson at length to reveal the full extent of his pro-British Empire views:

> Consider Uganda, pearl of Africa, as an example of the British record. Are we guilty of slavery? Pshaw. It was one of the first duties of Frederick Lugard, who colonised Buganda in the 1890s, to take on and defeat the Arab slavers. And don't swallow any of that nonsense about how we planted the 'wrong crops'. Uganda teems, sprouts, bursts with vegetation. You will find fruits rare and strange, like the jackfruit, hanging bigger than your head and covered with green tetrahedral nodules. Though delicately perfumed, it is, alas, more or less disgusting, and not even Waitrose is pretentious enough to stock it. So the British planted coffee and cotton and tobacco, and they were broadly right. It is true that coffee prices are currently low; but that is the fault of the

Vietnamese, who are shamelessly undercutting the market, and not of the planters of 100 years ago. If left to their own devices, the natives would rely on nothing but the instant carbohydrate gratification of the plantain ... the colonists correctly saw that the export market was limited.[123]

One way to boost African countries' economies, he suggested, is via British tourism: 'The best fate for Africa would be if the old colonial powers, or their citizens, *scrambled* once again in her direction; on the understanding that this time they will not be asked to feel guilty' (emphasis added).[124] As Policy Correspondent for *The Independent*, Jon Stone informs us, when approached by *The Independent* in 2020, Johnson's spokesperson declined to comment on the article.[125] There followed widespread condemnation from Opposition MPs. One of them, Labour MP Dawn Butler, commented:

I urge the PM to review his previous articles, books and statements and to re-examine them through the brutal lynching that he watched of George Floyd and say whether he regrets anything of what he has said, done or written in the past.[126]

She added that it was important not to

misrepresent or whitewash history. This Etonian attitude affects everyone who is not in that inner circle, no matter your colour. Instead of viewing history through rose-tinted glasses maybe it is time to look at history through the lenses of a very visible modern-day lynching.[127]

Slightly later the same year, Johnson said it was time to stop 'self-recrimination and general wetness' about the history of the British Empire.[128] This followed a row over the well-known nationalistic song 'Rule Britannia!' after the BBC declared that it would play only an orchestral version of it at a regular concert it holds in the Royal Albert Hall, London, 'often decked out in union flags for the occasion'.[129] True to form, Johnson responded:

I just want to say ... if it is correct, which I cannot believe that it really is, but if it is correct, that the BBC is saying that they will not sing the words of 'Land Of Hope And Glory' or 'Rule, Britannia!' as they traditionally do at the end of The Last Night of the Proms. I think it's time we stopped our cringing embarrassment about our history, about our traditions, and about our culture, and we stopped this general fight of self-recrimination and wetness. I wanted to get that off my chest.[130]

The then BBC Director General Tony Hall responded: 'I think ... [the organisers] have come to the right conclusion'.[131]

Johnson gets fascist support

In an article in *The London Economic*, early in 2021,[132] journalist Henry Goodwin asked, 'have the Tories become the party of the far-right?' He was referring to a remark by Jonathan Evans, a British life peer who formerly served as the Director General of the British Security Service.[133] In March 2020, according to Goodwin, 'in the heat of Britain's first salvoes with coronavirus', Evans made 'a remarkable intervention that, given the unfolding national crisis, slid somewhat under the radar'.[134] Evans suggested that the threat of far-right terrorism in Britain could be diminishing following Johnson's election victory. This was not because the ideological extremism which sustains the far-right was fading away, but 'because many of the "alienated" voters who are usually sucked into the British National Party (BNP) or English Defence League (EDL) felt as if their voices had been heard at the ballot box after the Conservative victory the previous December'.[135] Previously, Evans pointed out, 'Disaffected English nationalists were manifesting themselves at the extremes in things like the British National Party and National Action [the latter of which] which fed the undertone that articulated itself as extreme right-wing terrorism'.[136]

In the weeks after the election, it emerged that more than 5,000 supporters of far-right group Britain First − whose leaders Paul Golding and Jayda Fransen were jailed for hate crimes against Muslims in 2018[137] − had joined the Tories. In the words of the organization's spokesperson, 'We will support a party that is willing to take a firm stance against radical Islam and it looks like the Tories are willing to do that'.[138]

Islamophobia

In an incident in January 2022 that underlines the rampant Islamophobia and indeed sexism in the Tory Party under Johnson, MP Nusrat Ghani revealed that a Government Whip told her that her 'Muslimness was raised as an issue' in connection with her being sacked as a Minister in 2020,[139] and that her status as a 'Muslim woman…was making colleagues uncomfortable'.[140] Experiencing this, she said, was 'like being punched in the stomach. I felt humiliated and powerless'.[141] There were concerns 'that I wasn't loyal to the party as I didn't do enough to defend the party against Islamophobia allegations'.[142] Ghani had been appointed to a post at the Department for Transport in 2018, and become the first female Muslim minister to speak in the Commons, losing her job in a Cabinet re-shuffle in February 2020.[143] She disputed her dismissal but dropped it after being told that if she 'persisted' in asking about it she 'would be ostracised and her career and reputation would be destroyed':[144]

> When I challenged whether this was in any way acceptable and made clear there was little I could do about my identity, I had to listen to a

monologue on how hard it was to define when people are being racist and that the party doesn't have a problem and I needed to do more to defend it. It was very clear to me that the whips and No 10 were holding me to a higher threshold of loyalty than others because of my background and faith.[145]

Ghani concluded, 'I raised it several more times through official party channels ... I was extremely careful to follow procedure, and when the procedure ran out of road I had no choice but to get on with my career'.[146] She said that she welcomed a Cabinet Office Inquiry ordered by Johnson, saying all she wanted was for the matter to be taken seriously.[147] Tory Government Chief Whip Mark Spencer who was the Whip she was referring to, said the claims were completely false, and that he considered her allegations to be defamatory.[148] Number 10 said the Prime Minister had previously met with Ms Ghani to discuss her concerns. Johnson then 'wrote to her expressing to her his serious concern and inviting her to begin a formal complaint process. She did not subsequently do so'.[149] In response, according to *BBC News*, 'Ms Ghani said Mr Johnson "wrote to me that he could not get involved and suggested I use the internal Conservative Party complaint process."'[150] Ghani added that she did not do this because it was:

> very clearly not appropriate for something that happened on govern-ment business. I do not even know if the words that were conveyed to me about what was said in reshuffle meetings at Downing Street were by members of the Conservative Party. All I have ever wanted was for his government to take this seriously, investigate properly and ensure no other colleague has to endure this.[151]

Tory peer Sayeeda Warsi – who has frequently spoken about Islamophobia in the Tory Party – commented quite rightly that Ghani should never have been asked to go through the Party's complaint process, since this 'was not a party issue, this was a government issue',[152] adding that ... [Ghani's] experience had been 'an open secret in Westminster' and that Ghani had 'struggled to be heard' for nearly two years'.[153] Warsi went on to state that she believed there was a 'pattern' with Islamophobia in the Conservative Party, where 'Islamophobic racism is not viewed as seriously as other forms of racism' and 'action is rarely taken until the media is involved'.[154]

As the *BBC News* Political Correspondent Alex Forsyth explains, the latest allegations have once again drawn attention to the long-running issue of Islamophobia in the Tory Party and the way it handles such claims.[155] Almost four years ago, he goes on, the then-Chair of the Conservative Muslim Forum Mohammed Amin 'broke ranks and claimed the party was failing to take decisive action against anti-Muslim sentiment for fear of the political consequences'.[156] Amin was later expelled from his role and joined the Liberal Democrats. Moreover Warsi, who is in fact a former Tory Party

Chair and Cabinet Minister, has spoken of being 'ashamed' of her Party's approach to what she has repeatedly described as institutional racism.[157]

I have already referred to Johnson's 'letterbox and bank robber' comments about Muslim women. There have also been a number of other instances of Tory Party representatives and members making Islamophobic comments or sharing offensive material online that often goes unchecked. Forsyth refers to the Singh Inquiry in Spring 2021 that found 'discrimination and anti-Muslim sentiment' within the Tory Party.[158] Forsyth points out that there are now calls, including from the Muslim Council of Britain, for the Equality and Human Rights Commission to take action.[159]

Also early in 2022, in a stinging attack on Johnson, Chris Patten, former Tory Party chairman (sic) suggested the party had undergone 'fundamental change' with some sections having 'turned into an English nationalist populist, Johnsonian cult'.[160] Earlier Patten had said:

> What we're seeing is Boris Johnson on this runaway train of English exceptionalism and heaven knows where it is going to take us in the end. I want the best for my country, I fear for what's happening at the moment and I fear for our reputation around the world ... I hope that I'm wrong to feel so depressed about the outlook but I don't think that Mr Johnson is a Conservative, I think he is an English nationalist.[161]

Goodwin concludes his analysis of whether the Tories have become the party of the far right by noting that there are MPs in the Tory Party who veer dangerously close to extremism, and that the Johnson Government has swung hard to the right and is, among the most right-wing in living memory.[162]

SECTION 2: THE HOSTILE ENVIRONMENT AND THE POLICIES OF THE JOHNSON GOVERNMENT

Having looked at Johnson's own colour-coded racism, at his relationship with scientific racism and his denial of the existence of institutional racism in the UK; at his association with very right-wing figures, at the support he had from fascists, and at Islamophobia in the party, it is to the policies of this hard right populist government that I now turn in the remainder of this book. In Part 3 of the book, I examined immigration control and the birth and consolidation of Margaret Thatcher's 'Racecraft'. I began Part 4 with John Major's approach to multiculturalism and monoculturalism, before addressing the grassroots Tory backlash to ethnic diversity. I moved on to the origins, official launch, enactment, and impact of the hostile environment under Theresa May's watch. With the onset of the Johnson Government, unsurprisingly given the preceding analysis in this chapter, the hostile environment takes on a new dimension, ten years after its launch by Theresa May in 2012 (see chapter 9).

With my deadline for completing this book of May 2022 fast approaching, I am writing this section of the chapter in April/May at a time of considerable escalation in the hostile environment. I concentrate on three key policy initiatives: the Nationality and Borders Bill; the Police, Crime, Sentencing and Courts Bill; and curbing political topics in English schools. I also consider the Government's response to the 2022 Ukrainian refugee crisis and provide updates on the Windrush scandal and the Grenfell Tower disaster.

The Nationality and Borders Act (2022)

Having achieved the end of free movement from the EU following Brexit, the Johnson Government has been focusing its efforts to halt immigration by attempting to stop movement across the English Channel into the UK. These attempts have been accompanied by a series of 'moral panics' about the increase in the numbers of people coming to seek asylum in the UK, serving as a prelude to the Nationality and Borders Bill. Originally passed by 298 votes to 231 in the House of Commons in December 2021, it has been described by Home Secretary Priti Patel as the most significant overhaul of asylum system in over two decades.[163] According to the Government, the Bill seeks to:

- increase the fairness of the system to better protect and support those in need of asylum,
- deter illegal entry into the United Kingdom, thereby breaking the business model of people smuggling networks and protecting the lives of those they endanger,
- remove more easily those with no right to be in the UK.[164]

While the Bill is clearly an attempt to fulfil the third goal, but based on the Government's racist interpretation of 'no right', with respect to the first two goals it is likely to do the opposite. In the words of Amnesty International, Patel's 'attempt to paint this bill as targeting ruthless criminal gangs is a cynical distraction from her true intent' which is:

> to simply, and at whatever the cost, punish, penalise and deter people who seek asylum. The xenophobia that underpins this Bill is plain. It is as ruthless to victims of repression, torture and exploitation as it is exploitative of the racism and prejudice they face.[165]

After several months of 'ping-pong', the 'to and fro' amendments to Bills between the House of Commons and the House of Lords, the Act became law in April 2022. The United Nations High Commissioner for Refugees warned that Patel's Act could 'dramatically weaken' international systems for protecting those fleeing war and persecution, while Oxfam described it as a 'devastating blow for families fleeing conflict and persecution', and Médecins Sans Frontières (Doctors Without Borders) branded it 'despicable'.[166]

It will allow indefinite detention of refugees arriving in Britain, and intercepting refugees at sea, but not pushing them back towards France as Patel had wanted, accompanied by a new scheme for the Royal Navy rather than Border Control to take over anti-migrant operations in the English Channel. Following the threat of legal action from four organizations – the PCS (Public and Commercial Services union), Care4Calais,[167] Channel Rescue and Freedom from Torture – 'pushback' was abandoned. The Home Office Legal Department said the policy and procedures had been withdrawn and that the Ministry of Defence Joint Commander had not had permission to authorize the use of turnaround tactics.

The PCS General Secretary Mark Serwotka said:

> This humiliating climbdown by the government is a stunning victory for Home Office workers and for refugees. There is little doubt that lives have been saved. The pushbacks manoeuvre is extremely dangerous and represents a clear risk to life and limb. We were simply not prepared to allow our members to be placed in this horrendous position.

Clare Moseley, the founder of Care4Calais, said: 'I find it hard to believe that anyone within government thought that performing pushbacks in the Channel was a viable policy'

Sonya Sceats, the chief executive of Freedom from Torture, said:

> This momentous climbdown by the government shows that change is possible when we come together. But we should never have had to take this government to court in order to defend the sanctity of life – it is scandalous that it reached this point.

Steven Martin of Channel Rescue said: 'Pushbacks are a reckless endangerment to life and we have always maintained and reminded the government that they are unlawful. The violent forcing back of people seeking protection is abhorrent and deprives them of their right to asylum'.

Unsurprisingly, the Home Office letter made it clear that pushback had not been abandoned permanently, saying that if a decision were taken to use turnaround tactics in the future, it would only be after a full consideration of all relevant matters:

> The secretary of state for the home department [Patel] has determined that: the policy and procedures, which are the subject of the ongoing litigation, are withdrawn; if a decision were taken to use turnaround tactics in the future, it would only be after a full consideration of all relevant matters, including the evolving nature of the small boats threat, migrant behaviour and organised criminal activity; and new policies, guidance and operational procedures would need to be formulated at that point.[168]

It is right that we consider all safe and legal options to stop these unnecessary journeys, including turning boats around.

As we have set out previously, this tactic fully complies with both domestic and international law, however, there are extremely limited circumstances when you can safely turn boats back in the Channel.

The government's legal department acknowledged in a letter Patel announced, 'it would only be after a full consideration of all relevant matters, including the evolving nature of the small boats threat, migrant behaviour and organised criminal activity; and new policies, guidance and operational procedures would need to be formulated at that point'.[169]

The Act also makes it a criminal offence to 'knowingly arrive' in the UK illegally, that is to say without the required papers. Most refugees, of course, are fleeing war, poverty and environmental collapse and cannot go through all the obstacles of visas and visits to government offices.[170] It allows for asylum seekers to be treated differently based on how they entered the country and provides for offshore processing.[171]

Send them to Rwanda!

Offshore processing clearly reveals the Government's sinister plans and intent: allowing the UK to send asylum seekers to a so-called 'safe third country' and to submit claims at a 'designated place' determined by the Home Secretary. In a scarcely believable, even for Johnson and Patel, development of the hostile environment, the former appeared on TV screens at a press conference in Kent (the county most affected by so-called 'illegal channel crossings') on April 14, 2022 to announce plans to send 'unauthorized' asylum seekers on a one-way air ticket to Rwanda, 4,500 miles away in East Africa,[172] with those who are rejected by the Rwandan government being deported. The scheme involved an initial down-payment of £120 million to the Rwandan Government in return for accepting 'tens of thousands of asylum seekers'.[173] At the same time as Johnson's appearance at the press conference, Patel was in Rwanda sorting out the deal. Syal reports that in a visit to the Rwandan capital, Kigali:

> Patel was shown pristine accommodation that will be used to house people flown from the UK. The guest house has 50 rooms over four floors that can accommodate a maximum of 100 people. Two more blocks will be built that will provide a maximum capacity of 300. In a press conference with Rwanda's foreign minister, Vincent Biruta, Patel said: 'Our world-leading migration and economic development partnership is a global first and will change the way we collectively tackle illegal migration through new, innovative and world-leading solutions'.[174]

It has since been revealed that in the 'guest house', bedrooms are around 3.5 metres by 3.5 metres with two beds in each, and there are just 12 toilets and five showers for the 100 people.[175] As news correspondent for *Sky News*, Shingi Mararike points out Britain has a growing backlog of asylum claims which has reached a cost of £1.5 billion a year, and if the Government wants to use these accommodation blocks, it will need to find more of them imminently.[176] Rwandan Government officials, Mararike tells us, who took him around the accommodation told him they are planning to build two more 50-room blocks in the compound, but when asked when these would be finished, no definite answer was provided.[177]

Immediate widespread condemnation

In the words of Chief Executive of the Refugee Council Enver Solomon, 'Boris Johnson's administration in England has chosen to … offshore people seeking asylum to Rwanda; to treat them as no more than human cargo to be shipped thousands of miles away so they are out of sight and out of mind.[178] Patel had told the House of Lords Justice and Home Affairs Committee towards the end of 2021:

> All the data and evidence has shown this – that in the last 12 months alone, 70% of the individuals who have come to our country illegally via small boats are single men, who are effectively economic migrants. They are not genuine asylum seekers. These are the ones who are elbowing out the women and children, who are at risk and fleeing persecution.[179]

The reality is quite different. Solomon points out that the people the Government is seeking to offshore 'are not all illegal economic migrants, as it claims, but are mainly those who have escaped bloodshed and terror … exercising their right under the UN refugee convention, which the UK was a founding signatory of, to seek asylum in a country of their choosing'.[180] The Refugee Council analysed Channel crossings and asylum outcomes between January 2020 and June 2021 and found that '91% of people who travelled by boat across the Channel came from 10 countries where human rights abuses and persecution were common, namely Afghanistan, Iran, Syria, Iraq, Sudan, Vietnam, Kuwait, Ethiopia, Eritrea and Yemen'.[181] Moreover, about two-thirds are granted refugee status or protection in the UK.[182]

As Amnesty International UK argues, increasing criminal sentences, penalties and border controls (that will also apply to anyone helping someone to seek asylum in the UK, regardless of whether their help is for monetary gain or not) will allow smugglers to thrive since it 'will only increase the reliance of people, already vulnerable to exploitation, upon the gangs that remain the sole source of any prospect that people may have to ultimately escape their situations of insecurity, exploitation and deprivation by reaching a place of safety'.[183]

In a display of breath-taking hypocrisy, Theresa May, *the* architect of the hostile environment that split up thousands of families (see chapter 9), including my own (see the Appendix to chapter 9), attempted to seek assurance from Patel in the House of Commons 'if it is the case the families will not be broken up'.[184] As I pointed out in the Appendix to chapter 9, on November 28, 2017 the most popular website for supporting families divided by May's legislation and subsequent policies, I LOVE MY FOREIGN SPOUSE had 11,830 members on Facebook. As a demonstration of the hostile environment's ongoing disastrous impact, as of January 29, 2022 it had 19,988, meaning that membership has been increasing at an average of four per day. On April 20, 2022, the membership was 20,319, still an average of four new members a day. In the interchange between May and Patel, the latter said she understood the scheme was only for young men but did not tell the Commons if women and children would be sent to Rwanda.[185]

Human rights in Rwanda: migrants and refugees

When questioned about the poor human rights record in Rwanda, where some groups have logged the torture of detainees, Johnson, seemingly prepared for the question, replied: 'Rwanda has totally transformed. Over the last decades it has totally transformed from what it was',[186] describing Rwanda as 'one of the safest countries in the world, globally recognised for its record of welcoming and integrating migrants'.[187]

This is certainly not what freelance human rights journalist Nicola Kelly found when she spoke to small boat arrivals on the Kent coast who expressed fears about being sent to Rwanda.[188] A man from Eritrea told Kelly: 'Rwanda is like Eritrea, it does not keep human beings safe. Here in Europe, you are free'.[189] Jemel, another new arrival from Eritrea, told her:

> If they send me to Rwanda, I will not go. I will die here, I will take my life. Do you know how many thousands of miles I travelled to be here? How long I was in [the] desert ...? To reach this point, to be here, we all had to make so many sacrifices. A lot of [people] lost their lives on the sea. I left my country now – I cannot go back to Africa.[190]

Of the group of 22 migrants, she points out, 'all said they would take their own lives, rather than face removal from the UK to Rwanda'.[191]

Rwandan President Paul Kagame has been accused of seeking to assassinate opponents; the British police have warned critics of Kagame living in the UK that their lives may be in danger; and in 2018, Rwandan police killed 12 refugees after a demonstration outside UN High Commissioner's office, according to Peter Beaumont, writing for *The Guardian*.[192]

LGBT rights in Rwanda

Human Rights Watch report that in 2021 Rwandan authorities rounded up and arbitrarily detained over a dozen gay and transgender people, sex workers, street children and others in the months before a planned Commonwealth Heads of Government Meeting in June.[193] They were held in a transit centre known for its harsh and inhuman conditions.[194] People interviewed at the centre by Human Rights Watch who identified as gay or transgender said that security officials accused them of 'not representing Rwandan values' and informed the interviewer that other detainees beat them because of their clothes and identity, while other detainees held in the 'delinquents' room confirmed that fellow detainees and guards more frequently and violently beat people they knew were gay or transgender than others.[195] The day after Johnson's attempt to reassure the press and the public about Rwanda, Foreign and Commonwealth Office 'travel advice' on the Government website, that all UK citizens are urged to consult before travelling to any foreign country, had the following warning:

> Homosexuality is not illegal in Rwanda but remains frowned on by many. LGBT individuals can experience discrimination and abuse, including from local authorities. There are no specific anti-discrimination laws that protect LGBT individuals. See our information and advice page for the LGBT community before you travel.[196]

Challenges

In opposing the plans, the UN Hight Commission for Refugees Agency (UNHCR) noted that they could be challenged under the Refugee Convention. In the words of UNHCR's assistant high commissioner for Protection Gillian Triggs, the Agency:

> remains firmly opposed to arrangements that seek to transfer refugees and asylum seekers to third countries in the absence of sufficient safeguards and standards. Such arrangements simply shift asylum responsibilities, evade international obligations, and are contrary to the letter and spirit of the Refugee Convention. People fleeing war, conflict and persecution deserve compassion and empathy. They should not be traded like commodities and transferred abroad for processing.[197]

Warsi called the scheme inhumane and cynical, while the British Red Cross Executive Director Zoe Abrams said it was 'profoundly concerned' about the plans to 'send traumatised people halfway round the world to Rwanda'.[198] She added:

We are not convinced this drastic measure will deter desperate people from attempting to cross the Channel either. People come here for reasons we can all understand, like wanting to be reunited with loved ones, or because they speak the language. Making it harsher may do little to stop them risking their lives.[199]

Lucy Moreton, the Professional Officer of the ISU Immigration and Border Union, warned of further loss in the Channel (in 2021 at least 44 died or went missing in the attempt to cross over to England)[200] 'as people become desperate to reach the UK before any plans to send them Rwanda are implemented'.[201] The President of the Law Society of England and Wales Stephanie Boyce opined there were serious questions over whether the plans complied with international law: 'The government is announcing this scheme before parliament has approved the necessary powers. There are serious questions about whether these plans would or could comply with the UK's promises under international treaty'.[202] Outsourcing has also been condemned by the Church of England, with the Archbishop of Canterbury Justin Welby, saying it was 'ungodly', and the Archbishop of York Stephen Cottrell using his Easter sermon to call it 'depressing and distressing' and raising 'serious ethical questions'.[203] Labour pointed out that previous attempts by the Government to tackle the issue of sea crossings – such as by giving £54 million to France or considering the use of jet skis to push boats back – had failed.[204] Finally, Home Office staff have threatened to strike and drawn comparisons to working for the Third Reich over Patel's plan, with one anonymous civil servant drawing a comparison to serving under Adolf Hitler. In a reference to the post-World War II Nazi trials at Nuremberg, that person wrote: 'The words "I was only obeying orders" are echoing down through history to me and making me queasy'.[205]

The first migrants are due to be sent to Rwanda on a chartered flight in May 2022. However, it is likely to be delayed because of legal challenges.[206] Liz Wheatley, Unison Union Branch secretary in Camden, demonstrating against the Rwanda proposal, underlined the class nature of 'free movement', when talking to Isabel Ringrose of *Socialist Worker*: 'Anyone with a desire for a better life has a valid reason to be here. The rich get to decide where they want to live to make the most money out of us ... Our job is to make it possible to welcome them'.[207]

Safe routes?

It is long-time policy, confirmed in the Act, that asylum in the UK can only be claimed when someone arrives there. There is, therefore, no choice for almost all the refugees who seek asylum in the UK but to rely on dangerous journeys – and often dangerous people – to reach this country to make their claims. Moreover, only being allowed to seek asylum in the UK applies whatever the level of connection the person may have to the UK – including those with close family living here.[208]

In a joint article in *The Times* with Rwanda Foreign Minister Biruta, Patel expressed 'surprise that those institutions that criticise the plans fail to offer their own solutions', describing her controversial plans as 'bold and innovative'.[209] Energy minister Greg Hands reiterated the Government's challenge, stating 'What others – the critics of this plan – need to do is to show what their solution would be'.[210]

So, are there in fact other solutions? Are there safe routes for asylum seekers? As the Refugee Council correctly points out, for the vast majority of refugees there are currently no safe ways for them to seek asylum in the UK.[211] A humane government would, it goes on, increase the availability of 'Refugee Family Reunion', 'Refugee Resettlement' and 'Humanitarian visas'.

Refugee Family Reunion provides a safe way for family members to join someone who has already been granted refugee status in the UK. As the Refugee Council stresses, the Nationality and Borders Bill will all but destroy this vital route out of conflict for women and children. In the five years between 2017 and 2022, as many as 29,000 people have come to the UK safely under this route, over 90% of whom were women and children.[212]

Refugee resettlement refers to the transfer of refugees from an initial country of asylum. Resettlement to the UK nearly ground to a halt during the height of the Covid-19 pandemic in 2020. A new resettlement scheme introduced in 2021 has no targets. Furthermore, a scheme announced in August 2021 specifically for Afghans did not launch until January 2022, and then only for those already evacuated to the UK. The Refugee Council is calling for a commitment to the resettlement of 10,000 refugees a year.[213]

Humanitarian visas would allow people to apply for visas to enter the UK for the purposes of claiming asylum. Since people can only claim asylum in the UK when they are physically here is, of course, why people are crossing the Channel to reach the UK. It doesn't have to be this way – humanitarian visas would enable people in need of protection to travel to the UK in a safe manner.[214]

Instead of pursuing these safe routes, the Refugee Council concludes, the Johnson Government 'is trying to decrease the availability of these vital routes while also discriminating against those who make their own way here'.[215] We should, it goes on, 'be focused on safe routes and a warm welcome for refugees NOT criminalisation and cruelty'.[216] Whereas safe routes for refugees are referred to as 'safe and legal routes' or 'official routes', the Refugee Council refers to them as 'safe routes' since the alternative is to travel in an irregular manner to claim asylum in the UK. While this can be dangerous, it reminds us, claiming asylum is not illegal.[217]

The Police, Crime, Sentencing and Courts Act (2022)

Attempting to criminalize effective protest

Using the backlash against 'Insulate Britain', the Tory Government decided to toughen up the law by introducing a new bill, the Police, Crime,

Sentencing and Courts (PCSC) Bill.[218] Insulate Britain is an offshoot of the global environmental movement Extinction Rebellion (XR). Launched in July 2021, Insulate Britain had staged protests across England and Wales, demanding the Government retro fit all UK social housing homes to insulate the homes of the poorest people, thereby lowering energy bills, making homes warm and reducing carbon emissions. In September 2021, it protested on the M25 disrupting traffic as many glued themselves to the road. Seventy-eight people were arrested.[219] The PCSC Bill was an attempt to legislate for heavy-handed and oppressive police measures and draconian prison sentences. It was introduced in March 2021, sponsored by Patel, and passed in April 2022. The Act includes the following measures:

- Making it a criminal offence for protesters to cause 'serious distress, serious annoyance or serious inconvenience' without 'reasonable excuse' – carrying a penalty of up to ten years' prison.
- Allowing the police to impose restrictions on marches if 'noise' could cause 'serious disruption' to a nearby organization or government department.
- Police's power to contain a crowd for an indefinite period.

Criminalizing effective protest along with other Government measures represents a major lurch by Patel and Johnson in the direction of, in Guardian columnist, George Monbiot's words, 'an authoritarian state'.[220] Some measures were thrown out by the Lords in January 2022. These included attempts to make 'locking on' (people making it difficult for themselves to be removed from roads or buildings) a crime – a tactic at the core of XR's and Insulate Britain's strategy since they began.

However, in the Queen's speech in May 2022 that opens the new session of Parliament, in a new Public Order Bill, it will be now be illegal for protesters to lock themselves to buildings and large objects, with a maximum of six months imprisonment, while demonstrations that 'interfere with' infrastructure such as airports, railways and newspaper printing presses will also be outlawed, and anyone who blocks the construction of major transport projects such as HS2 (a major new rail network connecting Britain's major conurbations) could face 12 months in prison.[221]

Colour-coded racism

Damage to memorials

In response to the toppling of the statue of slave trader Edward Colston as part of the 2020 BLM protests following the murder of George Floyd, under the Act damage to memorials could lead to up to an incredible 10 years in prison.[222] This part of the Act is not only blatantly aimed at Black people, but also criminalizes antiracist protesters in general. A precursor to this is Johnson's lacklustre response to the BLM 2020 protests as discussed in the first section of this chapter. Patel described the protests as 'dreadful' and said that she opposes taking the knee as a symbol of support for antiracism.[223]

Stop and search

The Act also introduced what the Government refers to as 'Serious Violence Reduction Orders'. This entails 'new stop and search powers' for 'convicted knife offensive weapons offenders', that are 'designed', in the words of the Act, 'to ensure offenders are steered away from crime and if they persist in carrying a knife or an offensive weapon, that they are more likely to be caught and put in prison'.[224] Police and Criminal Evidence Act 1884 Code A states that 'a person's physical appearance, the fact that they are known to have a previous conviction, and assumptions about the likelihood of people from certain ethnic backgrounds being involved in criminal activity' must not be used as the reason for stopping and searching them or any vehicle they are in, 'unless there is information or intelligence giving a specific description of a person suspected of carrying an item for which there is a power to search'.[225] Nevertheless, as the National Stop and Search Learning Report of April 2022 points out, in the year ending March 2021, a Home Office Report showed people from a Black or Black British background were seven times more likely to be stopped and searched than those from a White ethnic background. People from an Asian or Asian British background, or mixed ethnic background, were approximately two and half times more likely to be stopped and searched than those from a White ethnic background.[226] In the words of Agnew-Pauley and Akintoye:

> The unjust use of stop and search causes innocent people to feel targeted and victimised by the police based on their ethnicity. In the long term, it eradicates trust and confidence in the police and alienates entire communities. Knife crime and violence are complex problems that require an evidence-informed approach. The available evidence suggests handing sweeping powers to the police to stop people and search them without strong justification is not an effective way to prevent crime. Meanwhile, it causes harm to people and damages their relationship with the police, particularly those from black and minority ethnic communities.

Under Section 60 of the Criminal Justice and Public Order Act 1994, a police officer *who has to be at least the rank of Inspector* can stop and search a person without suspicion, *only* if that officer reasonably believes that incidents involving serious violence might take place in the officer's area and authorization will help to prevent them, or an incident involving serious violence has taken place in the officer's area and that a weapon used in the incident is being carried in the area and authorization will help to find the weapon, or people are carrying weapons in the officer's area without good reason.[227] As criminology researcher Winifred Agnew-Pauley and PhD candidate in sociology Bisola Akintoye explain in an article in *The Conversation*, there is little evidence that extension of 'stop and search' solves this problem.[228] A 'super-complaint' (a system that allows designated organizations to raise issues on behalf of the public about 'harmful patterns or trends in policing')[229] submitted to the Government by the Criminal Justice Alliance (CJA)[230] found Section 60 to be highly ineffective, with only around 1% of searches leading to an arrest for weapons.[231] The CJA also argues that it is likely to cause more harm than good in the community.[232]

Echoing Monbiot's comments about the criminalization of protest, British journalist Moya Lothian-McLean writing for *The New York Times* notes that, undeterred by the pandemic, Johnson

> and his lieutenants are ... seizing control for themselves and stripping away the freedoms of others ... [setting] ... Britain, self-professed beacon of democracy, on the road to autocracy. Once in place, the legislation will be very hard to shift. For Mr. Johnson, it amounts to a concerted power grab.[233]

Like making locking on a criminal offence, Patel has now made stop and search easier. In a letter to police forces, she extended the length of time the powers can be in force from 15 to 24 hours and the period a Section 60 can be extended was upped from 39 to 48 hours. At the same time, the rank at which officers are able to authorize the deployment of stop and search was lowered from senior officer to inspector, while a superintendent can now extend the authorization. Authorizing officers now only need to anticipate that serious violence 'may' rather than 'will' occur, and no longer need to publicly communicate authorizations to communities in advance.[234]

Non-colour-coded racism: GRT communities

Monbiot argues correctly that as we focus on this serious threat to civil liberties, we must not forget 'something else buried in this monstrous bill'.[235] He is referring to the provision that turns trespass from a civil into a criminal offence, allowing the police to arrest people who are Gypsies, Roma and Travellers (GRT) and confiscate their homes, if they stop in places that have not been designated for them. As Monbiot points out, under the Act in another unbelievable use of incarceration as a punishment, any adult member of the communities can be put in prison for up to three months.[236] Given that authorized sites and stopping places cannot accommodate the GRT people who need them', Monbiot goes on, 'this is a deliberate attack on a vulnerable minority'.[237] It is also a manifestation of blatant non-colour-coded racism.

The Friends, Families and Travellers campaign group commented:

> We're aware of the darkness the criminalisation of trespass could bring to the nomadic way of life. It will not eradicate travelling. Instead, it will force those who have nowhere else to go into a direct confrontation with the law. A family seeking somewhere to bed down for the night will have to reckon with the possibility of their home being seized, their children thrown into care and their livelihoods torn apart.[238]

Gypsies, Roma and Travellers have been deprived of places where they can lawfully stop, and then punished for the absence of provision. Providing a brief history of anti-GRT racism, Monbiot informs us that, according to a study by the Community Architecture Group, between 1986 and 1993 roughly two-thirds of traditional Travellers' sites, some of which had been used for thousands of years, were blocked and closed under the Thatcher and Major Governments. Then, in 1994, Major's Criminal Justice Act granted the police new powers against people stopping without authorization.[239] 'With a cruel and perverse twist', he adds, 'the same act repealed the duty of local government to provide authorized sites, and removed the grant aid funding these sites'. Partly as a result, he concludes a 2020 study by Friends, Families and Travellers found that, out of 68 local authorities they looked at, only eight had met their own identified need for Gypsy and Traveller pitches.[240] Though there is a long waiting list of GRT households seeking authorized sites and stopping places, official pitches decreased by 8% between 2012 and 2022,[241] a period overseen by Tory Governments.

Monbiot again stresses the racist intent of the Act as well as its class nature:[242]

> It would put people who are Gypsies, Roma and Travellers in an impossible position. To apply for an official pitch, you must demonstrate 'proof of travelling'. But if you don't have access to official pitches, travelling will put you outside the new law. In other words, it is not a particular behaviour that is being criminalised. It is the minority itself … [This] harks back to an imagined world in which the peasants could be neatly divided into villeins (good) and vagrants (bad), where everyone knew their place, geographically and socially. Of course, the demonisation of mobile people, whether Roma or asylum seekers, does not extend to the government ministers and newspaper editors who might shift between their pads in London and their second homes in Cornwall or Tuscany. It's about the rich controlling the poor, as if democracy had never happened.[243]

Romany journalist Jake Bowers has examined the impact the Act will have on Britain's nomadic people.[244] As he argues, 'Home Secretary Priti Patel's Police, Crime, Sentencing and Courts Bill, which not only has profound implications for environmental protest but will also totally criminalise

Gypsy, Roma and Traveller (GRT) culture. Our culture is one that already faces multiple challenges'.[245] He continues:

> Legal stopping places are the foundation from which both travelling and access to mainstream services such as health and education spring. But a dramatic lack of such sites forces thousands of families to live at the side of the road, prompting conflict between GRT communities and local councils and communities.[246]

Bowers gives the example of one of the families forced to live at the side of the road, Gerry Connors. Connors' community which numbered 40 and included special needs children and a recent stroke survivor, were evicted three times.[247] The laws that lock them into a continuous cycle of trespass and eviction, he points out, are already draconian, but even evictions are not as bad as being split up and scattered in housing, where isolation and mental health problems have led to a suicide epidemic.[248] The hierarchy of the police force seems to agree about the real source of 'unauthorised encampments'. Early in 2021, Chair of the National Police Chiefs' Council (NPCC) Martin Hewitt said police leaders had not requested a change in the law, believing current powers to be sufficient. Hewitt told a parliamentary committee: 'The fundamental problem is that there is an insufficient provision of sites for Gypsy Travellers to occupy. That is what then causes the relatively small percentage where they end up in unlawful encampments'.

In another Guardian piece, Katherine Quarmby reports on Government-funded research by Margaret Greenfields and Carol Rogers at Buckinghamshire New University that found that Gypsy, Traveller and Roma communities are experiencing hate incidents on an almost daily basis, while mental health issues and suicide are leading to an 'epidemic of needless deaths',[249] with one Traveller telling researchers that her family had experienced four suicides within the previous one and a half years, the latest involving her sister-in-law, who left three young children.[250] Support workers were aware of 131 suicide attempts over a five-year period ending in 2020, a large proportion of whom said that over 90% of clients who had committed suicide or attempted to had previously experienced hate incidents. These incidents included social media abuse (87%), bullying of family members (78%) and racial hatred following media reports (82%).[251] Josie O'Driscoll, Chief Executive of GATE (Gypsy and Traveller Empowerment) said, 'One young person told us: "I've had enough, I can't take it anymore."'[252] Everywhere he turned, she explains, he felt he faced prejudice. 'A big part of Traveller life is attending funerals. By the time you get over one trauma, you are grieving for the next person'.[253] The report suggests a possible correlation between TV shows and hate speech, with reported increases in incidents following programmes such as 'My Big Fat Gypsy Wedding' on Channel 4 and the same channel's Dispatches programme, 'The Truth About Traveller Crime', in

April 2020.[254] O'Driscoll concluded: 'It's not just journalists writing, it's the pile-on after, referring to negative responses and language on social media after broadcasts.[255]

Connecting the anti-Insulate Britain aspect of the Act to its anti-GRT intents and referring to the part of the Act that targets anyone residing on land while causing noise that could be said to have damaged the environment, Bowers explains the close relationship of GRT communities with the environment. In so doing, he also challenges the popular misconception about 'leaving a mess', simply out of disregard for others or malice rather than because there are not enough authorized encampments:

> I find the defining of my community as an environmental hazard deeply offensive. I know that just as most of us aren't criminals or thugs, the vast majority of us never fly tip, and our homes are often fanatically clean. We see nature as something we are intimately connected to, whether that's as a place to forage or hunt, or a place to seek sanctuary. When we park up on roadside verges or commons or live on our own lands, we are simply re-asserting our rightful place in the British landscape; a landscape we shaped as agricultural labourers over the last 500 years and defended as soldiers in Britain's wars.

He then compares the GRT communities' affinity with indigenous peoples: 'the CO2 footprint of a caravan is far smaller than that of a house and our involvement in the scrap metal trade has made us huge recyclers ... but we exist in the here and now of Britain ... rather than in the Amazon or Arctic'.[256]

Given that a tradition of nomadic family life is a key non-negotiable part of GRT identity, Bowers continues: 'Priti Patel ... will have fundamentally altered our right, and the right of all British people, to access and defend the landscape ...We are, you see, the canary in the coal mine of liberty. If our culture is stamped out, then your freedoms are just one step behind, as evidenced by other parts of the ... [Act]'.[257] Bower concludes that 2021 marked exactly 50 years since Romany activists from across Europe met in London to give their transnational nation a flag, anthem, and a political direction. Today, many of the lives of Europe's 12 million Romany people are still blighted by 'racism, misperceptions, hatred and the denial that we are even a people at all'.[258]

Government 'objectively justifies' racism in the Act

In September 2021 the Home Office 'objectively justified' the fact that anti-GRT and anti-Black racism would be inherent in the Act by admitting that different groups would be disproportionately impacted by measures in it.[259] A Government Equalities Impact Statement claimed: 'There is no direct discrimination within the meaning of the Equality Act as the law will apply equally, regardless of any protected characteristic ... any discriminatory impact for those of a particular race or ethnicity will be indirect'. 'It is our view', it continued, 'that any indirect discrimination towards [Black and GRT] ... communities can be objectively justified'.[260]

The Government claimed it recognized the right to follow a nomadic way of life but that the proposed laws would 'apply to anyone who resides or intends to reside on land illegally', and that the plans were a 'proportionate means of achieving the legitimate aims of prevention and investigation of crime and the protection of the rights of others, notably those of the occupier and the local community'.[261]

To sum up, in response to the Equalities Impact statement, Liberty, the organization that 'challenges injustice, defends freedom and campaigns to make sure everyone in the UK is treated fairly' said the Government's plans would criminalize Gypsies and Travellers and cause the 'harassment' of Black people, while Jun Pang, its Policy and Campaigns Officer, told *The Independent*:

> The government's attempt to justify proposals it admits are discriminatory is an insult to the millions of people who will be affected by the policing bill. The government admission that these proposals are discriminatory means they shouldn't see the light of day, let alone be made into law.[262]

Curbing political topics in English schools

Following the publicity afforded to Johnson's aforementioned 2002 pro-imperialist article revealed by Stone in his 2020 piece in *The Independent*, the Shadow Secretary of State for Women and Equalities, Marsha de Cordova commented: 'Boris Johnson's past comments are an example of why we need to educate people about the impact of colonialism'.[263] She added, 'The legacy of British colonialism and its role in the slave trade is a scar on our society. To infer this is something to be proud of, and that African countries are worse off because they are no longer ruled by the empire, is an insult to millions'.[264]

Throughout the book I have made very many references to the British Empire and to British Imperialism. Indeed, Parts 1 and 2 have 'Empire' in their titles. I have discussed the connections between nation, racism and imperialism and how colour-coded racism directed towards Black and Asian communities in Britain has its origins in the British Empire. I have looked at slavery, primarily about profit, and how the transatlantic slave trade, the forced movement of enslaved Africans, was a major component of the British Empire. I have analysed how Tory Prime Ministers were dedicated to the growth, the preservation and championing of the Empire. I have described how British Imperial adventures were justified by institutional racism in popular culture and in the education system. I have shown how the Empire came home to roost in post-World War II Britain and have discussed in detail resultant ongoing colour-coded racism up to the second decade of the 21st century. Most of these issues will not have been addressed in schools.

However, within the Tory Party, there is a perceived need to maintain the narrative of 'Empire' espoused by Johnson. It should come as no surprise, therefore, that the Department of Education (DfE) under the Johnson administration, has issued Guidance entitled 'Political Impartiality in Schools' (February 2022).[265] As Richard Adams explains, the Guidance says that recent historical events 'which are particularly contentious and disputed', such as 'many topics relating to empire and imperialism', should be taught 'in a balanced manner'.[266] Education unions have described the Guidance as confusing and likely to deter teachers in England from tackling subjects such as racism.[267] Thus, Mary Bousted, Joint General secretary of the National Education Union, said that the guidance 'does not so much clarify existing guidance as add new layers of mystification and complexity to it' for teachers and school leaders, potentially fostering 'such a level of uncertainty and caution in schools about "political issues" that they are less likely to engage with them'.[268] She went on:

> The losers in the DfE's [Department for Education's] 34-page game of obfuscation about what is and is not a 'political' issue will be the students who are denied the opportunity to engage with the most challenging issues of our time. The warning lights that the government is flashing around climate change, racism, world poverty and the legacy of empire as topics of exploration are more likely to decrease students' engagement with learning than to stimulate it.[269]

The Guidance singles out Black Lives Matter, arguing that while teachers should be clear 'that racism has no place in our society', the demands of organizations like Black Lives Matter 'go beyond the basic shared principle that racism is unacceptable'.[270] To which I would add, 'and so they should'. As Adams points out, the Guidance avoids defining 'political issues', stating that ethical debates are not political issues if they are 'shared principles that underpin our society', such as freedom of speech or challenging racism.[271] Instead, according to the Guidance, school leaders and teachers should use 'reasonable judgment to determine what is and is not a "political issue"'.[272] Here my comments would be, 'there are no shared principles underpinning the UK'.

As to freedom of speech, this is a complex issue and again needs defining. There are and should be constraints on what people can say. Hate laws are an example. As far as challenging racism is concerned, racism takes many forms as discussed in the Introduction and exemplified throughout the book. As has been the theme of this book, far from challenging racism, the Tory Party has been at the forefront of promoting and exasperating it. With respect to what is a political issue, I would hold that education is in essence a profoundly *political* project. As Paulo Freire put it in 1985, educators must reconceptualize their labor as political work and 'must ask themselves for whom and on whose behalf they are working'.[273]

The Government response to the 2022 Ukrainian refugee crisis

Commenting on LinkedIn, one leading human rights lawyer and solicitor specializing in UK Immigration, Nationality, & Refugee law, Paul Ward wrote in March 2022 about the crisis for Ukrainians following the Russian invasion that started on February 24, 2022, revealing not just the late response to the huge numbers of women and children fleeing Ukraine, but the complexity of UK immigration law:

> So whilst the rest of Europe helps unlimited numbers of Ukrainian women and children (visa free) to flee to safety, the U.K. finally began to roll out parts of its visa scheme for Ukrainians yesterday afternoon, 8 days into the conflict. I'm now submitting applications under the scheme as fast as possible and what the U.K. lacks in speed it makes up for in complexity. A typical example this morning is a woman from Sussex who can't sponsor her elderly parents to come from Ukraine because she has only lived in the U.K. for 3 years and therefore doesn't meet the definition of a UK settled person. Fortunately she is saved by her British husband (who has only met those parents once) because with a little ingenuity and the uploading of documents which are tricky to find in a war-zone I can establish that he is an 'Immediate Family Member' of an 'Extended Family Member' of 'an Eligible Applicant', each of those words having specific meanings under the Guidance. There is absolutely no excuse whatever your political allegiance and attitude to immigration for such a mean response to a horrific war.[274]

About a week after Ward's intervention, the March 12 Leader in *The Economist* stated correctly that the British Government's response to Ukrainian refugees is typical.[275] It cited Johnson who stated, 'Of course we're going to take refugees. The UK is way out in front in our willingness to help'.[276] The Leader went on, 'You hardly dare imagine what unwillingness would look like. Britain's treatment of Ukrainian refugees so far has combined foot-dragging, hard-heartedness, ineptitude and dishonesty'.[277]

Expanding on Ward's point above on the response of other countries in Europe, the Leader explains that as the invasion began, European Union countries quickly agreed that all Ukrainians could enter without visas and 'could live, work and receive welfare for at least a year'.[278] By contrast, the Johnson Government 'came up with the meanest offer imaginable',[279] with Patel stating that Ukrainians might be granted refuge if they had close family members already in Britain, but they would have to obtain visas before being let into the country. They could not get visas in Calais, the nearest port to Britain, because, as she told Parliament using the typical language of anti-immigration politicians, this could result in a 'surge'. Instead incredibly, according to the *Economist* Leader, Ukrainians who arrive in Calais 'have been given a KitKat bar and a packet of crisps and told to apply online, then make their way to Paris, Brussels or Lille for an appointment a week later'.[280] Pointing out that offices there are thinly staffed and often closed, it quotes Tory Backbenchers, not known for their enlightened responses to immigration, as describing the response 'robotic'. Of the cold-hearted Patel and the Home Office, the Leader states that this is unfair to robots 'which are at least efficient'.[281] On a final note about Patel, it reminds us that in 2021 when the Taliban took over, she promised not to abandon Afghans 'living in terror', after the Taliban took over. When her visa scheme opened, it was revealed that many of the 5,000 or so slots in the first year would be filled by Afghans already living in Britain.[282] As we saw earlier in a discussion of the current Nationality and Borders Bill, the Johnson/Patel cabal is now trying to criminalist asylum-seekers who turn up without 'permission'. As the *Economist* Leader concludes:

> The Home Office has long been one of Britain's worst departments, partly because of its sprawling role. It manages both immigration and crime, so tends to view immigrants as actual or potential criminals. It should be cut in two. Neither arm should be run by the incompetent Ms Patel.[283]

On March 14, the Homes for Ukraine scheme allows individuals, charities, community groups and businesses in the UK to bring Ukrainians to stay in their home or in separate accommodation, including those with no family ties to the UK. Meanwhile, on March 18, *Guardian* writer Amelia Gentleman reported that refugees waiting to travel under a separate scheme for those with relatives voiced frustration at the length of time the Home Office was taking to process UK visas, despite Government promises to streamline the system.[284] Over 40,000, she points out, have applied for Ukraine family scheme visas and are waiting for their applications to be approved, with many of them staying in hotels in countries bordering Ukraine, 'repeatedly checking their emails to see if visa clearance has been granted.[285] For example, in Bucharest many of the hotels are crowded with refugees who have struggled to find accommodation for more than one night. When the MP of the son of one of them, a British citizen, asked the Home Office why the process was taking longer than anticipated, the reply was that further checks had been requested. 'I feel disappointed', he said. 'She has applied previously for a UK visa many, many times, so I'm not clear what they're actually checking'.[286] Underlining once again the true nature of UK attempts to keep out immigrants under the hostile environment, another UK citizen was still waiting for visas for her parents, 84 and 82, to be approved two weeks after they applied. She commented:

> Everything is done to make this process as difficult and complicated as possible. I was advised that my parents should fall into a priority category due to their age and health issues. We are surviving on a credit card as nobody could foresee being drawn into such a complicated red tape visa process. There is no communication with the [Home Office] and there is no mechanism allowing us to track our progress online.[287]

As we have seen in this book, in recent years many of the responses by the Tory and many other parties to (attempted) immigration have been xeno-racist while for refugees and asylum seekers more generally they have been hybridist (see the Introduction of explanations of these terms). This is due to the countries of origin of the former, mainly from central and eastern Europe since the fall of the Berlin Wall in 1989, and due to the various perceived 'ethnicities' of the latter. In the case of Ukraine, apart from the aforementioned perceived need by Johnson, Patel and the Home Office to keep out *all* immigrants in the hostile environment, clear instances of colour-coded racism are emerging in Ukraine.

A growing number of refugees are pointing out that the UK Government is ignoring them because they are Black.[288] One of them, Alani Iyanuoluwa fled the capital Kyiv in early March as the Russian invasion intensified. As she made her way across Europe, she hoped to be reunited with family in London. Yet for 10 days she was stranded in a French port because she is Nigerian. Staying in Boulogne-sur-Mer, all three fear returning to Nigeria because of the dangers of kidnapping and trafficking, but say that as non-Ukrainian nationals they are not eligible for the British schemes, despite two of them having family in the UK: 'We're coming from war and they are telling us that without a Ukrainian passport we can't come to the UK, but the UK should consider all residents living in Ukraine when the war started'.[289] Iyanuoluwa is among a large group identified by charities that appears to have been split up from other Ukrainians by authorities because they are Black. Clare Moseley, founder of the charity Care4Calais, said: 'The UK schemes to help Ukrainian refugees come to Britain are heavily biased towards Ukrainian nationals. But they are not the only people whose homes and lives have been destroyed by the conflict'.[290] In the words of Alba Kapoor, senior policy manager at the Runnymede Trust, the UK's response to the Ukrainian crisis had thrown up questions of parity amid claims that Black people fleeing the conflict tended to be 'dehumanized' and viewed as African migrants rather than Ukrainian refugees: 'There's an obvious question, which is why people of colour who are fleeing war and terror and persecution do not have the right to equal treatment to others'.[291] She went on:

We are still confronted by an inability to properly conceive people from the global south as humans if they are trying to flee war and persecution. That's a sad place to be – it's not just the government, but also the press.[292]

Jabeer Butt, chief executive of the Race Equality Foundation, concurred:

Devastatingly, race has undoubtedly been an issue in the level of support provided by the UK government for refugees from Ukraine ... This feels like being asked by the government to accept that in Britain we value the lives of people with a certain skin colour over others.[293]

Such revelations would surely gladden the heart of one ex-Tory MEP and journalist Daniel Hannan who wrote in *The Telegraph* towards the end of February:

They seem so like us. That is what makes it so shocking. Ukraine is a European country. Its people watch Netflix and have Instagram accounts, vote in free elections and read uncensored newspapers. War is no longer something visited upon impoverished and remote populations. It can happen to anyone.[294]

The Johnson Government's tardy and bureaucratic response to Ukrainian refugees is hardly surprising given the tightening of the hostile environment under which it operates, as it continues to play to its hard-line anti-immigration supporters, including its red wall voters (see earlier in this chapter). This is in direct contrast to the speed with which it tried to get the Nationality and Borders Bill passed.

MSF, who employ over 35,000 personnel across 70 countries, described Commons votes on March 22 as 'shameful" after Tory MPs 'ripped out amendments proposed by the House of Lords'.[295] As Stone notes, the votes come as three million people were fleeing Ukraine. Opposition MPs warned that the bill could criminalize these Ukrainians fleeing war and branded the new laws a 'traffickers charter'.[296] The Tories had reinserted the clauses that allow the Government to send refugees offshore and detain them indefinitely – a policy which aid groups say has caused 'terrible suffering' when tried by Australia.[297] Following the votes the bill gives the Government new powers to punish refugees for how they arrive in the UK. Proposals by the Lords to give people a safe route to join families in the UK were also rejected.[298] McCann referred to the criminalizing, detaining, pushing back and imprisoning refugees in offshore detention centres simply because of how they arrive in the UK,[299] while Pauline Chetcuti, head of policy at Oxfam, said the bill 'flagrantly undermines our obligations under international law':[300] 'The Ukrainian conflict painfully illustrates how innocent civilians everywhere have no choice but to flee conflict, persecution and violence. We need an asylum system that is based on the principle of protection, not punishment.'[301]

The House of Lords also voted to reject this clause of the bill, which would have given the Government powers to strip individuals of their British citizenship without notice. 'It's a complete nonsense, it's not workable and it diminishes this country in the eyes of the world', was the response of Alf Dubs, a Labour peer and refugee campaigner who escaped the Nazis in childhood.[302] Like the other Lords rejections outlined in the last section of this chapter, the bill now goes back to the House of Commons.

Grenfell Tower

Just before 1 a.m. on June 14, 2017, fire broke out in the kitchen of a fourth floor flat at the 23-storey tower block in North Kensington, West London, known as Grenfell Tower. As *BBC News* explains, within minutes the fire raced up the exterior of the building and then spread to all four sides. By 3 a.m., most of the upper floors were well alight.[303] It was the worst UK residential fire since World War II. As is well-known, Grenfell Tower was cladded with plastic-filled panels. Of the 72 people who died, a majority were people of colour in a working-class neighbourhood. In the words of Leslie Thomas QC, who represents bereaved families as well as the survivors:

> The Grenfell fire did not happen in a vacuum. A majority of the Grenfell residents who died were people of colour. Grenfell is inextricably linked with race. It is the elephant in the room. This disaster happened in a pocket of one of the smallest yet richest boroughs in London. Yet the community affected was predominantly working-class. That is the stark reality that cannot be ignored.[304]

He went on to compare the tragedy with the murder of George Floyd in the US, as well as the disproportionate number of Covid-19 deaths among people from minority ethnic backgrounds, noting the 'parallel themes' and adding 'Race and state obligation are at the heart of all three cases'.[305] The Grenfell Next of Kin group has called for an inquiry, formally set up on August 15, 2017, to 'investigate the extent of institutional racism as a factor' in the fire.[306] 'Legal submissions made to the inquiry', the Next of Kin group points out, 'explain there were four visitors to the tower among the dead and also stillborn Baby Logan Gomes. Of the remaining 67, 57 were from BAME [Black, Asian and other ethnic minority] communities',[307] while the English Housing Survey carried out at the time of the fire (2017–2018), found that 40% of those living in high-rise buildings in the social rented sector were from these backgrounds, compared to 14% of the population as a whole.[308] Disability Rights UK (DR UK) informs us that 'Fifteen of the 37 Disabled residents and 17 of the 67 children living in Grenfell Tower died in the fire'. As Fazilet Hadi, DR UK Head of Policy stated:

> Just read those figures again – almost half of those people who died in the Grenfell Tower fire were Disabled people or children. 41% of Disabled people who lived in the Tower died that night. A quarter of all the children who lived in the Tower died that night.[309]

Hadi underlined that the fire had serious disablist implications as well as racist ones:

> Disabled people knew they were sitting ducks should there be a disaster. They raised safety concerns which were dismissed time and again. The Inquiry has heard from residents who said they were 'bullied' and 'stigmatised' when they raised such concerns. The disproportionately high death rates of children and Disabled people in the Grenfell Tower fire is truly shocking and heart breaking. The evidence provided on the callous neglect of safety precautions by the Council and Management Company is breathtaking. Disability Rights UK is calling on the Government to urgently implement the Grenfell Tower Inquiry recommendations, requiring building owners and managing agents to prepare Personal Emergency Evacuation Plans for Disabled people who can't self-evacuate.[310]

In late March 2022, nearly five years after this unnecessary tragedy, London Labour Mayor Sadiq Khan pointed out that Tory Ministers had 'failed to complete a single recommendation' from the first phase of the public inquiry into Grenfell.[311] Sarah Haque notes that findings published in October 2019 urged changes to legislations:

> requiring owners of every high-rise residential building to carry out regular inspections of lifts and share details of the floorplans and cladding materials with their local fire and rescue service. It also urged the development of national guidelines for large-scale evacuations.[312]

According to the Mayor's office, as of March 2022, astonishingly none of these recommendations had been implemented, and no deadline had been provided by the Government for when they would be.[313] A spokesperson for the Justice4Grenfell campaign[314] commented:

> From the day of the fire, there has been no real political will for accountability or action. It is in the gift of the government to grant an inquiry; they agree to the terms of reference; they appoint the judge; yet there is no legal requirement for them to take on board recommendations and findings of [the] inquiries.[315]

Khan said he was 'extremely concerned' by the lack of progress made by the Government since the first phase of the inquiry was published more than two years ago. In contrast to the Tory Government, Khan announced that the London Fire brigade (LFB) had completed 26 out of 29 recommendations directed towards them and other fire and rescue services.[316] Khan rightly insisted that the Government and the housing and building industries act immediately rather than wait for the inquiry's phase 2 report – the hearing for which started in March 2022:

> Without faster action, the government is failing the Grenfell community, putting lives at risk and leaving residents feeling unsafe in their homes. The government, housing and building industries must not wait to implement the wholesale reforms that are needed to fix a broken system.[317]

In May 2022, it was revealed that Ministers have rejected a key recommendation from the Grenfell Tower public inquiry that all disabled tenants should be given personal emergency evacuation plans (Peeps), sparking anger from survivors and disability campaigners.[318] In 2019, Johnson had told Parliament, 'Where Sir Martin [Moore-Bick, the Chair of the Grenfell Tower Inquiry] recommends responsibility for fire safety to be taken on by central government, we will legislate accordingly', while Robert Jenrick, the Communities Secretary, at the time added, 'As the prime minister said in his opening remarks, the government will accept all of the findings of the report and accept them in full'.[319] Grenfell United, which represents bereaved people and survivors, said the decision 'has left us speechless. Outraged'.[320]

In its first phase, unsurprisingly the Inquiry concluded that the cladding fuelled the fire, while the second phase examined how it could have happened in the first place. As of the end of February 2022, according to Robert Booth, Social Affairs Correspondent for *The Guardian,* a senior official admitted that the Government knew in 2002, 15 years before the Grenfell Tower disaster, that plastic-filled cladding panels burned 'fast and fierce' and he believed they should not be used on tall buildings.[321] Arconic, the company that made the combustible polyethylene-filled panels on Grenfell, targeted the UK market because of less stringent requirements.[322] Taxpayer-funded tests 'showed the cladding panels failed "catastrophically", with flames reaching 20 metres into the air within five minutes'.[323] As well as Grenfell, similar panels went on to be used on more than 400 high-rise blocks. Under a European classification of combustibility, the panels were likely to be ranked as D, which meant they should not be used on tall buildings. The safest class is A.[324]

Who is responsible for Grenfell?

Between the outbreak of the fire until the time of writing (April 2022), the Government in power has, of course, been Tory, first that of Theresa May (see chapter 9; see also chapter 8 for May's policies before her premiership) and Boris Johnson. The owner of Grenfell Tower at the time of the fire up to April 2022 is Kensington and Chelsea London Borough Council. The Council has been controlled by the Tories since 1964. Construction of Grenfell Tower began in 1972 and was completed in 1974. Before and during the fire, it was managed by Kensington and Chelsea Tenant Management Organisation. After the fire, its contract was terminated, and it has been managed by the Council. It is awaiting demolition. So, who should be held responsible for Grenfell? While all the above constituencies must take their share of the blame, UK governments, Labour as well as Tory (Labour Governments were in power in 2002 when Arconic started targeting the UK until mid-2007; since then it has been all Tory) were ultimately responsible.

Hyland, has argued that when 'the list is drawn up of those criminally responsible for the Grenfell Tower fire in London, Boris Johnson's name should be at the top'.[325] Just after the fire when he was Foreign Secretary in Theresa May's Government, he described it as 'political game-playing' to suggest that 'this tragedy was somehow caused by fire service cuts'.[326] This is 'unbelievable', he declared.[327] At the same time, a video clip from 2013 was becoming widely viewed on YouTube.[328] In it he is seen telling a Labour Party London Assembly member to 'get stuffed' when he accuses Johnson of lying over the scale and consequences of cuts to the London Fire Brigade (LFB).[329] If Johnson is reacting so defensively, Hyland goes on, 'it is because in his capacity as mayor he forced through massive cuts in the LFB budget despite repeated warnings they would cost lives'.[330]

She explains that the London fire service at the time was the fifth largest in the world and covered a metropolitan area of nearly 14 million people. In addition to firefighting, it responds to emergency situations, including traffic accidents and terror incidents:

> Johnson took a sledgehammer to this vital provision. In 2012, he brought forward proposed cuts of £65 million, amounting to a 15 percent reduction in the LFB's £448 million annual budget. In words that should be branded on his forehead, he justified this on the grounds of 'the declining number of fire deaths'.[331]

Robert Booth, a major shareholder in Arconic, donated nearly £25,000 to Johnson and the Tory Party, with the most recent donation recorded in 2017, the year of the fire.[332] The bereaved and survivors have called on Johnson to return the money to Elliott Advisors UK, the British arm of a US private equity company that has a 10% holding in the $14 billion (£10.4 billion) annual turnover business, on the grounds that the 'cosy relationship' undermined trust in the Government and Grenfell.[333] As Karim Mussilhy, vice-chair of Grenfell United who lost his uncle, Hesham Rahman, in the fire, put it:

> How can we trust this government to deliver truth, justice and change when they themselves, including the prime minister, take donations from one of Arconic's major shareholders. Right now Arconic is getting away with not cooperating fully with the inquiry and the government appears not to be doing enough. Is this cosy relationship one of the reasons?[334]

Research by Grenfell United has revealed the British arm made donations to the Tories in 2008, 2016 and 2017, with the first being made directly to Johnson when he was the MP for Henley-on-Thames and before Elliott invested in 2015, at which point Arconic was part of Alcoa. The other two donations are believed to relate to Torty Party fundraising events.[335]

In December 2019, Johnson picked engineer Benita Mehra to sit on the Grenfell Tower Inquiry Panel, but she was forced to quit after some of the bereaved established she previously ran an organization that received a £71,000 grant from the charitable arm of Arconic.[336] Survivors pointed out that the grant created a clear conflict of interest and described Mehra's appointment as 'a slap in the face' for justice,[337] while lawyers for dozens of the Grenfell community complained her selection created 'a clear appearance of bias'.[338]

The Windrush scandal

In the second part of chapter 3, I discussed the beginnings of the existence of the Windrush Generation from 1948 with the arrival of the *Empire Windrush* at Tilbury Docks, while in chapter 4, I referred again to the Windrush Generation in the context of the anti-Black riots of 1958. In chapters 8 and 9, I showed the effects of the hostile environment on that group of people under Theresa May as Home Secretary and Prime Minister, respectively. No doubt members of that group of people will have been appalled as have many others by Boris Johnson's colour-coded racism as discussed at the beginning of this chapter and will also be disgusted at the racist policies that his Government is enacting.

Patel promises reform of the Home Office following *Windrush Lessons Learned Review*

In 2020 Patel promised significant cultural and systemic reform of the Home Office, as she accepted all 30 recommendations of an independent review into the Windrush scandal,[339] the *Windrush Lessons Learned Review*,[340] committing the Tory Government to undertake a 'scrupulous' evaluation of the risks and effectiveness of hostile environment legislation, and to introduce a new Home Office mission statement based on 'fairness, humanity, openness, diversity and inclusion', and force a change in culture to recognize that migration and wider 'Home Office policy is about people' and should be 'rooted in humanity'.[341] This 'decision' was made two days after Wendy Williams, the author of the review, stated that the risks posed by the hostile environment policy were flagged to the Home Office by 'other groups and stakeholders' but because ministers ignored the warnings, the outcome of the Windrush scandal was 'both foreseeable and avoidable',[342] and that 'The Home Office has a very stark choice. It can decide not to implement my recommendations and, if that happens, then I think there is a very grave risk of something similar happening again'.[343] In its conclusions, the review found that the Home Office displayed 'ignorance and institutional thoughtlessness' on the subject of 'race', in part consistent with institutional racism.[344] It also described the Home Office as characterized by a 'culture of disbelief and carelessness' and that there was a 'lack of empathy for individuals'.[345]

In a Commons statement, Patel said:

> I was clear when Wendy Williams published her Lessons Learned review that I would listen and I would act. I have heard what she has said and I will be accepting the recommendations she has made in full. I am committed to ensuring that the Home Office delivers for each part of the community it serves and I will come back to update the house on how we will be implementing the recommendations before the summer recess.[346]

Patel added: 'My determination to right the wrongs and the injustices suffered by the Windrush generation is undiminished and I will do all I can to make sure that more people are helped and more people are compensated in full. And if additional resources are needed, they will be provided'.[347]

Windrush compensation scheme

Since 2018, a compensation scheme has been 'operating' to recompense the many thousands of British residents who were denied healthcare, housing or the right to work: in theory 'righting the wrongs' of the Windrush scandal.[348] According to Jenna Macfarlane, writing for *The Scotsman,* towards the end of November 2021 it was expected that between £60 million and £260 million would be paid in compensation to around 11,500 people.[349] In that month, a cross-party Commons Home Affairs Committee revealed that it believed responsibility for the scheme should be transferred out of the Home Office, after discovering 'a litany of flaws' in how it was being managed.[350] As of the end of September, she points out, 'just 20.1% of the initially estimated 15,000 eligible claimants had applied, 5.8% had received ... [some] ... payment, and 23 individuals had died without receiving compensation at all'.[351] As the Committee put it: 'The treatment of the Windrush generation by successive governments and the Home Office was truly shameful'.[352] As if to add insult to injury, in January 2022 four Windrush generation descendants lost their High Court battle for the scheme for victims to be widened to include them.[353] Yvonne Williams, Yvonne Smith, Jennifer Ulett-Hall and Damian Gabrielle argued that the scheme should be extended beyond its current parameters to include descendants of the Windrush generation such as them.[354] As Diane Taylor explains, the current rules state that children who arrived as adults over the age of 18 after 1988 are excluded from the scheme. Moreover, this group do not have a path to citizenship through the scheme even if they have been resident in the UK for many years. Thus, all are at risk of removal from the UK, even though all four have Windrush families to whom they came to the UK to join, while the three women, Williams, Smith and Ulett-Hall, are all grandmothers.[355] Gabrielle, who arrived in the UK two months after his 18th birthday to join his father who came to the UK in 1961 and has lived there continuously since then, argued that it was because of the problems his father experienced due to Windrush Generation discrimination that he was unable to bring Gabrielle to the UK to join him until after that birthday.[356] Both Smith and Williams were detained at Yarl's Wood for several months because of Home Office plans to deport them to Jamaica. Grace Brown, counsel for the four, argued that discretion should be exercised based on the individual facts of the group, who arrived in the UK over the age of 18 to join Windrush generation family members, but Edward Brown, counsel for the Home Secretary, put the case that none of the claimants fell within any of the Windrush categories and that they had not suffered the injustices of the Windrush Generation.[357] Following the victory of the Home Secretary, Gabrielle responded:

> I am absolutely devastated by today's decision. Most of my adult life has been in limbo. For me, the UK is my home. It's where my mum, dad, brothers, sisters and extended family all live. I thought that today would have given me – and other Windrush descendants who are in a similar predicament – hope. But that has been taken away from us.[358]

Karen Doyle of Movement For Justice, which has campaigned for inclusion of Windrush descendants in the Windrush scheme, said:

> The damage done to the Windrush generation was not just to the individuals. It was damage done to whole families separated across borders. Families who came to rebuild Britain and were subject to brutal discrimination and racism. Many had to leave children behind they would otherwise have brought. Reuniting and offering security to those families now in the wake of the Windrush scandal would have been putting the government's apologies into action. Yet this government continues to fail the Windrush generation and their families at every stage. We are deeply disappointed in this decision but will continue to fight for the recognition and status of Windrush descendants.[359]

The Home Office response including the hypocrisy of the last sentence should come as no surprise to readers. Its spokesperson commented:

> We're pleased the court found in the department's favour. The Windrush scheme was designed to recognise the existing status and connection to the UK of members of the Windrush generation and their eligible children. The home secretary and the department remain steadfast in our commitment to members of the Windrush generation.[360]

Windrush: Home Office has failed

Inevitably, given the preceding analyses of the 'hostile environment' in this book, a progress report by Williams in March 2022 found that The Home Office had broken its promise to change its culture rendering completely hollow Patel's acceptance in full of Williams' recommendations.[361] Two years on, only eight of the 30 recommendations had been fully acted on. In Williams' words: 'The failure to complete the review of the compliant environment policy [as we saw earlier the meaningless changing of 'really hostile' to 'compliant' was announced by Sajid Javid when he became Home Secretary in March 2018] will fundamentally hamper the department's efforts to learn lessons and move on constructively'.[362] For example, the Home Office failed to appoint a migrants' commissioner, one of Williams' key measures. In addition, more efforts were needed to increase the number of Black, Asian and minority ethnic people at senior levels in the Home Office.[363] Williams was concerned in particular with the compensation scheme (discussed in the last paragraph) quoting a small poll of applicants that she had done that revealed that 76% said they had not been treated respectfully by Home Office staff, and 97% did not trust the Home Office to deliver on its commitments. Moreover, about 386 claimants had waited more than a year for their claims to be resolved, including 179 waiting more than 18 months:[364]

> I met people who were still in severe financial and personal difficulties two years on from my original review. Some were unable to find work after time away from the job market. Others were in temporary accommodation, having to live with families or facing eviction because of unpaid bills. Many still had unmet physical and psychological needs and had experienced a sense of loss and devastation which had fundamentally affected their ability to cope, undermining their sense of identity and feelings of self-worth.[365]

As Gentleman points out, 'Several anonymous Home Office staff interviewed by Williams expressed concern about the scheme. One told her: "Our approach does not scream 'righting the wrongs' or compassion, but 'how little can we get away with paying out'".'[366] Tellingly, although the Home Office had introduced a training programme to educate staff on the 'legacy of Empire and colonialism', only 163 people out of a total of about 38,000 had visited the Windrush learning hub on its internal intranet system.[367]

After his case was highlighted in *The Guardian*, one person affected by the Windrush scandal in similar ways to Paulette Wilson (discussed in chapter 9) was Anthony Bryan who was held in removal centres for five weeks and booked on a flight to Jamaica that he had left in 1965 when he was eight years old.[368] While officials have since acknowledged he was in the UK legally, as of April 2022 he had still not resolved his claim for compensation, and was appealing against the sum offered by the Home Office:

> Their offer doesn't reflect what I went through – it felt like an insult. I don't think the Home Office has changed; when the spotlight is on them they make promises, but once the public attention moves away nothing happens.[369]

Notes

1 Halliday, Josh and Goodman, Joe. 2019. 'Johnson accused of racial stereotyping with view on Nigerians', *The Guardian,* November 28. https://www.theguardian. com/politics/2019/nov/28/johnson-accused-of-racial-stereotyping-with-view-on-nigerians.

2 Johnson, Boris. 2000. 'Am I guilty of racial prejudice? We all are', *The Guardian*, February 21. https://www.theguardian.com/uk/2000/feb/21/lawrence. ukcrime3.

3 Ibid.

4 Johnson. 2000.

5 Stone, Jon. 2019. 'Boris Johnson said that seeing "bunch of black kids" makes alarm bells go off in his head, in old column', *The Independent,* November 22. https://www.independent.co.uk/news/uk/politics/boris-johnson-bunch-bla ck-kids-racist-column-guardian-a9213356.html.

6 Johnson. 2000.

7 Cited in Bloom, Dan. 2019. 'Boris Johnson said "bunch of black kids" made him "turn a hair" in old column', *Daily Mirror,* November 22. https://www. mirror.co.uk/news/politics/boris-johnson-said-bunch-black-20889302.

8 Cited in Bloom. 2019.

9 Ibid.

10 Bowcott and Jones. 2008.

11 Bowcott, Owen and Jones, Sam. 2008. 'Johnson's "piccaninnies" apology', *The Guardian*, January 23. https://www.theguardian.com/politics/2008/jan/23/ london.race.

12 Cited in Kuo, Lily. 2016. 'Britain's new foreign secretary once referred to Africa's "watermelon smiles" and "piccaninnies"', *Quartz Africa,* July 14. http s://qz.com/africa/731695/britains-new-foreign-secretary-once-referred-to-a fricas-watermelon-smiles-and-piccaninnies/.

13 Owen and Jones. 2008.

14 Bergman, Sirena. 2020. 'Boris Johnson just said "black lives matter"– let's remember the horrifyingly racist things he's said', *The Independent,* June 3. https://www. indy100.com/news/boris-johnson-racist-keir-starmer-pmqs-george-floyd-black-li ves-matter-9546586.

15 Kuo. 2016.
16 Learmouth, Andrew. 2020. 'Joe Biden remembers Boris Johnson's Barack Obama comments', *The Argus,* November 9. https://www.theargus.co.uk/news/18856809.joe-biden-remembers-boris-johnsons-racist-comments-barack-obama/.
17 Borger, Julian. 2018. 'Trump with better hair: how Obama White House saw Boris Johnson', *The Guardian,* May 31. https://www.theguardian.com/us-news/2018/may/31/trump-with-better-hair-how-obama-white-house-saw-boris-johnson.
18 Bergman, Sirena. 2020. 'Boris Johnson just said "black lives matter', *The Independent,* June 3. https://www.indy100.com/news/boris-johnson-racist-keir-starmer-pmqs-george-floyd-black-lives-matter-9546586.
19 Theodoracopulos, Taki. 2003. 'Thoughts on thuggery', *The Spectator,* January 11.
20 Ibid.
21 Ibid.
22 Ibid.
23 http://www.mlahanas.de/Greeks/NewLiteratur/TakiTheodoracopoulos.html.
24 Ibid.
25 Ibid.
26 Mudde, Cas. 2015. 'The Trump phenomenon and the European populist radical right', *The Washington Post,* August 28. https://www.washingtonpost.com/news/monkey-cage/wp/2015/08/26/the-trump-phenomenon-and-the-european-populist-radical-right/.
27 Ecarma, Caleb. 2020. 'Call it the Tucker Carlson wing of the GOP: The *American Conservative* wants to be the *Atlantic* of the Right'. https://www.vanityfair.com/news/2020/04/the-american-conservative-the-right-atlantic.
28 Hollander, Gavriel. 2013. 'Spectator editor defends column supporting Greek far-right party Golden Dawn', *PressGazette,* July 23. https://pressgazette.co.uk/spectator-editor-defends-column-supporting-greek-far-right-party-golden-dawn/.
29 McBain, Sophie. September 26, 2020. 'The rise of the Proud Boys in the US, Who are the self-styled gang of Western chauvinists Trump asked to "stand back and stand by"?' https://www.newstatesman.com/uncategorized/2020/10/rise-proud-boys-us.
30 JTA. Respected British magazine publishes defence of Nazi German troops Far-right Spectator columnist Taki says readers should feel sorry for Wehrmacht soldiers at Normandy, who were 'sitting ducks'. https://www.timesofisrael.com/respected-british-magazine-publishes-defense-of-nazi-german-troops/.
31 'Taki Theodoracopulos'. Undated.
32 Cited in *Evening Standard.* 2008. 'Boris says sorry over "blacks have lower IQs" article in the Spectator', *Standard,* April 2. https://www.standard.co.uk/news/mayor/boris-says-sorry-over-blacks-have-lower-iqs-article-in-the-spectator-6630340.html.
33 Ibid.
34 Ibid.
35 Ibid.
36 Ibid.
37 Ibid.
38 Stewart, Heather. 2019. 'Boris Johnson elected new Tory leader', *The Guardian,* July 23. https://www.theguardian.com/politics/2019/jul/23/boris-johnson-elected-new-tory-leader-prime-minister.
39 Cited in Stewart. 2019.
40 Stewart, 2019.
41 Ibid.

42   Elgot, Jessica. 2019. 'As government announces it will prorogue parliament, we answer the key questions', *The Guardian,* August 28. https://www.thegua rdian.com/politics/2019/aug/28/what-is-prorogation-prorogue-parliam ent-boris-johnson-brexit. Prorogation is a formal mechanism to end a session of Parliament, normally for only a short time until proceedings begin again with a new Queen's speech. It means Parliament's sitting is suspended and it ends all current legislation under discussion (Elgot. 2019).

43   Meredith, Sam. 2019. 'What is the Irish backstop? All you need to know about the border dispute blocking an orderly Brexit', CNBC, September 11. https://www.cnbc.com/2019/09/11/brexit-what-is-the-irish-backstop-and-why-is-it-so-contr oversial.html.

44   O'Carroll, Lisa. 2019. 'Boris Johnson's Brexit alternative to the Irish backstop: what's new?', *The Guardian,* October 2. https://www.theguardian.com/politics/2019/oct/02/boris-johnsons-brexit-alternative-to-the-irish-backstop-whats-new.

45   *BBC News.* 2019. 'Election results 2019: Boris Johnson hails "new dawn" after historic   victory',   December   13.   https://www.bbc.co.uk/news/election-2019-50776671.

46   Kanagasooriam, James and Simon, Elizabeth. 2021. 'Red wall: The definitive description', *Political Insight,* 12 (3). September 13. https://journals.sagepub.com/doi/10.1177/20419058211045127. Kanagasooriam coined this term 'red wall' to refer to what he defined in a tweet as a huge edifice 'stretching from N Wales into Merseyside, Warrington, Wigan, Manchester, Oldham, Barnsley, Notting-ham and Doncaster'. Kanagasooriam, James. 2019. 'When you talk about cultural barriers to voting Tory', he concluded, 'this is where it is' (Twitter). https://twitter.com/jameskanag/status/1161639307536457730?lang=en-GB.

47   Hyland, Julie. 2017. 'Boris Johnson and the Grenfell Tower Inferno'.

48   Ibid.

49   *BBC News.* 2019. 'Prime Minister Boris Johnson: Does his cabinet reflect "modern Britain?"', July 25. https://www.bbc.co.uk/news/uk-politics-49034735.

50   Clarke, Seán. 2019. 'How representative is Boris Johnson's new cabinet?', *The Guardian,* July 25. https://www.theguardian.com/politics/ng-interactive/2019/jul/25/how-representative-is-boris-johnsons-new-cabinet.

51   https://www.bbc.co.uk/news/uk-politics-49570682.

52   https://www.bbc.co.uk/news/uk-politics-49573555.

53   https://www.independent.co.uk/news/uk/politics/jo-johnson-resigns-boris-mp-conservative-party-protest-brexit-no-deal-parliament-family-latest-a9092751.html.

54   Helm, Toby, Savage, Michael, Rawnsley, Andrew and Boffey, Daniel. 2019. 'Amber Rudd quits cabinet and attacks PM for "political vandalism"', *The Guardian,* September 7. https://www.theguardian.com/politics/2019/sep/07/amber-rudd-resigns-from-cabinet-and-surrenders-conservative-whip.

55   Syal, Rajeev. 2020. 'Dominic Cummings calls for "weirdos and misfits" for No 10 jobs', *The Guardian,* January 2. https://www.theguardian.com/politics/2020/jan/02/dominic-cummings-calls-for-weirdos-and-misfits-for-no-10-jobs.

56   Proctor, Kate. 2020. 'Calls for Tory aide to be sacked over "enforced contra-ception" remarks', *The Guardian,* February 16. https://www.theguardian.com/politics/2020/feb/16/tory-aide-wants-enforced-contraception-to-curb-p regnancies. Clearly sexist as well as a scientific racist, Sabisky had also tweeted, using logic premised on a hierarchy of value that demeans women in general and people with physical and intellectual disabilities as inferior and, incompe-tent, using logic premised on a hierarchy of value that demeans women in general and people with physical and intellectual disabilities as inferior and incompetent 'I am always straight up in saying that women's sport is more comparable to the Paralympics than it is to men's'. In addition, Sabisky

described Labour MPs Angela Rayner, Rebecca Long-Bailey, and Yvette Cooper as 'dim' (Proctor. 2020).

57 *BBC News*. 2020a. 'No 10 refuses to condemn adviser's remarks', February 17. https://www.bbc.co.uk/news/uk-politics-51535367.

58 *BBC News*. 2020b. 'Andrew Sabisky: No 10 adviser resigns over alleged race comments', February 18. https://www.bbc.co.uk/news/uk-politics-51538493.

59 Cited in Proctor. 2020.

60 Mason, Rowena. 2020. 'No 10 refuses to comment on PM's views of racial IQ', *The Guardian,* February 17. https://www.theguardian.com/politics/2020/feb/17/no-10-refuses-to-comment-on-pms-views-of-racial-iq.

61 Mason, 2020.

62 Ibid.

63 Cited in Mason. 2020.

64 Ibid.

65 Ibid.

66 *BBC News*. 2000. 'School gap blamed on black culture', August 21. http://news.bbc.co.uk/1/hi/education/890214.stm.

67 *BBC News*. 2006. 'Schools "too feminine for boys"', June 13. http://news.bbc.co.uk/1/hi/5074794.stm.

68 'Charity boss Tony Sewell to head government race commission', *BBC News,* 16 July 2020.

69 Syal, Rajeev, Mason, Rowena and O'Carroll, Lisa. 2019. 'Sky executive among Johnson's first appointments', *The Guardian,* July 23. https://www.theguardian.com/politics/2019/jul/23/sky-executive-among-johnson-first-appointments-andrew-griffith-munira-mirza.

70 Walker, Peter, Siddique, Haroon and Grierson, Jamie. 2020. 'Dismay as No 10 adviser is chosen to set up UK race inequality commission', *The Guardian.* https://www.theguardian.com/world/2020/jun/15/dismay-over-adviser-chosen-set-up-uk-race-inequality-commission-munira-mirza

71 Cited in Walker, Peter, Aamna Mohdin and Alexandra Topping. 2021. https://www.theguardian.com/world/2021/mar/31/uk-an-exemplar-of-racial-equality-no-10s-race-commission-concludes.

72 Xinhua. 2021. 'UK government's race report accused of trying to downplay structural racism', April 1. http://www.xinhuanet.com/english/europe/2021-04/01/c_139850382.htm.

73 Cited in Walker, Mohdin, and Topping. 2021.

74 Walker, Mohdin, and Topping. 2021.

75 Cited in Walker, Mohdin, and Topping. 2021.

76 Gentleman, Amelia. 2021. 'Windrush campaigners alarmed by omissions of No 10 race report', *The Guardian,* April 2. https://www.theguardian.com/world/2021/apr/02/windrush-campaigners-alarmed-by-omissions-of-no-10-race-report.

77 Ibid.

78 Cited in Gentleman. 2021.

79 Ibid.

80 Ibid.

81 Ibid.

82 Ibid.

83 Iqbal, Nosheen. 2021. 'Downing Street rewrote "independent" report on race, experts claim', *The Guardian,* April 11. https://www.theguardian.com/uk-news/2021/apr/11/downing-street-rewrote-independent-report-on-race-experts-claim.

84 Iqbal. 2021.

85 Cited in Iqbal. 2021.

86 Ibid.

87 Ibid.

88   Ibid.

89   Iqbal. 2021.

90   Ibid.

91   Syal, Rajeev. 2021. 'No 10 race adviser Samuel Kasumu resigns', *The Guardian,* April 1. https://www.theguardian.com/politics/2021/apr/01/no-10-ra ce-adviser-resigns-day-after-uk-structural-racism-report-published.

92   UK Government. 2014. 'Child poverty strategy 2014 to 2017,' June 26. https://www.gov.uk/government/publications/child-poverty-strategy-2014-to-2017. The Child Poverty Strategy was the plan of the ConDem Coalition Government (2010–2015) for action needed to reduce child poverty between 2014 and 2017 towards their goal of ending child poverty by 2020. The Social Mobility Commission (SMC) was created in 2016 as an advisory non-departmental public body of the Department for Education (DfE) in England.

93   Bulman. 2020 May. 'UK's progress on social mobility "disappointing" despite pledges by Boris Johnson and Theresa May, says watchdog', *The Independent,* June 10. https://www.independent.co.uk/news/uk/politics/social-mobility-u k-inequality-boris-johnson-theresa-may-commission-report-a9558726.html.

94   Ibid.

95   Ibid.

96   Ibid.

97   Social Mobility Commission. 2021. *State of the nation 2021: Social mobility and the pandemic,* July 2021, p. xv. https://assets.publishing.service.gov.uk/gov ernment/uploads/system/uploads/attachment_data/file/1003977/State_of_ the_nation_2021_-_Social_mobility_and_the_pandemic.pdf.

98   Michaela Community School. 2016. 'Boris loves Michaela!', June 28. YouTube. https://www.youtube.com/watch?v=2TI42MJPk3c.

99   Carr, Flora. 2018, April 20. 'What it's like to study at the strictest school in Britain', https://time.com/5232857/michaela-britains-strictest-school/.

100 https://time.com/5232857/michaela-britains-strictest-school/.

101 Carr. 2018.

102 Ibid.

103 Ibid.

104 Ibid.

105 Cited in Carr. 2018.

106 Siddique, Haroon. 2021. 'UK's "strictest" headteacher Katharine Birbalsingh made social mobility chief', *The Guardian,* October 10. https://www.thegua rdian.com/society/2021/oct/10/uks-strictest-headteacher-ktharine-birba lsingh-made-social-mobility-chief.

107 According to Aja Romano, before 2014, the call to 'stay woke" was, for many people, unheard of. However, the idea behind it was common within Black communities – the notion that staying 'woke' and alert to the deceptions of other people was a basic survival tactic (Romano, Aja. 2020. 'A history of "wokeness"', *Vox,* October 9. https://www.vox.com/culture/21437879/stay-woke-wokeness-history-origin-evolution-controversy). But in 2014, following the police killing of Michael Brown in Ferguson, Missouri, '"stay woke" suddenly became the cautionary watchword of Black Lives Matter activists on the streets, used in a chilling and specific context: keeping watch for police brutality and unjust police tactics'. In the years since Brown's death, it has become 'a shorthand for political progressiveness by the left, and as a denigration of leftist culture by the right' (see Romano. 2020. for a thorough analysis).

108 Cited in Siddique. 2021.

109 Maidment, Jack. 2021. '"It is time to be proud of who we are": Foreign Secretary Liz Truss warns "woke" attacks on the UK's past and culture are a

gift to Britain's enemies as she says the nation should embrace "our history, warts and all"', *Daily Mail*, December 8. https://www.dailymail.co.uk/news/article-10287385/Liz-Truss-warns-against-woke-attacks-UKs-history-culture.html.

110 Cited in Siddique. 2021.

111 Ibid.

112 Bergman, Sirena. 2020.

113 Cited in Bergman. 2020. It should be noted here that hours after the statue of the slave trader Edward Colston was toppled in Bristol on June 7, 2020, as part of the protests, Home Secretary and close Johnson ally, Priti Patel appeared on *Sky News* to demand that police pursue those responsible, saying their behaviour was 'utterly disgraceful' (Syal. 2022d). She stated, 'It is right that the police follow up on that and make sure that justice is taken, under-taken, with those individuals that are responsible for such disorderly and law-less behaviour' (cited in Syal. 2022d). The day after the protests, she boasted, 'The thugs and criminals responsible are already being brought to justice', and the arrest total already stood at 135 (Bond. 2022). Two days after, according to Rajeev Syal, it emerged that she had also called the chief constable of Avon and Somerset police to demand an explanation. Nazir Afzal, the former chief prosecutor for northwest England, 'questioned why she appeared to have become so heavily involved in pursuing those involved instead of leaving decisions to police and prosecutors' (Syal. 2022d). Afzal told *The Guardian*, 'We have a tripartite regime for a reason and that is so that politicians do not get involved in the operational decisions taken by the police. It may be that she has overstepped the boundaries of that arrangement that we have had for nearly 200 years. It is not something that I think she would want to repeat' (cited in Syal. 2022d). As Paul Bond, writing for the World Socialist Website (WSWS) points out, between 1672 and 1689, Colston's Royal African Company shipped more than 84,000 enslaved West African men, women, and children. Some 19,000 died on route and were dumped at sea. Residents, Bond explains, 'had long complained that the statue was an affront', and campaigners had been calling for its removal for decades (Bond. 2022). The 'Colston Four' – Sage Willoughby, Rhian Graham, Milo Ponsford and Jake Skuse – were charged with 'others unknown' with damaging the statue and its plinth without lawful excuse. When they were charged in January 2021, police used Covid-19 lockdown restrictions to deter supporters from demon-strations outside the court. Although the defendants were told they could be tried in a magistrates' court, all four insisted on their right to be tried before a jury. The effect was to draw attention to Colston's record, and to the calls for the statue's removal. They did not deny involvement but argued that the presence of the statue was 'a hate crime' and so its removal was no offence. Denying that they were trying to edit history, Willoughby pointed out that others were 'whitewashing history' (cited in Bond). As Bond concludes, 'The statue's plaque described Colston as "virtuous and wise"' (Bond. 2022).

114 Cited in Bergman. 2020.

115 Bergman. 2020.

116 Ibid.

117 Mathers, Matt. 19 January 2021. 'What has Boris Johnson said about Trump? PM has attempted to distance himself from the president in recent weeks'. https://www.independent.co.uk/news/uk/politics/boris-johnson-donald-trump-comments-b1789384.html.

118 Mathers. 2021.

119 Cited in Mathers. 2021.

120   Stone, Jon. 2020a. 'Boris Johnson said colonialism in Africa should never have ended and dismissed Britain's role in slavery', *The Independent,* June 13. https://www.independent.co.uk/news/uk/politics/boris-johnson-colonialism-africa-brit ish-empire-slavery-a9564541.html?amp.

121   Cited in Stone. 2020a.

122   Ibid.

123   Ibid.

124   Ibid. For a discussion of the colonial powers' scramble for Africa, see chapter 2.

125   Stone. 2020a.

126   Cited in Stone. 2020a.

127   Ibid.

128   Stone, Jon. 2020b. 'Boris Johnson says time to stop "cringing embarrassment" about British history after BBC Proms drops Rule Britannia lyrics', *The Independent,* August 25. https://www.independent.co.uk/news/uk/politics/bor is-johnson-bbc-proms-rule-britannia-lyrics-row-british-history-black-lives-ma tter-a9687816.html?amp.

129   Ibid.

130   Cited in Stone. 2020b.

131   Ibid.

132   Goodwin, Henry. 2021. 'Have the Tories become the party of the far-right?', *The London Economic,* January 28. https://www.thelondoneconomic.com/poli tics/have-the-tories-become-the-party-of-the-far-right-218330/.

133   Jonathan Evans, Baron Evans of Weardale, Director General 2007–13, Security Service. Undated. https://www.mi5.gov.uk/sir-jonathan-evans.

134   Goodwin, Henry. 2021.

135   Ibid.

136   Cited in Goodwin. 2021.

137   Rawlinson, Kevin. 2018. 'Britain First leaders jailed over anti-Muslim hate crimes', *The Guardian*, March 7. https://www.theguardian.com/world/2018/mar/07/britain-first-leaders-convicted-of-anti-muslim-hate-crimes.

138   Cited in Goodwin. 2021.

139   Cited in Kuenssberg, Laura. 2022. 'Nusrat Ghani: PM orders Cabinet Office to investigate "Muslimness" claim', *BBC News,* January 24. https://www.bbc.co.uk/news/uk-politics-60108377.

140   Cited in *BBC News.* 2022. 'Nusrat Ghani: Muslimness a reason for my sacking, says ex-minister', January 23. https://www.bbc.co.uk/news/uk-p olitics-60100525.

141   Cited in *Sky News.* 2022. 'Chief whip denies claims he told Tory MP she was sacked as a minister due to her Muslim faith', January 23. https://news.sky.com/story/chief-whip-denies-claims-he-told-mp-she-was-sacked-as-a-minis ter-because-of-her-muslim-faith-12523176.

142   *Sky News.* 2022.

143   *BBC News.* 2022.

144   Cited in *BBC News.* 2022.

145   Cited in *Sky News.* 2022.

146   Cited in *BBC News.* 2022.

147   Kuenssberg. 2022.

148   Ibid.

149   Cited in *BBC News.* 2022.

150   Ibid.

151   Ibid.

152   Cited in Kuenssberg. 2022.

153   Ibid.

154   Ibid.

155 Forsyth, Alex. 2022. 'Nusrat Ghani: Ex-minister's claims reignite rows over Tories and Islam', *BBC News*, January 24. https://www.bbc.co.uk/news/uk-politics-60118044.

156 Ibid.

157 Ibid.

158 Ibid.

159 Ibid.

160 Cowburn, Ashley. 2022. 'Boris Johnson labelled "moral vacuum" over Savile comments by former Tory chairman', *The Independent,* February 4. https://www.independent.co.uk/news/uk/politics/boris-johnson-lord-patten-resigna tions-b2007801.html.

161 Littlejohn, Georgina. 2020. '"Boris Johnson isn't a Conservative, he's a nationalist", says former Tory chair Lord Patten', *The Independent,* December 12. https://inews.co.uk/news/brexit/boris-johnson-isnt-a-conservative-hes-a-nationalist-says-former-tory-chair-lord-patten-792618.

162 Goodwin. 2021.

163 Cited in Electronic Immigration Network (EIN). 2021. 'Nationality and Borders Bill heads for the Lords after passing its final third reading in the Commons', December 8. https://www.ein.org.uk/news/nationality-and-bor ders-bill-heads-lords-after-passing-its-final-third-reading-commons.

164 UK Parliament. 2022. 'Nationality and Borders Bill returns to the Lords', April 5. https://www.parliament.uk/business/news/2021/december-2021/ lords-debates-nationality-and-borders-bill/#:~:text=The%20Nationality% 20and%20Borders%20Bill%20seeks%20to%3A,lives%20of%20those%20they% 20endanger.

165 Cited in Kimber, Charlie. 2022. 'Use your right to protest – it's the best response to the Tory police bill', *Socialist Worker,* 2803, April 28. https://socialistworker. co.uk/news/use-your-right-to-protest-its-the-best-response-to-tory-police-bill/.

166 Cited in Woodcock. 2022.

167 Care4Calais is a volunteer-run refugee charity working with refugees in the UK, France, and Belgium.

168 Cited in Syal. 2022a.

169 Ibid. 'Priti Patel's refugee pushback policy withdrawn days before legal review', *The Guardian,* April 25. https://www.theguardian.com/uk-news/ 2022/apr/25/uk-refugee-pushback-policy-withdrawn-judicial-review-priti-patel? fr=operanews.

170 Kimber. 2022.

171 Woodcock, Andrew. 2022. 'Priti Patel's controversial immigration plans pass through parliament despite warnings of harm to refugees', *The Independent,* April 28. https://www.independent.co.uk/news/uk/politics/priti-patel-refu gees-immigration-unhcr-b2067028.html.

172 Syal, Rajeev. 2022b. 'UK Rwanda plan for asylum seekers decried as inhumane, expensive and deadly', *The Guardian,* April 14. https://www.theguardian. com/uk-news/2022/apr/14/uk-rwanda-plan-for-asylum-seekers-decried-as-inhumane-deadly-and-expensive?CMP=Share_iOSApp_Other.

173 Syal. 2022b.

174 Syal. 2022b.

175 Mararike, Shingi. 2022. 'Rwanda: First glimpse inside the centre that will house Channel migrants', *Sky News*. https://news.sky.com/story/rwanda-first-glimpse-inside-the-centre-that-will-house-channel-migrants-12589911.

176 Mararike. 2022.

177 Ibid.

178 Solomon, Enver. 2022. 'UK asylum seekers sent to Rwanda? That takes punishment of fellow humans to a new level', *The Guardian,* April 14. https://

www.theguardian.com/commentisfree/2022/apr/14/uk-asylum-seekers-rwanda -government.

179   Syal, Rajeev. 2021b. 'Most people who risk Channel boat crossings are refugees – report', *The Guardian*, November 17. https://www.theguardian.com/uk-news/ 2021/nov/17/most-people-who-risk-channel-boat-crossings-are-refugees-report.

180   Solomon. 2022.

181   Syal. 2021b. These countries being the origin of the asylum seekers exem-plifies the fact that the Act enshrines hybridist racism rather than xeno-racism, the latter of which was a major issue under the May administration. The dif-ference between these two forms of racism is addressed in the Introduction to this book.

182   Solomon. 2022.

183   Amnesty International. 2021. 'Nationality & Borders Bill: The truth behind the claims'. https://www.amnesty.org.uk/nationality-borders-bill-truth-behind-claims.

184   Syal, Rajeev. 2022c. 'Theresa May questions "legality and practicality" of Rwanda asylum plan'; and 'Theresa May says she does not support Rwanda asylum plan – video', *The Guardian*, April 19. https://www. theguardian.com/politics/2022/apr/19/theresa-may-questions-legality-and-practicality-of-rwanda-asylum-plan?CMP=Share_iOSApp_Other.

185   Cited in Syal. 2020c.

186   Cited in Syal. 2022c.

187   Hatton, Ben. 2022. 'Johnson defends Rwanda after concerns over "dismal" human rights record', *The Independent*, April 15. https://www.independent.co.uk/ news/uk/rwanda-boris-johnson-government-prime-minister-african-b2058037. html.

188   Kelly, Nicola. 2022. '"I will die here, I can't go back to Africa": migrants respond to Rwanda removal', *The Guardian*, April 15. https://www.thegua rdian.com/world/2022/apr/15/i-will-die-here-i-cant-go-back-to-africa-migra nts-respond-to-rwanda-removal?CMP=Share_iOSApp_Other.

189   Cited in Kelly. 2022.

190   Ibid.

191   Kelly. 2022.

192   Beaumont, Peter. 2022. 'Rwanda: human rights fears in nation whose leader faces murder claims', *The Guardian*, April 14. https://www.theguardian.com/ world/2022/apr/14/rwanda-human-rights-fears-paul-kagame.

193   Human Rights Watch. 2021. 'Rwanda: round ups-linked to commonwealth meeting', September 27. https://www.hrw.org/news/2021/09/27/rwanda-round-ups-linked-commonwealth-meeting.

194   Ibid.

195   Ibid.

196   GOV.UK. 2022, April 15. 'Foreign travel advice Rwanda'. https://www.gov. uk/foreign-travel-advice/rwanda/local-laws-and-customs.

197   Cited in Syal. 2022b.

198   Ibid.

199   Ibid.

200   https://www.infomigrants.net/en/post/37620/record-number-of-migrant-cha nnel-crossings-in-2021#:~:text=Last%20year%2C%20more%20than%2028% 2C000,went%20missing%20during%20the%20attempt.

201   Cited in Syal. 2022b.

202   Ibid.

203   *Sky News*. 2022, 'Come up with a better plan than Rwanda migrants scheme, Patel challenges critics', April 18. https://news.sky.com/story/come-up-with-a -better-plan-than-rwanda-migrants-scheme-patel-challenges-critics-12592743#.

204   Ibid.

205 Cited in Syal, Rajeev and Brown, Mark. 2022. 'Home Office staff threaten mutiny over "shameful" Rwanda asylum deal', *The Guardian,* April 20. https://www.theguardian.com/uk-news/2022/apr/20/home-office-staff-threaten-muti ny-over-shameful-rwanda-asylum-deal?CMP=Share_iOSApp_Other.

206 *Sky News.* 2022.

207 Cited in Ringrose, Isabel. 2022. 'Fight against Tory plan to deport refugees to Rwanda', *Socialist Worker.* https://socialistworker.co.uk/news/fight-against-tory-p lan-to-deport-refugees-to-rwanda/?mc_cid=1eae71084f&mc_eid=e49f0a2036.

208 https://www.amnesty.org.uk/press-releases/uk-priti-patels-racist-nationality-a nd-borders-bill-drags-uks-reputation-through-mud.

209 Cited in *Sky News.* 2022.

210 Ibid.

211 Refugee Council. 2022. 'Safe routes save futures'. https://www.refugee council.org.uk/get-involved/campaign-with-us/safe-routes-save-futures/.

212 Ibid.

213 Ibid.

214 Ibid.

215 Ibid.

216 Ibid.

217 Ibid.

218 Jones. 2022.

219 *ITV News.* 2021. 'Who are Insulate Britain, the group blocking M25 traffic, and what are they campaigning for?', September 20. https://www.itv.com/news/2021-09-20/who-are-insulate-britain-the-group-blocking-the-m25-and-what-do-they-want.

220 Monbiot, George. 2022. 'The UK is heading towards authoritarianism: just look at this attack on a minority', *The Guardian,* January 12. https://www.theguardian.com/commentisfree/2022/jan/12/uk-authoritarianism-minority-policing-bill-roma-gypsy-traveller.

221 Gye, Hugo. 2022. 'Protesters who chain themselves to buildings could face six months in prison under Queen's Speech plan', *Independent,* May 10. https://inews.co.uk/news/politics/protesters-who-lock-themselves-to-buildingscould-face-six-months-in-prison-under-queens-speech-plan-1620450.

222 *BBC News.* 2022. 'What is the Police and Crime Bill and how will it change protests?', April 29. https://www.bbc.co.uk/news/uk-56400751.

223 Kirby, Dean. 2021, 'Black Lives Matter: Priti Patel says the 2020 protests were "dreadful" and she opposes taking a knee', *iNews,* February 12. https://inews.co.uk/news/uk/black-lives-matter-priti-patel-2020-protests-dreadful-opposes-taking-knee-870528.

224 Raab, Dominic and Patel, Priti. 2022. 'Boost for public safety as four justice bills receive Royal Assent', Ministry of Justice, Home Office. April 28. https://www.gov.uk/government/news/boost-for-public-safety-as-four-justice-bills-receive-royal-assent.

225 Independent Office for Police Conduct. 2022. 'National Stop and Search learning report, April 2022'. https://www.policeconduct.gov.uk/national-stop-and-search-learning-report-april-2022.

226 Home Office. 2021. Police powers and procedures: stop and search and arrests, England and Wales, year ending 31 March 2021. https://www.gov.uk/governm ent/statistics/police-powers-and-procedures-stop-and-search-and-arrests-engla nd-and-wales-year-ending-31-march-2021/police-powers-and-procedures-stop -and-search-and-arrests-england-and-wales-year-ending-31-march-2021.

227 Liberty. Undated. 'Police Powers/Stop and Search', Police. https://www.lib ertyhumanrights.org.uk/advice_information/stop-and-search/.

228   Agnew-Pauley, Winifred and Akintoye, Bisola. 2021. 'Stop and search dis-proportionately affects black communities – yet police powers are being exten-ded', *The Conversation*. August 3. https://theconversation.com/stop-and-sea rch-disproportionately-affects-black-communities-yet-police-powers-are-being-extended-165477.

229   GOV.UK. 2022. 'Foreign travel advice: Rwanda', April 15. https://www. gov.uk/foreign-travel-advice/rwanda/local-laws-and-customs.

230   This is a network of 170 organizations working towards a fair and effective criminal justice system. Agenda. 2022. 'Government must tackle persistent racism and gender inequality in the criminal justice system', January 31. https://wear-eagenda.org/government-must-tackle-persistent-racism-and-gender-inequality-in-the-criminal-justice-system/#:~:text=The%20Criminal%20Justice%20Alli-ance%20(CJA,research%20institutions%20and%20staff20associations.

231   Cited in Agnew-Pauley and Akintoye. 2021.

232   Ibid.

233   Lothian-McLean, Moya. 2022. 'Boris Johnson is revealing who he really is', *The New York Times*. January 10. https://www.nytimes.com/2022/01/10/op inion/boris-johnson-britain-bills.html; see also https://www.opendemocracy. net/en/opendemocracyuk/british-democracy-is-under-attack-we-must-fight-to-protect-it/.

234   *The Guardian*. 2022. 'Met to stop recording ethnicity of drivers stopped by its officers', October 11. https://www.theguardian.com/law/2022/may/16/ restrictions-on-police-stop-and-search-powers-permanently-lifted.

235   Monbiot. 2022.

236   Ibid.

237   Monbiot. 2022.

238   Cited in Kimber. 2022.

239   Monbiot. 2022.

240   Nuttall, Emma, Gilmore, Victoria and Buck, Tommy. 2020. 'No place to stop: Research on the five year supply of deliverable Gypsy and Traveller sites in the South East of England', January. https://www.gypsy-traveller.org/wp-content/uploads/2020/02/Research-onthe-five-year-supply-of-deliverable-Gypsy-and-Traveller-sites-in-the-South-East-of-England.pdf.

241   Monbiot. 2022.

242   Ibid.

243   Ibid.

244   Bowers, Jake. 2022. 'Out of site: Britain's nomadic people', *Friends of the Earth*. https://friendsoftheearth.uk/system-change/out-site-britains-nomadic-people.

245   Ibid.

246   Ibid.

247   Ibid.

248   Ibid.

249   Quarmby, Katherine. 2020. 'Hate targeted at Gypsy, Traveller and Roma linked to rise in suicides – report', *The Guardian*, December 10. https://www.theguardia n.com/world/2020/dec/10/hate-targeted-at-gypsy-traveller-and-roma-linked-to-rise-in-suicides-report.

250   Ibid.

251   Ibid.

252   Cited in Quarmby. 2020.

253   Quarmby. 2020.

254   Ibid.

255   Cited in Quarmby. 2020.

256   Bowers. 2022.

257 Ibid.

258 Ibid.

259 Dearden, Lizzie. 2021. 'Government says discrimination against black people and Travellers "objectively justified" with new laws', *The Independent*, September 13. https://www.independent.co.uk/news/uk/home-news/policing-bill-discrimination-black-travellers-b1919272.html.

260 Cited in Dearden. 2021.

261 Ibid.

262 Ibid.

263 Stone. 2020a.

264 Cited in Stone. 2020a.

265 GOV.UK. 2022. 'Guidance: Political impartiality in schools'. https://www.gov.uk/government/publications/political-impartiality-inschools/political-impartiality-in-schools.

266 Cited in Adams, Richard. 2022. 'Guidance on political impartiality in English classrooms "confusing" say teachers' unions', *The Guardian*, February 17. https://www.theguardian.com/education/2022/feb/17/guidance-on-political-impartiality-in-english-classrooms-confusing-say-teachers-unions.

267 Adams. 2022.

268 Cited in Adams. 2022.

269 Ibid.

270 Cited in Adams. 2022. With respect to climate change, the guidance states that in teaching scientific facts around climate change, teachers should not provide balance in the form of misinformation or unsubstantiated claims, but 'where teaching covers the potential solutions for tackling climate change, this may constitute a political issue'.

271 Adams. 2022.

272 Cited in Adams. 2022.

273 Freire, Paulo. 1985. *The politics of education: culture, power, and liberation* (Donald Macedo, Trans.), South Hadley, MA: Bergin & Garvey, p. 80.

274 Personal correspondence.

275 *The Economist*. 2022. 'The British government's response to Ukrainian refugees is sadly typical', March 12. https://www.economist.com/leaders/the-british-governments-response-to-ukrainian-refugees-is-sadly-typical/21808100.

276 Cited in *The Economist*. 2022.

277 *The Economist*. 2022.

278 Ibid.

279 Ibid.

280 Ibid.

281 Ibid.

282 Ibid.

283 Ibid.

284 Gentleman, Amelia. 2022a. 'Ukrainian refugees with UK relatives frustrated by Home Office visa delays', *The Guardian*, March 18. https://amp.theguardian.com/uk-news/2022/mar/18/ukrainian-refugees-with-uk-relatives-frustrated-by-home-office-visa-delays.

285 Ibid.

286 Cited in Gentleman. 2022a.

287 Ibid.

288 Townsend, Mark. 2022. 'Stranded Nigerians accuse UK of ignoring pleas of black refugees fleeing Ukraine', *The Guardian*, March 19. https://www.theguardian.com/world/2022/mar/19/stranded-nigerians-accuse-uk-of-ignoring-pleas-of-black-refugees-fleeing-ukraine.

289 Cited in Townsend. 2022.

290   Ibid.

291   Ibid.

292   Ibid.

293   Ibid.

294   MEE staff. 2022. 'Russia-Ukraine war: Western media criticised for racist "blonde hair blue eyes" coverage of invasion', *Middle East Eye,* February 27. https://www.middleeasteye.net/news/russia-ukraine-war-criticised-racism-western-coverage.

295   Stone. 2022.

296   Ibid.

297   Ibid.

298   Ibid.

299   Ibid.

300   Cited in Stone. 2022.

301   Ibid.

302   Lester, Nick, Goodall, Sophie and Hatton, Ben. 2022. 'Government suffers series of defeats in Lords on immigration overhaul', *WalesOnline,* March 1. https://www.walesonline.co.uk/news/uk-news/government-suffers-series-defeats-lords-23246439.

303   *BBC News.* 2019. 'Grenfell Tower: What happened', October 29. https://www.bbc.co.uk/news/uk-40301289.

304   *BBC News.* 2020. 'Grenfell Tower inquiry: Fire "inextricably linked with race"', July 7, 2020. https://www.bbc.co.uk/news/uk-53320082.

305   Cited in *BBC News.* 2020. For the statistics and the reasons for this, see Butcher, Benjamin. and Massey, Joel. 2020. 'Why are more people from BAME backgrounds dying from coronavirus?', *BBC News,* June 19. https://www.bbc.co.uk/news/uk-52219070.

306   Cited in *BBC News.* 2020.

307   *BBC News.* 2020.

308   Ibid.

309   Disability Rights UK. 2021. 'Almost half of Grenfell fire deaths were disabled people and children', March 31. https://www.disabilityrightsuk.org/news/2021/march/almost-half-grenfell-fire-deaths-were-disabled-people-and-children.

310   Cited in Disability Rights UK. 2021.

311   Cited in Haque, Sarah. 2022. 'No Grenfell inquiry recommendations enacted by government, says Sadiq Khan', *The Guardian,* March 21. https://amp.theguardian.com/uk-news/2022/mar/21/grenfell-inquiry-no-recommendations-implemented-sadiq-khan.

312   Haque. 2022.

313   Ibid.

314   Justice4Grenfell (J4G) 2021. J4G in its own words is a 'community-led organisation, focused on the long-term goal of obtaining justice for the bereaved families, survivors, evacuated residents, and the wider local community, collaborating with representative organisations'. As it explains, along with many other local groups and individuals, J4G stepped into the void left by the authorities, to try to meet the urgent needs of those impacted. Its work continues because of the on-going failure of the authorities to respond adequately to the disaster. J4G's ultimate aim is to ensure that such an event never happens again. For a list of its core aims, see Justice4Grenfell. 2021. 'About'. https://justice4grenfell.org/about/.

315   Cited in Haque. 2022.

316   Ibid.

317   Ibid.

318   Booth, Robert. 2022a. 'Outrage as ministers reject post-Grenfell safety plans for disabled people', *The Guardian,* May 18. https://www.theguardian.com/uk-news/

2022/may/18/outrage-as-ministers-reject-post-grenfell-safety-plans-for-disabled-people.

319 Cited in Booth. 2022a.
320 Ibid.
321 Booth, Robert. 2022b. 'Fire safety official admits tests showed cladding danger 15 years before Grenfell', *The Guardian,* February 28. https://amp.theguardian.com/uk-news/2022/feb/28/cladding-danger-evidence-15-years-before-grenfell-tower-fire.
322 Booth. 2022b.
323 Ibid.
324 Ibid.
325 Hyland. 2017.
326 Cited in Hyland. 2017.
327 Ibid.
328 YouTube. 2013. 'Boris Johnson tells London Assembly's Andrew Dismore to "get stuffed"', September 12. https://www.youtube.com/watch?v=UN3e-aYUusc.
329 Hyland. 2017.
330 Ibid.
331 Cited in Hyland. 2017.
332 Booth, Robert. 2020. 'Tory donor was key shareholder in Grenfell cladding firm Arconic', *The Guardian,* December 23. https://www.theguardian.com/uk-news/2020/dec/23/tory-donor-was-key-shareholder-in-grenfell-cladding-firm-arconic.
333 Ibid.
334 Cited in Booth. 2020.
335 Booth. 2020.
336 Ibid.
337 Cited in Booth. 2020.
338 Ibid.
339 Gentleman, Amelia. 2020. 'UK government to act on all 30 Windrush recommendations', *The Guardian,* June 23. https://www.theguardian.com/uk-news/2020/jun/23/uk-government-to-act-on-all-30-windrush-recommendations.
340 Williams, Wendy. 2020. *Windrush Lessons Learned Review.* March. https://assets.publishing.service.gov.uk/government/uploads/system/uploads/attachment_data/file/876336/6.5577_HO_Windrush_Lessons_Learned_Review_LoResFinal.pdf.
341 Cited in Gentleman. 2020.
342 *BBC News.* 2020. 'Windrush: "Grave risk" of scandal repeat, warns review author', June 22. https://www.bbc.co.uk/news/uk-53129844.
343 *BBC News.* 2020.
344 Cited in Gentleman. 2020.
345 Ibid.
346 Ibid.
347 Ibid.
348 Macfarlane, Jenna. 2021. 'Windrush Scandal: Who is the Windrush generation in the UK and the Windrush history explained', *The Scotsman,* November 24. https://www.scotsman.com/news/politics/windrush-scandal-who-is-the-windrush-generation-in-the-uk-and-the-windrush-history-explained-3282065.
349 Macfarlane. 2021.
350 Cited in Macfarlane. 2021.
351 Macfarlane. 2021.
352 Cited in Macfarlane. 2021.
353 Taylor, Diane. 2022. https://www.theguardian.com/uk-news/2022/jan/14/windrush-descendants-lose-fight-to-expand-compensation-scheme.

354　Ibid.
355　Ibid.
356　Ibid.
357　Ibid.
358　Cited in Taylor. 2022.
359　Ibid.
360　Ibid.
361　Gentleman, Amelia. 2022b. 'Windrush: Home Office has failed to transform its culture, report says', *The Guardian,* March 31. https://www.theguardian. com/uk-news/2022/mar/31/windrush-home-office-has-failed-to-transform-its-culture-report-says.
362　Cited in Gentleman. 2022b.
363　Gentleman. 2022b.
364　Cited in Gentleman. 2022b.
365　Ibid.
366　Gentleman. 2022b.
367　Ibid.
368　See Cole. 2020, pp. 80–81 for a discussion of Bryan.
369　Cited in Gentleman. 2022b.

Conclusion

This book has demonstrated how deeply entrenched racism is in the Tory Party and how it has saturated the Party from the beginning of the 19th century to the second decade of the 21st. I began with the life and times of Benjamin Disraeli. His Jewish background was significant in his conception of what it means to be English: his steadfast conviction that the 'great Caucasian race' was the superior one was related to his belief that it was the 'Semitic' or 'Arabian' branch of the Caucasian 'race' that was superior to the other branches, and, among Semites, it was Jewish people at the pinnacle of the hierarchy. He was on the receiving end of antisemitism from his political opponents from the very beginning. At the same time, as we saw, as well as being up-front about his belief in the supremacy of the White 'race', he also openly acknowledged his own colour-coded racism towards Black people in the colonies and his non-colour-coded anti-Irish racism. At the heart of his worldview was also a belief in centrality of nation and Empire, as well as 'race'.

I pointed out that in the decade bridging the 19th and 20th centuries, Britain was governed by a unionist coalition of Liberals and Conservatives, headed by two Tory Prime Ministers, Robert Gascoyne-Cecil and Arthur Balfour. During that time, the country took part in the second Boer War. That war is infamous for the establishment by the British of 'White concentration camps' in southern Africa that entailed the racialization of White Boers, and of 'Black concentration camps' for Black Africans.

An analysis of the invocation of imperialism on the campaign trail between 1880 and 1914 with respect to the Liberals and the Tories determined which was the 'party of imperialism' of the period and which championed imperialism more in the elections that took place. I revealed that it was the Tories. The upsurge in antisemitism that occurred following the Russian pogroms and the migration of Jews to the UK was exacerbated by East End Tory MPs William Evans-Gordon, Samuel Forde Ridley, Claude Hay, Walter Guthrie, Spencer Charrington, Thomas Dewar and Harry Samuel. The result was the Aliens Act of 1905, passed under the premiership of Balfour, that drastically reduced the numbers of Jewish people entering the UK. Balfour was not only antisemitic, but a White supremacist, having argued around the same time

DOI: 10.4324/9781003198673-16

against enfranchising Black People in South Africa because White and Black 'races' are not born equal, and education cannot change that. About six months after the Act gained royal assent, in the 1906 General Election Campaign Tory MPs attempted to use Jewish immigration to win them votes. For example, David Hope Kyd told the electorate that the sitting Liberal MP Stuart Samuel was pro-alien and it was 'no good sending to Parliament a man who stands up... for the foreign Jews' and what was needed was 'someone who could speak for the English in Whitechapel'. Another Tory, William Joynson-Hicks, mounted a racist campaign appealing to 'the British working man' to vote against 'Pro-Alien Radical Jews' (Samuel was Jewish) and 'push back this intolerable invasion'.

I also addressed the imperial and 'racial' politics of Winston Churchill. The first section focused briefly on the period between his role in the British army fighting and killing for the Empire and supporting and setting up internment camps in Kenya and examined Churchill's colonial racist views from 1920s to the end of his first premiership. As we saw, Churchill also believed in the superiority of the White 'race'. In addition, he was Islamophobic, although his love of Empire transcended this. The Churchill Government in the 1950s was actively involved in trying to restrict immigration from the former Empire to preserve the 'racial character' of English people. Surprisingly, many might think, Churchill was an early admirer of fascism and a late convert to anti-Nazism, though, it is important to stress, never a supporter of Nazi 'racial' policies. With respect to non-colour-coded racism, as First Lord of the Admiralty during World War I, Churchill was responsible for the deaths of ill-prepared Irish troops in Gallipoli, and as Secretary of State for War in 1920, deployed the hated Black and Tans to support the Ulster Royal Constabulary in crushing the IRA.

In 1960, I pointed out, Tory Prime Minister Harold Macmillan gave his famous 'Wind of Change' speech in which he said that whether we like it or not, independence of the colonies was inevitable. As a direct result, some members of the Tory Party formed the right-wing racist Conservative Monday Club, an outfit that believed in the repatriation of immigrants from the Commonwealth, and is still in existence today, aligned with, though no longer endorsed by, the Party.

I also looked at the General Election of 1964 where in Smethwick local Tory members were accused of using the slogan, 'If you want a ni**er for a neighbour, vote Liberal or Labour'. I considered the rise of Powellism, after Enoch Powell gave his infamous hate-filled rant, known as his 'rivers of blood' speech, in which he described immigration as a 'preventable evil', and referred to a conversation 'a middle-aged, quite ordinary working man' who told him that within a couple of decades, the Black man will have the whip hand over the White man. I also referred to his lesser-known East-bourne speech where he stated, 'The West Indian or Indian does not, by being born in England, become an Englishman. In law, he becomes a United Kingdom citizen by birth; in fact he is a West Indian or Asian still'.

In the General Election of 1970, where the Tories beat the Labour Government, incoming Prime Minister Edward Heath refused to disown Powell, an important figure in the election campaign. Heath's premiership included his policy of internment without trial in Ireland and the 'Bloody Sunday' massacre of 1972, when British soldiers shot unarmed civilians during a protest march against it. I pointed out that the so-called 'Ugandan Asian crisis', where Britain was obliged to admit thousands of Asians holding British passports and living in Uganda, gave a major boost to the Conservative Monday Club and the fascist National Front.

Prime Minister Margaret Thatcher's 'racecraft' attempted to normalize racism. In 1978, she made her infamous 'swamping' remarks that brought racism to the heart of Tory politics. In Ireland, her Government also oversaw the hunger strikes and the 'Blanket' and 'Dirty' protests culminating in the death of hunger striker Bobby Sands in Belfast in 1981. I explored the links between the British Army and the loyalist paramilitaries, a connection with which Thatcher was involved, and looked at Thatcher's own anti-Irish racism.

In 1980/1981, there was a series of uprisings in Bristol, London, Liverpool and Manchester, the prelude of which was the New Cross house fire, in which 13 young Black people were killed. Following the uprisings, the Scarman Report highlighted 'racial' disadvantage, inner-city decline and heavy-handed police stop-and-search operations and warned of the need for urgent action. Thatcher objected to the Report's criticism of the police and contemplated arming them if things got much worse. In 1982, Thatcher resurrected imperial warfare in the Falklands/ Malvinas to booster her popularity. Less popular was the visit of hard-line South African Prime Minister and future President, P. W. Botha to Chequers at a time when he was facing global isolation. She described it as a 'natural reservoir of goodwill'. Her own solution to South Africa, I pointed out, was a White ethno-state, specifically a return to pre-1910 South Africa, with a White mini state partitioned from their neighbouring Black states. Comments on South Africa by Tory politicians include Teddy Taylor who said: 'Nelson Mandela should be shot', while according to Labour MP Brian Wilson, Federation of Conservative Students (FCS) conferences had been littered with slogans like 'Hang Nelson Mandela'. During Apartheid, and while future Black President Mandela was still in prison, rising Tory star and future Prime Minister David Cameron enjoyed a 'jolly' there on an all-expenses trip paid for by a firm that campaigned against the sanctions that had been imposed on that country.

John Major, often thought of as a multiculturalist, I suggested, was actually an entrenched monoculturalist believing in the promotion of 'British values'. Under his premiership, a Black candidate was adopted as a Tory candidate in the forthcoming 1992 General Election, after which local Tories tried unsuccessfully to stop him.

During Theresa May's time in office, we witnessed the origins, launch and enactment of the hostile environment. This began with some draconian changes in family migration rules and continued with May's infamous 'go home or face arrest' vans sent into parts of London with high minority ethnic populations, an endeavour that even Nigel Farage found 'nasty' and 'unpleasant'. May's premiership saw the consolidation and impact of the hostile environment. This included a pledge to kick out foreign students and to end free movement once and for all. Her 2018 White Paper on Immigration has been described as the biggest single attack on migrant rights in a generation. In 2018, Home Secretary Sajid Javid's acknowledged that the Home Affairs Select Committee accused the Home Office of setting up immigrants to fail.

Boris Johnson's own personal racism as well the ongoing march of the hostile environment were central issues in the last part of the book. I gave examples of his racism from 1999 to the present, drawing mainly on newspaper articles that he wrote. It was also revealed, following Johnson's General Election victory in 2019, that he had had the support of the far right. I noted how in February 2020, Number 10 refused to disassociate Johnson from scientific racism, and discussed Johnson's denial of the existence of institutional racism in the aftermath of the Report of the Commission on Race and Ethnic Disparities (CRED) in July 2020. I demonstrated the rampant Islamophobia, and indeed sexism in the Tory Party under Johnson. I concluded the book with the policies of the Johnson Government. These policies served to exacerbate and escalate the hostile environment. Specifically, two new Acts were introduced by the Johnson Government, the Nationality and Borders Act and the Police, Crime and Courts Act (PSCS). The former contains the widely condemned proposal to offshore asylum seekers to Rwanda. I considered human rights in Rwanda and found them to be lacking. I also discussed the Johnson Government's tardy and typically bureaucratic response to the 2022 Ukrainian refugee crisis. I concluded my discussion of the Nationality and Borders Act with a look at the issue of safe routes to the UK. With respect to the PSCS Act, I addressed both its attempts to criminalize effective protest and at its major project of non-colour-coded racism directed at the GRT communities, amounting to no less than an attempt to criminalize GRT cultures. I considered attempts to curb political topics in English schools by issuing Guidance entitled 'Political Impartiality in Schools'. Education unions argued that it was likely to deter teachers from tackling the subject of racism and the legacy of Empire. The end of the chapter on Johnson has updates on the Grenfell Tower disaster, including Johnson's role in this; and on the Windrush scandal, where despite promises from Home Secretary Priti Patel, an independent progress report found that the Home Office had failed to change its culture.

As I prepared to submit the manuscript for publication (late May/early June 2022), it was revealed by Amelia Gentleman that a Home Office-commissioned paper had been repeatedly repressed over the previous year. The paper reported what was documented in detail in this book, namely that the origins of the Windrush scandal lay in years of racist immigration legislation. Written by an unnamed historian, the paper described how 'the British Empire depended on racist ideology in order to function', and how this affected the laws passed in the post-war period.[1] It further noted that the origins of the 'deep-rooted racism of the Windrush scandal' lay in the fact that 'during the period 1950–1981, every single piece of immigration or citizenship legislation was designed at least in part to reduce the number of people with black or brown skin who were permitted to live and work in the UK'.[2] It goes on to state the cause of the scandal was a failure to recognize that changes to British immigration law over the past 70 years had a more negative impact on Black people than on other racial and ethnic groups.[3] In the words of the report:

> As a result, the experiences of Britain's black communities of the Home Office, of the law, and of life in the UK have been fundamentally different from those of white communities. Major immigration legislation in 1962, 1968 and 1971 was designed to reduce the proportion of people living in the United Kingdom who did not have white skin.[4]

According to Gentleman, the paper, named 'The Historical Roots of the Windrush Scandal', focused on 'the immigration legislation of the 20th century, rather than on more recent events, such as the effects of the hostile environment policies introduced by Theresa May'.[5]

On June 2, it was confirmed by Refugee Action, a charity that provides basic support for refugees to live with dignity and helps them build 'safe, happy and productive lives in the UK', and has a vision that 'refugees and asylum seekers will be welcome in the UK', and will get justice and live free of poverty, that on June 14, 2022, the Johnson Government aimed to march the first batch of refugees who sought asylum in the UK, numbering 100, onto a plane to be flown to Rwanda, a place where they face an unknown future, have no promise of safety, no family connections and no hope. This included Khaled, who fled Syria at 20 years old to avoid forced conscription into the army and being engaged in a bloody war. It is informative to quote at length the words of Mariam at Refugee Action:

> Khaled is a refugee who fled Syria at just 20 years old, rather than facing forced conscription into Assad's army. When news of the war in Syria first hit our headlines years ago, we saw with our own eyes the horror people were facing. It's the same horror we felt when we saw people throwing their children over fences to reach safety on planes evacuating Afghanistan … [in 2021]. When we saw desperate people lose their lives in the Channel. When we watched people clinging to their families in bunkers in Ukraine. Our hearts broke. Thousands, if not millions of us, desperately wondered, how can we help? How can we show these people some humanity? This Government's ugly plan to deport people thousands of miles away laughs in the face of all those who so desperately want to offer hope, help, and humanity to people

seeking safety. *Like the rest of the new anti-refugee laws, these plans are violent, racist and inhumane.*

The number of asylum seekers expected to be sent to Rwanda fell from 130 in the week beginning June 6, to 31 at the end of that week, to just seven on June 14. However, after an eleventh-hour ruling by the European Court of Human Rights (ECHR), Johnson and Patel's plan to send the inaugural flight was abandoned just an hour and a half before scheduled take-off, following the ECHR's decision on one of the seven cases allowed lawyers for the other six to make successful last-minute applications. Patel's response was predictable: 'We will not be deterred from doing the right thing and delivering our plans to control our nation's borders. Our legal team are reviewing every decision made on this flight and preparation for the next flight begins now.'

As if to add insult to injury, his first planned flight was scheduled five years to the day from the tragedy at Grenfell. The fire, Mariam at Refugee Action concludes, claimed the lives of Mohammed Alhaj Ali and his brothers Omar and Hashem, who like Khaled, had fled Syria. Though their circumstances are different, she goes on, they are victims of the same problem:

> It's no coincidence that most, if not all, people earmarked for depor-
> tation to Rwanda are racialised citizens of one of Europe's former
> colonies. Just like it's no coincidence that most of those who died at
> Grenfell were from a racialised minority.

My remit in this book was not to pose solutions to the horrific injustices detailed within it. However, I feel it is incumbent on me to end on a note of optimism. As I argued in the Introduction, 'race' is a social construct, not a biological reality. It is not an inevitable feature of societies. On the contrary, I believe that, in general we are socialized into accepting the norms, values and customs of the social systems in which we grow up. While in the short term, it is imperative to work towards the end of the Boris Johnson Government, if Johnson goes and given his current unpopularity among fellow Tories,[6] this is looking increasingly likely, he will be replaced by someone just as bad or worse. Longer term, we must continue to strive for antiracism, but, from my perspective, in the context of a socialist future. But we are told by the powers that be that no one wants this. Not so, in 2018, a major Ipsos survey was conducted in 28 countries around the world: Argentina, Australia, Belgium, Brazil, Canada, Chile, China, France, Germany, Great Britain, Hungary, India, Italy, Japan, Malaysia, Mexico, Peru, Poland, Romania, Russia, Saudi Arabia, Serbia, South Africa, South Korea, Spain, Sweden, Turkey and the United States. When asked the question, 'Do you agree or disagree with the following statements: – at present, socialist ideals are of great value for societal progress', half of the respondents globally think that at present socialist ideals are of great value for societal progress – Chinese people are most likely to agree, Japanese people least likely. In Britain the figure was 49%.[7] At the same time, almost half of all respondents worldwide thought that socialism is a system of political oppression, mass surveillance and state terror. This underlines the need for a socialism of the 21st century to be truly democratic in the way Marx intended. I have written elsewhere about what I think this should entail.[8] That socialism, I have argued, must be ecosocialist, ecofeminist, antiracist and fully inclusive.

Notes

1 Cited in Gentleman. 2022c. https://www.theguardian.com/uk-news/2022/may/29/windrush-scandal-caused-by-30-years-of-racist-immigration-laws-report?CMP=Share_iOSApp_Other.
2 Ibid.
3 Gentleman. 2022c.
4 Cited in Gentleman. 2022c.
5 Gentleman. 2022c.
6 Mason, Rowena. 2022. 'Boris Johnson wins no-confidence vote despite unexpectedly large rebellion', *The Guardian*, June 6. https://www.theguardian.com/politics/2022/jun/06/boris-johnson-wins-no-confidence-vote-despite-unexpectedly-large-rebellion. As Rowena Mason explains, as of early June 2022, following a confidence vote that delivered the worst verdict on a sitting Prime Minister by their own party in recent times – 148 of his own MPs voted against him – Johnson was clinging to his premiership, with many citing his lack of repentance over 'Partygate'. This refers to the revelation that having told the general public they must stay at home during Covid-19, he continued to 'party' at Downing Street.
7 IPSOS Global Advisor. 2018. 'Attitudes towards Socialist Ideals in the 21st Century'. https://www.ipsos.com/sites/default/files/ct/news/documents/2018-05/global_socialism_survey-ipsos.pdf.
8 See, for example, Cole. 2021, chapter 3; Cole. 2022. 'Public pedagogy, climate change activism and the case for ecosocialism', in Walsh, E. (ed.) *Equity and Social Justice in Climate Change Education*, London: Routledge; Cole, M. 2023b. 'Social class, neoliberal capitalism and the Marxist alternative', in Cole. M. (ed.) *Education, Equality and Human Rights: Issues of Gender, 'Race', Sexuality, Disability and Social Class*, 5th Edition, London: Routledge.

Postscript: the rise and fall of Boris Johnson

The rise

Alan McGuinness, Assistant Editor, and Tom Rayner, Digital Politics Editor, for *Sky News* have provided a detailed account of the rise and fall of Alexander Boris de Pfeffel Johnson.[1] As they explain, he was born in New York, and spent the first years of his life 'moving between countries with his family, as his father Stanley pursued a varied international career':[2]

> At the age of eight, it is said he declared his ambition was to become 'world king'. Schooled at Eton, he went on to Oxford University in 1983 to study Classics at Balliol College. He became president of the Oxford Union debating society, as well as a member of the notorious Bullingdon Club.[3]

While still a journalist, he entered parliament, eventually becoming Shadow Arts Minister in 2004. In 2008, he became Mayor of London. After two terms as mayor, he returned to the Commons in 2015, and according to McGuinness and Rayner, 'sparked speculation he was coming for David Cameron's job'.[4]

The fall

Given the endemic racism in the Tory Party as detailed in this book, readers may not be surprised that it was not racism that brought Johnson's downfall, but something quite different. During the time of the Covid-19 pandemic in 2020 and 2021 there were a number of scandals. These included questions over who paid for Johnson's holiday in Mustique and for the expensive refurbishments to his Downing Street flat; other questions were raised over the way in which contracts were awarded at the height of the pandemic, and whether Tory donors and associates were given preferential treatment. There was also his demand that the Tories voted against former Cabinet Minister Owen Paterson who had preached Tory Party rules on lobbying.[5]

DOI: 10.4324/9781003198673-17

Then there was 'Partygate'. After telling people to stay away from social events such as parties to 'save lives and save the NHS',[6] reports began to emerge of parties in Downing Street and Whitehall (that contains other government buildings). This was repeatedly denied until photos, videos and emails came to light. He first responded by once again repeating his denial. Then former Press Secretary Allegra Stratton resigned after 'a video was obtained by ITV News showing her joking about a party in Downing Street that was held in December 2020'.[7] Other revelations followed, and Johnson was eventually forced to apologize in January 2022, when he added that he attended one, but as far as he was aware, the Covid rules had always been adhered to.[8] Just days after the Metropolitan Policed launched an investigation into 'Partygate', the war in Ukraine began when Russia invaded in February 2022, shifting people's attention away from parties, so that even when it was revealed that Johnson and his wife had been issued a fixed penalty notice for celebrating his birthday in the cabinet room during lockdown 'did not create a sense his downfall was imminent'.[9] However in May 2022, it came to light that a scuffle broke out, one person attending was sick and excessive amounts of alcohol were drunk when workers at Downing Street held a party on June 18, 2020, in the middle of the Covid crisis.[10] Moreover, at another event, Johnson's former Principal Private Secretary Martin Reynolds boasted to colleagues on the WhatsApp messaging service that staff appeared to have 'got away' with drinks events in the Downing Street garden in May 2020.[11]

In June 2022, Graham Brady, chair of 1922 Committee, announced that he had enough letters of 'no confidence' in Johnson's leadership from Tory MPs to trigger a vote among them. Although it was lost, there were more 'no confidence' votes than expected. Under the rules at the time, that meant no further such votes for a year. In addition, Tories feared changing leader in the middle of the Ukraine war, and a cost-of-living crisis did not make it worthwhile. There followed two serious by-election defeats, with Party Chair Oliver Dowden resigning as the votes came in[12]. The final straw came in early July 2022 when it emerged that Chris Pincher had resigned as Deputy Chief Whip, writing to Johnson that he had 'drunk far too much' the night before.[13] Pincher was accused of groping two men at the Carlton Club, a private venue for Tories, in front of many MPs. In the next few days, Downing Street's account of what Mr Johnson knew about allegations around Mr Pincher changed repeatedly.[14] Ministers were sent out to do media interviews pushing the Government line, 'only to find they had been misled by Number 10 – and ultimately Mr Johnson'.[15] Chancellor Rishi Sunak and Health Secretary Sajid Javid resigned their posts, prompting 'a wave of departures from more junior ranks in government'.[16] McGuinness and Rayner conclude:

> The speed with which the situation became untenable was dizzying – most obviously for Mr Johnson himself as he appeared to be almost in

denial as his premiership fell apart around him. Few politicians would have been in the position he was and still remained resolute that they would continue. It was the chutzpah and self-certainty that perhaps explains the extraordinary story of his rise to power. But this time, the political magic did not work. The mischievous, blundering, charismatic persona that had once been his strength had become a weakness in the eyes of his MPs. Boris Johnson was no longer seen as the winner the Conservative Party had elected him to be.[17]

On July 7, 2022, Johnson resigned. Mary Elizabeth (Liz) Truss was elected leader of the Tory Party and hence Prime Minister by the Tory Party membership on September 6, 2022, becoming Britain's third female PM. Truss resigned after 44 days, making her the shortest serving PM in UK history. She was replaced on October 25, 2022 by Rishi Sunak, formerly Chancellor of the Exchequer, and the first person of colour to serve as Prime Minister. Sunak has made it clear that the hostile environment will be accelerated under his premiership.

Notes

1 McGuinness, Alan and Rayner, Tom. 2022. 'The rise and fall of Boris Johnson: the political magician who won power but lost control', *Sky News,* July 7. https://news.sky.com/story/the-rise-and-fall-of-boris-johnson-the-political-magician-who-won-power-but-lost-control-12519849.
2 Ibid.
3 Ibid.
4 Ibid.
5 Ibid.
6 Cited in McGuinness and Rayner. 2022.
7 McGuinness and Rayner. 2022.
8 Ibid.
9 Ibid.
10 Macaskill, Andrew and James, William. 2022. 'Drunkenness, vomiting and a scuffle at UK government lockdown parties', *Reuters,* May 25. https://www.reuters.com/world/uk/drunkenness-sickness-fighting-duringlockdown-party-uk-government-report-2022-05-25/.
11 Ibid.
12 McGuinness and Rayner. 2022.
13 Cited in McGuinness and Rayner. 2022.
14 McGuinness and Rayner. 2022.
15 Ibid.
16 Ibid.
17 Ibid.

References

Abortion Rights Campaign. Undated. 'Abortion law in Ireland'. https://www.abortionrightscampaign.ie/abortion-law-in-ireland/.

Adams, Richard. 2022. 'Guidance on political impartiality in English classrooms "confusing" say teachers' unions', *The Guardian*, February 17. https://www.theguardian.com/education/2022/feb/17/guidance-on-political-impartiality-in-english-classrooms-confusing-say-teachers-unions.

Addison, Paul. 2006. *Churchill: The Unexpected Hero*, Oxford: Oxford University Press.

Addison, Paul. 2011. 'Why Churchill lost in 1945', BBC, February 17. http://www.bbc.co.uk/history/worldwars/wwtwo/election_01.shtml.

Adkins, Frankie. 2021. '"13 dead, nothing said" – remembering the New Cross Fire', *News Shopper*, January 18. https://www.newsshopper.co.uk/news/19019348.13-dead-nothing-said—remembering-new-cross-tragedy/.

Agenda. 2022. 'Government must tackle persistent racism and gender inequality in the criminal justice system', January 31. https://weareagenda.org/government-must-tackle-persistent-racism-and-gender-inequality-in-the-criminal-justice-system/#:~:text=The%20Criminal%20Justice%20Alliance%20(CJA,research%20institutions%20and%20staff%20associations.

Agnew-Pauley, Winifred and Akintoye, Bisola. 2021. 'Stop and search disproportionately affects black communities – yet police powers are being extended', *The Conversation*, August 3. https://theconversation.com/stop-and-search-disproportionately-affects-black-communities-yet-police-powers-are-beingextended-165477.

Aitken, Jonathan. 2013. *Margaret Thatcher: Power and Personality*, London: Bloomsbury.

Alderman, Geoffrey. 1998. *Modern British Jewry*, Oxford: Clarendon Press.

Alibhai-Brown, Yasmin. 2014. 'Racism and the truth about the Ugandan Asians', *The Independent*, January 10. https://www.independent.co.uk/voices/commentators/yasmin-alibhai-brown/racism-and-truth-about-ugandan-asians-172084.html.

Alibhai-Brown, Yasmin. 2015. *Exotic England: The Making of a Curious Nation*, Edinburgh: Portobello Books.

Althusser, Louis. 1970. 'Ideology and ideological state apparatuses (Notes towards an Investigation)', in *"Lenin and Philosophy" and Other Essays*, transcribed: by Andy Blunden. https://www.marxists.org/reference/archive/althusser/1970/ideology.htm.

Ames, Jonathan. 2020. 'Would floating detention centres forasylum seekers work?', *The Times*, October 1. https://www.thetimes.co.uk/article/would-floating-detention-centres-for-asylum-seekers-work-bkldrv2zn.

Amnesty International. 2019. 'UK: domestic abuse bill risks failing migrant women'. www.amnesty.org.uk/press-releases/uk-domestic-abuse-bill-risks-faili ng-migrant-women.

Amnesty International UK. 2020. 'Northern Ireland: "Shameful" refusal to agree public inquiry in Finucane murder will undermine confidence in rule of law', November 30. https://www.amnesty.org.uk/press-releases/northern-ireland-sham eful-refusal-agree-public-inquiry-finucane-murder-will.

Amnesty International. 2021. 'Nationality & Borders Bill: The truth behind the claims'. https://www.amnesty.org.uk/nationality-borders-bill-truth-behind-claims.

Anderson, Benedict. 1987. *Imagined Communities: Reflections on the Origin and Spread of Nationalism*, London: Verso.

Anderson, Jon Lee. 2013. 'Neruda, Pinochet, and the Iron Lady', *New Yorker*, April 9. https://www.newyorker.com/news/daily-comment/neruda-pinochet-and-the-iron-lady.

Andrews, Kehinde. 2021. 'Forty years on from the New Cross fire, what has changed for black Britons?', *The Guardian*, January 17. https://www.theguardian.com/world/2021/jan/17/forty-years-on-from-the-new-cross-fire-what-has-changed-for-black-britons.

Anne Frank House. Undated. 'Antisemitism: Why did Hitler hate the Jews'. https://www.annefrank.org/en/anne-frank/go-in-depth/why-did-hitler-hate-jews/#source-392934.

AP. 1990. 'Conservative Party member apologizes for racist remark', December 11. https://apnews.com/article/fb84d210671f045606397e6e54261f86.

Ashe, Stephen D. and McGeever, Brendan. 2011. 'Marxism, racism and the construction of "race" as a social and political relation: an interview with Professor Robert Miles', *Ethnic and Racial Studies*, 34 (12).

Associated Press. 2016. 'Jackson blasts the status quo in US, Britain', *DeseretNews*, December 26. https://www.deseret.com/1994/12/26/19150027/jackson-blasts-the-status-quo-in-u-s-britain.

Asthana, Anushka, Mason, Rowena and Elgot, Jessica. 2017. 'Theresa May calls for UK general election on 8 June', *Guardian*, April 18. www.theguardian.com/poli tics/2017/apr/18/theresa-may-uk-general-election-8-june.

Atherton, Louise. 1994. 'Lord Lloyd at the British Council and the Balkan Front, 1937–1940', *The International History Review*, 16, (1).

Atkins, Richard A. 1974. 'The conservatives and Egypt, 1875–1880', *The Journal of Imperial and Commonwealth History*, 2 (2).

Attar, Samar. 2010. *Debunking the Myths of Colonization*, Lanham, Maryland: United Press of America.

Baig, Anila. 2021. 'Bradford race riots 20 years on as man recalls throwing stone "like bomb at my own life"', *The Mirror*, July 7. https://www.mirror.co.uk/news/uk-news/bradford-race-riots-20-years-24474030.

Baker, Colin. 1998. 'Macmillan's "Wind of Change" Tour, 1960', *South African History Journal*, May, 38 (1).

Baldwin, M. 2001. 'Subject to empire: Married women and the British Nationality and Status of Aliens Act', *Journal of British Studies* 40 (4).

Balfour, Arthur. 1905. 'Speech in the House of Commons', May 2. https://api.pa rliament.uk/historic-hansard/commons/1905/may/02/aliens-bill-1#S4V0145P0_19050502_HOC_228.

Ball, Stephen J. 1993. 'Education, Majorism and "the Curriculum of the Dead"', *Curriculum Studies*, 1 (2). https://www.tandfonline.com/doi/pdf/10.1080/0965975930010202.

Banton, Michael. 1977. *The Idea of Race*, London: Tavistock.

Bartlett, Roger. 2017. 'When Mosley men won elections'. http://britishguardian.blogspot.com/2017/05/when-mosley-men-won-elections.html.

Bartley, Paula. 2014. *Ellen Wilkinson: From Red Suffragist to Government Minister*, London: Pluto Press.

Bartley, Paula. 2016. 'Ellen Wilkinson and the Jarrow Crusade October 1936'. https://www.plutobooks.com/blog/ellen-wilkinson-and-the-jarrowcrusade-october-1936/.

Bates, Stephen. 2013. 'Two sides of the same party', *History Today*, 63, March 3. https://www.historytoday.com/archive/two-sides-same-party.

Bates, Stephen and Chaudhary, Vivek. 1994. 'Tim Yeo sacrificed to family values', *The Guardian*, January 6. https://www.theguardian.com/politics/2010/jan/06/tim-yeo-sacrificed-family-values.

BBC History. 2014. 'Family history research timeline: Migration'. http://www.bbc.co.uk/history/familyhistory/bloodlines/migration.shtml.

BBC News. 1969. '1969: Ulster's B Specials to be disbanded', October 10. http://news.bbc.co.uk/onthisday/hi/dates/stories/october/10/newsid_3146000/3146929.stm.

BBC News. 1998. 'UK politics: The Major scandal sheet', October 27. http://news.bbc.co.uk/1/hi/uk_politics/202525.stm.

BBC News. 2000. 'School gap blamed on black culture', August 21. http://news.bbc.co.uk/1/hi/education/890214.stm.

BBC News. 2001. 'Blair ahead in leadership ratings', May 3. http://news.bbc.co.uk/news/vote2001/hi/english/opinion_polls/newsid_1306000/1306664.stm.

BBC News. 2002. 'Local elections 2002'. http://news.bbc.co.uk/hi/english/static/vote2002/local_elections/atoz.stm.

BBC News. 2003a. '"Unite or die" warns Tory leader', 21 February. http://news.bbc.co.uk/1/hi/uk_politics/2403923.stm.

BBC News. 2003b. 'Tory leader: "Back me or get out"', October 9. http://news.bbc.co.uk/1/hi/uk_politics/3175680.stm.

BBC News. 2003c. 'Local elections: A-Z of results'. http://news.bbc.co.uk/1/shared/bsp/hi/vote2003/locals/html/atoz.stm.

BBC News. 2003d. 'Tory leader ousted', October 29. http://news.bbc.co.uk/1/hi/uk_politics/3225127.stm.

BBC News. 2003e. 'Howard crowned Tory leader', November 6. http://news.bbc.co.uk/1/hi/uk_politics/3245561.stm.

BBC News. 2004a. 'Thatcher's Class of '79'. http://news.bbc.co.uk/1/shared/spl/hi/uk_politics/04/thatchers_government/html/whitelaw.stm.

BBC News. 2004b. 'Q&A: The Scarman Report', April 27. http://news.bbc.co.uk/1/hi/programmes/bbc_parliament/3631579.stm.

BBC News. 2005a. '1959: Macmillan wins Tory hat trick', April 5. http://news.bbc.co.uk/1/hi/uk_politics/vote_2005/basics/4393287.stm.

BBC News. 2005b. '1957: Britons "have never had it so good"', July 20. http://news.bbc.co.uk/onthisday/hi/dates/stories/july/20/newsid_3728000/3728225.stm.

BBC News. 2006. 'Schools "too feminine for boys"', June 13. http://news.bbc.co.uk/1/hi/5074794.stm.

BBC News. 2008a. '1993: Minister resigns over business links', June 24. http://news.bbc.co.uk/onthisday/hi/dates/stories/june/24/newsid_2519000/2519201.stm.

BBC News. 2008b. 'Peer's apology over racist phrase', July 9. http://news.bbc.co. uk/1/hi/uk_politics/7497097.stm.

BBC News. 2010a. 'How Britain said farewell to its Empire', July 23. https://www. bbc.co.uk/news/magazine-10740852.

BBC News. 2010b. 'The Saville Inquiry 2003', June 11. https://www.bbc.co.uk/ news/10181619.

BBC News. 2010c. 'Bloody Sunday: PM David Cameron's full statement', June 15. https://www.bbc.co.uk/news/10322295.

BBC News. 2010d. 'Gordon Brown resigns as UK prime minister', May 11. http:// news.bbc.co.uk/1/hi/uk_politics/election_2010/8675913.stm.

BBC News. 2011a. 'Mau Mau uprising: Bloody history of Kenya conflict', April 7. https://www.bbc.co.uk/news/uk-12997138.

BBC News. 2011b. 'Profile: Lord Taylor of Warwick (Updated)', January 25. https:// www.bbc.co.uk/news/uk-politics-12175980.

BBC News. 2011c. 'State multiculturalism has failed, says David Cameron', February 5. https://www.bbc.co.uk/news/uk-politics-12371994.

BBC News. 2013. 'Farage attacks "nasty" immigration posters', July 25. https:// www.bbc.co.uk/news/uk-politics-23450438.

BBC News. 2014a. 'Margaret Thatcher's criticism of Brixton riot response revealed', December 30. https://www.bbc.co.uk/news/uk-30600064#:~i:text=Prime% 20Minister%20Margaret%20Thatcher's%20concerns,public%20for%20the%20first %20time.&text=A%20handwritten%20note%20by%20Mrs,highly%20critical% 20of%20the%20police.%22.

BBC News. 2014b. 'Lenny Henry racism row candidate quits UKIP', April 29. www.bbc.co.uk/news/uk-politics-27202753.

BBC News. 2014c. 'Norman Baker quits as Home Office minister', November 4. https://www.bbc.co.uk/news/uk-politics-29891132.

BBC News. 2015. 'Broadwater Farm riots: PC Keith Blakelock's 1985 murder recalled', October 6. https://www.bbc.co.uk/news/uk-england-london-34433752.

BBC News. 2018a. 'St Ann's riot: The changing face of race relations, 60 years on', August 25. https://www.bbc.co.uk/news/uk-england-nottinghamshire-45207246.

BBC News. 2018b. 'Margaret Thatcher was the "quintessential hate figure", says Mary Lou McDonald', December 28. https://www.bbc.com/news/uk-norther n-ireland-46611049.amp.

BBC News. 2018c. 'Brexit: backlash over May's EU nationals "queue jumping" vow', November 20. www.bbc.co.uk/news/uk-politics-4627411.

BBC News. 2019a. 'Election results 2019: Boris Johnson hails "new dawn" after historic victory', December 13. https://www.bbc.co.uk/news/election-2019-50776671.

BBC News. 2019b. 'Prime Minister Boris Johnson: Does his cabinet reflect "modern Britain?"', July 25. https://www.bbc.co.uk/news/uk-politics-49034735.

BBC News. 2019c. 'Brexit: Tory MP defects ahead of crucial no-deal vote', September 3. https://www.bbc.co.uk/news/uk-politics-49570682.

BBC News. 2019d. 'Brexit: Boris Johnson defeated as MPs take control', September 4. https://www.bbc.co.uk/news/uk-politics-49573555.

BBC News. 2019e. 'Grenfell Tower: What happened', October 29. https://www. bbc.co.uk/news/uk-40301289.

BBC News. 2020a. 'Pat Finucane: Labour urges Boris Johnson to order inquiry', October 27. https://www.bbc.co.uk/news/uk-northern-ireland-54698006.

BBC News. 2020b. 'No 10 refuses to condemn adviser's remarks', February 17. https://www.bbc.co.uk/news/uk-politics-51535367.

BBC News. 2020c. 'Andrew Sabisky: No 10 adviser resigns over alleged race comments', February 18. https://www.bbc.co.uk/news/uk-politics-51538493.

BBC News. 2020d. 'Charity boss Tony Sewell to head government race commission', July 16. https://www.bbc.co.uk/news/uk-politics-53428248.

BBC News. 2020e. 'Windrush: "Grave risk" of scandal repeat, warns review author', June 22. https://www.bbc.co.uk/news/uk-53129844.

BBC News. 2020f. 'Grenfell Tower inquiry: Fire "inextricably linked with race"', July 7. https://www.bbc.co.uk/news/uk-53320082.

BBC News. 2022a. 'Nusrat Ghani: Muslimness a reason for my sacking, says ex-minister', January 23. https://www.bbc.co.uk/news/uk-politics-60100525.

BBC News. 2022b. 'What is the Police and Crime Bill and how will it change protests?', April 29. https://www.bbc.co.uk/news/uk-56400751.

BBC Newsnight. 2019. 'Theresa May wanted to tighten every single screw she could find on the immigration system', YouTube, February 28. https://twitter.com/BBCNewsnight/status/1101254587309121537.

BBC World Service. Undated. 'The story of Africa: The middle passage'. https://www.bbc.co.uk/worldservice/specials/1624_story_of_africa/page53.shtml.

Bean, John. 2011. *Many Shades of Black*, Morrisville, North Carolina. lulu.com.

Beatty, Andrew. 2013. 'Thatcher's apartheid legacy still stirs anger in S. Africa', *Modern Ghana*, April 11. https://www.modernghana.com/news/458002/thatchers-apartheid-legacy-still-stirs-anger-in.html.

Beaumont, Peter. 2022. 'Rwanda: human rights fears in nation whose leader faces murder claims', *The Guardian*, April 14. https://www.theguardian.com/world/2022/apr/14/rwanda-human-rights-fears-paul-kagame.

Beckles, Hilary. 2017. 'On Barbados, the first Black slave society', *Black Perspectives*, April 8. https://www.aaihs.org/on-barbados-the-first-black-slave-society/.

Benneyworth, G. C. 2019. 'Land, labour, war and displacement: a history of four black concentration camps in the South African War (1899–1902)'. *Historia*, 64 (2). November, p. 6. http://www.scielo.org.za/pdf/hist/v64n2/01.pdf.

Bentley, Michael. 2001. *Lord Salisbury's World: Conservative Environments in Late-Victorian Britain*, Cambridge: Cambridge University Press.

Beresford, David. 2006. '"Great crocodile" of apartheid dies at 90', *The Guardian*, November 1. https://amp.theguardian.com/world/2006/nov/01/southafrica.davidberesford.

Bergman, Sirena. 2020. 'Boris Johnson just said "black lives matter"– let's remember the horrifyingly racist things he's said', *The Independent*, June 3. https://www.indy100.com/news/boris-johnson-racist-keir-starmer-pmqs-george-floyd-black-lives-matter-9546586.

Beveridge, William. 1942. *Social Insurance and Allied Services*, Cmd 6404, London: HMSO.

Bevins, Anthony. 1996. 'Nelson Mandela: From "terrorist" to tea with the Queen', *The Independent*, July 8. https://www.independent.co.uk/news/world/from-terrorist-to-tea-with-the-queen-1327902.html.

Bew, Paul and Maune, Patrick. 2020. 'The Great Advocate', *Dublin Review of Books*, 132, July. https://www.drb.ie/essays/the-great-advocate.

Bhabha, Homi K. 1990. (ed.) *Nation and Narration*, London: Routledge.

Bhalwani, Saarah and Zia Ud Din, Muhammed. 2021. 'The History of Paki-bashing: Educating on British BAME experiences', part of the Oxford Brookes University series of talks on 'Conversations on race, racism and anti-racism', April 13. https://bxtra. brookes.ac.uk/the-history-of-paki-bashing-educating-onbritish-bame-experiences/.

Bin Ahmad, Zakaria. 2022. 'Malaysia', October 20, *Britannica*. https://www.brita nnica.com/place/Malaysia.

Blake, Robert. 1967. *Disraeli*, New York: St Martins Press.

Blake, Robert. 1969a. 'Home letters' in Disraeli, London: University Paperbacks.

Blake, Robert. 1969b. *Disraeli*, Oxford: Oxford University Press.

Blake, Robert. 1970. *The Conservative Party from Peel to Churchill*, Colchester: TBS The Book Service Ltd.

Blake, Robert. 1982. *Disraeli's Grand Tour: Benjamin Disraeli and the Holy Land 1830–1831*, New York: Oxford University Press.

Blake, Robert. 2011. 'Disraeli and Gladstone: Opposing force'. http://www.bbc.co. uk/history/british/victorians/disraeli_gladstone_01.shtml.

Blake, Robert. 2022. 'Benjamin Disraeli, Prime Minister of United Kingdom', *Britannica*. https://www.britannica.com/biography/Benjamin-Disraeli.

Blaxill, Luke. 2017. 'The language of imperialism in British electoral politics, 1880-1910', *The Journal of Imperial and Commonwealth History*, 45 (3).

Blessing, Patrick J. 1980. 'Irish', in S. Thernstrom, A. Orlov and O. Handlin (eds.), Harvard Encyclopedia of American Ethnic Groups, Cambridge, MA: Harvard University Press.

Bloom, Dan. 2019. 'Boris Johnson said "bunch of black kids" made him "turn a hair" in old column', *Daily Mirror*, November 22. https://www.mirror.co.uk/ news/politics/boris-johnson-said-bunch-black-20889302.

Bloy, Marjie. 2003. 'William Ewart Gladstone', *The Victorian Web*. https://victoria nweb.org/history/wegchron.html.

Bloy, Marjie. 2016. 'A web of English history biography: Benjamin Disraeli (1804–1881)'. http://www.historyhome.co.uk/pms/dizzy.htm.

Bobby Sands Tribute. Undated. 'Dirty protest'. http://bobbysandstribute.weebly. com/maze—dirty.html.

Bobby Sands Trust. 2019a. 'Prison diary'. https://www.bobbysandstrust.com/wri tings/prison-diary/.

Bobby Sands Trust. 2019b. 'Bobby Sands MP'. https://www.bobbysandstrust.com/ bobbysands/ diary/.

Bond, Paul. 2022. 'UK: Colston Four acquittals fuel Johnson government's determination to intensify law-and-order agenda', World Socialist Website (WSWS), January 9. https://www.wsws.org/en/articles/2022/01/09/cols-j09. html.

Boon, Bruce. 2007. 'Malaysia: 50 years of independence: Colonialism at the root of the national question', *In Defence of Marxism*, August 31. https://www.marxist. com/malaysia-fifty-years-independence-part-one.htm.

Booth, Adam. 2019. 'The individual and the Marxist view of history', *In Defence of Marxism*, May 28. https://www.marxist.com/the-individual-and-the-marxist-view-of-history.htm#:~:text=The%20Marxist%20view%20of%20history%2C%20by% 20contrast%2C%20in%20the%20words,the%20history%20of%20class%20struggles% E2%80%9D.&text=History%2C%20then%2C%20is%20made%20up,own%20indivi-dual%20aims%20and%20interests.

Booth, Robert. 2020. 'Tory donor was key shareholder in Grenfell cladding firm Arconic', *The Guardian*, December 23. https://www.theguardian.com/uk-news/2020/dec/23/tory-donor-was-key-shareholder-in-grenfell-claddingfirm-arconic.

Booth, Robert. 2022a. 'Outrage as ministers reject post-Grenfell safety plans for disabled people', *The Guardian*, May 18. https://www.theguardian.com/uk-news/2022/may/18/outrage-as-ministers-reject-post-grenfell-safety-plans-for-disabled-people.

Booth, Robert. 2022b. 'Fire safety official admits tests showed cladding danger 15 years before Grenfell', *The Guardian*, February 28. https://amp.theguardian.com/uk-news/2022/feb/28/cladding-danger-evidence-15-years-before-grenfell-tower-fire.

Booth, Robert and Butler, Patrick. 2018. 'UK austerity has inflicted "great misery" on citizens, UN says', *The Guardian*, November 16. https://www.theguardian.com/society/2018/nov/16/uk-austerity-has-inflictedgreat-misery-on-citizens-un-says.

Borger, Julian. 2018. 'Trump with better hair: how Obama White House saw Boris Johnson', *The Guardian*, May 31. https://www.theguardian.com/us-news/2018/may/31/trump-with-better-hair-how-obama-white-house-saw-boris-johnson.

Borgstede, Simone, Beate. 2021. *All Is Race: Benjamin Disraeli on Race, Nation and Empire*, Hamburg: Lit Verlag.

Borrell-Verdu, Stephanie. 2018. 'Belgium, U.S. involvement in World War I', *USAG Benelux Public Affairs*, February 16. https://www.army.mil/article/200760/belgium_u_s_involvement_in_world_war_i#:~:text=Germany%20declared%20war%20on%20France,4%2C%201914.

Bowcott, Owen. 2004. 'Inquest begins into 14 victims of 1981 fire', *The Guardian*, February 3. https://www.theguardian.com/uk/2004/feb/03/ukcrime.owenbowcott.

Bowcott, Owen and Jones, Sam. 2008. 'Johnson's "piccaninnies" apology', *The Guardian*, January 23. https://www.theguardian.com/politics/2008/jan/23/london.race.

Bowers, Jake. 2022. 'Out of site: Britain's nomadic people', *Friends of the Earth*. https://friendsoftheearth.uk/system-change/out-site-britains-nomadic-people.

Boyle, Danny, Wilkinson, Michael, Dominiczak, Peter, Swinford, Steven, Riley-Smith Ben and Chan, Szu Ping. 2016. 'Conservative leadership election: Theresa May wins more than half of MPs' votes as Stephen Crabb pulls out and Liam Fox is eliminated', *Telegraph*, July 5. www.telegraph.co.uk/news/2016/07/05/boris-johnson-backs-andrea-leadsom-tory-mps-vote-leadership-race/.

Bradford, Sarah. 1983. *Disraeli*, New York: Stein & Day.

Bradshaw, Peter. 2022. 'Hostile review – documentary highlights nastiness of UK immigration policy', *The Guardian*, January 19. https://www.theguardian.com/film/2022/jan/19/hostile-review-documentary-highlights-nastiness-of-uk-immigration-policy.

Brady, Robert A. 1950. *Crisis in Britain; plans and achievements of the Labour government*, Berkeley: University of California Press.

Brantlinger, Patrick. 2011. *Taming cannibals: Race and the Victorians*, Ithaca, New York: Cornell University Press.

Bratton, J. S. 1986. 'Of England, home, and duty: The image of England in Victorian and Edwardian juvenile fiction', in J. MacKenzie (ed.), Imperialism and Popular Culture, Manchester: Manchester University Press.

Braudel, Fernand. 1992. *The Perspective of the World, Vol III of Civilization and Capitalism*, California: University of California Press.

Brignell, Victoria. 2010. 'The eugenics movement Britain wants to forget', *New Statesman*, December 9. https://www.newstatesman.com/society/2010/12/british-eugenics-disabled.

Broadberry, Stephen and Burhop, Carsten. 2010. *Real Wages and Labor Productivity in Britain and Germany, 1871–1938: A Unified Approach to the International Comparison of Living Standards.* https://core.ac.uk/download/pdf/1353371.pdf.

Brodie, Marc. 2004. 'William Evans-Gordon', *Oxford Dictionary of National Biography.* https://doi.org/10.1093/ref:odnb/58246.

Brooke, Stephen. 1996. 'The Conservative Party, immigration and national identity, 1948–1968', in Martin Francis, Martin and Ina Zweiniger-Bargielowska (eds.), The Conservatives and British Society 1880–1990, Cardiff: University of Wales Press.

Brown, Derek. 2001a. 'Suez and the end of empire', *The Guardian*, March 14. https://amp.theguardian.com/politics/2001/mar/14/past.education1.

Brown, Derek. 2001b. '1945–51: Labour and the creation of the welfare state', *The Guardian*, March 14. https://www.theguardian.com/politics/2001/mar/14/past.education.

Browne, Anthony. 2002. *Do We Need Mass Immigration?: The Economic, Demographic, Environmental, Social and Developmental Arguments against Large-Scale Net Immigration to Britain*, London: Civitas.

Brunner, Edouard. 2001. *Lambris dorés et coulisses Broché [Gilded Panels and Corridors]*, Georg.

Bulman, May. 2018. 'Yarl's Wood: inside the crisis-hit immigration detention centre', *Independent*, 28 February. www.independent.co.uk/news/uk/home-news/yarls-wood-inside-experience-hunger-strike-immigration-detention-scandal-a8230056.html.

Burton, Richard Francis. 1855–56. 'Life Works Gallery: More personal narrative of a pilgrimage to Al-Madinah and Meccah: The Nile Steamboat – The "Little Asthmatic"', Burtoniana.org. https://burtoniana.org/books/1855-Narrative%20of%20a%20Pilgrimage%20to%20Mecca%20and%20Medinah/1893-Memorial%20Edition/HTML/chapter3.html.

Butcher, Benjamin, and Massey, Joel. 2020. 'Why are more people from BAME backgrounds dying from coronavirus?', BBC News, June 19. https://www.bbc.co.uk/news/uk-52219070.

Butler, David and Stokes, Donald. 1969. *Political Change in Britain: Forces Shaping Electoral Choice*, New York: St Martin's Press.

Byrne, Philippa. 2017. 'Why were the Jews expelled from England in 1290?'. https://www.history.ox.ac.uk/why-were-the-jews-expelled-from-england-in-1290.

CAIN Web Service. 1972. '"Bloody Sunday", Derry, 30 January 1972: Circumstances in which people were killed', compiled by Martin Melaugh. https://cain.ulster.ac.uk/events/bsunday/circum.htm.

CAIN Web Service. 2021a. 'Internment – Summary of main events'. https://cain.ulster.ac.uk/events/intern/sum.htm.

CAIN Web Service. 2021b. 'Anglo-Irish Agreement – Chronology of events'. https://cain.ulster.ac.uk/events/aia/chron.htm.

Campbell, Denis and Kollewe, Julia. 2022. 'Javid tells NHS England to give private hospitals up to £270m in case of Omicron surge', *The Guardian*, January 13. https://www.theguardian.com/society/2022/jan/13/sajid-javid-nhs-england-private-hospitals-omicron.

Campbell, John. 1993. *Edward Heath: A Biography*, London: Jonathan Cape.

Campbell, Kenneth L. 2013. *Ireland's History: Prehistory to the Present.* London: A & C Black.

Campbell, Scott. 2017. 'Real reason why Donald Trump and Theresa May held hands is revealed: US president "is frightened of STAIRS"', *Daily Mirror*, January 29. www.mirror.co.uk/news/world-news/real-reason-donald-trump-theresa-9716450.

Cannadine, David. 1990. *The Decline and Fall of the British Aristocracy*, New Haven and London: Yale University Press.

Cardaun, Sarah K. 2015. *Antisemitism in England and Britain: A History of Prejudice and Divided Responses Countering Contemporary Antisemitism in Britain*, Leiden: Brill.

Carr, Flora. 2018, April 20. 'What it's like to study at the strictest school in Britain', *Time*, April 20. https://time.com/5232857/michaela-britains-strictest-school/.

Carroll, Rory. 2020. 'Pat Finucane's murder: a pitiless act and a political storm', *The Guardian*, November 30. https://www.theguardian.com/uk-news/2020/nov/30/pat-finucane-murder-a-pitiless-act-and-a-political-storm.

Carter, Bob, Harris, Clive, and Joshi, Shirley. 1987. 'The 1951-55 conservative government and the racialisation of black immigration', Policy Papers in Ethnic Relations 11, Centre for Research in Ethnic Relations, University of Warwick. https://warwick.ac.uk/fac/soc/crer/research/publications/policy/policyp_no.11.pdf.

Casalicchio, Emilio. 2017. '*Vince Cable: Theresa May suppressed up to nine reports showing immigration benefits*', *Civil Service World*, September 7. www.civilserviceworld.com/articles/news/vince-cable-theresa-may-suppressed-nine-reports-showing-immigration-benefits.

Castle, Blair Stephen. 1995. 'Thatcher praises "formidable" Blair', *The Independent*, May 28. https://www.independent.co.uk/news/thatcher-praises-formidable-blair-1621354.html.

Cathcart, Brian. 1993. 'History gets a handbagging from Thatcherite scholars: John Charmley caused a stir with his criticism of Churchill', *The Independent*, January 10. https://www.independent.co.uk/news/uk/history-gets-handbagging-thatcherite-scholars-john-charmley-caused-stir-his-criticism-churchill-brian-cathcart-explores-why-attacks-come-right-1477675.html.

Cazamian, Louis. 1903. *The Social Novel in England, 1830–1850: Dickens, Disraeli, Mrs. Gaskell, Kingsley*. Translated by Martin Fido, 1973. London: Routledge & Kegan Paul.

Cesarani, David. 1989. 'The anti-Jewish career of Sir William Joynson-Hicks, Cabinet Minister', *Journal of Contemporary History*, 24.

Cesarani, David. 2013. 'Disraeli the cad, Disraeli the bounder', *The Jewish Chronicle*, November 17. https://www.thejc.com/disraeli-the-cad-disraeli-thebounder-1.50964.

Chakra, Hayden. 2018. 'Norman invasion of Ireland', May 16. https://abouthistory.com/norman-invasion-of-ireland/.

Chancellor, Valerie. 1970. *History for Their Masters*, Bath: Adams & Dart.

Charmley, John. 1988. *Lord Lloyd and the Decline of the British Empire*, New York: St Martin's Press.

Charmley, John. 1996. *A History of Conservative Politics, 1900–1996*, Basingstoke: Macmillan.

Chessum, Michael. 2017. 'War is deeply political, and the way we commemorate it even more so', *New Statesman*, November 11. https://www.newstatesman.com/politics/uk/2017/11/war-deeply-political-and-way-we-commemorate-it-even-more-so.

Child Protection and Rescue Society of Ireland (CPRSI). 1955. 42nd Annual Report, Dublin.

Chrisafis, Angelique. 2001. 'I'm a normal Conservative with perfectly normal views', *The Guardian*, August 25. https://www.theguardian.com/politics/2001/aug/25/uk.conservatives.

Chuhan, Kuljit. Undated. 'The development of racist theories and ideas', *Revealing Histories: Remembering Slavery*. http://revealinghistories.org.uk/legacies-stereotypes-ra

cism-and-the-civil-rights-movement/articles/the-development-of-racist-theories-an
d-ideas.html.

Churchill Book Collection. Undated. 'Mr. Winston Churchill on the Aliens Bill'.
https://www.churchillbookcollector.com/pages/books/001777/win
stons-churchill/mr-winston-churchill-on-the-aliens-bill.

Churchill, Winston. Undated. 'The Greatest Briton'. https://www.parliament.uk/
globalassets/documents/parliamentary-archives/Churchill-for-web-Mar-2014.pdf.

Churchill, Winston. 1920. 'Zionism versus Bolshevism: A struggle for the soul of the
Jewish People', *Illustrated Sunday Herald* (London), February 8. https://en.wiki
source.org/wiki/Zionism_versus_Bolshevism.

Churchill, Winston. 1938. 'The defence of freedom and peace (The lights are going
out)', *International Churchill Society*, October 16. https://winstonchurchill.org/resour
ces/speeches/1930-1938-the-wilderness/the-defence-of-freedom-and-peace/.

Clark, Alan. 2011. *Diaries: In Power 1983–1992*, London: Hachette.

Clark, Christopher. 2013. *Balkan Entanglements. The Sleepwalkers: How Europe Went to
War in 1914*, Glasgow: HarperCollins.

Clark, Colin. 2006a. 'Introduction', in Colin Clark and Margaret Greenfields (eds.),
Here to Stay: The Gypsies and Travellers of Britain, Hatfield: University of
Hertfordshire Press.

Clark, Colin. 2006b. 'Who are the Gypsies and Travellers of Britain?' in Colin Clark
and Margaret Greenfields (eds.), Here to Stay: The Gypsies and Travellers of
Britain, Hatfield: University of Hertfordshire Press.

Clarke, Seán. 2019. 'How representative is Boris Johnson's new cabinet?', *The
Guardian*, July 25. https://www.theguardian.com/politics/ng-interactive/2019/
jul/25/how-representative-is-boris-johnsons-new-cabinet.

CNN. 2019. 'Economic control recognized as domestic abuse in new UK draft law:
offenders may face lie-detector tests'. https://edition.cnn.com/2019/0w1/21/hea
lth/uk-domestic-abuse-bill-gbr-scli-intl/index.html.

Coates, Ta-Nehisi. 2015. *Between the World and Me*, New York: Spiegel and Grau.

Coben, Diana. 1999. 'Common sense or good sense: ethnomathematics and the
prospects for a Gramscian politics of adults' mathematics education', in Mieke van
Groenestijn and Diana Coben (eds.), *Mathematics as Part of Lifelong Learning. The
Fifth International Conference of Adults Learning Maths – A Research Forum, ALM-5*,
London: Goldsmiths College, University of London, in Association with ALM.
www.nottingham.ac.uk/csme/meas/papers/coben.html.

Coben, Diana. 2002. 'Metaphors for an educative politics: "common sense", "good
sense" and educating adults', in Carmel Borg, Joseph A. Buttigieg and Peter
Mayo (eds.), Gramsci and Education, Lanham: Rowman & Littlefield.

Cohen, Stanley. 1972. *Folk Devils and Moral Panics*, London: MacGibbon and Kee Ltd.

Cohen, Steve. 1985a. 'British Brothers' League: Birth of British fascism?', Jewish
Socialist 3.

Cohen, Steve. 1985b. 'Antisemitism, immigration controls and the welfare state',
Critical Social Policy, 13 (Summer).

Cole, Mike. 1989. '"Race" and class or "race", class, gender and community?: A
critical appraisal of the racialised fraction of the working-class thesis', *The British
Journal of Sociology*, 40 (1).

Cole, Mike. 2008. *Marxism and Educational Theory: Origins and Issues*, London:
Routledge.

Cole, Mike. 2011. *Racism in the UK and the US: Towards a Socialist Alternative*, New York: Palgrave Macmillan.

Cole, Mike. 2012. 'Introduction: human rights, equality and education', in Mike Cole (ed.), Education, Equality and Human Rights, 3rd Edition, London: Routledge.

Cole, Mike. 2016. *Racism: A Critical Analysis*, London: Pluto Press.

Cole, Mike. 2017. *Critical Race Theory and Education: A Marxist Response*, Revised 2nd Edition, New York: Palgrave Macmillan.

Cole, Mike. 2018a. 'Racism in the UK: continuity and change', in Mike Cole (ed.), Education, Equality and Human Rights: Issues of Gender, 'Race', Sexuality, Disability and Social Class, 4th Edition, London: Routledge.

Cole, Mike. 2018b. 'Racism and Education: from Empire to May', in Mike Cole (ed.), Education, Equality and Human Rights: Issues of Gender, 'Race', Sexuality, Disability and Social Class, 4th Edition, London: Routledge

Cole, Mike (ed.). 2018. *Education, Equality and Human Rights: Issues of Gender, 'Race', Sexuality, Disability and Social Class*, 4th Edition, London: Routledge.

Cole, Mike. 2019. *Trump, the Alt-Right and Public Pedagogies of Hate and for Fascism: What Is to Be Done?*, London: Routledge.

Cole, Mike. 2020a. 'US Election 2020 Alerts! Democracy under threat; coronavirus catastrophe; climate change destruction, war', *Journal for Critical Education Policy Studies*, 18 (2). http://www.jceps.com/archives/9259.

Cole, Mike. 2020b. *Theresa May, the Hostile Environment and Public Pedagogies of Hate and Threat: The Case for a Future Without Borders*. London: Routledge.

Cole, Mike. 2021. *Climate Change, the Fourth Industrial Revolution and Public Pedagogies: the Case for Ecosocialism*, London: Routledge.

Cole, Mike. 2022. 'Public pedagogy, climate change activism and the case for ecosocialism' in Walsh, E. (ed.), Equity and Social Justice in Climate Change Education, London: Routledge.

Cole, Mike. 2023a. 'Race' and racism in the UK: Through history and today', in Mike Cole (ed.), *Education, Equality and Human Rights: Issues of Gender, 'Race', Sexuality, Disability and Social Class*, 5th Edition, London: Routledge.

Cole, Mike. 2023b. 'Social class, neoliberal capitalism and the Marxist alternative', in Mike Cole (ed.), Education, Equality and Human Rights: Issues of Gender, 'Race', Sexuality, Disability and Social Class, 5th Edition, London: Routledge.

Çolson, Thomas and Bienkov, Adam. 2018. 'Theresa May told officials to "toughen up" controversial "go home" immigration vans', *Business Insider*, April 20. https://www.businessinsider.com/theresa-may-nick-timothy-home-office-go-home-vans-windrush-2018-4?r=US&IR=T.

Cooke, Alistair. 2011. *Founders of the Primrose League*, Oxford: Oxford University Press.

Cooke, Alistair. 2016. 'Harold Macmillan's resignation', Lord Lexden. September 21. https://www.alistairlexden.org.uk/news/harold-macmillans-resignation.

Copping, Robert. 1972. *The Story of the Monday Club: The First Decade*, London: Ilford.

Cousins, Emily. 2010. 'Nottingham Riots (1958)', *Blackpast*, August 30. https://www.blackpast.org/global-african-history/nottingham-riots-1958/.

Cowburn, Ashley. 2016. 'Margaret Thatcher's government tried to prevent Nelson Mandela being honoured by British university, documents reveal'. *The Independent*, January 25. https://www.independent.co.uk/news/uk/politics/margaret-thatcher-s-government-tried-prevent-nelson-mandela-being-honouredbritish-university-documents-reveal-a6831986.html.

Cowburn, Ashburn. 2017. 'Election 2017: Theresa May's immigration policy in "chaos" following confusion over timetable for target reductions', *Independent*, June 2. www.independent.co.uk/news/uk/politics/election-2017-theresa-may-immigration-policy-timetable-targets-conservative-manifesto-prime-minister-a7768371.html.

Cowburn, Ashley. 2022. 'Boris Johnson labelled "moral vacuum" over Savile comments by former Tory chairman', *The Independent*, February 4. https://www.independent.co.uk/news/uk/politics/boris-johnson-lord-patten-resignations-b2007801.html.

Creegan, M. F. 1967. 'Unmarried mothers: An analysis and discussion of interviews conducted in an Irish mother and baby home', unpublished M. Soc. Sc. Dissertation, University College Dublin.

Crick, Martin. 1994. *History of the Social-Democratic Federation*, Edinburgh: Edinburgh University Press.

Cultural India: History of India History of India. Undated. https://www.culturalindia.net/indian-history/index.html#:~:text=%20History%20of%20India%20%201%20India%20Timeline.,the%20third%20emperor%20of%20the%20Mughal…%20More%20.

Curtis, Mark. 2017. 'Britain's role in the war in Palestine, 1948', British foreign policy declassified, March 16. http://markcurtis.info/2017/03/16/britains-role-in-the-war-in-palestine-1948/.

Daniel, W. W. 1968. *Racial Discrimination in England: Based on the P.E.P. Report*. Harmondsworth: Penguin.

Darby, Graham. 1999. *Hitler, Appeasement and the Road to War*, Munich, Germany: AbeBooks.

Darder, Antonia and Torres, Rodolfo D. 2004. *After Race: Racism After Multiculturalism*, New York: New York University Press.

Davin-Power. David. 2015. 'Gallipoli: Churchill's folly must be remembered 100 years on', *The Irish Times*, April 20. https://www.irishtimes.com/culture/heritage/gallipoli-churchill-s-folly-must-be-remembered-100-years-on-1.2182702.

Davis, L. E. and Huttenback, R. A. 1986. *Mammon and the Pursuit of Empire: The Political Economy of British Imperialism, 1860–1912*, Cambridge: Cambridge University Press.

Davis, Wes. 2007. 'When English eyes are smiling', *New York Times*, March 11. https://www.nytimes.com/2007/03/11/opinion/11davis-sub.html.

Dawson, Sarah. 2017. 'A brief history of Blenheim Palace', *The Culture Trip*, August 22. https://theculturetrip.com/europe/united-kingdom/england/articles/a-brief-history-of-blenheim-palace/.

Dearden, Lizzie. 2015. 'Tory conference 2015: Theresa May says she will overhaul asylum seeker process – as it happened', *The Independent*, October 6. https://www.independent.co.uk/news/uk/politics/tory-conference-2015-theresa-may-to-tell-conservative-party-mass-immigration-is-bad-for-britain-live-a6681231.html.

Dearden, Lizzie. 2021. 'Government says discrimination against black people and Travellers "objectively justified" with new laws', *The Independent*, September 13. https://www.independent.co.uk/news/uk/home-news/policing-bill-discrimination-black-travellers-b1919272.html.

de Cecco, Marcello. 1975. *Money and Empire: International Gold Standard, 1890-1914*, Hoboken, New Jersey: Wiley–Blackwell.

Dejevsky, Mary. 2009. 'Cameron's freebie to apartheid South Africa', *The Independent*, April 26. https://www.independent.co.uk/news/uk/politics/cameron-s-freebie-to-apartheid-south-africa-1674367.html.

Demby, Gene. 2014. 'The ugly, fascinating history of the word "racism"', *Codeswitch*, January 6. https://www.npr.org/sections/codeswitch/2014/01/05/260006815/the-uglyfascinating-history-of-the-word-racism?t=1614602816933.

Diniejko, Andrzej. 2018, 'Benjamin Disraeli and the Two Nation Divide', *The Victorian Web*. http://www.victorianweb.org/authors/disraeli/diniejko3.html.

Dirk-Uys, Pieter. 1987. *P.W. Botha: In His Own Words*, Harmondsworth: Penguin.

Disability Rights UK. 2021. 'Almost half of Grenfell fire deaths were disabled people and children', March 31. https://www.disabilityrightsuk.org/news/2021/march/almost-half-grenfell-fire-deaths-were-disabled-people-and-children.

Disraeli, Benjamin. 1847. *Tancred; or The New Crusade*, Vol I., London: M. Walter Dunne.

Disraeli, Benjamin. 1852. *Lord George Bentinck: A Political Biography*, Ithaca, New York: Cornell University Library Press.

Disraeli, Benjamin. 2016. *Delphi Complete Works of Benjamin Disraeli* (Illustrated) (Delphi Series Seven Book 4), Delphi Classics. https://tmbukz.ga/read.php?id=F7dKDAAAQBAJ.

Disraeli, Benjamin. 2017. '*Speech at the opening of Shaftesburgh Park Estate (18 July 1874)*', *in* Wit and Wisdom of Benjamin Disraeli: Collected from his Writings and Speeches (1881), Andesite Press, p. 38.

Domestic Abuse Act. 2021. 'Overarching factsheet', July 11. https://www.gov.uk/government/publications/domestic-abuse-bill-2020-factsheets/domestic-abuse-bill-2020-overarching-factsheet.

Dorey, Peter. 1995. *The Conservative Party and the Trade Unions*, London: Routledge.

Dorling, Danny. 2016. 'Brexit: the decision of a divided country', *British Medical Journal*, 354:i3697, July 6. www.bmj.com/content/354/bmj.i3697.

Dorney, John. 2012a. 'The Irish War of Independence – A brief overview', *The Irish Story*, September 18. https://www.theirishstory.com/2012/09/18/the-irish-war-of-independence-a-brief-overview/#.YRYG7IhKgUU.

Dorney, John. 2012b. '9 August 1971, internment is introduced in Northern Ireland', *The Irish Story*. https://www.theirishstory.com/2012/08/10/today-in-irish-history-9-august-1971-internment-is-introduced-in-northern-ireland/#.YRTixIhKgUU.

Dorney, John. 2015. 'Ireland and the Spanish Armada 1588', *The Irish Story*. August 19. https://www.theirishstory.com/2015/08/19/ireland-andthe-spanish-armada-1588/#.YK-r9flKhGN.

Douglass, Frederick. 1845. *Narrative of the Life of Frederick Douglass, an American Slave, Written by Himself*, Boston, MA: Anti-Slavery Office.

Dovidio, John F. and Gaertner, Samuel L. 1986. 'The aversive form of racism', in John F. Dovidio and Samuel L. Gaertner (eds.), Prejudice, Discrimination and Racism, Cambridge, MA: Academic Press. https://research.pomona.edu/sci/files/2017/08/dovidio-et-al-2017-cambridge-proof.pdf.

Dresser, Madge and Fleming, Peter. 2007. *Bristol: Ethnic Minorities and the City 1000–2001*, Chichester: Phillimore and Company.

Duffield, Charlie. 2020. 'Was Winston Churchill racist? Why some people accused the wartime PM of racism after his London statue was defaced', *The Independent*, June 25. https://inews.co.uk/news/winston-churchill-racist-pm-racism-accusations-london-statue-protest-blm-explained-440668.

Duffy, Ryalla and Tomlinson, Andy. 2009. 'Education on the hoof'. Paper presented to the first seminary of the Centre for Education for Social Justice, in the English Centre, Bishop Grosseteste University College Lincoln, Monday January

19.   https://s3.eu-west-1.amazonaws.com/bishopg.ac.uk/documents/Centre-for-Education-for-Social-Justice.pdf.

Ecarma, Caleb. 2020. 'Call it the Tucker Carlson wing of the GOP: The American Conservative wants to be the Atlantic of the Right', *Vanity Fair*, April 27. https://www.vanityfair.com/news/2020/04/the-american-conservative-the-right-atlantic.

Eccleshall, Robert and Walker, Graham. (eds). 2002. *Biographical Dictionary of British Prime Ministers*, London: Routledge.

EIN (Electronic Immigration Network). 2014a. 'Movement Against Xenophobia meeting: Immigration Act codifies racism into British law and will become untenable'. www.ein.org.uk/news/movement-against-xenophobia-meeting-immigration-act-codifies-racism-british-law-and-will-become.

EIN (Electronic Immigration Network). 2014b. 'Yvette Cooper says Labour would scrap net migration target, Miliband forgets section of speech on immigration', September 24. www.ein.org.uk/news/yvette-cooper-says-labour-would-scrap-net-migration-target-miliband-forgets-section-speech-immi.

EIN (Electronic Immigration Network). 2021. 'Nationality and Borders Bill heads for the Lords after passing its final third reading in the Commons', December 8. https://www.ein.org.uk/news/nationality-and-borders-bill-heads-lords-after-passing-its-final-third-reading-commons.

Elgot, Jessica. 2019. 'As government announces it will prorogue parliament, we answer the key questions', *The Guardian*, August 28. https://www.theguardian.com/politics/2019/aug/28/what-is-prorogation-prorogue-parliament-boris-johnson-brexit.

Elgot, Jessica and Walker, Peter. 2019. '*Javid under fire over "illegal" cross-Channel asylum seekers claim*', *Guardian*, January 2. www.theguardian.com/politics/2019/jan/02/people-crossing-channel-not-genuine-asylum-seekers-javid.

Elkins, Caroline. 2005. *Britain's Gulag: The Brutal End of Empire in Kenya*, London: Jonathan Cape.

Elman, Peter. 1951. 'The Beginnings of the Jewish Trade Union Movement in England', Transactions, JHSE 17.

Engels, Friedrich. 1845. *The Condition of the Working Class in England*. https://www.marxists.org/archive/marx/works/1845/condition-working-class/ch00.htm.

Engels, Friedrich. 1890. 'Engels to J. Bloch in Königsberg', Marx-Engels Correspondence. https://www.marxists.org/archive/marx/works/1890/letters/90_09_21.htm.

English, Otto. 2019. 'A Churchill history lesson for Brexit Britain', *Politico*, February 14. https://www.politico.eu/article/winston-churchill-history-lesson-for-brexit-britain/.

English, Otto. 2020. 'The Churchill factor: Boris would rather everyone talked about Winston', *Politico*, June 16. https://www.politico.eu/article/the-churchill-factor-boris-johnson-would-rather-everyone-talked-about-winston/amp/.

Ensor, Robert. 1936. *England 1870–1914*, Oxford: Oxford University Press.

Erlanger, Steven. 2015. 'Release of 1985 race riots memo prompts apology from Cameron aide', *New York Times*, 30 December. https://www.nytimes.com/2015/12/31/world/europe/oliver-letwin-riots.html?_r=0.

Equality and Human Rights Commission (EHRC). 2018. 'Asylum seekers in Britain unable to access healthcare', November 29. www.equalityhumanrights.com/en/our-work/news/asylum-seekers-britain-unable-access-healthcare.

Erwin, Alan. 2019. '"Hooded men": court rules treatment of men would be torture if deployed today', *The Irish Times*, September 20. https://www.irishtimes.com/news/crime-and-law/hooded-men-court-rules-treatment-of-men-would-be-torture-if-deployed-today-1.4024773.

Evening Standard. 2008. 'Boris says sorry over "blacks have lower IQs" article in the Spectator', *Standard*, April 2. https://www.standard.co.uk/news/mayor/boris-says-sorry-over-blacks-have-lower-iqs-article-in-the-spectator-6630340.html.

Faulkner, Neil. 2012. 'A Marxist history of the world part 56: The Indian Mutiny', *Counterfire*. https://www.counterfire.org/articles/a-marxist-history-of-theworld/15384-a-marxist-history-of-the-world-part-56-the-indian-mutiny.

Feder, Don. 1998. 'Enoch Powell spoke the truth on immigration', *Jewish World Review*. http://www.jewishworldreview.com/cols/feder021698.html.

Fekete, Liz. 2001. 'The emergence of xeno-racism', Institute of Race Relations, September 28. https://irr.org.uk/article/the-emergence-of-xeno-racism/.

Felsenstein, Frank. 1990. 'Jews and devils: antisemitic stereotypes of late medieval and renaissance England', *Literature and Theology*, 4 (1), March. https://www.jstor.org/stable/23927203?seq=1.

Fhlathúin, Máire Ní. 2008. 'The British Empire in the nineteenth century', *19th Century UK Periodicals*, Detroit: Gale. https://www.gale.com/intl/essays/maire-ni-fhlathuin-british-empire-nineteenth-century.

Financial Times. 1985. 'Tory minister faces row over race remark', February 7.

Finestein, Israel. 1959. 'Anglo-Jewish opinion during the struggle for emancipation (1828–1858)', *Transactions (Jewish Historical Society of England)*, 20, https://www.jstor.org/stable/29777970.

Finucane, John 2020. 'The British government is still hiding the truth about my father's murder', *The Guardian*, December 4. https://www.theguardian.com/commentisfree/2020/dec/04/british-government-father-murder-boris-johnson-pat-finucane-loyalist-northern-ireland.

Fletcher, T. W. 1973. 'The Great Depression of English agriculture 1873–1896', in P. J. Perry (ed.), British Agriculture 1875–1914, London: Methuen.

Foot, Paul. 1965. *Immigration and Race in British Politics*, Harmondsworth: Penguin.

Foot, Paul. 1995. 'Tearing up the race card', *London Review of Books*, 17 (23).

Foot, Paul. 2003. 'Brian Nelson', *The Guardian*, April 17. https://www.theguardian.com/news/2003/apr/17/guardianobituaries.northernireland.

Forrest, Adam. 2020. 'US politicians urge Boris Johnson to set up public inquiry into murder of human rights lawyer', *The Independent*, November 26. https://www.independent.co.uk/news/uk/politics/boris-johnson-finucane-murder-us-congress-b1762173.html.

Forsyth, Alex. 2022. 'Nusrat Ghani: Ex-minister's claims reignite rows over Tories and Islam', BBC News, January 24. https://www.bbc.co.uk/news/uk-politics-60118044.

Forward to Freedom. 1984. 'Demonstration against PW Botha, 2 June 1984'. https://www.aamarchives.org/archive/history/1980s/pic8433-demonstration-against-pw-botha-2-june-1984.html.

Francis, Matthew. 2013. 'Harold Wilson's "white heat of technology" speech 50 years on', *The Guardian*, September 19. https://www.theguardian.com/science/political-science/2013/sep/19/haroldwilson-white-heat-technology-speech.

Frankel, J. 1997. '"Ritual murder" in the modern era: The Damascus Affair of 1840', *Jewish Social Studies*, 3, Winter.

Frankel, Robert. 2007. *Observing America: The Commentary of British Visitors to the United States, 1890–1950 (Studies in American Thought and Culture)*, Madison, Wisconsin: University of Wisconsin Press.

Fraser, Giles. 2015. 'The Lutfur Rahman verdict and the spectre of undue spiritual influence', *The Guardian*, April 29. https://www.theguardian.com/commentis free/2015/apr/29/lutfurrahman-tower-hamlets-mayor-verdict-undue-spiritual-influence.

Fraser, Nancy. 2000. 'Rethinking recognition', *New Left Review*, 3, May/June.

Freedland, J. 2003. 'The trailblazer', *The Guardian*, October 31. https://www.theguardian.com/politics/2003/oct/31/conservatives.politicalcolumnists.

Freedland, J. 2014. 'Scrapping Human Rights Law is an act of displaced fury', *The Guardian*, October 3. www.theguardian.com/commentis free/2014/oct/03/scrapping-human-rights-law-european-court-ukip.

Freedland, J. 2016. 'Disraeli by David Cesarani review – the Jewish prime minister and antisemitism', *jt*The Guardian, June 11. https://www.theguardian.com/books/2016/jun/11/disraeli-the-novel-politician-by-david-cesarani-review.

Free Movement. 2018. 'The immigration white paper is a charter for the wealthy', December 21. www.freemovement.org.uk/immigration-white-paper-wealthy-migrants/.

Freire, Paulo. 1985. *The Politics of Education: Culture, Power, and Liberation*. Translated by Donald Macedo. South Hadley, MA: Bergin & Garvey.

Frothingham, Mia Belle. 2021. 'Folk devils and moral panics (Cohen 1972)', *Simply Psychology*, October 28. www.simplypsychology.org/folk-devils-and-moral-panics-cohen-1972.html.

Fryer, Peter. 1984. *Staying Power: The History of Black People in Britain*, London: Pluto Press.

Garden Court Chambers. https://www.gardencourtchambers.co.uk/.

Gardner, Bill. 2014. 'From "shrill" housewife to Downing Street: the changing voice of Margaret Thatcher', *The Telegraph*, November 25. https://www.telegraph.co.uk/news/politics/11251919/From-shrill-housewife-to-Downing-Street-the-changing-voice-of-Margaret-Thatcher.html.

Garrett, Paul Michael. 2000. 'Responding to Irish "invisibility": anti-discriminatory social work practice and the placement of Irish children in Britain', *Adoption & Fostering*, 24 (1).

Garrett, Paul Michael. 2002. '"No Irish need apply": Social work in Britain and the history and politics of exclusionary paradigms and practices', *The British Journal of Social Work*, 32 (4). https://www.jstor.org/stable/pdf/23716328.pdf?refreqid=excelsior%3A404450420bfd56776eb67b3e38a01de5.

Garrett, Paul Michael. (2010). 'The hidden history of the PFIs: The repatriation of unmarried mothers and their children from England to Ireland in the 1950s and 1960s', *Immigrants & Minorities*, 19 (3).

Garton Ash, Timothy. 2017. 'UK PM's private secretary composed the "little list" of alleged German qualities', *Financial Times*, January 3. https://www.ft.com/content/222d2562-cec2-11e6-864f-20dcb35cede2.

Gatewood Jr., Willard B. 1981. 'Frederick Douglass and the building of a "Wall of Anti-Slavery Fire" 1845–1846. An essay review', *The Florida Historical Quarterly*, 59 (3).

Gathara, Patrick. 2019. 'Berlin 1884: Remembering the conference that divided Africa', *Aljazeera*, November 15. https://www.aljazeera.com/opinions/2019/11/15/berlin-1884-remembering-the-conference-that-divided-africa/.

Geddes, Andrew. 2003. *The politics of migration and immigration in Europe*, London: Sage Publications.

Gellner, Ernest. 1964. *Thought and Change*, London: Weidenfield and Nicholson.

Gentleman. Amelia. 2017. '"I can't eat or sleep": the woman threatened in Britain', *The Guardian*. November 28. https://www.theguardian.com/uk-news/2017/nov/28/i-cant-eat-or-sleep-the-grandmother-threatened-with-deportation-after-50-years-in-britain.

Gentleman, Amelia. 2020. 'UK government to act on all 30 Windrush recommendations', *The Guardian*, June 23. https://www.theguardian.com/uk-news/2020/jun/23/uk-government-to-act-on-all-30-windrush-recommendations.

Gentleman, Amelia. 2021. 'Windrush campaigners alarmed by omissions of No 10 race report', *The Guardian*, April 2. https://www.theguardian.com/world/2021/apr/02/windrush-campaigners-alarmed-by-omissions-of-no-10-race-report.

Gentleman, Amelia. 2022a. 'Ukrainian refugees with UK relatives frustrated by Home Office visa delays', *The Guardian*, March 18. https://amp.theguardian.com/uk-news/2022/mar/18/ukrainian-refugees-with-uk-relatives-frustratedby-home-office-visa-delays.

Gentleman, Amelia. 2022b. 'Windrush: Home Office has failed to transform its culture, report says', *The Guardian*, March 31. https://www.theguardian.com/uk-news/2022/mar/31/windrush-home-office-has-failed-to-transform-its-culture-report-says.

Gentleman, Amelia. 2022c. 'Windrush scandal caused by "30 years of racist immigration laws" – report', *The Guardian*, May 29. https://www.theguardian.com/uk-news/2022/may/29/windrush-scandal-caused-by-30-years-of-racist-immigration-laws-report?CMP=Share_iOSApp_Other.

Gentleman, Amelia and Campbell, Lucy. 2020. 'Windrush campaigner Paulette Wilson dies aged 64', *The Guardian*, July 23. https://amp.theguardian.com/uk-news/2020/jul/23/windrush-campaigner-paulette-wilson-dies-aged-64.

Gilbert, Martin. 1977. *Winston S. Churchill, 1922–1939, Vol. 5*, Boston: Houghton and Mifflin.

Gilbert, Martin. 1991. *Churchill: A Life*. London: Pimlico.

Gilbert, Martin. 1993. 'Churchill and the Holocaust: The possible and impossible', Speech at the International Churchill Society Conference, U.S. Holocaust Memorial Museum, Washington, November 8. https://winstonchurchill.org/the-life-of-churchill/war-leader/churchill-and-the-holocaust-the-possible-and-impossible/.

Gilbert, Martin. 2007. 'Myth and reality – What did Churchill really think about the Jews?', Washington DC: International Churchill Society. https://winstonchurchill.org/publications/finest-hour/finest-hour-135/myth-and-reality-what-did-churchill-really-think-about-the-jews/.

Gilmore, Peter. 2016. 'United Electrical, Radio and Machine Workers of America', March 16, https://www.ueunion.org/ue-news-feature/2016/easter-rising-1916-labor-and-the-irish-independence-struggle.

Glendenning. F. J. 1973. 'History textbooks and racial attitudes: 1804–1969', *Journal of Educational Administration and History*, 5.

Global Justice Now. 2018. 'Campaigners call immigration white paper "biggest attack on rights in Britain in a generation"', December 19. www.globaljustice.org.uk/news/2018/dec/19/campaigners-call-immigration-white-paper-biggest-attack-rights-britain-generation.

Glover, D. 2009. 'Imperial Zion: Israel Zangwill and the English origins of territorialism' in E. Bar-Yosef and N. Valman (eds), 'The Jew' in Late-Victorian and Edwardian Culture: Between the East End and East Africa, Houndsmill: Palgrave Macmillan.

Godrej, Dinyar. 2008. 'A short history of Burma', *New Internationalist*, April 18. https://newint.org/features/2008/04/18/history.

Godwin, Richard. 2018. 'Sajid Javid's cynical headline-grabbing epitomises yet another year of anti-immigrant hysteria', *Independent*, 30 December. www.independent.co.uk/voices/home-office-sajid-javid-migrants-refugees-kent-beach-donald-trump-caravan-a8704521.html.

Goldsmiths. 2017. '"13 dead, nothing said" exhibition at Goldsmiths', 16 May 2017–27 May 2017. Exhibition notes by Professor Les Back'. Exhibition video, 10 March. https://www.youtube.com/watch?v=ypfcqyj-FiM.

Goodchild, Sophie and Dillon, Jo. 2001. '"Hundreds" of Conservatives are in the BNP', *The Independent*, August 26. https://www.independent.co.uk/news/uk/politics/hundreds-of-conservatives-are-in-the-bnp-9134986.html?amp.

Goodfellow, Maya. 2019. 'Keeping Britain White', *Tribune*, November 18. https://tribunemag.co.uk/2019/11/keeping-britain-white.

Goodwin, Henry. 2021. 'Have the Tories become the party of the far-right?', *The London Economic*, January 28. https://www.thelondoneconomic.com/politics/have-the-tories-become-the-party-of-the-far-right-218330/.

Goonewardena, Kanishka. 2020. 'Populism, nationalism and Marxism in Sri Lanka: from anti-colonial struggle to authoritarian neoliberalism', *Human Geography*, 102 (3).

Goveia, Elsa V. 1965. *Slave Society in the British Leeward Islands at the End of the Eighteenth Century*, Caribbean Series, Number 8, New Haven, CT: Yale University Press.

GOV.UK. 2010. 'Immigration: Home Secretary's speech of 5 November 2010'. https://www.gov.uk/government/speeches/immigration-home-secretarys-speech-of-5-november-2010.

GOV.UK. 2013. 'Speech by Home Secretary on second reading of Immigration Bill'. https://www.gov.uk/government/speeches/speech-by-home-secretary-on-second-reading-of-immigration-bill.

GOV.UK. 2016. 'Statement from the new Prime Minister Theresa May'. www.gov.uk/government/speeches/statement-from-the-new-prime-minister-theresa-may.

GOV.UK. 2022a. 'Foreign travel advice: Rwanda', April 15. https://www.gov.uk/foreign-travel-advice/rwanda/local-laws-and-customs.

GOV.UK. 2022b. 'Police super-complaints', June 13. https://www.gov.uk/government/collections/police-super-complaints.

GOV.UK. 2022c. 'Guidance: Political impartiality in schools'. https://www.gov.uk/government/publications/political-impartiality-inschools/political-impartiality-in-schools'.

Gramsci, Antonio. 1971. *Selections from Prison Notebooks*, edited and translated by Quintin Hoare and Geoffrey Nowell Smith, London: Lawrence and Wishart.

Gray, Robert. 1966. *The Factory System and Industrial England 1830–1860*. Cambridge: Cambridge University Press.

Greaves, Andrew. 2009. 'Gorilla picture Tory suspended', *The Bolton News*, February 26. https://www.theboltonnews.co.uk/news/4155201.gorilla-picture-tory-suspended/.

Green, E. E. H. 1985. 'Radical conservatism: The electoral genesis of tariff reform', *The Historical Journal*, 28 (3), September.

Green, E. E. H. 1996. *The Crisis of Conservatism: The Politics, Economics and Ideology of The British Conservative Party*, 1880–1914, London: Routledge.

Greenfields, Margaret. 2006. 'Stopping places', in Colin Clark and Margaret Greenfields (eds.), Here to Stay: the Gypsies and Travellers of Britain, Hatfield: University of Hertfordshire Press.

Greenslade, Roy. 1997. 'It's the Sun wot's switched sides to back Blair', *The Guardian*, 18 March. https://www.theguardian.com/politics/1997/mar/18/past.roy greenslade.

Grice, Andrew. 2015. 'David Cameron rules out third term as PM and reveals favourites for next Tory leader', *The Independent*, March 23. www.independent. co.uk/news/uk/politics/david-cameron-admits-he-wont-serve-beyond-2020-10128858.html.

Grierson, Jamie. 2018. 'Hostile environment: anatomy of a policy disaster', *The Guardian*, August 27. https://www.theguardian.com/uk-news/2018/aug/27/hostile-environment-anatomy-of-a-policy-disaster.

Griffiths, Peter. 1966. *A Question of Colour*, London, Leslie Frewin.

Günes, Zeynep. 2005. 'A Marxist approach to the problem of Cyprus', *In Defence of Marxism*, July 18. https://www.marxist.com/cyprus-marxist-approach201201.htm.

Gye, Hugo. 2022. 'Protesters who chain themselves to buildings could face six months in prison under Queen's Speech plan', *Independent*, May 10. https:// inews.co.uk/news/politics/protesters-who-lock-themselves-to-buildingscould-face-six-months-in-prison-under-queens-speech-plan-1620450.

Hadden, Peter. 1980. 'Divide and rule'. https://www.marxists.org/history/etol/wri ters/hadden/1980/divrule/introduction.html.

Hanke, Philip. 2011. *Bobby Sands – An Irish Martyr?* Munich: GRIN Verlag.

Hall, M. P. 1960. *The Social Services of Modern England*, London: Routledge & Kegan Paul.

Haller, John S. 1970. 'The species problem: nineteenth-century concepts of racial inferiority in the origin of man', *American Anthropologist*, 72 (6), pp. 1319–1329. https://www.jstor.org/stable/672850.

Halliday, Josh and Goodman, Joe. 2019. 'Johnson accused of racial stereotyping with view on Nigerians', *The Guardian*, November 28. https://www.theguardian. com/politics/2019/nov/28/johnson-accused-of-racial-stereotyping-with-view-on-nigerians.

Hannan, Martin. 2021. 'Northern Ireland: Impact of internment still felt by many 50 years on', *The National*, August 14. https://www.thenational.scot/news/19513550. northern-ireland-impact-internment-still-felt-many-50-years/.

Hanning, James and Elliott, Francis. 2009. *Cameron: The Rise of the New Conservative*, updated edition, New York: Harper Perennial.

Hansard. 1848. 'Supply–Navy estimates'. *Speech in the House of Commons*, 9 August 1848. http://hansard.millbanksystems.com/commons/1848/aug/09/supply-navy-estimates.

Hansard. 1803–2005 → 1840s → 1847 → December 1847 → 16 December 1847 → 'Commons sitting disabilities of the Jews', Volume 95: HC Deb 16 December 1847, cc1234–332. https://api.parliament.uk/historic-hansard/commons/1847/dec/16/disabilities-of-the-jews#S3V0095P0_18471216_HOC_26.

Hansard. 1803–2005 → 1980s → 1986 → October 1986 → 24 October 1986 → Written Answers (Commons) → Home Department. Visitors HC Deb, 24 October 1986, vol 102 cc1013–21W. https://api.parliament.uk/historic-hansard/written-answers/1986/oct/24/visitors#S6CV0102P0_19861024_CWA_125.

Hansard. 2018. 'Immigration: Hostile environment', Volume 791: debated on Thursday 14 June 2018. https://hansard.parliament.uk/lords/2018-06-14/debates/4EB5AD24-87B4-43E9-908F-1DE447952889/ImmigrationHostileEnvironment.

Hansard's Parliamentary Debates. 1857. Third series 147 (20 July 1857–28 August 1857). London: Thomas Curson Hansard et. al., pp. 440–545.

Happold, Tom. 2003. 'Heath gives Bloody Sunday evidence', *The Guardian*, January 14. https://www.theguardian.com/politics/2003/jan/14/northernireland.devolution1.

Haq, Riaz. 2018. 'Post-Truth partition narrative delegitimizes Pakistan', *PakAlumni Worldwide: The Global Social Network*, April 20. http://www.pakalumni.com/m/blogpost?id=1119293%3ABlogPost%3A120277.

Haque, Sarah. 2022. 'No Grenfell inquiry recommendations enacted by government, says Sadiq Khan', *The Guardian*, March 21. https://amp.theguardian.com/uk-news/2022/mar/21/grenfell-inquiry-no-recommendations-implemented-sadiq-khan.

Hari, Johann. 2020. 'Not his finest hour: The dark side of Winston Churchill', *The Independent*, June 8. https://www.independent.co.uk/news/uk/politics/not-his-finest-hour-dark-side-winston-churchill-2118317.html.

Harlow, V. T. 1926. *The History of Barbados, 1625-1685*, Oxford: Clarendon Press.

Harman, Chris. 1981. 'The summer of 1981: a post-riot analysis (Autumn 1981)', *International Socialism*, 2 (14), Autumn. https://www.marxists.org/archive/harman/1981/xx/riots.html.

Harman, Harriet. 2017. 'Labour's 1997 victory was a watershed for women but our gains are at risk', *The Guardian*, April 10. https://www.theguardian.com/commentisfree/2017/apr/10/labour-1997-victory-women-101-female-mps.

Harrison, J. F. C. (John Fletcher Clews). 1985. *The Common People of Great Britain: A History from the Norman Conquest to the Present* (1st Midland book ed.). Bloomington: Indiana University Press.

Harvey, Fiona. 2021. 'Tories accused of corruption and NHS privatisation by former chief scientist', *The Guardian*, April 13. https://www.theguardian.com/politics/2021/apr/13/tories-accused-of-corruption-and-nhs-privatisation-by-former-chief-scientist.

Hattenstone, Simon. 2018. 'Why was the scheme begind May's "Go Home" vans called Operation Vaken?', *The Guardian*, April 26. https://www.theguardian.com/commentisfree/2018/apr/26/theresa-may-go-home-vans-operation-vaken-ukip.

Hattenstone, Simon. 2020. '"The man who shot my mum is still living his life": Cherry Groce's son on life after police brutality', *The Guardian*, September 5. https://www.theguardian.com/books/2020/sep/05/the-man-who-shot-my-mum-is-still-living-his-life-cherry-groces-son-on-life-after-police-brutality.

Hatton, Ben. 2022. 'Johnson defends Rwanda after concerns over "dismal" human rights record', *The Independent*, April 15. https://www.independent.co.uk/news/uk/rwanda-boris-johnson-government-prime-minister-african-b2058037.html.

Hayton, Richard. 2012. *Reconstructing Conservatism? The Conservative Party in opposition, 1997–2010*, Manchester: Manchester University Press.

Hearth Tax Rolls, cited in toppr. Undated. 'How many Irish people emigrated between 1815 and 1845?', *Toppr.com*. https://www.toppr.com/ask/question/how-many-irish-people-emigrated-between-1815-and-1845/.

Heath, Anthony F., and Ridge, John M. 1983. 'Social mobility of ethnic minorities', *Journal of Biosocial Science*, 8.

Heath, Edward. 1998. *The Course of My Life: The Autobiography of Edward Heath*, London: Hodder and Stoughton.

Heinrich-Heine University Dusseldorf. 2021. '64 human genomes as new reference for global genetic diversity', *Science Daily*, February 25. https://www.sciencedaily.com/releases/2021/02/210225143855.htm.

Helm, Toby. 2019. 'End game: the fall of Theresa May', *The Guardian*, May 26. https://www.theguardian.com/politics/2019/may/26/end-game-fall-of-theresa-may.

Helm, Toby, Savage, Michael, Rawnsley, Andrew and Boffey, Daniel. 2019. 'Amber Rudd quits cabinet and attacks PM for "political vandalism"', *The Guardian*, September 7. https://www.theguardian.com/politics/2019/sep/07/amber-rudd-resigns-from-cabinet-and-surrenders-conservative-whip.

Hennessy, Mark. 2014. 'British ministers sanctioned torture of NI internees', *The Irish Times*, June 5. https://www.irishtimes.com/news/politics/british-ministers-sanctioned-torture-of-ni-internees-1.1820882.

Hennessy, Patrick. J. 2004. 'Blair calls for quotas on immigrants from "New Commonwealth"', The Telegraph, June 6.

Hennessy, Peter. 2007. *Having It So Good: Britain and the Fifties*, London: Penguin.

Herrnstein, Richard and Murray, Charles. 1994. *The Bell Curve: Intelligence and Class Structure in American Life*, New York: Free Press.

Heyden, Tom. 2015. 'The 10 greatest controversies of Winston Churchill's career', *BBC News Magazine*, January 26. https://www.bbc.co.uk/news/magazine-29701767.

Hibbert, Christopher. 2004. *Disraeli: A Personal History*. London: HarperCollins.

Hickman, Kennedy. 2019. 'Mahdist War: Siege of Khartoum', *Thought.Co*, December 2. https://www.thoughtco.com/mahdist-war-siegeof-khartoenum-2361378.

Hickman, Mary J. 1997. *Religion, Class and Identity: the Irish in Britain: The State, the Catholic Church and the Education of the Irish in Britain*, Aldershot: Avebury.

Hickman, Mary J. and Walter, Bronwen. 1995. 'Deconstructing Whiteness: Irish women in Britain', *Feminist Review*, 50 (Summer), pp. 5–19. https://www.jstor.org/stable/i260654.

Higham, Nick. 2016a. 'Margaret Thatcher concerned over "second wives"', BBC News, July 21. https://www.bbc.co.uk/news/uk-36838760.

Higham, Nick. 2016b. 'National Archives: Thatcher's poll tax miscalculation', BBC News. December 30. https://www.bbc.co.uk/news/uk-38382416.

Hill, Dave. Undated. 'The Hillcole group of radical left educators'. http://www.ieps.org.uk/media/1043/hillcole_group_chapter.pdf.

Hindell, Keith. 1965. 'The genesis of the Race Relations Bill', *Political Quarterly*, 34 (October-December).

Historic Hansard. 1987. 'Prison ships', Written-Answers. https://api.parliament.uk/historic-hansard/written-answers/1987/oct/21/prison-ships#S6CV0120P0_19871021_CWA_309.

History.com Editors. 2017. 'Palestine', *History.com*, August 11. https://www.history.com/.amp/topics/middle-east/palestine.

History.com Editors. 2018. 'Social Darwinism', *History.com*, August 21. https://www.history.com/topics/early-20th-century-us/social-darwinism#:~:text=Social%20Darwinism%20is%20a%20loose,%2C%20social%2C%20or%20economic%20views.

History.com. 2022a. 'June 28, 1914: Austria's Archduke Ferdinand assassinated'. https://www.history.com/this-day-in-history/archduke-ferdinand-assassinated#:~:text=The%20assassination%20set%20off%20a,France%20and%20possibly%20Great%20Britain.

History.com. 2022b. '3 August, 1914: Germany and France declare war on each other'. https://www.history.com/this-day-in-history/germany-and-france-declare-waron-each-other.

History Workshop. 2014. 'The Thatcher-Botha Papers', January 5. https://www. historyworkshop.org.uk/the-thatcher-botha-papers/.

History of England. Undated. 'Ireland – The first colony'. https://www.histor yofengland.net/british-empire/ireland-the-first-colony.

HM Government. 2019. 'Transforming the response to domestic abuse consultation response and draft bill, January'. https://assets.publishing.service.gov.uk/government/ uploads/system/uploads/attachment_data/file/772247/Transforming_the_response_ to_domestic_abuse_-_consultation_response_and_draft_bill_-print.pdf.

HM Inspectorate of Prisons. 2017. 'Report on an unannounced inspection of Yarl's Wood Immigration Removal Centre'. www.justiceinspectorates.gov.uk/hmiprisons/ wp-content/uploads/sites/4/2017/11/Yarls-Wood-Web-2017.pdf.

Hobbsbawm, Eric. 1983. *The Invention of Tradition*, Cambridge: Cambridge University Press.

Holmes, Colin. 1979. *Anti-Semitism in British Society 1876–1939*, London: Edward Arnold.

Holocaust Encyclopedia. Undated. 'Invasion of Poland, Fall, 1939'. https://encyclopedia. ushmm.org/content/en/article/invasion-of-poland-fall-1939.

Holocaust Encyclopedia. Undated. 'Protocols of the Elders of Zion'. Washington DC: United States Holocaust Memorial Museum. https://encyclopedia.ushmm. org/content/en/article/protocols-of-the-elders-of-zion.

Holland, Evangeline. 2010. 'Anti-racism in 19th century Britain', *Beyond Victorina*, June 13. #30 Anti-Racism in 19th Century Britain–Guest Blog by Evangeline Holland.

Hollander, Gavriel. 2013. 'Spectator editor defends column supporting Greek far-right party Golden Dawn', *PressGazette*, July 23. https://pressgazette.co.uk/specta tor-editor-defends-column-supporting-greek-far-right-party-golden-dawn/.

Home Affairs Select Committee. 2018. 'House of Commons Home Affairs Committee: The Windrush Generation, sixth report of session 2017–19', June 27. https:// publications.parliament.uk/pa/cm201719/cmselect/cmhaff/990/990.pdf.

Holt, Andrew. 2014. 'British Foreign Policy in the shadow of a general election: The Douglas-Home Government', Exeter: CIGH, April 15. https://imperia lglobalexeter.com/2014/04/15/british-foreign-policy-in-the-shadow-of-a-general- election-the-douglas-home-government/.

Holton, Kate and Smout, Alistair. 2018. 'May apologises for saying EU workers can't "jump the queue"', *Reuters*, edited by William Schomberg. https://uk.reuters. com/article/uk-britain-eu-may-migration-idUKKCN1NV24U.

Home Office. Undated. 'Immigration Act 1971'. https://www.legislation.gov.uk/ ukpga/1971/77/contents.

Home Office. 2013. 'Proscribed terrorist groups or organisations', July 12. https:// web.archive.org/web/20100118084213/http://security.homeoffice.gov.uk/legislation/ current-legislation/terrorism-act-2000/proscribed-groups.html.

Home Office. 2021a. 'How many people do we grant asylum or protection to?', November 25. https://www.gov.uk/government/statistics/immigration- statistics-year-ending-september-2021/how-many-people-do-we-grant-asylum- or-protection-to.

Home Office. 2021b. 'Police powers and procedures: stop and search and arrests, England and Wales, year ending 31 March 2021'. https://www.gov.uk/government/ statistics/police-powers-and-procedures-stop-and-search-and-arrests-england-and- wales-year-ending-31-march-2021/police-powers-and-procedures-stop-and-search- and-arrests-england-and-wales-year-ending-31-march-2021.

Hooper, David. 2004. 'The injustice of Betsygate', *The Guardian*, March 31. https://www.theguardian.com/politics/2004/mar/31/conservatives.uk1.

Hope, Christopher and Willgress, Lydia. 2016. 'Margaret Thatcher had deep misgivings over reunification of Germany, National Archives reveal', *Telegraph*, December 30. https://www.telegraph.co.uk/news/2016/12/30/margaret-thatcher-had-deep-misgivings-reunification-germany/.

Hopkins, Nick and Norton-Taylor, Richard. 2001. 'Police talk to ex-minister Hogg about Ulster killing', *The Guardian*, June 13. https://www.theguardian.com/uk/2001/jun/13/northernireland.richardnortontaylor.

Howkins, Alun. 1991. *Reshaping Rural England. A Social History 1850–1925*, London: HarperCollins Academic.

Hughes, Laura. 2017. 'PMQs: Theresa May says immigration has depressed wages in wake of leaked Brexit paper' *Telegraph*, September 6. www.telegraph.co.uk/news/2017/09/06/pmqs-live-home-office-plans-curb-migration-leaked/.

Human Rights Watch. 2021. 'Rwanda: round ups-linked to commonwealth meeting', September 27. https://www.hrw.org/news/2021/09/27/rwanda-round-ups-linked-commonwealth-meeting.

Hunt, Alex and Wheeler, Brian. 2017. 'Theresa May: 10 reasons why the PM blew her majority', *BBC News*, June 14. https://www.bbc.co.uk/news/election-2017-40237833.

Hunt, James. 1864. 'On the Negro's place in nature', *Journal of the Anthropological Society of London*, (2), pp. xv–lvi. https://www.jstor.org/stable/i351664.

Hyland, Julie. 2017. 'Boris Johnson and the Grenfell Tower inferno', World Wide Socialist Website (WSWS), June 24. https://www.wsws.org/en/articles/2017/06/24/john-j24.html.

Imperial War Museum. 2022. 'How Kaiser Wilhelm II changed Europe forever'. https://www.iwm.org.uk/history/how-kaiser-wilhelm-ii-changed-europe-forever.

In Defence of Marxism. Undated. 'World War 11'. https://www.marxist.com/theory-world-war-ii.htm.

Independent Office for Police Conduct. 2022. 'National Stop and Search learning report, April 2022'. https://www.policeconduct.gov.uk/national-stop-and-search-learning-report-april-2022.

Inside the Games. 2021. '1986 – Edinburgh'. https://www.insidethegames.biz/articles/5285/1986-edinburgh.

Institute for Economics & Peace. 2018. 'Global Peace Index, 2018: Measuring peace in a complex world', June. http://visionofhumanity.org/app/uploads/2018/06/Global-Peace-Index-2018-2.pdf.

IPSOS Global Advisor. 2018. 'Attitudes towards socialist ideals in the 21st century'. https://www.ipsos.com/sites/default/files/ct/news/documents/2018-05/global_socialism_survey-ipsos.pdf.

Iqbal, Nosheen. 2021. 'Downing Street rewrote "independent" report on race, experts claim', *The Guardian*, April 11. https://www.theguardian.com/uk-news/2021/apr/11/downing-street-rewrote-independent-report-on-race-experts-claim.

ITV News. 2021. 'Who are Insulate Britain, the group blocking M25 traffic, and what are they campaigning for?', September 20. https://www.itv.com/news/2021-09-20/who-are-insulate-britain-the-group-blocking-the-m25-and-whatdo-they-want.

Jackson, T. A. 1922. 'The British Empire', The Communist Party of Great Britain. Marxists Internet Archive, 2007. https://www.marxists.org/archive/jackson-ta/pamphlets/british_empire.htm.

Jacobs, Joseph. 1906. 'England'. https://www.jewishencyclopedia.com/articles/5764-england.

Jaffe, Benjamin. 1978. 'A reassessment of Benjamin Disraeli's Jewish aspects', *Transactions & Miscellanies* (Jewish Historical Society of England), 27. http://www.jstor.org/stable/29778900.

James, Robert Rhodes. 1970. 'The Conservative Party and the Empire', *The Round Table: The Commonwealth Journal of International Affairs*, 60 (240).

Jayanetti, Chaminda. 2018. 'NHS denied treatment for migrants who can't afford upfront charges', *Guardian*, November 13. www.theguardian.com/society/2018/nov/13/nhs-denied-treatment-for-migrants-who-cant-afford-upfront-charges.

JCWI (Joint Council for the Welfare of Immigrants). 2016. 'What's next for the Hostile Environment: The Immigration Act 2016 and the Queen's Speech', May 23. https://jcwi.org.uk/blog/2016/05/23/what%E2%80%99s-next-hostile-environment-immigration-act-2016-and-queen%E2%80%99s-speech.

Jeffries, Stuart. 2014a. 'Britain's most racist election: the story of Smethwick, 50 years on', *The Guardian*, October 15. https://www.theguardian.com/world/2014/oct/15/britains-most-racist-election-smethwick-50-years-on.

Jeffries, Stuart. 2014b. 'Swamped' and 'riddled': the toxic words that wreck public discourse', *The Guardian*, October 27. https://www.theguardian.com/uk-news/2014/oct/27/swamped-and-riddled-toxic-phrases-wreck-politics-immigration-michael-fallon.

Jenkins, Gareth. 1999. 'The badge of prejudice', *Socialist Review*, 234. http://pubs.socialistreviewindex.org.uk/sr234/jenkins.htm.

Jenkins, Simon. 2013. 'How Margaret Thatcher's Falklands gamble paid off', *The Guardian*, April 9. https://amp.theguardian.com/politics/2013/apr/09/margaret-thatcher-falklands-gamble.

Jewish Telegraphic Agency. 1989. '*British TV show explores government anti-semitism: the Jewish chronicle'*, *November 3*. https://www.jta.org/archive/british-tv-show-explores-government-anti-semitism-the-jewish-chronicle.

Jewish Telegraph Agency. 1926. 'Sir Stuart Samuel dies; brother of Sir Herbert', May 16. https://www.jta.org/archive/sir-stuart-samuel-dies-brother-of-sir-herbert.

John Major Archive. 1993a. 'Mr Major's speech to the Carlton Club', February 3. https://johnmajorarchive.org.uk/1993/02/03/mr-majors-speech-to-the-carlton-club-3-february-1993/.

John Major Archive. 1993b. 'Mr Major's speech to Conservative Group for Europe', April 22. https://johnmajorarchive.org.uk/1993/04/22/mr-majors-speech-to-conservative-group-for-europe-22-april-1993/.

Johnson, Boris. 2000. 'Am I guilty of racial prejudice? We all are', *The Guardian*, February 21. https://www.theguardian.com/uk/2000/feb/21/lawrence.ukcrime3.

Johnson, R. W. 1989. 'Is this successful management?', *London Review of Books*, 11 (8). https://www.lrb.co.uk/the-paper/v11/n08/r.w.-johnson/is-this-successful-management.

Jonathan Evans, Baron Evans of Weardale, Director General 2007–13, Security Service. Undated. https://www.mi5.gov.uk/sir-jonathan-evans.

Jones, Dan. 2010. 'Becoming a Victorian', *The Spectator*, March 20. https://www.spectator.co.uk/article/becoming-a-victorian.

Jones, Elizabeth. 2018. 'The Bristol bus boycott of 1963', *Black History Month 2021*, October 7. https://www.blackhistorymonth.org.uk/article/section/bhm-heroes/the-bristol-bus-boycott-of-1963/.

Jones, Maldwyn A. 1980. 'Scotch-Irish', in Stephan Thernstrom, Ann Orlov and Oscar Handlin (eds.), Harvard Encyclopedia of American Ethnic Groups, Cambridge, MA: The Belknap Press of Harvard University Press.

Jones, Nigel. 2012. 'Cameron, Churchill, race… and a historical howler', *Daily Mail*, March 15. https://www.dailymail.co.uk/debate/article-2114950/amp/Cameron-Churchill-Race–historical-howler.html.

Jones, Nicholas. 2016. 'My father and Enoch Powell', Weekend supplement, Shropshire Star, October 8.

Jones, Rupert. 2016. 'My grandparents, Enoch Powell and the day they fell out over his "rivers of blood" speech', *The Guardian*, October 26. https://amp.theguardian.com/lifeandstyle/2016/oct/22/my-grandparents-enoch-powell-andthe-day-they-fell-out-over-his-rivers-of-blood-speech.

Jones, Sara and Goodwin, Kinga. 2021. 'Lost in the storm: Arts venues re-open too late for some migrant artists', *Byline Times*, May 17. https://bylinetimes.com/2021/05/17/lost-in-the-storm-arts-venues-re-open-too-late-for-some-migrant-artists/.

Jones, Scott. 2021. 'Lessons from history: 1920s-30s Britain: A working-class movement fighting unemployment and capitalism', *The Socialist*, April 14. https://m.socialistparty.org.uk/articles/32371/14-04-2021/1920s-30s-britain-a-workingclass-movement-fighting-unemployment-and-capitalism.

Jones, Steve. '1956 Suez Crisis: the death of an empire', *Socialist Appeal*, November 7. https://www.socialist.net/1956-suez-crisis-the-death-of-an-empire.htm.

Jordan. Undated. 'The making of Transjordan'. http://www.kinghussein.gov.jo/his_transjordan.html.

JTA. 2018. 'Respected British magazine publishes defense of Nazi German troops', *Times of Israel*, May 18. https://www.timesofisrael.com/respected-british-magazine-publishes-defense-of-nazi-german-troops/.

Justice4Grenfell. 2021. 'About'. https://justice4grenfell.org/about/.

Kaminer, Reuben. 2003. 'The Palestine question analyzed in the light of Marxist politics', Third International Conference on the work of Karl Marx and its challenges in the twenty-first century. Marxists.org. https://www.marxists.org/subject/jewish/kaminer.pdf.

Kanagasooriam, James. 2019. '"When you talk about cultural barriers to voting Tory", he concluded, "this is where it is"' (Twitter). https://twitter.com/jameskanag/status/1161639307536457730?lang=en-GB.

Kanagasooriam, James and Simon, Elizabeth. 2021. 'Red Wall: The definitive description', *Political Insight*, 12 (3). September 13. https://journals.sagepub.com/doi/10.1177/20419058211045127.

Kareem, Abdul. 2017. 'September 24, 1992: Mellor resigns amid scandals', *Gulf News*, September 23. https://gulfnews.com/today-history/september-241992-mellor-resigns-amid-scandals-1.2094643.

Kavon, Eli. 2022. 'Why did Benjamin Disraeli's father convert his son?' *The Jerusalem Post*, March 5. https://www.jpost.com/opinion/article-700402.

Kelly, Nicola. 2022. '"I will die here, I can't go back to Africa": migrants respond to Rwanda removal', *The Guardian*, April 15. https://www.theguardian.com/world/2022/apr/15/i-will-die-here-i-cant-go-back-to-africa-migrants-respond-to-rwanda-removal?CMP=Share_iOSApp_Other.

Kelly, Stephen. 2021a. *Margaret Thatcher, the Conservative Party and the Northern Ireland Conflict, 1975-1990*, London: Bloomsbury Publishing.

Kelly, Stephen. 2021b. 'Margaret Thatcher, state collusion, and the murder of Pat Finucane', *LSE British Politics and Policy*, March 3. https://blogs.lse.ac.uk/politicsandpolicy/margaret-thatcher-state-collusion-and-the-murder-of-pat-finucane/.

Kentish, Benjamin. 2018. 'Theresa May accused of fuelling hate crime over claims EU migrants "jump the queue"', *Independent*, November. 29. www.independent.co.uk/news/uk/politics/theresa-may-eu-migrants-hate-crime-jump-queue-cbi-speech-conservatives-a8643456.html.

KESSE. 2020. 'Takyi, the Ghanaian king who led a slave rebellion in Jamaica', *Ghanaian Museum*, April 6. https://ghanaianmuseum.com/the-story-of-takyi-the-ghanaian-king-who-led-a-slave-rebellion-in-jamaica-in-1760/.

'Key dates in Working Conditions, Factory Acts Great Britain 1300–1899'. Undated. http://www.thepotteries.org/dates/work.htm#:~:text=1874%20Factory%20Act%20raised%20the,working%20week%20to%2056%C2%BD%20hours.

Kidd, Alan. 1999. *State, Society and the Poor: In Nineteenth-Century England* (Social History in Perspective), London: Springer.

Kiernan, V. G. 1969. *Lords of Human Kind: European Attitudes Towards the Outside World in the Imperial Age*, London: Weidenfeld & Nicolson.

Kimber, Charlie. 2022. 'Use your right to protest – it's the best response to the Tory police bill', *Socialist Worker*, 2803, April 28. https://socialistworker.co.uk/news/use-your-right-to-protest-its-the-best-response-to-tory-police-bill/.

Kinealy, Christine. 2011. *Daniel O'Connell and the Anti-Slavery Movement*, London: Pickering and Chatto.

King, Oliver. 2015. 'The poll tax riot 25 years ago was the day I woke up politically', *The Guardian*, March 31. https://www.theguardian.com/commentisfree/2015/mar/31/poll-tax-riots-25-years-ago-political-awakening-carnage-trafalgar-square.

Kirby, Dean. 2021, 'Black Lives Matter: Priti Patel says the 2020 protests were "dreadful" and she opposes taking a knee', *iNews*, February 12. https://inews.co.uk/news/uk/black-lives-matter-priti-patel-2020-protests-dreadful-opposes-taking-knee-870528.

Kirkup, James. 2015. 'Theresa May's immigration speech is dangerous and factually wrong', *Telegraph*, October 6. www.telegraph.co.uk/news/uknews/immigration/11913927/Theresa-Mays-immigration-speech-is-dangerous-and-factually-wrong.html.

Kirkup, James and Winnett, Robert. 2012. 'Theresa May interview: "We're going to give illegal immigrants a really hostile reception"', *Telegraph*. October 6. https://www.telegraph.co.uk/news/0/theresa-may-interview-going-give-illegal-migrants-really-hostile/.

Kohn, Hans. 1955. *Nationalism: Its Meaning and History*, Princetown: Van Nostrand.

Kovel, Joel. 1970. *White Racism: A Psychohistory*, New York: Pantheon.

Kraft, Dina. 2020. 'When did Hitler start hating Jews? New evidence may change what we know', *Haaretz*, February 16. https://www.haaretz.com/amp/jewish/holocaust-remembrance-day/.premium.MAGAZINE-whendid-hitler-start-hating-jews-new-evidence-may-change-what-we-know-1.8529591.

Kuenssberg, Laura. 2022. 'Nusrat Ghani: PM orders Cabinet Office to investigate "Muslimness" claim', *BBC News*, January 24. https://www.bbc.co.uk/news/uk-politics-60108377.

Kundnani, Arun. 2001. 'From Oldham to Bradford: the violence of the violated', *Institute of Race Relations*, October 1. https://irr.org.uk/article/from-oldham-to-bradford-the-violence-of-the-violated/.

Kuo, Lily. 2016. 'Britain's new foreign secretary once referred to Africa's "watermelon smiles" and "piccaninnies"', *Quartz Africa*, July 14. https://qz.com/africa/731695/britains-new-foreign-secretary-once-referred-to-africas-watermelon-smiles-and-piccanninies/.

Kushner, Tony. 2102. 'The impact of the holocaust on British society and culture', *Contemporary British History*, 5 (2).

LA Times Archives. 1985. 'European Community approves sanctions on S. Africa', September 11. https://www.latimes.com/archives/la-xpm-1985-09-11-mn-7171-story.html.

Laskey, John. 2003. 'Marx & Engels on the Civil War', Crossfire, 73 (December).

Lamb, Richard. 1987. The Failure of the Eden Government, London: Sidgwick & Jackson.

Lamb, Richard. 1995. *The Macmillan years 1957–1963: The Emerging Truth*, London: John Murray.

Lambert, Tim. 2019. 'Ireland in the 18th century'. *Local Histories*. http://www.localhistories.org/ireland18th.html.

Langdon, Julia. 2020. 'Terry Dicks obituary', *The Guardian*, June 22. https://www.theguardian.com/politics/2020/jun/22/terry-dicks-obituary.

Langworth, Richard M. 2019. 'Was Churchill a White supremacist?', *The Churchill Project*, May 7. https://winstonchurchill.hillsdale.edu/white-supremacy/.

Larres, Klaus W. 2020. 'When a winner becomes a loser: Winston Churchill was kicked out of office in the British election of 1945', *The Conversation*, July 27. https://theconversation.com/when-a-winner-becomes-a-loser-winston-churchill-was-kicked-out-of-office-in-the-british-election-of-1945-129746.

Lassalle, Didier. 1997. *Les minorités ethniques en Grande-Bretagne: Aspects démographiques et sociologiques contemporains*, Paris: L'Harmattan.

Latour, Vincent. 2009. 'Multiculturalism upheld? Immigration, "race relations" and diversity management under John Major (1990-1997)', *Observatoire de la société britannique*, 7. https://journals.openedition.org/osb/804.

Latour, Vincent. 2012. 'Muscular liberalism: surviving multiculturalism? A historical and political contextualisation of David Cameron's Munich speech', *La nouvelle donne politique en Grande-Bretagne (2010–2012)*, 12. https://journals.openedition.org/osb/1355.

Latour, Vincent. 2017. 'Between consensus, consolidation and crisis: immigration and integration in 1970s Britain', *French Journal of British Studies*. https://journals.openedition.org/rfcb/pdf/1719.

Lawrence, Errol. 1982. 'Just plain common sense: the "roots" of racism', in Centre for Contemporary Cultural Studies (ed.), Empire Strikes Back: Race and Racism in 70's Britain, London: Routledge.

Lawrence, Jon. 2009. *Electing Our Masters: The Hustings in British Politics from Hogarth to Blair*, Oxford: Oxford University Press.

Lawrence, Stephen. 2000. 'Am I guilty of racial prejudice? We all are', *The Guardian*. February 21. https://www.theguardian.com/uk/2000/feb/21/lawrence.ukcrime3.

Lawson, Dominic. 2014. 'Alan Clark was not "wonderful". He was sleazy and cruel', *The Independent*, July 8. https://www.independent.co.uk/voices/commentators/dominic-lawson/alan-clark-was-not-wonderful-he-was-sleazy-and-cruel-1787343.html.

Layton-Henry, Zig. 1992. *The Politics of Immigration*, Oxford: Blackwell Publishers.

Lea, Sian. 2016. 'The Immigration Act 2016 in plain English', *Human Rights News, Views & Info*, May 31. https://rightsinfo.org/immigration-act-2016-plain-english/.

Learmouth, Andrew. 2020. 'Joe Biden remembers Boris Johnson's Barack Obama comments', *The Argus*, November 9. https://www.theargus.co.uk/news/18856809. joe-biden-remembers-boris-johnsons-racist-comments-barack-obama/.

Lenin, Vladimir Ilyich. 1916. *Imperialism, the Highest Stage of Capitalism*. https://www.marxists.org/archive/lenin/works/1916/imp-hsc/imperialism.pdf.

Lester, Nick, Goodall, Sophie and Hatton, Ben. 2022. 'Government suffers series of defeats in Lords on immigration overhaul'. *WalesOnline*. March 1. https://www.walesonline.co.uk/news/uk-news/government-suffers-series-defeats-lords-23246439.

Lewis, Gail. 1996. 'Welfare settlements and racialising practices', Soundings *4 (Autumn)*. http://banmarchive.org.uk/collections/soundings/04_109.pdf.

Lewis, Paul. 2011. 'Tottenham riots: a peaceful protest, then suddenly all hell broke loose', *The Guardian*, August 7. https://www.theguardian.com/uk/2011/aug/07/tottenham-riots-peaceful-protest.

Lewontin R. C. 1972. 'The apportionment of human diversity', Evolutionary Biology, 6:381–3986:381–398.

Liberal History: The website of the Liberal Democrat History Group. Undated. 'Liberal unionists'. https://liberalhistory.org.uk/history/liberal-unionists/.

Lindsay, Caron. 2017. 'In full: Tim Farron's speech: I love my country and I want it back from the nationalists', *Liberal Democratic Voice*, March 19. www.libdemvoice.org/in-full-tim-farrons-speech-i-love-my-country-and-i-want-it-back-from-the-nationalists-53681.html.

Linning, Stephanie. 2016. 'Margaret Thatcher feared the fall of the Berlin Wall could herald return of Nazis as aides told her Germans were aggressive, egotistical and bullying', *DailyMail*, December 30. https://www.dailymail.co.uk/news/article-4074992/Margaret-Thatcher-feared-fall-Berlin-Wall-herald-return-Nazis-aides-told-Germans-aggressive-egotistical-bullying.html.

Littlejohn, Georgina. 2020. '"Boris Johnson isn't a Conservative, he's a nationalist", says former Tory chair Lord Patten', *The Independent*, December 12. https://inews.co.uk/news/brexit/boris-johnson-isnt-a-conservative-hes-anationalist-says-former-tory-chair-lord-patten-792618.

Liu, H., Prugnolle, F., Manica, A., and Balloux, F. August 2006. 'A geographically explicit genetic model of worldwide human-settlement history', *American Journal of Human Genetics*, 79 (2).

Livingston, Grace. 2020. 'Torture "for your amusement": How Thatcher's government misled MPs and public about its dealings with the Pinochet regime', *Daily Maverick*, April 21. https://www.dailymaverick.co.za/article/2020-04-21-torture-for-your-amusement-how-thatchers-government-misled-mps-and-public-about-its-dealings-with-the-pinochet-regime/.

Lofchie, Michael F. 1972. 'The Uganda coup – class action by the military', *The Journal of Modern African Studies*, 10 (1) May.

Longford, Elizabeth. 2019. *Queen Victoria*, Orion Publishing Group.

Lord Scarman. 1981. *The Brixton Disorders 10–12 April 1981*, report of an inquiry, Cmnd 8427, HMSO.

Lorimer, Douglas A. 1978. *Colour, Class and the Victorians: English Attitudes to the Negro in the Mid-nineteenth Century*, Leicester University Press.

Lorimer, Douglas A. 2013. *Science, race relations and resistance: Britain, 1870–1914*, Manchester: Manchester University Press.

Lothian-McLean, Moya. 2022. 'Boris Johnson is revealing who he really is', *The New York Times*, January 10. https://www.nytimes.com/2022/01/10/opinion/boris-johnson-britain-bills.html.

Lowe, Josh. 2014. 'Tory crisis: The most famous defectors in British politics', Prospect, September 29. httpsv://www.prospectmagazine.co.uk/other/tory-crisis-british-politicss-most-famous-defectors-mark-reckless.

Lowe, Norman. 2013. *Mastering Modern World History*, New York: Red Globe Press.

Lyons, Kate, Thöne, Eva, Kirchgaessner, Stephanie, Baumard, Marilyne and Galarraga, Naiara. 2017. 'Britain is one of worst places in western Europe for asylum seekers', *Guardian*, March 1. www.theguardian.com/uk-news/2017/mar/01/britain-one-of-worst-places-western-europe-asylum-seekers.

Macaskill, Andrew and James, William. 2022. 'Drunkenness, vomiting and a scuffle at UK government lockdown parties', *Reuters*, May 25. https://www.reuters.com/world/uk/drunkenness-sickness-fighting-duringlockdown-party-uk-government-report-2022-05-25/.

MacDonald, Malcolm. 1972. *Titans & Others*, London: Collins.

Macfarlane, Jenna. 2021. 'Windrush Scandal: Who is the Windrush generation in the UK and the Windrush history explained', *The Scotsman*, November 24. https://www.scotsman.com/news/politics/windrush-scandal-who-is-the-windrush-generation-in-the-uk-and-the-windrush-history-explained-3282065.

MacGregor, Marion. 2022. 'Record number of migrant Channel crossings in 2022', *Infomigrants*, April 1. https://www.infomigrants.net/en/post/37620/record-number-of-migrant-channel-crossings-in-2021#:~:text=Last%20year%2C%20more%20than%2028%2C000,went%20missing%20during%20the%20attempt.

MacKenzie, J. M. (ed.). 1984. *Propaganda and Empire: The Manipulation of British Public Opinion 1880–1960*, Manchester: Manchester University Press.

Mackie, Lindsay and Phillips, Mike. 1981. 'How smouldering tension erupted to set Brixton aflame – archive', *The Guardian*, April 13. https://www.theguardian.com/theguardian/1981/apr/13/fromthearchive.

Macmillan, Harold. 1960. 'The Wind of Change speech', delivered to Members of both Houses of Parliament of the Union of South Africa, Cape Town, 3 Feb. https://web-archives.univ-pau.fr/english/TD2doc1.pdf.

MacShane, Denis. 2008a. 'Fear and loathing in Westminster', *Total Politics*, October 27. https://www.totalpolitics.com/articles/culture/fear-and-loathing-westminster.

MacShane, Denis. 2008b. *Globalising Hatred: The New Antisemitism*, London: Weidenfeld and Nicolson.

Madeley, Peter. 2018. 'A fit country for heroes: 100 years since Lloyd George made legendary speech in Wolverhampton', *Express and Star*, November 23. https://www.expressandstar.com/news/politics/2018/11/23/a-fit-country-forheroes-100-years-since-lloyd-georges-legendary-wolverhampton-speech/.

Maguire, Kevin. 2002. 'Switzerland? Keep it white – a classic case of the DT's', *The Guardian*, March 14. https://amp.theguardian.com/uk/2002/mar/14/conservatives.politics.

Maidment, Jack. 2021. '"It is time to be proud of who we are": Foreign Secretary Liz Truss warns "woke" attacks on the UK's past and culture are a gift to Britain's enemies as she says the nation should embrace "our history, warts and all"', *Daily Mail*, December 8. https://www.dailymail.co.uk/news/article-10287385/Liz-Truss-warns-against-woke-attacks-UKs-history-culture.html.

Mair, John, Keeble, Richard and Fowler, Neil. 2013. *What Do We Mean by Local? The Rise, Fall – and Possible Rise Again – of Local Journalism*, Bury St Edmunds: Arima Publishing.

Maisuria, Alpesh. 2021. 'Antonio Gramsci – hegemony', in Themelis, Spyros (ed.), Critical Reflections on the Language of Neoliberalism in Education Dangerous Words and Discourses of Possibility, London: Routledge.

Maisuria, Alpesh. 2022. 'Introduction to Marxism for critical educators', in Maisuria, Alpesh (ed.), Encyclopaedia of Marxism and Education, The Netherlands: Brill Publishing.

Maisuria, Alpesh and Cole, Mike. 2017. 'The neoliberalization of higher education in England: an alternative is possible', *Policy Futures in Education*, 15 (5).

Malik, Nuzhat. 2008. 'Europe: Overview of public benefit status defining "charity" and "charitable purposes"' in the United Kingdom', *The International Journal of Not-for-Profit Law*, 11 (1). https://www.icnl.org/resources/research/ijnl/defi ning-charity-and-charitable-purposesin-the-united-kingdom.

Mangan, J. A. 1986. 'The grit of our forefathers: invented traditions, propaganda and imperialism', in J. MacKenzie (ed.), Imperialism and Popular Culture, Manchester: Manchester University Press.

Manjapra, Kris. 2018. 'When will Britain face up to its crimes against humanity?', *The Guardian*, March 29. https://www.theguardian.com/news/2018/mar/29/slavery-abolition-compensation-when-will-britain-face-up-to-its-crimes-against-humanity.

Mararike, Shingi. 2022. 'Rwanda: First glimpse inside the centre that will house Channel migrants', *Sky News*. https://news.sky.com/story/rwanda-first-glimpsein side-the-centre-that-will-house-channel-migrants-12589911.

Marks, Kathy. 2013. 'Margaret Thatcher an "unabashedly racist": The view of the Australian Foreign Minister', *The Independent*, April 10. https://www.independent. co.uk/news/world/australasia/margaret-thatcher-unabashedly-racist-view-australian-foreign-minister-8567946.html?amp.

Marx, Karl. 1844. 'On the Jewish question'. https://www.marxists.org/archive/marx/works/1844/jewish-question/.

Marx, Karl. 1852. *The Eighteenth Brumaire of Louis Bonaparte*. https://www.marxists. org/archive/marx/works/1852/18th-brumaire/ch01.htm#:~:text=Men%20make %20their%20own%20history,the%20brains%20of%20the%20living.

Marx, Karl. 1860. '*Marx to Engels, after 11 January 1860*', *in* Marx and Engels Collected Works, Vol 41, London: Lawrence and Wishart.

Marx, Karl. 1862. 'A London workers meeting', *Marx and Engels Collected Works* (Vol. 19). https://wikirouge.net/texts/en/A_London_Workers%E2%80%99_Meeting_ (1862).

Marx, Karl. 1870. 'To Paul and Laura Lafargue', March 1870, in Marx and Engels. 1987. *Ireland and the Irish Question*, Moscow: Progress Publishers.

Marx, Karl. 1887. *Capital Vol. 1*, Moscow: Progress Publishers. https://www. marxists.org/archive/marx/works/download/pdf/Capital-Volume-I.pdf.

Marx, Karl and Engels, Friedrich. 1948. *Manifesto of the Communist Party*. https:// www.marxists.org/archive/marx/works/download/pdf/Manifesto.pdf.

Marx, Karl and Engels, Friedrich. 1955. 'Letter from Marx to Engels' in Manchester, Abstract, London, November 30, 1867. *Selected Correspondence*, Moscow: Progress Publishers; Transcribed and HTML markup by Tim Delaney, 1999. https:// www.marxists.org/archive/marx/works/1867/letters/67_11_30-abs.htm.

Marx, Karl and Engels, Friedrich. 1975. *Selected Correspondence*, Moscow: Progress Publishers.

Mason, Rowena. 2019. 'Tory candidate faces calls to quit over "disgusting racism"', *The Guardian*, November 11. https://www.theguardian.com/politics/2019/nov/11/tory-candidate-anthony-browne-faces-calls-quit-over-disgusting-racism.

Mason, Rowena. 2020. 'No 10 refuses to comment on PM's views of racial IQ', *The Guardian*, February 17. https://www.theguardian.com/politics/2020/feb/17/no-10-refuses-to-comment-on-pms-views-of-racial-iq.

Mason, Rowena. 2022. 'Boris Johnson wins no-confidence vote despite unexpectedly large rebellion', *The Guardian*, June 6. https://www.theguardian.com/politics/2022/jun/06/boris-johnson-wins-no-confidence-vote-despite-unexpectedly-large-rebellion.

Mathers, Matt. 2021. 'What has Boris Johnson said about Trump? PM has attempted to distance himself from the president in recent weeks', *The Independent*, January 19. https://www.independent.co.uk/news/uk/politics/boris-johnson-donald-trump-comments-b1789384.html.

Matthew, H.C.G. 1987. 'Rhetoric and politics in Great Britain, 1860–1950', in P. J. Waller (ed.), *Politics and Social Change in Modern Britain*, Brighton: Harvester.

Mayor of London. 2018. 'Mayor calls to protect victims of serious crime with insecure status', 15 August. www.london.gov.uk/press-releases/mayoral/protect-victims-of-crime-with-insecure-status.

McBain, Sophie. 2020. 'The rise of the Proud Boys in the US, Who are the self-styled gang of Western chauvinists Trump asked to "stand back and stand by"?', *NewStatesman*, September 26. https://www.newstatesman.com/uncategorized/2020/10/rise-proud-boys-us.

McCarthy, Terry. 2017. *A Short History of the British Labour Movement*, Labour History Movement Publications, pp. 48–50.

McClements, Freya. 2021. 'What Bobby Sands means to me: "The hunger strikers chose to die. Daddy didn't"', *The Irish Times*, April 3. https://www.irishtimes.com/culture/heritage/what-bobby-sands-means-to-me-thehunger-strikers-chose-to-die-daddy-didn-t-1.4525223.

McCracken, John. 2012. *A History of Malawi, 1859–1966*, Melton: James Currey.

McGeever, Brendan, and Virdee, Satnam. 2017. 'Antisemitism and socialist strategy in Europe, 1880–1917: An Introduction', *Patterns of Prejudice*, 51 (3–4).

McGuinness, Alan and Rayner, Tom. 2022. 'The rise and fall of Boris Johnson: the political magician who won power but lost control', *Sky News*, July 7. https://news.sky.com/story/the-rise-and-fall-of-boris-johnson-the-political-magician-whowon-power-but-lost-control-12519849.

McIntyre, Niamh and Taylor, Diane. 2018. 'Britain's immigration detention: how many people are locked up?', *The Guardian*. https://www.theguardian.com/uk-news/2018/oct/11/britains-immigration-detention-how-many-people-are-locked-up.

McKay, James. 2008. 'The passage of the 1962 Commonwealth Immigrants Act, a case-study of backbench power', *Observatoire de la société britannique*. https://journals.openedition.org/osb/433.

McKenzie, Robert and Silver, Allan. 1968. *Angels in Marble: Working Class Urban England*, London: Heinemann Educational.

McKie, R. 2020. 'The search for Eden: in pursuit of humanity's origins', *The Guardian*, January 5. https://www.theguardian.com/world/2020/jan/05/the-search-for-eden-in-pursuit-of-humanitys-origins.

McSmith, Andy and Dillon, Jo. 2003. 'Tory MPs line up to deal death blow to IDS', *The Independent*, February 23. https://www.independent.co.uk/news/uk/politics/tory-mps-line-up-to-deal-death-blow-to-ids-120094.html.

Mead, Matthew. 2007. 'Empire Windrush: cultural memory and archival disturbance', *MoveableType*, Vol. 3. http://discovery.ucl.ac.uk/1572362/1/Matthew%20Mead.pdf.

MEE staff. 2022. 'Russia-Ukraine war: Western media criticised for racist "blonde hair blue eyes" coverage of invasion', *Middle East Eye*, February 27. https://www.middleeasteye.net/news/russia-ukraine-war-criticised-racism-western-coverage.

Melaugh, Martin and McKenna, Fionnuala. 1916. 'Proclamation of the Irish Republic', CAIN Web Service, Conflict and Politics in Northern Ireland, Ulster University, April 24. https://cain.ulster.ac.uk/issues/politics/docs/pir24416.htm.

Meredith, Sam. 2019. 'What is the Irish backstop? All you need to know about the border dispute blocking an orderly Brexit', *CNBC*, September 11. https://www.cnbc.com/2019/09/11/brexit-what-is-the-irish-backstop-and-why-is-it-so-controversial.html.

Merrick, Rob. 2018. 'Jo Johnson resigns: Minister quits in protest and demands new Brexit referendum', *The Independent*, November 9. https://www.independent.co.uk/news/uk/politics/jo-johnson-resigns-boris-mp-conservative-party-protest-brexit-no-deal-parliament-family-latest-a9092751.html.

Merrick, Rob. 2019. 'Students wrongly caught up in Theresa May's "hostile environment" still being detained and "living in terror"', *Independent*, February 17. www.independent.co.uk/news/uk/politics/students-theresa-may-hostile-environment-immigration-detention-deport-english-tests-a8781731.html.

Michaela Community School. 2016. 'Boris loves Michaela!', June 28. YouTube. https://www.youtube.com/watch?v=2TI42MJPk3c.

Miles, Robert. 1982. *Racism and Migrant Labour: A Critical Text*, London: Routledge and Kegan Paul.

Miles, Robert. 1987. *Capitalism and Unfree Labour: Anomaly or necessity?*, London: Tavistock.

Miles, Robert. 1988. 'Racism, Marxism and British politics', *Economy and Society*, 18 (3).

Miles, Robert. 1989. *Racism*, London: Routledge.

Miles, Robert. 1990. 'The Racialization of British Politics', *Political Studies*, 38 (2).

Miles, Robert. 1993. *Racism After 'Race Relations'*, London: Routledge.

Milmo, Cahal. 2016. 'Margaret Thatcher's aides stopped her from condemning apartheid', *The Independent*, February 19. https://www.independent.co.uk/news/uk/politics/margaret-thatcher-aides-buried-plan-make-her-condemn-apartheid-a6882706.html.

Mishra, Pankaj. 2007. 'Exit wounds: the legacy of Indian partition', *The New Yorker*, August 6. https://www.newyorker.com/magazine/2007/08/13/exit-wounds.

Mohdin, Aamna. 2021. 'How the New Cross fire became a rallying cry for political action', *The Guardian*, January 15. https://www.theguardian.com/uk-news/2021/jan/15/how-the-new-cross-fire-became-a-rallying-cry-for-political-action.

Momodu, Samuel. 2021. 'Tacky's War (1760–1761)', *BlackPast*, December 3. https://www.blackpast.org/global-african-history/tackys-war-1760-1761/.

Monbiot, George. 2016. 'Neoliberalism – the ideology at the root of all our problems', *The Guardian*, April 15. https://www.theguardian.com/books/2016/apr/15/neoliberalism-ideology-problem-george-monbiot.

Monbiot, George. 2022. 'The UK is heading towards authoritarianism: just look at this attack on a minority', *The Guardian*, January 12. https://www.theguardian.com/commentisfree/2022/jan/12/uk-authoritarianism-minority-policing-billroma-gypsy-traveller.

Monday Club. 1970. 'The aims of the Monday Club', Executive Council publication, Monday Club.

Monypenny, William Flavelle, and Buckle, George Earle. 1929. *The Life of Benjamin Disraeli, Earl of Beaconsfield. Volume I. 1804–1859*, London: John Murray.

Moore, Diana. 2020. 'Romances of no-popery: transnational anti-Catholicism in Giuseppe Garibaldi's The Rule of the Monk and Benjamin Disraeli's Lothair', *Catholic Historical Review*, 106 (3).

Moore, Michael and Ramsay, Gordon. 2017. 'UK media coverage of the 2016 EU Referendum campaign', London: Centre for the Study of Media, Communication and Power. The Policy Institute, King's College London, May. www.kcl.ac.uk/sspp/policy-institute/CMCP/UK-media-coverage-of-the-2016-EU-Referendum-campaign.pdf.

Moore, Rowan. 2014. 'Margaret Thatcher began Britain's obsession with property. It's time to end it', *The Guardian*, April 6. https://amp.theguardian.com/society/2014/apr/06/margaret-thatcher-britains-obsession-property-right-to-buy.

Moriarty, Gerry. 2019. 'Internment explained: When was it introduced and why?', *The Irish Times*, August 9. https://www.irishtimes.com/news/politics/internment-explained-when-was-it-introduced-and-why-1.3981598.

Morgan, R. 1985. 'Setting the PACE (Police and Criminal Evidence Act 1984) Police Community Consultation Arrangements in England and Wales', NCJ Number, US Department of Justice: Office of Justice Programs. https://www.ojp.gov/ncjrs/virtual-library/abstracts/setting-pace-police-and-criminal-evidence-act-1984-police-community.

Mougel, Nadège. 2011. 'World War I casualties', REPERES. http://www.centre-robert-schuman.org/userfiles/files/REPERES%20%E2%80%93%20module%201-1-1%20-%20explanatory%20notes%20%E2%80%93%20World%20War%20I%20casualties%20%E2%80%93%20EN.pdf.

MSI. 2020. 'Abortion and your rights'. https://www.msichoices.org.uk/abortion-services/abortion-and-your-rights/.

Mudde, Cas. 2015. 'The Trump phenomenon and the European populist radical right', *The Washington Post*, August 28. https://www.washingtonpost.com/news/monkey-cage/wp/2015/08/26/the-trump-phenomenon-and-the-european-populist-radical-right/.

Mullins, Bill. 2021. 'How militant trade unionism defeated the 1971 Industrial Relations Act', *The Socialist*, February 24. https://www.socialistparty.org.uk/issue/1122/32086/24-02-2021/how-militant-trade-unionism-defeated-the-1971-industrial-relations-act.

Munayyer, Yousef. 2017. 'It's time to admit that Arthur Balfour was a white supremacist – and an anti-Semite too" *Institute for Palestine Studies*, November 1. https://www.palestine-studies.org/en/node/232119.

Munnion, Christopher. 1972. 'The African who kicked out the Asians, who said Hitler was right, who has made his country a state sinister', *The New York Times*,

November 12. https://www.nytimes.com/1972/11/12/archives/if-idi-amin-of-uganda-is-a-madman-hes-a-ruthless-and-cunning-one.html.

Nairn, Tom. 1981. *The Break-up of Britain: Crisis and Neonationalism*, London: Verso.

Natarajan, Radhika. 2013. 'Ties of blood: how Thatcher altered "British"', *Open Democracy*, April 17. https://www.opendemocracy.net/en/opendemocracyuk/ties-of-blood-how-thatcher-altered-british/.

Newsinger, John. 2006. *The Blood Never Dried – A People's History of the British Empire*, London: Bookmarks.

Newsinger, John. 2007. 'Falklands: war and lies', *Socialist Worker*, 2042, March 17. https://socialistworker.co.uk/art/10711/Falklands:%20war%20and%20lies#:~:text=It%20is%2025%20years%20since%20Thatcher%20launched%20the,Malvinas%20%E2%80%93%20plunging%20Britain%E2%80%99s%20Tory%20government%20into%20crisis

New World Encyclopedia Contributors. 2021. 'Sri Lanka', *New World Encyclopedia*, January 2. https://www.newworldencyclopedia.org/p/index.php?title=Sri_Lanka&oldid=1030045.

Nicholson, Frances. 1997. 'Implementation of the Immigration (Carriers' Liability) Act 1987: Privatising immigration functions at the expense of international obligations?', *The International and Comparative Law Quarterly*, 46 (3). https://www.jstor.org/stable/pdf/761276.pdf?refreqid=excelsior%3A1a7b79c510813005f87c87e84c9dfa82.

Nicolson, J. 1968. *Mother and Baby Homes*, London, George Allen & Unwin.

Nkrumah, Kwame. 1965. 'Neo-Colonialism, the last stage of imperialism: Introduction'. https://www.marxists.org/subject/africa/nkrumah/neo-colonialism/introduction.htm.

Northern Ireland Elections. Undated. 'Fermanagh and South Tyrone 1973–1982'. https://www.ark.ac.uk/elections/cfst.htm.

Norton-Taylor, Richard and Evans, Rob. 2005. 'UK held secret talks to cede sovereignty', *The Guardian*, June 28. https://www.theguardian.com/uk/2005/jun/28/falklands.past.

Norton-Taylor, Richard and Milne, Seumas. 1999. 'Racism: Extremists led Powell marches', *The Guardian*, January 1. https://www.theguardian.com/uk/1999/jan/01/richardnortontaylor2.

Nuttall, Emma, Gilmore, Victoria and Buck, Tommy. 2020. 'No place to stop: Research on the five year supply of deliverable Gypsy and Traveller sites in the South East of England', January. https://www.gypsy-traveller.org/wp-content/uploads/2020/02/Research-onthe-five-year-supply-of-deliverable-Gypsy-and-Traveller-sites-in-the-South-East-of-England.pdf.

O'Carroll, Lisa. 2019. 'Boris Johnson's Brexit alternative to the Irish backstop: what's new?', *The Guardian*, October 2. https://www.theguardian.com/politics/2019/oct/02/boris-johnsons-brexit-alternative-to-the-irish-backstop-whats-new.

O'Connell, Hugh. 2013. '6 key moments that defined Margaret Thatcher's relationship with Ireland', *The Journal*, April 9. https://www.thejournal.ie/margaret-thatcher-ireland-haughey-north-861575-Apr2013/.

O'Day, Rosemary. Undated. 'The Jews of London: From diaspora to Whitechapel'. http://fathom.lse.ac.uk/Features/122537/.

O'Dowd, Niall. 2013. 'Margaret Thatcher was anti-Irish – my encounter with the British PM in Texas', *Irish Central*, April 13. https://www.irishcentral.com/op

inion/niallodowd/margaret-thatcher-was-anti-irish-my-encounterwith-the-british-pm-in-texas-202833091-238178111.

O'Dowd. Niall. 2020. 'Winston Churchill ordered Black and Tans into Ireland in 1920'. *Irish Central*, June 16. https://www.irishcentral.com/roots/history/winston-churchill-black-tans-ireland.amp.

Office of the Historian, Foreign Service Institute, US Department of State. Undated. 'The Spanish-American War, 1898'. https://history.state.gov/milestones/1866-1898/spanish-american-war.

O'Garro, Laurie. Undated. 'The 1980 St Paul's "Riots"', *Everyday Magazine*. https://theeverydaymagazine.co.uk/opinion/the-bristol-riots.

Ó Gráda, Cormac. 1995. *Ireland: A New Economic History 1780–1939*, Oxford: Oxford University Press. https://academic.oup.com/book/7117.

O'Hearn, Denis. 2006. *Nothing But an Unfinished Song: The Life and Times of Bobby Sands*, New York: Nation Books.

Ohlinger, Gustavus A. 1966 (2015). 'WSC: A midnight interview, 1902', *Finest Hour 159*, Washington, DC, The International Churchill Society, March 15, p. 33. https://winstonchurchill.org/publications/finest-hour/finest-hour-159/wsc-a-midnight-interview-1902/.

O'Kane, Maggie and Pallister, David. 2000. 'Heath "approved Londonderry massacre"', *The Guardian*, November 23. https://amp.theguardian.com/politics/2000/nov/23/uk.bloodysunday.

Olusoga, David. 2018. 'TheWindrush story was not a rosy one even before the ship arrived', *The Guardian*, April 22. https://amp.theguardian.com/commentisfree/2018/apr/22/windrush-story-not-a-rosy-one-even-beforeship-arrived.

O'Malley, J.P. 2016. 'Churchill and his uneasy Irish legacy', *Irish Independent*, May 9. https://m.independent.ie/entertainment/books/churchill-and-his-uneasyirish-legacy-34691865.html.

Operation Black Vote (OBV). 2021. 'Remembering the New Cross fire', January 21. https://www.obv.org.uk/news-blogs/remembering-new-cross-fire.

Oppenheim, Maya. 2017. '"Winston Churchill is no better than Adolf Hitler," says Indian politician Dr Shashi Tharoor', *The Independent*, March 21. https://www.independent.co.uk/news/world/world-history/winston-churchill-adolf-hitler-no-better-shashi-tharoor-indian-politician-post-colonialist-author-inglorious-empire-nazi-a7641681.html.

Owen, Paul. 2013. 'The life of Margaret Thatcher – timeline', *The Guardian*, April 8. https://www.theguardian.com/politics/2013/apr/08/life-of-margaret-thatcher timeline.

Pannick, David. 1993. 'The primary purpose rule: a rule with no purpose', *Young Justice*, London. https://files.justice.org.uk/wp-content/uploads/2015/01/06171917/Primary PurposeRuleRuleWithNoPurpose.pdf.

Parry, Gareth, Tirbutt, Susan, and Rose, David. 1985 (2009). 'From the archive: Riots in Brixton after police shooting', *The Guardian*, September 30. https://www.theguardian.com/theguardian/2009/sep/30/brixton-riots-1985-archive.

Parry, Jonathan. 2016. 'Benjamin Disraeli, Earl of Beaconsfield', 4 May. https://history.blog.gov.uk/2016/05/04/benjamin-disraeli-earl-of-beaconsfield/.

Parry, Marc. 2016. 'Uncovering the brutal truth about the British empire', *The Guardian*, August 18. https://www.theguardian.com/news/2016/aug/18/uncovering-truth-british-empire-caroline-elkins-mau-mau.

Patterson, Orlando. 1969. *The Sociology of Slavery*, Madison, New Jersey: Fairleigh Dickinson University Press.

Paul, Diane. 1981. '*"In the Interests of Civilization": Marxist views of race and culture in the nineteenth century*', *Journal of the History of Ideas*, 42 (1). https://www.jstor.org/stable/2709420?origin=crossref.

Pearce, Malcolm and Stewart, Geoffrey. 1992. *British Political History, 1867–2001*, London: Routledge.

Pearce, Tom. 2017. 'UK budget steps up attacks on education', World Socialist Web Site (WSWS), March 21. www.wsws.org/en/articles/2017/03/21/educ-m21.html.

Perraudin, Frances. 2019. 'Home Office criticised for accelerating removals to Zimbabwe', *Guardian*, 12 February. www.theguardian.com/world/2019/feb/12/home-office-criticised-for-accelerating-removals-to-zimbabwe?CMP=Share_iOSApp_Other.

Philp, A. F. and Timms, N. 1957. *The Problem of the Problem Family*, London: Family Service Units.

Peoplepill. Undated. 'British Politician: Crispin Blunt'. https://peoplepill.com/people/crispin-blunt.

Perkins, Anne and Quinn, Ben. 2018. 'May's immigration policy seen as "almost reminiscent of Nazi Germany"', *The Guardian*, April 19. https://www.theguardian.com/uk-news/2018/apr/19/theresa-may-immigration-policy-seen-as-almost-reminiscent-of-nazi-germany.

Petter, Olivia and Cockburn, Harry. 2019. 'Who was Christine Keeler? The true story behind BBC drama about Profumo affair', *The Independent*, December 30. https://www.independent.co.uk/life-style/christine-keelertrial-profumo-affair-bbc-true-story-real-yevgeny-ivanov-a8095576.html.

Pike, E. Royston. 1968. *Britain's Prime Ministers*, London: Odhams.

Pilger, John. 1994. Documentary: *Death of a Nation: The Timor Conspiracy*. https://johnpilger.com/videos/death-of-a-nation-the-timor-conspiracy [Video].

Pimlott, Daniel, Giles, Chris, and Harding, Robin. 2010. 'UK unveils dramatic austerity measures', *Financial Times*, October 20. https://www.ft.com/content/53fe06e2-dc98-11df-84f5-00144feabdc0.

Pionke, Albert. 2007. 'Representations of the Indian Mutiny in Victorian higher journalism', *The Victorian Web*. http://www.victorianweb.org/history/empire/1857/intro.html.

Pitman, Isaac. 1901. *King Edward History Reader (for Juniors)*, UK: Sir Isaac Pitman & Sons, Ltd.

Plumb, J.H. 1973. *England in the 18th Century: The Irish Empire*, London: Pelican.

PoliticalNews.co.uk. 2001. '1970 Conservative Party General Election Manifesto'. http://www.conservativemanifesto.com/1970/1970-conservative-manifesto.shtml.

Polyani, Karl. 1944 [2001]. *The Great Transformation*, Boston: Beacon Press.

Ponting, Clive. 1994. *Winston Churchill*, London: Sinclair-Stevenson Ltd.

Portes, Jonathan. 2018. 'Austerity really has hit poor people hardest – the figures prove it', *The Guardian*, March 14. https://www.theguardian.com/commentisfree/2018/mar/14/austerity-poor-disability-george-osborne-tories.

Pottins, Charlie. 2007. 'Book review: The Man Who Might Have Been', *Jewish Socialist*, 53, Spring. https://www.jewishsocialist.org.uk/reviews/item/the-man-who-might-have-been.

Powell, Enoch. 1968a. 'Rivers of Blood speech', delivered to a Conservative Association Meeting in Birmingham, April 20. https://anth1001.files.wordpress.com/2014/04/enoch-powell_speech.pdf.

Powell, Enoch. 1968b. 'Speech to London Rotary Club, Eastbourne', November 16. https://www.enochpowell.net/fr-83.html.

Prabhat, Devyani. 2021. 'Stripping British citizenship: the government's new bill explained', *The Conversation*, December 14. https://theconversation.com/stripping-british-citizenship-the-governments-new-bill-explained-173547.

Press Association. 2019. 'Javid questions whether cross-Channel migrants are "genuine" asylum seekers', *Isle of Wight County Press*, January 2. www.iwcp.co.uk/news/national/17330284.javid-questions-whether-cross-channel-migrants-are-genuine-asylum-seekers/.

Proctor, Kate. 2020. 'Calls for Tory aide to be sacked over "enforced contraception" remarks', *The Guardian*, February 16. https://www.theguardian.com/politics/2020/feb/16/tory-aide-wants-enforced-contraception-to-curb-pregnancies.

Quakers in the World. Undated. 'Quakers against racism: Catherine Impey and the Anti-Caste Journal'. https://www.quakersintheworld.org/quakers-in-action/362/Quakers-against-racism-Catherine-Impey-and-the-Anti-Caste-Journal.

Quarmby, Katherine. 2020. 'Hate targeted at Gypsy, Traveller and Roma linked to rise in suicides – report', *The Guardian*, December 10. https://www.theguardian.com/world/2020/dec/10/hate-targeted-at-gypsy-traveller-and-roma-linkedto-rise-in-suicides-report.

Raab, Dominic and Patel, Priti. 2022. 'Boost for public safety as four justice bills receive Royal Assent', Ministry of Justice, Home Office, April 28. https://www.gov.uk/government/news/boost-for-public-safety-as-four-justice-bills-receiveroyal-assent.

Ramachandra, Guha. 2019. 'Churchill, the greatest Briton, hated Gandhi, the greatest Indian', *The Atlantic*, April 6. https://www.theatlantic.com/international/archive/2019/04/churchill-gandhi-briton-indian-greatest/584170/.

Ramdin, Ron. 1987. *The Making of the Black Working Class in Britain*, London: Verso.

Rawlinson, Kevin. 2018. 'Britain First leaders jailed over anti-Muslim hate crimes', *The Guardian*, March 7. https://www.theguardian.com/world/2018/mar/07/britain-first-leaders-convicted-of-anti-muslim-hate-crimes.

Reader, John. 2011. Missing Links: In Search of Human Origins, Oxford University Press.

Redfern. Neil. 2018. *Social-Imperialism in Britain: The Lancashire Working Class and Two World Wars (Historical Materialism)*, Leiden, Netherlands: Brill.

Refugee Council. 2022. 'Safe routes save futures'. https://www.refugeecouncil.org.uk/get-involved/campaign-with-us/safe-routes-save-futures/.

Rehman, Asad. 2021. 'The relationship between imperialism, racism, and the environmental crisis', Santa Rosa, CA: Post Carbon Institute. https://www.postcarbon.org/great-unraveling/imperialism/.

Reynolds, Sile. 2018. 'This is what the hostile environment did to asylum seekers', *Politics.co.uk*, May 8. www.politics.co.uk/comment-analysis/2018/05/08/this-is-what-the-hostile-environment-did-to-asylum-seekers.

Richard Chambers Immigration Barristers. 2012. 'Summary of key changes in family Immigration Rules on 9 July 2012'. https://immigrationbarrister.co.uk/summary-of-key-changes-to-immigration-rules-on-9-july-2012/.

Ringrose, Isabel. 2021. 'Blood money—how wealth created by slavery bankrolled capitalist Britain', *Socialist Worker*, March 6. https://socialistworker.co.uk/art/51426/Blood+money+how+wealth+created+by+ry+bankrolled+capitalist+Britain.

Ringrose, Isabel. 2022. 'Fight against Tory plan to deport refugees to Rwanda', *Socialist Worker.* https://socialistworker.co.uk/news/fight-against-tory-plan-to-dep ort-refugees-to-rwanda/?mc_cid=1eae71084f&mc_eid=e49f0a2036.

Rix, Kathryn. 2018. 'Tackling electoral corruption: how Victorian Britain reformed the trial of election petitions in 1868', July 31. https://thehistoryofparliament. wordpress.com/2018/07/31/tackling-electoral-corruption-how-victorianbrita in-reformed-the-trial-of-election-petitions-in-1868/.

Roberts, Matthew. 2006. '"Villa Toryism" and popular conservatism in Leeds, 1885–1902', *The Historical Journal*, 41 (1).

Roberts, Michael. 2016. *The Long Depression: How It Happened, Why It Happened, and What Happens Next*, Chicago, Il: Haymarket Books.

Robinson, Abby. 2019. 'Peaky blinders, Oswald Mosley – the real story behind Tommy Shelby's new foe', *Digital Spy*, August 27, Hearst UK Entertainment.

Robinson, Nick. 2013. 'Economy: there is no alternative (TINA) is back', BBC News, March 7.

Rodan, Garry and Robison, Richard (eds). 2006. *The Political Economy of South-East Asia: Markets, Power and Contestation*, Melbourne: OUP Australia & New Zealand.

Rodgers, Lucy and Ahmed, Maryam. 2018. *'Windrush: Who exactly was on board?'*, BBC News, *April* 27, 2018.

Rodney, Walter. 1970. 'The imperialist partition of Africa'. https://www.marxists. org/subject/africa/rodney-walter/works/partition.htm.

Romano, Aja. 2020. 'A history of "wokeness"', *Vox*, October 9. https://www.vox. com/culture/21437879/sta y-woke-wokeness-history-origin-evolution-controversy.

Rose, Steven, and Rose, Hilary. 2005. 'Why we should give up on race', *The Guardian*, April 9. https://www.theguardian.com/world/2005/apr/09/race.science.

Rosenberg, David. 2011. *Battle for the East End: Jewish Responses to Fascism in the 1930s*, Nottingham: Five Leaves Publications.

Rosenberg, David. 2015. 'Ukip is nothing new: The British Brothers' League was exploiting immigration fears in 1901', *The Guardian*, 4 March. https://www.theguardian.com/ uk-news/2015/mar/04/ukip-nigel-farage-immigrants-british-brothers-league.

Routledge, Paul. 2019. 'Why Margaret Thatcher's advisor Airey Neave became an INLA target 40 years ago', *The Mirror*, March 29. https://www.mirror.co.uk/ news/uk-news/margaret-thatchers-advisor-airey-neave-14205986.

Royle, Edward and Walvin, James. 1982. *English Radicals and Reformers 1760–1848*, Brighton: Harvester.

RTÉ (Raidió Teilifís Éireann). 2022. 'Explainer: What was the Easter Rising?'. https:// www.rte.ie/centuryireland/index.php/articles/what-was-the-easter-rising.

Runnymede Trust. 2019. 'The struggle for race equality: British Nationality Act 1981'. https://www.runnymedetrust.org/histories/race-equality/61/british-nationality- act-1981.html.

Russell, M. 1964. 'The Irish delinquent in England', *Studies: An Irish Quarterly Review*, 53 (210). https://www.jstor.org/stable/30088825.

Russell, Neil. 2018. 'As an NHS doctor, this "hostile environment" has made me reject my medal', *The Guardian*, July 23. https://www.theguardian.com/comm entisfree/2018/jul/23/nhs-doctor-ebola-medal-migrant-patients.

Rutherford, Adam. 2020. 'How to fight racism using science', *The Guardian*, January 26. https://www.theguardian.com/world/2020/jan/26/fight-racism-using-science-race- genetics-bigotry-african-americans-sport-linnaeus.

Saad-Filho, Alfredo. 2008. 'Marxian and Keynesian critiques of neoliberalism', in Panitch, Leo and Leys, Colin Leys, *Socialist Register*. https://www.researchgate.net/publication/282184624_MARXIAN_AND_KEYNESIAN_CRITIQUES_OF_NEOLIBERALISM.

Sacks, Jonathan. 1997. *The Politics of Hope*, London: Jonathan Cape.

Saini, Angela. 2019. *Superior: The Return of Race Science*, London: HarperCollins.

Salmon, Rachel. 2014. 'The 2014 Immigration Act 2 June 2014', LGiU Policy Briefing. www.lgiu.org.uk/wp-content/uploads/2014/06/The-2014-Immigration-Act.pdf.

Sartre Jean-Paul. 1960. *The Search for Method (1st Part): Introduction to Critique of Dialectical Reason*. https://files.libcom.org/files/jean-paul-sartre-critique-of-dialectical-reason-volume-1.compressed.pdf.

Sassoon, Donald. 2012. 'To understand this crisis we can look to the Long Depression too', *The Guardian*, April 29. https://www.theguardian.com/commentisfree/2012/apr/29/long-depression-crashes-capitalism-history.

Schaffer, Gavin. 2008. *Racial Science and British Society, 1930–1962*, London: Palgrave Macmillan.

Schoen, Douglas, E. 1977. *Enoch Powell and the Powellites*, London: Palgrave Macmillan.

Schoppmann, Claudia. 1996. *Days of Masquerade: Life Stories of Lesbians During the Third Reich*, New York: Columbia University Press.

Semmel, Bernard. 1968. *Imperialism and Social Reform*, Sydney: George Allen and Unwin.

Shannon, Richard. 1996. *The Age of Salisbury, 1881–1902: Unionism and Empire*, London: Longman.

Sharma, Ruchira. 2018. 'Here's every single public immigration failure under Theresa May since 2016', *The iNewsletter*, April 19. https://inews.co.uk/news/politics/windrush-immigration-theresa-may/amp/.

Sharma, Swati. 2018. 'Ta-Nehisi Coates on Cornel West's one-sided war', *The Atlantic*, January 17. https://www.theatlantic.com/entertainment/archive/2018/01/ta-nehisi-coates-cornel-west/550727/.

Sherwood, Marika. Undated. 'Murder in Notting Hill', *Our Migration Story*. https://www.ourmigrationstory.org.uk/oms/murder-in-notting-hill.

Shiner, Michael. 2015. 'Stop and search: the police must not revive this discredited tactic', *The Guardian*, October 19. https://www.theguardian.com/commentisfree/2015/oct/19/stop-and-search-riots-2011-section-60-knife-crime-police-chiefs.

Shivdasani, Siddy. 2021. 'We must acknowledge the legacy of the Brixton Riots', *Metro*, April 10. https://metro.co.uk/2021/04/10/40-years-later-we-must-acknowledge-the-legacy-of-the-brixton-riots-14353854/.

Shoppmann, Claudia. 1995. 'The position of lesbian women in the Nazi period', in Günter Grau and Claudia Shoppmann (eds.), Hidden Holocaust? Gay and Lesbian Persecution in Germany, 1933-1945.

Siddique, Haroon. 2020. 'Mark Duggan police shooting: can forensic tech cast doubt on official report?', *The Guardian*, June 10. https://www.theguardian.com/uk-news/ng-interactive/2020/jun/10/mark-duggan-shooting-can-forensic-tech-cast-doubt-on-official-report.

Siddique, Haroon. 2021. 'UK's "strictest" headteacher Katharine Birbalsingh made social mobility chief', *The Guardian*, October 10. https://www.theguardian.com/society/2021/oct/10/uks-strictest-headteacher-ktharine-birbalsingh-made-social-mobility-chief.

Siegel, Eric. 2017. 'The real problem with Charles Murray and "The Bell Curve"', *Scientific America*, April 12. https://blogs.scientificamerican.com/voices/the-real-problem-with-charles-murray-and-the-bell-curve/.

Simkin, John. 2020a. 'Benjamin Disraeli', *Spartacus Educational*. https://spartacus-educational.com/PRdisraeli.htm.

Simkin, John. 2020b. 'Winston Churchill', *Spartacus Educational*. https://spartacus-educational.com/PRchurchill.htm.

Simkin, John. 2020c. 'The General Strike', *Spartacus Educational*. https://spartacus-educational.com/TUgeneral.htm.

Simkin, John. 2021. 'Was Winston Churchill a supporter or an opponent of Fascism?', *Spartacus Blog*. https://spartacus-educational.com/spartacus-blogURL118.htm.

Simkin, John. 2022. 'James Connolly', *Spartacus Educational*. https://spartacus-educational.com/Sconnolly.htm.

Sinn Féin. Undated. 'History of the Conflict'. https://www.sinnfein.ie/history.

Sivanandan, A. 1990. 'Sri Lanka: A case study', in Communities of Resistance: Writings on Black Struggles for Socialism, London: Verso.

Sivanandan, A. 2009. 'Foreword', in L. Fekete, *A Suitable Enemy: Racism, Migration and Islamophobia in Europe*, London: Pluto Press.

Skibba, Ramin. 2019. 'The disturbing resilience of scientific racism', *Smithsonian Magazine*. https://www.smithsonianmag.com/science-nature/disturbing-resilience-scientific-racism-180972243/.

Sky News. 2022. 'Chief whip denies claims he told Tory MP she was sacked as a minister due to her Muslim faith', January 23. https://news.sky.com/story/chief-whip-denies-claims-he-told-mp-she-was-sacked-as-a-minister-because-of-her-muslim-faith-12523176.

Slater, E. and McDonough, T. 1994. 'Bulwark of landlordism and capitalism: the dynamics of feudalism in nineteenth-century Ireland', Research in Political Economy, 14.

Smith, D. J. 1977. *Racial Disadvantage in Britain*, Harmondsworth: Penguin.

Smith, David. 2007. 'What Churchill said about Britain's immigrants', *The Guardian*, August 5. https://amp.theguardian.com/uk/2007/aug/05/race.past.

Smith, Natalie. 2018. 'The Tottenham 3: the legacy of the Broadwater Farm riot', *The Justice Gap*, July 13. https://www.thejusticegap.com/the-tottenham-3-the-legacy-of-the-broadwater-farm-riot/.

Social Mobility Commission. 2021. 'State of the nation 2021: Social mobility and the pandemic', July. https://assets.publishing.service.gov.uk/government/uploads/system/uploads/attachment_data/file/1003977/State_of_the_nation_2021_-_Social_mobility_and_the_pandemic.pdf.

Solomon, Enver. 2022. 'UK asylum seekers sent to Rwanda? That takes punishment of fellow humans to a new level', *The Guardian*, April 14. https://www.theguardian.com/commentisfree/2022/apr/14/uk-asylum-seekers-rwanda-government.

Solomos, John. 1993. *Race and Racism in Britain*, 2nd edition, London: Macmillan.

South African History Online (SAHO). Undated. 'The people armed, 1984–1990'. https://www.sahistory.org.za/article/people-armed-1984-1990.

South African History Online (SAHO). 1956. 'Ghana demands independence from Britain', August 3. https://www.sahistory.org.za/dated-event/ghana-demandsindependence-britain.

South African History Online (SAHO). 2019. 'Women and children in white concentration camps during the Anglo-Boer War, 1900–1902'. https://www.sahistory.

org.za/article/women-and-children-white-concentration-campsduring-anglo-boer-war-1900-1902.

South African History Online (SAHO). 2020. 'Hendrik Verwoerd's response to the "Winds of Change" speech'. https://www.sahistory.org.za/archive/hendrikverwoerds-response-winds-change-speech.

Southwark, Andy. 2011. 'Tottenham riots: A community on the edge', *Socialist Appeal*, August 8. https://www.socialist.net/tottenham-riots-a-community-on-the-edge.htm.

Spartacus Educational. 2020a. 'William Evans-Gordon'. https://spartacus-educational.com/William_Evans-Gordon.htm.

Spartacus Educational. 2020b. 'Anti-semitism in Britain'. https://spartacus-educational.com/U3Ahistory45.htm.

Spartacus Educational. 2021. '1945 general election'. https://spartacus-educational.com/GE1945.htm.

Sparrow, Andrew. 2001. '"I refuse to keep quiet on race", says rebel MP', *The Telegraph*, March 29. https://www.telegraph.co.uk/news/uknews/1328295/I-refuse-to-keep-quiet-on-race-says-rebel-MP.html.

Spencer, Ian R. G. 1997. *British Immigration Policy since 1939: The Making of Multi-Racial Britain*, London: Routledge.

Spinley, B. M. 1953. *The Deprived and the Privileged*, London, Routledge & Kegan Paul.

Springhall, John. 1986. '"Up Guards and at them!"; British imperialism and popular art, 1880–1914', in J. MacKenzie (ed.), Imperialism and Popular Culture, Manchester: Manchester University Press.

Stanley, Tim. 2013. 'Peter Griffiths and the ugly Tory racism of the 1960s killed rational debate about immigration', *The Telegraph*. https://web.archive.org/web/20131201001553/http:/blogs.telegraph.co.uk/news/timstanley/100248091/peter-griffiths-and-the-tory-racism-of-the-1960s-killed-rationaldebate-about-immigration/.

Stanton, Philip. 2000. *Britain 1905–1951*, Oxford: Nelson Thornes.

Starkey, P. 2000. 'The feckless mother: women, poverty and social workers in wartime and post-war England', *Women's History Review*, 9 (3).

Stevens, Robert. 2013. 'UK Prime Minister Cameron plays the anti-immigrant card', World Socialist Web Site (WSWS), November 29. www.wsws.org/en/articles/2013/11/29/came-n29.html.

Stevens, Robert. 2021. 'UK government crisis deepens as lorry driver shortage leaves fuel stations empty', World Socialist Web Site, September 28. https://www.wsws.org/en/articles/2021/09/29/ukfu-s29.html.

Stewart, Heather. 2016. 'Theresa May appeals to centre ground but cabinet tilts to the right', *The Guardian*, July 14. www.theguardian.com/politics/2016/jul/13/theresa-may-becomes-britains-prime-minister.

Stewart, Heather. 2019. 'Boris Johnson elected new Tory leader', *The Guardian*, July 23. https://www.theguardian.com/politics/2019/jul/23/boris-johnson-elected-new-tory-leader-prime-minister.

Stone, Jon. 2016. 'What Theresa May said about immigration in her infamous speech to Tory conference', *Independent*, August 25. www.independent.co.uk/news/uk/politics/theresa-may-immigration-policies-speech-conference-2015-tory-conservative-party-views-a7209931.html.

Stone, Jon. 2019. 'Boris Johnson said that seeing "bunch of black kids" makes alarm bells go off in his head, in old column', *The Independent*, November 22. https://

www.independent.co.uk/news/uk/politics/boris-johnson-bunch-black-kids-racist-column-guardian-a9213356.html.

Stone, Jon. 2020a. 'Boris Johnson said colonialism in Africa should never have ended and dismissed Britain's role in slavery', *The Independent*, June 13. https://www.independent.co.uk/news/uk/politics/boris-johnson-colonialism-africa-british-empire-slavery-a9564541.html?amp.

Stone, Jon. 2020b. 'Boris Johnson says time to stop "cringing embarrassment" about British history after BBC Proms drops Rule Britannia lyrics', *The Independent*, August 25. https://www.independent.co.uk/news/uk/politics/boris-johnson-bbc-proms-rule-britannia-lyrics-row-british-history-black-lives-matter-a9687816.html?amp.

Stone, Jon. 2022. 'Borders bill makes UK "one of the most anti-refugee countries in the world", says Médecins Sans Frontières', *The Independent*, March 22. https://www.independent.co.uk/news/uk/politics/borders-nationality-bill-refugees-msf-b2041671.html.

Stratton, Allegra. 2010. 'David Cameron condemns Bloody Sunday killings and makes apology', *The Guardian*, 15 June. https://www.theguardian.com/commentisfree/2010/jun/15/david-cameron-bloody-sunday-apology.

Summerfield, Penelope. 1986. 'Patriotism and empire: music-hall entertainment, 1870–1914', in J. MacKenzie (ed.), Imperialism and Popular Culture, Manchester: Manchester University Press.

Summers, Deborah. 2009. 'David Cameron warns of "new age of austerity"', *The Guardian*, April 26. https://www.theguardian.com/politics/2009/apr/26/david-cameron-conservative-economic-policy.

Swift, Roger and Gilley, Sheridan (eds.). 1999. *The Irish in Victorian Britain: The Local Dimension*, Dublin: Four Courts Press.

Swinford, Steven. 2015. 'Election 2015: *How David Cameron's Conservatives won*', *Telegraph*, May 8. www.telegraph.co.uk/news/general-election-2015/11592230/Election-2015-How-David-Camerons-conservatives-won.html.

Syal, Rajeev. 2020. 'Dominic Cummings calls for "weirdos and misfits" for No 10 jobs', *The Guardian*, January 2. https://www.theguardian.com/politics/2020/jan/02/dominic-cummings-calls-for-weirdos-and-misfits-for-no-10-jobs.

Syal, Rajeev. 2021. 'No 10 race adviser Samuel Kasumu resigns', *The Guardian*, April 1. https://www.theguardian.com/politics/2021/apr/01/no-10-race-adviser-resigns-day-after-uk-structural-racism-report-published.

Syal, Rajeev. 2022a. 'Priti Patel's refugee pushback policy withdrawn days before legal review', *The Guardian*, April 25. https://www.theguardian.com/uk-news/2022/apr/25/uk-refugee-pushback-policy-withdrawn-judicial-review-priti-patel#:~:text=Priti%20Patel's%20refugee%20pushback%20policy%20has%20been%20officially%20withdrawn%20by,heard%20in%20the%20high%20court.

Syal, Rajeev. 2022b. 'UK Rwanda plan for asylum seekers decried as inhumane, expensive and deadly', *The Guardian*, April 14. https://www.theguardian.com/uk-news/2022/apr/14/uk-rwanda-plan-for-asylum-seekers-decried-as-inhumane-deadly-and-expensive#:~:text=After%20the%20prime%20minister%20outlined,a%20waste%20of%20public%20money.

Syal, Rajeev. 2022c. 'Theresa May questions "legality and practicality" of Rwanda asylum plan', *The Guardian*, April 19. https://www.theguardian.com/politics/2022/apr/19/theresa-may-questions-legality-and-practicality-of-rwanda-asylum-plan.

Syal, Rajeev. 2022d. 'Did Priti Patel cross a line in urging pursuit of the Colston

Four?' *The Guardian*, January 5. https://amp.theguardian.com/global/2022/jan/05/did-priti-patel-cross-a-line-in-urging-pursuit-of-the-colston-four.

Syal, Rajeev and Brown, Mark. 2022. 'Home Office staff threaten mutiny over "shameful" Rwanda asylum deal', *The Guardian*, April 20. https://www.theguardian.com/uk-news/2022/apr/20/home-office-staff-threaten-mutiny-over-shameful-rwanda-asylum-deal?CMP=Share_iOSApp_Other.

Syal, Rajeev, Mason, Rowena and O' Carroll, Lisa. 2019. 'Sky executive among Johnson's first appointments', *The Guardian*, July 23. https://www.theguardian.com/politics/2019/jul/23/sky-executive-among-johnson-firstappointments-andrew-griffith-munira-mirza.

'Taki Theodoracopulos'. Undated. http://www.mlahanas.de/Greeks/NewLiteratur/TakiTheodoracopoulos.html.

Taylor, Diane. 2022. 'Windrush descendants lose high court fight to expand scheme', *The Guardian*, January 14. https://www.theguardian.com/uk-news/2022/jan/14/windrush-descendants-lose-fight-to-expand-compensation-scheme.

Taylor, Diane, and Perraudin, Francis. 2019. 'Couples face "insulting" checks in sham marriage crackdown', *The Guardian*, April 14. https://www.theguardian.com/uk-news/2019/apr/14/couples-sham-marriage-crackdown-hostile-environment.

Taylor, Pablo. 2021. 'We need to ask why: Cousin of Mark Duggan speaks out 10 years after riots', *ITV News*, October 28. https://www.itv.com/news/central/2021-10-28/cousin-of-mark-duggan-speaks-out-10-years-after-riots.

Taylor, Peter. 1997. *Behind the Mask: The Ira and Sinn Fein*, TV Books Inc.

Taylor, Peter. 1999. *Loyalists*. London: Bloomsbury Publishing Plc.

Taylor, Peter. 2021. 'Bobby Sands: The hunger strike that changed the course of N Ireland's conflict', *BBC News*, May 1. https://www.bbc.co.uk/news/stories-56937259.

Taylor, Ros. 2017. 'The interregnum: 11 years without free movement from 1962 to 1973', *London School of Economics*, May 25. https://blogs.lse.ac.uk/brexit/2017/05/25/the-interregnum-11-years-without-free-movement-from-1962-to-1973/.

Tempest, Matthew. 2001. 'Duncan Smith backs action against Iraq', *The Guardian*, November 29. https://www.theguardian.com/politics/2001/nov/29/conservatives.uk.

Terrill, Richard J. 1989. 'Margaret Thatcher's Law and Order Agenda', *The American Journal of Comparative Law*, 37 (3), Summer, 1989. https://www.jstor.org/stable/pdf/840088.pdf?refreqid=excelsior%3A04e01cfffafce6cb813bd899793ae74e.

Tharoor, Ishaan. 2015. 'The dark side of Winston Churchill's legacy no one should forget', *The Washington Post*, February 3. https://www.washingtonpost.com/news/worldviews/wp/2015/02/03/the-dark-side-of-winston-churchills-legacy-no-one-should-forget/.

Tharoor, Ishaan. 2016. 'The angry letter Bernie Sanders wrote to Margaret Thatcher', *The Washington Post*, February 19. https://www.washingtonpost.com/news/worldviews/wp/2016/02/19/the-angry-letter-bernie-sanders-wrote-to-margaret-thatcher/.

Tharoor, Shashi. 2017. 'The Partition: The British game of "divide and rule"', *Aljazeera*, August 10. https://www.aljazeera.com/opinions/2017/8/10/the-partition-the-british-game-of-divide-and-rule.

Tharoor, Sashi. 2018. *Inglorious Empire*, Penguin.

Thatcher, Margaret. 1978. 'TV interview for Granada World in Action ("rather swamped")', Margaret Thatcher Foundation, January 27. https://www.marga retthatcher.org/document/103485.

Thatcher, Margaret. 1981. 'Speech in Belfast', Margaret Thatcher Foundation, March 5. https://www.margaretthatcher.org/document/104589.

Thatcher, Margaret. 1982. 'Falkland Islands', Margaret Thatcher Foundation, April 3. https://www.margaretthatcher.org/document/104910.

Thatcher, Margaret. 1985. 'Remarks on murder of PC Keith Blakelock (Broadwater Farm riot)', Margaret Thatcher Foundation, October 8. https://www.margarettha tcher.org/document/106143.

Thatcher, Margaret. 1993. *The Downing Street Years*, London: HarperCollins.

Thatcher, Margaret. 2011. *Statecraft*, London: HarperCollins.

The Children's Society. 2016. www.childrenssociety.org.uk/sites/default/files/ma king-life-impossible.pdf.

The Churchill Project. 2016. 'Hillsdale & Statesmanship'. https://winstonchurchill. hillsdale.edu/about-the-churchill-project/.

The Commonwealth. 2021. 'Our History'. https://thecommonwealth.org/aboutus/ history.

The Daily Telegraph. 2013. 'Peter Griffiths – obituary', November 27. https://www. telegraph.co.uk/news/obituaries/10479104/Peter-Griffiths-obituary.html.

The Economist. 2008. 'Race and the police. No quick fix', September 18. https:// www.economist.com/britain/2008/09/18/no-quick-fix.

The Economist. 2022. 'The British government's response to Ukrainian refugees is sadly typical', March 12. https://www.economist.com/leaders/the-british-go vernments-responseto-ukrainian-refugees-is-sadly-typical/21808100.

The Editors of Encyclopaedia Britannica. Undated. 'Balfour Declaration United Kingdom [1917]'. https://www.britannica.com/event/Balfour-Declaration.

The Editors of Encyclopaedia Britannica. Undated. 'East India Company'. https:// www.britannica.com/topic/East-India-Company.

The Editors of Encyclopaedia Britannica. Undated. 'Henry Mayers Hyndman British Marxist'. https://www.britannica.com/biography/Henry-Mayers-Hyndman.

The Editors of Encyclopaedia Britannica. Undated. 'Slave rebellions'. https://www. britannica.com/topic/slave-rebellions.

The Editors of Encyclopaedia Britannica. 2021. 'Anglo-Irish agreement'. https:// www.britannica.com/event/Anglo-Irish-Agreement.

The George Padmore Institute. Undated. 'New Cross Massacre Campaign, 1980–1985'. https://catalogue.georgepadmoreinstitute.org/records/NCM.

The Guardian. 1990. 'Cheltenham Tory rebels challenge black candidate', *The Guardian*, December 23.

The Guardian. 2004. 'Basingstoke's ex-Tory MP Hunter joins DUP', December 10. https://www.theguardian.com/politics/2004/dec/10/northernireland.devolution.

The Guardian. 2021. 'Tory leadership timeline', September 14. https://www.thegua rdian.com/politics/2001/sep/14/conservatives.uk.

The Guardian. 2022. 'Met to stop recording ethnicity of drivers stopped by its officers', October 11. https://www.theguardian.com/law/2022/may/16/restrictions-on-police-stop-and-search-powers-permanently-lifted.

The Health Foundation: Policy Navigator. 2022. 'Workhouses and the Poor Law Amendment Act 1834'. https://navigator.health.org.uk/theme/workhouses-and-poor-law-amendment-act-1834.

The Independent. 2013. 'Margaret Thatcher's timeline: From Grantham to the House of Lords, via Arthur Scargill and the Falklands War', April 9. https://www.indep endent.co.uk/news/uk/politics/margaret-thatcher-s-timeline-grantham-house-lords-arthur-scargill-and-falklands-war-8564555.html.

The Irish Times. 1998. 'Powell right – Thatcher', November 23. https://www.irish times.com/news/powell-right-thatcher-1.217653?mode=amp.

The Irish Times. 2013. 'Thatcher believed the Irish were "all liars"', April 18. https:// www.irishtimes.com/news/thatcher-believed-the-irish-were-all-liars-1.1363098.

The Irish Times. 2021. 'More than half in North want vote on a united Ireland, poll finds', January 24. https://www.irishtimes.com/news/politics/more-than-half-in-north-want-vote-on-a-united-ireland-poll-finds-1.4466547.

The Library of Congress. Undated. 'Churchill and the Great Republic: The finest hour'. https://www.loc.gov/exhibits/churchill/wc-hour.html.

The National Archives. Undated. 'Chamberlain and Hitler 1938'. https://www. nationalarchives.gov.uk/education/resources/chamberlain-andhitler/#:~:text=At% 20Munich%2C%20Chamberlain%20got%20an,demands%20to%20make%20in %20Europe.

The National Archives. 2021. 'Power, Politics and Protest'. https://www.nationala rchives.gov.uk/education/politics/g7/#:~:text=Chartism%20was%20a%20working %20class,main%20aims%20of%20the%20movement.

The National Archives: The Cabinet Papers. Undated. 'The IMF and Bretton Woods Conference'. https://www.nationalarchives.gov.uk/cabinetpapers/them es/bretton-woodsconference.htm.

The Newsroom. 2020. 'Taoiseach Micheal Martin wants Boris Johnson to hold full public inquiry into at Finucane murder, family say', *News Letter.* https://www.news letter.co.uk/news/crime/taoiseach-micheal-martin-wants-boris-johnson-hold-full-public-inquiry-pat-finucane-murder-family-say-3048470.

The New York Times. 1985. 'Commonwealth leaders agree on sanctions against South Africa', October 21. https://www.nytimes.com/1985/10/21/world/comm onwealth-leaders-agree-on-sanctions-against-south-africa.html.

Theodoracopulos, Taki. 2003. 'Thoughts on thuggery', *The Spectator,* January 11. http://archive.spectator.co.uk/article/11th-january-2003/46/thoughts-on-thuggery.

The Week. 2016. 'Theresa May rejects calls to increase Indian visa quota', November 7. https://www.theweek.co.uk/60665/theresa-may-rejects-calls-to-in crease-indian-visa-quota/page/0/4.

Tomlinson, Sally. 2019. *Education and Race from Empire to Brexit,* Bristol: Policy Press.

Topping, Alexandra. 2011. 'Rioters were "unruly mob" claims Theresa May', *The Guardian,* December 18. https://www.theguardian.com/uk/2011/dec/18/lon don-riots-theresamay.

The Political Quarterly. 1993. 'Ethnic minority candidates in general elections', January-March.

The Royal Household. 2022. 'Victoria (r. 1837–1901)'. https://web.archive.org/ web/20020202023604/http://www.royal.gov.uk/output/Page118.asp.

The Times. 1872. 'Mr. Disraeli at Sydenham'.

The Times. 2014. 'Peter Griffiths', December 11. https://www.thetimes.co.uk/arti cle/peter-griffiths-qdlkzggcbbq.

The Troubles: A Chronology of the Northern Ireland Conflict (magazine). 1971, December. Issue #8, Glenravel publications. https://issuu.com/glenravel/docs/issue_08.

The Week Staff. 2020. 'Winston Churchill: antifascist hero or racist warmonger – or both?', *The Week*, June 9. https://www.theweek.co.uk/62209/winston-churchill-british-antifascist-hero-or-racist-warmongering-villa.

Thoburn, Ethan. 2020. 'Airey Neave: The man who helped make Margaret Thatcher', The Bruges Group, April 3. https://www.brugesgroup.com/blog/airey-neave-the-man-who-helped-make-margaret-thatcher.

Thompson, Andrew. S, 2000. *Imperial Britain: The Empire in British Politics c. 1880–1932*, Harlow: Longman.

Thompson, Paul. 1967. *Socialists, Liberals and Labour: the Struggle for London, 1885–1914*, Toronto: University of Toronto Press.

Thorn, Lyka. 2013. 'Factory life'. https://rikowski.wordpress.com/2013/12/04/factory-life-by-lyka-thorn/.

Thorpe, Andrew. 2001. *A History of the British Labour Party*, London: Palgrave.

Timms, Elizabeth Jane. 2019. 'Primroses for her Prime Minister: Benjamin Disraeli and Queen Victoria', July 11. https://royalcentral.co.uk/features/primroses-for-her-prime-minister-benjamin-disraeli-and-queen-victoria-126648/.

Toczek, Nick. 2016. *Haters, Baiters and Would-Be Dictators: Anti-Semitism and the UK Far Right*, Abingdon: Routledge.

Townsend, Mark. 2022. 'Stranded Nigerians accuse UK of ignoring pleas of black refugees fleeing Ukraine', *The Guardian*, March 19. https://www.theguardian.com/world/2022/mar/19/stranded-nigerians-accuse-uk-of-ignoring-pleas-of-black-refugees-fleeing-ukraine.

Toye, Richard. 2015. *Churchill's Empire*, Basingstoke: Pan Macmillan.

Toye, Richard. 2020. 'Yes, Churchill was a racist. It's time to break free of his "great white men" view of history', *CNN Opinion*, June 10. https://edition.cnn.com/2020/06/10/opinions/churchill-racist-great-white-men-view-toye-opinion/index.html.

Travis, Alan. 1992. 'Major raises horror spectre', The Guardian, March 31.

Travis, Alan. 2001. 'Asylum issue takes election centre stage', *The Guardian*, January 5. https://www.theguardian.com/society/2001/jan/05/asylum.socialcare.

Travis, Alan. 2002a. 'Senior officers tried to play down reports of race riots but police on street witnessed attacks by White mobs', *The Guardian*, August 24. https://www.theguardian.com/uk/2002/aug/24/artsandhumanities.nottinghillcarnival2002.

Travis, Alan. 2002b. 'Ministers saw law's "racism" as defensible', *The Guardian*, January 1. https://www.theguardian.com/politics/2002/jan/01/uk.race.

Travis, Alan. 2007. 'Officials launch drive to seek out illegal migrants at work', *The Guardian*, May 16. https://www.theguardian.com/uk/2007/may/16/immigration.immigrationandpublicservices.

Travis, Alan. 2013. 'Tory immigration language "like National Front of 1970s"', *The Guardian*, September 25. https://www.theguardian.com/uk-news/2013/sep/25/tory-immigration-language-national-front-yvette-cooper.

Travis, Alan. 2015. 'Oliver Letwin blocked help for black youth after 1985 riots: Cameron's policy chief makes apology over advice to Thatcher that assistance would benefit "disco and drug trade" and Rastafarian crafts', *The Guardian*, 30 December. https://www.theguardian.com/politics/2015/dec/30/oliver-letwin-blocked-help-for-black-youth-after-1985-riots.

Travis, Alan. 2017a. 'May pressured NHS to release data to track *immigration* offenders', *Guardian*, February 1. www.theguardian.com/uk-news/2017/feb/01/home-office-asked-former-nhs-digital-boss-to-share-data-to-trace-immigration-offenders.

Travis, Alan. 2017b. 'UK asylum seekers' housing branded "disgraceful" by MPs', *Guardian*, January 31. www.theguardian.com/uk-news/2017/jan/31/uk-asylum-seekers-housing-branded-disgraceful-by-mps-yvette-cooper.

Trent, Noelle. 2021. 'Frederick Douglass United States official and diplomat', *Britannica.com*, April 5. https://www.britannica.com/biography/Frederick-Douglass.

Trewin, Ion. 2009. *Alan Clark – The Biography*, London: Orion.

Trilling, Daniel. 2013. 'Thatcher: the PM who brought racism in from the cold', *Verso Blog*, April 10. https://www.versobooks.com/blogs/1282-thatcher-the-pm-who-brought-racism-in-from-the-cold.

UK Government. Undated. 'Benjamin Disraeli, the Earl of Beaconsfield'. https://www.gov.uk/government/history/past-prime-ministers/benjamin-disraeli-the-earl-of-beaconsfield.

UK Government. Undated. 'Past Prime Ministers: 21st century, Winston Churchill'. https://www.gov.uk/government/history/past-prime-ministers/winstonchurchill.

UK Government. 1993. 'Asylum and Immigration Appeals Act 1993'. https://www.legislation.gov.uk/ukpga/1993/23/contents.

UK Government. 1996. 'Asylum and Immigration Act 1996'. https://www.legislation.gov.uk/ukpga/1996/49/introduction.

UK Government. 2014. 'Child poverty strategy 2014 to 2017', June 26. https://www.gov.uk/government/publications/child-poverty-strategy-2014-to-2017.

UK Parliament. Undated. 'C.O.1028/22, STU 91/143/01, CWP (53) 15, 28 September 1953'.

UK Parliament. 1867. 'Second Great Reform Act'. https://www.parliament.uk/about/living-heritage/evolutionofparliament/houseofcommons/reformacts/from-the-parliamentary-collections/collections-reform-acts/great-reform-act111/.

UK Parliament. 2014. 'The work of the Immigration Directorates (January – June 2014) – Home Affairs Committee Contents'. https://publications.parliament.uk/pa/cm201415/cmselect/cmhaff/712/71204.htm.

UK Parliament. 2021. 'The 1922 Committee (the 22)'. https://www.parliament.uk/site-information/glossary/1922-committee-the-22/.

UK Parliament. 2021a. 'What are early day motions?'. https://www.parliament.uk/about/how/business/edms/.

UK Parliament. 2021b. 'Race Relations Act 1965'. https://www.parliament.uk/about/living-heritage/transformingsociety/private-lives/relationships/collections1/race-relations-act-1965/race-relations-act-1965/.

UK Parliament. 2022. 'Nationality and Borders Bill returns to the Lords', April 5. https://www.parliament.uk/business/news/2021/december-2021/lords-debates-nationality-and-borders-bill/#:~:text=The%20Nationality%20and%20Borders%20Bill%20seeks%20to%3A,lives%20of%20those%20they%20endanger.

UK Parliament. 2022. 'King George V'. https://www.parliament.uk/about/living-heritage/transformingsociety/privatelives/yourcountry/collections/the-outbreak-of-the-first-world-war/kinggeorge-v/.

UK Parliament, Erskine May. 2022. 'Peers of Ireland'. https://erskinemay.parliament.uk/section/4515/peers-of-ireland/.

UKPOL.CO.UK. 2015. 'David Cameron – 2014 Speech to Conservative Party Conference'. https://www.ukpol.co.uk/david-cameron-2014-speech-to-conservative-party-conference/.

UK Polling Report. 1974–1979. http://ukpollingreport.co.uk/voting-intention-1974-1979.

United States Holocaust Memorial Museum. Undated. 'Nazi racial science'. https://www.ushmm.org/collections/bibliography/nazi-racial-science.

United States Holocaust Memorial Museum. 2020. 'Documenting numbers of victims of the holocaust and Nazi persecution'. https://encyclopedia.ushmm.org/content/en/article/documenting-numbers-of-victims-of-the-holocaust-and-nazi-persecution.

UN WOMEN. 2016. 'Global database on violence against women'. http://evaw-global-database.unwomen.org/en/countries/europe/united-kingdom-of-great-britain-and-northern-ireland/2002/domestic-violence-concession-under-the-immigration-rules.

Usborne, Simon. 2018. 'How the hostile environment crept into UK schools, hospitals and homes', *Guardian*, August 1. www.theguardian.com/uk-news/2018/aug/01/hostile-environment-immigrants-crept-into-schools-hospitals-homes-border-guards.

Vallely, Paul. 2009. 'A short history of Anglo-Jewry: The Jews in Britain, 1656–2006', *The Independent*, April 1. https://www.independent.co.uk/news/uk/thisbritain/short-history-anglo-jewry-jews-britain-1656-2006-6098403.html.

van Bockhaven, Vicky. 2009. 'Leopard-men of the Congo in literature and popular imagination', *Tydskr. letterkd*, 46 (1). http://www.scielo.org.za/scielo.php?script=sci_arttext&pid=S0041-476X2009000100006.

Van Hartesveldt, Fred R. 1983. 'Race and political parties in Britain, 1954-1965', *Phylon*, 44, (2). https://www.jstor.org/stable/pdf/275024.pdf?refreqid=excelsior%3A237ddf2329d393408015371524efdae2

Vassiliou, John. 2019. 'Media pressure saved my clients from removal – but now come the crippling fees', Freemovement.org.uk, February 25. https://www.freemovement.org.uk/media-pressure-saved-my-clients-from-removal-but-now-come-the-crippling-fees/.

Video RTÉ Investigations Unit. 2014. 'The torture files'. https://www.rte.ie/news/player/prime-time-web/2014/0604/.

Viney, M. 1966. 'No birthright: A study of the Irish unmarried mother and her child', *Irish Times*, Dublin.

Virdee, Satnam. 2014. *Racism, Class and the Racialised Outsider*, London: Red Globe Press.

Virdee, Satnam and McGeever, Brendan. 2017. 'Racism, crisis, Brexit', *Ethnic and Racial Studies*, 41 (10). https://doi.org/10.1080/01419870.2017.1361544.

Wahl, Asbjørn. 2021. 'Class struggle built the welfare state', *Jacobin*, May 2. https://jacobinmag.com/2021/05/welfare-state-class-struggle-confrontationcompromise-labor-union-movement.

Walker, Martin. 1977. *The National Front*, London and Glasgow: Fontana.

Walker, Peter, Aamna Mohdin and Alexandra Topping. 2021. 'Downing Street suggests UK should be seen as model of racial equality', *The Guardian*, March 31. https://www.theguardian.com/world/2021/mar/31/uk-an-exemplar-of-racial-equality-no-10s-race-commission-concludes.

Wallace, J. 1995. 'Unmarried mothers in Ireland in the middle decades of the twentieth century', unpublished M. Phil Dissertation, Dublin, Trinity College.

Wallenfeldt, Jeff and Lotha, Gloria. 2020. 'The Troubles: Northern Ireland history', *Britannica*, August 21. https://www.britannica.com/event/The-Troubles-Northern-Ireland-history.

Walsh, Pat. 2017. 'The Eugenics Congress, London 1912', *History and Politics Analyst*, May 26. https://drpatwalsh.com/2017/05/26/the-eugenics-congress-london-1912/.

Walter, Bronwen. 2001. *Outsiders Inside: Whiteness, Place and Irish Women*, London: Routledge.

Walters, Simon. 2001. *Tory Wars: Conservatives in Crisis*, London: Politicos.

Walters, Simon. 2018. 'Margaret Thatcher "wanted a whites-only South Africa": Diaries of one of the Iron Lady's top diplomats also reveal she wanted to "push" Vietnamese boat people into the sea and "loathed" Germans', *MailOnline*, January 21. https://www.dailymail.co.uk/news/article-5292859/Margaret-Thatcher-wanted-whites-South-Africa.html.

War Cabinet, 276 (40). National Archives, 24 October 1940. https://discovery.nationalarchives.gov.uk/details/r/C9110640.

Watson, James L. 2004. 'Presidential address: Virtual kinship, real estate, and diaspora formation: The Man Lineage revisited', *The Journal of Asian Studies*, 63 (4).

Watt, Nicholas. 2001a. 'Stalled Portillo hustles for votes', *The Guardian*, July 13. https://www.theguardian.com/politics/2001/jul/13/uk.conservatives2.

Watt, Nicholas. 2001b. 'Furious Thatcher rounds on Portillo', *The Guardian*, July 16. https://www.theguardian.com/politics/2001/jul/16/uk.conservatives1.

Watt, Nicholas. 2001c. 'Duncan Smith sacks backer with BNP link', *The Guardian*, August 24. https://www.theguardian.com/politics/2001/aug/24/uk.conservatives.

Watt, Nicholas. 2014. 'Norman Baker resigns as Home Office minister with parting shot at May', *The Guardian*, November 3. https://www.theguardian.com/politics/2014/nov/03/norman-baker-resigns-home-office-minister.

Watts, Carl Peter. 2011. 'The "Wind of Change": British decolonisation in Africa, 1957–1965', History Review (71).

Weale, Sally. 2018. 'Children denied free school meals because of parents' immigration status', *The Guardian*, May 9. www.theguardian.com/education/2018/may/09/children-denied-free-school-meals-because-of-parents-immigration-status?CMP=share_btn_tw.

Welford, John. 2017. 'The rivalry between Benjamin Disraeli and William Ewart Gladstone', *Owlcation*. https://owlcation.com/humanities/The-Rivalry-Between-Benjamin-Disraeli-and-William-Ewart-Gladstone#:~:text=Although%20they%20were%20both%20highly%20intelligent%20and%20ambitious%2C,of%20life%2C%20whereas%20Gladstone%20was%20seriousminded%20and%20unimaginative.

West, Cornel. 2017. 'Ta-Nehisi Coates is the neoliberal face of the black freedom struggle', *The Guardian*, December. https://www.theguardian.com/commentisfree/2017/dec/17/ta-nehisi-coates-neoliberal-black-struggle-cornel-west.

Wheeler, W. 1998. *Imagining Home: Gender, 'Race' and National Identity 1945–64*, London: UCL.

White, Michael. 2001. 'Demoralised Tories face lengthy leadership battle', *The Guardian*, June 9. https://www.theguardian.com/politics/2001/jun/09/uk.conservatives1.

White, Michael and Watt, Nicholas. 2001. 'Clarke takes pole position as shocked Portillo quits the race', *The Guardian*, July 18. https://www.theguardian.com/politics/2001/jul/18/uk.conservatives7.

Whitfield, Kate. 2018. 'Theresa May speech in full: read the PM's punchy Tory conference speech', *Express*, October 3. www.express.co.uk/news/politics/1026247/theresa-may-speech-in-full-read-prime-minister-tory-conference-speech/amp.

Whitney, Craig. 1990. 'Man in the news: John Major; a Tory of humble origins', Special to the *New York Times*, November 28. https://www.nytimes.com/1990/11/28/world/man-in-the-news-john-major-a-tory-of-humble-origins.html.

Wilkins, Chris. 1992. 'Freedom of speech in the multicultural society', in James Lynch, Celia Modgil and Sohan Modgil (eds), Cultural Diversity and the Schools. Vol. 3 Equity or Excellence? Education and Cultural Reproduction, London: The Falmer Press.

Williams, Elizabeth M. 2015. *The Politics of Race in Britain and South Africa: Black British Solidarity and the Anti-apartheid Struggle*, London: I. B. Tauris.

Williams, Jack. 2001. *Cricket and Race*. Oxford: Berg.

Williams, Raymond. 1961. *The Long Revolution*, London: Chatto and Windus.

Williams, Wendy. 2020. *Windrush Lessons Learned Review*, March. https://assets.pub lishing.service.gov.uk/government/uploads/system/uploads/attachment_data/file/876336/6.5577_HO_Windrush_Lessons_Learned_Review_LoResFinal.pdf.

Wilson, Jamie. 1999. 'Who will listen to his story now?', *The Guardian*, December 22. https://www.theguardian.com/uk/1999/dec/22/hamiltonvalfayed.jamiewilson3.

Wohl, Anthony S. 1990. 'Racism and anti-Irish prejudice in Victorian England'. HYPERLINK "https://victorianweb.org/history/race/Racism.html"https://vic torianweb.org/history/race/Racism.html.

Wolpert, Stanley, A. 'British Raj: Indian and Pakistani history', *Britannica*. https://www.britannica.com/event/British-raj.

Womack, Amelia. 2018. 'Theresa May – meet with the Yarl's Wood hunger strikers before it's too late', *News.co.uk*. https://inews.co.uk/opinion/comment/yarls-wood-amelia-womack-hunger-strike/.

Wood, Marcus. 2002. *Slavery, Empathy, and Pornography*, Oxford: Oxford University Press.

Wood, Michael. 2018. 'It was a visionary idea born out of postwar optimism and fairness', *BBC History Magazine*, January 25. https://www.pressreader.com/uk/bbc-history-magazine/20180125/281981787997579.

Wood, Mike. 2018. 'His darkest hour: 12 times Winston Churchill was far from being a hero', *History Collection*, February 12. https://historycollection.com/darkest-hour-12-times-winston-churchill-far-hero/3/.

Woodcock, Andrew. 2022. 'Priti Patel's controversial immigration plans pass through parliament despite warnings of harm to refugees', *The Independent*, April 28. https://www.independent.co.uk/news/uk/politics/priti-patel-refugees-imm igration-unhcr-b2067028.html.

Woods, Alan. 2019. *The First World War: A Marxist Analysis of the Great Slaughter*, London: Wellred. HYPERLINK "https://www.marxist.com/first-world-war-a-ma rxist-analysis-of-thegreat-slaughter/1.-assassination-in-sarajevo.htm" https://www.marxist.com/first-world-war-a-marxist-analysis-of-thegreat-slaughter/1.-assassination-in-sarajevo.htm.

Worsley, P. 1964. *The Third World*, Chicago: Chicago University Press.

Wragg, Ted. 2016. 'Education policy and class inequality', *Sociology Review*. https://www.longroad.ac.uk/wp-content/uploads/2016/06/Sociology-Education-policy-and-class.pdf.

Wright, Oliver. 2016. 'David Cameron resigns: Prime Minister announces resignation after vote for Brexit', *The Independent*, June 24. www.independent.co.uk/news/uk/politics/david-cameron-resigns-resignation-brexit-eu-referendum-result-live-latest-prime-minister-general-a7099936.html.

Wright, Patrick. 2018. *Behind Diplomatic Lines: Relations with Ministers*, Hull: Biteback Publishing.

Wright, Robert. 2018. 'Home Office tells couple it divided to stay together on Skype', *Financial Times*, May 15. https://www.ft.com/content/38dfc2bc-575e-11e8-bdb7-f6677d2e1ce8.

Xinhua. 2021. 'UK government's race report accused of trying to downplay structural racism', April 1. http://www.xinhuanet.com/english/europe/2021-04/01/c_139850382.htm.

Yarl's Wood Immigration Removal Centre. 2019. www.yarlswood.co.uk/.

Yeung, Peter. 2016. 'Theresa May "to further scrutinise student visas" in immigration crackdown', *The Independent*, July 25. https://www.independent.co.uk/news/uk/politics/theresa-may-immigration-student-visas-brexit-uk-degrees-foreign-students-a7153246.html.

Younge, Gary. 2020. 'In these bleak times, imagine a world where you can thrive', The Guardian, January 10.

Your Dictionary. Undated. 'Benjamin Disraeli'. https://biography.yourdictionary.com/benjamin-disraeli.

YouTube. 2013. 'Boris Johnson tells London Assembly's Andrew Dismore to "get stuffed"', September 12. https://www.youtube.com/watch?v=UN3e-aYUusc.

Zaheer, Mohammad. 2021. 'Defining Islamophobia is the first step toward addressing it', *Foreign policy.com*, January 29. https://foreignpolicy.com/2021/01/29/islamophobia-united-kingdom-anti-racist-definitions/.

Zimmermann, Moshe. 1986. *Wilhelm Marr: The Patriarch of Anti-Semitism*, Oxford: Oxford University Press.

Index

Printed in Great Britain
by Amazon

17026495R00278